The Glorious Foods of Greece

The

GLORIOUS FOODS

of

Diane Kochilas

GREECE

Traditional Recipes from the Islands, Cities, and Villages

WM WILLIAM MORROW *An Imprint of* HARPERCOLLINS*Publishers*

Portions of this book have appeared in somewhat different forms in *Saveur* magazine, *Cooks Illustrated, Eating Well, Slow: the International Herald of Tastes, Odyssey* magazine, *Proceedings of the Oxford Symposium on Food and Cookery 1999*, and the *New York Times*.

Several recipes have been reprinted from other books by arrangement:

False Soufflé with Meat (Pikantino), page 98, is from the *Cookbook of the Jews of Greece* © Nicholas Stavroulakis 1986 with permission from the publisher, Lycabettus Press.

Meat-Stuffed Carrots Constantinople Style, page 250, is from *Politiki Kouzina (The Cuisine of the Constantinople Greeks)* © Ekdoseis Asterismos and Soula Bozi 1994. With permission of the author, Soula Bozi.

Cheese- and Bread-Filled Tomatoes, page 315; Mashed Potato Pie from Tinos, page 328; and Sweet Chard Crescents with Rice, Walnuts, and Raisins from Tinos, page 345, are all from *Paradosiakes Syntages apo tin Tino (Traditional Recipes from Tinos)* © Nikoleta Foskolou, 1996, with permission from the author.

Easter Bread Ring Kneaded with Milk and Cream, page 437, is from *Kritiki Paradosiaki Kouzina (Traditional Cretan Cuisine)* © Nikos and Maria Psilakis, Karmanor Publishers, Herakleion 1995, with permission from the authors.

HarperCollins books may be purchased for educational, business, or sales promotional use. For information please write: Special Markets Department, HarperCollins Publishers Inc., 10 East 53rd Street, New York, NY 10022.

FIRST EDITION

Designed by Fritz Metsch

Printed on acid-free paper

LIBRARY OF CONGRESS CATALOGING-IN-PUBLICATION DATA

Kochilas, Diane.
    The glorious foods of Greece / Diane Kochilas.—1st ed.
      p.   cm.
    Includes bibliographical references and index.
    ISBN 0-688-15457-3
    1. Cookery, Greek.   2. Food habits—Greece. I. Title.

  TX723.5.G8 K595 2000
  641.59495—dc21   00–028158

01   02   03   04   05/QW   10 9 8 7 6 5 4 3 2 1

for three women who influenced everything:
my mother, Zoe, who taught me to hold on;
my sister Athena, who brought me to Greece;
and my daughter, Kyveli, who keeps me here, smiling.
For Vassili, too, who knows how to dream.

Other books by Diane Kochilas

The Food and Wine of Greece
The Greek Vegetarian

Contents

Acknowledgments

Sitting down to thank those who helped me with this book means that I can indulge in memories of trips taken, meals cooked and shared, and friendships forged all in the name of research.

My husband, Vassilis Stenos, lived through all the traveling, the writer's turmoil, the cook's experiments, and the highs and lows, and was always both flawlessly generous in his support and mercilessly honest. I love him for that.

I owe a great deal to Eric Moscahlaidis, who extended a generous, unquestioning hand when I really needed one and has remained a good friend since. Thanks to the Greek Food and Wine Institute, which Eric founded as a resource for anyone seeking information on the subject. I am also indebted to the newspaper I work for in Athens, *Ta Nea,* without which half the doors in Greece would have been closed. Much of the material in this book was first presented in one form or another, in Greek, in my weekly column for the paper. The International Olive Oil Council supported my work and the Culinary Institute of America gave me the opportunity to share a passion for Greece and Greek cuisine.

This book has gone through a series of adventures before arriving at publication, and its arrival would surely not have been possible without the faith that my agent par excellence, Doe Coover, showed in me and in the project from the start. I want to thank three editors, all of whose pens have been felt between the lines: Pam Hoenig, who believed in the book and gave me a very lengthy tow on which to lean while writing it; Harriet Bell, who inherited the book, liked and respected it, and made sure the best would come of it; I don't have enough kind words with which to shower gratitude on Elizabeth Crossman, the good angel whose erudite and meticulous mind and sensible approach to organization really rescued my manuscript. And, I am still in awe that the onerous task of copyediting was handled with such care and inquisitiveness by Chris Benton, one of the best in the business. And thanks to the proofreader, Jayne Lathrop. I would like to thank the production editor, Ann Cahn, the production manager, Karen Lumley, and the cookbook design manager, Leah Carlson-Stanisic, for pulling all the pieces of the book together in a creative and precise way. I would like to thank the designer, Fritz Metsch, for the book's graceful but serious look. I was fortunate to have found another godsend, Brigitte Bernhard Fatsio, who put her great cooking skills to work testing every recipe.

The list of friends and acquaintances whom I want to thank has no beginning or end. I've met and befriended too many home cooks who shared knowledge, recipes, tales, to list them all here. In a general way, I'd like to say thank you to them all, because it was in their homes and kitchens that I encountered the real spirit of Greece and the glow of unfailing hospitality.

In various parts of the country, specific individuals ushered me through the labyrinth of local mores and customs. In the Peloponnesos, I owe thanks to Maria and Epaminondas Spyropoulos, wine makers in Arcadia, who provided the introductions and more that led me to many local cooks. Angelos Rouvalis, another wine maker, in Aigio, also helped me find local cooks and others with whose help I patched together the region's culinary composite. Fritz Blauel, an olive oil producer in the Mani, did much the same in his neck of the woods deep in the southern Peloponnesos.

My journeys through the Ionian Islands would not have been fruitful had it not been for several individuals. I owe thanks to Nicos Manessis, who made his native Corfu accessible. He led me to Ninetta Laskari, who made the island's history and its rich food culture come alive as we chatted during endless afternoons in her ancient ancestral house. In Cephalonia, Spyros Cosmetatos, scion of an old Cephalonian dynasty, and his wife greeted me with hospitality and help. In Ithaca, Mihalis Maghoulas, another local son whose home and work is now in Athens, shared his archives of self-collected recipes, providing much of what I know regarding the foods of Odysseus's island. In Lefkada, the wine maker Yiannis Halikias provided me with the names of home cooks and artisanal food producers who offered great food and recipes.

The mainland, dense and impenetrable for many reasons, would not have been an easy place to move around in were it not for the generosity of many helpful people. In the southern reaches of Roumeli, I owe special thanks to Eric Moscahlaidis, an olive merchant in Itea, who brought me to home cooks and local food producers. Zafeiris Trikalinos, botargo king, ushered me up and down the western coast of Greece, ever ready to share his knowledge of local fishing customs and to find cooks who could teach me the region's specialties. Lefteris Theodorou, a local artist who lives in the mountains near Karpenissi, sent me off into the woods, literally, on many fruitful recipe reconaissance expeditions. On the other side of Roumeli, in Larissa, I found my way thanks largely to the help of Eleni Polykandriotou, president of the local folklore museum, who, together with a group of women gathered over a few long afternoons, initiated me into the intricacies of all sorts of unusual local foods.

The north: in Epirus, Macedonia, and Thrace I sought and found the guidance of many kind people. Epirus would have been incomprehensible were it not for Vassilis and Eleni Paparounas, Athenian restaurateurs with roots in Greece's majestic northwestern reaches, who took me in over a long summer and taught me the ways of Greece's isolated mountain cuisine. The Tossitsa Foundation in Metsovo many moons ago provided me with shelter and introductions to local Vlach cooks, shepherds, and cheese makers, all of whom made Greece's alpine enclave one of the most pleasant places visited for this book.

In Macedonia, Greece's most complex region, I am grateful to countless people: Yiannis Boutaris, one of the region's most famous sons and wine maker par excellence, for making the pivotal calls that sent me off in all sorts of beneficial directions; Evgenia Zalou and Sofia Mourafetli, Naoussa's self-proclaimed welcome committee, whose knowledge of local foods provided me with indispensible information and many sweet memories; Nerantza Boutari and Popi Kontogianni in Nymphaio, who lifted the lid on Vlach cookery by sharing many unusual dishes with me; Maria Kabesi in Kastoria, in whose kitchen I spent several afternoons; Stelios Samaras, for sending me off on the Macedonian pepper trail well armed; my colleague Yiannis Drenogiannis, for leading me to Vassilis Arabatzis and Yiorgos Haskos, two great food lovers in the remotest regions of Prespes, Greece's pristine northern lakes; Evangelia Iota, a young cook from Grevena; Theophilos Yiorgiades, a walking encyclopedia of all things Pontian; Victoria Benozilio and Andreas Sefika, for providing much useful insight into the Jewish traditions of Thessaloniki. Thrace without Nena Ismirnoglou would have been a tepid experience.

In the Aegean, the list of people who opened their homes and notebooks is a long one. My time in Limnos would have provided much less had it not been for the oenologist Petros Honas, who knows everyone. In Chios, local artist Yiorgos Moutsatsas shared his extensive knowledge of his native island.

My source of information for most things Cycladic was Yiorgos Hatziyiannakis and his wife, Evelyn, who know Santorini like the backs of their hands and shared every detail with me. Yiannis Koulelis also introduced me to many of the lost foods of Santorini through his extensive network of acquaintances. Syros came to light thanks to Nikos Halavatzis, Antonis Roussos, and Eva Marini. In Tinos, I had the world's best guide in the local cook and cookbook writer Nicoletta Delatolla Foskolou. In Naxos, Yiorgos Margaritis, in the mountain village of Apirantho, led me to some great food and great cheese. In Kalymnos, Yiorgos Yiannikouris, who works at the local mayor's office, took it as a personal responsibility to introduce me to every island cook he could think of. In Rhodes, my colleague Yiorgos Zahariades was the best guide anyone could ask for.

Crete, the end of the journey, was a continuous feast of food and fun thanks to so many generous people. My good friend Christoforos Veneris, an excellent chef, has taken me under his wing more than once and has taught me most of what I know about Crete. Zaharias Kypriotakis was my formidable guide through Crete's fields of greens. Nikos Stavroulakis in Hania looked at the introductory material on Crete and was fair and honest. Victoria Athanasiades, sister of the Archbishop of Hania and a great cook, helped me in more ways than she ever imagined. The journalist Nikos Psillakis and his wife, Maria, introduced me to cooks all over the island.

Paula Wolfert was always there to answer every e-mail query on the arcana of anything and everything Mediterranean. Colman Andrews and Nancy Harmon Jenkins extended friendly hands on more than one occasion. I spent endless hours at the Gennadius Library in Athens, and without the academic acumen of the librarians Aliki Asvesta and Andreas

Sideris, I would not have uncovered half the books I did. I am indebted, too, to Stathis Finopoulos, a collector of rare books in Athens, who opened his personal library to me and let me sift my way through his formidable collection. Thanks to my friends Christos Carras and Dimitris Portolos, who provided me with great olive oil and olives and answered endless questions. Ilias Mamalakis, a fellow food writer in Greece, was always generous with his knowledge of Greek cheeses. I am grateful to Costas Spiliades for giving me a toehold at Milos and more.

Many thanks to truly good friends: to my pal Eleanna Rozaki, mostly just for being the best friend anyone could be blessed with, and to Andy, Daniel, Lizzy, Clare, Yiorgos, Stamatis, Mary, and Stratis, willing cohorts who tasted many of the recipes with a good appetite and a keen critical palate. My friend Kiki Birtaha accompanied me on more than one trip and is a walking accessible encyclopedia of things Greek.

Finally, I count my blessings for having a great family: my mom, Zoe, whose will has always been an inspiration; my sisters, Athena and Kostia, their husbands, Paul and Trifon, and all the kids—Kristi, Katharine, George, Tom. I owe much to my in-laws Sappho and Yiorgos Stenos, who never said no to taking care of my daughter whenever my work became overwhelming. Although she's still too young to know it, my own little one, Kyveli, is my muse and the best traveling companion anyone could ask for. She was on most of the expeditions with me, and I only hope she remembers a fraction of them someday.

Introduction

Journeys are always personal.

This book is a reflection of my own travels through Greece, mainly over the eight years it took to research and write it but really over the course of a lifetime, ever since, as a young girl, I first stepped foot in the island village where my father was born. Without being able to define it then, I knew that I had tapped something valuable there, elemental and very human. Food, somehow, was a part of it, included in every interaction. From the simplest snacks, like almonds just off the tree in July and sour-cherry syrup mixed with cool mountain water, to the elaborate family meals with aunts and cousins and neighbors that defied all sense of time, my earliest memories of Greece are intertwined with images of food being offered and accepted, of dishes shared and glasses clinked and people just being people, with no airs and lots of joy.

It was a little trick of fate that I, a born and bred New Yorker, ended up a cook and chronicler of Greece's food. Greeks say the psyche is an abyss, a great dark unknown, and somehow mine, in its own mysterious ways, guided me to cooking as a way to discover my roots and to complete a cycle. My dad was a cook. He left Greece by talking his way into the galley of an English tanker in 1937, never to see his birthplace again because the circumstances of his life were such that he couldn't make it back. I lost him as a child, and my image of him has always been sketchy, a composite pieced together from disparate bits and hearsay. Mostly I recall smells and sounds and minor tactile things: the woody scent of bay leaf simmering in the big iron pots brought home from some ship; of lentils that I seem to recall him cooking often; the blare of the transistor on the kitchen table, always on when he cooked, blasting tinny Greek popular music. I remember the general chaos of his presence in our kitchen at home, the piles of pots in the sink and the palpable air of someone lost among them, absorbed by the rituals of preparing food and by his own thoughts in that most utilitarian, public of rooms. He filled the gregarious role of cook well. Everyone loved him, and everyone loved his food. He was the undenied choreographer of every holiday. My mother, thin and spry, had none of his sonorous energy. On this odyssey I found a part of him in the kitchen and in the country he loved and left but always yearned to go back to, because I went back, the reverse of the immigrant's tale.

I married an artist who happens to trace his ancestry to the same island village as my own. We lived in New York for a decade then "moved back" to Greece in the early 1990s, partly so that Vassili could practice his craft more easily and partly so I could start on this book. In the time since then, we've set down roots, mostly in Athens, where I work as a food reporter for a large Greek daily, but also in Ikaria, where we farm and find refuge.

Over the last decade, my meanderings through Greece brought me great pleasure and led me to understand the nature of the country in a way I never would have been able to otherwise. In Greece history links everything. After reading through my own manuscript, written over about eight years, I realize that almost every chapter begins by noting that such and such a place has always been a cross-roads. This is Greece's story. It has absorbed and co-opted and shunned and embraced three thousand years of people's fortunes and follies. That is still what makes it so fascinating. Even now, as Greece gorges on the detritus of the late twentieth century and enters the twenty-first, it has a soul, and I encountered it, alive and well, in every village I spent time in and almost every cook I met.

It always took some effort and a little ingenuity to get people to open up and share a bit of their lives. Food in Greece has a unique place in the culture, and the home cooks, almost always women, who stoke the proverbial fire are proprietary about their recipes. Greek villages are both welcoming and daunting places, where everyone speaks to you but few people really talk, even about a subject as innocuous as dinner. Most, though, are willing to share a meal. Cooking, for Greek women of a certain generation, is a source of power and an outlet for their creativity. Their ability to do it well, to nourish and please, is also part and parcel of their ability to control a large part of family life, to draw the family in, to keep the children, young and grown alike, in tow, to keep their husbands close. Divulging the secrets of their foods in a way dilutes that power, so it was always with great discretion that I approached them, treading lightly or circuitously, as I navigated my way around the details of their tables. But real cooks are also givers by nature, and in the end taking an interest in someone and in her talents is the ultimate compliment. Most shared their knowledge.

I met cooks in many different places. Sometimes I'd travel to a town or village with a litany of official introductions, usually from the local mayor's office, using my job as a journalist from Greece's largest daily newspaper, *Ta Nea,* to help open doors. I am very grateful for these opportunities. Sometimes I traveled with my young daughter. Women with children are persona grata everywhere in this country, and with Kyveli at my side I could break the ice anywhere. I talked to untold numbers of women at markets all over Greece and picked up little old ladies on their way back from their daily expeditions to the fields, usually for wild greens.

Once, in Crete, I offered an old woman a ride up a steep hill. She was weighed down with three plastic bags full of greens. She peered into the car, found my face a trusting one, and got in. I spent the whole afternoon with her, after she insisted on offering me a cup of coffee. She called me "daughter" and told me about her son in Chicago and her own daughter and grandchildren in Athens. Her house was an ancient assemblage of wood and stone. There was a small refrigerator, but mostly she kept food in a screen-covered triangular old blue cupboard that looked as if it had been standing in the corner of the kitchen for a hundred years. Pictures of her family were curled into cups on top of the cupboard, together with pencils and pens. On the walls faded sepia photographs of her parents and grandparents posed in large oval wooden frames. She insisted I eat something and made a delicious omelet and a plate of greens and sliced thick pieces of her own bread. Then, after a few hours of talking about everything and nothing, and managing in between to record about a dozen local recipes, I told her I had to get going. She motioned to me to wait, opened a floorboard door, descended beneath it into the cellar, and brought up a small wheel of her cheese as a gift. I can still feel her dry leathery hands as she took mine, and the dusty, almost honeylike scent of her skin as she kissed me. "*Sto kalo,*" she said—"Go toward the good," which is how Greeks say good-bye.

In my travels I also stopped in tavernas and *cafeneia* in the most unlikely places, where only natives go, to see what kind of food derives from the immediate environs when people gather together to be sociable. I found some of the best little *mezethes* (appetizers) that way. Once, in Crete again, I walked alone into a *cafeneion* in the middle of the day. I was the only woman, and within about two seconds every face in the room had turned, in utter astonishment, to see who this strange, bold foreigner was. Then I spoke Greek, and I could see a little shock ripple through about fifteen stone-faced men. They all had mustaches, black shirts, and dark pants, the Cretan macho garb. I told them I was lost (which I was). The owner offered me something to drink, and as soon as I sat down they began to interrogate me: What was I doing alone? Was I married? Did I have children? I told them what I was looking for, and within minutes they were sending me off in every direction to find their mothers, wives, sisters, and arguing over where I should go first. I spent two days in the village, traveling from house to house like an honored guest.

Working my way into every region of Greece, I also found the local, usually self-taught history buff or folklorist, someone who loves his or her particular pocket of the country and who typically has spent years documenting everything there is to know about it. These people were often great sources of information about dishes, especially ritualistic ones, that have been lost and about old agrarian food customs. I also visited farmers and cheesemakers and bakers, eking out pearls of gustatory wisdom from them all.

This book aims to be as much a compilation of recipes, most of which I hope will be enticing to American cooks, as it is a look at the long, sinuous, and multifaceted history of a country and its people through its food. I got caught in the quagmire of it a little, wanting to track down every last recipe, before realizing that I had to rein myself in, choose what I liked best, what I thought had symbolic or historic merit, and what I thought represented the places at hand. Thus the recipes are a combination of good, accessible food, ritualistic food, and food tied so indelibly to one place or another that omitting it would have been an oversight. Because many of the classics of the cuisine are easy to find in other cookbooks, including my own first one, I opted to omit most of them here, concentrating on dishes that had a connection to a specific place.

Despite the fact that Greece is a small country, the diversity from north to south and east to west is impressive. Trying to make sense of those differences is what still keeps me here.

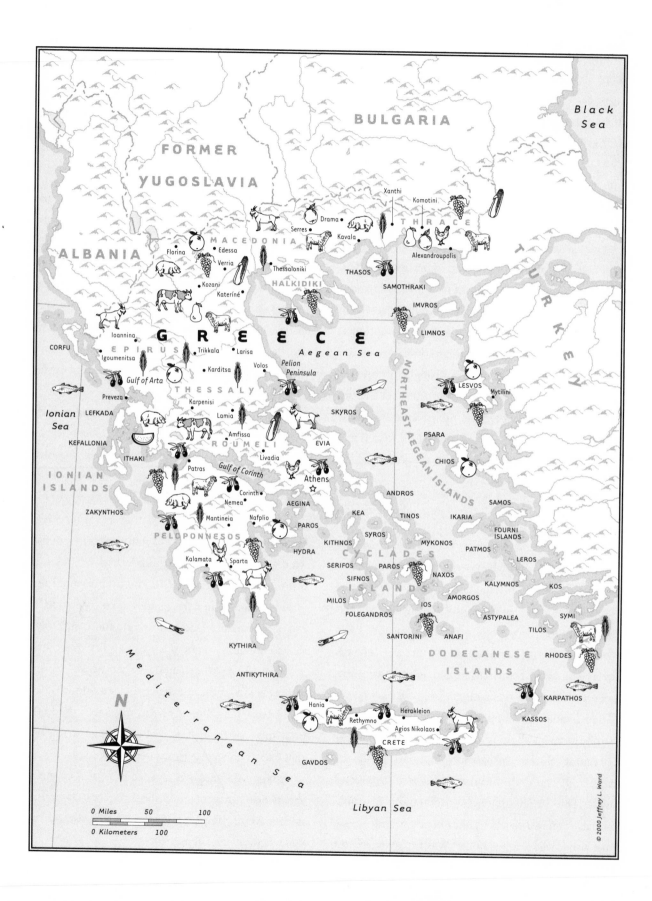

Greece's Culinary Lineage

It is impossible to delineate all the strands of Greek regional food, because nothing is ever that cut and dried. The boundaries drawn in this book, the regions themselves, are organized here more for practical reasons than anything else. Instead of following the borders of prefectures, and so on, I could have just as easily divided the book more loosely, using the physical contours of the land and sea as my guide. It isn't as though boundaries exist that carve up the culinary map into clear, distinct cooking styles. Instead there are many place-specific recipes that came to exist because of the confluence of history and geography. In places where that conjunction has been strongest, such as Macedonia, Crete, and the Ionian Islands, so is the cuisine more vivid than elsewhere. On the other hand, there is also an equal number of dishes that are made all over the country and that defy regional limitations, lending instead a sense of unity to the whole of Greek cooking.

The more I delved into the origins of Greek food and lore, the more I became entangled in the web of this country's long, complex history. Greece, from its most remote past, has always been a crossroads between East and West. It has endured invaders and absorbed settlers from neighboring lands. Much of its history is a history of migrations and resettlements. One has only to think of the long colonial arm of the ancient Greek world and then to think of Greeks today, in places as far apart as Toronto, New York, and Melbourne, to understand that the wanderer's instinct runs deep in the Greek spirit. Most migrations, of course, were forced upon them; threats from the outside—from pirates to earthquakes to Ottoman Turks, Venetians, and others (from the fifteenth to the twentieth centuries) to economic hardship in more recent decades—have often pushed Greeks out of their homelands. Sometimes, the villages and towns left behind were reinhabited, either by neighboring Greeks, such as the mainlanders who settled in parts of the northern Peloponnesos, or by others, such as Christianized Albanians fleeing the Ottomans five hundred years ago. In the Aegean, whole islands have been abandoned and repopulated for one reason or another over the course of history. The country's sinuous history has played itself out

1

on her table, too, for Greek cuisine is an amalgam of influences. The ancient, Byzantine, Balkan (Slavic), Turkish, and Venetian are among the most tangible. Like the Greek language itself, alive and well at work on many different levels concurrently, a beautiful, complicated, yet surprisingly clear mixture of the ancient, the modern, the colloquial, the formal, and the foreign, so, too, is this country's cuisine an entity at once whole yet in a constant state of change.

The country's own geography has dictated what local peoples cultivated and consumed throughout history, and so the palette of ingredients and flavors has often gone unchanged, as in Crete, for example, where, in many respects, the modern table overflows with ancient foods, with the same basic ingredients that sustained the Minoans in 3000 B.C. Olive oil, wine, grains such as barley and wheat, lentils, chickpeas, broad beans, herbs such as wild fennel, so loved here, wild greens, fish, rabbit, simple goat's and ewe's milk cheeses, certain fruits, sesame, and honey are as much a part of the contemporary Greek larder as they were in the Golden Age. The ancient Greeks had achieved a high level of culinary sophistication, characterized by a profound understanding of their natural environs and the specific regional foods that derived from them. Until recent times, when pollution and modernity sullied the lands and waters, many of the same regional foods were still revered, among them delicacies such as small fish from the Bay of Phaleron (now a busy marina, buttressed by stadiums, apartment blocks, and so on, four or five miles from downtown Athens), tunny from the Bosphorous, Attica honey, and much, much more.

In "deconstructing" the cuisine, one can see clearly that three arteries run through the Greek kitchen: the shepherds' traditions; the laconic cook-

ing of the Aegean Islands; and the urbane, fragrant cuisine of the Asia Minor Greeks.

The shepherds' cuisine, is, to a large extent, pan-Balkan. It grew out of the needs of seminomadic peoples who moved with their animals and with the seasons in and among the remote, breathtaking peaks and valleys of the Pindus, the Rhodope, and other northern Greek mountain ranges. These are places that share almost nothing with the sparse, geometric landscape of the Greek islands, the Greece of blue and white that most non-Greeks are familiar with. In the mountain cooking of Epirus, Roumeli, and Thessaly, where most of the Greek shepherd tribes eventually settled, all the ingredients of a once movable larder still form the backbone of the cuisine: milk, cheese, yogurt, some grains or grain products, such as corn- and milk-based pasta, *trahana,* easy-to-forage greens, and meat. It is also a cuisine where butter traditionally has been more important than olive oil, because butter is a dairy—a shepherd's—product and the olive tree does not flourish in high altitudes.

An itinerant lifestyle meant that shepherds had to develop foods they could prepare and carry. The result: among other things, such as whole roasts, a vast array of savory pies, which could be baked in ersatz ovens wherever camp was set up and which could be packed away as part of a midday snack to be eaten while out grazing the flocks. It is no surprise that such pies exist not only in the north of Greece but also in parts of the former Yugoslavia, in Albania, and in Bulgaria. The fluidity with which shepherds moved meant that a hundred years ago, before the present-day boundaries were drawn, they lived all over these mountains and had contact with one another. Today their cuisine still reflects those nomadic connections and necessities.

The Greek Islands and the cuisine that developed there could not be more different. There is a certain lucidity and simplicity that characterizes Greek island cooking, a characteristic born of places where the struggle for the most basic necessities, such as groundwater, marked every aspect of life. For example, as an American kid in Ikaria in the summers, I remember very well the way my aunts and others used to wash dishes. They'd dampen the sponge with a minimum of water and soap it well. Once the dishes were lathered up, they would rinse them under the barest trickle. "My mother used to wash a stack of dishes with a cup of water," my father-in-law once told me. It's a lesson that's embedded now in my own cook's ways, and I'll never be able to take precious water for granted again.

With the exception of Crete and the Ionian Islands, most Greek Islands are dry with sparse vegetation. Islanders had to carve out arable parcels from the mountains, and even now, in the majority of Aegean Islands, the landscape is sculpted with long, narrow steps where people farm to meet the immediate needs of their families. Raw ingredients are limited—a few garden vegetables, pulses, greens, some fish, and less meat—but they have evolved into countless and diverse dishes, paeans to inventiveness.

The islands were also places that were constantly threatened, in distant times by pirates, which forced populations away from the coastal areas and into the interior, and in more recent times by economic hardship. Many families, even now, disperse for large chunks of the year. The husbands usually go off to work at sea. Years ago they might have emigrated to other countries, mainly America and Australia. A few generations ago the young, unmarried women also left home, to work in the households of wealthy Greeks in Egypt or Asia Minor. So the island stories are stories of people longing to return home, echoes of the ancient mariner's tale. But despite the loneliness and burdens of typical island life, there is a sweetness in most Greek Islands that defies description. The islands have none of the heavy, solemn energy of Greece's mainland mountain areas. The stories villagers tell in the *cafeneia* and around the fireplace today move almost surreally across generational boundaries, as people recall the feats of great grandfathers or admonish the slyness of long-dead uncles or praise the strength of mothers and grandmothers. In my own life these stories, retold all the way across the world in New York City, among a small immigrant community of people with ancestry from the island of Ikaria, became the source of much strength. In a society like America that encourages mobility, having a strong sense of place, of belonging, shielded me, I think, from the alienation that often comes as a result of such unbridled freedom to move.

Aegean cooking is old, elemental Greek cooking. Its foundation is the three pillars of the Mediterranean—grains, grapes, and olives. The Aegean is the place to find ancient customs side by side with modern life. I'll never forget the first time I went to Santorini, one of the most visited places in Greece. About a five-minute drive from our very plush hotel in Fira was an old threshing ground still in use, where mules turned the stones and wheat was ground as it had been in Neolithic times. In the cooking of the Aegean, the lack of embellishment is its most telling characteristic. There is a kind of no-nonsense simplicity, a respect for ingredients and for leaving them as is or as close to their natural state as possible. This simplicity and economy culminates, in my mind at least, in the cuisine of Crete, where ingredients play themselves out in an endless fugue enriched by the island's great agricultural wealth.

Diametrically opposed to the pared-down cooking of the Aegean is the complex cuisine of the Asia Minor Greeks who settled mostly in Macedonia and Thrace but are also dispersed throughout the mainland and islands. These Greeks were the heirs to a whole different set of culinary traditions. In the vast expanses of Asia Minor, where Greeks lived for more than two millennia and where, during those two thousand years four great empires (Persian, Byzantine, Arabian, and Ottoman) flourished, the cuisine evolved into a mosaic of contradicting elements: There were the aromatic hues imparted from the East and South, from Persian cookery, and a legacy that eventually played itself out in such "classic" Greek dishes as rice-stuffed vegetables and leaves, and more. Some historians support the notion that even the nut-filled pastries that are so closely associated with Greek—and Turkish—cuisine trace their roots to multilayered nut confections of the Persian kitchen.

Byzantine cuisine, which evolved over the thousand-year course of the Byzantine Empire, was an amalgam of ornate, sophisticated foods whose roots lay not only in the cosmopolitan riches of cities such as Constantinople and Smyrna, where ingredients from every corner of the world were readily available, but also in the deepest past, for the Byzantines inherited and advanced many of the culinary practices of the ancient Greeks. Then, the Ottoman Turks, nomads with an unsophisticated cuisine at first but with an uncanny knack for co-opting, absorbing, and finally disseminating the cooking styles and ingredients from all over their vast empire, took the legacies of Byzantine cookery, of Persian, Arabian, and Balkan cuisines, and interwove them into the complex Turkish cookery we know today. The Asia Minor Greeks were privy to all these currents, and their cuisine is as complex as

their heritage, a reflection not only of the urban and urbane cuisines of the cultivated cities in which they lived but also of the simple peasant cooking of the countryside, for many were farmers, too. Among the most interesting and "non-Mediterranean" Greek regional cuisines is that of the Pontioi, or Pontian Greeks, whose homeland was the Black Sea. Theirs is an agrarian cuisine based mainly on dairy and is part of the tapestry of Asia Minor Greek cookery.

Yet when Greeks today think of the cooking of the Asia Minor Greeks, who settled in the islands and mainland en masse after the political upheavals of the 1920s, what we mostly think of is their bourgeois cuisine. So many different people lived side by side in places like Constantinople and Smyrna—Greeks, Turks, Armenians, Jews, and more—making the sharing of recipes and the blurring of lines inevitable. For example, butter and oil both were seminal in Asia Minor cooking. Many of the wealthy Greek merchant families either employed cooks or traveled frequently back and forth to France. They had as a point of reference—and reverence—the hierarchical cuisine of the French, the complicated sauces and other preparations. In recipe books dating from the late nineteenth and early twentieth centuries, for example, one begins to see mention of such things as béchamel, rosto (roast beef), ragout, poached fish with mayonnaise, soufflés, and more.

In the early 1920s, when political tensions forced the mass exodus of about a million Greeks from their homes in Asia Minor, they flooded into Greece proper. Once they were settled, it was only a matter of time before the riches of their cuisine—*tzatziki*, stuffed vegetables, eggplant caviar, smoked fish, kebabs, *pastourma*, and so much more—would be found side by side with the unadorned, essentially peasant cuisine that had characterized mainland and island Greek cooking until then. One sterling example of their legacy drives home the importance of their contribution to the whole of Greek cooking: Before the arrival of these Greeks from Asia Minor, the mainland did not know the likes of moussaka, the one dish, perhaps more than any other, that is the cliché icon for all of Greek cuisine.

The Mikrasiates, as these Asia Minor Greeks are known in Greece, really changed the face of the Greek table, and no understanding of Greek cooking, regional or otherwise, would be complete without due credit to them.

Regional Flavors

Now, to get the heart of the matter at hand: the cooking of Greece as one moves from one corner of the country to another.

Looking at Greek regional cuisine now, after having traveled the length and breadth of the country, I find a clear image of the food from place to place emerging. In organizing the book, I decided to begin the regional foray with the Peloponnesos for several reasons. Most important, Greece's southern "hand" comprises elements of both the mainland and the islands. Its mountains are formidable, but its coastline is equally important, and both have shaped the cuisine. Peloponnesian cookery is probably the simplest of all Greek cuisines, an olive oil cuisine from the land that produces the majority of Greece's liquid gold and some of its most famous olives, such as the Kalamata.

The cooking of the Peloponnese is peasant cuisine at its very best. Most Peloponnesian dishes fall into the category of one-pot meals. Vegetables, which grow profusely in the region, are, together

with olive oil, the mainstay of the local diet. The region is also a potpourri of influences, a kind of litmus test in miniature of the migrations and resettlements and goings back and forth that have marked the entire history of the country.

The book moves from there westward into the Ionian Islands and then into Roumeli and Epirus. There are many common threads between the Peloponnesian table and that of the Seven Islands in the Ionian Sea, on Greece's western coast, but the Ionian region also has one of the most complete cookeries, one that can easily stand on its own, with few other points of reference.

In Roumeli and Epirus, the cuisine is again the distinct product of a specific environment. Here mountains define everything. Most of Roumeli and Epirus are shepherds' domains, and the cuisine is one that reflects hardship but also ingenuity. The reigning food is *pita,* as in savory pie—hundreds, if not more, of them. But one also finds some unusual combinations of greens and dairy products from this part of Greece, again reflecting the pastoral traditions.

Thessaly, where the cuisine is also a reflection of pastoral ways, is a kind of bridge for all the cuisines of continental Greece, combining Macedonian traditions with shepherds' traditions and both of those with its own unique geography of coasts, plains, and lush, fruitful mountains. Thessaly is Greece's grain belt and, together with Roumeli, probably the one place in the whole country where meat played a fairly prominent role in the local diet.

Macedonia and Thrace comprise Greece's great North. Here the culinary leitmotivs include things such as peppers (hot and sweet, fresh and dried), pickled vegetables, especially cabbage, and many other vegetables, but especially leeks. The cuisine of the North is spicier than any other local cuisine in

Greece and shares a lot with greater Balkan cuisine, but it is also the reflection of an extremely complex and multilayered society.

The Aegean Islands are a different story. Here the cuisine is sparse and exceedingly simple. Greek island cooking—that of the Cyclades and the Dodecanese—culminates in the cuisine of Crete, which, together with that of the Ionian and of Macedonia, is, to my mind at least, complete and whole in its own right, more so than any other region's cuisine. Crete offers the best example of a unified, perfect Mediterranean cuisine. It is, in its way, the heart and soul of all Greek cooking.

I chose to end this book with Athens, because there, in the country's capital, every regional thread is woven together. The city is experiencing a culinary renaissance and is the weather vane for the direction modern Greek cooking is bound to take.

Ritual, Folklore, and Religion

The folklore of food is a subject too vast to touch on in any real way here. But Greece is a culture where food is still steeped in ritual, and I thought it might be useful to understand a little about how the cuisine is also a reflection of a deeper part of the national psyche beyond the necessity to stave off hunger and be nourished.

The simplest examples of ritualistic foods are things many non-Greeks are already familiar with: the twisted, braided, red-egg-laden breads of Easter; the nut-and-honey sweets made in vast quantities at Christmas and New Year's (nuts being symbolic of fertility and prosperity); the Saint Basil's bread—*vassilopita*—prepared at New Year's

with a coin inserted for good luck. Bread in Greece is a vast subject; space has allowed me to touch upon it only in the most perfunctory way. For one thing, the kind of grain used in breads has always been indicative of its importance. Holiday breads and the *prosforon*—or offering, brought to church—were always made from the finest white flour, while daily bread in many parts of the country was usually a rough hardtack made of barley, not the more expensive wheat. In Crete, Karpathos, and other Aegean islands, the custom of preparing ornate, sculpted breads to celebrate a birth, engagement, or marriage still exists. These beautiful breads, made by groups of women within the family, are often decorated with symbolic motifs, such as birds, snakes, and flowers. Grains—especially whole wheat—appear in other symbolic dishes. One such dish is the ancient grain dish called *kolyva* that symbolizes rebirth and regeneration and, to this day, is prepared at funerals and memorials. It is made with boiled, sweetened whole wheat kernels. On certain holidays, especially around the fall harvest, sweetened porridgelike dishes made with a variety of grains and pulses are prepared and left as offerings in church.

Some ritualistic foods have become icons of the whole cuisine. One such preparation is the whole roasted Easter lamb, a practice that harks back to pagan sacrificial rites and to the feasts of ancient Greek heroes as they prepared for war or celebrated victory. Another is the *kourbani,* or ritualistic bull slaughter and ensuing festival. The rooster is also important, and is cooked for special occasions. Custom has it, for example, that when one breaks ground for a new home, a rooster is slaughtered and cooked for the celebratory feast.

One of the most fascinating array of ritualistic dishes are those prepared for nursing mothers. I have had to leave them out of the body of recipes, mostly because I thought they would not appeal to American cooks, but they include a bevy of sweetened pasta dishes believed to bestow strength on mother and child alike. They are generally made with noodles boiled in milk and sugar and served up either brothlike or as something akin to puddings.

There are many, many more obscure ritualistic foods that are still prepared in Greece today: breads, pies, bean and pulse dishes, pasta, sweets, and more. Every milestone, from birth to death, is usually celebrated with or represented by a specific dish, which may or may not vary regionally. There are also plants and fruits that are considered highly symbolic in and of themselves. Nuts and dried fruits, for instance, are among the edible symbols of prosperity, while grains symbolize regeneration and the cycle of life. The pomegranate, with its hundreds of ruby-colored seeds, is a more specific symbol of fertility. It used to play an important role in the wedding ceremony; in some parts of Greece the young bride would toss a pomegranate into her new house. As the fruit split open and the seeds poured out, their numbers represented fecundity, prosperity, happiness, etc. Farmers in some parts of Greece would do the same thing—toss a pomegranate into their fields—before planting. Today the custom has died out, but the pomegranate is still a symbol of prosperity, and renditions of it, in glass, ceramic, and other materials, are part of the holiday decorations in many homes at Christmas.

Another fascinating ritualistic food is the *fanouropita,* usually a walnut-filled cake that is made at the end of the summer on the name day of Saint Fanourios, who is the patron saint of lost or unrevealed fortunes. People still bake the cake, but one old folk belief dictates that if young girls place a piece under their pillow at night, they'll dream of their future husbands. There are lots of similar recipes for Saint Fanourios cake from all over Greece. I included the one I liked the most, from Ikaria.

I suppose I need to touch on one last thing within the general framework of food endowed with some kind of meaning or specific place on the table: the great wealth of vegetarian dishes in Greece, which I have tried to do justice to in the pages that follow. Greek cuisine lays claim to a great variety of vegetable- and grain-based dishes, maybe more than any other traditional cuisine in the Mediterranean. There are several reasons for this. The first is simple economy. Until a generation ago families just couldn't afford to eat meat regularly. More important, though, the religious calendar dictated frequent abstention not only from meat but also from dairy.

The fasting periods in Greek Orthodoxy, in fact, account for about half the year. As a result, over generations, of course, people have developed myriad ways to cook vegetables, grains, and pulses. Olive oil has always played a seminal role in these dishes, many of which are one-pot, stovetop preparations. Their name, *lathera,* derives from the Greek word for olive oil, *lathi.*

In the spirit of Lent and abstention, a slew of endearing recipes evolved locally that are named for what they are not: For example, Lenten fish, which are nothing more than fried leeks, are said to resemble small fried fish, forbidden during the fast. There are dozens of such ersatz dishes all over Greece, and I have included a few of them.

In this book I have tried to draw the image of a cuisine that few people, Greek and non-Greek alike, know very much about. Although Greece is a small country, its mountain and island geography has long prohibited easy communication and travel from one part of the country to another. Even today, in many remote parts of the mainland or the islands, what locals call a road would strike fear in the hearts of most drivers. And although flora and fauna do not differ dramatically from one place to another, there are specific regional identities. It is these, as reflected in the cuisine, that I have tried to capture.

Still, what you'll find here is as complete a picture as is possible to give. One of the great lessons I learned during my research and writing is that there is really no such thing as a "comprehensive" book. I hope what I have served up makes you want to turn the pages and cook, cook, cook and read, read, read.

The Peloponnesos

A Sense of Place and Palate

Pelops's Island is really a peninsula, the southernmost part of continental Greece, which was separated from the mainland in 1893 when the Corinth Canal was dug. The ancients referred to it as the Acropolis of Greece, meaning the "edge of Greece."

Seven large counties make up the region: Corinth, Achaia, Ilia, Arcadia, Argolida, Messinia, and Laconia. Each has a character all its own, shaped equally by the region's complicated history, by her people, and by her landscape—the dominant, masculine Taygetus Mountains from the center to the south; the sea; the wetlands on the northwestern coast, which looks out toward the Ionian Islands; the "fruitless Arcadian mountains," as they were described by a Greek traveler to the region in 1958; the fertile Messinian plain, where "even umbrellas would grow if you planted them," as Charilaos Trikoupi, the nineteenth-century Greek prime minister, once said of the place; the rock-strewn Mani, austere, poor, and breathtaking.

In many ways, Greece begins here. It was Pelops's grandson, Menelaus, who was married to Helen, for whom the whole Trojan War was fought. It was the region's most powerful king, Agamemnon, who agreed to amass the army necessary to sail off and fight at Troy. It was in the Peloponnesos that Hercules enacted his trials, and here that the ancient Olympic games were held, and, here, too, that the modern Greek state was born, on March 25, 1821, when Bishop Germanos of Patras hoisted the Greek flag at the Monastery of Agias Lavras, sparking the Greek War of Independence. Nafplion, a beautiful fortressed city on the Peloponnese's eastern coast, was the country's first capital. "The Peloponnesos has always been regarded as the cradle of Hellenism: sacred, fruitful earth, with all the delights of both island and mainland . . . A journey to Greece must always begin from the Peloponnesos, the old mother," as Nikos Kazantzakis wrote in *Journey to the Morea.*

Yet, for all its "Greekness," the history of the Peloponnesos, like that of all of

Greece, is a history of migrations, invasions, and population exchanges that date back in time to the most ancient days and continue up through living memory. The more I tried to delve into the origins of the region's food and lore, the more I became entangled in the web of different peoples who at times have inhabited this fertile, mountainous place, many, in their way, leaving a mark on her culinary traditions.

In the southeast, for example, especially around Monemvassia, there are dishes such as *rafiolia*, a nut-filled sweet, which take at least an etymological cue from the Venetian legacy; others, such as *yioulbasi* and *atzem pilaf,* from the central and northern parts of the region, which are remnants of the Turks. Others state their provenance plainly, as in a dish called, simply, "Albanian chicken," which is nothing but stewed chicken with the very Balkan combination of vinegar and garlic. Along the northern coast, where one expects the traditional table to be centered around the bounty of the sea, the influences seem oddly pastoral. It makes sense, since this part of the Peloponnesos was largely settled by the mainland mountain shepherds. So, instead of a rich fish tradition, there flourishes the taste for real shepherd's food—things such as boiled old goat and ram, and milk-and-pasta pies.

The foundations of Peloponnesian cookery are rooted in the region's formidable agriculture. First and foremost, no doubt, are table olives and olive oil, for here lies Kalamata (in Messinia), home to the mahogany-black, tight, almond-shaped eponymous olive—perhaps the world's most famous. Here, too, is Nafplion (in Argolida), well known for its slim, green, cracked olives. All the way south, on the tip of the third Peloponnesian finger is Coroni, birthplace of the Coroneiki olive, the most significant oil olive in Greece, no small encomium for a country

whose impressive output of olive oil is composed of more than 75 percent extra-virgin.

In the regions where olives grow, figs grow, too, and in modern-day Kalamata the two are often packaged at the same warehouses. I remember visiting one of the large cooperative oil bottlers and seeing the odd machines for stringing figs, like mechanized hole-punchers, lined up at the front. Kalamata figs are sun-dried and flattened, then strung garlandlike on thin pieces of reed. They come to market seasoned with sesame seeds (which used to be another local crop and the main ingredient in the local sweet, *pastelli*), and bay leaf.

The Peloponnese's other historically significant raw ingredient is, without a doubt, the grape. Wine figures prominently in the glass and in sauces, but, in cooking, nowhere near as prominently as vinegar. There are numerous dishes that call for the strong puckish combo of red wine vinegar and crushed garlic, or the sweet-sour combination of vinegar, tomatoes, and raisins (*savoro*).

If vinegar is on one end of the scale of a grape's life, then raisins are its rudimentary sibling. Raisin grapes have been crucial to the economy of the region for eons. Both the blond sultanas from Corinth and the tiny dark currant, called *bostizza,* from Achaia and elsewhere, have been an essential part of the agricultural economy for at least five hundred years. The Venetians took currants from Corinth and replanted them in the Ionian, thereby establishing other places such as Zakynthos as veritable centers of trade and production. Toward the end of the nineteenth century, and well into the twentieth, the English, too, found a handsome business in buying raisins in exchange for salt cod, which they could procure in vast amounts from the North Sea. English-Greek trade statistics from the end of the nineteenth century corroborate the importance of the tiny dried fruit and also offer insight into the possible reason why salt cod is so much a part of the local Peloponnesian table. In many places, raisins enter the savory repertory in a slew of unusual (for Greece) dishes. But as a wine-producer friend along the northern coast told me, in recent times raisin production has been waning, replaced by wine grapes because the landscape is more conducive to vineyards, and wine is more lucrative.

The Peloponnesos produces many prized garden vegetables. Most of Greece's artichokes are cultivated here, and the area around Nafplion is famous for them. The region abounds in eggplants, too, including a long and thin, light purple local variety called *Tsakoniki,* which comes from around Leonidio, where an eggplant festival is held every August.

Lemon groves—indeed, citrus groves of every sort—seem to be everywhere one looks all over the region, so it is not surprising that the lemon, and then, second to that, the orange, should play such a major role in the kitchen. There is even a place on the eastern coast, across from the island of Poros, called Lemon Forest. Lemons appear in the savory kitchen as a marinade for the tiny green olives that one finds in the south, and then mainly in the form of thick avgolemono sauce, sometimes married with tomatoes. Oranges season the sausages and cured pork of the Mani and are widely used in baking—holiday breads, biscuits, cookies, cakes.

Another staple crop is the tomato. Through late autumn, truckloads of sweet ripe tomatoes wobble along what seems like every road in the region, heading to some point of delivery or debarkation. In small villages, where old ways are still maintained, one still can see tomatoes sun-drying on planks. In the middle of the Peloponnesos, tomato canning is a huge business, and the local crop is almost exclusively the small plum tomato.

Cooks in the Peloponnesos almost always make their sauces with tomato paste, which they in turn almost always make themselves at the end of summer to keep on hand all year-round. It is a staple in the Peloponnesian pantry, even today. This concentrated tomato paste, coupled with unsparing amounts of ubiquitous, exquisite local olive oil, gives great character to a bevy of local dishes, from simply stewed green beans, to medleys of aromatic wild greens simmered with a tablespoon or two of tomato paste added to the pot, to meat awash in a sea of delicious sauce. In fact many recipes come in two versions—red and white—in other words, with and without tomatoes. One of the characteristic things about the tomato sauces of the Peloponnese is that they so often are perfumed with cinnamon. Frequently, they are partnered with the region's other characteristic sauce, *avgolemono* (egg-and-lemon). Even fresh tomato salads are dressed with a few drops of lemon juice (and olive oil) in the Peloponnese.

The Peloponnesian Pantry

OLIVES AND OLIVE OIL

"Climate, soil, variety," my friend and oil expert Paraskevas Tokousbalides said emphatically when I asked him what makes the olive oil from this part of Greece so good. The Peloponnesos has everything it takes to make perfect oil and, indeed, an impressive 95 percent of the 100,000 to 120,000 tons a year of oil that it produces is extra-virgin. The Peloponnesos is probably the single most important region in Greece for olive oil (followed by Crete); it accounts for more than a third of the country's entire production.

The summers are hot and dry, the winters mild, and the sunshine blessedly relentless at about three thousand hours annually. It rains enough and at the right time of the year, in the early fall, when the fruit needs moisture in its first stages of growth.

The landscape is mountainous, which means that the almighty tractor can't plough its way into the olive groves so that, like it or not, most olive farmers have to do the arduous work of harvesting them by hand. And, by and large, the soil is chalky and rich with phosphorous, just right for olive cultivation.

Peloponnesian olive oils vary a fair amount from place to place within the region. The oils of the southern Peloponnesos are probably the most highly regarded, and especially that from the Mani. Peloponnesian oil tends generally to be a little heavier than that of Crete, with a more pronounced olive taste. For an American cook, Greek olive oil in general is the best bet on the market in terms of value for the money, and there are many oils available in the States from the Peloponnesos, as well as from Crete, another stellar oil producer.

Generous amounts of olive oil are poured over greens, beans, bread; used in a wealth of one-pot dishes, usually added toward the end; heated in the skillet for frying; and revered for baking, even for pastry making. It is this copious use of excellent, extra-virgin olive oil that is one of the characteristic elements of the food here, and in all my recipes from the region I have tried to maintain a level of authenticity by calling for extra-virgin olive oil to be used freely, in quantities that might raise some eyebrows.

OIL OLIVE VARIETIES

There are several main varieties of olives used to produce oil in the Peloponnesos:

CORONEIKI. This is the king of all Greek oil olives and one of the most significant varieties in the whole Mediterranean. The name derives from Coroni, the stunning medieval town a few hours' drive south of Kalamata on the southeastern tip of the Messinian peninsula at Cape Akritas. The Coroneiki is cultivated all over Greece now, and in some places it has acquired local names, too. In Crete, for example, the tiny Coroneiki is also called *lianolia* or *psilolia*. It is a lovely olive: small, long, and slim, with a pointy tip. The Coroneiki, when properly tended, harvested, and pressed, and depending, of course, on the microclimate and soil in which it is cultivated, tends to produce fruity, astringent, and often peppery oils.

MANAKI. After the Coroneiki in commercial importance is the Manaki, an olive as small as the Coroneiki that produces equally low-acid oils. The Manaki is most widespread in and around Corinth, Argolida, and Arcadia. Sometimes it is cured and consumed as a table olive, but mostly it is cultivated as an oil olive.

ATHINOLIA. This is an olive found mainly in Laconia and on the taste scale is quite different from the Coroneiki and Manaki. The Athinolia produces low-acid oils that are distinguished by a round, fresh, fruity, sweet, and mellow taste.

CHEESE

Although cheese makers in the Peloponnesos make a variety of cheeses found all over Greece—*graviera, myzithra, kefalotyri* (an especially sharp variety of this common hard yellow cheese comes from the mountain villages of Parnona)—several regional cheeses stand out. Among them:

THE MANI, A JOURNEY INTO THE FOODS OF HARDSHIP

"The place in which they live is waterless and inaccessible, but has olives from which they gain some consolation." So wrote the Byzantine emperor Constantine Porphyrogenitus about the Mani in A.D. 950.

In my sojourn deeper into the Peloponnesos, I knew there wouldn't be much in the way of embellished tables from the Mani, a land whose hardship and poverty were, throughout most of its history, proverbial—so poor and isolated that even coffee and coffee shops were unknown in many villages until the end of the nineteenth century. But I wanted to see and feel for myself this place where the ancients believed lay the entrance to Hades—in a cave at the bottom tip near Cape Tenaron, where Hercules had brought up Cerberus. I wanted to thread my way around this bony middle finger of the Peloponnesos, the southernmost tip of the Balkans and indeed second southernmost tip of Continental Europe after Tarifa in Spain. The mountains do not taper into the sea with grace or subtleness; nothing is subtle in the Mani. The Taygetus range ends as a profusion of rocks thrust toward the sea, as if the gods had meant them to disappear. The Mani—with its countless Byzantine churches, caves, mountains, blood feuds within living memory, and feudal towers—is masculinity exalted. To this day, parents still voice that age-old bias in favor of male offspring. Ask a Maniot how many children he or she has and you're likely to get an answer something like this: "three children and one daughter"; four offspring in all, in other words, but somehow not of equal status!

I descended into the contradicting landscapes of the Mani, like most tourists, by driving southeast along the coast from Kalamata. It was the start of spring, and my introduction was gentle. Poppies, daisies, chamomile, and lavender carpeted the hillsides, giving the false impression that all of Mani's earth is plush and soft. Yellow mullein erupted, unexpectedly large, like loud laughter, everywhere.

But the backdrop to everything, to sea and slopes and vegetation, is unmistakably the olive tree. That is true, of course, for all of Messinia and much of Laconia and the rest of the Peloponnesos, but here the trees are different. The trees in Mani, mostly host to the small, slender Coroneiki variety of olive, are low and thin regardless of their age, nourished on pure rock. The oil that derives from them is some of the best olive oil in the world. And if there is anything you leave Mani with, besides the desire to return, it is the taste of that oil in your mouth.

Olive oil is rampant in the cuisine of the entire Peloponnesos, but in the Mani it was the maintainer of life. To this day it is everywhere. I had it raw, emulsified with lemon as a marinade for the tasty little olives themselves, and raw over toasted bread in a tourist taverna in Gythion. I dipped into it in a typical Maniot dish of boiled *horta* topped with black-eyed peas at the home of Christos and Chryssa Koukoutsi in Doloi. "Go on, go on, don't be afraid to pour the oil," implored my host. "Here oil is more plentiful than water." I had it in the form of fried—drenched—bread served with slices of the local brine cheese *sfela* and some of Mani's famous cured pork (also preserved in olive oil) as I whiled away the afternoon with an old-timer at the local *cafeneion* in Thalames. I crunched into it in the region's famed *lalangia,* the finger-thick, curled dough fritters (kneaded with olive oil, then fried in olive oil) traditionally served at Christmas but now widely available and served either hot with grated *sfela* or cold like pretzels. I followed the trail of oil to the olive wood–burning baker's oven in Areopolis that everyone all over the peninsula raves about, to sample the crisp bites of *paximathia* (rusks) made with the olive's thick green juice. I recorded it in the recipes for *anevata koulourakia* ("floating biscuits," made with one water glass of oil per kilo, 2.2 pounds, of flour and so called because you test their readiness for the oven by first dropping one in a cup of water; if it floats, it has been allowed to rise sufficiently). I had it in *kourambiethes* (shortbread cookies) and *melomakarona* (syrup-soaked cookies) made with oil that melt in your mouth and in olive oil–fried *thiples,* the dessert of joy, mandatory at weddings.

Feta The flagship Greek cheese is associated mostly with the mountainous regions of Continental Greece, but the Peloponnesos has a special, honored place in its production, for it is here that most of the last barrel-aged feta is still produced.

Sfela Another local specialty from the southern Peloponnesos. It is a sheep's milk brine cheese, not unlike feta but saltier, shaped into thin bricks, and almost always aged in tins.

Zalaka Found in the southeast mountain villages between Sparta and Monemvassia. It is a soft, white goat's milk cheese preserved in goatskins, not unlike the *touloumotyri* of the northeastern Aegean. It is difficult to find, and is procured mainly by befriending a local shepherd who makes it.

THE LAST BARREL FETAS

Everything is damp and moist at Taki Langas's feta factory in ancient Mantineia, a cool mountain plateau in the center of Peloponnesos. The strange, thick, sweet-and-sour smell of fermenting milk permeates the whole place. Hoses snake across the wet cement floors carrying milk and whey. Salt cracks under your feet as you walk around. In the front yard, balls of the whey cheese *myzithra* are strung from red and green ribbons and dangle like Christmas ornaments from the rafters. On the ground, barrels are everywhere: some empty, piled pyramid-style outside, some new, being washed down with whey, some in use, filled with feta at various stages of maturity.

The Peloponnesos is the main producer of barrel-aged fetas in Greece, and Langas's place is the real thing, one of the last small, family-run, traditional cheese factories left in the region—there

are about 800 all over Greece. The number might seem vast, but these factories are a dying breed, choked more and more by European Union regulations and ever prey to the vagaries of the market. Here, during the production season from December to mid-June, Langas's 250 annual tons of feta are handmade by a wiry, unshaven cheese master named Gerasimos Theodoratos. His fifty years' experience is worth more than any single piece of machinery. Theodoratos learned the cheese craft from his father and grandfather on his native island, Cephalonia, which is where most of Greece's old-time, empirically trained fetameisters come from.

It was noon when I arrived, and the day's production cycle was well under way. The four tons or so of sheep's and goat's milk that Mr. Langas buys from the sixty-three shepherds he works with had already arrived hours earlier. It had long been checked for safety, skimmed slightly, heated—pasteurized—and cooled through a radiatorlike contraption. By midday, the milk was already in the three enormous vats in the center of the feta room. You couldn't tell by looking—it seemed so deceptively still—but the milk was in the midst of ferocious activity. Every few minutes, Theodoratos ran his arm and a thermometer through each vat. The temperature has to remain steady, somewhere between 35°C and 38°C (95°F and 100°F). "It's a delicate balance. One degree off and you've ruined the cheese," he explained. Next, he took a slotted cup and scooped up big crystal salt that he first rinsed in a barrel of water. "I can't tell you how much I add. I just know by looking," he said, but Mr. Langas interrupted: "It's about four kilos for the vat—for 1,500 kilos of milk." Theodoratos had already added the rennet and starter necessary for it to set. The rest was up to nature and skill.

It would take about forty-five minutes to be

transformed into "pasta"—a substance thick and white like yogurt, about as tenuously solid as Jell-O, but afloat in deep yellow liquid, the whey. The "pasta" is bland and warm, and feels strange on the tongue. The curds have to be cut at this stage, so Theodoratos took a long, stainless steel paddlelike frame outfitted with rows of wire evenly spaced about an inch apart and ran it horizontally, then vertically, through each vat, forming a grid. "If you want very firm cheese, you coagulate the milk at a slightly higher temperature and you cut the curds very small. If you want soft feta, you do the opposite—lower temperature, bigger curds." Moving across the room, he reached for another tool, this one a long wooden oar docked with several large holes with which he stirred up the curds. Finally, he ran his hands through all the pasta, breaking up the mass from the bottom to make sure the curds were indeed small.

As the cheese set, he weighed down the thickened curds in each vat with as many as could fit of the round slotted molds that the feta would eventually be shaped in. Then he pumped out the green-gold whey, and the volume in each vat dropped by half. He filled the molds with the pasta, patting each down and distributing the curds evenly so that each filled to exactly the same height. "If the pasta is too hard, it won't drain properly." He salted every mold, then, about an hour later, flipped them, salted them again, and, using a special cutter, divided each wheel into three triangular wedges, which he put carefully back into the molds in exactly the same position. The curds are flipped and salted by hand three times over the course of the day. By morning the cheese is solid enough to be placed for the first time in the barrel.

The first barreling is called *lanza* in Greek. The feta is placed in five salted layers in the barrel (which holds fifty kilos or about 110 pounds of cheese), where it remains, unsealed, from three to five days, depending on the weather. Then it is removed, washed down with brine, and placed in other barrels, whose interiors are first rubbed with soft *myzithra* "to keep the cheese from acquiring the taste of wood." There, the feta will stay for anywhere from two weeks to forty days, depending on the temperature, to ferment, mature, and exude its own brine. Finally, it is refrigerated for a minimum (by Greek law) of two months before it can be sold.

To feta aficionados there is no comparison between artisanal, barrel-aged feta and the tinned feta produced in huge automated factories all over the Balkans. Wood breathes, and the barrel can't be hermetically sealed, so the skill of the cheese master determines the quality of the final product.

While all this was happening, in the next room the whey was being put to other uses. In different vats, it was being heated, then strained in cheesecloth—destined to become those dangling balls of *myzithra.* It was also being used, steaming hot, to hose down new barrels, a protective measure that helps the feta from later developing unwelcome bacteria. In the meanwhile, neighboring farmers had lined up tins and demijohns to be filled with whey that they buy and mix with flour to use as natural hog feed. And so, the cycle goes on. As I watched the whole process, I kept thinking about what Theodoratos told me on my way out: "Isn't it amazing—a few hours ago all this was just milk." Cheese making, to the uninitiated, is alchemy.

CHARCUTERIE

All over Greece the pork slaughter traditionally has been a time of revelry. In most places it takes place around Christmas, the idea being that the felled animal will be savored all winter long, usually as the only source of meat. In certain parts of the Peloponnesos, the pork slaughter is even called *gourouno-hara* ("pig joy").

Sausages and large pieces of cured pork kept either like *confit,* in lard or in the region's omnipresent olive oil, are the two charcuterie specialties of the Peloponnesos, but they vary considerably from one end of the region to the other. The basic difference has to do with whether the meat is smoked.

The cured pork, which is called either *pasto* (meaning salted) or *singlino,* is still made in mountain villages and in the Mani, the middle southern "finger" of the Peloponnesos. In the mountain plateau of Arcadia, the pig, once slaughtered and cleaned, is cut into relatively large pieces—about the size of half a dinner plate. Usually only the thigh is used. The pieces are salted for four to eight days, boiled for several hours, sometimes in wine, removed, then browned in olive oil or lard to which allspice, cinnamon, and pepper are often added, "to rid the meat of its heavy pork smell," as one local connoisseur told me. Once the meat is well browned, it is stored in large clay jugs and preserved, usually in olive oil but traditionally in rendered lard. In Arcadia it is from this meat that sausages are made, seasoned with salt, pepper, orange rind, and allspice. Once the sausages are filled, they are boiled again in the original broth left over from simmering the *pasto.* They are preserved together with *pasto* in olive oil.

The most renowned *pasto* and sausages come from the Mani. There the meat is layered and salted in large clay vessels for about five days (in a meat-to-salt ratio of ten to one by weight). Then it is removed and hung to drain. Afterward it is smoked, only for a few hours, over sage or cypress wood. At this point many butchers and local producers sell it, but one more step is needed before the *pasto* is considered edible: It must be boiled, usually with oregano and whole orange rinds. Sausages are flavored with garlic, nutmeg, and wine and almost always boiled with large pieces of orange rind.

In the meat emporiums of Kalamata one can find *pasto* and sausages from the Mani, often sold in the traditional way—put up in glass jars and preserved in olive oil. The meat is eaten either alone, as a *meze,* especially with ouzo, or cooked into omelets or with rice.

BREAD

One has only to travel around the Peloponnesos a little and visit the dozens of old flour mills that dot the region to realize how important wheat and all its products have been to the local diet. The Peloponnesos gave birth to most of the wheat-milling dynasties of Greece. To this day, the biggest names in flour production come from here.

The Peloponnesos, like all of Greece, is rife with bread traditions steeped in symbolism and superstition. One of the most delicious local breads is the *Christopsomo,* made at Christmastime and traditionally eaten on Christmas Eve. It was always made with the most expensive ingredients: highly sifted white flour, sesame seeds, and spice mixtures such as aniseed, orange, bay, cinnamon, and cloves. It was decorated with a cross and thus sometimes referred to colloquially as *stavropsomo* (cross bread), garnished with walnuts or almonds, dried figs, and sometime eggs, a custom that exists in Crete as well. Sometimes, too, the home cook who prepared it would score it five times, like a hand—the hand of Christ.

In the pastry shops all over Kalamata and farther south in the Mani, one of the first things visitors notice are the baskets full of *lalangia,* dough fritters as thin as fingers, sometimes coiled into an unusual, oblong shape, fried in the region's ubiquitous olive oil. Traditionally these were made only on Christmas Eve, as a food meant to ward off the impish little spirits that were said to descend and wreak chaos on the holiday revelry.

There is a bevy of fried dough specialties indigenous to the region. *Milopites,* or miller's pies, after the many flour mills, were the thin, crepelike precursors to what today are called *tiganithes.* Fried in olive oil, *tiganithes* are still served either with honey or as a *meze* with skin-aged goat's cheese and wine.

On New Year's Day, cooks still make *thiples,* delicious, light, and airy dough fritters drizzled with honey and sprinkled with cinnamon. They are common throughout Greece, but what sets them apart in the Peloponnesos is their shape: flat and wide like a wallet. The word comes from the Greek word for "double," as in doubling one's years—enjoying a long life. They are also made at weddings.

The region's New Year's bread, *vassilopita,* or *vassilokouloura,* has become the benchmark for all such breads in urban Greece, seasoned lavishly with orange, bay, and spices and rich with butter and eggs. You will find a recipe for it in my book *The Food and Wine of Greece.* In the mountain plateau of Mantineia in Arcadia, New Year's bread is called *bogatsa* and is usually, but not necessarily, sweet. When it is, ouzo and sugar provide its main aromas.

At Easter, the traditional festive bread came in different shapes depending on the age and sex of the person it was being made for. If meant for a grown man, it was shaped like an arc—the arc of a bow, for example—and decorated with little nodes of dough like pine nuts and three requisite red Easter eggs, symbolic of the blood of Christ; for women, the bread was invariably round, symbolic of the perpetuity of life. Children got fish-shaped Easter breads with a dyed red egg in the mouth of the fish (the fish is a symbol of Christianity) or breads shaped like little dolls.

In older times several breads were said to be conduits for fortune telling, to inspire clairvoyant dreams, especially about future husbands, and to help one see into money matters. A special sweet pumpkin pie made on the first Saturday of Lent was an omen for the farmer's almanac: If the crust turned a beautiful golden color, it was sure to be a good year for crops. On August 27, Saint Fanourios Day, the patron saint of lost articles and untold fortunes, people made and ate *glykopita*—or *fanouropita*—another sweet pie, filled with raisins, allspice, and sesame seeds.

Last but not least is the formidable bread tradition surrounding the milestones of life, especially engagements and weddings. Local women, young and old, recounted to me the number of *kouloures* they had had at their weddings or engagements. These are large round loaves sculpted of dough, decorated, usually with walnuts and sesame seeds, and sometimes stuffed with coins for good luck. Female friends and relatives traditionally get together at the home of the groom on the night before the bride's *proikia*—the equivalent of our American bridal shower. A young boy on the groom's side would sift the flour. The groom tossed coins into it, and with that the starter was made. The next day, women on both sides of the family got together to make the breads, an act symbolic of friendship and unity. During the *proikia,* which was usually on Friday, the young women on both sides would play a kind of game, gently tugging at the bread rings to pull them apart. Whoever's side got the biggest piece would end up with the most children.

Bread is basic throughout all of Greece, indeed fundamental to the whole Mediterranean. In the following bread recipes, I have tried to give a small selection of the region's many ceremonial breads.

⅔ cup extra-virgin olive oil
5 pounds tomatoes, grated (see page 459)
Salt and freshly ground black pepper to taste
6 to 8 cups water or chicken broth, as needed
½ pound small Greek egg noodles, or sweet
     trahana (page 456)
1 cup crumbled Greek feta cheese

Heat ¼ cup of the olive oil in a large pot over medium heat and cook the tomatoes for 5 minutes. Season with salt and pepper and pour in 6 cups of the water or broth. Bring to a boil and add more salt if necessary. Add the pasta to the boiling soup and cook until tender. Add more of the water or broth if the soup is too thick. Pour in the remaining olive oil at the end. Serve warm, topped with the crumbled feta.

The Recipes

SOUP

Tomato Soup with Rustic Pasta

TOMATOSOUPA ME HILOPITES Y ME
TRAHANA

 Makes 6 to 8 servings

Tomato soup with grains is found in many agrarian communities around Greece. The dish provides for a simple, filling meal that doesn't take much time to prepare. In Crete a similar dish is made with bulgur wheat. In the Peloponnesos, noodles are the preferred pasta. Egg noodles come in several shapes in the Peloponnesos: flat and wide like fettuccine or cut into small squares of varying sizes. This recipe calls either for the small squares or for trahana.

Cranberry Bean Soup with Chervil and Onions

FASOLATHA ME BARBOUNIA KAI
KAFKALITHRES

 Makes 6 to 8 servings

This is one of many Peloponnesian dishes combining beans and greens.

½ pound dried cranberry or borlotti beans,
     picked over and rinsed
⅔ to 1 cup extra-virgin olive oil, to taste
2 medium red onions, finely chopped
2 cups fresh chervil, coarsely chopped
4 plum or other small tomatoes, peeled, seeded,
     and coarsely chopped (canned are fine)
Salt and freshly ground black pepper to taste
Fresh lemon juice to taste

1. Soak the beans overnight in ample water. Drain and discard the water. Place the beans in a clean pot with enough cold water to cover by 2 inches. Bring to a boil and drain again, discarding the water. Set the beans aside and wipe the pot dry.

2. Heat ⅓ cup of the olive oil in the same pot and cook the onions, stirring, over medium heat until wilted, about 7 minutes. Add the beans and enough water to cover by 2 inches. Bring to a boil, reduce the heat and simmer, partially covered, 35 to 40 minutes, or until the beans are about half cooked. Add the chervil and tomatoes, season with salt and pepper, and simmer, partially covered, until the beans are tender, another 30 to 40 minutes or longer if necessary, adding more water to keep the mixture liquid. Just before removing from the heat, add the remaining ⅓ cup olive oil or more, as desired, and adjust the seasoning with salt, pepper, and lemon juice.

VEGETABLES

Artichokes and Rice with Egg-Lemon Sauce

ANGINARES KAI RIZI AVGOLEMONO

 Makes 4 to 6 servings

1 bowl of acidulated water (see page 458)
2 lemons, halved
6 medium artichokes, cleaned (see page 459)
½ cup extra-virgin olive oil
1½ cups snipped fresh dill or wild fennel leaves
1 cup peeled, seeded, and chopped tomatoes
   (canned are fine)

Salt and freshly ground black pepper to taste
3 cups water
½ to 1 teaspoon sugar (optional), to taste
1 cup long-grain rice, rinsed and drained
2 large eggs
Juice of 1 large lemon, or more to taste

1. Have a bowl filled with acidulated water (see page 458) and two cut lemons ready: Clean the artichokes as described on page 459, keeping at least 1 inch of the stem intact. As you clean each artichoke, cut it in half lengthwise, rub the surface with a lemon half and drop into the bowl of acidulated water. This keeps the artichokes from discoloring.

2. Heat the olive oil in a large stewing pot. Rinse and drain the artichokes and place them carefully in the hot oil. Stir with a wooden spoon, and as soon as they begin to brown lightly, add the dill or fennel and the tomatoes and season with salt and pepper. Add 2 cups of the water, cover, and bring to a boil. Reduce the heat to low and simmer for about 10 minutes. Taste and adjust the seasoning with the sugar and additional salt, if desired. Add the rice and the remaining cup water. Stir gently, adjust the seasoning, cover, and simmer until the rice is tender, another 20 to 25 minutes.

3. Make the egg-lemon sauce: Whisk together the eggs and lemon juice in a bowl. Pour a ladleful of the pot juices into the egg-and-lemon mixture in a slow, steady stream, whisking all the while. Add a second ladleful and do the same. Immediately pour the mixture back into the artichokes and rice, stir, and remove from the heat. Taste and adjust the seasoning with additional salt and lemon juice, if desired. Serve sprinkled with a little freshly ground pepper.

Artichokes Stuffed with Rice, Oregano, and Fennel

ANGINARES YEMISTES ME RIZI, RIGANI KAI MARATHO

 Makes 4 to 5 main-course servings or 8 to 10 *meze* servings

8 to 10 large artichokes, cleaned (see page 459)

2 large lemons, halved

1 bowl of acidulated water (see page 458)

⅔ cup extra-virgin olive oil

3 large onions, finely chopped

3 garlic cloves, minced

⅔ cup long-grain or basmati rice

Salt and freshly ground black pepper to taste

1 cup water

¼ cup chopped fresh oregano or 2 teaspoons dried

1½ cups snipped wild fennel leaves (see Note)

1. Wash and trim the artichokes as explained on page 459, but leave the tender inner leaves intact so that the artichokes are like cups that can be filled. Trim the stems so that they can sit upright in the pot. Immediately rub the artichokes with lemon and drop into the bowl of acidulated water.

2. Heat ⅓ cup of the olive oil in a large skillet and cook the onions over medium heat until soft, about 8 minutes. Add the garlic and stir. Add the rice and stir. Season with salt and pepper and pour in the water. Cover and simmer the rice over very low heat until all the water has been absorbed, about 7 minutes. Remove the rice mixture from the heat and toss in the oregano, 1¼ cups of the fennel, and 3 tablespoons of the remaining olive oil. Adjust the seasoning with additional salt and pepper and let the mixture cool.

3. Fill each artichoke with about 2½ to 3 scant tablespoons of the mixture, patting it down tightly.

4. Pour the remaining olive oil in the bottom of a medium pot and place the artichokes upright so that they fit snugly against each other without falling over. Add enough water to come almost to the top of the artichokes. Cut a sheet of wax paper or parchment to the circumference of the pot and fit it snugly over the artichokes. Place a plate on top to keep the artichokes from moving. Cover the pot and simmer the artichokes until they and the rice are tender, 25 to 30 minutes. Just before serving, sprinkle with the remaining ¼ cup of fennel leaves. Serve warm or at room temperature.

✳ NOTE If wild fennel is unavailable, use only 2 large onions and combine with 1 cup chopped fennel bulb. To enhance the fennel flavor even more, add 3 tablespoons ouzo to the mixture after sautéing.

ARTICHOKES IN THE PELOPONNESOS

Artichokes, known and savored since antiquity, are indigenous to the Mediterranean. The ancients called the artichoke *Cynara* (which is now used as its Latin genus name), and Theophrastus, the Golden Age chronicler of Greece's flora, recognized two varieties: the globe artichoke and its close relative, the cardoon.

Today Greece produces somewhere in the vicinity of 27,000 tons of artichokes every year, and the center for cultivation is the Peloponnesos. Although about a dozen varieties of artichoke are found all over the Mediterranean, in Greece, and especially in the Peloponnesos, two reign supreme: the Argos artichoke, which is essentially a globe artichoke, all green with tightly closed leaves; and the Iodine of Attica variety, which is smaller with light purple leaves. There are also the small, wild, thorny artichokes, which are enjoyed almost exclusively locally, since they rarely come to market in Athens or other big cities. These are savored raw with olive oil and lemon juice or grilled over coals.

The vegetable is much loved throughout the Peloponnesos, and there is no shortage of recipes calling for it.

Fried Artichokes in Garlic Sauce

ANGINARES TIGANITES MESA SE
SKORDALIA

 Makes 4 servings

10 small artichokes, cleaned (see page 459)
2 lemons, halved
1 bowl of acidulated water (see page 458)
1 cup all-purpose flour
Salt and freshly ground black pepper to taste

Olive or other oil for frying
Two ½-inch-thick slices stale rustic bread,
    crusts removed
1 small head garlic, cloves peeled
½ to ⅔ cup extra-virgin olive oil
2 to 4 tablespoons red wine vinegar, to taste
2 cups water

1. Wash and trim the artichokes as explained on page 459. Immediately rub the artichokes with lemon and drop into the bowl of acidulated water.

2. Bring a pot of salted water to a boil and blanch the artichoke hearts until cooked al dente, about 5 minutes. Remove to a colander and rinse under cold running water.

3. Combine the flour with a little salt and pepper in a bowl or on a dinner plate. Dredge the artichokes in the seasoned flour, tapping off any excess. Heat about ½ inch of olive oil in a large heavy skillet. When very hot, fry the artichokes until browned and golden on all sides. Remove with a slotted spoon to paper towels to drain. Strain and reserve the olive oil from the skillet for another use or discard. Wipe the skillet dry.

4. Run the stale bread under the tap and wring dry lightly. In a mortar, crush the garlic with a little salt and add the dampened bread, little by little, working it in with the pestle. As you work in the bread, add ½ to ⅔ cup of extra-virgin olive oil and the vinegar, alternating between them until the mixture is thick and pasty. Slowly add the water, again working it in with the pestle. The mixture will be like a thick porridge.

5. Pour the garlic sauce into the skillet and heat it, stirring, over medium-low heat for about 5 minutes. Add the artichokes to the sauce and continue cooking, stirring gently, for another 3 to 4 minutes to heat through. Serve immediately.

Artichokes Stewed with Spinach

ANGINARES ME SPANAKI

 Makes 4 to 6 servings

This recipe, from Pyrgo Lefktrou—the Mani—falls somewhere between a stew and a cooked salad.

1 bowl acidulated water (see page 458)
2 lemons, halved
4 to 6 large artichokes
⅔ cup extra-virgin olive oil
8 large scallions, white and tender, green parts finely chopped
2 pounds fresh spinach, trimmed, coarsely chopped, and washed well
1 cup snipped fresh dill
Salt to taste
Juice of 2 large lemons
Freshly ground black pepper to taste

1. Clean the artichokes (see page 459) retaining the hearts and an inch or so of the stems. As you clean each artichoke, rub the surface with a lemon half and drop into the bowl of acidulated water.

2. Heat ⅓ cup of the olive oil in a large pot and cook the scallions over low heat, stirring, until wilted and soft, 8 to 10 minutes. Add the spinach and dill, season with salt, and toss. When the spinach has cooked down to about half its volume, place the artichokes on top, sprinkling them with salt, too. Add half the lemon juice to the pot. Cover and reduce the heat to low. Let the vegetables cook in their own juices until the spinach is completely soft and the artichokes tender, 25 to 30 minutes. Adjust the seasoning with salt, pepper, and the remaining lemon juice. Drizzle in the remaining ⅓ cup olive oil and serve.

Asparagus Omelet

OMELETA ME SPARANGI

 Makes 4 to 6 servings

2 tablespoons extra-virgin olive oil
Coarse salt to taste
6 to 8 asparagus spears, woody bottoms trimmed
6 large eggs
2 teaspoons all-purpose flour
Freshly ground white pepper to taste

1. Heat a large, well-seasoned cast-iron or non-stick skillet for about a minute over high heat. Add the olive oil and sprinkle in a little salt. Add the asparagus, cover, reduce the heat to medium, and cook, shaking the skillet back and forth to make sure the asparagus cooks evenly, until wilted and lightly charred all around, about 10 minutes.

2. Meanwhile, break the eggs into a bowl and beat lightly with a fork or whisk, adding the flour, salt, and pepper. Pour the eggs over the asparagus and tilt the pan so that the eggs cover the whole surface of the skillet. Using a rubber spatula, push the coagulating egg toward the center of the pan and continue tilting so that all the loose egg can cook through and set. Cover and cook the omelet over low heat until the eggs are set but still loose. Slip the omelet out onto a large round plate and flip the omelet back into the skillet to cook for a minute or two on the other side. To serve, cut the omelet into pieces or wedges.

I missed the opportunity to go asparagus picking late one March in Nemea with Vassilis Paparounas, a restaurateur in Athens who knows everything there is to know about foraging. But I reaped the harvest at his restaurant, Symposium, enjoying every inch of the tiny emerald-green strands that he had prepared. "They don't need anything but a few minutes of boiling, olive oil, and salt. For God's sake, don't put lemon on them," he admonished, convincing me that the way I had learned to eat asparagus my whole life was, plain and simple, wrong. Dinner with Vassilis is an education, and that night the lesson was mainly about seasonality, the cycle of life, and, of course, asparagus, the tender young shoots of a European perennial called *Asparagus officinalis,* which grows into a four-foot-tall, fernlike plant with vivid red berries—if the goats don't get to it first.

Wild or not, the vegetable is in season in early spring in Greece—anywhere from around February 15 if you're foraging for it as far south as Crete, up through the end of May if you're picking in Epirus, where the season starts later but lasts longer. Generally, asparagus as nature intended is with us for about a month out of the year. It grows wild in many parts of the country, but in the Peloponnesos it is held in high esteem, and one of the best local recipes is a simple one for asparagus cooked in an omelet. Acknowledging the fact that wild asparagus is hard to come by at American greengrocers, I've had to replace it with the cultivated variety, which has a grassier taste and tougher texture. Look for the best asparagus—green, thin, tender.

Black-Eyed Peas Stewed with Wild Greens

MAVROMATIKA FASOLIA ME MYRONOLAHANA

 Makes 4 to 6 servings

Except for the addition of the black-eyed peas, this dish essentially falls into the category of myronolahana *or* tsigarta—*essentially greens, mostly chervil, stewed with tomato paste and olive oil, a common way to cook them in the Peloponnesos, as well as in parts of the Ionian.*

½ pound dried black-eyed peas, picked over and rinsed
⅔ to 1 cup extra-virgin olive oil, to taste
1 large onion, finely chopped or grated
3 garlic cloves, finely chopped
1½ pounds mixed greens (spinach, chervil, collards, chard), trimmed, chopped, and washed well
2 tablespoons tomato paste
Salt and freshly ground black pepper to taste

1. Bring the black-eyed peas to a boil in ample water, then drain. Place the peas back in the pot with fresh cold water and bring to a boil again. Reduce the heat to medium-low and simmer over medium heat until tender, 35 to 40 minutes.

2. Meanwhile, prepare the greens: In a large, deep skillet or Dutch oven, heat ⅓ cup of the olive oil and cook the onion and garlic over medium heat, stirring, until wilted. Add the greens and tomato paste and season with salt and pepper. Cover and cook the greens in their own juices over low heat for about 20 minutes; they should be soft.

3. Drain the black-eyed peas and add them to the greens, stirring gently with a wooden spoon to combine. Cover the pot and cook the beans and greens together over medium-low heat for another 5 to 10 minutes for the flavors to meld. Adjust the seasoning with salt and pepper. Just before removing from the heat, pour in the remaining olive oil. Serve warm or at room temperature.

BEANS AND GREENS

Beans and greens are a combination found all over Greece, but in the Peloponnesos they make for a kind of national dish. In a small village in the Mani, I was served the simplest version of this combination: a plate of freshly picked and boiled wild greens topped with a ladleful of black-eyed peas and doused in the region's magnificent olive oil. At a taverna in Sparta, I ordered a plate of greens stewed with black-eyed peas. In Mantineia, one local housewife gave me her recipe for giant beans (similar to what Americans call butter beans) baked with celery and another for cranberry beans cooked in a soup with chervil and tomatoes.

Of all the wild greens in the region, chervil is the most beloved. It appears in countless stews, as well as in pies. The local kitchen boasts two types—*kafkalithres*, whose leaves are as big as clover but soft, almost downy, and *mironia*, what we recognize in America as the herb chervil. In these recipes they are interchangeable.

Black-Eyed Peas with Vegetables and Small Pasta

MAVROMATIKA FASOLIA ME ZARZAVATIKA KAI HILOPITES

 Makes 4 servings

We drove to the town of Molaous, in Laconia, on a gorgeous Saturday morning in February during the end of the olive harvest only to find that all the women we were to meet, members of the local Club of Ladies and Maidens, were not available to see us. They were taking the opportunity to pick their olives under the warm winter sun. In good faith, though, they left a packet of recipes for us with Matoula Ritsou, the club's president, who also happens to run the local pharmacy, and this was one of them.

As I talked with the president and flipped through the pages, the scene in the pharmacy began to change. I was there with my friend Kiki, an archeologist, and our presence stirred up some curiosity. Sure enough, one by one, whoever walked in was drawn into our conversation. In that pharmacy we met one of the local schoolteachers as well as the province's educational director. Both were walking encyclopedias of the region's gastronomy, farming, and folkways. We talked for hours, then we drove off to nearby Monemvassia together and, later, down to Neapoli, the southern tip of the first finger of the Peloponnesos. En route, as Haralambos (the schoolteacher) expounded on the etymology of certain food terms and on his theories about the mysterious ancient Spartan soldier's dish, melanos zomos, or black broth, (no scholar has ever been able to discern exactly what it was made with), I remembered something I had read in Kazantzakis's Journey to the Morea: "Where else is Darwin's theory alive today, the philosophy of Taine or Spencer, the poetry of Achilles Paraschos? In *the quiet, languid enchanted provinces—where doctor philosophers sit in the pastry shops or pharmacies and debate the great issues."*

½ pound dried black-eyed peas, picked over and rinsed
1 large onion, finely chopped
1 large carrot, finely chopped
1 leek, white part only, washed well and finely chopped
1 large red bell pepper, seeded and chopped
1 large green bell pepper, seeded and chopped
1 small hot green pepper, seeded and chopped, or more to taste
¼ cup tomato paste
1 bay leaf
⅔ to 1 cup extra-virgin olive oil, to taste
½ cup small pasta (tubettini or small square Greek egg noodles, if available)
2 tablespoons red wine vinegar

1. Bring the black-eyed peas to a boil in ample water, then drain and set aside.

2. Place all the chopped vegetables, the tomato paste, bay leaf, and black-eyed peas in the same pot, add ½ cup of the olive oil and enough water to cover by 2 inches, cover the pot, and bring to a boil. Reduce the heat to medium-low and simmer until the vegetables and beans are tender, about 50 minutes. Add the pasta, increase the heat to high, and, as soon as the mixture begins to boil, reduce the heat to medium-low and simmer until the pasta is cooked, 10 to 12 minutes. Most of the liquid should have been absorbed, but the dish should be moist, with ample pot juices. Pour in the remaining olive oil, season with vinegar, let the dish cool for about 10 minutes, and serve.

Giant Beans with Celery

GIGANTES ME SELINO

 Makes about 4 to 6 servings

Gigantes, giant beans, are similar to what Americans know as butter beans. This recipe comes from Ioanna Brotsi, who opened her Arcadian home to us, invited ten of her neighbors, and served us up a feast of old recipes and handwritten cooks' notebooks.

½ pound dried Greek giant beans (see Note), picked over and rinsed
½ cup plus 2 tablespoons extra-virgin olive oil, or more to taste
5 cups chopped celery, with leaves
3 garlic cloves, minced
Salt to taste
3 tablespoons tomato paste diluted with 1¼ cups water
Freshly ground black pepper to taste
1 bunch flat-leaf parsley, finely chopped
Juice of 1 to 2 lemons, to taste

1. Place the beans in a large pot with water to cover by several inches. Leave to soak for 8 hours or overnight, then drain the beans. Place the beans back in the pot with enough water to cover by 2 inches. Bring to a boil, reduce the heat to medium-low, and simmer until the beans are tender but not thoroughly cooked, 1 to 1½ hours.

2. Meanwhile, heat 2 tablespoons of the olive oil in a large skillet over medium heat and cook the celery and garlic, stirring, for a few minutes, just to soften. Season lightly with salt. Remove from the heat.

3. Preheat the oven to 350°F. Drain the beans and place in a large baking pan. Toss with the sautéed celery and garlic, the remaining ½ cup olive oil, and the diluted tomato paste. Cover the pan with aluminum foil and bake until the giant beans are soft and creamy, 1 to 1½ hours. This is the whole secret to this dish—the beans have to soak properly and cook enough so that they are creamy, almost the texture of roasted garlic, without disintegrating. About 15 minutes before removing from the oven, season with salt and pepper and toss in the parsley. When they are ready, adjust the seasoning with the lemon juice and additional salt, pepper, and olive oil.

✳ **NOTE** *Gigantes* can be found in Greek and Middle Eastern food shops or at some specialty retailers.

Chard Stewed with Celery and Feta

SESKOULA YIAHNI ME FETA

Makes 4 to 6 servings

It was dark and late, and my friend Kiki and I were heading from Arcadia to the Mani. The road was much worse than we'd anticipated, so we made an impromptu stop in Sparta. The hotel owner sent us to a big, bustling "family" restaurant on the edge of town. The place was more or less a hasapotaverna, *specializing in meat, but in a corner of the menu there was a heading for "locul plats" [sic], and through the kitchen window I could see the family matriarch keeping watch over her food. This dish came to us in a large clay pot, and it was really good. Once back in my own kitchen, I reconstructed it.*

2 pounds green chard, trimmed, coarsely chopped, and washed well
½ cup extra-virgin olive oil, plus oil for drizzling on
3 large onions, finely chopped
2 cups finely chopped celery
2 cups grated tomatoes (see page 459) or coarsely chopped plum tomatoes (canned are fine)
Salt and freshly ground black pepper to taste
¾ pound Greek feta cheese, crumbled

1. Bring a large pot of salted water to a boil and blanch the chard for 15 minutes. Drain in a colander.

2. In a large pot, heat the olive oil over medium heat and cook the onions and celery for about 7 minutes, stirring, until wilted. Add the chard and toss to coat with the oil. Add the tomatoes and season with a little salt and pepper. Let the greens simmer, uncovered, until most of the pot juices have boiled off, about 20 minutes.

3. Add the crumbled feta, stir, and continue simmering until the cheese is completely melted and the sauce very thick, another 7 minutes or so. Serve warm or at room temperature, drizzled, if desired, with additional olive oil.

Fresh Green Beans with Onions and Fresh Cream

FASOLAKIA FRESKA ME ANTHOGALA

 Makes 4 to 6 servings

Anthogala, which is what the original recipe calls for, are the billows of cream that float atop fresh milk. Its Greek name translates as "milk blossom"; the French know it as fleur de crème. *In the U.S. the best substitute is heavy cream. I found this recipe in a collection of old regional Greek dishes, and it surprised me because cream in any form is not something Greeks traditionally cook with.*

½ cup extra-virgin olive oil
2 large onions, finely chopped
2 pounds fresh green beans, ends trimmed
Salt and freshly ground black pepper to taste
½ cup heavy cream

1. Heat the olive oil in large casserole or Dutch oven over medium-high heat. Add the onions, reduce the heat to medium-low, and cook the onions until lightly golden and translucent, 12 to 15 minutes. Add the beans, season with salt and pepper, toss to coat with the oil, and cover the pot. Keep the heat low so that the beans steam in the hot oil for about 10 minutes.

2. Add enough water to cover the beans by 1 inch, cover, and cook until the beans are very tender, practically limp, which is how Greeks like them, and most of the water has evaporated, about 30 minutes. Add the cream to the pot, toss to coat the beans, and continue cooking, with the cover askew, until the cream has thickened. Serve hot.

PASTA, RICE, AND TWO SAVORY PIES

Like everywhere in Greece, in the Peloponnesos there used to be a wealth of homemade pasta products that were part of every household's larder. Some, such as *trahana* (hard, pebblelike pasta made with milk, yogurt, buttermilk, or vegetable pulp), were dried; others were made fresh for immediate consumption. There were *striftades,* or little twists that looked like little rice pellets; *toutoumakia,* tiny square egg noodles; and *gongides,* shaped like curled little shells and made in the villages east of Sparta and down to Neapoli on the southeastern tip. Except for the three or four different sizes and shapes of *hilopites*—egg noodles—still made, and *trahana,* which in the Peloponnesos is mostly sweet, made with whole milk, not buttermilk, most handmade pasta varieties have disappeared together with the dire poverty that once made them a necessity on the weekly table. To this day, though, the national dish of the Peloponnesos continues to be *kokkora me hilopites*—rooster stewed in a tangy tomato sauce and served with soft egg noodles. I have not included a recipe for this dish here, because many similar dishes appear throughout the country, and my own favorites come from the Ionian Islands. Nevertheless, there are several simple, interesting Peloponnesian dishes still made with pasta, and those follow.

The popularity and inexpensiveness of pasta, especially when it used to be made at home, eclipsed the use of rice in the local kitchen, so rice appears sparingly, usually reserved for Sunday or festive meals, turned into broth-soaked pilafs that are molded into decorous little cups, or used, as elsewhere in Greece, in stuffings. There isn't a great tradition of savory pies in the Peloponnesos. Sure, there are greens pies, and some delicious pumpkin pies, which are mostly sweet.

Strained Egg Noodles with Brown Butter and Cheese

STRANGISTES HILOPITES

 Makes 4 to 6 servings

This dish is a quick and steadfast country dinner in many parts of Greece. I include it here, in the foods of the Peloponnesos, because it was mentioned by every local cook I spoke with, leading me to realize that even if the dish isn't unique to the region, it is so commonly cooked that it is considered a local specialty. I was told, too, that the best noodles are homemade and served with ewe's milk butter. Now there's a novel idea for some American entrepreneur.

1 pound Greek or other egg noodles
½ pound (2 sticks) unsalted butter or sheep's
   milk butter
2 cups grated kefalotyri cheese or any hard
   yellow cheese

1. Bring a large pot of salted water to a rolling boil and cook the egg noodles until well done.

2. Just before the noodles are drained, melt the butter in a skillet over low heat until the butter bubbles up and browns. Timing is the secret to this very simple dish. Drain the noodles very well.

3. Spread a third of the drained noodles on a large serving platter and sprinkle with a third of the cheese. Pour a third of the melted butter on top. Add a second layer of noodles, cheese, and butter and then the final third. Serve immediately.

Fresh Pasta with Lots of Garlic

SKORDOMAKARONA

 Makes 2 to 4 servings

My friend Haralambos, the district education counselor from Molaous near Sparta, is a walking encyclopedia of local history, gastronomy, and folkways. He shared this simple recipe with me, explaining that it was the workers' lunch during the summer threshing period as well as during the fig harvest. The tremendous amount of garlic—3 whole heads or more—acted as a replacement for more expensive cheese, which was reserved for the family to eat, not for its hired, usually migrant, help. Another version was sometimes made with the local cured pork. In an effort to replicate the fresh homemade pasta described, I have simply called for fresh fettuccine or egg noodles. As for the garlic, don't be daunted by the amount. Boiling garlic is to the Greeks what roasting it is to the Italians—a way to mitigate the sharpness of the stinking rose and bring out its inherent sweetness.

3 large heads garlic, cloves peeled and coarsely
   pounded in a mortar
½ pound fresh egg noodles or fettuccine
½ cup extra-virgin olive oil

Bring enough salted water to cover the pasta by about 1 inch to a boil. Add the pounded garlic and pasta and boil all together until the pasta is cooked as desired (traditional Greek cooks like it soft, not al dente). Remove with a slotted spoon, making sure some of the liquid and all of the garlic end up in the serving bowl. Toss the pasta with the olive oil and serve.

Beef with Egg Noodles and Egg-Lemon Sauce

VRASTO ME HILOPITES

 Makes 6 to 8 servings

Another classic on the region's Sunday table.

⅓ cup extra-virgin olive oil, plus a little for the
noodles
2 medium onions, finely chopped
7 cups water
4 to 5 pounds whole bone-in beef shank,
trimmed of fat
Salt and freshly ground black pepper to taste
1 pound Greek *hilopites* or other egg noodles
4 large eggs
Juice of 2 large lemons

1. Heat the olive oil in a large pot over medium heat and add the onions. Cover, reduce the heat to medium-low, and steam the onions in the oil until very soft, about 15 minutes. Without removing the onions, add 3 cups of the water to the pot and bring to a boil. Add the meat, season with salt and pepper, cover, and simmer until the meat is very tender and almost falling off the bone, about 2 hours. Skim the foam off the surface of the water as the meat cooks.

2. Remove the meat and onions from the pot with a slotted spoon and set aside. Add the remaining 4 cups water to the pot, season with salt, and bring to a boil. Add the noodles and simmer until tender. Do not drain. Remove the noodles with a slotted spoon and spread on a serving platter, tossing with a little olive oil to keep them from clumping together. Place the meat on top of the noodles in the center of the platter.

3. Make the egg-lemon sauce: Beat together the eggs and lemon juice in a bowl until frothy. Add a ladleful of the broth to the egg-and-lemon mixture in a slow, steady stream, beating all the while. Repeat with another ladleful of broth, then pour the mixture into the pot and stir to combine. Pour the *avgolemono* over the meat and noodles and serve immediately.

Pilaf

PILAFI

 Makes 4 to 6 servings

The simple Sunday and festive meal eaten in most of the Peloponnesos and elsewhere.

⅔ cup extra-virgin olive oil
2½ pounds boneless beef chuck, cut into large
stewing pieces
Salt and freshly ground black pepper to taste
2 tablespoons tomato paste
1 cup long-grain rice
Juice of 1 lemon
1 large onion, finely chopped
2 to 3 tablespoons unsalted butter, to taste

1. Heat ⅓ cup of the olive oil in a pot over high heat and sear the meat until browned on all sides. Remove from the pot, set aside, and season with salt and pepper. Add the tomato paste to the pot and stir into the olive oil. Place the meat back in the pot and add enough water just to cover. Simmer, covered, over low heat until very tender, 1½ to 2 hours.

2. About 25 minutes before the meat is done, prepare the rice: Rinse and drain the rice and toss by hand with the lemon juice in a bowl. In a flameproof casserole or Dutch oven, heat the remaining ⅓ cup olive oil over medium heat and cook the onion, stirring, until soft and pearly.

3. Measure out 3 cups of broth from the pot. Add the rice to the casserole and stir to combine with the onion and oil. Pour in the hot broth, reduce the heat to medium-low, and simmer the rice until tender, 12 to 15 minutes, adding more broth if necessary.

4. To serve: Spread the rice on a large serving platter and pour the meat and all its pot juices over the rice. Melt the butter until it bubbles up and turns a golden brown and pour the melted butter over the meat just before serving.

Macaroni Pie

MAKARONOPITA

 Makes 6 to 8 servings

This dish, typical of shepherd communities, which always had ample butter, egg-and-milk pasta, and other dairy products on hand, comes from Achaia in the north of the Peloponnesos. The area is both mountainous and coastal. This recipe comes from Angelos Rouvalis, a respected local vintner, who shed light on why so many of Achaia's dishes have little to do with the nearby sea but much to do with shepherd culture. The local population, he says, traces its roots to the mountainous mainland across the Gulf of Corinth.

1 pound thick tubular spaghetti, like bucatini
6 to 8 tablespoons unsalted butter, cut into
    small pieces, as needed

½ pound Greek feta cheese, crumbled
Salt and freshly ground black pepper to taste
½ teaspoon ground cinnamon
10 large eggs
Milk

1. In a large pot, bring ample salted water to a boil, add the pasta, and boil until it is about half cooked. Drain, return to the pot, and toss with 3 to 4 tablespoons of the butter, the cheese, salt, pepper, and cinnamon. Preheat the oven to 350°F.

2. Lightly beat 6 of the eggs together and toss them with the pasta. Place in a large, 12- or 14-inch round by 3-inch deep lightly oiled baking pan. Pour in enough milk to barely cover the pasta. Beat the remaining 4 eggs and pour on top. Dot the surface with 3 to 4 more tablespoons of butter and bake until the surface is golden and the pasta set, about 50 minutes.

Fresh Cheese Pie with Fennel from Kalavryta

MYZITHROPITA KALAVRYTON

 Makes 6 to 8 servings

This dish calls for local myzithra, *a fresh whey cheese made from the residuals of feta production. It is possible to find fresh* myzithra *in Greek food shops across America. It has the consistency of fresh farmer's cheese or good ricotta, which can easily be substituted. The original recipe also calls for wild fennel. I have reworked it to include dill and some fennel seeds instead, since wild fennel is generally available only in specialty shops or via mail order.*

1½ pounds fresh *myzithra* or ¾ pound farmer's
    cheese mixed with ¾ pound fresh whole-milk
    ricotta
4 large eggs, well beaten
1 cup snipped fennel leaves or dill mixed with
    1 teaspoon ground fennel seeds
Salt to taste
¼ cup extra-virgin olive oil

1. Preheat the oven to 350°F. Place the cheese in a bowl and crumble it with a fork until it is mealy and soft. Add the beaten eggs, fennel or dill and fennel seeds, and a little salt. Knead together for several minutes.

2. Oil a 6- by 8-inch tart pan and spread the cheese mixture evenly in the pan. Bake until set and golden, about 45 minutes. Serve hot.

MEAT

In the Peloponnesos the majority of meat dishes are home-spun stews, the kind of food that calls for unsparing amounts of olive oil, which the region produces plenty of. The recipes are by and large simple and the seasonings and spices minimal.

Peloponnesian cooks disparage the use of rich spices, and one finds recipes here that are usually cooked slowly, in a single pot, with tomato—another regional staple—and a few herbs or cinnamon. Artichokes, cultivated extensively in the Peloponnesos, are a favorite addition to meat and chicken dishes, too.

I have tried to stay true to the flavors of the region in the handful of meat, poultry, and game dishes that follow; if my own liking for generous amounts of olive oil is too much for the average American cook, feel free to reduce it. The texture will be different, but the recipes will taste just as

good. You should be privy, though, to the one piece of advice that almost every cook in the region shared with me concerning these and other stewed dishes. By the end of the cooking, they say, the liquid content in the pot should be reduced to the point where the food, whatever it is, "remains only with its oil."

Stuffed Chicken in a Pot

KOTOPOULO YEMISTO STIN KATSAROLA

 Makes 6 servings

Proximity has made the cooking of the Peloponnesos share much in common with that of the Ionian Islands and this dish, just slightly varied, is also found in parts of the Seven Islands.

6 to 8 tablespoons extra-virgin olive oil, as needed
1 chicken liver (optional), trimmed and chopped
2½ cups of 1-inch bread cubes cut from rustic
    bread, crusts removed
3 garlic cloves, finely chopped
Salt and freshly ground black pepper to taste
1 tablespoon dried Greek oregano
¾ cup water
1 tablespoon tomato paste
½ cup grated *kefalotyri* or aged *myzithra* cheese
One 3- to 3½-pound chicken
1½ cups grated tomatoes (see page 459) or
    chopped canned plum tomatoes

1. If using the chicken liver, heat 2 tablespoons of the olive oil in a large, heavy skillet over medium heat and cook the liver, stirring, until brown, 6 to 7 minutes. Remove from the skillet and set aside.

Heat another 2 tablespoons of the oil over medium heat and brown the bread cubes and garlic until both are lightly golden. Season with salt, pepper, and ½ tablespoon of the oregano. Stir for 1 minute. Add the water, return the chicken liver to the skillet, and simmer for another 5 to 7 minutes. Stir the tomato paste into the mixture and cook for 3 to 4 more minutes. Remove from the heat and toss with the grated cheese.

2. Rinse the chicken inside and out with cold running water and fill loosely with the bread stuffing. Sew or skewer closed and season with salt and pepper. Heat the remaining ¼ cup olive oil over medium-high heat in a pot large enough to hold the chicken. Place the chicken in the pot and sear to brown on all sides. Add the tomatoes and enough water to come about a third of the way up the chicken. Cover and simmer until the chicken is tender, about 1½ hours. About 2 minutes before removing, sprinkle in the remaining ½ tablespoon oregano.

3. To serve, place the chicken on a large serving platter and spoon out the stuffing all around it. Pour the pot juices over the bird and stuffing and serve.

One-Pot Chicken Simmered with Artichokes and Served with Tomato-Egg-Lemon Sauce

KOTOPOULO ME ANGINARES

 Makes 4 to 6 servings

I found several recipes, especially in the northern and western Peloponnesos, for chicken or Cornish game hens stewed with artichokes. Some cooks marry this dish with the ubiquitous (in the Peloponnesos) combination of tomatoes and egg-lemon sauce. Others opt for a white version, with plain avgolemono. *I've chosen the former.*

One 3- to 3½-pound chicken, cut into serving
    pieces
Salt and freshly ground black pepper to taste
All-purpose flour for dredging
½ cup extra-virgin olive oil
1 large red onion, finely chopped
2 garlic cloves, finely chopped
1 tablespoon tomato paste
Juice of 1 large lemon
1 teaspoon ground cinnamon, or more
    to taste
1 cup brandy or dry white wine
6 artichokes, cleaned and halved (see page 459)
2 large eggs, lightly beaten
Juice of 2 lemons

1. Season the chicken with salt and pepper and dredge lightly in flour, tapping off any excess. Heat the olive oil in a large, shallow pot such as a Dutch oven over medium-high heat and brown the chicken on all sides. Remove the chicken from the pot, add the onion and garlic, and cook over medium heat, stirring, until wilted, 10 to 12 minutes. Add the tomato paste and stir. Add the lemon juice and stir. Return the chicken pieces to the pot, season with the cinnamon, salt, and pepper, and add the brandy or wine and enough water to come about halfway up the chicken. Cover and simmer over low heat for 35 minutes.

2. Add the artichokes to the pot. Adjust the seasoning with additional salt, pepper, and cinnamon and add more water if necessary to cover the artichokes partially. Cover the pot and simmer the stew over low heat until the artichokes and chicken are both tender, another 25 to 30 minutes.

3. Before serving, make the egg-lemon sauce. Using a wire whisk, beat the eggs and lemon juice in a bowl until frothy. Slowly drizzle in 2 ladlefuls of the pot juices from the chicken, whisking all the while. Pour the mixture into the pot, over and around the chicken, and tilt the pot so that it is distributed evenly. Remove from the heat and let stand for 3 to 5 minutes to thicken. Serve hot.

⊙ Try adding a little chopped fresh rosemary to the sauce in step 2 with the other seasonings; also, with Cornish game hens (*frangokota*) black olives are sometimes added.

Chicken Smothered with Onions and Feta from the Barthounohoria

KOTOPOULO BARTHOUNIOTIKO TOU YIORGOU ZERVOULAKOU

 Makes 6 servings

This recipe is indigenous to the Barthounohoria, a small belt of mountain villages between Sparta and Gythion, in the southern Peloponnesos. For several hundred years before the Greek Revolution these villages were home to Muslim Albanians who had descended into Greece and settled in several places, largely in the Peloponnesos. They evacuated en masse on the eve of the Greek Revolution in 1821. I don't know whether this unusually rich dish is a remnant of their kitchen or if it is inherently Greek. I do know that it is found nowhere else.

This particular recipe comes from a family friend, Yiorgos Zervoulakos, whose native village is one of the Barthounohoria and who considers himself as proud and diehard a Maniot as they come. He has cooked this for me on several occasions, each time imparting the same secret: practically no water. Everything should cook in the onions' own juices. This is a heavy, hearty dish.

One 3- to 3½-pound chicken, cut into serving
    pieces
Salt to taste
¼ cup red wine vinegar
1½ cups extra-virgin olive oil
6 large red onions, finely chopped
Freshly ground black pepper to taste
½ pound Greek feta cheese, crumbled

1. Trim the chicken of excess fat. Place in a large bowl and sprinkle with salt and the vinegar. Set aside.

2. Heat the olive oil in a large pot over medium heat and add the onions. Reduce the heat to very low, cover the pot, and let the onions steam in the oil for about 25 minutes. Check and stir occasionally to keep them from burning or sticking to the bottom of the pot.

3. Drain the chicken and pat dry with paper towels. Remove the onions from the pot with a slotted spoon, leaving as much olive oil behind as possible. Raise the heat a little and brown the chicken pieces, in batches if necessary. Remove from the pot and set aside. Return the onions to the pot, place the chicken pieces on top, and season with salt and pepper. Stir a little so that the onions are all around and on top of the chicken. Cover, reduce the heat to very low, and simmer until the chicken is very well cooked and almost falling off the bone, about 1 hour. During cooking, add a little water if necessary to keep the chicken and onions from burning. Add the crumbled feta to the pot. Cover and cook until the feta is completely melted and the sauce is very thick, another 8 minutes or so. Remove from the heat and serve.

Goat with Onions and Olive Oil
KREAS ASPROYIAHNI

 Makes 6 servings

*P*ast Corinth, *in any direction, the landscape changes dramatically. Along the northern coast, toward Aigio for example, the water is a constant companion, and across the Gulf of Corinth one can see the nearby mainland clearly. Surprisingly, the mainland on the other side has shaped the table of the northern Peloponnesos more than the sea has, mostly because of the many people who emigrated here from Roumeli generations ago. Most were shepherds, so they took to the nearby mountain villages better than to the coast. It is not unusual to find along the northern shores of the Peloponnesos a wealth of dishes for boiled goat, offal, and ram. The shepherd's wisdom runs deep here and is evinced in the most unexpected details. As we sat in a taverna overlooking the sea, the local cook shared with me what seemed like his most cherished advice: "Eunuch rams and virgin goats are the best meat," he whispered.*

Indeed, in this recipe from Aigio, local cooks prefer ewes, rams, or old female goats, none of which is in great supply in America. Plain goat, whatever the butcher has available, will have to do. As for the rest of the title, yiahni *in Greek usually refers to one-pot preparations of meat, beans, or vegetables that are cooked with a plenitude of onions and often with tomatoes.* Asproyiahni *literally translates as "white onions" because the onions are cooked without tomato in this recipe. They simmer for a long time so that they practically melt into the pot juices.*

You'll also notice an interesting and seemingly bizarre technique in this recipe. The meat and onions are boiled together to the point where all the pot juices are cooked off, and then they are browned, basically the opposite of what I have always taken for granted—searing first, to brown, then braising. A lot of Greek cooks use the boil-then-brown method because they say it makes the dish lighter. I'm still not sure if I agree. The onions aren't as sweet when they're boiled. Anyway, I have stayed true to the recipe as it was recounted to me, not because I take a particular stand one way or the other but in the name of preserving old country ways.

2 to 2½ pounds goat meat (shoulder, bone in), preferably from a ewe, cut into stewing pieces

4 large red onions, finely chopped

⅔ cup extra-virgin olive oil

Salt and freshly ground black pepper to taste

1. Trim off the fat and rinse the meat.

2. In a large, wide pot, place the onions and meat with about 3 inches of water. Bring to a boil, reduce the heat to medium-low, and simmer, uncovered, until all the liquid has boiled off, about 45 minutes.

3. Pour the olive oil into the pot, increase the heat to medium, and continue cooking the onions and meat, stirring, until the meat is browned, about 15 minutes. Season generously with salt and pepper and add enough water to the pot to barely cover the meat. Cover and simmer until the meat is very tender and the onions are practically disintegrated, about 1 hour.

Goat Stewed with Onions and Whole Garlic

GITHA STIFATHO

 Makes 6 to 8 servings

Greeks in agrarian communities hold the meat of old female goats in high esteem. No longer fit for rearing kids, their meat is sometimes tough, which means it is perfect for the stew pot or for boiling. In parts of the Peloponnesos and elsewhere, goat stewed simply with onions and garlic is wedding food, prepared in huge cauldrons over vinewood fires by village cooks who specialize in the recipes associated with large communal feasts. This recipe comes from one such cook, Vassilis Papayiorgiou, in a small village in Mantineia, the central mountain plateau of the Peloponnesos. His advice to me was simple enough and direct: "Goat meat stifatho without cumin just doesn't happen," he said. As for the abundance of vinegar poured into the pot: "Go outside and take a deep breath. If you don't get a strong whiff of vinegar from far away, you need to add more."

The proportions in this recipe have been changed to fit the meal plan of an average family.

2½ pounds goat meat (shoulder, bone in), cut into large stewing pieces

1 cup extra-virgin olive oil

2 pounds small boiling onions (about 1 inch in diameter), peeled

10 cloves garlic, peeled

3 small cinnamon sticks

20 allspice berries

2 teaspoons cumin seeds

3 to 4 fresh rosemary sprigs, to taste

3 bay leaves

Salt and freshly ground black pepper to taste
1 cup red wine vinegar
½ cup tomato paste diluted with ½ cup water

1. Wash the goat meat, pat dry with paper towels, and trim off excess fat. Heat about ⅓ cup of olive oil in a large, heavy flameproof casserole over medium-high heat and brown the meat on all sides. Add enough water to cover the meat and bring to a boil. Reduce the heat to medium-low, cover the pot, and simmer the goat for 35 to 40 minutes. Drain, reserving the broth.

2. Add another ⅓ cup of the olive oil to the pot. Place a layer of onions in the bottom of the pot and sprinkle 6 to 7 garlic cloves all around. Toss in a cinnamon stick, about a third of the allspice berries, and a third of the cumin seeds. Add a sprig of the rosemary and one of the bay leaves. Layer some of the meat on top of this, seasoning it lightly with salt and pepper as you go. Continue layering the onions, spices (but save the remaining bay leaves and rosemary) and meat, making sure that the top, last layer is onions.

3. Pour in the remaining olive oil, the vinegar, and diluted tomato paste. Add the remaining 2 bay leaves and rosemary and enough of the reserved goat broth to cover the contents of the pot. Put the lid on, bring the stew to a boil, reduce the heat to low, and simmer very slowly until the meat is completely tender and the onions are practically disintegrated, 1½ to 2 hours. Serve hot.

Arcadian Pork Baked with a Tangy Garlic Sauce

LAGOTO TIS ARCADIAS

Makes 6 servings

This dish is found widely throughout the Peloponnesos, but especially in Arcadia and farther south, in the villages around Sparta. The name is confusing, because lagos *in Greek means "hare," but the dish is made with pork. No one I spoke with in the region could come up with an explanation for the mix-up. A similar recipe calls for rabbit, and my guess is that somehow, over time, the two became interchangeable. Names are misleading in Greece anyhow. There is also a dish by the same name from Cephalonia that calls for rabbit but is entirely different from the one here.*

In any event, the Arcadian lagoto *that follows is an interesting and pungent recipe.*

2 pounds pork shoulder, with bones, trimmed of
    fat and cut into stewing pieces
¼ cup extra-virgin olive oil
3 tablespoons unsalted butter
Salt and freshly ground black pepper to taste
3 tablespoons tomato paste
1 cinnamon stick
1 small head garlic, cloves peeled
⅓ cup red wine vinegar

1. Place the pork in a large pot with enough water to cover it. Bring to a boil, reduce the heat to medium-low, and simmer, covered, skimming the foam off the surface of the water, for 40 minutes. Drain, reserving the broth.

2. In the same pot, heat the olive oil and butter together over medium-high heat. Place the meat back in and brown on all sides. Season with salt and pepper. Add the tomato paste and enough of the reserved broth to almost cover the meat. Add the cinnamon stick, stir, cover, and simmer over low heat for another hour.

3. Meanwhile, using either a mortar and pestle or a food processor, work the garlic to a pulp with a little salt, slowly adding the vinegar and a little of the remaining broth. Pour this mixture into the pot, shake a little, and continue simmering the meat, uncovered, until almost all the pot juices are evaporated, another 20 minutes. There should not be more than about ⅓ cup liquid left in the pot. Remove from the heat and serve immediately.

Pork and Cabbage Stew

HOIRINO ME MAPA

 Makes about 6 servings

Throughout the Peloponnesos, cabbage is referred to colloquially as mapa—*mop!*

½ cup extra-virgin olive oil
2 to 2½ pounds boneless pork, trimmed of fat
 and cut into stewing pieces
2 large onions, grated
2 tablespoons tomato paste diluted with
 3 tablespoons water
Salt and freshly ground black pepper to taste
 (see note)
1 small cabbage

1. Heat ¼ cup of the olive oil in a large stewing pot or Dutch oven and brown the meat on all sides. Remove with a slotted spoon and set aside. Add the

onions to the pot and reduce the heat to low. Cover and steam in the oil until wilted, about 10 minutes. Add the diluted tomato paste and stir.

2. Place the meat back in the pot. Season with salt and pepper. Pour in enough water to cover the meat. Cover the pot and increase the heat to high. As soon as the liquid comes to a boil, reduce the heat to low and simmer for 1 hour.

3. Meanwhile, cut the cabbage in half, remove the core, and cut each half into strips about 1½ inches wide. Break apart the leaves, then wash and drain the cabbage thoroughly. Add to the pot and toss to combine thoroughly with the meat. Adjust the seasoning with additional salt and pepper and add the remaining olive oil. Cover and simmer until the cabbage and meat are very tender, another 45 minutes or so.

✳ **NOTE** Because the cabbage makes this dish relatively sweet, it tends to need a fair amount of salt.

Roasted Leg of Lamb with Wine, Garlic, Allspice, and Cheese

ARNI KRASATO

 Makes 4 to 6 servings

This is another Sunday and festive specialty of the Peloponnesos. It is usually made in the spring with young lambs, not more than three or four months old.

One 3- to 4-pound leg of spring (baby) lamb,
 bone in, trimmed of fat
3 to 4 garlic cloves, to taste, peeled and minced

1 teaspoon ground allspice

¼ pound *kefalotyri* or any hard yellow cheese, coarsely grated

Salt and freshly ground black pepper to taste

1 cup extra-virgin olive oil

1 cup dry white wine, or more as needed

2 to 3 pounds small all-purpose potatoes, such as Yukon Gold, peeled and halved

1. Preheat the oven to 375°F. With a sharp paring knife, make small incisions all over the surface of the lamb.

2. Grind the garlic and allspice together in a mortar or an electric spice mill, then combine in a bowl with the cheese. Press a pinchful of the mixture deep into each of the incisions until the spice-and-cheese mixture is used up and all the incisions are stuffed. Season generously with salt and pepper.

3. Heat ½ cup of the olive oil in a large, wide roasting pan (something big enough to fit the leg) over medium-high heat and sear the lamb until golden, turning frequently to brown on all sides. Pour in the wine. As soon as it steams, remove the pan from the heat.

4. Place the potatoes around the lamb and season generously with salt and pepper. Drizzle the remaining ½ cup olive oil over the potatoes. Roast until the lamb is cooked to the desired doneness, 45 minutes to 1 hour. Remove from the oven and cover with aluminum foil to keep warm. If necessary, continue roasting the potatoes, adding water or wine to the pan to keep them from burning. Carve the lamb and serve.

Easter Lamb Roasted with Artichokes and Potatoes from the Mani

PASCHALIATIKO ARNI ME ANGINARES STO FOURNO

 Makes 4 to 6 servings

What is unusual about this recipe is the conspicuous absence of garlic and the addition of artichokes to the roasting pan. Christos Koukoutsis, from the small village of Doloi, was adamant about the garlic when he explained to me how to make his village's Easter specialty. Olive oil—lots of it—is essential.

3 to 4 fresh rosemary sprigs, to taste

Salt and freshly ground black pepper to taste

1 cup extra-virgin olive oil

One 3- to 4-pound leg of spring lamb, bone in, trimmed of fat

2 pounds all-purpose potatoes, such as Yukon Gold, peeled and quartered

Juice of 4 to 6 lemons, to taste

12 artichokes, cleaned (see page 459)

1. Preheat the oven to 375°F. In a mortar, crush together the leaves from one rosemary sprig, a scant teaspoon salt, a little pepper, and about ⅓ cup of the olive oil. Rub this mixture all over the lamb, then season generously with additional salt and pepper.

2. Place the lamb on a rack in a large roasting pan. Place the potatoes in the pan, toss with the remaining olive oil, add a cup of water, and season generously with salt and pepper. Add the remaining rosemary sprigs and half the lemon juice and mix in. Roast for about 30 minutes, tossing the potatoes occasionally and basting the lamb with the pan juices. Add the cleaned artichokes and a little more of the lemon juice and toss with the potatoes in the pan. Continue roasting, basting every 10 to 15 minutes, until the lamb is cooked to the desired doneness, 30 to 40 minutes. Greeks like their lamb medium-well, which will take about 1 hour and 10 minutes from start to finish. Season with additional salt, pepper, or lemon juice. Remove from the oven, let the meat stand for 20 minutes to settle the juices, then carve.

Rabbit with Creamy Garlic Sauce

KOUNELI SKORDALIA

 Makes 4 to 6 servings

The combination of meat—especially rabbit or, better yet, hare—with copious amounts of garlic is much loved throughout the central and southern Peloponnesos. My friend Takis Petrakos, a Spartan by birth, first described this dish to me, which he remembered fondly from his childhood in the 1930s and 1940s. As I traveled around the mountainous region of Arcadia, then down into Sparta and other parts of Laconia, mention of this dish came up again and again. It is traditionally made with wild hare, not rabbit. I finally got to taste the gentrified version (with rabbit) in a small taverna outside of Sparta. It is strong stuff, redolent of garlic and thick with tomato sauce.

1 rabbit, about 2½ pounds, cut into serving
    pieces
Red wine vinegar
Salt and freshly ground black pepper to taste

½ cup extra-virgin olive oil
½ cup tomato paste diluted with ½ cup water
1 cinnamon stick
½ teaspoon whole cloves

For the garlic sauce
Three 1-inch-thick slices stale rustic bread,
    crusts removed
½ cup walnut halves
½ cup blanched almonds
4 to 6 garlic cloves, to taste, peeled
Salt to taste
⅔ cup extra-virgin olive oil
⅓ to ½ cup red wine vinegar, to taste

1. Wash the rabbit and place it in a large bowl with enough red wine vinegar to cover. Refrigerate for at least 3 hours or overnight. Remove from the vinegar, pat dry with paper towels, and season with salt and pepper.

2. Heat the olive oil in a large, deep ovenproof skillet or Dutch oven over medium-high heat and brown the rabbit pieces on all sides, in batches if necessary. Add enough water to the pot to come about halfway up the rabbit and simmer over medium heat until about two thirds of the liquid has boiled off, about 25 minutes. Strain the liquid, and reserve.

3. Add the diluted tomato paste, cinnamon, and cloves to the pot with the rabbit. Add enough water to cover the rabbit, cover the pot, and bring to a boil. Reduce the heat to medium-low and braise the meat for 45 minutes.

4. Preheat the oven to 350°F. Make the garlic sauce: Dampen the bread under the tap and squeeze dry. Break into crumbs and set aside. Place the nuts and garlic in a food processor and pulse on and off until mealy. Add the bread and pulse to combine. Season with salt. Add the olive oil, vinegar, and reserved rabbit broth in alternating streams a little at a time, pulsing until the mixture is thick and creamy, adding water if necessary to achieve the consistency of a very thick batter.

5. Pour the *skordalia* over the rabbit. Transfer the pot to the oven and bake until the sauce is very thick, almost set, 15 to 20 minutes more. Remove from the oven and serve.

Quails in Bread

ORTYKIA STO PSOMI

 Makes 4 servings

There is something medieval about this old hunter's recipe that calls for whole (unboned) quails baked in a loaf of fresh bread, which was essentially made with leftover dough from the weekly or biweekly home cooks' routine of baking a quantity of bread for the family. I wish I could have heeded the advice of Christos Koukoutsis, the avid Maniot hunter who gave me the recipe and who warned that "only August quails should be used. They're fat then, and it's their fat that makes the bread taste so good." I wish, too, that I could recommend one keep on hand a ball of Maniot sourdough, made with flour from local wheat and baked in an olive wood–burning oven. As with so many old and truly regional dishes, replicating them in a modern kitchen inevitably means compromising.

Nevertheless, after thinking that I had discovered one of the most unusual recipes in all of Greece, I learned from my colleague and fellow Greek cookbook author Evy Voutsina that this dish also goes by the name kozouna, *which refers to the bread itself.*

Unique bread traditions exist in almost every pocket of the Mani. Kozouna is made into either anthropomorphic loaves or round ones, which are stuffed.

For the bread
6 cups bread flour, or more if needed
One envelope active dry yeast
2½ cups warm water
1 scant tablespoon salt
2 to 3 tablespoons extra-virgin olive oil, as needed

For the quail
4 quail
½ cup extra-virgin olive oil
Salt and freshly ground black pepper to taste
Juice of 1 lemon

1. Make the bread: Start early in the day. Place 1 cup of the flour in a medium bowl. Add the yeast and mix in 1 cup of the warm water. Let stand in a warm, draft-free place until the mixture bubbles and swells, about 1 hour.

2. In the bowl of a stand mixer fitted with a dough hook, combine the remaining 5 cups flour and the salt. Make a well in the center and add the yeast mixture and the remaining 1½ cups warm water. Mix and knead with the dough hook until the dough is solid and silky to the touch, about 10 minutes at medium speed. Add a little more flour during kneading if necessary for the dough to be smooth. Remove from the bowl, knead a little by hand on a lightly floured work surface, and shape into a ball.

You can also mix the dough by hand. Mix the remaining 5 cups of flour and salt together in a large bowl and make a well in the center. Add the yeast mixture and remaining 1½ cups of warm water. Work the flour into the well from the perimeter inward using a fork or large wooden spoon. Knead, either in a bowl or on a lightly floured surface, adding flour if necessary, until the dough is smooth and dense. It will take 10 to 15 minutes to prepare. Shape into a ball.

Pour the olive oil into a large bowl and turn the dough in the oil to coat. Cover with a clean cloth and let rise in a warm, draft-free place until doubled in bulk, about 2 hours.

3. Meanwhile, prepare the quail: With tweezers, remove any feathers that may still be attached to the birds. Wash and pat dry the birds with paper towels. Using a sharp boning knife, split the breast lengthwise and open the quail so they are butterflied. Remove the backbone and as many of the tiny rib bones as possible. Remove the innards. Place the quail in a small bowl and toss with the olive oil, salt, pepper, and lemon juice. Leave them to marinate in the refrigerator until the dough has risen.

4. Divide the dough into 2 equal balls and punch down on a lightly floured work surface. Flatten each half with your hands, pushing the dough outward with the tips of your fingers to form a large circle about 10 inches in diameter and 1 inch thick. Place the quail over one of the dough circles and pour the marinade over them. Cover with the second dough circle, joining the edges by kneading them or folding them under to close. Place in an oiled baking pan and let stand at room temperature for 30 minutes. Meanwhile, preheat the oven to 400°F. Bake the quail in bread until the bread is golden, 45 to 55 minutes. Remove from the oven, let cool for 20 minutes, and cut into wedges as you would a pie.

QUAIL IN THE MANI

For eons, quail have captured the Maniot imagination as much as Maniots have captured quail. Game in the southern Peloponnesos, especially small birds, has always been an important way for locals to enrich their impoverished diets with much-needed protein. At the southern tip of the Mani there is a tiny old fishing village and port called Porto Kagio—Bay of Quail—so named because here, until DDT and other twentieth-century chemicals ravaged the ecosystem, the tiny birds would stop to rest by the hundreds of thousands on their yearly migration back and forth from Africa. They were so tired that locals could forgo the shotgun in favor of the net to catch them. Villagers ran a bustling if seasonal business in quail, putting them up in salt and olive oil, packing them in tins or amphorae, and sending them off for export, usually to Italy.

The whole business ground to a halt in the 1960s, but the local appetite for game is apparent in the many dishes one still finds in homes and tavernas all over the region. I drove to Porto Kagio to see for myself the place once so renowned for its quail, but it was the return journey north that gave me the opportunity firsthand to realize how important the hunt continues to be for the local table and for local trade. The dull thump of shotgun fire followed us everywhere as we drove north. It was early evening by the time we stopped at a *cafeneion* in Melissa, a small village a few kilometers outside Gythion. There a table full of hunters who had just returned from their late-afternoon sojourn were discussing the day's catch and the price each bird fetches at the butcher shops in Sparta, where they sell their bounty. The prices were dear—anywhere between six and nine dollars a bird.

Quail Preserved in Olive Oil

ORTYKIA PASTA

Makes 4 servings

8 quail
Coarse kosher or sea salt
Zest of 1 orange, cut into thick strips
Extra-virgin olive oil

1. Rinse the quail and remove any feathers that still might be attached to the birds. Using a sharp boning knife, butterfly the birds by slitting them slightly down the center, running the knife along the breastbone. Place in layers in a colander, set in a large bowl and sprinkle ample salt, enough to cover the birds like snow, over each layer. Let the birds drain overnight in the refrigerator.

2. The next day, shake off any excess salt. Place the quail in a large pot with enough water to cover by several inches. Add the orange zest. Bring to a boil, reduce the heat to medium-low, and simmer the quail for about 45 minutes. Drain.

3. Place the quail in a large glass jar together with the orange zest. Pour in enough olive oil to cover them. Let the birds cool with the jar lid off, then keep in the refrigerator. They will keep this way for at least a month.

To serve, remove them from the oil and place on a plate. Serve with bread, olives, cheese, or any other simple *mezethes*.

FISH AND SEAFOOD

Salt cod has always played a seminal role in this region's cooking, and I will corroborate that statement by including many of the local dishes that use cod. It might seem odd that a preserved fish claims its place as a protagonist on the local table, since the Peloponnesos has a long and fertile coast, and fish in the villages and towns along the coast was never scarce. But inland, where dense, impassable mountains made access to the sea difficult, roving merchants would often sell lots of preserved seafood; first among them, mainly because traditionally it was cheap, was cod. The way it is cooked—with raisins, with greens, with beans, etc., and always with lots of olive oil—mirrors the way other dishes are prepared in this part of Greece as well. As I have said throughout these pages, and as any researcher of regional food customs anywhere in the world would attest, local culinary customs evolve out of what is most readily available. Raisins, olive oil, and vegetables were always staples in the Peloponnesian kitchen.

There are some unusual recipes here, too, for fish and seafood cooked *en papillote;* the term used locally comes from the Turkish, *yioulbasi.*

I have included two recipes for one of the classics of Greek fish cookery, *savoro,* which is essentially small fried fish preserved in a sweet-and-sour sauce. It isn't unique to the Peloponnesos by any means, but it is cooked more here than perhaps anywhere else in Greece, so I thought it fitting that it should be included in this chapter.

All the fish dishes are simple and easy to prepare. You might consider looking for some regional wines to accompany them, from the areas of Nemea or Mantineia. Several are now being exported.

Salt Cod Cooked with Tomatoes, Onions, and Raisins

BAKALIARO PLAKI

 Makes 4 to 6 servings

1 piece salt cod fillet, about 2 pounds
½ to ⅔ cup extra-virgin olive oil, to taste
1½ pounds red onions, chopped
2 to 3 garlic gloves, to taste, chopped
2 tablespoons tomato paste, diluted with
  ¼ cup water
1 cup dark raisins
1 cinnamon stick
10 to 15 whole cloves, to taste
10 allspice berries
Freshly ground black pepper to taste

1. Rehydrate the salt cod as on page 463 and cut into 2-inch squares.

2. Heat the olive oil in a large casserole or Dutch oven over medium heat and cook the onions, stirring, until wilted, about 10 minutes. Add the garlic and stir for a minute. Add the diluted tomato paste, raisins, and spices. Add enough water to cover the onions. Reduce the heat to medium-low and simmer the onions, covered, for 15 to 20 minutes, until very tender. Place the fish on top, cover, and simmer until the cod is fork-tender, another 15 to 20 minutes. Serve immediately.

Salt Cod with Vegetables and Greens

BAKALIARO ME LAHANIKA KAI HORTA

 Makes 4 to 6 servings

Cod stewed with greens is a dish found throughout both the Peloponnesos and the Ionian Islands. This recipe comes from Molaous, a town in the southern Peloponnesos between Sparta and Monemvassia.

1 piece salt cod fillet, about 2 pounds
½ cup extra-virgin olive oil
1 bunch scallions, white and tender green parts,
  chopped
1 medium leek, white part only, washed well
  and chopped
1 large carrot, peeled and chopped
1 large green bell pepper, seeded and
  chopped
2 tablespoons tomato paste, diluted with
  2 tablespoons water
2 pounds mixed greens (spinach, chard, wild
  celery, wild fennel, dill, parsley), trimmed,
  coarsely chopped, and washed well
1 tablespoon all-purpose flour mixed with
  3 tablespoons water
Freshly ground black pepper and salt to taste

1. Rehydrate the salt cod as on page 463 and cut into 2-inch squares.

2. Heat the olive oil in a large pot over medium heat. Add the scallions, leek, carrot, and pepper, cover the pot, reduce the heat to very low, and cook until tender, 12 to 15 minutes.

3. Add the diluted tomato paste and stir together with the wilted vegetables for a minute. Add the greens to the pot and stir with a wooden spoon. Keep the cover askew and cook over low heat until the greens are wilted and tender about 10 minutes. Add the cod to the pot, tossing it gently with the greens and vegetables, and cook, with the cover askew, over medium-low heat until the cod is fork-tender and the greens extremely soft, about 15 minutes. Add the flour slurry to the pot, stirring well but gently to combine with the cod, greens, and vegetables. Simmer until the pot juices thicken, another 5 to 8 minutes. Season with pepper and salt if necessary (it may be salty enough from the cod) and serve hot.

Salt Cod Stewed with Garden Vegetables

BAKALIARO ME ZARZAVATIKA

 Makes 4 to 6 servings

In several parts of the Peloponnesos, but most notably in Kalamata, there are many recipes for dried salt cod served up with either legumes or vegetable stew. I've seen the fish cooked with spinach, with squash or squash blossoms, with chard, and with fresh green beans. The recipe that follows calls for the long thin light-purple eggplant that is native to the Peloponnesos and similar to what we know in America as Japanese eggplant.

1 piece salt cod fillet, about 2½ pounds
1 cup all-purpose flour for dredging
Salt and freshly ground black pepper to taste
Olive oil for frying plus 3 tablespoons
1 pound large green bell peppers, seeded and cut into ¼-inch-wide strips
1 pound long, thin eggplant, cut into ½-inch cubes

2½ pounds tomatoes, peeled, seeded, and chopped
Pinch of sugar (optional)

1. Rehydrate the salt cod as on page 463 and cut into 2-inch squares.

2. Season the flour with salt and pepper and dredge the salt cod pieces in it, tapping off any excess. Heat ½ inch of olive oil in a large, heavy skillet over medium-high heat. When the oil is very hot, fry the cod, in batches if necessary, until golden, about 5 minutes. Remove with a slotted spoon and drain on paper towels.

3. In a large clean skillet, heat 3 tablespoons olive oil over medium heat and cook the peppers and eggplant together, stirring, until soft, about 10 minutes. Add the tomatoes, season with salt and pepper, and bring to a boil. Reduce the heat to medium-low, cover, and simmer for 15 to 20 minutes. Taste the vegetable mixture; if the eggplant is a little bitter, add the sugar.

4. Place the fried cod on top of the vegetables, shaking the skillet a little so that the fish and vegetables combine slightly. Simmer the fish and vegetables together for about 5 minutes so that the flavors meld. Remove from the heat and serve hot.

Vine Leaves Stuffed with Salt Cod and Served with Tomato-Flavored Egg-and-Lemon Sauce

DOLMATHES ME BAKALIARO KAI
TOMATENIO AVGOLEMONO

 Makes about 70 *dolmathes*; enough for 8 to 10 servings

In the interior of the Peloponnesos, where fresh fish was rare, dried fish such as cod became staples. This is an interesting dish from Sparta that generally is found in the whole of Laconia. Seldom in other parts of Greece is fish used as filling for vine leaves, although vine leaves are used to wrap fish such as sardines destined for the grill.

1 piece salt cod fillet, about 2½ pounds
One 22-ounce jar vine leaves in brine
½ cup extra-virgin olive oil
3 cups finely chopped white and tender green parts of scallions
½ cup long-grain rice, preferably basmati
3 large firm, ripe tomatoes, peeled, seeded, and finely chopped or grated (see page 459)
Salt and freshly ground black pepper to taste
½ cup finely chopped fresh mint
½ cup finely chopped fresh flat-leaf parsley
3 large eggs
Juice of 2 lemons

1. Rehydrate the salt cod as on page 463.

2. When ready, rinse the vine leaves in a colander. Blanch in batches if necessary for about 3 minutes to soften. Drain, rinse under cold running water, and snip away the tough stems.

3. Shred the cod. Heat ¼ cup of the olive oil in a large, heavy skillet over medium heat and cook the scallions, stirring, until wilted. Add the shredded cod and rice. Reduce the heat to low and stir to combine. Add one third of the grated tomatoes and ½ cup water and cook the mixture over very low heat until the liquid has been absorbed, 5 to 7 minutes. Remove from the heat and let cool slightly. Season with salt and pepper, add the chopped mint and parsley, and stir in one egg, lightly beaten.

4. Remove the shredded or torn vine leaves and place enough of them on the bottom of an oiled pot to cover the surface. To expedite the rolling, place as many of the remaining leaves as will fit on a table or work surface. Make sure the leaves are vein side up. Place a scant tablespoon of the filling in the bottom center of each of the vine leaves. Fold up the bottom to cover the filling, then fold in the sides and roll up. Place the stuffed vine leaves seam side down in the pot so that they fit snugly next to one another either in rows or concentrically.

5. Pour in the remaining ¼ cup olive oil, the remaining chopped tomatoes, half the lemon juice, and as much water as needed to barely cover the rolled leaves. Cut a piece of parchment paper to the circumference of the pot and place it over the *dolmathes*. Gently slip one or two plates on top to keep them secure in their place. Cover the pot and bring to a boil. Reduce the heat to low and simmer the vine leaves until both leaves and rice are tender, about 45 minutes.

6. Prepare the egg-lemon sauce: Whisk together the remaining 2 eggs and the remaining lemon juice in a small bowl. Uncover the pot and remove the plates and parchment. Tilt the pot and dip a ladle into it to collect the juices. Slowly add the ladleful of the pot juices to the egg-and-lemon mixture, whisking all the while. Repeat with a second ladleful of juices. Pour the mixture back into the pot, shaking gently from side to side to distribute the *avgolemono* everywhere, and serve hot.

Fish Stew with Onions and Pepper

BOURIETO

 Makes 4 servings

*B*ourieto *to the denizens of the northern coast of the Peloponnesos is* bourtheto *to the Seven Islanders. The recipes differ substantially for this savory fish stew, but in both cases they take their names from the Italian* brodetto, *broth. There has always been a lot of trade and contact between the Ionian Islands and the Peloponnesos, and many recipes found in one place are also found in the other, even if in a slightly different version. In the Ionian the traditional* bour-theto *can be made with almost any creature of the sea—from cod to octopus, which is much revered. It is a juicy stew redolent of red pepper—either sweet paprika or cayenne—and it often calls for an abundance of leeks. In the northern Peloponnesos, the rendition is decidedly simpler. First, it is almost always made with small fresh cod—whiting to Americans. It also calls for black, not red, pepper, and its fieriness is very much a matter of taste. There is a small fish taverna in Aigio that locals claim makes the best* bourieto *in the world. The owner wouldn't part with her recipe, but I was lucky enough to find her friend, Dina Varthaki, who did, claiming she'd seen it made a thousand times. Dina's only caveat: "The success of* bourieto *depends on the amount of onions and the degree to which they are boiled."*

1½ to 2 pounds fresh whiting, gutted and
    washed
Salt and freshly ground black pepper to taste
1 cup extra-virgin olive oil
3 cups coarsely chopped red onions

⅓ cup fresh lemon juice
1 cup water

1. Season the fish with salt and pepper and set aside. Heat the olive oil in a large pot over medium heat and add the onion. Reduce the heat to medium-low and cook the onion in the oil until softened, 5 to 7 minutes. Sprinkle with salt, pepper, and half the lemon juice. Add ½ cup of the water. Cover and simmer the onion over very low heat until very soft, about 15 minutes.

2. Place the whiting on top of the onion in the pot. Add the remaining lemon juice and water. Cover and simmer over low heat until the fish are cooked, about 25 minutes. The sauce should be thick from the disintegrated onions and rich with the flavor of the fish. Remove from the heat and serve.

Small Fish in a Sweet and Savory Sauce

PSARI SAVORO

 Makes 4 servings

*S*avoro, *from the Italian for "savory" or "tasty," is a name given to small fried fish that are marinated in a pungent sauce. Red mullet is the most common fish for* savoro, *but in the northern coastal parts of the Peloponnesos, especially around Aigio, a mix of fish—mullet, small mackerel, whiting, bogue, and anchovy—is preferred. Depending on the region, the sauce may or may not contain tomatoes. In some versions rosemary is the dominant seasoning; in others, bay leaf; onion and garlic appear; raisins are a standard in certain parts of the Peloponnesos but not in others. The one constant, regardless of where the* savoro *is from, is vinegar. The tangy, pungent sauce probably evolved as a way to preserve fried fish for a few days, even weeks. In the Peloponnesos, especially in the vineyards of Mantineia,* savoro *was the traditional workers' lunch during the grape harvest. No matter where it is made,* savoro *is always eaten at room temperature.*

1½ pounds small fish (red mullet, whiting, small
    mackerel, anchovy, or bogue)
Salt and freshly ground black pepper to taste
All-purpose flour for dredging and thickening
Olive oil for frying, plus ⅓ cup extra-virgin olive
    oil for sauce
2 large red onions, chopped
2 to 3 garlic cloves, to taste, minced
4 large tomatoes, grated (see page 459)
1 cup water
1 fresh rosemary sprig
½ cup red wine vinegar

1. Wash and gut the fish, then pat dry with paper towels. Season with salt and pepper. Dredge the fish lightly in flour, tapping off any excess. Heat about ¾ inch of olive oil in a large, heavy skillet over medium-high heat and, when the oil is very hot, fry the fish until golden on both sides, 8 to 12 minutes, depending on the size. Remove with a slotted spoon and set aside on paper towels to drain.

2. Pour the oil from the skillet, scrape out any burned flour, and wipe the skillet dry. Heat the extra-virgin olive oil over medium heat and cook the onions and garlic, stirring, until soft, 8 to 10 minutes. Sprinkle in 1 scant tablespoon of flour and stir continuously until the flour turns a light golden. Be careful not to burn. Add the grated tomatoes and season with salt and pepper. Add the water and rosemary and bring to a boil. Reduce the heat to low and simmer, stirring with a wooden spoon, for 8 to 10 minutes. Stir in the vinegar and remove from the heat. Let the sauce cool to room temperature.

3. Place the fish in a large container with a tight-fitting lid and cover with the sauce. Refrigerate overnight before serving. Serve at room temperature.

⊙

Savory "White" Marinated Fish from Aigio

SAVORO ASPRO

 Makes 4 servings

1 pound mixed small fish (whiting, bogue,
    anchovy, red mullet, etc.)
Salt and freshly ground black pepper to taste
All-purpose flour for dredging and thickening
Olive oil for frying, plus ⅓ cup extra-virgin
    olive oil for sauce
3 garlic cloves, peeled and crushed
1 cup water
1 fresh rosemary twig
2 bay leaves
1 cup white wine vinegar

1. Gut and wash the fish, then pat dry with paper towels. Season with salt and pepper and dredge lightly in flour. Heat about ¾ inch of olive oil in a large, heavy skillet over medium-high heat and, when the oil is very hot, fry the fish in batches until golden on both sides. Remove with a slotted spoon and set aside on paper towels to drain. Pour off the oil.

2. Scrape any burned flour from the skillet. Wipe dry. Heat the extra-virgin oil over medium heat and add the garlic. Cook for a minute. Sprinkle in 1 scant tablespoon of flour and stir constantly until the flour turns light golden. Add the water, rosemary, and bay leaves and bring to a boil. Reduce the heat to low and simmer, stirring, for 5 minutes. Add the vinegar, simmer for 1 to 2 minutes, and remove from the heat. Let the marinade cool to room temperature.

3. Place the fish in a large container with a tight-fitting lid and pour the marinade over them. Let set overnight or for several days in the refrigerator before removing bay leaves and serving at room temperature.

Bonito Baked in Paper

PALAMITHA YIOULBASI

 Makes 4 to 6 servings

I got this recipe from an old cruise ship chef in Neapoli, a town on the southern coast of the Peloponnesos known for, among other things, the predominant profession of its local sons: A whole generation of sailor-cooks came from here.

1½ to 2 pounds bonito or other small tuna,
    boned
½ cup extra-virgin olive oil
Salt and freshly ground black pepper to taste
4 to 5 garlic cloves, to taste, minced
1 cup chopped fresh flat-leaf parsley
½ pound *kefalotyri* cheese or any hard yellow
    cheese, diced
2 large tomatoes, each cut into 8 wedges

1. Cut as many sheets of parchment paper and aluminum foil as there are fish, each big enough to wrap one up in. Place each sheet of parchment on top of a sheet of aluminum foil. Preheat the oven to 350°F.

2. Rub each fish with a little of the olive oil and season with salt and pepper. Place one fish in the center of each sheet of parchment. Top the fish with a little garlic, parsley, and cheese. Place several pieces of the cut tomatoes on top of each. Fold up the parchment so that it encloses the fish entirely, almost like an envelope. Wrap each in aluminum foil, place in a shallow baking pan, and bake until the fish is completely cooked and fork-tender, about 35 minutes. Immediately serve on individual plates.

Octopus Baked in Paper

OCTOPUS YIOULBASI

 Makes 4 to 8 *meze* servings

Traditionally this recipe calls for hanging a fresh octopus out to dry in the sun for a day so that its liquid drains and its flavor intensifies. One can do this easily enough if the weather is warm and sunny. If not, hang the octopus over the kitchen sink for a day or two or cook it in a dry pot until it exudes all its juices.

1 medium octopus (about 2½ pounds)
¼ cup olive oil
3 garlic cloves, very thinly sliced
⅓ cup chopped fresh flat-leaf parsley
Freshly ground black pepper to taste

1. Wash the octopus and pat dry. Rub the octopus with a little olive oil and hang on a clothesline outdoors in hot weather for 24 hours. If this is impossible, clean the octopus (remove the hood and beak, page 462) and place it in a dry pot. Heat over a very low heat until the octopus has exuded all its liquid, about 45 minutes. Drain well.

2. Have a large sheet of parchment or wax paper ready. Preheat the oven to 350°F. Place the octopus on the parchment. Sprinkle it with the garlic, parsley, and pepper and wrap it in the parchment. Place in a lightly oiled baking pan and bake the octopus until tender, 35 to 45 minutes. Transfer to a serving platter and serve immediately, cutting it into pieces along its tentacles.

BREAD

Traditional New Year's and Wedding Bread from Mantineia

BOGATSA

 Makes one 18-inch round loaf

8 to 10 cups all-purpose flour, as needed
3 cups sugar
1 teaspoon baking powder
1 teaspoon baking soda
8 large eggs
½ cup plus 2 tablespoons extra-virgin olive oil
1 cup warm water
⅓ cup ouzo
Sesame seeds or slivered blanched almonds for
    garnish

1. Combine 8 cups of the flour, the sugar, baking powder, and baking soda in a large bowl or basin. Make a well in the center and add the eggs, ½ cup of the olive oil, the water, and the ouzo. Stir with a wooden spoon to combine. Start kneading, adding more flour if necessary, until a smooth, firm dough forms. Knead for 10 to 12 minutes, or until the dough is silky. Form into a ball, and let the dough rest in the bowl, covered, for a half hour.

2. Preheat the oven to 400°F. Lightly oil an 18-by 3-inch round baking pan with the remaining 2 tablespoons olive oil. Roll the dough out to the circumference of the pan on a lightly floured work surface. The dough shouldn't be more than about 1 inch thick. Fit it into the pan. Using the backs of 2 spoons, or simply your fingers, pinch the surface of the *bogatsa* decoratively. Sprinkle with sesame seeds or almonds and bake until golden, 45 to 50 minutes. Remove from the oven and cool on a rack.

Cheese Bread from Laconia

PROTSOUMA

 Makes 6 to 8 servings

Haralambos, my schoolteacher friend in Molaous, told me all about the breads of his childhood as we drove south from Monemvassia to Neapoli in Laconia. I drove, he talked. It is hard to absorb information while concentrating on making it past the hairpin turns of most Greek country roads, but I did manage to glean a sense of some of the old dishes that have been lost in the name of convenience. Not everything dies so easily, though. In Neapoli, he took us to a tiny taverna owned by a friend whose mother still makes a few of the region's bygone dishes. This cheese bread was one of them. It used to be prepared either for breakfast or as an early evening snack. Now its place has been moved up to the meze *table, together with a host of other small plates served as appetizers.*

6 to 7 cups all-purpose flour, as needed
1⅓ cups extra-virgin olive oil
1 teaspoon baking soda
1 cup warm water
⅔ pound *kefalotyri* or any hard yellow cheese, coarsely grated

1. Place 6 cups of the flour in a large bowl or basin and drizzle with the olive oil. Using your fingertips, work the oil into the dough until it becomes coarse and mealy.

2. Dissolve the baking soda in the water. Make a well in the center of the flour and add the soda mixture. Add the cheese and knead all together until a soft, smooth dough forms. Add a little more flour as you knead if dough is too sticky.

3. Preheat the oven to 450°F. Oil a large baking pan or sheet pan. Shape the dough into a large ball and spread it into the pan with your fingertips to form a circle about 15 inches in diameter. Make indentations in the surface as you go. Bake the cheese bread until golden, 30 to 40 minutes. Remove from the oven and the pan and cool on a rack. Serve warm or at room temperature.

Christmas Bread

CHRISTOPSOMO APO TIN PELOPONNISO

 Makes two 12-inch round loaves

For the starter
1 teaspoon active dry yeast
1 cup warm water
3 cups unbleached all-purpose flour

For the dough
8 to 10 cups all-purpose flour, as needed
1 cup sugar
Salt
¾ cup extra-virgin olive oil
1½ cups warm water, or more if necessary
½ cup ouzo
1½ cups coarsely chopped walnuts
1½ cups coarsely chopped golden raisins
10 whole unshelled walnuts for garnish

1. Begin to make the starter 1 to 2 days ahead: In a large bowl, dissolve the yeast in ½ cup of the warm water and mix to combine. Let stand until creamy, about 10 minutes. Add the remaining ½ cup water and stir in the flour. Mix until a dough mass forms, adding a little more flour if necessary to make it smooth. Cover with plastic wrap and let the starter stand at room temperature for 1 to 2 days; it will rise and then fall back on itself and turn slightly sour.

2. Prepare the dough for the bread: Combine 8 cups of the flour, the sugar, and salt in a large bowl or basin. Add the olive oil and work the mixture with your fingertips until it is coarse and mealy. Make a well in the center and pour in the warm water, ouzo, chopped nuts, and raisins. Break the starter up into small pieces, adding them to the well. Mix to combine with a wooden spoon, then knead well on a lightly floured work surface until the dough is smooth and soft, about 12 minutes, adding more flour if needed to achieve the proper texture. Cover and let rise in a warm, draft-free place until doubled in bulk, about 2½ hours.

3. Punch the dough back down. Remove a fist-size piece and set aside. Shape the remaining dough into 2 equal balls, flatten each a little with your hands, and place in 2 oiled 12-inch round pans. Press 5 walnuts, forming a cross, into each of the loaves. Take the fistful of dough you've set aside and roll it into thin, round (not flat like fettuccine) strips. Cut and wrap around each of the walnuts to secure. Let the dough rise again. Meanwhile, preheat the oven to 400°F. When the dough is swollen and almost doubled, place in the oven and bake until golden, about 45 minutes. Remove from oven and pans and cool completely on a wire rack.

Pencil-Thin Dough Fritters

LALANGIA

 Makes about 120 fritters

These are the signature fritters of the southern Peloponnesos, piled high in bakeries and sweet shops, made at home around Christmas, and savored with either honey or grated cheese. They are made with a basic bread dough, leavened with homemade starter. It is a process that requires some time, but overall it is easy.

For the starter
1 teaspoon active dry yeast
1 cup warm water
3 cups unbleached all-purpose flour

For the dough
8 to 10 cups all-purpose flour, as needed
1 teaspoon salt
2 teaspoons baking powder
1½ cups extra-virgin olive oil
1 cup warm water, or more if necessary

To fry and serve
Olive oil and/or vegetable oil
Honey or grated sharp cheese

1. Begin to make the starter 1 to 2 days ahead: In a large bowl, dissolve the yeast in ½ cup of the warm water and mix to combine. Let stand until creamy, about 10 minutes. Add the remaining ½ cup warm water and stir in the flour. Mix until a dough mass forms, adding a little more flour if necessary. Cover with plastic wrap and let the starter stand at room temperature for 1 to 2 days; it will rise and then fall back on itself and turn slightly sour.

2. Prepare the dough for the fritters: Combine 8 cups of the flour, the salt, and baking powder in a large bowl or basin. Drizzle in the olive oil and rub with your fingertips, working the oil into the flour until it is coarse and mealy. Make a well in the center. Add the water and the starter, broken up into small pieces. Mix with a wooden spoon to combine. Remove the dough to a lightly floured work surface and knead, adding more flour if necessary until a smooth, firm dough forms. Cover and leave to rise in a warm, draft-free place until doubled in bulk, about 2 hours.

3. When the dough has risen, break it up into fist-size balls and knead them gently. Let rest, covered, until swollen, about 30 minutes. Roll a little piece of dough, about the size of a child's fist, into a long, pencil-thin, rounded (not flat like fettuccine) strip. Repeat with the rest of the dough and set aside, covered.

4. In a large, deep pot over medium-high heat, heat ample olive oil or a combination of olive and vegetable oil—there should be 4 to 6 inches of oil in the pot and it should be very hot. Deep-fry the dough strips in batches until puffy and golden, remove with a slotted spoon, and drain on paper towels. Drizzle with honey or sprinkle with grated cheese and serve either hot or at room temperature.

Dough Fritters Drizzled with Honey and Nuts

THIPLES

 Makes about 36 pieces

*T*hiples—*sometimes called* xerotygana—*are not unique to the Peloponnesos, but they are very much a part of the region's culinary life. "A wedding without* thiples *would be like a wedding without a bride," one woman told me. While the sweet is made all over Greece, it is shaped differently from place to place. In Crete, for example, strips of dough about 2 feet long are twirled into decorative coils as they fry in hot oil; elsewhere* thiples *are shaped like bows or left to take their own amorphous shape as the dough hits the hot oil. In the Peloponnesos* thiples *are folded and large—as big as wallets. They are the dessert of joy throughout the region, served not only at marriages but also at baptisms and on holidays. Their name comes from the Greek for "to double," in reference both to the way they are folded and to the wish that all good things should last long—"twice as long."*

7 to 8 cups all-purpose flour, as needed
2 scant teaspoons baking soda
10 large eggs, separated
2 teaspoons pure vanilla extract
Olive or vegetable oil for frying
Honey for drizzling
Chopped walnuts and ground cinnamon for
　garnish

1. Combine 7 cups of the flour and the baking soda in a large bowl.

2. Beat the egg yolks with the vanilla in a bowl until creamy and pale. In a large bowl, beat the whites until stiff peaks form. Fold the yolks into the whites and slowly add the flour mixture, folding vigorously until a dough mass begins to form. Moisten the palms of your hands with olive oil and knead the dough until it is smooth and firm, adding more flour if necessary.

3. Divide the dough into 6 or 8 balls and on a lightly floured work surface roll out each ball to a large, very thin sheet. Using a pizza cutter, cut the dough into large strips, about 6 inches wide and 8 inches long.

4. Heat about 6 inches of olive or vegetable oil in a large, heavy pot over medium-high heat. When the oil is very hot, deep-fry the *thiples,* one or two at a time, for a few seconds, until they puff up and are light and pale gold. As they fry, try to fold them like a flat *s,* using two long forks and gathering up the ends of each piece of dough as it fries. Remove with a slotted spoon and drain on paper towels. When cool, drizzle with honey and sprinkle with chopped nuts and cinnamon. Serve warm or at room temperature.

SWEETS

One of the common characteristics of many of the pastries in the Peloponnesos is the widespread use of olive oil in doughs, cookies, and cakes.

Walnut-Filled Crescents

RAFIOLIA

  Makes about 3 dozen

In the pastry shops of Monemvassia, the beautiful Venetian fortressed port on the east coast of the Peloponnesos, these little crescents are a main attraction. I love the name—clearly Venetian, although the pastry itself is as Greek as one can get. Rafiolia *are a specialty throughout this whole southeastern region of the Peloponnesos, all the way down to Neapoli. This recipe comes from a local cook in Molaous.*

For the dough
3 large eggs
1 scant teaspoon baking powder
¾ cup fresh orange juice
3 tablespoons extra-virgin olive oil
4 cups pastry flour

For the cinnamon dipping water
2 cinnamon sticks
2 cups water

For the filling
½ pound ground walnuts
2 to 3 tablespoons plain bread crumbs or ground
   Greek rusks, as needed
1 scant teaspoon ground cinnamon
¼ teaspoon mastic crystals pounded with
   1 teaspoon sugar (see page 458)
¼ cup honey
¼ cup granulated sugar
¼ cup water

To finish
Confectioners' sugar for dusting

1. Prepare the dough: Beat the eggs in a large bowl until fluffy. Dissolve the baking powder in the orange juice and add it to the eggs, together with the oil. Beat together for several minutes until smooth and viscous. Add the flour in increments, mixing with a wooden spoon as you go, until a dough mass begins to form. Reserve about ½ cup and sprinkle onto a clean, dry work surface. Knead the dough until smooth, cover with plastic wrap, and let it rest for at least 30 minutes at room temperature. (The dough may be made ahead of time, covered, and refrigerated for up to 2 days. Bring to room temperature before using.)

2. Prepare the cinnamon water: Place the cinnamon sticks in the water in a small saucepan and bring to a boil. Reduce the heat to medium-low and simmer for 10 minutes. Remove from the heat and let cool completely.

3. Prepare the filling: Combine the ground walnuts, crumbs or rusks, cinnamon, and mastic mixture. Heat the honey, granulated sugar, and water in a small saucepan over medium heat. Simmer the syrup until thick and bubbly, 8 to 10 minutes. Remove from the heat and immediately mix in the nuts. Let the filling cool.

4. Preheat the oven to 375°F and lightly oil several baking sheets. Divide the dough into 6 little balls. Lightly sprinkle your work surface with flour and roll the first ball into a thin circle 12 to 15 inches in diameter. Using a 4-inch round cookie cutter or glass, cut circles out of the dough. Place a scant teaspoon of filling in the center and fold over to form a crescent. Dampen your fingertips with a little water and pinch the edges together to close completely. With the tines of a fork, make a decorative pattern along the edge. Continue until all the dough and filling are used up, rekneading, rerolling, and recutting the excess dough as you go. Bake until lightly golden, 15 to 18 minutes. Remove from the oven and let cool slightly.

5. Have a plate ready with ample confectioners' sugar. When the *rafiolia* are more or less cooled, dip them with a slotted spoon into the cool cinnamon water and immediately roll in the sugar. Serve or store in a closed cookie tin in a cool place. They will keep for about a week.

Almond- and Sesame-Stuffed Pastries from Laconia

SAMOUSATHES

 Makes about 30 pieces

*T*raveling *from Sparta south toward Neapoli, I saw and heard about these "countryside" sweets everywhere. They require a fair amount of dexterity to make. The pastry is opened into thin sheets and then, once filled, rolled around a dowel, shirred or gathered and cut so that the* samousathes *end up like wrinkled little nuggets. They are not unique to the Peloponnesos, but they are so much a part of the local foodscape that I include them here. You will need an 18-inch-long, ¼-inch-thick dowel or other smooth rod.*

For the pastry
¾ cup strained fresh orange juice
4 large eggs
3½ to 4½ cups all-purpose flour, as needed

For the filling
¾ cup sesame seeds
3 cups finely ground walnuts or almonds (not blanched)
1 teaspoon ground cinnamon
½ teaspoon ground cloves

For the syrup
2 cups sugar
2 cups honey
2 cups water
1 cinnamon stick
5 to 6 whole cloves, to taste
1 strip lemon zest

To finish
½ cup (1 stick) unsalted butter, melted
¼ cup olive oil

1. Prepare the dough: Beat the orange juice and eggs together in a large bowl until frothy. Add the flour in ½-cup increments, beating vigorously with a wooden spoon after each addition, until a dough mass begins to form. Knead by hand, adding enough flour to form a firm, smooth dough. Cover with plastic wrap and set aside to rest while you prepare the filling and syrup.

2. Prepare the filling: Pound the sesame seeds in a mortar or in a food processor until coarse and mealy. Combine with the ground nuts, cinnamon, and cloves.

3. Make the syrup: Heat the sugar, honey, and water in a medium saucepan. Bring to a simmer and add the cinnamon stick, cloves, and zest. Simmer over low heat for 15 minutes. Remove from the heat and set aside to cool.

4. Lightly oil a baking sheet or jelly roll pan. Combine the melted butter and olive oil. Divide the dough into 4 equal balls. Lightly flour a clean work surface. Flatten the first ball of dough with your palm and shape into a rectangle about 8 inches wide and 10 to 12 inches long. Using a rolling pin, roll it out, alternately working it vertically, then horizontally, so that it retains its rectangular shape. Place it horizontally in front of you. Brush the surface with some of the butter-and-oil mixture. Sprinkle a quar-ter of the nut mixture over the entire surface of the pastry, leaving about an inch clear on the bottom and sides.

5. Fold the bottom flap of pastry over the filling so that it is covered by about 2 inches. Place the dowel across the bottom and carefully roll up the dough tightly around the dowel. When you get to the top, push the pastry in, toward the center, from both sides to shirr or wrinkle it. Remove the dowel. Cut the roll into 1½-inch nuggets and place seam side down on the baking sheet. Repeat with the remaining dough and filling. Brush the tops with the remaining butter and oil and bake until light golden, about 30 minutes.

6. While the *samousathes* are still hot, submerge them, in batches, in the cooled syrup. If desired, place them in individual paper confection cups or between sheets of wax paper in several cookie tins. These keep up to two weeks stored in a cool, dry place.

Sesame-Seed Brittle

PASTELLI

 Makes about 50 pieces

The Peloponnesos used to produce enough sesame to cover its needs for the production of one of its most famous local confections, pastelli. *The sesame-seed brittle is a sweet whose roots clearly go back to the seed-and-honey and nut-and-honey desserts of the ancients. In these parts the confection is bound indelibly to one old local producer, Pastelli Lambo, who has a factory in the region and a pastry shop but whose candy is also sold everywhere, from kiosks to ouzo emporiums. One of the pleasant culinary idiosyncrasies of the region is the taste for ouzo and* pastelli *together. The confection used to be served up in place of the more usual olives or cheese or other small* mezethes *to accompany a carafe of the potent, anise-flavored distillation. While most people don't make their own* pastelli *any longer, the sweet was a standard in the old recipe books of local housewives.*

3 cups sesame seeds
1½ cups sugar
½ cup water
¾ cup honey
Juice of 1 lemon

1. In a large dry skillet over medium heat, toast the sesame seeds lightly. Set aside. Butter or oil a jelly roll pan and set aside.

2. Heat the sugar, water, and honey in a saucepan, bring to a boil, reduce the heat to medium-low, and simmer until the mixture reaches 250°F on a candy thermometer. Stir in the lemon juice and sesame seeds and mix vigorously with a wooden spoon.

3. Spread the *pastelli* over the buttered jelly roll pan and flatten with a metal spatula, spreading it evenly over the surface of the pan. While the *pastelli* is still warm, cut it into strips and then into diagonal wedges. Let it sit to cool for several hours or overnight. Remove the pieces from the tray and store in between layers of wax paper in several cookie tins. Keep in a cool, dry place. *Pastelli* will keep for at least 2 weeks.

Small Phyllo Logs Filled with Dried and Candied Fruit from Levithi

PASTA PHYLLO APO TO LEVITHI

 Makes about twenty-four 2-inch pieces

For the syrup
4 cups sugar
3 cups water
1 medium cinnamon stick
5 whole cloves
Juice of ½ lemon
1 strip lemon zest

1½ to 2 cups well-drained Greek citrus fruit spoon sweets (bitter orange, lemon, bergamot), to taste
6 large eggs, separated
1 cup sugar
⅓ cup ouzo
1 cup coarse dried bread crumbs from stale bread
2 cups chopped blanched almonds

1 pound commercial phyllo, defrosted and at
    room temperature (see page 455)
1 cup (2 sticks) unsalted butter, melted

1. Make the syrup: Heat the sugar and water in a medium saucepan over medium heat. When the sugar dissolves, add the cinnamon, cloves, lemon juice, and zest. Simmer for 10 minutes, remove from the heat, and cool completely.

2. Finely chop the spoon sweets.

3. Beat the egg yolks with the sugar in a large bowl until creamy. Add the ouzo and mix well. Combine the bread crumbs with the almonds and mix into the egg-yolk mixture. Beat the whites separately in a large bowl until stiff peaks form, then fold vigorously into the bread crumbs and almonds with a rubber spatula, so that the mixture is completely combined.

4. Preheat the oven to 350°F and lightly oil a large jelly roll pan. Unroll the phyllo. Keep covered with a cloth and work quickly. Take 4 sheets at a time, brushing each with melted butter, and stack vertically in front of you. Spread about 3 tablespoons of the chopped spoon sweets in a straight thin line starting about an inch from the bottom, leaving an inch on both sides. Top with 2 to 3 tablespoons of the egg-and-nut mixture. Fold in the sides and roll up carefully into a tight cylinder. Place on the baking sheet, seam side down. Repeat with the remaining phyllo and filling until all the ingredients are used up. Place the cylinders next to one another on the pan. Pierce the surface of the phyllo at random intervals with a fork or a toothpick. Bake until the phyllo is golden, but not too dark, about 45 minutes.

5. As soon as the pastry comes out of the oven, let cool slightly, cut into 2-inch pieces, and dip with a slotted spoon into the cooled syrup. Store the individual pieces in pastry cups inside a cookie tin and keep in a cool, dry place. The pasta phyllo will keep for about a week.

SWEETS FROM LEVITHI IN ARCADIA

My hostess in Arcadia, Maria Spyropoulou, runs a large local winery in the village of Kakouri with her husband, Epaminondas. The two know Arcadia, and especially the plateau of Mantineia, very well. Epaminondas is a local son, scion of one of the area's old families. It was from them that I learned about Levithi and with them that I went to visit the lovely town perched high in the mountains above Mantineia overlooking the whole plateau. "The Levithiotisses [women from Levithi] are known for being persnickety," Maria told me. "They're picky about everything—in Levithi you see lots of bachelors and lots of unmarried women because they consider themselves too good for just anyone!" For some reason—maybe because pastry making requires a certain fussiness—this town is known for its excellent desserts. "The *karythopita* [walnut cake] is famous. The baklava is sought after. The olive-oil *kourambiethes* (shortbread cookies) are the best in the world. Not to mention their own, totally local dessert—phyllo-covered spoon sweets."

My hostess was right on the mark. It was just after Christmas when she took me to Levithi and we visited the home of the local school principal, a lovely woman with a warm but aristocratic mien, who is also the wife of the town mayor. She had invited a group of women for me to meet, local women dressed in their Sunday best, who waxed poetic about the nuances of *pasta phyllo* and indulged with caution, their figures a concern, in the hostess's offerings of holiday sweets. Indeed the *kourambiethes,* as well as the roster of other cookies and biscuits set on old porcelain plates and served with crystal glasses full of cool water, were divine.

Olive Oil—and–Walnut Shortbread Cookies from Levithi

KOURAMBIETHES ME ELAIOLATHO APO TO LEVITHI

 Makes about 72 shortbread cookies

2 cups extra-virgin olive oil
⅔ cup granulated sugar
⅓ cup ouzo
½ teaspoon baking soda dissolved in
    2 tablespoons fresh lemon juice
1 cup finely chopped walnuts
Grated zest of 1 lemon
1 teaspoon ground cinnamon
4 to 5 cups all-purpose flour, as needed
3 to 4 cups confectioners' sugar for dusting

1. Preheat the oven to 350°F. Using an electric mixer set at high speed, whip the oil with the sugar in a large bowl until smooth. Add the ouzo, the dissolved baking soda, and mix well. Add the walnuts, zest, and cinnamon and mix vigorously with a wooden spoon. Add 3 cups of the flour, a little at a time, mixing by hand or with a wooden spoon until a dough begins to form. Keep adding and kneading in the flour in ½-cup increments until the dough is tight, firm, and smooth, 10 to 15 minutes.

2. Line several lightly greased cookie sheets with parchment. Take a little piece of dough about the size of an unshelled walnut and shape it into a mounded oblong. Place on the cookie sheet. Continue until all the dough is used, setting the *kourambiethes* about an inch apart on the baking sheet. Bake until very light golden, 10 to 12 minutes. Let cool on wire racks, then place on a serving platter and sift the confectioners' sugar over them. Store in cookie tins and keep in a cool, dry place. They will keep for up to two weeks.

Syrup-Drenched Nut-and-Spice Cookies with Olive Oil

MELOMAKARONA ME ELAIOLATHO

 Makes 4 to 5 dozen *melomakarona*

This is one Peloponnesian version of a traditional Christmas cookie. The region's telltale ingredient, olive oil, replaces butter in this recipe. Sometimes, Greek cooks will do that—replace butter with oil, that is—to transform a sweet into something permissable for fasting. In the Peloponnesos, though, the use of olive oil is the norm rather than the exception.

For the syrup
1 cup sugar
1 cup honey
½ cup water
1 medium cinnamon stick
One inch-wide strip lemon zest

For the cookies
3 to 3½ cups all-purpose flour, as needed
1 scant teaspoon baking powder
1 teaspoon ground cinnamon
½ teaspoon ground cloves
1 cup extra-virgin olive oil
½ cup sugar
½ teaspoon baking soda
½ cup fresh orange or lemon juice
¼ cup brandy
1 cup chopped walnuts
Grated zest of 1 orange

1. Make the syrup: Bring the sugar, honey, and water to a boil in a medium-size saucepan. Add the cinnamon and lemon zest and simmer over medium heat for 10 minutes. Let cool completely.

2. For the cookies: Sift together 3 cups of the flour, the baking powder, cinnamon, and cloves in a small bowl and set aside. In a large bowl, beat the olive oil with the sugar until creamy. Stir the baking soda into the citrus juice and add to the oil-and-sugar mixture. Add the brandy, walnuts, and grated zest and continue mixing vigorously until combined. Slowly add the flour to the mixture, beating vigorously with a wooden spoon until a stiff dough forms.

3. Preheat the oven to 325°F. Lightly oil 2 large baking sheets. One at a time, break off pieces of dough the size of an unshelled walnut and shape into a small, mounded oblongs. Place 1 inch apart on the baking sheets and bake until lightly browned, about 20 minutes. Remove from the oven and submerge in the cooled syrup to soak for a few minutes. Drain them, if desired, on racks.

⊙ Olive Oil–Fried Melomakarona from Neapoli: Prepare the recipe as directed. Shape the *melomakarona* into small, oval mounds, about 1 inch long, and deep-fry in very hot olive oil. Remove when golden with a slotted spoon, drain on paper towels for about a minute, then submerge in the same syrup.

A SHORT HISTORY OF THE ROSE

The noble rose has had a place in Greece's kitchen and in the kitchens of neighboring countries for eons, tantalizing, seducing, intoxicating people more than any other flower. Roses, which were used as a seasoning, were sold by the roadside in fourth-century B.C. Athens. In ancient Greece, the symposia were occasions in which all the senses were engaged, and the perfumes used were as important as the foods served. Rose fragrance was considered appropriate for a drinking party. Rose essence was also sometimes used to season wine in both ancient Greece and Rome. From Apicius we learn of the fondness for rose petals crushed with *garum* (the ancient Greek fish sauce) and cooked with eggs and wine as a sauce for lamb's brains. Later the rose appears in confections. The Byzantines were probably the first to make rose sugar, which was also a popular medieval sweetmeat. Rose water also was mixed with *salep* (a thick, sweet drink made from ground orchid bulbs) and drunk as a fortifying beverage as early as the seventh century in Constantinople. The Byzantines also mixed rose syrup with crushed mountain ice to make sorbet. Throughout its long, exotic history the rose was considered good for the stomach and the monks at the Taxiarhon Monastery just outside of Aigeon in the northern Peloponnesos made—and still make—rose sugar for the same purpose. Rose sugar, an exotic rare spoon sweet made from the macerated petals of pink, aromatic roses, and rose petal jam have been made here for at least one hundred years from some eighty acres of rose bushes around the monastery.

MONKS AND ROSES AT THE TAXIARHON MONASTERY IN AIGEON

It's not the kind of thing we think of every day, eating roses, that is. It's just that here, high in the mountains above Aigeon on the central northern coast is the Taxiarhon Monastery, known throughout Greece for the monks' unique food product, which they sell in order to help the monastery survive. The sign read "rose jam factory," and I knew we had arrived in the right place. Sheltered from the sun under a corrugated tin roof, four somber monks and a handful of workers sat around a long narrow table gently twisting the petals off of thousands of velvety, iridescent, pink roses. The first thing that hits you is the aroma, at once heavy, obviously floral, almost intoxicating, but ultimately ephemeral. The scent of so many roses pervades everything within its reach yet is as fleeting as the breeze.

Rose petal jam has been made at the Taxiarhon Monastery for at least the last one hundred years. No one could say for sure how or when the tradition began. By one brother's account, the roses and the secrets of making the spoon sweet were brought to the monastery by a Bulgarian monk during the Turkish occupation. It's a story that makes sense given the tradition in the Rodopi Mountains (along the border of Bulgaria and Greece) of growing roses and of producing things like rose water and rose oil.

Whatever the story of the sweet's origins at the monastery, the natural environment is conducive to the monks' traditions. "We have a lot of water, good water, and rich red soil," explained Brother Christostomo, an elder monk who has been making the rose petal jam since he arrived at the monastery in 1935. As the most experienced brother, he oversees production. But the process is shrouded in mystery. First, ironically, as you approach the monastery up a long winding road, you get no inkling of the occupation at hand. There isn't one rosebush to be seen, and the monks are politely evasive when asked to point out the gardens. "They're spread out all over there," said Brother Christostomo, gesturing with a wave of his hand to fields or gardens that are obviously hidden from view. The brothers seemed equally reticent about telling us the name of the rose itself. "There is no name. It is just the real rose, the one with thirty petals."

We sat at the table to help the monks clean the mounds of flowers. In an average day, together they collect and clean about 200 pounds. By 5:00 A.M., the monks and their workers are out harvesting. By midmorning they have to be back to beat the heat. The petals have to be separated within hours of collecting, lest they wilt and turn brown, which renders them useless. Color is as important as aroma in the making of this elegant sweet. With a quick gentle twist, the petals are dislodged and spread over a large screen, so that the stamens and pollen and everything else except the petals themselves fall through. As the petals are separated, they are collected in barrels and weighed out into 10-kilo (22-pound) batches. Then Brother Christostomo pours one barrelful of petals at a time into the wooden trough at the other end of the work area, sprinkles them with a little water, a kilo (2.2 pounds) of sugar, and three grams of citric acid. His hands are swollen from the work, but he is good-humored, almost jolly, stopping even to pose for pictures. He rolls up his sleeves and starts the kneading, working the sugar into the petals, almost massaging them, until they turn into a dark, violet pulp. It takes him about 20 minutes to knead about 20 pounds of petals to the desired consistency. Then, he gently squeezes the pulp a little at a time to strain it, and places it back inside the barrels, which in turn are stored in the refrigerator and taken out when the time comes to actually make the sweet.

During the harvest, Brother Christostomo boils and bottles the sweet every other day, but he explained that the rose petal jam is made all year round, as orders come in. The preliminary kneading process and subsequent refrigeration is a way of preserving the supply. The basic recipe is a one-to-six ratio of flowers to sugar, so about 20 pounds of petals call for about 120 pounds of sugar. The two ingredients are simmered together in a huge cauldron over a wood-burning fire, but the trick is to get the color right. "The final product has to have the same color as the flowers when they are raw," says Brother Christostomo, and therein lies the art. "You can't boil it for too long, otherwise the sugar will caramelize and darken and the sweet will be ruined. The color of the sweet is indeed light and opaque, nothing like the pulp from which it derives. "It has taken me fifty years to perfect the color," says the monk. "There are many, many secrets."

Rose Petal Jam

ROTHOZAHARI

½ pound unsprayed young pink rose petals
2 pounds sugar
1 cup water
Juice of 2 lemons

1. Place the petals, in batches, in a large sieve or colander and shake so that any excess dirt, pollen, and stamens fall out. Place the cleaned petals in a large basin and sprinkle with the sugar. (This may also have to be done in batches.) Knead them with the sugar, rubbing the petals vigorously with your fingertips, until they wilt and become a pulplike mass. Let stand for 2 hours.

2. Place the rose petal pulp in a stockpot or other large pot, add the water, and stir continuously over very low heat for 10 to 15 minutes, until the sugar becomes a thick syrup. Just before removing from the heat, stir in the lemon juice.

3. While the jam is simmering, bring eight 6-ounce bottles to a boil to sterilize. Remove just before use. Place the jam in the bottles and seal when cooled completely.

The Ionian Islands

A Sense of Place and Palate

Where to begin this foray into the history and cuisine of the Seven Islands? With Odysseus, Ithaca's mythic king? With Corfu's fabled gardens of King Alcinoos, immortalized in Homer's *Odyssey*? Or with the Corinthians, then the Romans, then the Byzantines, the Venetians, and, finally, the Russians, French, and British, all of whom at one time or another over the nearly two and a half millennia from the eighth century B.C. to the nineteenth century A.D. have occupied the rich, fertile, economically strategic Seven Islands?

The islands themselves haven't always numbered exactly seven. For several centuries Kythira—geographically situated not among the Ionian Islands in the Ionian Sea but off the southeastern tip of the Peloponnesos—was administered by Venice as part of the Seven Islands. For a time, when the Russians controlled the territory at the end of the nineteenth century, they were referred to as the Ionian State. Modern Greeks recognize Kythera as historically and nostalgically "belonging" to the Ionian, but officially count the *Eptanyssa*—Seven Islands—as such: Corfu, the northernmost island; the two tiny Paxis just south of Corfu; Ithaca; Cephalonia; Zakynthos; and Lefkada.

From their earliest history, the Seven Islands have been an important way station for trade between East and West. Barely a hint, though, is left of illustrious antiquity anywhere in the Seven Islands. Jolted by frequent, violent earthquakes—the islands teeter along not one but two fault lines—and scavenged by fortune hunters, the islands bear few traces of the distant past today.

After the fall of Rome, the Ionian Islands were absorbed by the Byzantine Empire. During the eleven-hundred-year duration of Byzantium, the islands continued to attract the attention of almost every other power of the times whose economic interests were intertwined with the trade routes between Europe and the East. The islands were difficult to protect from the Byzantine Empire's seat in far-off Constantinople, so the emperors turned to Venice, offering trading privileges to the formidable superpower in return for help fending off would-be marauders. By the early fifteenth century Venice had wrested complete control of all the Seven Islands, save for Lefkada, which had been seized by and remained in the hands of the Ottoman Turks for two hundred years before falling again to Venice.

These were turbulent times, rife with wars and whirling from the vast changes that were taking place thanks largely to the imminent discovery of America and the opening of new sea routes to the Orient. Mediterranean trade dwindled, and so did Venice's empire, though it maintained its grip in the Ionian Islands until Napoleon routed it in 1797. The French were temporarily ousted by the Russians, who, alarmed by Napoleon's conquests, had formed an unlikely alliance with their longtime enemy, the Turks. But in 1807 the French regained control of the islands and remained there until 1815, when Napoleon was finally defeated. The islands became a British protectorate, and the English ruled there until 1864, when Queen Victoria peacefully signed the islands over to Greece.

With such a long history of foreign—mostly Western—domination, it is hard not to see the stamp of conquest on the foods of the Seven Islands. The first palpable traces of Ionian cookery begin, like those of most of Greece, with the Byzantine Empire. Techniques such as *avgolemono*—the egg liaison enlivened with lemon that is now so characteristically Greek—the penchant for expensive foods seasoned generously with black pepper, the array of vegetables slowly stewed in olive oil, and much else began during the Byzantine Empire.

More than any other single factor, though, it was the four hundred years of Venetian control, and shorter stays by the French, Russians, and English,

that left its mark on the cooking of the Seven Islands. The food here is distinct. Although there are differences in the cuisine from island to island, and some dishes found in one place are completely absent in another, many common threads run through the Ionian kitchen. The most obvious is in the Latin names of dishes and of ingredients, even those that are commonly found in other parts of Greece. In Lefkada, for example, the rice-shaped pasta known as orzo in English (*kritharaki* everywhere else in Greece) is called *nioki*, like the Italian gnocchi. In Corfu, pasta makers of yore used to be called *manestropoiia*, and even today throughout the islands small pasta is often referred to by its Italian name, *manestra*. *Keftedes*, the little meatballs ubiquitously enjoyed throughout Greece, also go by the Italian *polpetes* in Corfu. *Sofrito, pastitsatha, sartsa, bourtheto, savori*, and dozens of other dishes take their etymological and culinary cue from the Venetians, who either brought them or named them.

However, few of the grandiose dishes that made Venetian cuisine renowned throughout the world are in evidence in the cooking of the Ionian Islands. The anchovy, sage, and rosemary that season the Venetian palate were never adopted by Greek cooks, rich or poor, in the Seven Islands, but almost all of the vegetables that came to Europe from the New World found their way to the Ionian Islands via the Venetians. Among them, of course, were tomatoes, as well as peppers (*Capsicum*), green beans, corn, and pumpkins, which in Zakynthos are still called Venetian squash. The most important New World crop to reach Europe, the potato, arrived late in the Ionian Islands and in the rest of Greece. It was first imported by the French at the end of the eighteenth century, but no Greek would go near it. It took a clever young Russian-educated Greek aristocrat of Corfiote descent named Ioannis

Capodistrias to reintroduce the potato to his fellow Greeks. Knowing their suspicious natures, one afternoon he ordered sacks of the humble tuber be placed under lock and key in the middle of Nafplion, a small city in the eastern Peloponnesos that was Greece's first capital. By morning the lock had been broken and the potatoes stolen. The rest is Greek history. Capodistrias went back to Russia only to return to Greece in 1828 as the first governor of a free nation.

As far as sweets, there isn't much of a pastry culture in this part of Greece, nothing certainly akin to the great phyllo pastries or the profusion of spoon sweets and rose-water-scented confections that are made in the northern and eastern parts of the country, where the cooking is influenced by the proximity to Asia Minor. In the Ionian Islands, the best-known confection is the Italian-influenced *mandolato,* a kind of nougat redolent of local honey and almonds. Two other specialties from the Ionian (mainly Corfu) are caramelized nuts and candied kumquats. There is also a wealth of puddings and some tarts and a local interpretation of the great Piedmontese and Venetian dessert sauce, zabaglione.

CORFU

Corfu is really a world apart from the rest of the country, which Corfiotes refer to nonchalantly as the "other" Greece. Many still use the word *Romios*—a Greek of the Byzantine Empire—to refer to their fellow countrymen on the mainland. They talk nostalgically of the island at its peak in the seventeenth and eighteenth centuries.

In Corfu, as in many of the other places in Greece that fell under the Venetian yoke, such as Santorini, the disparity between the landed gentry and the poor was enormous. There are two distinct cuisines, that of the rich, or *nobili,* and that of their feudal subjects.

The four best-known dishes of the Corfiote upper classes all have been influenced by the Venetians: *sofrito* (from *fritto,* for "fry"), made by lightly frying sliced veal, then cooking it with vinegar, garlic, and parsley; *bourtheto* (from the Italian *brodetto*) traditionally a paprika-based sauce that now denotes a peppery fish stew; *bianco,* the island's white, garlicky fish stew; and *pastitsatha,* the hearty Sunday meal of the island's well-to-do, a pasta-and-meat dish that was made traditionally with cock-and-tomato sauce over thick macaroni. Today *pastitsatha* has become decidedly more mundane and usually refers to spaghetti and beef in red sauce.

Many of the island's sweets also date to its illustrious Venetian past. *Pasta frolla* (called *pasta flora* elsewhere in the country) is the most popular dessert, filled alternately with apricot or peach jam or with figs. Until about the 1960s, women who had just given birth were sent gifts of *pan di spagne* (literally "bread of Spain"), which also found its way to the island from Venice. In some historical texts, there is mention as well of the *bianco maniar* (*bianco mangare* in Italian)—or all-white sweets table—which was a wedding custom among the rich, especially when sugar was a new and dear ingredient. Corfu, as well as the other Seven Islands, also lays claim to a number of bread-and-fruit puddings, which also might be legacies of the Venetians.

The Venetians exited Corfu in 1797, and on their heels came the Russians, then Napoleon, and, finally, in 1815 and for fifty years afterward, the British. While the island's culinary inheritance from Venice is unrivaled to this day, the Russians and British both managed to leave a few things behind on Corfu's table. Little culinary trace remains of the French, who were hated among the island's ruling class because they brought with them the seeds of democratic revolution.

One dish survives from the Russian imperial forces. It was recounted to me by Ninetta Laskari, daughter of one of the island's oldest families and a local historian. It is a simple recipe for fish fried in butter, with lots of black pepper, parsley, potatoes, and milk. It might seem easy and common enough to us now, but in its time the recipe was revolutionary. First, butter was rare on the island since most families preferred to make cheese with what little cream they could garner. Also, because Corfu is covered with olive trees—thanks to the Venetians, who planted them in systematic groves—oil was always easily available. It would have seemed completely extravagant then to fry fish in butter. This one recipe survives, though even today butter is reserved only for the most delicate fish, usually trout.

When Napoleon fell in 1815, the French garrison in Corfu surrendered to the English, who, in the five decades that followed, established a university, built roads and waterworks, organized the postal service, and brought cricket, ginger beer, and plum pudding to the island. The cafés along the Liston, bordering Corfu town's Esplanade, are just about the only place left where you can still find ginger beer or, as it is called here, *tzitzibeera*. It's a strange brew, indeed, first made for the British army. *Tzitzibeera* is a little bit like American ginger ale, but it is at once much sweeter and slightly sour with the taste of fermentation. It is a pearly, grayish white color, has a pronounced lemon taste, and is extremely gaseous. It isn't exactly thirst-quenching, but it is pleasantly anachronistic to sip it and watch cricket, which is still played on the Esplanade.

The culinary heritage from Corfu's imperial overlords is rich, indeed, but most of what the Venetians and everyone after them brought to the island could be savored by the aristocracy alone. While the upper classes were busy carving their Christmas turkey, the poor, if they were lucky, were eating salt cod, which is linked indelibly to the tables of Corfu's peasants. At Christmas it was cod baked with tomatoes and potatoes. During Carnival time they made pie with cod, potatoes, rice, goat's cheese, eggs, and milk. Even the Sunday meal for those employed in the houses of the rich was salt cod stewed with leeks and paprika. The latter, in fact, was the seasoning by default on the tables of Corfu's villagers; only the *nobili* could afford black pepper and other exotic and imported spices.

Until late-twentieth-century tourism brought affluence to Corfu's natives, the peasants subsisted on a paltry but healthful diet of wild greens cooked with onions and olive oil and *barbarella,* or corn bread (the word may come from the Italian *barbari,* as in Barbary Coast, since corn was long believed to have originated in Africa).

Corfu is lush with all sorts of wild greens, most called by local names. Among them are watercress, wild celery, mustard greens, sorrel, dandelion, poppy, nettles, white radish, and mâche. Despite the wealth of greens, though, savory pies were never a great tradition on the island. There are some squash pies and a meat pie eaten during Carnival made with lamb, rice, onions, and cinnamon, baked in a thick yeasty crust. Most greens and vegetables are stewed or simply boiled.

Sweet potatoes also appear regularly in the local diet. They are cooked in several different ways: baked with syrup, the way the English and Americans like them; fried and dusted with cinnamon and sugar; or grilled or boiled and dressed with olive oil and salt.

KUMQUATS AND THE CORFIOTES

▼

The small, fragrant kumquat has become part and parcel of Corfu's culinary lore almost by historical accident. It happened during the 1950s, when an Englishman named Merlin returned to the island and, for purely commercial reasons, planted the first groves of the fruit in the northern town of Thasia. Now the island produces about sixty tons of kumquats annually. To most Greeks, kumquats, and everything made with them, from the bright liqueur almost the color of Mercurochrome, the marmalades, spoon sweets, and candied fruits, are synonymous with Corfu, but locals are of another opinion. "No one eats candied kumquats in Corfu," Ninetta Laskari, a local food historian told me, brushing the notion aside. "All that stuff is only for the tourists." Nevertheless, Corfu does a handsome business in marketing its tiny, fragrant kumquats, and the shops along the Esplanade are stocked full of them in all their edible transformations. The liqueur is sharp and surely an acquired taste, but I rather like the candied fruits and the marmalade.

In the fall, drying on windowsills throughout Corfu Town, and all over the countryside, are tray after tray of *tzitzifes,* known in English either as the Trebizon date or the Russian olive or as oleaster. They are small, reddish brown acorn-size fruits that have a mealy texture like an apple but resemble dates in flavor. Islanders store the sun-dried fruit in jars filled with ouzo. Of all the recipes on the island, whether from the peasant kitchens or from the well-stocked larders of the rich, the most ethereal combination of flavors can be found in the autumn preparation *sikomaitha,* a kind of fig paste. It is, in fact, a recipe that crosses economic lines—traditionally made by the poor and sold in Corfu Town's farmer's market for anyone to enjoy. Fresh figs are left to dry, then chopped and kneaded with ouzo and black pepper (or sometimes with fennel seeds and grape must). The fig pies are shaped like a good-size hamburger, wrapped in either grape leaves or chestnut leaves, and left to set for a few weeks. The pies are dark and rich and the trio of flavors positively unearthly.

The Venetians and others who passed through

THE JEWS OF CORFU

♦

Until World War II, the Jewish community in Corfu and throughout the Ionian Islands was a thriving one with about seven thousand Jews in Corfu Town alone. Today the community numbers around seventy.

The Jews in the Ionian Islands (and in Epirus and the Peloponnesos) were not part of the wave of Sephardic Jews who arrived from Spain during the Inquisition. Most are Romaniote Jews who have lived in Greece, in some cases for more than two thousand years. In Corfu many of the Jews have close ties to Italy, something that is reflected in at least one recipe I got from a shopkeeper in Corfu Town, for pasta (ziti) with beans. The dish, which calls for red beans, greatly resembles the chocolate-colored *pasta e fagioli* of the Veneto region, where the soup is made with borlotti beans and bacon. The Corfiote Jewish version calls for celery, carrots, tomatoes, and small tubular macaroni.

Other dishes common in the Jewish community in Corfu are chickpeas with spinach; *pikadinio,* something between a soufflé and a meat loaf, made with ground beef, matzo meal, and eggs and eaten at Passover; and *polpetes,* which, among Corfiote Jews are not meatballs but meat-stuffed spinach leaves. The sweets include the Passover dish *kouvelo,* a kind of cake similar to the syrup-soaked *revani* (page 257) but made with matzo; and the Amman's teeth, pencil-thin dough strips fried in oil and served with honey.

the Ionian Islands left their traces in the cookery pots, architecture, dialect, and culture of every island. It's not that the rest of the Seven Islands pale in comparison to Corfu. It is just that the island was unharmed by the terrible earthquake that rocked the Ionian region in 1953 and devastated Cephalonia and Zakynthos. By default, it's the grandest of the Seven Islands, and so, by extension, is its cuisine.

CEPHALONIA

Cephalonia is the largest of the Ionian Islands, lush and green, blessed with great stretches of white-sand beaches, and known throughout Greece for its idiosyncratic inhabitants. Cephalonians are the raconteurs and jokesters of the Ionian Islands.

Life in Cephalonia (as well as in Zakynthos), though, was irrevocably transformed one fateful day in 1953 when an earthquake leveled both islands. Only the fishing village of Fiskardo in the north of Cephalonia was left standing. The quake changed the very fabric of life. Thousands of people lost their lives. Churches and monasteries were destroyed. After 1953 many islanders simply left to begin life anew elsewhere. Those who remained rebuilt the island with the help of the streams of Epirotes and others, poor but eager to work in the scurry of construction that burgeoned in the quake's aftermath.

The local cuisine miraculously survived, however. Cephalonia is known for its savory pies, unique among Greek *pites* because they almost always contain rice. Its feta and *kefalograviera* cheeses are famous throughout Greece, and so are its cheese makers. Invariably, at most feta factories, not only in Greece but in Sardinia, America, Den-mark, and Germany, the cheese master will be the scion of generations of cheese makers from one of Cephalonia's mountain villages. The island's feta is extremely creamy.

Cephalonia (as well as Ithaca) also has the *tserepa,* a portable oven made of gray clay and goat's hair that is still in use in villages. Local cooks still prepare chicken in the *tserepa.*

Something savored all over Greece, but raised to a kind of cult status in Cephalonia, is the garlic sauce *skordalia,* called here (and throughout the Ionian Islands) by its Latin-influenced local name, *aliatha* (similar to aioli). In the rest of Greece the sauce can be made with either bread or potatoes, but here it is always made with potatoes. Cephalonians say that the best potatoes for *aliatha* are the ones planted in the winter and watered only by the rain. *Aliatha* is served with codfish croquettes. In April and May it also comes to the table alongside a salad of vine shoots—*ambelovlastara* in Greek—that are blanched and served with olive oil and salt.

ZAKYNTHOS

To the south of Cephalonia lay Zakynthos, *il fiori di Levante*—the flower of the East—as the Venetians called it. In dialect and in dishes, they left much behind.

The food in Zakynthos, or Zante, the Italian name still sometimes used, is more visceral than in other parts of the Ionian. The sauces are thick and the meals hearty. The national dish is *sartsa,* a garlicky tomato-based stew made with either chicken, guinea fowl—for which Zanteans have a particular fondness—or beef. Beef stew is the communal meal (unusual for Greece, where goat and lamb eclipse most other meats in the traditional diet), served at some of the island's *panigyria,* or saints' feasts. *Skalt-sotseta*—thin slices of veal rolled with peppers and cheese and baked in tomato sauce—is another well-known Zantean specialty, sometimes found at tavernas on the island. Eggplant is cooked in tomato sauce with plenty of garlic and some vinegar. Even sunny side up eggs are served on a lake of thick red sauce.

The Venetians brought their *mostarda,* or sweet mustard, to Zakynthos (as well as to Corfu), where the condiment survives to this day. Here, though, it is usually made with quince and not with the variety of dried fruits we find in the recipes from Corfu. But, as in Corfu, it is served at Christmas with the holiday pork or turkey and at Easter with another island specialty, *pancetta,* cured breast of pork seasoned with peppercorns, garlic, and bay leaf.

Zakynthos is also known for its cheeses, currants—the "black gold" of the Venetians who reintroduced the crop to the island as well as to Cephalonia—and some fruits and vegetables not found anywhere else in Greece.

Of the fruits and vegetables indigenous and unique to Zakynthos, probably the most revered are the island's native onions, called *belousiotika,* because they come from the town of Belousi in the Northeast. They are sweet, flat, large, and white, similar in taste to the Vidalia onions of Georgia. Kohlrabi flourishes in Zakynthos, and the island's melons and wild strawberries are in demand all over Greece.

More than anything else, though, Zakynthos is synonymous with two sweets, the *mandolato,* which is similar to nougat, and *pastelli,* a kind of brittle made here with sesame seeds and almonds. One of the most unusual sweets on the island is the *fytoura,* which is made in a skillet and resembles fried polenta. It is made with semolina flour, baked into a thin cake, then lightly fried and sprinkled with

sugar. *Fytoura,* together with the local *pastelli,* is served at several of the feasts honoring local saints.

ITHACA

I suppose a purist would say that the cuisine of Ithaca begins with the *Odyssey,* with Homer's descriptions of the island's wine, of its blood sausages and roasted meats, its fruits and vegetables. Ithacans will tell you about Laertes's olive tree, in the village of Agios Yiannis, with its enormous girth, some forty feet in diameter, which is reputed to be more than two thousand years old.

Ithaca, although poorer than nearby Cephalonia and Zakynthos, is also a reflection of its European past, of the Venetians and others who occupied the island for the better part of the last millennium. But there is also a whole other cuisine here, brought back to the island by so many of its immigrants who returned, like their mythic king, from faraway shores. Some of the culinary souvenirs they picked up in their wanderings, usually to America and Australia, and introduced to the island are strange, indeed. Curried shrimp and lobster, for example, have been cooked on the island for at least the last forty years, bequeathed perhaps by some sailor-made-good who encountered it on an odyssey all his own.

The signature of Ithaca's cookery, though, is garlic. Islanders so revere it, they even pinpoint the village that the best is said to come from—Anogi.

Ithacans use oregano with alacrity, but here whole twigs are added to a dish while it cooks and then are removed, the way bay leaf is used in other parts of the country. Rosemary and basil are the other two herbs found most readily in the island's pots. Rosemary is so popular, in fact, that villages often have a communal bush or two, plucked and primed by all the neighbor-cooks who share it.

Octopus in every form—stewed, dried, grilled, pickled, in soups, in pies, and fried—appears in the island's traditional repertory, and so do many other fish and seafoods. Ithaca is one of the few places in Greece where squid is cooked in its ink.

The pastry tradition is meager, although there are a few local specialties. Ithacans make spoon sweets with small apples and with unripe figs. There are a number of recipes for biscuits like the kinds found all over the country, as well as for fried biscuits, which is unusual. Quince appears in several confections, and there are puddings made on the island similar to those found throughout the Ionian. One extremely unusual Ithacan dish is the local rendition of *revani,* the thick, honey-soaked cake found all over Greece and the East. *Revani* elsewhere in Greece is made almost exclusively with semolina flour. In Ithaca, oddly, it is made with rice slowly cooked in syrup, then baked, and it is known in the local dialect as *rovani.*

LEFKADA

The last major island of the Ionian Sea—barring the smaller Paxis and Antipaxi—is Lefkada, the only one of the Seven Islands accessible by bridge from the mainland, the only Seven Island that passed through two hundred years of Ottoman domination, and the poorest of the lot. Lefkada's traditional cookery is founded on the island's wealth of indigenous fish, on a number of breads and bread dishes, and on lentils, for which the island is reputed, and other legumes. But there are also a number of completely local preparations that are unique, simple, and ingenious.

For example, one of the most unusual condiments in all of Greece is Lefkada's rosewater vinegar. Like so many other local specialties, this one can't be found in any shop. It is made at home, and the only requisites for preparing it are a fragrant, pesticide-free rose bush (forget about using scentless commercially grown flowers) and a good bottle of red wine vinegar, which in Lefkada is made from the dark, heady wine of the local *vartzami* grape that came to the island with the Venetians and can still be found in markets in Italy under the name *vartza-mino.* Rose petals are placed in a bottle in the sun and left to wilt over several days, during which time their liquid is drawn out. The petals are discarded, and the remaining essence is mixed with vinegar. Rosewater vinegar is used to flavor the island's famous *riganatha,* a snack of toasted and then moistened bread or rusks dressed with Lefkada's yellow olive oil, salt, oregano, and this rare vinegar. *Riganatha* is sometimes served with a side of salted sardines.

Lefkadian cooks turn simple bread dishes into an art. *Paximathia,* or rusks, in Lefkada are quite unique. The local *paximathia* are as thin as toast and are flavored with fennel seeds, cumin seeds, cloves, and coriander seeds, something not encountered often elsewhere. Although it is difficult to find nowadays, the *panatha,* a meal made with sautéed bread, tomato paste, olive oil, salt, and pepper, was long another of the island's foods of sustenance, basic and delicious, even if it was poor man's food. There is the local version of the pan-Ionian *zuppa,* a concoction of dried bread drizzled with olive oil and dark red wine from the *vartzami* grape. *Tiganopsomo* (fried bread served with grape must syrup), *tiganithes* (a kind of pancake), and *thiples* (made with the same dough as *tiganopsomo* but filled with cheese) are just a few of the lunchtime preparations that used to be made especially to eat while working in the fields.

There are at least three dishes made with corn-meal in Lefkada and several local varieties of pasta called by Italian names. *Bazina,* for example, is the island's rendition of polenta, served here either with oil and garlic or with olive oil and grape must syrup. There are two kinds of corn bread, called *rokissa:* leavened corn bread made in a large pan and a flat corn bread seasoned with raisins, olive oil, and cinnamon.

As for the pasta dishes that sound uncannily Italian, there is the *niokos* or *birbilonia,* which is nothing other than the rice-shaped pasta orzo, as well as the *timatsi,* egg noodles that are cooked as soup, in meat broth or sometimes with milk.

Fish and seafood abound on the island, culled from the dozens of lagoons that curve in and out along the coast. There is a tiny indigenous shrimp called *sernikares,* which is fried whole and served in many of the local fish tavernas. Clams, sea urchins, limpets, and mussels abound, as do crabs, which are barbecued. Other seafood specialties are the island's dried octopus, which is cooked either with pasta or with potatoes, paprika, and olive oil—a dish similar to the Corfiote *bourtheto*—and the *kofisi,* a transliteration of the English stockfish, which is nothing more than air-dried (as opposed to salt-cured) cod.

The Ionian Pantry

CHEESE

Artisanal cheese makers throughout the Seven Islands all make their supply of typical Greek country cheeses. Some cheeses, though, are unique to the region, and others, while made elsewhere, too, stand out because of their superior quality and taste.

Corfu That's the eponymous name of a cheese, first produced in 1965 in Corfu, of course. Corfu is modeled after the Italian pecorino and is one of the few cow's milk cheeses made in Greece. Aged for at least three months, Corfu is both a lovely grating cheese and a table cheese. It has a characteristic black paraffin skin and a sharp taste, but a relatively soft texture for a hard cheese. Unfortunately, it is being fast eclipsed by myriad other, cheaper, grating cheeses.

Cephalonian Feta Although in the eyes of Greek agronomy officials, feta is a name that should be reserved for the sheep's milk brine cheese of Continental Greece, some of the best feta is made in Cephalonia. It is distinguished mainly because of its creaminess.

Cephalonian Kefalotyri Cephalonia is reknowned for her cheese makers, the best in Greece. One of their specialties is the island's peppery *kefalotyri.* Here, this otherwise common Greek grating cheese is made into unusually large wheels, about six inches high. My friend and cheese expert Elias Mamalakis says the cheese owes its flavor to the area's rich flora on which the sheep and goats graze, but also to its size. Cephalonia's *kefalotyri* is creamier than most. It is made in the high-altitude area called Pilarou, in the northern part of the island.

Lathograviera Zakynthou As its name suggests, this is a typical *graviera* steeped in olive oil *(lathi)* and a specialty of Zakynthos. Once made, it is left to mature for about two weeks until it develops a slight rind, then it is placed in large barrels filled with local olive oil. It has a pleasantly sharp taste and a nice, toothsome texture.

Lathotyri Zakynthou This "oil cheese" is quite unlike that of Lesvos, which is better known and more widely available. Zakynthos's *lathotyri* is a small fez-shaped feta, not a hard yellow cheese as is Lesvos's. It is steeped in salt brine for anywhere from two weeks to a month, removed and dried for twenty-four hours, and then stored in local olive oil. The cheese ferments in the oil so that, once mature, it is very pungent and peppery. Each fez-shaped head weighs between three and four pounds.

Pretza The name is probably a transliteration of the English "to press." *Pretza,* a specialty of Cephalonia, is nothing more than the residuals on the bottom of the feta barrel collected and mixed with a little crumbled *myzithra* cheeses and sometimes a little of the salty, creamy brine in the feta barrel, then with olive oil and dried thyme. The result is a soft, pungent cheese spread that is delicious on toasted bread with a little tomato, which is exactly how Cephalonians savor it.

OLIVES AND OLIVE OIL

In speaking about Ionian Island oil, one must go straight to Corfu and to the Paxis, just south of the island, for here, more than anywhere else in the region, the olive has been the salve of life. For natives on the other Ionian Islands, the olive was extremely important, but there were other ways to earn a living—shipping and raisin farming, mostly. Corfu was different. Thanks to an early Venetian policy of offering gold for every hundred trees planted, the island quickly grew into one enormous olive grove. The Venetians encouraged the planting of an Italian variety, the *lianolia,* to supplement the native trees. By the end of the seventeenth century there were more than two million olive trees on the island. Oil exports ran to about sixty thousand barrels every two years. Growing dependence on one crop meant that the island could no longer feed itself. It had become an importer of many of the foods—grains, meats, vegetables—it once provided for itself.

For centuries the olive crop was absolutely essential to life in Corfu and in the Paxis. Land value was often measured by the number of olive trees on a given property; no estate was ever without its olives. For the peasants the olive was one of the sole foods of sustenance; together with corn bread and greens it formed the dietary trinity that kept whole families alive.

Despite the island's affinity, whether willing or imposed, for the olive, one thing is unique here: The harvest in Corfu is noticeably different from that in other parts of Greece. The trees are rarely pruned. They look different from the olive trees in and around Kalamata, or in Crete, for example. In Corfu they are tall and wide, not conducive to climbing or stoking with long poles to facilitate the harvest. So, native practice when it comes to reaping the fruit is just to let it fall to the ground. This has been the source of numerous snubs about islanders' innate indolence. I can't pass judgment on that, although it is odd that, as a result, the harvest lasts months. Often there is still fruit on the tree when it flowers in April. The truth is that Corfu's oil is more acidic than the oil in other parts of the country, and this is a direct result of the bruising that occurs as the olives fall to the ground, waiting to be collected.

CHARCUTERIE

Several cured meats are unique to the Ionian Islands.

Noumboulo, made with pork tenderloin, traditionally is prepared in Corfu in the winter, around the time of the pig slaughters, and is ready to eat at Easter. Although today it is manufactured locally and often found all year-round in the island's supermarkets, a few artisans still prepare it the old-fashioned way. First, the casing is washed with red wine. Then the meat is marinated in wine and black pepper for three days. It is fitted into the casing together with a single long strip of pork fat. The whole thing is about one to two inches wide and three inches long. Once in the casing, the *noumboulo* is tied up with reeds, which help to keep it straight during the long smoking process. Aromatic woods and sprigs—olive, laurel, rosemary, oregano, and sage—are used to smoke it. *Noumboulo* takes about three months to prepare.

The *Salami Lefkados,* salami of Lefkada, is less esoteric. It is an air-dried, fairly fatty salami with a very pronounced pork taste. On the island it is eaten as a *meze* or as an accompaniment to bean soups and stews. It is widely available all over Greece now and carried by all Athens's large supermarkets.

Zakynthos lays claim to two interesting cured pork preparations. The first is the *hiromeri,* which is a cured ham similar to prosciutto but saltier. It still is a prominent feature of the Easter menu.

The *pancetta* of Zakynthos is quite different. Despite its name, it is not bacon (like the same word in Italian) but rather a kind of cured, smoked sparerib. There is also a cooked dish called *pancetta* on the island that is pork belly stuffed with cheese and herbs.

SWEETS

There used to be dozens of workshops turning out plank after plank of chewy *mandolato*—the Ionian sweet made with meringue, honey, and almonds that once was the standard gift of every prospective groom in Zakynthos to his bride and her parents when he went courting. The sweet has always been associated with Zakynthos—and, to a lesser degree, with Lefkada, where, of all things, its production was monopolized by local barbers, who put their apprentices' idle time to good use by making them chop almonds. As a tribute to that tradition, some old barber shops in Lefkada still stack and sell boxes of local *mandolato.*

Zakynthos has everything it takes to make great *mandolato*—eggs, exquisite honey, and plenty of almonds. According to Anastasios Kokkonis, owner of one of the handful of old *mandolato* workshops still left on the island, when the confection arrived with the Venetians it was first made with bitter almonds. Today, although the confection is still considered a Seven Islands tradition, it is rarely made with any local ingredients, because they are too expensive. Cheaper honey and almonds are imported from elsewhere. There is a difference, too, in the *mandolato* of Zakynthos and that of Lefkada. The former likes a straightforward, chewy bar, similar to nougat; in Lefkada, the nougatlike confection is twisted with wafers and shaped into amorphous clumps.

Pastelli, the sesame brittle found in many versions all over Greece, also has a long-standing tradition in the Ionian, except that sometimes here it is flavored with anise. Zakynthos also makes *mandoles,* or candy-covered almonds, a local version of confetti, which are used in wedding favors and as a topping for ice cream.

The Recipes

MEZETHES

Throughout the rest of Greece old bread is usually cooked into porridgelike dishes or fried with a little olive oil to stave off hunger. It is never, of course, wasted or thrown away. *Paximathia,* or rusks—twice-baked bread usually made from barley or chickpea flour—are dampened and eaten in place of bread as the midday snack if you are out working your fields. In Crete and in Santorini, rusks are served with tomatoes and olive oil in a kind of salad. But nowhere else in the country do we find dried bread served as it is in the Ionian, spread with olive oil or cheese or tomatoes and revered as a tasteful *meze.*

In the Corfiote pantry, up until the years following World War II, everyone ate *rimbolitho,* the light evening meal that was basically nothing more than slices of leftover bread rubbed with garlic, topped with whatever the day's lunch was—from fish to beans—and warmed briefly in the oven. There was *panatha,* in Corfu a concoction of dried bread cubes soaked in water, then cooked to a thick gruel, to which eggs, paprika, butter, and grated cheese were added. In Lefkada *panatha* is a simpler affair: old bread cooked in olive oil with onions and tomatoes. Following are a few of the Ionian's traditional, unusual bread *mezethes.*

Crumbled Feta Spread on Bread from Zakynthos

PRETZA ME PSOMI

  Makes 6 to 10 pieces

Pretza is a local feta cheese product made in Zakynthos and Cephalonia, something akin to cream cheese but pungent and peppery (see page 71). You can find it in several cheese shops in Athens, but it is nowhere to be found in America. You can make an ersatz version by mixing crumbled feta with a little ricotta or fresh Greek myzithra *cheese, olive oil, and thyme. This is a wonderful breakfast meal, and indeed that's how it is eaten on the island, but it also serves well as an opener to any hearty Mediterranean meal.*

1½ cups crumbled Greek feta cheese

⅓ cup ricotta or *myzithra* cheese

3 to 4 heaping tablespoons thick Mediterranean-style yogurt or plain yogurt, drained (see page 459), to taste

3 to 4 tablespoons extra-virgin olive oil, plus more to taste, for drizzling on the bread

2 teaspoons dried thyme
Good bread, preferably sourdough with a thick
    crust, cut into six to ten ½-inch-thick slices
1 to 2 firm, ripe tomatoes, as needed, sliced
Freshly ground black pepper to taste

1. Combine the feta, ricotta or *myzithra*, yogurt, olive oil, and thyme in a small bowl or whip together in a food processor. You can make the spread several days ahead.

2. To serve, toast the bread on both sides under the broiler until golden. Drizzle a little olive oil on each slice. Spread a tablespoon or two of the cheese mixture on each slice, top with a slice of tomato, and sprinkle with pepper.

Bread or Rusks with Vinegar, Olive Oil, and Salted Sardines from Lefkada

RIGANATHA APO TIN LEFKADA

This is another simple bread snack that was the traditional afternoon meal among field hands and farmers in Lefkada. Islanders will tell you proudly that riganatha *isn't made anywhere else in Greece, and they are right. Unique to this dish is its dressing—rose water vinegar.*

For the rose water vinegar: The traditional way of making this was to extract the rose essence by placing petals of the flower in a glass jar and letting it stand in the sun for several days. You can try it (see page 69) only if you have unsprayed garden roses; otherwise, combine ¼ cup mild red wine vinegar with 2 teaspoons rose water and let it sit for at least a day before using. It's an ersatz version, to be sure; nonetheless,

the flavored vinegar is also delicious with tender greens and salad.

Slices stale sourdough bread or several whole
    wheat or barley rusks
Extra-virgin olive oil
Salt to taste
Dried oregano
Rose water vinegar or any good fragrant red wine
    vinegar
Salted sardines

If using rusks, run them quickly under the tap to dampen slightly, then pat dry, break apart, place on a platter, and drizzle with olive oil. If using stale bread, dampen only if it is extremely hard; otherwise, just drizzle with olive oil. (You don't need to break it apart since it isn't as hard as the rusks.) Sprinkle with salt and oregano and, finally, with a few drops of the rose water or other fragrant vinegar. Serve accompanied by salted sardines.

Sautéed Bread with Onion and Tomato from Lefkada

PANADA

 Makes 2 to 4 servings

Kitchen economy in Greece, indeed in the whole Mediterranean, once required that home cooks make use of every last bit of food. There are lots of old dishes made with leftover bread. Most call for simmering small bits of stale bread in some kind of broth or milk or sometimes just in plain water with a little olive oil and salt. I like this old dish, which calls for

sautéing cubes of stale bread with a few other ingredients. Panada is one more dish from Lefkada, culled from the island's impressive repertory of simple country recipes.

6 tablespoons extra-virgin olive oil

2 cups 1-inch bread cubes without crusts

1 medium red onion, coarsely chopped

3 tablespoons tomato paste

Salt to taste

Freshly ground black pepper to taste

1. Heat 2 tablespoons of the olive oil in a large skillet over medium-low heat and sauté the bread until golden and crisp. Remove bread and set aside.

2. Add 2 more tablespoons of olive oil and cook the onion, stirring, just until the onion begins to color, about 10 minutes. Add the tomato paste and swirl around with the onion. Season with a little salt. Add the bread and toss all together in the skillet until the bread is warmed through. Remove from the heat, drizzle with the remaining 2 tablespoons olive oil, season with salt and pepper, and serve.

Garlic-and-Potato Sauce from Cephalonia

ALIATHA TIS KEFALONIAS

 Makes 6 to 8 servings

This is nothing more than the island's own skordalia, *the pungent dipping sauce made with potatoes and lots of garlic. Two things define the Cephalonian version:* Aliatha *is always made with potatoes and always with fish broth, preferably made from cod bones. It has a strong, acidic flavor since Greeks are not shy about using either garlic or lemon juice in generous quantities. The taste will vary, however, depending on the time of year you make this dish: In spring, when garlic is fresh, its flavor is delicate; in the fall and winter, garlic is dry and brittle and its flavor harsh and more bitter.* Aliatha *is a good match on a* meze *table for the greens cooked with tomato on page 79 or with cod croquettes, page 254, a popular duo throughout Greece.*

4 to 5 large waxy potatoes, to taste, scrubbed well

6 to 8 garlic cloves, to taste, peeled and crushed

Salt to taste

Juice of 2 to 3 lemons, to taste

1 to 2 cups fish broth, as needed

Extra-virgin olive oil, as needed

1. Boil the potatoes whole in salted water to cover. When they are tender and begin bursting out of their skins, remove the pot from the heat.

2. In a large mortar, crush one or two garlic cloves together with a little salt and lemon juice until the mixture becomes a thick paste.

3. Remove one potato from the hot water and peel quickly. Pound it in the mortar until it becomes part of the garlic paste and drizzle in a little fish broth (about ¼ cup) and olive oil as you go. Continue doing this, transferring some of the *aliatha* to a bowl as you go, until all the ingredients are used. The final consistency of the *aliatha* should be creamy and smooth. It will keep for up to 2 days, covered and refrigerated. After that the garlic starts to turn bitter.

⊙

Garlic Sauce from Corfu

AYIATHA TIS KERKYRAS

 Makes 6 to 8 servings

Another take on the pan-Mediterranean garlic sauce that accompanies fried fish and boiled vegetables. But Corfu's version of ayiatha, *as it is pronounced in the local dialect, calls for bread and almonds, as opposed to potatoes, as the base. Vinegar makes this garlic sauce slightly harsher in flavor than those that call for lemon juice. Locals tend to use strong red-wine vinegar, which will give the final dish a dark grayish-rose color.* Ayiatha *will keep for up to 2 days in the refrigerator, but it is best to eat it fresh.*

1 small head garlic (about 6 small cloves)

Three 1-inch-thick slices stale rustic bread, crusts removed

Salt to taste

1 cup finely chopped blanched almonds

1 cup extra-virgin olive oil

3 to 5 tablespoons red wine vinegar, to taste

Separate the garlic cloves and peel. Run the bread under the tap, wring dry, and crumble. In a large mortar, crush the garlic with a little salt until it is like a thick paste. Slowly add the bread, almonds, oil, and vinegar in alternating increments. Pound very well after each addition. The *ayiatha* must be creamy. The whole process will take 10 to 12 minutes.

A NOTE ON POUNDING GARLIC SAUCES

Pounding *aliatha, ayiatha,* or *skordalia* in a mortar takes time and energy. You'll need a large mortar, made of either granite or wood. I prefer wooden ones because they impart another, albeit subtle, flavor component to the finished sauce. If pounding manually isn't your cup of tea, you can simulate the action by pounding the sauce in a stand mixer with the paddle mechanism—not the blade, which breaks down the potato or bread too quickly and causes the *aliatha* to become gummy. That's why I would never recommend a food processor.

Sweet Mustard

MOSTARDA DOLCE

 Makes about 4 cups

Zakynthos and Corfu both make sweet mustards, vestiges of English and Venetian rule. The mustards, made either with quince, as in this recipe, or with dried fruits, are eaten at Christmas with roast turkey, game, pork, or other meats.

3 quinces, peeled and cored

1 quart Mavrodaphne wine or sweet port

1 teaspoon ground cloves

½ teaspoon freshly grated nutmeg

2 teaspoons dry mustard

1. Cut the quinces into cubes. Place in a large saucepan with the wine, bring to a boil, reduce the heat to low, and simmer, covered, until the quinces are very soft and the mixture is thick, about 40 minutes.

2. Combine the quinces with the spices and mustard and keep stored in a glass jar in the refrigerator. *Mostarda dolce* is excellent spread on bread.

SOUP

The World's Most Basic Soup

ZOUPA

 Makes 4 servings

This dish is the apotheosis of the trinity of Mediter-ranean flavors—wheat, wine, and olive oil. I was first led to it in Cephalonia by Siora Eleni Cosmetatou, an Englishwoman who has lived on the island for most of the last fifty years and whose son produces some of the best wines in Greece. "It's just like the akraton—*the breakfast of bread and undiluted wine—that the ancients used to eat." At first I thought it was one of those dishes, like so many others, lost to time, but I found it in Pylaro, the island's cheese-making area in the North, where it is the lunchtime meal during the olive harvest.* Zoupa *is still eaten in Lefkada, too, where the wine used is the dark and tannic local vari-ety made from the* vartzami *grape. I don't know if anyone would actually make this in America, although I did attempt to serve it once at an olive-oil tasting I organized at Milos restaurant in New York. People lapped it up. I wanted to include it for histori-cal reasons.*

Four 1-inch slices stale rustic bread
1⅓ cups dark, dry red wine
1½ cups extra-virgin olive oil

1. Toast the bread, preferably over coals or on a grill. Warm the wine slightly.

2. Place each piece of bread in a dish, pour on ample olive oil (4 to 5 tablespoons per slice), and then drizzle into each bowl about ⅓ cup of warmed wine. Let the bread soak a bit and serve.

Turkey Soup with Egg-Lemon Sauce

GALOPOULA AVGOLEMONO

 Makes 8 to 10 servings

Sometime after the sixteenth century, turkey arrived in Corfu from the West. There is some disagreement as to who first brought it. If its name is any indica-tion, then the turkey came with the French, since its name in Greek, galopoula, *translates literally as "French bird." Regardless of its provenance, today it is still the Christmas meal in Corfu. In fact islanders distinguish between the male and female birds. The female turkey is turned into* avgolemono *soup, while the male is stuffed (either with pasta or with bread) and roasted with potatoes. The turkey would not be complete, though, without the candied fruit-filled* mostarda dolce, *or sweet mustard (see page 76), which almost certainly came with the Venetians.*

1 turkey carcass, divided into several large
    pieces
3 quarts water
2 large carrots, peeled
1 large onion, peeled
2 celery stalks
⅔ cup short-grain rice
2 cups peeled, seeded, and diced firm, ripe
    tomatoes
Salt and freshly ground black pepper to taste
3 large eggs, separated
Juice of 2 lemons, or more to taste
½ cup grated *kefalograviera* cheese or any hard
    yellow cheese

1. Preheat the oven to 450°F. Place the turkey carcass on a large sheet pan and place in the oven. Leave for 10 minutes, then reduce the oven temperature to 375°F. Leave the carcass in the oven until browned, another 30 to 40 minutes. Remove from the oven and let cool.

2. Place the bones in a large stockpot with the water. Bring to a boil, then add the carrots, onion, and celery. Reduce the heat to medium-low and simmer for about 2 hours, skimming the foam off the top. Strain the broth through a fine-mesh sieve and discard the bones and vegetables. Return the broth to the pot, add the rice and tomatoes, and season with salt and pepper. Simmer until the rice is tender, another 20 minutes, then turn off the heat.

3. Meanwhile, make the egg-lemon sauce: Beat the egg yolks in a large bowl until pale and creamy. Beat in the lemon juice. Whip the egg whites separately in a medium-size bowl with an electric mixer until stiff peaks form. Fold the whites into the yolks. Slowly pour a ladleful of the hot broth into the eggs, whipping all the while with a wire whisk to temper them. Do this with several ladlesful of the soup. Pour the eggs into the stockpot, stir well, and serve immediately, topped with the grated cheese. Squeeze in more lemon juice if desired when the soup is served.

Lenten Fresh Clam Soup from Lefkada

LEFKADITIKI HAVIAROSOUPA

Makes 8 servings

5 pounds cockles or any other small fresh clams
½ cup extra-virgin olive oil
4 fresh green garlic stalks, coarsely chopped, or
    3 scallions, white and tender green parts,
    chopped, combined with 2 garlic cloves,
    minced
Salt and freshly ground black pepper to taste
½ cup medium-grain polished rice
Juice of 2 large lemons

1. Place the clams in a large basin filled with water and soak all day, changing the water frequently to rid them of as much sand as possible. Place in a large soup pot and add water to cover by 4 inches. Bring to a boil and remove from the heat as soon as the shells have opened. Drain the clams in a colander set over a large bowl to catch the broth. Let the clams cool slightly and remove from their shells, discarding any clams whose shells haven't opened.

2. Heat the olive oil in the soup pot and cook the fresh garlic or the scallions and garlic over medium heat, stirring, until wilted, 5 to 7 minutes.

3. Strain the broth through cheesecloth to catch any remaining sand and pour back into the soup pot. Bring to a boil, season with salt and pepper, and add the rice. Reduce the heat to medium-low and simmer until tender, about 20 minutes. Add the clams back to the pot and season with the lemon juice. Simmer until the clams are heated through. Remove from the heat and serve.

Octopus Soup

HTAPODOSOUPA

 Makes 6 to 8 servings

This soup traditionally calls for dried octopus, not the easiest thing to find either in America or in urban Greece, so I have reworked it a little for fresh octopus.

1 medium fresh or frozen (see Note) octopus
    (about 3 pounds), cleaned if necessary
    (see page 462)
½ cup extra-virgin olive oil
1 cup dry white wine
2 medium yellow or red onions, halved and finely
    chopped
1 cup grated firm, ripe tomatoes (see page 459)
    or chopped canned plum tomatoes
1 to 2 fresh oregano sprigs, to taste
Freshly ground black pepper to taste
⅔ cup tiny pasta stars or pastina
Aged *myzithra* cheese or any hard white cheese
    for grating
Salt, as needed (see Note)

1. Place the octopus in a large pot. Pour in ¼ cup of the olive oil and ¼ cup of the wine. Cover and cook over very low heat until the octopus has a deep pink color and is fairly tender, 25 to 30 minutes. The octopus will have exuded its own juices. Remove from the pot and cut into pieces small enough to manage with a soupspoon. Reserve the pot juices.

2. In another large pot, heat the remaining ¼ cup olive oil and cook the onions over medium heat, stirring, until lightly browned, 8 to 10 minutes. Add the octopus pieces, the remaining ¾ cup wine, and the tomatoes. Pour the reserved octopus juices into the pot together with about 8 cups of water. Add the oregano and season with pepper. Cover,

bring to a boil, reduce the heat to medium-low, and simmer for another 30 minutes. Add the pasta to the pot. Continue simmering until the pasta is tender. If the pasta makes the soup too thick, dilute it with a little more water. Remove from the heat and serve hot, with freshly grated cheese and black pepper on top.

✴ **NOTE** If using frozen octopus, defrost in the refrigerator overnight.

Because octopus is naturally salty, most dishes made with it rarely require additional salt. Taste and adjust seasoning as needed.

VEGETABLES

Sautéed Greens with Onions and Tomatoes

TSIGARELLI

 Makes 4 servings

In spring, certain tender greens, both bitter and sweet, are picked to make tsigarelli, *a dish of blanched greens sautéed with onions, herbs, olive oil, and—traditionally—reddened with paprika or chile pepper. Today the dish has been modified considerably and is more likely to get its color mainly from tomatoes. Tsigarelli is not exclusive to Corfu—it is found throughout the Ionian Islands, and, indeed, stewed greens are popular in many other parts of Greece. One thing unique, though, about the greens in Corfu, whether simply boiled as for salad or cooked for tsigarelli, is that they are always served hot.*

An old acquaintance, Nico Manessi, a Corfiote by

birth, remembers this dish from his childhood and acted as my gauge when I tried to replicate the recipe. One should look for tender greens. Most local cooks prefer bitter young greens, but today there seems to be no rule of thumb. Tomato paste is added in the modern-day rendition of this dish, but traditional island cooks use paprika to lend red color and cayenne to spice it up.

2½ pounds fresh, preferably mixed tender greens, such as spinach, sorrel, and dandelion, trimmed and washed well
¼ cup extra-virgin olive oil, or more to taste
2 large onions, halved and sliced
1¼ cups snipped fresh wild fennel leaves or 1 large fennel bulb, trimmed, quartered, and thinly sliced, plus 1 scant teaspoon ground fennel seeds
2 garlic cloves, minced
¼ cup tomato paste or 1 heaping tablespoon sweet paprika
2 teaspoons sweet paprika
1¼ cups snipped fresh dill
Salt and cayenne pepper to taste

1. Steam or blanch the greens until wilted, then drain completely.

2. Heat the olive oil in a large skillet and cook the onions, stirring, over medium heat until soft, 5 to 7 minutes. If using sliced fennel bulb and seeds, add them here and wilt together with the onions. Add the garlic, tomato paste, and paprika and stir for about 3 minutes. Add the wilted greens, dill, and wild fennel leaves (if using), and simmer over low heat, uncovered, until the greens are soft and all the pan liquids have cooked off, about 20 minutes. The dish should be fairly dry. Adjust the seasoning with salt and cayenne and serve either hot or warm. Pour a little fresh olive oil over the greens once they are cooked, if desired.

Zucchini Blossoms and Greens Cooked with Garlic and Celery Root from Lefkada

KOLOKITHOKORFATHES ME SKORTHO KAI SELINORIZA

 Makes 4 to 6 servings

In Greece in the late spring, zucchini flowers fill up the markets. There are 2 kinds: the large sturdy flowers that grow on the stalk of the zucchini plant and the smaller, more fragile ones that sprout out of the actual zucchini. Greeks generally prefer the sturdier ones because they're easier to work with. These are sold together with the stalks and the leaves in Greek markets. This unusual recipe is one more addition to the endless litany of lathera, *basically stewed vegetables with ample olive oil. As for finding the zucchini stalks, leaves, and blossoms, they are available at some ethnic markets in America and through several specialty mail-order houses.*

2 pounds zucchini stems, leaves, and blossoms
⅔ cup extra-virgin olive oil, or more to taste
1 large celery root, peeled, cut into 1-inch cubes (1½ to 2 cups), and placed in acidulated water (see page 458)
4 large garlic cloves, thinly sliced
Salt and freshly ground black pepper to taste
Juice of 1 large lemon

1. Trim the root ends off the zucchini stems. Cut the stems into 2-inch pieces; coarsely chop or julienne the leaves and blossoms, keeping them separate.

2. Heat half the oil in a stewing pot or Dutch oven over medium heat, add the cubed celery root, toss to coat in the oil, cover, and steam in the oil for 5 minutes. Add the garlic and stir to mix. Add the zucchini stems and leaves, again tossing to coat. Pour in just enough water to come about halfway up the contents of the pot. Season with salt and pepper, cover, and simmer over low heat until all the vegetables are soft, about 25 minutes. Add the flowers to the pot and continue cooking, covered, for another 10 to 15 minutes, until all the vegetables are very tender. Just before removing from the heat, pour in the lemon juice and the remaining olive oil.

Garlicky Eggplant from Zakynthos

MELITZANES SKORDOSTOUMBI

 Makes 4 to 6 servings

This simple dish is a paean to the robust flavors that mark so much of Greek—and Ionian—cooking. Garlic and vinegar are a combination we find on country tables all over Greece, but usually it is one reserved for seasoning meat. Its use here with eggplant is what makes it unique.

2 large or 3 medium eggplant (about 2 pounds total), sliced into ½-inch-thick rounds

Salt to taste

½ to ⅔ cup extra-virgin olive oil, as needed

8 to 10 garlic cloves, to taste, peeled and crushed

4 to 5 large tomatoes, to taste, grated (see page 459)

Freshly ground black pepper to taste

3 tablespoons sherry vinegar or red wine vinegar, or to taste

1 teaspoon sugar (optional)

1. Place the eggplant slices in layers in a colander, salting each layer lightly. Place a plate and a weight on top of them and leave to drain for 1 hour. Rinse and pat dry.

2. Heat 2 to 3 tablespoons of the olive oil in a large, heavy skillet over medium-high heat and lightly brown the eggplant slices on both sides, in batches, replenishing the olive oil if necessary. Drain on paper towels.

3. Preheat the oven to 350°F. Heat 2 tablespoons olive oil in another large skillet and cook the garlic over medium heat, until soft and lightly browned, about 10 minutes. Add the grated tomato pulp and season with salt and pepper. Add the vinegar and adjust the seasoning after a few minutes by adding a little sugar if the sauce is too acidic. Simmer, uncovered, over low heat for 10 minutes.

4. Lightly oil a 10-inch square ovenproof glass or ceramic baking dish. Place the eggplant slices in layers in the dish and pour a little of the sauce over each layer, reserving a bit for the top. Sprinkle the top with a few more drops of vinegar. Bake until the eggplant is tender and the sauce thick, 40 to 45 minutes. Serve hot, lukewarm, or at room temperature.

Sweet Potatoes with Onions and Cayenne

GLYKOPATATES BOURTHETO

 Makes 4 servings

Sweet potatoes probably came to Corfu with the Venetians, as did many other New World crops, sometime during the sixteenth century, where they remained poor man's fodder for hundreds of years. It took the English to popularize them, by showing Corfiote aristocrats the virtues of serving them with syrup. Nevertheless, they have long been cooked on a grill or in a pan in the classic Greek way, with olive oil and garlic. Roasted sweet potatoes were the classic accompaniment to Christmas turkey. There is also one great old recipe for sweet potatoes cooked with onions and cayenne, in a countryside rendition of bourtheto.

3 tablespoons extra-virgin olive oil

2 large red onions, peeled, halved, and thinly sliced

2 garlic cloves, finely chopped

1 heaping tablespoon sweet paprika

1 teaspoon cayenne pepper, or more or less to taste

1 tablespoon tomato paste

3 pounds sweet potatoes, peeled and quartered lengthwise

1 cup dry white wine

Salt and freshly ground black pepper to taste

1. Heat the olive oil in a large, heavy skillet and sweat the onions and garlic over low heat, covered, until softened, 5 to 7 minutes. Add the paprika, cayenne, and tomato paste and stir with a wooden spoon for about a minute.

2. Add the sweet potatoes and stir for another minute. Pour in ½ cup of the wine and enough water to barely cover the potatoes. Bring to a gentle boil, lower the heat to medium-low, and simmer, covered, until the sauce is thick and dark, about 15 minutes. Season with salt and pepper.

3. Add the remaining ½ cup wine, cover the pot, and simmer until the potatoes are very tender, another 10 to 15 minutes.

4. Remove from the heat, let stand for about 5 minutes, and serve.

PASTA, RICE, AND POLENTA

It was some years ago that I first met Ninetta Laskari in her fabulous ancestral home in the town of Agio Marko in Corfu. I had gone in search of the island's traditional cuisine, and all roads seemed then to lead to her. Mrs. Laskari, a self-taught expert on Corfu's social and culinary history, daughter of an old and illustrious family with Venetian roots, had embarked on a book about the island she was born and raised on and loves so dearly. Her house, a seventeenth-century building heaving under the patina of so much history, was recessed into the hills, nestled by Corfu's lush greenery, by the cyprus and pine and olive trees that sweep over the whole island. The sitting room overlooked an operatic panorama of sea and sky, a view as grand as Mrs. Laskari herself. She was well into her seventies when I visited her and as lordly as one can be in Greece. Mrs. Laskari, a heavy-set woman with a sonorous voice and a certain dolefulness about her that seemed at odds with her patrician ways, invited me to sit on one of the plush velvet couches in her sitting room. Her servant poured us tea from a silver samovar and served us sweets on delicate gold-rimmed china. The whole house was filled with antiques, family heirlooms stretching back seven and eight generations.

After a lengthy conversation—the kind of give and take that serves as a litmus test for trust—she must have realized my motives for visiting her were innocuous and my interest in the island's food genuine. After about three hours of lecturing me ever so gently on Corfu and its unique social history, she rose and led me to the oldest part of the house, explaining that very few guests were ever invited back there. I had to duck my head as we passed under a three-hundred-year-old doorway. On the other side was the original kitchen, still perfectly intact. She had managed to collect and keep in mint condition almost all the culinary paraphernalia that had been used by her and her husband's families over the generations. She had a whole array of antique molds, one of which, as tall as a top hat but narrower, was specifically for making one of the best dishes I found and tasted in all the Seven Islands, and one I first learned about from Mrs. Laskari. It is the *pastitsio Venetsianiko,* a grand composition of pasta, boiled eggs, and all the residual meats, cheeses, and charcuterie that would have been typically produced on an old Corfiote estate. She told me of another, even more baroque version, the *pastitsio dolce,* which calls for a sweet pastry shell. In the recipes that follow, I offer a version of both, but in their modern transformation; nowadays *pastitsio Venetsianiko* and its sweeter cousin are not the tall, dramatic dishes they were in the days when Venetian aristocrats ruled the island. But it is still a delicious, rich combination of pasta and charcuterie encrusted in a delicate pastry, and one could certainly make it as it was originally intended to be, an amalgam of all the week's leftovers metamorphosed. It is still made in Corfiote homes on festive occasions.

Pastry-Cloaked Pasta from Corfu

PASTITSIO VENETSIANIKO

 Makes 10 to 12 servings

For the pastry
3¼ cups all-purpose flour
1 teaspoon salt
1½ teaspoons sugar
1½ cups (3 sticks) cold unsalted butter
⅓ to ½ cup ice water, as needed

For the filling
1 pound thick tubular spaghetti, like bucatini
2 to 3 tablespoons unsalted butter, to taste
2 cups shredded, cooked chicken
½ pound boneless smoked ham or cooked pork chop, diced
½ pound salami or mortadella, diced
2 to 3 small fresh sausages, sautéed, cooked through and chopped
2 to 3 cups diced yellow cheese (*graviera, kasseri,* etc.), to taste
4 hard-cooked eggs, peeled and halved
Freshly ground black pepper to taste
Pinch of cayenne pepper

For the béchamel
¼ cup (½ stick) unsalted butter
3 tablespoons all-purpose flour
3 cups milk
1 cup heavy cream
Salt to taste
2 large egg yolks

1. Make the pastry: In a food processor fitted with the pastry blade, pulse together the flour, salt, and sugar. Cut the butter into small pieces and add to the flour. Pulse on and off until the flour is mealy, about 30 seconds. Add the ice water a little at a time and pulse on and off just until a dough begins to form. Remove and shape the dough into 2 balls, one slightly larger than the other. Flatten each into a disk, cover with plastic wrap, and refrigerate for at least an hour but no longer than one day before using. Before rolling the dough out, let it rest at room temperature for 30 minutes.

If making the pastry by hand, mix the flour, salt, and sugar together in a large bowl. Add the butter, cut into small pieces, and cut it into the flour using either a pastry cutter or 2 knives, stopping when the mixture is the consistency of coarse meal. Add the ice water a little at a time and mix the dough quickly by hand until a mass takes form. Shape the dough into 2 balls, one slightly larger than the other, then flatten each into a disk, cover with plastic wrap, and refrigerate.

2. Boil the pasta in salted water until it is softened but not completely cooked through. Drain, place back in the pot, and mix with the butter.

3. Make the béchamel: In a medium saucepan, heat the butter over medium heat. When it begins to bubble, add the flour and stir vigorously with a wire whisk for several minutes until the flour turns pale gold. Add the milk, stirring all the while; add the heavy cream. Continue stirring the béchamel over medium heat until very thick, 10 to 12 minutes. Season with salt. Remove from the heat, cool slightly, and add the egg yolks, stirring vigorously.

4. Preheat the oven to 375°F. Lightly butter a 12-inch springform pan. Roll out the larger ball of dough to a circle big enough to fit up the sides of the pan and to hang over the edge a little. Place it in the pan.

5. Mix half the buttered pasta with half of the meats and cheese, season with pepper and cayenne, and toss with about one-third of the béchamel. Place in the bottom of the pan. Place

the hard-cooked eggs (8 halves) on top of the pasta so that they are evenly spaced. Combine the remaining pasta with the remaining meats and cheese, season with additional pepper and cayenne as desired, and toss with a little more béchamel. Spread evenly in the pan over the eggs. Pour in the remaining béchamel. Press the filling down with a plate or a big spoon.

6. Roll out the second dough ball and place it over the filling. Press the edges together and fold inward to form a decorative rim around the *pastitsio.* Bake until the pastry is golden, about 1 hour and 15 minutes. Remove from the oven, let cool for 20 to 30 minutes, and serve.

⊙ For *pastitsio dolce,* use the sweetened pastry *pasta frolla.*

3¾ cups all-purpose flour
¾ cup sugar
½ teaspoon salt
½ teaspoon baking powder
15 tablespoons unsalted butter, chilled
1 large egg
1 large egg yolk
6 tablespoons water

1. In a food processor fitted with the pastry blade, pulse together the flour, sugar, salt, and baking powder. Cut the butter into small pieces and add to the flour. Pulse on and off until the flour is mealy, about 30 seconds. Add the whole egg and pulse, then add the egg yolk and pulse on and off to combine. Add the water and pulse just until a dough begins to form.

2. Remove and shape the dough into 2 balls, one slightly larger than the other. Flatten each into a disk, cover with plastic wrap, and refrigerate for at least an hour but no longer than one day before using. Before rolling the dough out, let it rest at room temperature for 30 minutes.

To make the pastry by hand: Combine the dry ingredients in a large bowl. Cut the butter into small pieces and work it into the flour using your fingertips, rubbing the flour and butter together until the whole mixture is mealy. Do this quickly and thoroughly, so that all the flour has been mixed with the butter, about 2 minutes. Using a fork, lightly beat the egg, egg yolk, and water together in a small bowl and pour into the flour mixture. Mix all together with a fork until a dough mass begins to form. Turn out onto a lightly floured work surface and squeeze the dough together until it is smooth. Be careful not to overwork it, or it will be tough. Shape the dough into 2 balls, one slightly larger than the other, and then flatten each into a disk. Wrap in plastic and chill for at least 1 hour.

Proceed with the *pastitsio* recipe from step 2.

Shrimp and Curry Pilaf from Ithaca

GARIDES PILAFI ME KARI

 Makes 4 to 6 servings

A strange and very un-Greek recipe, since this unusual dish has existed in Ithaca for the last three decades. It is the product of two historical forces—the British domination of the island from the end of the nineteenth century to the middle of the twentieth and the economic circumstances that forced husbands, brothers, and sons to take to the seas as merchant marines. The British brought with them their beloved curries from India, and the ever-flowing tide of returning sailors who encountered the spice mix in their own travels brought it back to the island, too. Both helped give curry a permanent place in the larder of every island cook. This dish is also made with lobster in Ithaca.

3 tablespoons unsalted butter
1 tablespoon extra-virgin olive oil
2 medium red onions, finely chopped
2 garlic cloves, minced
4 teaspoons curry powder
2 cups peeled, seeded, and chopped plum
    tomatoes (canned are fine)
1 cup dry white wine
Salt and freshly ground black pepper to taste
1 teaspoon sugar (optional)
4 cups water
2 cups long-grain rice
2½ pounds medium shrimp, cleaned and deveined

1. In a large skillet, heat 1 tablespoon of the butter and the olive oil over medium heat and cook the onions, stirring until soft, 5 to 7 minutes. Add the garlic, stir it for a minute, then add the curry and stir with a wooden spoon for 1 minute. Add the tomatoes, bring to a boil, and pour in the wine. Season with salt and pepper and sugar if necessary. Reduce the heat to a simmer and cook, covered, until the sauce thickens, 15 to 20 minutes.

2. Meanwhile, prepare the rice: Bring the water to a boil, salt lightly, and add the rice. Reduce the heat to medium-low and simmer, partially covered, until the water is absorbed and the rice tender, 15 to 20 minutes. Toss the rice with the remaining 2 tablespoons butter. You can prepare it ahead to this point.

3. About 5 minutes before serving, add the shrimp to the sauce and cook until bright pink. Serve the sauce over the rice on a serving platter or on individual plates.

Pilaf with a Head of Garlic from Ithaca

ITHAKIANO PILAFI ME ENA KEFALI SKORDO

 Makes about 4 servings

I *took a couple of liberties with this old Ithacan dish. First, believe it or not, I reduced the amount of garlic from one head per serving to one head for 4 servings. The garlic is poached first, an old Greek method for ridding it of its bitter edge. I also replaced the original short-grain polished rice, which turns mushy easily, with aromatic, long-grain rice, preferably basmati. The dish makes a nice side to various meat and poultry dishes. I like it very much with* sofrito *(page 95) and with quail and fava bean stew (page 94).*

1 medium head garlic, cloves very thinly sliced
    lengthwise
5 tablespoons extra-virgin olive oil
1 cup dry white wine
1 cup peeled, seeded, and chopped plum
    tomatoes (canned are fine)
Salt and freshly ground black pepper to taste
1 cup long-grain rice (preferably basmati)

1. Bring about 1 inch of water to a simmer in a small skillet and poach the garlic for 1 minute. Remove the garlic, pour off the water, and dry the skillet. Heat it again with 3 tablespoons of the olive oil. Add the poached garlic back to the skillet and cook it over low heat until it begins to soften, about 3 minutes.

2. Add the wine to the skillet and, as soon as it steams up, pour in the tomatoes. Season with salt and pepper. When the sauce begins to boil, add the rice and keep stirring it over low to medium heat until it swells and softens, slowly adding another cup or so of water to the skillet to keep the pilaf moist. This should take 12 to 15 minutes. When the rice is cooked and the water absorbed, adjust the seasoning, toss with the remaining 2 tablespoons olive oil, and serve.

Polenta from Lefkada

LEFKADITIKI POULENTA

 Makes 6 servings

M*uch of my wanderings for this book took me to older women, and their husbands, who would usually sit near them in the family armchair and impose their opinions on almost every aspect of the cooking arts. Whenever the subject of polenta came up, it was as though I were inciting revolution. They'd raise their palms in the typical Greek gesture of disbelief, furrow their eyebrows, and utter a high-pitched "pa-pa-pa-pa-pa," the Greek for "no-no-no."*

Most older Greeks cringe at the thought of eating what to many Americans has become synonymous with Italian comfort food, because it was just about the only thing, together with some hardtack, chicory coffee, and maybe a little olive oil, if they were lucky, that kept them alive during the long hard years of World War II. People were very hungry then, and when the war was finally over, the national psyche spurned anything that reminded it even vaguely of the years when so many Greeks were lost to starvation. Most younger Greeks have never even tasted it because their parents have shunned it, as one woman told me, "like the devil shuns church incense."

So why include it here? First, because it is familiar

food to so many Americans. Second, because many people love it. And third, because I found some interesting versions of the dish prepared in the kitchens of old Greek cooks.

Cornmeal still figures prominently in some Greek dishes. In the North of Greece, in both Epirus and Macedonia, it is still used to make easy and fast crusts for savory pies. It is also still used to make bobota, usually a sweet cornmeal cake filled with raisins. The cake is so popular in so many places in Greece that sometimes cornmeal itself is referred to as bobota. As for the mush, which mainland Greeks, especially in the western part of the country, call bazina but Lefkadians and other Seven Islanders know as poulenta, obviously a transliteration of the Italian, it is made into both savory and sweet dishes. I serve polenta with the sofrito from Corfu (page 95) and also with the guinea hen sartsa from Zakynthos (page 93).

As for the sweeter variation that follows, with onions and raisins, I usually serve it together with a host of other dishes on the table. It is an unusual accompaniment to stewed greens, such as the tsigarelli (page 79). The last variation, with grape must, honey, or molasses, is a hit with kids and a filling breakfast on cold mornings.

A word about the cornmeal itself: Greek cornmeal is usually a coarse grind, which is what I recommend in the recipe that follows. The ratio of water to cornmeal varies depending on the final texture one wants to achieve. In the old Greek dishes, the cornmeal was cooked to a medium consistency, which means a 4:1 ratio of water to cornmeal.

½ cup extra-virgin olive oil
4 to 6 garlic cloves, to taste, very finely chopped
2 quarts water
1 tablespoon salt
2 cups coarse stone-ground yellow cornmeal, preferably organic
2 tablespoons unsalted butter, melted

1. Heat 2 tablespoons of the olive oil in a small skillet over medium heat and cook the garlic until soft but not browned, about 3 minutes. Remove from the heat and set aside.

2. Bring the water and salt to a boil in a large saucepan. Add the cornmeal slowly, in a very thin stream, keeping the heat high enough so that the water continues to boil. Stir the cornmeal with a large, long whisk the entire time you are pouring it in. Once it has been incorporated, pour in ¼ cup of the olive oil and add the cooked garlic. Reduce the heat to low and keep stirring the mixture with a wooden spoon until it is thick and creamy, 30 to 40 minutes. When the mixture begins to pull away from the pot, it is ready. Serve immediately, drizzled with the remaining 2 tablespoons olive oil and the butter.

⊙ Polenta from Ithaca (Ithakiani Poulenta): Prepare the polenta as directed, but omit the garlic. In a separate skillet, heat 2 tablespoons of butter or olive oil and cook 2 finely chopped red onions over medium heat, stirring, until they are very soft, 5 to 7 minutes. Place 1 cup seedless dark raisins in a bowl with warm water to cover for 10 minutes, to plump, then drain. Combine the raisins and onions with the polenta as it is cooking and serve the same way.

⊙ Sweet Polenta with Grape Must or Honey (Poulenta me Petimezi): Prepare as directed, but omit the garlic. Once the polenta is ready, spread it on a plate to serve and drizzle with either petimezi, which is available in Greek and Middle Eastern food shops, or with honey or molasses.

SAVORY PIES

There isn't a great *pita* tradition in the Ionian Islands. *Pita,* savory pie, is more a mainland and northern Greek specialty, its making elevated to an art, in fact, in Epirus. But there are unusual pies in the Ionian Islands and combinations of ingredients, such as fish or shellfish and cheese, that are not found anywhere else in the country. Tomatoes are often among the ingredients in the filling, and in Cephalonia no pie is ever made without a handful of rice tossed in.

Pumpkin and Carrot Pie from Cephalonia

KEFALONITIKI PITA ME KOLOKYTHA KAI KAROTA

 Makes 6 to 8 servings

One finds recipes in the most unusual places, in this case from Spiros Bazigos, the accountant at the Coridalenio Library in Argostoli, Cephalonia's capital. I had just spent a day looking for books on old island customs and food habits. He had come in to say good night to the rest of the staff, and all fingers pointed in his direction. "He's the one you should be talking to, a walking encyclopedia, and his belly's the proof," the librarian said. Sure enough, he knew much about the island's traditional recipes, and I have him to thank for the following three pita *dishes.*

1 recipe Basic Homemade Phyllo Dough (page 455), commercial phyllo, or *Afrato* phyllo, at room temperature

½ cup extra-virgin olive oil
3 medium-large yellow onions, finely chopped
2 cups shredded carrots
4 cups shredded pumpkin
½ cup long-grain rice
1 cup peeled, seeded, and chopped plum tomatoes (canned are fine)
1 cup packed snipped fresh dill
2 large eggs
Salt and freshly ground black pepper to taste

To bake
Olive oil for brushing

1. Make the filling: Heat ¼ cup of the olive oil in a large skillet and cook the onions over medium heat, stirring constantly with a wooden spoon, until wilted, 5 to 7 minutes. Add the carrots and continue cooking until the carrots are very soft, about 10 minutes. Transfer to a large bowl.

2. Heat another 2 tablespoons of the olive oil in the same skillet and add the pumpkin. Cook, stirring, until it is soft and most of its liquid has evaporated, 12 to 20 minutes, depending on the pumpkin. Place in the bowl with the carrots and onions. Let the mixture cool slightly.

3. Add the rice, tomatoes, dill, and eggs to the mixture. Season with salt and pepper and mix in the remaining 2 tablespoons olive oil.

4. Preheat the oven to 375°F. Oil a 15-inch-round baking pan that is 2 inches deep. Divide the phyllo into 4 balls. Lightly flour your work surface and roll out the first ball into a circle slightly larger than the diameter of the pan. Place it in the pan and brush it generously with olive oil. Do the same with the next ball. Spread the filling evenly over the phyllo and roll out and layer the remaining 2 balls of phyllo the same way, brushing each generously with olive oil. Join the top and bottom rims by pinching them together and roll around the pan to form a thick perimeter. Score the pie into diamond-shaped wedges or into squares without cutting through to the bottom of the pan and bake until golden, about 50 minutes. Remove from the oven, let cool for at least 30 minutes, and serve, either warm or at room temperature.

✳ **NOTE** You may reduce the ingredients by half and bake the pie in an 8-inch or 10-inch round pan.

The pie may also be made with commercial phyllo. For every sheet of homemade phyllo use 3 to 4 sheets of commercial phyllo. See directions (page 455) for more details on how to work with frozen phyllo.

Codfish Pie from Ithaca

BAKALIAROPITA TIS ITHAKIS

 Makes 8 to 10 servings

Codfish pies are found throughout the Ionian Islands. The Ithacan version includes both rice and cubed potatoes, testimony to the fact that this originated as poor man's food, a dish that needed to be as filling as possible. Cod pie is a classic Lenten dish not only in Ithaca but in Cephalonia and in Corfu too, where it is also sometimes made with a batter crust, not with the more bread-textured homemade phyllo.

3 pounds boneless salt cod, trimmed of any
    excess skin

2 tablespoons extra-virgin olive oil, plus extra
    for brushing
1 large yellow onion, chopped
½ cup short-grain rice
2 medium waxy potatoes, peeled and cubed
1½ cups peeled, seeded, strained, and chopped
    plum tomatoes
4 to 6 garlic cloves, to taste, chopped
⅔ cup chopped fresh flat-leaf parsley
Freshly ground black pepper to taste
Salt to taste
1 recipe Basic Homemade Phyllo Dough
    (page 455) or commercial phyllo, at
    room temperature

1. Rehydrate cod as on page 463 and break apart into large pieces.

2. Bring 2 to 3 inches of water to a boil in a large skillet or saucepan, add the cod, reduce the heat to medium-low, and poach the cod just until it becomes slightly pearly, about 5 minutes. Drain, reserving the water. Shred the cod.

3. Heat the olive oil in a skillet and cook the onion over medium-low heat until wilted, 5 to 7 minutes.

4. In a large bowl, combine the cod, onion, rice, potatoes, tomatoes, garlic, parsley, and pepper. Taste the filling before adding salt, since the cod is naturally salty.

5. Preheat the oven to 375°F. Oil a 15-inch round or square pan that is about 2 inches deep. Divide the phyllo into 4 balls. Lightly flour a work surface and roll out the first ball into a circle slightly larger than the pan. Place it in the pan and brush it generously with olive oil. Do the same with the next ball. Spread the filling evenly over the phyllo and pour in ½ cup of the reserved poaching liquid. Roll out the remaining 2 balls of phyllo and cover the pie with them, brushing each with oil. Trim the top and bottom edges if necessary and fold them in decoratively to create a rim. Make several incisions in the top of the pie and bake until golden brown, about 50 minutes. Let cool for at least 30 minutes but preferably 40 to 45 minutes before cutting. Serve warm or at room temperature.

⊙ Cod pie exists in several variations throughout the Ionian Islands. Sometimes it is made with stock-fish, which is air-dried (as opposed to salt-cured) cod. Cheese may be added, as it is in both Cephalonia and Corfu. Try the same recipe with the addition of cubed *graviera* or grated *kefalotyri* cheese, but adjust the seasoning; with cheese, the filling does not need any salt.

✳ NOTE You may reduce the ingredients by half and bake the pie in an 8-inch or 10-inch round or square pan.

The pie may also be made with commercial phyllo. For every sheet of homemade phyllo use 3 to 4 sheets of commercial phyllo. See directions (page 455) for more details on how to work with frozen phyllo.

Picarel Pie from Lefkada

MARITHOPITA TIS LEFKADAS

 Makes 8 to 10 servings

Of the Ionian fish pies, this is my favorite.

4 pounds small picarel, gutted and washed
2 medium onions, finely chopped
1 cup short-grain rice

Salt and freshly ground black pepper to taste
2 tablespoons tomato paste diluted with ¼ cup water (optional)
¼ cup extra-virgin olive oil, plus extra for brushing
1 recipe Basic Homemade Phyllo Dough (page 453), at room temperature

1. Remove and discard the heads and back-bones from the picarel. Finely chop the fish. Combine the fish, onions, rice, salt, pepper, diluted tomato paste if using, and olive oil in a large bowl.

2. Preheat the oven to 350°F. Divide the phyllo into 4 equal balls. Oil a 13- by 9-inch baking pan. Lightly flour your work surface and roll out the first ball into a rectangle slightly larger than the pan. Place it in the pan and brush it generously with olive oil. Do the same with the next ball. Spread the filling evenly over the phyllo, then roll out and layer the remaining 2 phyllo balls the same way, brushing each generously with olive oil. Join the top and bottom edges by pinching them together and rolling around the pan to form a thick rim. Score the pie into diamond-shaped wedges or into squares without cutting through to the bottom of the pan and bake until golden, 50 minutes to 1 hour. Let cool for at least 30 minutes before cutting.

✳ NOTE I don't recommend commercial phyllo for this recipe because it changes the texture of the dish completely. There are some commercial phyllo products available, however, that resemble the thick homemade pastry this recipe calls for. You can find them in Greek and Middle Eastern food shops under the name *horiatiko* or *spitiko* phyllo.

Meat Pie from Cephalonia

KEFALONITIKI KREATOPITA

 Makes 8 to 10 servings

This recipe, from native Cephalonian Roussa Meleti, originally appeared in my first book, The Food and Wine of Greece.

5 tablespoons extra-virgin olive oil, plus extra
    for brushing
½ pound boneless lamb, trimmed of fat and cut
    into ½-inch pieces
½ pound lean boneless pork, cut into ½-inch
    pieces
½ pound lean boneless beef, cut into ½-inch
    pieces
2 large onions, finely chopped
3 cloves garlic, minced
¼ cup medium-grain rice
1½ cups peeled, seeded, and chopped tomatoes
    (canned are fine)
½ teaspoon ground cinnamon
½ teaspoon freshly grated nutmeg
½ cup water
1 large egg, lightly beaten
½ cup grated *kefalotyri* cheese or any hard
    yellow cheese
Salt and freshly ground black pepper to taste
½ cup chopped fresh flat-leaf parsley
1 recipe *Afrato* phyllo (page 453), or commercial
    phyllo, at room temperature

1. Heat 3 tablespoons of the olive oil in a large, heavy skillet over medium-high heat and brown the meats, in batches if necessary. Remove from the heat and let cool enough to handle. Shred the meats by hand.

2. Add the remaining 2 tablespoons olive oil to the skillet and cook the onion over medium heat, stirring, until translucent, about 10 minutes. Add the garlic, then the rice, and stir for 1 to 2 minutes. Add the tomatoes, cinnamon, and nutmeg and stir together. Add the water, reduce the heat to medium-low, and cook the mixture until most of the liquid has been absorbed, about 10 minutes. Remove from the skillet and let cool.

3. Preheat the oven to 350°F. In a large bowl, combine the meat mixture with the egg, cheese, salt, pepper, and parsley. Oil a 15-inch-round baking pan that is 2 inches deep. Divide the phyllo into 4 equal balls. Lightly flour your work surface and roll out the first ball into a circle slightly larger than the pan. Place it in the pan and brush it generously with olive oil. Do the same with the next ball. Spread the filling evenly over the phyllo, then roll out and layer the remaining 2 phyllo balls the same way, brushing each generously with olive oil. Join the top and bottom edges by pinching them together and roll around the pan to form a thick rim. Score the pie into diamond-shaped wedges or into squares without cutting all the way to the bottom of the pie and bake until golden, about 50 minutes. Let cool for at least 35 minutes before cutting. Serve warm or at room temperature.

✳ **NOTE** You may reduce the ingredients by half and bake the pie in an 8-inch or 10-inch round or square pan.

The pie may also be made with commercial phyllo. For every sheet of homemade phyllo use 3 to 4 sheets of commercial phyllo. See directions (page 455) for more details on how to work with frozen phyllo.

MEAT

There is something luscious, almost opulent, about many of the meat dishes in the Ionian Islands. Meat is often cooked in highly aromatic sauces or served with thick, buttery pasta. Many of these dishes, to my mind at least, are for weekends or festive meals. The following recipes, as always, represent my own personal favorites culled from the extensive Ionian repertoire.

1 teaspoon freshly grated nutmeg
1 teaspoon sweet paprika
½ teaspoon ground cloves
Cayenne pepper to taste
2 cups peeled, seeded, and chopped tomatoes (canned are fine)
1 cinnamon stick
4 to 6 allspice berries, to taste
Salt to taste
2 tablespoons tomato paste diluted with 2 tablespoons water
2 to 3 tablespoons red wine vinegar, to taste
Freshly ground black pepper to taste
Pinch of sugar
1 pound tubular spaghetti, like bucatini
Grated *kefalotyri* or any hard yellow cheese

Chicken Stewed in Fragrant Tomato Sauce with Thick Pasta

KOTOPOULO PASTITSATHA APO TIN KERKYRA

 Makes 4 to 6 servings

Pastitsatha was the traditional Sunday meal of Corfu's well-to-do. It was almost always made with free-range cock or with turkey, which Corfiotes hold in particularly high esteem. Thick tubular spaghetti is needed for this dish. According to island cooks, a proper pastitsatha *requires no fewer than 9 spices: allspice, cinnamon, cloves, cumin, nutmeg, paprika, cayenne, salt, and black pepper.*

½ cup extra-virgin olive oil
One 3- to 3½-pound chicken, cut into stewing pieces (fat trimmed and skin removed, if desired)
3 cups coarsely chopped red onions
4 garlic cloves, finely chopped
1½ teaspoons ground cumin

1. In a large stewing pot, heat the olive oil over medium-high heat, then brown the chicken pieces on all sides in batches. Remove from the pot and drain on paper towels to remove excess oil.

2. Add the onions to the pot, reduce the heat to medium-low, and stir until wilted, about 7 minutes. Add the garlic, cumin, nutmeg, paprika, cloves, and cayenne and stir for a minute, just enough to open up their aroma. Add the chicken back to the pot and pour in the tomatoes. Add the cinnamon stick, allspice, salt, and enough water to cover the chicken. Cover and simmer over medium-low heat until the chicken is tender, about 40 minutes. Before removing the chicken from the heat, stir in the diluted tomato paste and add 2 tablespoons of the vinegar and the black pepper. Taste the sauce and adjust the seasoning as desired, with a bit more vinegar or with the sugar if it is too pungent.

3. While the chicken is cooking, heat a large pot of salted water for the pasta. Boil the pasta until al dente and drain. To serve, place pasta on individual plates or on a large serving platter with the chicken and sauce over it. Sprinkle with grated cheese.

Guinea Hen Cooked with Tomato Sauce and Cheese from Zakynthos

SARTSA

 Makes 4 servings

Guinea fowl in the Ionian region might have an interesting history—or, at the least, an interesting etymology, if one is to believe historian Waverley Root. The Zakynthians call it frangokota, *or "French chicken," while in Corfu it is called* faraona, *after the Italian* gallina faraona, *or pharaoh's turkey. Root says that the bird, indeed a native of Guinea in West Africa, was known to the Greeks as early as 500 B.C. They were buying it via Egypt, which might account for its Corfiote name. It slipped into obscurity after the fall of the Roman Empire and resurfaced again in Europe sometime in the 16th century when the merchants of Portugal, then in charge of Guinea, began selling them to France, which explains why Zakynthians refer to the delicious but tough-fleshed bird as "French." Maybe it's a bit far-fetched, but Root is always fun to read. In any event, this dish is little more than a simple, hearty red stew for which the mysterious bird is favored among islanders. Indicative of the heartiness of Zakynthian cooking, chunks of local cheese are tossed into the pot a few minutes before serving.*

¼ cup extra-virgin olive oil

2 medium red onions, finely chopped

4 garlic cloves, chopped

2 cups peeled, seeded, and chopped plum tomatoes (canned are fine)

Salt to taste

¼ cup good-quality red wine vinegar

2 small guinea fowls (about 1½ pounds each and preferably the hen, not the male) (see Note)

½ teaspoon freshly ground black pepper

¾ cup cubed *graviera* or *kefalograviera* cheese

1. Heat the olive oil in a large, heavy skillet over medium heat and cook the onions and garlic, stirring, until wilted, 5 to 7 minutes. Add the tomatoes and season with salt. Simmer over medium-low heat, covered, until the sauce begins to thicken, about 20 minutes. Add the vinegar and simmer for another 5 minutes.

2. Preheat the oven to 350°F. Season the guinea hens with salt and pepper. Place them in a deep clay or ovenproof ceramic baking dish and pour the sauce over and around the birds. Add enough water so that the sauce comes a third of the way up the birds. Bake until the hens are tender, 45 to 55 minutes, basting the birds with the sauce every 10 minutes. Ten minutes before removing from the oven, stir the cubes of cheese into the dish. The cheese should be in oozing chunks when the dish is served. Serve hot, accompanied by mashed potatoes or, better still, Polenta from Lefkada (page 86).

⊙ If guinea hen is unavailable, a 3-pound chicken, preferably free-range, cut-up, will do.

Quail Stewed with Fava Beans

ORTYKIA ME KOUKIA

 Makes 6 to 8 servings

Quail appear in many varied dishes all over Greece, from the preserved quail (see page 42) so revered in the Mani to the quail-stuffed bread (page 41), also from the southern Peloponnesos. From the eastern Aegean, we find another unusual quail dish, in which the tiny birds are stuffed into eggplants (the recipe is included in my first book, The Food and Wine of Greece). *This recipe comes from a cluster of tiny Ionian islands called Othoni.*

12 quail
Salt to taste
½ cup extra-virgin olive oil
4 garlic cloves, peeled and crushed
5 pounds fresh fava beans, shelled, or 2 pounds
    frozen shelled fava beans, defrosted
Freshly ground black pepper to taste
1 cup dry white wine
1 bunch fresh dill, snipped
Sugar to taste (see Note)

1. Clean the quail if necessary: Chop off and discard the necks and pluck off any remaining feathers. Season with a little salt.

2. Heat the olive oil in a large Dutch oven or flameproof casserole over medium-high heat and cook the quail, in batches if necessary, until browned lightly on all sides, about 3 to 5 minutes. Add the garlic and toss together with the birds. Add the fresh fava beans and season with a little more salt and pepper. Add the wine and enough water to barely cover the birds. Cover and simmer over medium-low heat until the beans are very tender and the flesh is almost falling off the quail, 45 to 50 minutes.

If using frozen fava beans, add them later: Simmer the quail with the garlic, wine, and water for 35 minutes, then add the defrosted favas and continue cooking until both the birds and favas are tender. About 15 minutes before removing from the heat, add the dill to the pot.

✳ **NOTE** Fava beans can sometimes be bitter. Taste the pan juices and adjust the seasoning by adding a little sugar if necessary.

Rabbit Stew with Tomato, Lemon, and Garlic from Cephalonia

KEFALONITIKO LAGOTO

 Makes 4 servings

This dish is traditionally made with wild hare in Cephalonia, but in its absence rabbit is often used. The name lagoto (lago *means "hare" in Greek) is also found in parts of the Peloponnesos, where it refers either to a dish of hare or rabbit thickened with* skordalia *or, oddly, to pork stewed with* skordalia. *The Cephalonian version of* lagoto *is a good example of some of the similarities in the cuisines of the Ionian and the Peloponnesos. Cephalonia, especially, since it is the closest island, shares much in common with the tables of the western Peloponnesos. One such common thread is the use of tomato paste, rather than fresh tomatoes, as seen in the recipe below. Another is the marriage of the lemon to the tomato, a combination unusual for almost all of Greece except the Ionian Islands and the Peloponnesos. As for the boiled gar-*

lic, that is a technique that appears to be unique in the Ionian. Boiling mellows the garlic, making the use of two whole heads easier to understand.

One 3- to 3½-pound rabbit
2 cups red wine vinegar
2 tablespoons black peppercorns
2 heads garlic, unpeeled
½ cup extra-virgin olive oil
⅓ cup tomato paste diluted with ¼ cup water
Salt and freshly ground black pepper to taste
Juice of 3 to 4 lemons, to taste

1. Wash the rabbit and cut into serving pieces. Marinate it in the vinegar and peppercorns in a glass bowl or dish, covered, in the refrigerator overnight.

2. Remove the rabbit from the marinade and pat dry. Set aside. Meanwhile, place the unpeeled heads of garlic in a small saucepan with just enough water to cover and bring to a boil. Simmer until the garlic is soft, 15 to 20 minutes. Remove from the water (do not discard the garlic water), let cool slightly, separate the cloves, and squeeze out the pulp.

3. Heat the olive oil in a large Dutch oven or flameproof casserole over medium-high heat and add the rabbit, turning to brown on all sides. Remove from the pan. Add the garlic pulp to the hot oil and stir for a few seconds. Add the diluted tomato paste and stir for a minute. Return the rabbit to the pot, together with the reserved garlic water. Add enough additional water to cover the rabbit. Season with salt and pepper. Bring to a boil, then reduce the heat to medium-low and simmer the meat for 30 minutes. Add ½ cup of the lemon juice, cover, and continue to simmer until the rabbit is tender, another 30 to 40 minutes or so. Just before removing from the heat, adjust the seasoning with several tablespoons of the remaining lemon juice and salt and pepper.

Pan-Fried Veal with a Tangy Vinegar Sauce from Corfu

KERKYREIKO SOFRITO

 Makes 4 to 6 servings

Sofrito gets its name from the Italian fritto, *or "fried." The dish is traditionally made with veal, but beef can be substituted.*

⅓ cup all-purpose flour
Freshly ground black pepper to taste
Dash of cayenne pepper
2 pounds boneless veal, preferably top round, cut into 6 slices
6 tablespoons extra-virgin olive oil
4 garlic cloves, finely chopped
¼ cup white wine vinegar, or slightly more to taste
1½ cups beef broth
Salt to taste
½ cup finely chopped fresh flat-leaf parsley

1. Spread the flour over a large plate and season with black pepper and cayenne. Lightly dredge the veal slices, tapping off any excess.

2. Heat 4 tablespoons of the olive oil in a large nonstick skillet over medium-high heat. Add the meat and brown lightly on both sides. Transfer to a plate.

3. In a separate large, deep skillet or casserole, heat the remaining tablespoons of the olive oil over medium heat. Add the garlic and stir for a minute. Add the veal. Pour in the vinegar, which will steam up and lose some of its pungency. Add the broth and season with salt. Simmer the *sofrito* over low to medium heat until the meat is tender and the sauce thick, 15 to 20 minutes. About 5 minutes before removing from the heat, stir in the parsley and add more vinegar if desired for a more pungent flavor. Serve the *sofrito* hot over mashed potatoes.

Stuffed Veal Cooked in Aromatic Tomato Sauce

SKARTSOTSETTA

 Makes 4 to 6 servings

Here's a dish that some claim was the invention of Zakynthian and Corfiote taverna owners, but others, more wisely, point to Venice as the source of its provenance. (Skartsotsetta—at least etymologically—probably derives from the Italian scartocetti for "packets" because of the way the thinly sliced veal is stuffed, rolled, and braised.) Regardless of its origins, the dish has evolved to become one of the Seven Islands' Sunday lunchtime classics, as well as a standard on many taverna menus.

For the sauce

2 tablespoons extra-virgin olive oil

1 medium-large onion, very finely chopped

2 garlic cloves, finely chopped

2½ cups peeled, seeded, and chopped plum tomatoes (canned are fine)

1 cup dry red wine

Salt and freshly ground black pepper to taste

Dried oregano to taste

For the filling

½ cup finely chopped fresh flat-leaf parsley

2 garlic cloves, minced

½ cup finely crumbled Greek feta cheese

½ cup grated *graviera* cheese

⅓ cup plain bread crumbs from stale bread

Salt and freshly ground black pepper to taste

Pinch of freshly grated nutmeg

2 large egg yolks

To make the rolls and cook

2 pounds veal cutlets, pounded thin

3 to 4 tablespoons olive oil, as needed

1. Make the sauce: Heat the olive oil in a medium pot over medium heat and cook the onion and garlic, stirring, until soft, about 5 minutes. Add the tomatoes and bring to a boil. Add the wine and bring to a boil again. Season with salt, pepper, and oregano. Reduce the heat to medium-low and simmer the sauce, uncovered, until thick, about 30 minutes.

2. Make the filling: In a large bowl, combine the parsley, garlic, cheeses, bread crumbs, salt, pepper, and nutmeg. Mix in the egg yolks well.

3. Season the cutlets with salt and pepper. Spread each of the cutlets with 2 to 3 tablespoons of the filling, leaving a little room around the edges. Following the grain of the meat, roll up each cutlet and secure closed with several toothpicks or small metal skewers. Heat the olive oil in a large, heavy skillet and cook the rolled cutlets over high heat, turning, to brown on all sides. As soon as the rolls are browned, pour the tomato sauce into the skillet, reduce the heat to medium-low, cover, and simmer until the meat is cooked through and tender, 20 to 25 minutes. Serve hot.

Stuffed Little Meatballs

POLPETES APO TIN KERKYRA

Makes about 24 meatballs

What the rest of Greece knows as keftedes *or by the diminutive,* keftedakia, *Seven Islanders call pol-petes, delicate little meatballs. In the Ionian area these days they are apt to be the mint-doused rendition common throughout all of Greece. This particular recipe, borrowed from Ninetta Laskari's excellent book on Corfu, harks back to an older, more glorious time, when the Venetians ruled the palaces and palates of the Ionian Islands and taught local cooks to make these little meatballs stuffed with anchovies and hard-cooked eggs.*

1 pound finely ground beef

½ cup (1 stick) unsalted butter, melted

1 large egg

½ cup chopped fresh flat-leaf parsley

½ cup grated *kefalotyri* cheese or any hard
    yellow cheese

Salt to taste

2 large hard-cooked eggs, peeled and chopped

3 to 4 anchovies, preserved in coarse salt, not
    oil, to taste, chopped

2 slices Canadian bacon, very finely chopped

1 scant teaspoon curry powder

All-purpose flour for dredging

Olive oil for frying

1 cup dry red wine

1 cup peeled, seeded, and chopped tomatoes
    (canned are fine)

1 teaspoon sugar

1. Place the ground beef, melted butter, egg, parsley, cheese, and salt in a medium bowl and knead until all the ingredients are mixed thoroughly. Set aside, covered, in the refrigerator for 1 hour.

2. In a small bowl, using a fork, crush the hard-cooked eggs, anchovies, bacon, and curry to a pulp.

3. Remove the ground meat from the refrigerator. Take a heaping tablespoon at a time and shape into meatballs. Using your thumb, make an indentation in the center and fill with a little of the anchovy-and-egg mixture. Press closed. Continue until all the meat and filling are used up.

4. Spread ample flour onto a plate and dredge the meatballs in it, tapping off any excess. Meanwhile, heat about 1 inch of olive oil in a large, heavy skillet over medium-high heat until very hot, then brown the floured *polpetes* on all sides, in batches if necessary. Remove with a slotted spoon and drain on paper towels. Replenish the oil if necessary as you fry them, making sure always to bring it to a high heat before placing the *polpetes* in the skillet.

5. Strain the hot oil and pour about ½ cup of it back into the skillet. You can also use fresh oil if desired, especially if the oil left over after frying has acquired the harsh aroma of burned flour. Heat the oil over medium-high heat, then add the wine, tomatoes, and sugar to the skillet. As soon as it starts to boil, add the meatballs back to the pan, reduce the heat to low, and cook in the sauce for 10 minutes. Remove from the heat and serve, either hot or at room temperature with plenty of fresh bread.

False Soufflé with Meat (a Corfiote Jewish Recipe)

PIKANTINO

 Makes 6 servings

I first learned of this recipe from Rebecca Aaron in Corfu. I found it again in Nicholas Stavroulakis's book The Cookbook of the Jews of Greece *and borrow it almost verbatim from there. According to Stavroulakis, the dish falls under the general category of a* frittada, *basically a baked omelet, and was made for Shavuoth, the Feast of Weeks. It is one of the more unusual dishes from the Jewish larder of Corfu.*

1 cup extra-virgin olive oil
1¼ pounds ground beef, veal, or lamb
Salt and freshly ground black pepper to taste
½ cup pine nuts
1 tablespoon matzo meal
12 large eggs, separated

1. Preheat the oven to 450°F. Heat the olive oil in a large, heavy pot over medium-high heat, add the ground meat, salt, and pepper, and fry until the meat is well browned, breaking it up with a spoon to facilitate browning, 7 to 10 minutes. Add the pine nuts and cook for 5 minutes more. Remove from the heat and mix in the matzo meal.

2. Beat the egg yolks in a large bowl until creamy. In a separate large bowl, whip the whites with an electric mixer until stiffened but not forming peaks. Fold the whites into the yolks, then fold this into the meat mixture and mix well.

3. Pour the mixture into a well-oiled deep baking pan and bake for 5 minutes. Reduce the oven temperature to 300°F and bake until the top is golden and crusty, 30 to 45 minutes. Cut into wedges and serve either hot or at room temperature.

FISH AND SEAFOOD

Fried Octopus from Ithaca

TIGANITO HTAPOTHAKI APO TIN ITHAKI

 Makes 8 to 10 *meze* servings

Octopus is the Lenten fare par excellence in Ithaca. There is plenty of it, it is rich and filling despite its associations with the fast, and it is cooked in several unusual ways. The following recipes were given to me by Mihalis Maghoulas, an Ithacan native who tinkers in the kitchen in his spare time and who has recorded his island's rich culinary heritage in a self-published book called, simply, Ithacan Cuisine. *This is a beautiful dish and an excellent* meze *with red wine and with ouzo.*

2 pounds fresh or frozen (see Note) small
   octopuses, cleaned if necessary
   (see page 462)
¼ to ⅓ cup extra-virgin olive oil, as needed
1 cup dry white wine
8 to 10 slices rustic bread, ¾ inch thick
Salt and freshly ground black pepper to taste
½ cup finely chopped fresh flat-leaf parsley

1. Place the octopuses in a large saucepan, cover, and cook over very low heat until they are tender, 30 to 40 minutes. They will exude their own juices; reserve them to make *skordalia* (page 216) Remove the octopuses with a slotted spoon and divide by their tentacles so that you have at least 16 pieces. Preheat the broiler.

2. Heat 4 to 5 tablespoons of the olive oil in a large skillet and fry the octopuses in the oil over medium-high heat until they turn dark pink,

5 to 7 minutes. Pour in the wine and simmer over medium-high heat until the wine has evaporated.

3. While the octopuses are frying, toast the bread on both sides under the broiler, about 6 inches from the heat. To serve, place the toast on a platter and drizzle with the remaining olive oil. Top each piece of toast with one or two tentacles and any juices left from the skillet. Season with salt and pepper and garnish with parsley.

✳ **NOTE** If using frozen octopus, defrost in the refrigerator overnight.

Garlic Sauce with Octopus Broth from Ithaca

SKORDALIA APO HTAPOTHOZOUMO

 Makes 4 to 6 *meze* servings

This garlic dip is served just as aliatha, ayiatha, *and others are—as an accompaniment to boiled greens, fried vegetables or fish, plain on bread, or as a side with Ithacan Fried Octopus (page 98).*

Four 1-inch-thick slices stale rustic bread
Pan juices from cooking 2 small or 1 large
　octopus (see step 1, Fried Octopus from
　Ithaca, page 98)
4 to 6 garlic cloves, to taste, peeled and crushed
Salt to taste
½ to ¾ cup extra-virgin olive oil, as needed
¼ to ⅓ cup red wine vinegar, as needed

1. Remove the crusts from the bread and dampen the bread slightly under the tap. Squeeze out the excess water. Crumble the bread a little and place it in the octopus juices to absorb them.

2. Put 2 cloves of the garlic and a little salt in a large mortar and begin to pound them into a paste. Add one more garlic clove and a little of the crumbled, soaked bread. Continue pounding. Alternately add a little olive oil and vinegar and any excess octopus juice. Add more garlic, then more bread, pounding all the while and loosening the mixture with alternating additions of oil and vinegar. Do this until the bread and garlic and as much olive oil and vinegar as are needed to make the mixture thick but smooth are used up. The *skordalia* should be dense like mashed potatoes but creamy. You may need to dilute it a little by adding some water. It will have an odd mauve color from the octopus juice, but it will be pungent and delicious.

Ithacan Octopus Ragout with Tomatoes and Celery

HTAPOTHI CAPAMA TIS ITHAKIS

 Makes 4 servings

The word capama *comes from the Turkish for "to cover." It is a name given to many different kinds of stew all around Greece. Sometimes it refers to beef or chicken dishes cooked with tomatoes and cinnamon, other times to simple ragouts. This* capama *includes celery. What is unusual about it is that celery is usually cooked with white (lemon-based) sauces in the rest of Greece. But as in so many dishes in the Ionian, here the tomato reigns.*

¼ cup olive oil

2 cups coarsely chopped cultivated celery (with leaves) plus 1 teaspoon ground celery seeds, or 2 cups coarsely chopped wild celery (with leaves)

2 large red onions, halved and thinly sliced

4 garlic cloves, peeled and crushed

1 medium fresh or frozen (see Note) octopus (about 3 pounds), cleaned if necessary (see page 462)

1 cup dry white wine

2 bay leaves

1 cup peeled and chopped plum tomatoes (canned are fine)

Freshly ground black pepper to taste

Heat the olive oil in a large, heavy pot and cook the celery (and celery seeds, if using), onions, and garlic over medium heat, stirring, until soft, about 8 minutes. Add the octopus, cover, reduce the heat to low, and cook for 25 minutes. Remove the octopus from the pot and cut into 8 pieces. Return to the pot. Add the wine, bay leaves, and tomatoes and bring to a boil. Reduce the heat to medium-low and cook covered, until the octopus is very tender and the sauce thick, another 45 minutes or so. Remove the bay leaves. Season with pepper and serve hot.

✳ NOTE If using frozen octopus, defrost in the refrigerator overnight.

Peppery Fish and Leek Casserole from Corfu

TO BOURTHETO TIS KERKYRAS

 Makes 6 servings

The name comes from the Italian brodeto, for "broth," a legacy of Corfu's Venetian past. A similar dish, at least in name, is the bourieto of the northern Peloponnesos, where it refers to a fish stew redolent with onions but not colored with paprika or tomato paste. On Corfu, bourtheto is one of the island's four signature dishes. Before tomatoes entered the island's larder, bourtheto used to get its deep reddish brown color from a combination of paprika and cayenne, which still appear in the recipe.

As for the fish itself, any firm, white-fleshed fish can be used for this recipe. The most beloved on the island is the local scorpina—the scorpionfish. Its drawback are its many bones, which make it difficult to eat, but this deep-water rockfish is one of the premier soup and stewing fish in Greece because it is so tasty. Another favorite fish for this recipe is grouper.

There are other variations, too. Octopus bourtheto, for example, is a common menu item in Corfu's many taverns. Fresh cod is also much used and, in fact, makes for one of the island's standard Sunday lunch dishes.

2 pounds fresh whole white-fleshed fish (grouper, scorpionfish, cod, etc.), gutted and cleaned

Salt and freshly ground black pepper to taste

3 tablespoons extra-virgin olive oil

1 large leek, white and tender green parts, washed well and thinly sliced

2 garlic cloves, finely chopped

1 heaping tablespoon sweet paprika

1 scant teaspoon cayenne pepper, or more or less to taste

1 tablespoon tomato paste

1 cup dry red wine

1 cup water

1. Season the fish with salt and pepper and place in the refrigerator until ready to use.

2. Heat the olive oil in a large, heavy skillet, add the leek and garlic, and sweat over low heat until the leek is very soft, about 20 minutes. Add the paprika and cayenne and with a wooden spoon for about a minute. Add the tomato paste and stir for another minute. Pour in ½ cup of the wine and the water. Bring to a gentle boil, reduce the heat to low, and simmer, covered, until the sauce is thick and dark, about 15 minutes. Season with salt and pepper.

3. Place the fish over the leeks in the skillet. Add the remaining ½ cup wine, cover the skillet, and simmer until the fish is flaky and tender, another 15 minutes or so, depending on the size of the fish. Remove from the heat, let stand for about 5 minutes, and serve.

⊙ Octopus Casserole *(Htapothi Bourtheto)*: Substitute one 3-pound cleaned octopus for the fish and 2 cups finely chopped onions for the leek. In a separate pot with a heavy bottom, place the whole cleaned octopus and 2 tablespoons olive oil. Cover the pot and cook over very low heat until the octopus is bright pink and has exuded its juices, about 30 minutes. Remove, let cool slightly, and cut into serving pieces. Reserve all the juices. In the same pot, heat 2 more tablespoons olive oil and cook the onions and garlic, stirring, over medium heat until soft, about 5 minutes. Add the paprika and cayenne, then add the tomato paste and wine. Place the octopus in the pot, pour in any remaining juices, cover, and simmer until the octopus is very tender and the sauce thick, another 45 to 50 minutes.

Garlicky Fish Stew from Corfu

BIANCO

 Makes 4 to 6 servings

Another Corfiote fish recipe with an Italian-sounding name. Bianco *is pungent with garlic and is called "white" because it is made without tomatoes.*

2 tablespoons unsalted butter

3 tablespoons extra-virgin olive oil

2 medium onions, halved and thinly sliced

8 to 10 garlic cloves, to taste, chopped

6 to 8 medium waxy potatoes, to taste, peeled
  and cut into large cubes

Salt and freshly ground black pepper to taste

2½ to 3 pounds grey mullet or whiting, cleaned
  and gutted

Juice of 1 lemon

3 tablespoons chopped fresh flat-leaf parsley
  for garnish

1. Heat the butter and 1 tablespoon of the olive oil together in a large stewing pot or Dutch oven. Add the onions and garlic and cook over medium-low heat, stirring, until softened, about 5 minutes. Add the potatoes, season with salt and pepper, and cook, stirring gently, until the potatoes are about half cooked, 10 to 12 minutes.

2. Place the fish in the pot over the potatoes, drizzle with the remaining 2 tablespoons olive oil, and add enough water just to cover the fish. Season with salt and pepper. Place the lid partially over the pot and simmer over medium-low heat until the fish is flaky and the liquid almost gone, about 20 minutes. Adjust the seasoning, pour in the lemon juice, and garnish with chopped parsley. Serve hot.

Mullet Stew from Lefkada

STRADIA

 Makes 4 to 6 servings

This is an "urban" summer dish in Lefkada, savored in its capital. It calls for the grey mullet, which spawn at the end of summer. The female, called bafa, *is swollen with eggs, and the male is at the height of his sperm production—details, granted, that are difficult to appreciate out of context. The secret of this dish is to cook it without water but with a fair amount of olive oil. As the fish simmers, it exudes its own liquid, and as the potatoes cook—slowly and for a long time—the starch in them breaks down, which helps give this dish its final thick consistency.*

Salt to taste

3 pounds grey mullet, cleaned, gutted, and cut into 2-inch-wide pieces

½ cup extra-virgin olive oil, or more if desired

1 large onion, minced or grated

3 to 4 large waxy potatoes, to taste, peeled, halved lengthwise, and cut into 1-inch-thick slices

3 large firm, ripe tomatoes, grated (see page 459)

Freshly ground black pepper to taste

1. Salt the fish and refrigerate until ready to use. In a large, wide pot, heat the olive oil over low heat, add the onion, and cook until wilted and translucent, about 7 minutes. Add the potatoes, pour in the tomatoes, and season with salt and pepper. Cover and simmer until the potatoes are about half cooked, about 15 minutes.

2. Place the fish over the vegetables, cover, and simmer over low heat for about 25 minutes, until the *stradia* is a thick, hearty consistency, somewhere between a soup and a stew.

BREAD

The Christmas and Easter breads of the Ionian Islands and the customs that surround them are considerably different from those in the rest of Greece.

More than anywhere else in the Ionian, in Cephalonia and in Zakynthos, Christmas is a celebration of hearth and home and is manifested in the three breads that are made over the fifteen days from December 24 to January 7. Although almost everywhere else in Greece the custom of baking festive breads with a coin inside for good luck is reserved for New Year's Day, in Cephalonia and Zakynthos a coin-stuffed bread ring is made and broken on Christmas Eve. Traditionally the ring is decorated with sesame seeds, raisins, almonds, and walnuts and baked in the hearth over a combination of olive wood, vinewood, and rush, hence the local name for the tradition, which is "Baptism by Fire" (*baptisma tou Pirros*). The Christmas Eve bread ring is also called *koulouri tis gonias,* or the "bread ring of the corner," since the fireplace is usually situated in a corner of the home. (In Ithaca, too, the hearth is referred to as the corner.) Before the bread is broken apart and eaten, the head of the household pours wine and oil over it and into the fire. The meal that follows is traditionally a fasting menu made up of cooked greens, olive oil, and sweet dough fritters.

On Christmas Day, together with the traditional pork and cabbage or pork and cauliflower that is found in many parts of Greece, Cephalonians make an enormous Christmas bread (called *Christopsomo*) shaped either like an X or a double-necked violin, crowned in the center with an unshelled walnut, one of the pan-Greek symbols of prosperity. It is eaten over the remainder of the holidays. In Zakynthos the Christmas bread is tall and fluffy, like the Italian *panettone.*

Only in recent years has the custom of making *vassilopita,* the yeasty, egg-rich New Year's bread found in the rest of Greece, taken root in the Ionian Islands. The traditional Cephalonian New Year's bread is called *vassilitsa,* another yeasty and egg-rich ring-shaped loaf with a cross in the center and walnuts all around.

The end of the Christmas festivities on January 7, the Day of the Epiphany, is also marked by a special bread, sometimes passed from godparent to godchild, called the *fotitsa,* or "little light." It is a solid, round loaf with a dough cross on top and four whole almonds or walnuts in each quadrant.

Easter Bread with Citrus Spoon Sweet from Corfu

FOGATSA

 Makes 2 large round loaves

In Corfu the Venetian influence is echoed in the island's Easter bread, which is called fogatsa. *Unlike the braided* tsoureki *eaten everywhere else in Greece, here the Eastern spices* mahlepi *and mastic are nowhere to be found. Instead,* fogatsa *is a dense, high, round loaf, with a cross slashed into its center and flavored with bergamot spoon sweet. Whereas* tsoureki *is sprinkled with either blanched almonds or sesame seeds, in Corfu the bread can be topped with caraway seeds.*

2 cups milk

Three ¼-ounce envelopes active dry yeast

8 to 10 cups all-purpose flour, as needed

1½ cups plus 2 tablespoons sugar

3 large eggs, separated

1 cup well-drained, chopped orange or bergamot spoon sweet

2 teaspoons pure vanilla extract

¼ cup kumquat or orange liqueur

1 cup (2 sticks) unsalted butter, melted

½ cup caraway seeds

1. Heat the milk in a small saucepan until it is just warm. Pour it into a very large glass or ceramic bowl and stir in the yeast, 1 cup of the flour, and ¾ cup of the sugar. Place the bowl in a warm, draft-free place, lightly covered with a cloth, and allow to stand until the yeast starts to bubble up, about 30 minutes.

2. With an electric mixer in a medium bowl, beat the egg yolks with ¾ cup of the remaining sugar until pale and creamy. Pour this mixture into the yeast mixture. Stir in the drained orange or bergamot spoon sweet, vanilla, kumquat or orange liqueur, and melted butter. Slowly add flour, 1 cup at a time, mixing it in with a wooden spoon, until a mass begins to form. Turn this out onto a lightly floured work surface and knead, adding more flour if necessary to form a very smooth, large ball of dough. Cover, place in a warm, draft-free place, and allow to stand until the dough has doubled in bulk, about 2 hours.

3. Punch the dough down and knead again for about 7 or 8 minutes. Shape into 2 equal round loaves and place each on a buttered baking sheet. Make 2 sharp slashes like an X on the surface of the dough, cover with a cloth, and let rise again until doubled for about 1 hour.

4. Preheat the oven to 350°F. With an electric mixer, beat the egg whites with the remaining 2 tablespoons sugar in a medium bowl until they are frothy without forming peaks. Brush the surface of each loaf with the mixture, sprinkle with caraway seeds, and bake until the *fogatsa* has swelled and browned, about 1 hour. Remove from the oven, let cool on a wire rack, and serve.

SWEETS

No doubt, many of the desserts that are native to the Ionian Islands take their gustatory cue from the Venetians, whose influence is still obvious both in the actual dishes and in the names of them. The puddings, the candied-fruit-filled breads, the sweet wine sauces, and more are all seemingly more Italian than they are Greek. If the beauty—or one of the beauties—of Greek cuisine is its ability to absorb all sorts of influences, to co-opt them, and ultimately to make them Greek, then the sweets of the Ionian Islands are the perfect example of such a process. Here we find dishes that are a marriage of East and West. On the one hand there are desserts such as Corfu's pudding with a local interpretation of zabaglione sauce or the fried cake that resembles pan-fried polenta, at least in spirit. On the other hand, though, there is a bevy of undeniably Greek confections, mainly in the form of spoon sweets. In the following dishes I have tried to give a good sense of the gamut of Ionian sweets.

Cornmeal Fritters from Corfu

TSALETIA

 Makes about 12 pieces

From the Venetian zaleti, *these little fritters have long been an adopted specialty of Corfu. They are usually served as a snack.*

1 cup fine yellow cornmeal
1 cup all-purpose flour
¼ teaspoon salt
¾ cup hot water
2 tablespoons fresh orange juice
Finely chopped zest of ½ orange
¾ cup currants
½ cup (1 stick) unsalted butter or extra-virgin olive oil for frying, or more as needed
Sugar for sprinkling or honey or *petimezi* for drizzling

1. Combine the cornmeal, flour, and salt in a large bowl and make a well in the center. Add the hot water, orange juice, zest, and currants and mix together to form a thick, dense batter with the consistency of cooked oatmeal.

2. Heat 2 tablespoons of the butter or oil in a large skillet over medium heat and drop 3 tablespoons at a time of the batter for each *tsaleti* into the skillet. Fry the *tsaletia* over medium heat until nicely browned, 3 to 4 minutes on each side—the trick is to cook them relatively slowly so that the inside cooks through. Replenish the butter or oil as you go. Remove and either sprinkle with sugar or drizzle with honey or *petimezi.* Serve hot.

Steamed Pudding from Corfu with a Local Rendition of Zabaglione

KERKYREIKI POUTINGA

 Makes about 12 servings

Puddings are found readily in several parts of Greece, and whether by accident or not, they seem to be most popular in the places long controlled by Venice. Corfiotes say, though, that the English showed them pudding in the nineteenth century. The puddings are made with either lady fingers or crumbled rusks, layered with candied fruits, raisins, and pine nuts and moistened with eggs and milk. Steamed pudding, so very English, is served up with a local version of that famous Italian dessert sauce, zabaglione.

½ pound coarse bread crumbs from stale bread
   or rusks
3 cups chopped mixed dried fruits (apricots,
   figs, candied orange)
1 cup golden or dark raisins
2 large eggs
3 cups milk
1 cup sugar
1 recipe Zabaglione (recipe follows)

1. Combine the bread crumbs, dried fruits, and raisins in a large bowl. Butter a 10-inch square oven-proof glass or ceramic baking dish.

2. In a medium bowl, beat together the eggs, milk, and sugar until frothy and pour the liquid over the bread crumb–and–dried fruit mixture. Toss to combine thoroughly and press the surface down a little so that all the liquid is absorbed. Allow to sit for a half hour. Preheat the oven to 350°F.

3. Place the bread crumb mixture in the buttered baking dish and set the baking dish inside another, larger pan. Pour enough water into the larger pan to come halfway up the sides of the baking dish. Bake until the pudding is golden and set, 45 to 50 minutes.

4. To serve: Using a large round cookie cutter, cut circles out of the pudding. Spoon a little zabaglione onto a plate, place the pudding on top, and spoon a little more zabaglione over it.

Zabaglione

ZABAYION

 Makes about 1½ cups

Make the zabaglione just before serving the pudding.

Ninetta Laskari imparted the Corfiote secret for zabayion to me: For every egg yolk, measure out 2 half-eggshells of Mavrodaphne wine and one half of sugar. Here goes:

6 large egg yolks
6 tablespoons sugar
¾ cup Mavrodaphne wine or sweet port

1. Bring 3 inches of water to a boil in a medium saucepan or in the bottom of a double boiler. Place the egg yolks in a metal bowl or pot or the top of the double boiler on top of the boiling water and whip with a wire whisk until the mixture is liquid.

2. Add the sugar in a slow stream, whisking all the while. Add the Mavrodaphne. Continue whisking vigorously until the zabaglione is thick, about 5 minutes. Spoon immediately over the hot pudding and serve.

Bread Pudding from Ithaca
ITHAKANIANO BOUTINO

 Makes 10 to 12 servings

This Ithaca recipe also comes from Mihalis Maghoulas. It is another variation on the bread-pudding theme, but here the result is more like a sponge cake than a pudding. It is light and delicious.

8 large eggs, separated
¾ cup sugar
½ cup ground rusks or bread crumbs from stale bread
1 cup ground blanched almonds
1 teaspoon freshly grated nutmeg
1 teaspoon ground cinnamon
½ teaspoon ground cloves
Grated zest of 1 lemon
2 teaspoons baking powder
1 recipe Zabaglione (page 105)

1. Preheat the oven to 400°F. Beat the egg yolks and sugar together in a large bowl until they are smooth and pale. Place the whites in a separate large bowl and whip with an electric mixer until stiff peaks form.

2. In a separate bowl, combine the ground rusks or bread crumbs, almonds, spices, lemon zest, and baking powder. Using a spatula, fold the dry ingredients into the egg yolk–and-sugar mixture and then fold in the egg whites. Mix quickly and thoroughly, making sure the whites leave no streaks. Pour the mixture into a buttered 10-inch-square ceramic or ovenproof glass dish. Bake until the pudding is set, 35 to 40 minutes. Cut out individual servings with a 2½-inch round or square cookie cutter. Have the zabaglione ready. To serve, place on a plate and spoon a little of the sauce over and around it.

Marzipan Pears from Ithaca
APITHAKIA

 Makes 72 pieces

There are dozens of variations on this theme in Greek confectionary—sweets shaped like pears or balls or little logs made with liquor-dampened ground nuts. Generally they are made during Lent, although the ones here wouldn't qualify as a Lenten specialty because of the butter they require. Throughout the book are recipes for similar sweets from different places in Greece.

1 cup (2 sticks) unsalted butter
1 pound finely ground blanched almonds
12 rusks or bread crumbs from stale bread, finely ground
2 tablespoons ground cinnamon
1 tablespoon ground cloves
½ cup orange blossom water
1 cup brandy
5 cups granulated sugar
2 teaspoons pure vanilla extract
72 whole cloves
Confectioners' sugar

1. Melt the butter in a large saucepan, then add the almonds, ground rusks, cinnamon, cloves, orange blossom water, and brandy. Stir over low heat just long enough to bring out the aromas and to warm. Remove from the heat and add the granulated sugar and vanilla. Mix thoroughly to combine. You just put in 5 cups of sugar!

2. Break off a golf ball–size piece of dough and form into a pear. Insert a whole clove on the top to simulate a stem. Repeat with the remaining dough and cloves. Place the *apithakia* on several large serving platters or trays and sprinkle generously with confectioners' sugar.

Almond Cookies from Corfu

MOUSTATSONIA

 Makes about 50 cookies

1 pound blanched almonds
2 large eggs
1 cup sugar
1 teaspoon pure vanilla extract
1 teaspoon fresh lemon juice

1. Preheat the oven to 300°F. Pulverize the almonds in a food processor fitted with a steel blade until they are like fine meal. Add the eggs, sugar, vanilla, and lemon juice and process until thoroughly combined.

2. Line 2 cookie sheets with parchment paper. A spoonful at a time, shape the almond mixture into 1-inch balls and flatten each with your palm to form a small ½-inch-thick disk. Place on the cookie sheets and bake until firm, about 12 minutes. They should not turn golden. Remove from the oven and let cool on a rack. As they tend to crumble easily, serve them with care.

Pears and Almonds Preserved in Syrup

ACHLADI GLYKO TOU KOUTALIOU

5 pounds firm small pears
Acidulated water (see page 458)
6 cups sugar
3 cups water
Juice of 3 lemons
1 cup whole blanched almonds

1. Peel, halve (lengthwise), and core the pears, then submerge them in the acidulated water to keep them from discoloring.

2. In a large pot, bring the sugar and the water to a boil over medium heat. When the sugar dissolves, add half the lemon juice. Add the pears to the syrup, reduce the heat to medium-low, and simmer for 15 minutes. Remove from the heat. Let the pears cool, cover the pot with plastic wrap, and let the pears remain in the thick syrup in the refrigerator overnight.

3. The next day, return the pot to the heat and simmer over medium-low heat until the syrup is thick and viscous, about 1 hour. About 10 minutes before removing from the heat, add the almonds and stir in the remaining lemon juice. Let the mixture cool, then place in sterile jars. Let cool completely and keep stored in the refrigerator, tightly closed. As long as the pears are completely submerged in the syrup, they will last indefinitely.

Roumeli

A Sense of Place and Palate

To an islander like me, Roumeli seems intangible. "It is not found on present-day maps of Greece. It isn't a political or administrative delineation," as Patrick Leigh Fermor writes of it in his renowned book *Roumeli, Travels in Northern Greece*. It is, rather, a colloquial name, just as one might say "the South" or "the East." A few centuries ago, Roumeli meant roughly the whole of continental Greece, from the Bosphorous to the Adriatic and from Macedonia to the Gulf of Corinth. After the War of Independence in the nineteenth century, Roumeli shrank, and the name referred only to the southern part of this great area, the mountainous strip of territory between the Gulf and the unredeemed lands that remained part of the Ottoman Empire. On modern Greek lips, Roumeli refers to almost that same broad swath of land that stretches from the eastern to the western coasts encompassing now five entire principalities—Fokida, Boetia, Evritania, Fthiotida, and Aitoloakarnania. To non-Greeks, Roumeli is familiar territory, for here lay Delphi, seat of the famous ancient oracle, and Messolongi, where Byron died.

Although the wetlands along the western mainland coast of Greece belong, administratively, to Roumeli, most of the rest of the region is extremely mountainous, and that more than anything else has shaped its people and table. To understand the region, one has to understand the shepherd's way of life, and to dig deep into the nomad's culture—especially that of the Sarakatsans—who had settled in great numbers here (as well as in Thessaly, Epirus, and Macedonia) by 1960.

Many people still herd sheep and goats in Roumeli, but they have adapted their transhumant lifestyle to modern times. Although shepherds still spend their winters in the lowlands, in places such as Thebes and Livadia, they do so not in makeshift abodes but in real homes and organized towns and villages. In the summer, they still move with their flocks to the cooler mountain reaches in Evritania and elsewhere, not on footpaths that take weeks to traverse but by car and pickup truck. The stamp of their pastoral ways is still clear.

It is not by chance, for example, that in most of Roumeli, cheese and other dairy products embellish many foods, or that lard and butter traditionally were more common than olive oil. In precipitous, impenetrable Roumeli, olive oil was scarce, since most of the region was not—and still isn't—conducive to its cultivation. As a result, oil had to be purchased with hard cash, so it was used sparingly. Only along the southern reaches, around Delphi, is the olive prevalent; indeed, one of Greece's largest groves is here, a million trees strong, majestically filling the beautiful valley below the oracle's ancient seat.

Dairy is probably the single most important aspect of Roumeli's table. It was in Roumeli that I first witnessed a home cook pour two cups of milk into a spinach pie before baking it, asking almost rhetorically, "How else is the spinach supposed to cook?" Ironically, she was the mother-in-law of one of Itea's largest olive merchants, and from her, I also first learned of another local specialty, *lepothies,* a kind of green similar to small tender spinach, simmered in milk, a custom found all over the shepherding communities of the north of Greece. Milk, yogurt, and cheese find their way into another regional specialty, the array of savory pies. Eggplant pie with milk and *trahana,* wild greens pies with yogurt, onion pie with *myzithra* cheese and yogurt, potato and feta pie, feta and cornmeal or semolina pies—all these and much more belong to the region's culinary traditions.

The most stereotypical image of Roumeli is that of the meat-eating Easter feasts of rows of whole lambs on spits in the streets of every town and village. In some parts of the region, though, namely in Evritania, the Easter feast is not a skewered lamb, but rather a stuffed lamb cooked in a pot and from whose juices a riceless *mageiritsa,* the traditional Easter soup, is made.

But it is the cliché image that captures the imagination. The *souvla*—spit—harks to very ancient ways, and belongs almost exclusively to the wandering shepherds who had no other means of cooking a feast of meat. (See more on the wandering shepherds' communities of northern Greece in the chapter on Epirus.)

One distinction, though, is that "meat" in this region refers almost exclusively to either lamb or goat. Pork, some beef, poultry, and small game were and are widely eaten, but it is the flocks of lamb and mountain goats that have given rise to Roumeli's image as Greece's meat capital. The region boasts an enormous variety of lamb dishes. I had never had a proper *kontosouvli* (literally "short skewer," made with lamb, not pork) before coming to Roumeli; or a real *kokkoretsi,* the national dish, made with lamb offal wrapped in intestines and rotisserie-grilled; or *garthoumbes,* a kind of mini *kokkoretsi* baked (not rotisserie-grilled) with tomatoes and herbs. I would never have ventured to try a spleen stuffed with walnuts, pine nuts, feta, and *trahana,* which was delicious, had I not been at the epicenter for such dishes. Local connoisseurs even distinguish the taste of lamb or goat by the age of the animal. The best *kontosouvli* is either from spring lamb or *provatina*—an older female lamb—one cook told me. The best *sarmades* (cabbage *dolmas*) are made with ground ram meat, another cook advised. *Zigouria* (year-old lambs), *mounoukia* (eunuched lambs or goats), *kriaria* (rams), and more all have their place on the local table.

The Roumeli table, of course, is enhanced by

vegetables, many farmed locally. Thebes, for example, produces some of the best potatoes in Greece. Whether by sheer coincidence or not, there have always been ample ways to cook them in Roumeli: stewed, roasted, fried among them. One interesting but simple old dish, *patates grouboulias,* calls for boiling, salting, and ricing them—one way to fool the eye and fill the belly in a place where rice normally was dear. I have come across other recipes, too, that called for cooking potatoes and rice together, something few people still do.

Eggplants are another favorite, cooked in myriad ways, too: baked in the clay dish called *gastra;* layered with onions and herbs and baked; stewed with tomatoes; fried, for a quick snack; and, finally, stuffed with rice or bulgur. The latter, in fact, was always economically more accessible, and as a result there are many recipes for bulgur-stuffed vegetables in the region. Even the Christmas pork sausage *maties* traditionally is enriched with bulgur, not rice, as it is when prepared elsewhere.

In some parts of Roumeli, locally grown beans and pulses are considered among the best in Greece. One such place is Karpenissi, known for its *gigantes,* or butter beans. Unfortunately, they are cultivated less and less, making room for other more profitable crops. As one local cook jokingly told me, "You have to have a bean merchant for a boyfriend to find them now!"

Homemade *trahana* (see page 456), noodles, and other pasta provide some of the most sating raw ingredients in the Roumeli larder. Corn, too, appears often in various traditional dishes. The best known is the local version of polenta, called either *katsamaki* or *mamalinga,* which is simmered into a mush like polenta and served with butter, cheese, or honey.

The Roumeli Pantry

AMFISSA AND ITS OLIVES

We visited the million-tree olive grove—or so they say—that produces the famed, plump Amfissa olive and stretches the length of the whole valley below Delphi, a breathtaking sight. Many of the trees are hundreds of years old.

The Amfissa olive is really the Conservolia variety, one of the three most commercially important table olives in Greece. Since the naming of olives is a confusing ordeal in Greece, and often has more to do with place rather than variety, it is important to note that the Conservolia is also recognizable at markets under the names Volos, Agrinio, Stylida, and Atalanti, as well as Amfissa. It is a large, oval olive that starts off a rich dark green when it is unripe and changes into a whole spectrum of different colors as it matures: greenish yellow, greenish red, mahogany, and, finally, dark bluish black.

Conservolia is the most versatile Greek olive, processed with equal success as both a green and black olive. When harvested green, the Conservolia can be stuffed, cured in salt brines of varying strength, and finally turned into what the Greeks call *tsakistes,* or "cracked" greens (the small, taut-skinned olives that traditionally are cracked with a stone before being cured). Harvested black and mature, it is cured in a vinegar brine, or as a black "slit" olive (olives that are scored almost down to the pit on both sides before being cured). These are also called *haraktes* in Greek. The Conservolia accounts for the majority of table olive production in the country. In recent years, however, the area has also gained ground as one of Greece's most important olive oil–producing regions.

CURED MEATS

Despite the meat traditions in Roumeli, the region isn't particularly well known for any kind of specialty charcuterie. Traditional farm families did all the things other farm families throughout Greece did with pork to preserve it for the winter. Salt pork, cut into strips and kept in barrels between layers of coarse salt, was one typical preparation; smoked pork was also prepared, usually at home, near the hearth. There was also an old local preparation called *lourides,* literally "strips," made from the pork skin, which was salted and smoked, then cooked with cabbage. Local sausages, almost exclusively pork, are a fairly simple affair, too, and like much of the rest of northern Greece they are seasoned with leeks.

CHEESE AND OTHER DAIRY PRODUCTS

The cheeses of Roumeli are shepherd's cheeses. Here, some of the best Greek yellow cheeses, *kasseri* and *kefalotyri,* are made. From here, too, comes some of the best-known feta on the American market, from Parnassus and Arahova. But there are other local cheeses produced on a small scale and often difficult to find outside the region.

Apsimotyri or **Psomotyri** This is essentially salted strained sheep's milk yogurt. It is made from three-day old yogurt, which is then mixed with salt and left to ferment for about three weeks. It is absolutely delicious, thick and sharp and surprisingly refreshing.

Formaella *Formaella* is a mild, semihard sheep's milk cheese, shaped in cylindrical basket molds, and a little like mozzarella in texture, but chewier. It is an appellation-of-origin cheese made exclusively in Arahova near Delphi. It is also one of the few Greek cheeses that taste better cooked and, in fact, it is mostly eaten pan-fried as *saganaki.* One special local treat calls for skewering the whole cylinder and roasting it in the fireplace.

Katiki Another appellation-of-origin cheese from Domokou in Roumeli, but also found in parts of Epirus and Macedonia, sometimes by the name *tsalafouti.* It is one of many naturally fermented sheep's and goat's milk cheeses, soft like mascarpone but pleasantly sour and slightly grainy. (For more, see *tsalafouti,* in the Thessaly cheese section, page 175.)

Klotsotyri Literally, "kick" cheese. Its name supposedly comes from the stunned face one makes upon eating too much of it. In order to snap out of the stupor of overeating you have to be kicked! *Klotsotyri* is made by boiling the whey (essentially buttermilk) left over after the production of butter. *Klotsotyri* is used to make *zymaropita,* a savory, phylloless *pita* made with zucchini, cornmeal, and the cheese.

Tripsana This is milk cooked with salt and cooled, and it makes for a shepherd's beverage all over the region, especially in summer.

Tyri Tsantillas Literally, "bag" cheese, this is a fresh, unsalted soft cheese made from whey.

Voustina This is an unusual cheese made from goat's milk. It is very sour and soft, almost like a fermented ricotta.

SALT-FISH

From as early as the fifth century B.C. Greeks have been making *tarihos,* or salt-fish, as a way to preserve a vital source of nourishment. Salted fish had a place in ancient medicine as well, and medical writers such as Hippocrates attributed different curative properties to such products.

Although salted fresh sardines and anchovies are found in many parts of Greece, the greatest variety of salt-fish is made along the melancholy western coast of the mainland, perhaps because salt has always been part and parcel of this region's lifeblood—Greece's main salt beds are here—and perhaps, too, because the fish conducive to preservation swim in abundance here.

The most prized local fish for salting is the *tsipoura,* a kind of bream. It is gutted and salted whole and, because it tends to be large, needs to sit for anywhere between twelve and eighteen days in salt. Then it is skinned and filleted and served with freshly squeezed lemon and olive oil. Small bream (about five ounces) are also prized. These aren't even scaled before salting, and they take just a few hours to be readied for consumption.

One of the local salt-fish specialties and best *mezethes* is called *petali,* or butterfly, and it can be made with several different kinds of fish. Large summer mullet *(kefalos)* is considered best, although large bream and smaller *lavrakia* (bass) are also used to make it. The fish is cracked at the head and split open down the middle from the spine, not the gut side, so that it is butterflied. The guts and brains are removed and the fish is boned. Then it is lightly salted and skewered across the top width so that it stays open. Finally it is hung for about a day to dry and served with a sprinkling of lemon juice

and olive oil. *Petali* is one of Messolongi's most renowned *mezethes.*

Salt plays a crucial role in the preparation of another local delicacy—eel. For one, eels always have to be cleaned with salt. They are rubbed with rock sea salt, *afrina* to the Greeks, to clear away their slippery, mucouslike skins. The best-known local specialty, *principato,* also necessitates the use of salt. Here, large eels (anywhere between one and a half to two pounds and sometimes up to three feet long) are preferred. The eel is split down the middle along the spine, sprinkled with coarse salt, and hung to drain and dry for anywhere from thirty minutes to several hours. The salt helps dislodge the fat between the skin and flesh. Then the eel is skinned from head to tail, but the skin is not removed. Instead, its flesh is sprinkled with cinnamon and cloves, the eel is dressed again and hung upside down from its tail for another half hour or so, then, finally, grilled.

GREY MULLET ROE, BOTARGO

It is a late August day, about four P.M., when we arrive at the *ybari,* one of the many natural fisheries set up as labyrinthine systems of netted walls throughout the wetlands all over the western coast of Greece. Late August is an important time here, when the shoals of grey mullet, *bafa* in the local dialect, are swollen with eggs and trying to move back to the sea to spawn. Instead, they are trapped, and fished.

It is their eggs, though, that are prized much more than their flesh, because they provide the essential material in the making of *botargo,* the amber bars of salted, sun-dried roe that is one of the most expensive delicacies in the world.

BOTARGO

▼

Little is known about exactly where or by whom *botargo* was first eaten. According to the English classicist Andrew Dalby, in *Siren's Feast*, *botargo* was appreciated in classical Byzantium, first mentioned by the Byzantine physician Simeon Seth circa 1025, in his survey of the dietary traditions of his era, *On the Properties of Foods*. The name is Greek in origin, from *oiotarikhon*, meaning "egg pickle."

Botargo is known throughout the rest of the Mediterranean, and it is almost always made from the roe of the grey mullet, because, as Yiorgos Trikalinos explained, the grey mullet's eggs are very compact and dense and do not fall apart when salted. In Venice, however, *botargo* is made from tuna eggs.

In my opinion, *botargo* is best savored as it is, like caviar, with as little embellishment as possible. Slice it paper-thin and then peel off the wax rind. Place it on a small serving plate. Serve plain, or sprinkle with a little freshly ground pepper, a drizzle of olive oil, and a little bit of fresh lemon juice. It is also delicious with ripe fresh figs.

The five fishermen working that day have finished lunch and are just emerging after their siesta from the simple prefabricated huts they call home most of the year. I am with Zafeiris Trikalinos and his uncle Yiorgos, Greece's premier *botargo* merchants.

We all wait for the tide to rise. I look around at the landscape—I've never been in wetlands before, and there is something interminably sad but beautiful about the place. Everything is a pale, grayish blue. The still water stretches for a distance inland, giving you the false impression that the stillness is infinite. In reality the whole marsh is shrinking as progress encroaches on it continuously.

"Stop there," Zafeiris says, almost scolding me for heading toward the wooden walkways above the traps. "If they sense you, they don't approach," he explains. By five o'clock, the work begins. The fishermen bring their pails and nets to the walkway and start pulling up the day's first catch. Besides female mullet there are males, of course, and *skaros* (parrotfish), small bream, and a few crabs here and there. The fish are separated, and then the first stage in the making of *botargo* begins. The equipment is deceptively simple—just a few small inexpensive paring knives, sharpened anew every day. Each fish is slit and gutted, and the two soft, long egg sacs are lifted out. To detach them completely, the mullet is slashed across the point in its belly right where the egg sacs are joined. There's a little piece of flesh that comes out with them, the *fkari*, which is, according to the younger Trikalinos, the fishermen's favorite *meze*, salted lightly and savored with ouzo.

The roe can range in color from an almost ivory shade of white to a deep amber. The yellower the eggs, the more mature. Once they are removed, the egg sacs are placed in coarse salt for a few hours, "to tighten them," says Zafeiris. Then they are rinsed and left on planks in special screened cages outdoors to dry for several days. Experience and personal taste dictate when the *botargo* is ready. "The fishermen like it dark and hard," says the younger Trikalinos, "but the taste makers in Athens like it light and soft." When fresh, the egg sacs weigh anywhere between three and eight ounces each, depending on the size of the fish. By the time they are dried, they weigh about half that. Once ready, they are dipped in beeswax to preserve them.

The Recipes

MEZETHES

Pan-Fried Formaella Cheese

FORMAELLA SAGANAKI

 Makes 4 to 6 servings

*F*ormaella *is a sheep's milk cheese formed in cylindrical baskets and unique to Arahova, a mountain village near Delphi. The town is filled with artisanal cheese makers who produce* formaella *and other dairy products, but there is reputedly (at least at the time of this writing) only one old-timer left who still knows how to weave the baskets in which the cheese is shaped. The baskets are said to last a good five years, and nowadays they tend to be longer and thinner than they were a few decades ago, when* formaella *was made by almost every family in stout, wine-glass-size baskets, and reserved either for very special occasions or given as gifts. It is still hard to find the real thing, made by artisan cheese makers, in Athens and other big cities. However, commercially produced* formaella *is available in the States at specialty Greek shops. A drive to Arahova revealed not only the cheese but this simple delicious recipe for grilling it.*

One ½-pound cylinder *formaella* cheese, cut
    into ¼-inch-thick rounds
½ cup all-purpose flour for dredging
2 to 3 tablespoons unsalted butter,
    as needed
1 lemon (optional), halved or quartered

1. Lightly dampen each round of cheese by running it under the faucet. Dredge it lightly in the flour and shake off the excess.

2. Melt the butter in a large nonstick skillet over medium-high heat and fry the cheese slices a few at a time until they begin to soften and melt. Remove, place on a plate, and serve, sprinkled, if desired, with lemon juice.

Pork-Stuffed Eggplants with Bulgur or Trahana and Herbs

MELITZANES PAPOUTSAKIA ME HOIRINO
KAI MYRODIKA

 Makes 6 servings

*I*n the past ground meat wasn't ground at all but finely chopped with a huge knife, a technique that Greek cooks today often look back on nostalgically. This recipe attempts to revive that old world technique. The dish itself comes from the western reaches of Roumeli, near the Agrafa mountains.*

6 medium eggplants, ends trimmed
¾ cup extra-virgin olive oil
½ pound boneless lean pork, preferably from the
    thigh
6 to 8 scallions, to taste, white and tender green
    parts only, chopped
Salt and freshly ground black pepper to taste
1 cup peeled, seeded, and chopped plum
    tomatoes (canned are fine)
¼ cup bulgur or sweet *trahana* (see page 456)
½ cup snipped fresh dill
½ cup finely chopped fresh flat-leaf parsley

1. Lay the eggplant down horizontally and cut out a rounded hollow that stretches the length of the eggplant, leaving about 1½ inches on both ends. The idea is to make a "pot hole" in the middle of the eggplant, which will be filled. Chop and reserve the pulp.

2. Heat ½ cup of the olive oil in a large skillet over medium heat and cook the hollowed eggplants until their skins soften and brown lightly in some places. Do this in batches if necessary. Remove from the skillet and set aside.

3. Using a knife, finely chop the pork into very small cubes. Heat the remaining ¼ cup olive oil in a large skillet over medium heat and cook the scallions, stirring, until wilted, about 3 to 5 minutes. Add the pork and cook until lightly browned on all sides. Add the eggplant pulp and season with salt and pepper. Add the tomatoes and *trahana* and simmer until the mixture begins to thicken, about 5 minutes. Remove from the heat and set aside to cool. Mix in the dill and parsley and adjust the seasoning with more salt and pepper.

4. Preheat the oven to 350°F. Fill the eggplants with the meat mixture and place side by side in a lightly oiled large ovenproof glass baking dish. Bake the eggplants until the meat is cooked, the *trahana* soft, and the eggplants tender, about an hour. Remove from the oven and serve hot or at room temperature.

Onions Stuffed with Ground Goat Meat from Galaxidi

KELEMIA APO TO GALAXIDI

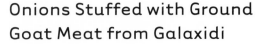   Makes 6 to 7 servings

This dish is usually made with ground ram's meat, for which Greeks, especially in Roumeli, have an affinity. Difficult to find in the United States, it can be replaced with more accessible goat or lamb.

12 very large yellow onions
½ pound ground goat or lamb
½ pound lean ground beef
½ cup grated *kefalograviera* cheese or any hard yellow cheese
1 cup finely chopped fresh flat-leaf parsley
¼ cup short-grain rice (see Note)
Salt and freshly ground black pepper to taste
⅓ cup extra-virgin olive oil
1 cup dry white wine

1. Peel the onions and cut off the tops and bottoms so that both ends are level, reserving the cut ends. Bring a large pot of salted water to a boil and blanch the onions for about 5 minutes to soften. Drain in a colander and rinse with cold water. Using a teaspoon, hollow out the inside of the onions, leaving a ¼- to ½-inch shell. Finely chop the inner sheaves, together with the reserved tops and bottoms.

2. Combine the ground meats, cheese, and parsley in a large bowl. Add the chopped onions and rice, season with salt and pepper, and add the olive oil. Knead together very well.

3. Fill each of the onions with the ground meat mixture. Place in a single layer in a large, wide pot. Pour in the wine and enough water to just cover the onions. Place a sheet of parchment paper over the onions and weigh it down with a plate. Cover the pot, bring to a boil, reduce the heat to medium-low, and simmer until the onions are very tender and the filling cooked, about 40 minutes. Remove from the heat and let cool slightly. Serve.

✳ **NOTE** Short-grain polished rice, called *nihaki* in Greek, is available at Greek food shops.

SOUP

Corn and Cabbage Soup

LAHANOSOUPA ME KALAMBOKALEVRO

 Makes 6 to 8 servings

*S*oup in Roumeli is a markedly simple affair—there are many old bread-based soups and vegetable-and-rice soups much like what one finds in the rest of the traditional Greek larder. I came across this very northern recipe and liked it, even though it is a dish that has all but disappeared from the region's table today. It went the way of the dinosaur sometime in the 1960s, a kind of turning point in the annals of the traditional Greek kitchen, when much of the country's simple fare disappeared in favor of the foods of affluence. I have changed the recipe slightly to include chicken stock instead of plain water as the base.

3 cups cored and shredded green cabbage, washed and drained
½ cup extra-virgin olive oil
2 large red onions, chopped
6 to 8 cups chicken stock, as needed
¾ cup fine yellow cornmeal
Salt and freshly ground black pepper to taste

1. Bring a large pot of salted water to a boil and blanch the cabbage. As soon as the water comes back to a boil, remove the cabbage and drain. Set aside.

2. Heat the olive oil in a large, deep skillet over medium heat and cook the onion, stirring, until wilted, about 8 minutes. Add the cabbage and cook, stirring, for about 8 minutes.

3. In another large pot, bring 6 cups of the stock to a boil. Add the cornmeal in a slow, steady stream, stirring constantly, to keep it from clumping. Simmer it until thick and creamy but liquid, about 15 minutes. Add the sautéed vegetables and simmer for another 10 minutes. If the soup is too dense, dilute it with some or all of the remaining stock and simmer to warm through. Adjust the seasoning with salt and pepper and serve.

SAVORY PIES

On the drive down from Granitsa deep in the Agrafa Mountains, we stopped in Domani, another small mountain village forgotten by time but not by tourism, since many Greeks come here to kayak on the region's rushing streams and rivers. Our connection in Granitsa, Lefteris Theodorou, had arranged for us to visit a relative and good local cook. Sure enough, when we knocked on the door of Kyria Peryla, she was waiting for us at the kitchen table together with her husband and son. We went through all the typical Greek niceties that I have come to love so much: the where-are-you-froms served up with an offering of a homemade spoon sweet, in this case a local wild berry called *krana* (actually they're Cornelian cherries), and coffee. The whole kitchen was suffused with the aroma of eggs and cheese, and the light in Kyria's small oven

A WORD ON PHYLLO

⏥

There are many different recipes for homemade phyllo in Greece. In Macedonia, for example, one of the traditional phyllo recipes resembles puff pastry for the way the butter is pounded into the dough, which is then stacked and rolled out. In my travels through Roumeli, I kept running into two basic phyllo recipes: The first, which calls for olive oil and vinegar or lemon juice, is a pretty standard recipe and doesn't differ from the way phyllo is handmade in most of the rest of the country. The other recipe, though, calls for the addition of vegetable shortening, together with olive oil, and makes for a very light, crisp pastry. See page 453 for phyllo recipes.

shone dimly over the round pan that was the source of that mouthwatering perfume. A pie. One of Roumeli's famous pies. One of its unique ones at that: all yellow and green and gurgling, it was made with cornmeal and zucchini and eggs, but no phyllo. I took out my notebook and settled in, prepared to spend the afternoon listening, imbibing, eating, and asking. In the end, I went away with the recipe for her *zymaropita* as well as recipes for much more.

Roumeli, together with Epirus and Thessaly, is one of the regions of Greece where savory pies play a vital role in the local kitchen. Indeed, all three areas have much in common, for the pastoral traditions in each run deep. Although nowadays most shepherds move their flocks by truck from their cool summer retreats in the mountains to their winter shelters in the plains, their foodways have remained, by and large, intact. *Pita,* as the Greeks call savory pie, evolved from their traditional way of life, from the need to create dishes that could be made with ingredients on hand such as cheeses,

milk, certain grains, which were always part of the shepherd's larder, or wild greens, which could be foraged from wherever they camped or lived.

Cheese and milk pies are especially common in Roumeli. The cheese pies traditionally were the most difficult to make because they often called for upwards of eighteen sheets of phyllo, which was hand-rolled and had to be very thin lest the pie become stodgy or the inner sheets not bake completely. Similar multilayered pies are found in Epirus. Although the ingredients were sparse, the variety of cheese pies was—and is—daunting. Feta, butter, and phyllo might be the basic ingredients for four or five different pies, distinguished mostly by shape. Other cheeses, such as *myzithra,* also appear. Sugar or honey is sometimes added to the filling, and milk and eggs might be used to enrich the mixture, as well as various grains such as rice and *trahana.* In many parts of Roumeli, and especially among the Sarakatsan populations, milk pies (with milk, eggs, and usually rice) were considered feast food, prepared especially to celebrate Saint George, their patron saint whose name day falls just after Easter, and right around the time of their spring migration.

The greens pies are just as unique in Roumeli because they often call for substantial amounts of dairy products, in the form of cheese, milk, or yogurt. Greens in this part of Greece consist largely of a variety of local spinach, sorrel, nettles, wild leeks, and several kinds of chervil. There are a number of other lovely vegetable pies from this part of Greece, too, especially with eggplant.

The third category of *pita* seems more like a stuffed bread than a pie, since there is no phyllo. Many of these dishes contain either cornmeal or wheat flour that is made into a batter, mixed with the other ingredients, and baked all together.

Whatever the pie in question, one thing remains constant: *Pita* is just about the only Greek food never eaten with bread on the side.

Rich Egg and Cheese Pie

AVGOPITA

 Makes 12 servings

Every cook in Greece has his or her little secrets concerning phyllo and how to work with it. An acquaintance in Itea, Erse Moscahlaides, passed this recipe along to me. She said that seltzer sprinkled over the phyllo helps to keep it fluffy and also helps to keep it from drying out and cracking when baking.

6 large eggs, lightly beaten
3 cups milk
1½ pounds Greek feta cheese, crumbled
½ pound *kefalograviera* cheese or any hard
    yellow cheese, grated
Freshly ground white pepper to taste
¾ cup extra-virgin olive oil
1 pound commercial phyllo, defrosted and at
    room temperature (see page 455)
⅓ cup soda water

1. Beat the eggs and milk together well in a large bowl either by hand or with an electric mixer until frothy. Mix in the feta and *kefalograviera* cheeses and season with pepper. Add 3 tablespoons of the olive oil and stir to combine.

2. Preheat the oven to 400°F. Lightly oil a 12- by 18-inch baking pan. Open the phyllo and keep the stack covered with a kitchen towel to keep it from

drying out. Layer 8 to 10 sheets on the bottom of the baking pan, brushing each with a little of the remaining olive oil. Spread the filling evenly over the phyllo. Top with the remaining phyllo sheets, brushing each with the oil. Do not score the pie into serving pieces, but rather puncture the surface all over with a sharp paring knife. Sprinkle the soda water over the top. Bake the pie until the phyllo is golden and the filling is set, 1 to 1¼ hours. Remove from the oven, let cool, and cut into serving pieces. Serve warm or at room temperature.

Twisted Cheese Pie

STRIFTOPITA

 Makes 12 servings

Another classic, and one way to take the most ordinary ingredients and, using shape and form, turn them into something extraordinary.

1 pound Greek feta cheese, crumbled
½ pound *myzithra* cheese, grated
4 large eggs
1 cup milk
1 recipe Roumeli phyllo (page 453) or
    commercial phyllo, at room temperature
1 cup (2 sticks) unsalted butter, melted

1. Combine the cheeses in a large bowl. Beat the eggs and milk together and add to the cheeses, combining thoroughly.

2. Lightly oil an 18-inch round baking or pizza pan and preheat the oven to 375°F. Divide the dough into 10 equal balls. On a lightly floured work surface, pat down the first ball with your palms and shape into a circle. Using a floured rolling pin or dowel, roll it out to a circle about 15 inches in diameter. Brush generously with the melted butter and sprinkle generously with the cheese mixture. Starting from the bottom edge, roll up the dough over the cheese to form a long, loose cylinder. Holding the cylinder in both hands, gently twist it almost the way one wrings wet laundry. Place one end of the twisted cylinder in the center of the pan, and coil it tightly. Repeat with the remaining balls of dough, melted butter, and filling, placing each twisted cylinder next to the other, working your way coil-like toward the rim of the pan.

3. Bake until the phyllo is golden, 1 to 1½ hours. Remove from the oven and let cool slightly. To serve, cut into wedges like a pie, so that each piece is comprised of part of several cylinders.

✳ **NOTE** You may reduce the ingredients by half and bake the pie in a 9-inch or 10-inch round baking pan.

Greens Pie with Milk and Eggs

HORTOPITA AMFISSIS

  Makes 12 servings

Milk and cheese, staple foods of shepherds, appear often in combination with greens in the pies of Roumeli.

2 pounds fresh flat-leaf spinach, trimmed,
    chopped, and washed well
1 large leek, trimmed, chopped, and washed well
4 scallions, white and tender green parts, chopped
4 large eggs
1¾ cups milk
1 pound Greek feta cheese, crumbled
½ pound *kefalograviera* cheese or any hard
    yellow cheese, grated
3 tablespoons sweet *trahana* (see page 456)
1 cup olive oil
Salt and freshly ground black pepper to taste
1 recipe Roumeli phyllo (page 453) or
    commercial phyllo, at room temperature

1. Wash the spinach very well and drain thoroughly. Place in a large bowl with the leek and scallions. Beat the eggs lightly and add them to the spinach mixture. Pour in the milk and add the cheeses, *trahana,* and ¾ cup of the olive oil. Season with salt and pepper and toss together to combine well.

2. Preheat the oven to 375°F. Lightly oil a large rectangular baking pan (18 by 12 by 3 inches). Lightly flour your work surface and divide the dough into 4 equal balls. Pat down the first ball with your palms and shape into a rectangle. Using a floured rolling pin or dowel, roll it into a large rectangle, slightly larger than the pan. Fit it inside the pan and brush with some of the remaining ¼ cup olive oil. Roll out the second ball in the same way, place it on top of the first sheet, and brush with olive oil.

3. Spread the filling evenly over the phyllo. Continue with the last 2 pieces of dough, layering and brushing each generously with oil. Pinch the top and bottom phyllo sheets together and roll up to form a decorative rim. Score the pie into diagonal wedges without running the knife through to the bottom of the pie and bake in a hot oven until the phyllo is golden and the filling set, 1 to 1½ hours. Remove from the oven, let cool, and serve either warm or at room temperature.

"Kneaded" Pie with Cornmeal and Squash

ZYMAROPITA

 Makes 12 to 15 servings

Zymi is the Greek word for "dough." This and the next few recipes are among the many for easy batter pies made without a crust, hence without the fuss of phyllo, found all over the region, and generally all over northern Greece. This was fast food for working women when work consisted of tending animals, fields, home, and family. These recipes, and similar ones from Epirus, often call for a soft, sour local cheese that goes by different names depending on where one is from. It is not easy to find substitutes for these cheeses in the United States, and to the best of my knowledge, they are not imported. I've done the next best thing: By combining feta, strained yogurt, and fresh ricotta, I have tried to simulate both the sour flavor and tartness of these local farmhouse cheeses.

4 medium-large zucchini, peeled and grated (about 6 cups)
1 tablespoon salt
⅔ pound goat's milk feta cheese, crumbled
⅓ pound fresh whole-milk ricotta or fresh Greek *myzithra* cheese
1 cup yogurt, preferably Greek or Mediterranean style, drained (see page 459)
½ cup extra-virgin olive oil
5 large eggs, lightly beaten
1 cup milk
Freshly ground black pepper to taste
3 to 4 cups fine yellow cornmeal, as needed

1. Place the zucchini in a colander and toss with the salt. Let stand for an hour, weighed down in the colander with a plate and a weight on top. Take a little at a time of the mixture and squeeze between the palms of your hands to rid the squash of as much liquid as possible.

2. Preheat the oven to 375°F. Combine the feta, ricotta or *myzithra*, and yogurt in a large bowl. Add the zucchini and toss very well to combine. Add the olive oil. Mix the eggs and milk together and pour into the zucchini mixture. Season with salt and pepper. Slowly add the cornmeal, kneading until the mixture is dense like a wet dough.

3. Oil either an 18-inch round or an 18- by 12- by 3-inch rectangular baking or pizza pan. Spread the mixture in the pan and pat it down with your fingers. Bake until the pie is set and golden on top, 50 minutes to 1 hour. Remove from the oven, let cool, and cut into serving pieces. Serve either warm or at room temperature.

✳ **NOTE** You may reduce the ingredients by half and bake the pie in a 9-inch or 10-inch round or square baking dish.

MEAT BEYOND LAMB ON A SPIT— EASTER TRADITIONS FROM ROUMELI

More than any place in the entire country, Roumeli stands out in every Greek's mind for Easter. Roumeli is where the *foustanellas,* the white pleated skirts of traditional Greek soldiers, flutter, where whole lambs turning on spits have become the national symbol. The cliché no doubt still captures our imaginations, or it would not be copied all over the country the way it is.

The *souvla* (spit), or *lako* (for pit) as Roumeliotes call it, harks back to very ancient ways and taps into the primordial memories bottled up inside every Greek—warrior feasts, sacrifices, manliness, honor. To this day the animals are always roasted with their heads intact. "A decapitated lamb is very bad luck," says Maria Polymeropoulou, president of the Women's Club of Lamia, which, in conjunction with the Folklore Museum, published a book on traditional recipes from Roumeli. Cooking whole animals on a spit also is a custom that belongs to the wandering shepherds.

In Amfissa, as my friend and guide there, Eric Moscahlaidis, told me, "Meat here is synonymous with lamb." In Granitsa, though, a village high in the mountains of Agrafa, goat is the preferred meat, thanks largely to necessity. (Lambs can't pasture easily on craggy slopes; goats can.) The tenderest meat is considered to come from the *mounouchia,* castrated young goats.

Easter begins after the midnight liturgy on Holy Saturday. While most of the rest of the country breaks the fast with a hot bowl of *mageiritsa* (the traditional offal soup), most of Roumeli does not. "*Mageiritsa* is a new phenomenon for us," says Mrs. Polymeropoulou. "We consider it too heavy a dish with which to break the fast, something that will bring on a stomachache. If we want soup, more than likely we'll make it with the [lamb's] head," she adds. So, instead of *mageiritsa,* the fast is broken with any number of local offal dishes. In Desfina, for example, "there isn't a family who does not prepare the *psmarni,*" says Loukia Stefou, a philologist and folklorist whose heritage lies there. *Psmarni* is an unusual dish that calls for very young lamb— never more than a few weeks old. Once it is butchered and cut into large pieces, washed well, and marinated in olive oil, salt, pepper, lemon juice, and wine, it is baked over a huge amount of fresh green garlic and fresh scallions in an outdoor oven. The dish takes about 4 hours to cook and usually is put in the oven at about 8:30 in the evening to be ready by the time the family gets home from church after midnight.

The next day, Easter Sunday, is marked by the spit-roasted lamb except in the high mountain reaches around Karpenisi and all the way to Granitsa. In this part of Roumeli, most cooks stuff the cavity of a whole baby lamb and cook it in a large pot on top of the stove, reserving the pan juices to make a soup. In the last few years, too, many cooks have traded the traditional spit-roasted lamb for goat. "It's healthier," notes Mrs. Polymeropoulou. "Goats run wild. Lambs are fed on animal feed and have become very fatty."

The men almost always roast the animal, and while they do, an array of *mezethes* flows from the Roumeli kitchen, most rooted in every country cook's sensibility of not letting a single part of the animal go to waste. In Desfina, according to Ms. Stefou, sautéed liver is the morning *meze.* (Similar recipes appear in the chapter on Epirus.) Elsewhere, *koilitses riganatha,* lamb stomachs cooked with tomato and oregano, feed the men while they tend to the rotisserie. Spleen wrapped in intestine—*spleenantero*—is another favorite *meze.* Among the most unusual dishes is the *giomidia*—chopped intestines, liver, and stomachs simmered with stewed spinach. In Amfikleia, Fthiotida, locals make what they call *frigadelia,* liver wrapped in caul fat and cooked over coals on a skewer.

Not everyone in Roumeli makes *kokkoretsi,* the rotisseried offal-and-intestine sausage for which the region has become famous within Greece. In Desfina, which claims some notably different customs, locals prefer to reserve the innards for their much-loved little *garthoumbes* (miniature stuffed intestines), which are also rife with fresh garlic and scallions, baked with local rosé wine, and eaten on the second day of Easter. Soup made with the tripe is reserved for later in the week, usually Wednesday, and as the week progresses all the leftovers are gradually consumed, culminating in the local version of fricassee, the dish eaten on Friday, Zoodohou Pigi Day (which means "life-giving source" and is a celebration of the Virgin Mary). It is made with the leftover bones and trimmings, together with lettuce, dill, parsley, scallions, and wine.

The meat dishes of Roumeli are formidable, indeed, and together with them comes the whole bevy of dairy specialties that tie both to the shepherd's life and to the Easter table. For example, all over the region many of these meat dishes are savored with a side dish of thick, salted yogurt cheese, called either *tsalafouti* or *psimotyri.* Dessert is almost always some kind of milk pie or the semolina custard pie, *galaktoboureko.*

Goat or Lamb Baked on a Bed of Spring Onions and Garlic
PSIMARNI

 Makes 6 to 8 servings

The practice of baking goat or lamb on a bed of vegetables is followed all over Roumeli and in parts of central Macedonia as well. This dish comes from Desfina, just above Thebes.

1 cup extra-virgin olive oil
1 cup fresh lemon juice
½ cup water
Salt and freshly ground black pepper to taste
1 leg of goat or lamb, fat trimmed, bone in, 7 to 8 pounds
3 pounds spring onions or scallions
15 fresh green garlic stalks (see Note), or 8 garlic cloves, peeled and crushed
2 pounds fresh spinach, trimmed, coarsely chopped, and washed well
1 cup snipped fresh dill
1 cup finely chopped fresh flat-leaf parsley

1. In a large bowl, combine 6 tablespoons of the olive oil with ½ cup of the lemon juice, the water, salt, and pepper and whisk until smooth. Add the meat to the bowl and coat with the marinade. Marinate for 1 hour, covered and refrigerated.

2. Preheat the oven to 400°F. Lightly oil a baking pan large enough to fit the meat. Trim and wash the spring onions or scallions and garlic, leaving as much of the greens as possible if using fresh garlic.

3. Heat ¼ cup of the remaining olive oil over medium heat in a large, deep skillet and add the spinach. Cook, stirring, until wilted, about 5 minutes. Remove from the heat. Cut the stalks of both the spring onions or scallions and fresh garlic in half across the width, then in half lengthwise. Toss in the pan with the spinach (and its juices), dill, and parsley and mix in the remaining 10 tablespoons olive oil and ½ cup lemon juice.

4. Spread the mixture evenly over the bottom of the pan. Season with salt and pepper. Place the goat or lamb over the vegetables. Pour the marinade over the meat. Roast until the meat browns, 35 to 40 minutes. Cover the pan with aluminum foil, reduce the oven temperature to 350°F, and continue to bake until the meat is tender, another 45 to 50 minutes. Add a little water to the vegetables if necessary during baking to keep them from burning. Test for doneness by cutting into the fleshiest part of the leg. It should have a faint pink color. (Roast for less time if you prefer rare goat; Greeks, for better or worse, tend to like their goat well done.) Remove from the oven, let rest for 20 minutes, and carve. Spoon the vegetables and pan juices around the meat on a large serving platter.

✳ **NOTE** Fresh garlic is available in spring from some specialty greengrocers.

Goat or Lamb with Garlic and Cheese Baked in Paper

KLEFTIKO

 Makes 6 servings

The word klephtiko *comes from the Klephts, or mountain rebels of the Greek Revolution, who used to cook their food underground so that no steam or aromas would escape which could divulge their positions. Nowadays,* klephtiko *has come to refer to any food that is somehow wrapped or sealed during cooking.*

6 tablespoons unsalted butter
3 pounds boneless goat or lamb, preferably
    shoulder, fat trimmed and cut into 1½-inch
    cubes
Salt and freshly ground black pepper to taste
4 to 6 garlic cloves, to taste, peeled and crushed
½ pound tin-aged Greek feta cheese, cut into
    ½-inch cubes
⅓ pound *kefalotyri* cheese, cut into ½-inch
    cubes
2 cups chopped fresh or canned tomatoes
½ cup water

1. Preheat the oven to 325°F. Butter six 12-inch squares of parchment paper or heavy aluminum foil each with 1 tablespoon of butter.

2. Season the goat with salt and pepper and toss with the garlic, cheeses, and tomatoes in a large bowl. Place a little goat, about 5 or 6 pieces, plus a handful of the tomato-cheese mixture in the center of each parchment sheet. Carefully fold up the sheets to seal, like a package. Place side by side in a deep ovenproof clay, ceramic, or glass baking dish. Pour the water over the packets and bake until the goat is very tender and all the ingredients have melded together, about 2 hours.

3. Remove from the oven, let cool for about 5 minutes, and place each individual packet on a plate. Cut open the parchment and serve.

⊙ The same dish can be prepared with a whole leg of lamb. You'll need one large sheet of parchment, buttered. Using the tip of a sharp paring knife, make incisions all over the leg of lamb and stuff each with some crushed garlic and small cubes of *kefalotyri* cheese (you'll need about 8 garlic cloves and about 1½ cups cheese cubes for a leg). Season with salt and pepper. Wrap the leg carefully in the buttered paper and place in a large, deep, preferably clay, glass, or ceramic baking dish. Bake at 350°F until the lamb is tender but pink on the inside, about 2 hours. Remove from the oven, let cool slightly, and serve.

Goat Meatballs Served with Trahana

GIDINOI KEFTEDES ME TRAHANA

 Makes 4 to 6 servings

This unusual recipe calls for 2 typical mountain ingredients—goat meat and trahana. It comes from an isolated corner of Roumeli, near Tzoumerka in the Agrafa Mountains.

1½ pounds ground goat meat (see Note)
2 large red onions, finely chopped
2 garlic cloves, minced
1 cup chopped fresh mint or 3 tablespoons dried
1 cup chopped fresh flat-leaf parsley

½ pound rustic bread, crusts removed
Salt and freshly ground black pepper to taste
½ cup extra-virgin olive oil
¼ cup (½ stick) unsalted butter
½ cup sweet *trahana* (see page 456)
2 cups water, or more as needed

1. Combine the goat meat, onions, garlic, and herbs in a large bowl. Run the bread lightly under the tap to dampen and squeeze dry. Crumble it into the meat mixture. Season with salt and pepper and knead to combine all the ingredients thoroughly. Shape into balls the size of golf balls. Set aside.

2. In a large, deep skillet, heat the olive oil over medium-high heat and fry the *keftedes* until browned and cooked through, turning them to cook on all sides. This will have to be done in batches. Remove the *keftedes* with a slotted spoon and set aside to drain on paper towels. Let the skillet cool and scrape it clean.

3. Add the butter to the same skillet, heat over medium-low heat, and when it melts and bubbles up, pour in the *trahana.* Cook, turning constantly, for 5 minutes. Add the water to the skillet, reduce the heat to low, and simmer the *trahana,* stirring, until all the water has been absorbed and the *trahana* is tender, 12 to 15 minutes. Add another ½ to 1 cup water if necessary. About 5 minutes before the *trahana* is done, return the *keftedes* back to the skillet and heat everything together. Serve hot.

✳ **NOTE** *Gida* refers to a large, old female goat. The meat is tougher and gamier—and tastier—than that of a young animal. If your butcher cannot provide it, use regular goat. Lamb will also do.

Greek Easter Innards Sausage

KOKKORETSI

 Makes 10 to 12 *meze* servings

In a culture where shepherding and husbandry have always been the trade by which people earned their livelihoods, little is shunned when it comes to savoring meat of any kind. I have omitted the majority of organ-meat recipes that I've collected from all around Greece, because American cooks don't relish them with the same enthusiasm as Greek cooks do. But in Roumeli, because meat is so important, it would have been inaccurate to ignore them altogether. Here is one representative recipe. After the beef scares in Britain and other parts of Europe in 1997, a European Union law was passed forbidding the sale of offal from animals more than a year old. It was a few months before Easter, and all of Greece went up in arms. Headlines read, "No Kokkoretsi." The public outcry was so strong that the law was changed to permit the sale of ingredients that went into Greece's famous Easter sausage, kokkoretsi. *All of Greece eats* kokkoretsi *at Easter, but in Roumeli it is a treat year-round, found in tavernas and savored as a local* meze. *Making it is man's work, and a good rotisserie is needed for proper grilling.*

Viscera of 1 young lamb (liver, heart, spleen,
    lungs, sweetbreads), washed very well
Salt and freshly ground black pepper to taste
3 to 4 teaspoons dried Greek oregano, to taste
6 to 8 garlic cloves, to taste, chopped
1 lamb's intestine
Several lemons, halved
Caul fat from 1 lamb, washed and chopped into
    1-inch pieces

1. Chop the liver, heart, spleen, and lungs into about 2-inch pieces. Season with salt, pepper, and oregano and toss with the garlic. Set aside, refrigerated, until ready to use.

2. Wash the intestine very well: Turn it inside out and run under the tap, rubbing it clean. Rub with lemon and place in a bowl of ice water until ready to use.

3. Skewer the cut viscera onto the long metal skewer of a rotisserie, alternating between types and adding the cut caul fat intermittently between pieces.

4. Take the intestine, pierce it onto the tip of the skewer to secure, and begin to wrap the meats, winding the intestine tightly around them to cover completely. Tuck in the end once finished, to secure closed. Season with salt. Place the skewer about 8 inches from the heat source and roast, turning, until the *kokkoretsi* is browned and crisp and completely cooked, about 2 hours.

5. To serve, remove from the skewer, cut into 1-inch rings, and sprinkle with lemon juice.

FISH AND SEAFOOD AND ROUMELI'S WESTERN COAST

Politically, the western coast of central Greece is considered part of Roumeli, but geographically the area is unique. Greece's wetlands lie here, stretching from the western coast of the Peloponnesos in the South all the way up to Aitoloakarnania in the North, near Epirus.

The best known town along the Roumeli coast is Messolongi, which means "in the middle" and is where Lord Byron died, a hero of the Greek Revolution. Commercially, the region is still important, for here are some of Greece's largest salt basins. Almost all year round the stark white mounds of sea salt sculpt the coast near Messolongi like dunes, and in August and early September, when the beds are filled with seawater and dried, and the salt harvested, the whole area is abuzz with activity. Salt also plays a major role in the area's cooking, as the large number of preserved fish dishes easily testifies.

Dozens of natural fisheries dot the marshy coast. Unlike the rest of Roumeli—with the exception of Galaxidi and other towns laced along the Gulf of Corinth—fish reigns supreme here, but the cuisine is also an interesting blend of mountain and coastal customs. There is a wealth of savory pies, which attests to the Roumeliote—the mountain—influence, and several meat dishes that clearly seem to derive from a pastoral tradition: one is the local *giouvetsi* (clay pot) of lamb, butter, rice (not pasta), and yogurt, a dish also found in parts of Epirus; another is the *tsoubleki,* a kind of stew that was prevalent until the 1960s, when local butchers would cook up and sell all their leftover cuts, including ram and large sheep and beef, at the week's end. The local version of *capama,* a kind of meat casserole that can be made with anything from beef to chicken, is here (in Amfilohia, specifically) made with lamb's tongue.

There is, of course, also a large number of fish dishes similar to those found in the Ionian Islands, just across the water. One of the most unusual is *bourgieto,* the peppery Seven Island fish stew that is one of the classics of the Ionian Islands, made here with eel, a local specialty.

After the Greek Revolution in the early nineteenth century, large numbers of people from the Peloponessos, which is just on the other side of the Gulf of Corinth, settled here in droves, and many local dishes such as the *asproyiahni* reflect their influence, too. Generally, whether in dishes derived from the shepherd's or the seaman's traditions, the food in this part of the country is plain. At one time

A CALENDAR OF LOCAL FISH

In Roumeli, from around November through April, it is the season for *lavraki* (sea bass), the rockfish *govios* (goby), and a tiny local shrimp, about an inch long, that is fried and eaten whole.

November also marks the beginning of the saltwater eel season, which is a very important local fish commercially—most of it is exported directly to Italy, and there much of it is consumed in Comoccio, south of Venice, where eel is the national dish. Eel is one of the most difficult fish to catch. Eels, great migrant international creatures that they are, swimming all the way to the Bermuda Triangle to spawn, are hermaphrodite during their sojourn in Greek waters. While here, they never have eggs. Local preparations vary according to how big or small the eel is.

Early spring marks the height of the shellfish season, which is consumed in great quantities during Lent. Local shellfish include species of clams such as the *havara* (carpet shell clams), *solines* (razor clams), which are usually used as bait in Greece but are also sometimes grilled or simmered, *nyhaki* wedge shell clams, and, finally, *ahivada,* a kind of small carpet shell, which is boiled and served with olive oil and lemon juice or with rice or served raw, all specialties of Lent. By far, though, the most prized local shellfish is the large (roughly three ounces), one-eyed shrimp (nature's way of keeping it from eating its young) called *gambari,* found in the Aitoliko Gulf. Locals consider them so delicious that they prepare them very simply, seasoned with coarse salt and cooked live, in a dry skillet.

June and July mark the time of year when locals enjoy the tiny cuttlefish and squid, which are fried. Mullet, perhaps the region's most important fish, are just beginning to prevail. Together with the local sea bass, these fish provide the best flesh for light salt preserving and for the making of *petali,* or butterflied, salted fish.

Bream *(tsipoures)* are at their peak in September. The small ones, known as *ligdes,* which weigh in at five to six ounces, are preserved lightly in salt and olive oil.

almost the entire local population, especially in Messolongi, was employed as fishermen. Now only about 10 percent of the population works the marsh; in Messolongi, a town of about fifty or sixty thousand inhabitants, there are only 120 fishermen left.

Several fish are extremely important to the local economy. Among them are eel, mullet, and bream, and there is a virtual calendar for catching them as well as others, and many unique preparations for each. One caveat: The fish in this part of Greece generally tend to be fattier than elsewhere because they don't need to hunt that much for their food; the nutrient-rich marsh and regional waters have made the fish here lazy!

Gilthead Bream and Wild Celery Stew

TSIPOURES ME SELINO

 Makes 2 to 4 servings

Gilthead bream are in season in the fall in the waters around the western and northwestern coasts of Greece, where this dish is a local favorite. Bream also appears in the local rendition of savoro, *fried fish preserved in a sweet-sour sauce made of vinegar, tomato, garlic, onions, and bay leaf, something found in many other parts of Greece.*

Salt
2 pounds gilthead bream, cleaned and gutted
1 cup extra-virgin olive oil
3 large onions, coarsely chopped

2 large carrots, cut into ¼-inch-thick rounds
1½ pounds cultivated celery, coarsely chopped, plus 1 teaspoon ground celery seeds, or 2 pounds thin-stalked wild celery (see Note)
Freshly ground black pepper to taste
Juice of 2 lemons
2 large eggs

1. Salt the fish inside and out and refrigerate for an hour.

2. Meanwhile, prepare the vegetables: Heat the olive oil in a large pot and cook the onions over low heat, stirring until wilted, about 10 minutes. Add the carrots, celery, and celery seeds, if using, and toss to coat with the oil. Season with salt and pepper and pour in half the lemon juice and enough water to cover the vegetables by ½ inch. Cover and simmer over low heat until the vegetables are tender, about 45 minutes, adding water if necessary to keep the mixture from burning. Place the fish on top of the vegetables in the pot. Cover and simmer until flaky, about 15 minutes.

3. Prepare the egg-lemon sauce: Beat the eggs and remaining lemon juice together with a wire whisk in a small bowl. Slowly add a ladleful of the pan juices from the fish, whisking all the while, and immediately pour the *avgolemono* into the pot. Stir gently, remove from the heat, and serve.

✳ **NOTE** Wild celery is available at some specialty greengrocers. The dish may be made a little ahead of time, reheated slightly, and the *avgolemono* prepared at the last minute, just before serving.

Pan-Fried Salmon Trout with Cornmeal and Sheep's Milk Butter

PESTROFA STO TIGANI ME PROVEIO VOUTYRO

 Makes 6 servings

The rivers of northern Greece teem with both rainbow and salmon trout. Most of it is prepared simply as in this recipe. The key, though, is in the sheep's milk butter, which has a very distinct, almost musky aroma.

6 small whole fresh rainbow or salmon trout
   (about ½ pound each), gutted
1 to 2 tablespoons coarse salt, to taste
Juice of 6 lemons
⅔ cup fine yellow cornmeal
1 cup sheep's milk butter (see Note)
Lemon wedges for garnish

1. Rinse the trout. Place in a plastic container and sprinkle with the coarse salt. Pour in the lemon juice. Cover and refrigerate for 12 hours.

2. Remove the trout from the marinade. Spread the cornmeal on a large plate, dredge the trout lightly in it, and shake off the excess. Set aside.

3. In a large, heavy skillet, heat the butter until it bubbles. Place the trout in the skillet and cook over low heat, turning once, to brown on both sides. Remove and serve, garnished with lemon wedges.

✳ **NOTE** Sheep's milk butter is available at some specialty retailers. If unavailable, use unsalted cow's milk butter.

Fresh Anchovies in Brine

GAVROS XITHATOS

 Makes 8 to 10 *meze* servings

This simple, pungent, exquisite meze *is found in many parts of Greece. I've placed it here among the seaside dishes of Messolongi and the western coast of Roumeli only because here the light salting and quick preserving of small fish and seafood is a practice completely entrenched in local culinary customs. While elsewhere only vinegar, salt, and olive oil go into the marinade for* gavros, *in this part of Greece the dish is enhanced with parsley and garlic.*

2 pounds small fresh anchovies
Salt
Red wine vinegar
4 garlic cloves, cut into very thin slivers
1 cup chopped fresh flat-leaf parsley
Extra-virgin olive oil

1. Gut the anchovies and remove the heads. Wash the fish thoroughly.

2. Place the fish in layers in a plastic container, salting each layer generously. Pour in enough vinegar to cover. Leave the fish to marinate, covered, in the refrigerator for 15 hours.

3. Drain off the vinegar. Remove the spine from the fish by pulling it gently but firmly from the tail end. The whole backbone should come out this way. Place the fish back in the container in neat layers and sprinkle a little garlic and parsley between layers. Pour in enough olive oil to cover. Let stand for several hours before serving. Refrigerate the fish and it will keep for several weeks.

Crabs Cooked with Peppers

PIPERONATA ME KAVOURIA TOU GLYKOU
NEROU

 Makes 6 servings

This unusual dish comes from the northwestern corner of mountainous Roumeli, not too far from Lake Kremaston. Traditionally it calls for local freshwater crabs that have first been cooked in embers and their flesh removed. I've reworked it to include Atlantic crabs.

4 to 6 large saltwater crabs (frozen are fine)
½ cup extra-virgin olive oil
2 large red onions, halved and thinly sliced
8 large green bell peppers, cut into ¼-inch strips
Two 1-inch-long, thin hot fresh peppers, seeded and chopped
½ cup long-grain rice
1 cup water
Salt and freshly ground black pepper to taste
½ cup snipped fresh dill
½ cup chopped fresh flat-leaf parsley
½ cup chopped fresh mint

1. If a fireplace is available, build a fire and let it settle. Meanwhile, bring a large pot of salted water to a rolling boil and blanch the crabs until they turn bright red. Remove immediately and let cool. Wrap the crabs in aluminum foil and place under the burning embers. Roast until the shells have charred and the meat is tender, about 20 minutes. To simulate this in an oven, simply preheat the broiler. Blanch the crabs, let them cool, then individually wrap them in foil. Place about 6 inches from the broiler and roast until the shells are charred. Let cool. Crack open the crabs and remove their sweet, white flesh. Shred it and set aside.

2. Heat the olive oil in a wide, deep pot over low heat and cook the onions until wilted and translucent, about 10 minutes. Add the bell and hot peppers and cook until softened, about 5 minutes. Add the rice and pour in the water. Season with salt and pepper and cover. Simmer over low heat until most of the liquid has been absorbed, about 8 minutes.

3. Add the herbs and shredded crabmeat, stir and cook for about 5 minutes for the flavors to meld. Adjust the seasoning with salt and pepper and serve, either hot or at room temperature.

☉ It is entirely possible to prepare this dish with packaged crabmeat. It won't have any of the same smoky flavor that grilling the crabs achieves, but it saves time and reduces the hassle of having to crack and clean the crabs. Substitute 2 cups shredded crabmeat, picked over for cartilage and shells, and skip step 1.

Large Shrimp Seared in a Dry Skillet

GAMBARI STO TIGANI

 Makes 4 to 6 servings

The large, one-eyed shrimp called **gambari** *is native to the gulf and coastal waters all along the northwestern part of Greece. It is considered one of the country's most prized seafoods, and locals so esteem it that they cook it minimalistically—seared whole and unshelled in a skillet with nothing but salt, a technique that helps preserve the flavor of the shrimp. You can substitute other large shrimp for the* **gambari**.

2 pounds large *gambari* or other large shrimp
   (about 3 ounces each)
2 teaspoons coarse salt
2 large lemons, cut into wedges

1. Wash and pat the shrimp dry. Do not peel, but, using a sharp paring knife, remove the string-like intestine from the underside.

2. Sprinkle the coarse salt in a large, heavy nonstick skillet over medium-high heat and heat until the salt begins to "dance" on the metal. Add the shrimp, in batches if necessary, and sear until bright red, 6 to 8 minutes total. Flip to cook on both sides. Remove from the skillet and serve with lemon wedges.

BREAD

Corn Bread with Leeks and Cheese

LAHANOPSOMO OR PLASTO

 Makes 10 to 12 servings

This recipe, from Granitsa, a mountain village in the western part of Roumeli, harks back to another era. Traditionally, plasto *was made in a* gastra *or* sini, *a metal—usually copper—dome that was placed over the pan, which in turn sat on a bed of embers, making for a kind of makeshift oven. Roving gypsies used to hammer out the* gastras *and hawk them, and quasi-nomadic peoples such as the shepherds of northwestern Greece used to count them as part of their necessary kitchen accoutrements; nowadays a regular electric oven is the most likely place to find these old-fashioned pies baking. They are common from*

Karpenisi west throughout Roumeli and north into Epirus.

¾ cup extra-virgin olive oil, or as needed
2 pounds leeks, white and all but toughest green
   parts, finely chopped and washed well
2 cups boiling water
1 teaspoon salt
2 cups fine yellow cornmeal
6 large eggs, lightly beaten
2½ pounds Greek feta or *vlachotyri* cheese
   (see page 139), crumbled
3 tablespoons unsalted butter, cut into small
   pieces

1. Heat 3 tablespoons of the olive oil in a large skillet over medium heat and cook the leeks until wilted. Remove from the heat and let cool.

2. Preheat the oven to 350°F. Rub a 15-inch-round or a 12 by 18 by 2-inch rectangular baking pan with olive oil. Place the hot water and salt in a large bowl. Slowly add the cornmeal in a steady stream, stirring with a wooden spoon to combine. Mix in the remaining olive oil. Stir in the eggs, cheese, and sautéed leeks, combining well. The mixture should be the consistency of a very thick batter. Pour into the prepared baking pan. Bake for 45 minutes, dot with the butter, then continue baking until golden and set, about 45 minutes longer. Remove from the oven, let cool, and cut into serving pieces. Serve either warm or at room temperature.

SWEETS

No claims to patisserie greatness can be boasted in this part of Greece. The sweets are, by and large, simple and unexceptional, but some desserts are unique to the region.

Sweet Crustless Pie with Angel Hair Pasta, Milk, and Cheese

PIGOULOPITA

 Makes 6 to 8 servings

One among a surprisingly long list of sweet pasta dishes that once were common on the Greek table.

½ pound angel hair pasta

4 large eggs

½ cup sugar

¾ cup evaporated milk

1 pound fresh unsalted *myzithra, anthotyro,* or whole-milk ricotta cheese

1 teaspoon ground cinnamon or grated zest of 1 lemon

½ cup (1 stick) unsalted butter, melted

1. Bring a large pot of lightly salted water to a boil and cook the pasta until al dente. Drain.

2. Preheat the oven to 350°F. In a large bowl, beat together the eggs and sugar. Add the evaporated milk and continue beating until smooth. Crumble the cheese and stir it into the mixture, together with the cinnamon or zest, to combine well. Add the pasta and melted butter and mix thoroughly.

3. Lightly butter a 12-inch round baking pan. Spread the mixture evenly in the pan and bake until golden and set, about 1 hour. Remove from the oven, cool slightly, cut into serving pieces, and serve, either warm or at room temperature.

Coiled Baklava Filled with Roasted Chickpeas

STRIFTOPITA ME STRAGALIA

 Makes 10 to 12 servings

In Itea and its environs, there are no walnut trees; hence baklava was always an ersatz affair. One finds it with almonds but also with ground stragalia, *the hard roasted chickpeas that have long been a snack food in Greece. This dish was always made as a kind of faux baklava at Christmas and New Year's and served to children and gypsies who went from house to house singing the* kalanda, *the Greek equivalent of Christmas carols.*

For the syrup

2½ cups sugar

2 cups water

One 1-inch strip lemon zest

For the filling

½ pound *stragalia* (skinned, roasted chickpeas) (see Note)

¼ cup sugar

2 teaspoons ground cinnamon

1 scant teaspoon ground cloves

2 cups (4 sticks) unsalted butter or sheep's milk butter

1 pound commercial phyllo, defrosted and at room temperature (see page 455)

1. Make the syrup: Place the sugar and water in a medium saucepan and heat. When the sugar dissolves, add the lemon zest. Bring the syrup to a boil over medium heat, reduce the heat to low, and simmer for 10 minutes. Remove from the heat and let cool.

2. With either a large mortar and pestle or a food processor fitted with a steel blade, pulverize the *stragalia* until finely ground. They should be mealy. You will have to do this in batches, and don't be dismayed by the furious sound of the processor as it pulverizes the *stragalia.* Place in a bowl and combine with the sugar, cinnamon, and cloves.

3. Preheat the oven to 350°F. Butter a 15-inch round baking pan. Melt the butter.

4. Open the phyllo. Place a kitchen towel on top to keep the phyllo moist. Place 2 sheets horizontally in front of you. Brush the first sheet lightly with melted butter, place the second sheet on top, and lightly brush with melted butter, too. Sprinkle about 3 tablespoons of the chickpea filling in a neat line along the bottom of the phyllo, 1 inch from the edge. Fold the edge over the filling and fold in the sides. Carefully roll up the phyllo to form a long, narrow cylinder. Place in the center of the baking

pan, seam side down, and coil. Continue with the remaining phyllo and filling, working your way around the pan as you go, until the whole pan is filled with a large coil, the *striftopita.* Pour any remaining melted butter over the top and sprinkle with a little cold water. Bake until golden, 1 to 1½ hours.

5. Remove the *striftopita* from the oven and pour the cold syrup over the hot pie. Let it stand to absorb the syrup for at least 2 hours. To serve, cut into small pieces.

✳ **NOTE** *Stragalia* are available in Greek and Middle Eastern food shops. They usually are eaten as a snack in Greece, tossed with some raisins or nuts, and served as an accompaniment to ouzo or other alcohol.

Epirus

A Sense of Place and Palate

In mid-April, when the weather warms in the valleys and the greenery begins to dry up, shepherds are on the move. It used to be that April, at least in much of the northwestern part of Greece, belonged to the nomads' peregrinations. Vlachs and Sarakatsans, the two dominant itinerant shepherds' tribes in Greece's northern climes, moved on foot with wives and kin and their often thousand-strong flocks of sheep and goats from their traditional winter grazing lands on the lower plains and lumbered northward to summer abodes high in the Pindus Mountains. For centuries these seasonal migrations were like the slow, undulating pulse of Epirus, Greece's isolated, pristine, vast northwestern frontier. Now the flocks are apt to be moved by truck, and the sight of a lone, black-caped shepherd and his herds is as distant as a dream.

This is not the Greece familiar to most foreigners. Although Epirus has a coast and looks across the Ionian Sea westward toward Corfu, the sea figures little in its culture. It is the imposing mountains that have defined Epirote life for eons. It is the mountains that have forged the customs and mores of the local people.

Epirus is an isolated, melancholy, beautiful place, still overwhelmingly rural and sparsely populated, still poor and barren. Farming has always been exceptionally difficult; only ten percent of the land is level, but pastureland has always been ample, so the age-old professions of shepherding and dairy production are still going strong.

In the cities and coastal towns, though, the picture is different. Ioannina, the region's capital, has been a commercial center for centuries. The southern parts of the region saw their day in the commercial limelight, too. Preveza, a misty, oblique town along the coast, was once a bustling port.

But still, its mountains loom large. The region's history—and its cuisine—is indelibly tied to that of the rest of the Balkans, for before the area was returned to Greece in 1912 (after the Balkan Wars, when the last remnants of the Ottoman

Empire finally collapsed) its mountains knew no national boundaries. Greek, Vlach, and Albanian shepherds used to cross the mountains freely with their flocks. The villages on the other side of the Albanian border were inhabited by Greeks (and they still are). That region is known colloquially among Greeks as northern Epirus. It is no coincidence that Epirus's cuisine is largely a shepherd's cuisine and that, throughout the neighboring Balkans, people sustain themselves on many of the same dishes.

And so Epirus is a land of butter eaters much more than of olive oil aficionados, because nature made it that way. Except in the region's southern reaches, and all along the coast, the inland climate is too cold and harsh to provide a good home for the olive tree.

What the land does offer, though, is ample pasture for thousands of sheep and goats; thick forests inhabited by deer, wild boar and goats, pheasant, partridge, and other game birds; lakes and rivers that abound in trout, eel, and other freshwater fish; a coast that lays claim to some of the best seafood in Greece, including an indigenous species of shrimp; and, finally, an incredibly rich flora that has long provided fodder for animals and bees (Epirote honey, especially its sage honey, is delicious), fillings for pies, and ingredients for what was once the region's famed herbal medicine tradition. The Vikos Gorge is like Greece's own Amazon, a place teeming with plant life, with greens and herbs and leaves and seeds that once formed the backbone of an exceptionally complex pharmacopoeia.

Epirus is poor, but its cuisine isn't. Certainly, there are many dishes that belong uniquely to the Vlachs, dishes that cross boundaries from Epirus into western Macedonia, where many Vlach families also settled, and that seem Balkan in their ori-

gins, relying on all kinds of peppers and cabbage and other such Balkan staples. There are distinct dishes, too, that belong to an urban rather than to a rural tradition. But, by and large, the cuisine of Epirus is homogeneous; certainly, there are differences in the foods that one finds from village to village and among specific groups, but the differences seem insignificant compared to the similarities.

The unique demands of an itinerant shepherd's life, coupled with the harshness of a mountain life, forged a cuisine that at once catered to the needs of a mobile people and found versatility even in a dearth of ingredients. It is not by accident that the mainstay of the Epirote kitchen is its countless savory pies, dishes that sustain local, Vlach, and Sarakatsan shepherds alike and that run like a leitmotiv throughout the culinary tapestry up here. It is not by accident, either, that some of the tastiest meats—lamb and goat especially—in Greece come from Epirus, where animals have a cornucopia of edible weeds in their pastureland. Lamb and goat are savored differently according to their age (see more on this in the chapter on Roumeli, which shares many of the same customs), but they are not, traditionally, eaten often, mainly because animals were valued more for their milk, which, together with the cheese and butter made from it, formed the basis of the shepherd's income. It is not coincidence either that the number of dairy preparations is probably greater here than anywhere else in the country, save perhaps among the Pontian Greeks (see the chapter on Macedonia). Those are the products nature provided, the raw ingredients people had to work with for centuries and that have remained, regardless of whether their nomadic lifestyles have disappeared, the foundation of the Epirote kitchen.

Nature has blessed Epirus with a host of supplementary raw ingredients as well. Fruit trees, from citrus along the temperate coast to apples, pears, cherries, peaches, apricots, and mulberries, abound in almost every village. The almonds and walnuts from this part of Greece are the delicious outcome of the rainiest climate in the country. Although the famed oak forests mentioned by Homer have long since dwindled, victims of fires and uprooting, woodland is still ample (much of Epirus claims an alpine climate) and provides the necessary natural environment for the region's feast of mushrooms. Chanterelles, morels, and, by some accounts, even white truffles, are savored up here, although they almost never make it out of the region and into the hands of urban Greeks. (As of this writing, no one has yet thought of exporting them.)

The cuisine here, like the environment, is somber. There is a kind of no-nonsense economy inherent in many dishes, and very little fanfare. The tomato traditionally doesn't prevail in many sauces or dishes, but paprika, the Balkan spice, does. Stews and baked bean dishes tend not to include a lot of different ingredients. Sorrel, nettles, spinach, and a much revered local green called *nanes*—Good King Henry—that grows on the peaks of mountains where it is fertilized by the sheep and goats that graze are the greens of choice among Epirote cooks. These few culinary notes play themselves out in a wide spectrum of local dishes.

VLACHS AND SARAKATSANS

Many people confuse the Vlachs and the Sarakatsans, the two previously nomadic peoples who roamed all of northern Greece. Although they once shared a certain way of life, moving with the seasons and their flocks from winter pastures in the lowlands to summer pastures in the mountains, the two groups have never mixed and have little else in common besides their once-itinerant way of life. The Vlachs are said to have descended from Roman guards; their native language was never Greek but a latinized tongue related to Romanian. They have been settled in Greece for centuries and long since hellenized. They settled in permanent villages long before the Sarakatsans did, and many abandoned the traditional itinerant profession a few hundred years ago in favor of trade. The Vlachs became avid merchants, and many count as some of the oldest and wealthiest families in Greece.

The Sarakatsans are different. For one, they are Greek, some say the purest, oldest Greeks, and the only extant Greek nomadic peoples. Their native dialect is Greek, and it was the same wherever they lived and wandered—mainly in Epirus, in central Greece, in Thessaly, in Macedonia, in Thrace, in the northern Peloponnesos. With the exception of the island of Evia, most Greek islands never saw a Sarakatsan shepherd. But until the seventeenth century, their cradle was the central and southern Pindus Mountains of Epirus. Their days of traveling with their flocks are a living memory. The last ones settled in the 1960s.

METSOVO AND THE VLACHS

There are two ways to access Metsovo by car. One is via Ioannina, on a road known for its harrowing, hairpin turns, so much so that the precipitous mountain it crosses is called Katara, or "the curse"; the other is to cross the vast plain of Thessaly, which is like sailing through a sea of golden wheat punc-

tured in the distance by the jagged, mat-black protuberances known as the Meteora. There are monasteries built on these crests, hundreds of meters straight up off the ground, places so inaccessible that until fairly recently the monks used baskets and pulleys to get themselves up and down. In the early spring the plain of Thessaly swelters in a relentless, dust-bowl kind of heat. The road turns inward toward the Vlach capital, and the landscape changes decisively. Metsovo, at over three thousand feet above sea level, has an alpine clime. It is known as the "Switzerland of Greece," and when we arrived one afternoon in mid-April, the town's cobblestone streets and ceramic, slated rooftops were under a blanket of snow.

The place smelled of the wood burning in every fireplace. In the town square, despite the cold, a handful of mustached old men sat dressed in the garb from days gone by: black pantaloons and thick cummerbunds, with their carved shepherds' staffs in hand. There weren't many tourists, despite the fact that Metsovo is a popular ski resort, so the old-timers seized the chance to pose for us. Metsovo exists in a curious time warp. Its traditional stone and wood houses are perfectly preserved; the local population is able to carry on with traditional professions such as wood carving, weaving, and the shepherd's métier, and the town, despite its remote location, has been able to thrive even in hard times.

Metsovo means "amid the mountains," so named, a very long time ago, because of its location in the heart of the Pindus range, between Epirus, Thessaly, and Macedonia, at the point where the five main rivers of Epirus find their source. It is also situated right at the Zygos Pass, which was the key thoroughfare of the region's itinerant shepherds, Vlach and Sarakatsan alike, as they made their way between summer and winter pasturage.

The town was saved from the obscurity and desertion that plagues so many other Greek mountain villages by its local oligarchs, the Tossitsa and Averoff families, two of Greece's oldest, richest dynasties. Today Metsovo, thanks mainly to the Averoff family, is home to one of Greece's most respected wineries and, thanks to the Tossitsa fam-

ily, also to a state-of-the-art cheese-making facility that has helped keep many local sons employed and, by extension, has helped stem the tide of emigration.

Its gastronomic claims to fame are no doubt its cheeses and wines, but the shops and tavernas also serve a bevy of local fare that make up the basics of Epirote shepherd's cuisine. Delicious greens and cheese pies, many made with the ubiquitous cornmeal crust; *trahana,* made from the wheat and milk again essential to all shepherding communities; *hilopites,* or egg noodles; and excellent meat and game can be found in every taverna in Metsovo.

IOANNINA

Ioannina is a city of ironies. It is a bustling, modern university town flooded with thousands of students and studded with cafés and fast-food emporiums, but where the streets jangle with the wares of the city's traditional craftsmen, their silver and bronze and copper hammered into trays and dishes and cups and bowls and belt buckles and more, evincing the continuity of age-old professions that took root when Ioannina was a flourishing trade center. Small, tight old Turkish houses with their wood trim and inner courtyards nestle up against Bauhaus boxes, shrugging off any hint of incongruity. The old city walls contain the pristine relic of Ioannina, the old city: Ali Paşa's streets winding and wending within the confines of the stone perimeter, minarets jutting overhead, motorbikes and cars whizzing by. Then, there is the legacy of Ali Paşa himself, the Lion of Ioannina, a powerful, Machiavellian eighteenth-century overlord of Albanian descent who managed to turn Ioannina into an autonomous province and whose dominion extended beyond Epirus well into

Thessaly, Aitoloakarnania, and the Peloponnesos, who had grand plans to create a Greek-Albanian state, whose court was the breeding ground from which many of the heroes of the Greek Revolution emerged, and who, finally, was beheaded by the Ottomans for treason in 1822. There is nature in the midst of Ioannina: the lake on which it was built, still the heart and soul of the city, even though pollution has eaten away at its economic importance and most of the marine life has disappeared from its once teeming waters.

Ioannina is an interesting city for food. Here the shepherd's cooking of Epirus is distilled into an urbanized cuisine. The basic ingredients are, for the most part, the same. Savory pies are popular but hardly the mainstay. Meat and offal are served aplenty. The *gastra,* which is either a large zeppelin-shaped clay pot or a copper dome-shaped ersatz oven, quintessential cooking gear among the region's itinerant shepherds, here in its clay-pot form becomes a restaurant tradition, almost in the same way that the famed *parilla* of the Argentine pampas became a tradition in chic Buenos Aires eateries. There is even a well-known local place called Gastra that prepares lamb in the eponymous fired-up, makeshift clay oven.

Ioannina is known for its freshwater fish and shellfish, even though almost none come from the lake itself anymore but from farms. Trout is one specialty, but more interesting is the tiny *tsima,* a freshwater sandsmelt that is either salted and dried and then rehydrated or eaten fresh and fried; the freshwater prawns, which are easy to find in local restaurants and are usually boiled and served with *skordalia* or made into a pilaf; and the eels, renowned in a local dish called *heli sto keramidi* (eel in clay). The dish is another paean to local ingenuity, for the eels are baked in the U-shaped red

ceramic tiles that enclose traditional rooftops all over Greece. The two ends are sealed with dough and the eel baked, usually with just a few bay leaves and lemons for flavor. Finally, there are the frogs: In the middle of the lake of Ioannina is a small island, where, as the story goes, Italian soldiers during World War II popularized the previously unheard of practice of pan-frying frogs' legs. The dish is now a local specialty, offered in all the island's tavernas.

More than anything else, though, Ioannina is famed for its sweets. A couple of generations ago many a local son found work in Poli (Constantinople, or present-day Istanbul) as pastry chefs, and many returned to open sweet shops of their own. The main city square is lined with pastry shops, all of which serve *yianniotiko baklava,* the local version of Greece's best-known phyllo dessert. What distinguishes the local version are the manifold layers and the use of almonds, not walnuts, in the filling. Local pastry makers also prepare another regional specialty, simply called *yianniotiko,* which is baklava enclosed in shredded wheat pastry and baked in a clay dish. The local *bogatsa*—a buttery, custard- or cheese-filled phyllo pastry—is also delicious.

The Epirus Pantry

MILK

In Epirus, nature's cycle, especially the myriad greens that erupt and then ebb like a seasonal tide over mountain slopes, is linked to the single most important aspect of the local table: milk production. The quantities and variety of greens that sheep and goats graze on directly affect the flavor and quality of their milk.

FROM GREEK OUTLAWS, UNDERGROUND FOOD AND OTHER UNUSUAL COOKING PRACTICES

Across the mainland of Greece, people have been digging holes for their dinner for centuries. This manner of cooking, in a shallow, dirt-covered pit over smoldering coals, is called *steen hovoli,* or "in embers." But more often than not it is referred to as *klephtica*—"of thieves"—after the Klephts, rebel bands who fought in the Pindus Mountains and elsewhere during the Greek War of Independence. The Klephts are folk heroes, with ballads praising their feats and tales of their hardship and glory ingrained in the national psyche.

They survived by encamping themselves in the rugged, inaccessible northern Greek mountains, acting by night and hiding by day. They cooked underground, digging shallow pits, filling them with burning embers, placing a copper or clay pot on top, and covering the whole thing with dirt. Nothing escaped—no aroma, no steam or smoke that might betray their positions. Their simple survival tactic managed to capture the popular imagination, and to this day anything that is sealed and cooked, especially lamb baked in paper or enclosed in pastry, is called *klephtico.*

Legend aside, the practice of baking over embers was hardly invented by nineteenth-century revolutionaries. It is an ancient way to cook and one that survives all over Epirus. Shepherds always carried with them a makeshift oven that was essentially a dome-shaped cover. It was easy to build a fire wherever they happened to be; once the flames died and the embers remained, they would place a large round pan, usually containing a savory pie, over the embers and cover the whole thing with the *sini,* or copper dome-shaped cover. This, in turn, was covered with hot ash and embers. The dome-shaped cover contained the heat and helped circulate it, hence acting as an oven.

Despite the demise of the nomads' lifestyle, many local Epirote cooks prefer to bake pies and breads under the *sini.* Most village homes have a small shack outside especially for such baking.

Milk is consumed as an ingredient in its own right. Slightly salted milk is the shepherd's drink. Milk also goes into fillings for savory pies, usually mixed with grains or cheeses. *Trahana* is simmered in milk, and so are greens and other vegetables, such as zucchini, an unusual practice found in only a few other shepherds' communities throughout Greece, namely in Roumeli. These are old dishes that reflect the need to use every available foodstuff and, in the process, create some unexpected marriages.

Milk is also used to make butter, which has been the predominant fat for eons. Olive oil was and is used in the kitchen, but sparingly, since it always had to be purchased, imported, or bartered for from other areas. At home, butter is made in the summer, when the milk production slows down.

Nothing is wasted. The liquid that remains after butter is made—the buttermilk—was and is considered a great delicacy. It is served with many of the cornmeal-based pies, specifically one called *blatsaria,* and it is also boiled to make a cheese called *giza,* which in turn is the main ingredient in a local cheese pie. These are the kinds of dishes, obviously, that are impossible to translate for an American or even an urban Greek kitchen, because there are no appropriate substitutes for the specific agrarian ingredients.

Milk has its cycles. In the winter, around February, when the ewes and sheep have given birth, their first milk, called *kouliastra,* is rich and thick and is considered a special treat. By the time the young lambs and goats are weaned, nature is bursting with greens, which means the animals have plenty to feed on and thus produce plenty of milk. The best cheeses are made in the spring, their production peaking in May. Ironically, though, shepherds don't produce cheeses for themselves then; they sell their milk to big dairies and cheese makers. Not too long ago, though, specialized cheese makers, usually Vlachs, would set up their cauldrons and fires and other basic equipment on the periphery of the itinerant shepherds' summer encampments, producing cheeses daily from the constant supply of spring milk. Production usually ended in summer, when the flora and hence the milk supply dwindled. Then it would be time for the families to make their own yearly supply of cheeses.

CHEESE

In Epirus, as in the mountainous parts of Roumeli, and really as in all the rest of Greece, the best cheeses are the obscure artisanal cheeses. But it is no accident, either, that the biggest names in commercial cheese making are found in Epirus, for here, thanks mainly to the terrain and the traditional profession of shepherding, is Greece's cheese-making Mecca.

Following is a description of Epirus cheeses, both common and obscure. Many are synonymous with the cheeses made in Thessaly as well as in Roumeli, because the shepherds moved freely between these places with the seasons.

Feta The quintessential shepherd's cheese. While most feta from Epirus is no longer aged in barrels, most of the barrel makers are still in Epirus.

There is one name that has surpassed all others in the production of the best-known Greek cheese: Dodoni, named for the town in which it is located. Dodoni is the oldest cheese cooperative in Greece, and still one of the most technologically advanced. The best feta in Epirus (and all over Greece) is made in May, when the flora is richest.

Galotyri Literally "milk cheese," *galotyri* is soft, creamy, and beautifully sour. It is one of many naturally fermented sheep's milk cheeses (made without starter or rennet, in other words, by first boiling the milk to about 176°F and leaving it to sour and thicken on its own). It is made in late summer. Traditionally *galotyri* was fermented and stored in goatskins, but nowadays it is kept in jugs. Like so many of these soft, pungent cheeses, one finds *galotyri* as readily in Thessaly and Roumeli as in Epirus.

Kefalotyri Hard, salty, and pale yellow, *kefalotyri* is usually reserved for grating. It is one of the oldest shepherd's cheeses, made almost exclusively with sheep's and goat's milk. It is found all over Greece, but some of the best comes from Epirus.

Manouri One of the oldest whey cheeses made in the Mediterranean and very similar to ricotta salata. *Manouri* is dense and creamy, the color of alabaster, and shaped in large, compact loaves. It is rich and sweet, and is excellent as a dessert cheese, drizzled with honey, or served with poached fruits. *Manouri* is made from sheep's whey or a combination of sheep's and goat's milk whey, enriched with whole milk or cream. The cheese is lightly salted and very well drained to achieve its characteristic compact texture. It is not unique to Epirus; rather, it is made all over the north, from Thessaly onward. But some of the best comes from Epirus, produced from the whey left after making the hard yellow cheese *kefalograviera*.

Vlachotyri The "Vlachs' cheese," which is essentially a goat's milk *kefalograviera*—a hard, tangy, yellow table and grating cheese—from Metsovo, the Vlach capital.

Xynogalo The Greek word for buttermilk (literally "sour milk") made with the residuals of sheep's or goat's milk butter. It is consumed as a refreshing drink, and is a favorite accompaniment with a wedge of local greens-and-cornmeal pie. *Xynogalo* also sometimes refers to a primitive, deliciously sour, yogurtlike cheese, made by placing raw buttermilk inside a sheepskin and agitating it over several days. This used to be the itinerant shepherd's cheese; the "agitation" was little more than the movement of the shepherd's back as he moved with his flocks from grazing place to grazing place. It is as common in Thessaly as it is in Epirus.

Xynomyzithra A buttermilk cheese made by boiling *xynogalo* (buttermilk) and allowing it to set. Deliciously pungent and soft, almost like cream cheese, it is commonly used in pies.

BREAD

Bread in Epirus begins from the simplest cornmeal loaves and culminates in the complex rituals at Christmas, at Easter, and at weddings in which it plays a seminal role. From the time New World corn first appeared in the local diet—Epirus has always been especially conducive to its cultivation—sometime in the early seventeenth century, it captured the local palate and pocket. Easy to grow and less expensive than wheat, it quickly became the region's main grain and the shepherd's grain. Most of the daily bread of the Sarakatsans and the Vlachs was corn bread, often made on the spot at camp and grilled over a bed of embers. Wheat grows in Epirus, too, of course, but, the yield per acre is fairly low. It makes sense that wheat flour would then be used sparingly, either to make one of

---

THE TOSSITSA CHEESES

One of the best-known dairies in Epirus is the one established a few decades ago by the Tossitsa Foundation in Metsovo. In an effort to keep native sons on native soil, the family began a modern dairy. Interestingly, the Tossitsa cheese facility does not specialize in local Vlach cheeses but instead produces Italian-style and other European cheeses. They have been tremendously successful.

Graviera Although *graviera* is made in many parts of Greece, the Tossitsa *graviera* stands out mainly because it is made exactly in the manner of Swiss Gruyère, except with sheep's milk. The result is a highly aromatic cheese with a lovely, pocketed texture.

Katsikisio Its name means goat's milk cheese and it is a take on the traditional French chèvre. There are two kinds of Greek chèvre, both from Epirus. The first, made at the Tossitsa dairy, is a hard, strong cheese flavored with black pepper. The cooperative at Dodoni also makes a chèvre, but it is milder and softer than the Tossitsa cheese. Both are strictly seasonal, made at the end of the summer.

Metsovella A cow's milk cheese that falls somewhere between *kasseri* and *graviera*. It has a sweet, subtle flavor and a semisoft texture.

Metsovone A cheese made in the manner of Italian provolone, with a combination of cow's milk and sheep's milk. It is then smoked. It is eaten as a table cheese and is also sautéed to make *saganaki,* which is served with a sprinkling of paprika.

---

the region's myriad savory pies (in phyllo a little flour goes a long way) or to make specialty breads for important holidays.

At Christmas, for example, bread is the most important part of the holiday preparations, and

Christmas Eve is still one of the busiest days of the year for bread making. What the rest of Greece calls *Christopsomo*—the large, round, usually spiced Christmas loaves—in Epirus is called *kouloura*—ring. Tradition dictates that *kouloures* for the family be decorated with dough motifs depicting the family's occupation: For farmers, ploughs, sheaths of wheat, and cows are shaped out of dough and set on the surface of the loaves; for shepherds, sheep and goats top the loaf. Tradition also dictates that special *kouloures* be prepared in honor of the animals—for the cow, the donkey, and the sheep. Then there are the smaller loaves called *koliantines,* which are made especially for children and are either ring shaped or shaped like a figure eight, or like a figure eight with part of the top clipped off.

A bevy of other dough-based sweets are also made at Christmas. In the rest of Greece, for example, *thiples* (fried dough strips drizzled with honey) are one of the standards sweets. In Epirus traditional cooks make something similar, called *melinta* (after the Greek word *meli,* for "honey"), except that they aren't fried but grilled on a heavy metal griddle.

New Year's was, and is, another occasion for frenzied baking, but in Epirus the traditional *vassilopita* is either a savory meat pie or a cheese or cheese-and-bulgur pie and not the fragrant, yeast-risen loaf that it is almost everywhere else in the country.

In a few short paragraphs it is nearly impossible to cover the breadth of breads in Epirus or anywhere else. As is generally the case all over Greece, specialty breads are made for many important occasions throughout the year. One quaint old bread custom is the small buns baked and distributed as wedding invitations in many villages throughout Epirus. Then there is the *kouloura tis nyfis,* the bride's bread ring, which, at least among the Sarakatsans, is baked by the women in the groom's family and offered to the bride's family as a symbol of kinship and communion. Epirus, with its isolated villages and its different populations, is home to countless other customs surrounding bread and its rituals.

The Recipes

SOUP

Lamb Soup with Potatoes and Egg-Lemon Sauce

KREAS SKETO

 Makes 6 to 8 servings

This dish is traditionally made with lamb's neck, but since that is not always easy to find in the United States, I've substituted shank or shoulder. The dish is something between a soup and a stew, "eaten with both a spoon and a fork," as Eleni Skourti, a native of the Zagorohoria, told me when she passed along the recipe to me.

3 tablespoons unsalted butter or sheep's milk
    butter (see Note)
2 lamb shanks or 1½ pounds lamb shoulder,
    trimmed of fat and cut into 1-inch cubes
8 cups water
1 large red onion, peeled
Salt to taste
½ cup chopped fresh flat-leaf parsley
4 large waxy potatoes, peeled and cut into
    1½-inch cubes

2 large eggs, well beaten
Juice of 1 to 2 lemons, to taste
Freshly ground black pepper to taste

1. Heat the butter in a large soup pot over medium-high heat and brown the lamb on all sides. Pour in the water. Add the onion to the pot and season lightly with salt. Bring to a boil, reduce the heat to medium-low, and simmer slowly, skimming off the foam from the surface, for 1½ hours. Add water as needed to keep the level constant.

2. Stir in the parsley and simmer another half hour. Add the potatoes and simmer another hour or so, until both the meat and potatoes are tender to the point of disintegration. Again, more water may need to be added to the soup as it simmers. Remove the onion with a slotted spoon.

3. Make the egg-lemon sauce: Whisk the eggs and lemon juice together in a medium bowl. Slowly drizzle a ladleful of the soup into the egg-lemon mixture, whisking all the while. Pour the *avgolemono* into the hot soup, turn off the heat, and tilt the pot back and forth so that the mixture works its way into the whole pot. Adjust the seasoning with salt and pepper. Serve immediately.

✳ **NOTE** Sheep's milk butter is available at specialty retailers.

VEGETABLES

Most vegetables in Epirus find their culinary use as filling for any one of hundreds of savory pies. There are, though, a number of place-specific vegetable dishes found in Epirus and in parts of Roumeli as well. Among them are recipes for vegetables cooked in milk and for beans—especially giant beans—baked with greens.

Onions, squash, sorrel, and spinach are probably the most revered and common vegetables in the Epirote larder. Corn, another staple, is used mostly in the form of flour. The region produces some excellent beans, and greens are there for the picking for well over half the year; the ravines and gorges and mountain slopes of Epirus, like those of Crete, are blanketed by a seemingly endless variety of wild greens. Mushrooms, too, are an important supplement to the local table, and many, many varieties are found up here, among them morels, chanterelles, and, according to some mycologists, even white truffles. They are cooked in simple ways, grilled or fried or preserved in brine, and since I have included descriptions or instructions for very similar preparations elsewhere in this book, I have omitted mushrooms from the Epirote recipe repertoire. Nevertheless, there should be enough here to satisfy most herbivorous appetites.

Spring Onion Greens in a Salad

KREMMYDOSALATA

 Makes 2 to 4 servings

My friend and colleague Evy Voutsina, in her book on Greek food, describes this salad from Epirus and explains its existence: Spring onions were not uprooted, she writes. They were left in the ground to mature so that locals would be sure to have onions in the winter. Their greens, though, were ripe for the picking and made into a simple, tasty salad. This is a classic Vlach dish.

3 cups of coarsely chopped greens from spring
onions (reserve the bulbs for another use)
⅓ cup extra-virgin olive oil, or more to taste
2 to 4 tablespoons red wine vinegar, to taste
Salt to taste

Wash and drain the greens. Toss together with
the oil and vinegar. Season with salt and serve.

Giant Beans Baked with Spinach and Feta

GIGANTES STO FOURNO ME SPANAKI KAI
FETA

 Makes 4 to 6 servings

*This is a classic dish from Epirus, found both at home
and in tavernas all over the region. Epirus produces
some of the best giant beans in Greece. In America
they can be found either packaged or sold in bulk at
Greek and Middle Eastern grocery stores. Butter
beans come closest to the Greek giant beans and
make an acceptable substitute.*

½ pound dried giant beans, picked over, rinsed,
soaked overnight in water to cover, and
drained
2 pounds flat-leaf spinach, trimmed, chopped,
and washed well
½ cup snipped fresh dill
½ cup chopped fresh flat-leaf parsley
1 medium leek, white and tender green parts,
coarsely chopped and washed well
Salt to taste
1 cup extra-virgin olive oil
2 large onions, coarsely chopped, or 2 cups
chopped white and tender green parts of
scallions

1½ cups crumbled hard Greek feta cheese,
preferably goat's milk (see Note)
2 cups peeled, seeded, and chopped plum
tomatoes (canned are fine)
Freshly ground black pepper to taste
⅓ cup plain bread crumbs from stale bread

1. Place the drained beans in a large pot with
enough water to cover by 3 inches and bring to a
boil. Reduce the heat to medium-low and simmer
the beans until al dente, about 1 hour.

2. Meanwhile, place the spinach, herbs, and
leek in a colander and sprinkle lightly with salt. Rub
and press the mixture between the palm of one
hand and the holes of the colander, almost in a
kneading motion, so that the greens exude liquid.
Do this for 10 minutes, then place a weighted plate
over the greens and leave them to drain for an hour.

3. Heat 2 tablespoons of the olive oil in a
medium skillet over medium heat and cook the
onions, stirring, until wilted, about 7 minutes. Preheat the oven to 350°F.

4. Combine the drained greens with the cooked
onions and 1 cup of the feta. Drain the beans, reserving 4 cups of the hot liquid. Toss the beans with the
greens and 1 cup of the tomatoes. Taste and adjust
the seasoning with salt, if desired, and pepper. Place
the beans-and-greens mixture in a large ovenproof
glass or ceramic baking dish and mix in a ½ cup of
the remaining olive oil and 2 cups of the hot cooking
liquid. Pour the remaining 1 cup tomatoes over the
surface of the beans and sprinkle the remaining ½
cup feta and the bread crumbs on top. Drizzle the
remaining 6 tablespoons olive oil over the surface
and bake, covered with a sheet of aluminum foil,
until the beans are very creamy and soft but not disintegrating. Depending on the age and condition of
the dried beans, this could mean anywhere between

1 and 2½ hours of cooking. Add more liquid to the pan if necessary during baking to keep it moist. Serve hot, lukewarm, or at room temperature.

✳ **NOTE** There is a lot of variation in the flavor and texture of feta cheese. I recommend hard feta in this recipe because I like the generally sharper flavor of hard feta and its ability to hold up a little better in the oven. Hard fetas tend to be those aged in tins, not barrels. Ask the cheesemonger for a sample taste of several before choosing.

☉ Giant beans are also baked with sorrel in Epirus. Follow the directions through step 3, substituting sorrel for the spinach, and omitting the dill and parsley. Proceed with step 4, omitting the feta and, later on, the bread crumbs.

You could also omit greens and step 2 completely and bake the beans instead with 4 large leeks, washed and coarsely chopped.

Baked Onion and Paprika Relish

KREMMYDIA PSITA

 Makes about 4 cups

Baked onions, baked leeks, baked scallions, all seasoned with paprika, are found throughout Epirus and parts of Macedonia, especially in the western reaches where the cuisines are similar. This is a wonderful side dish for grilled meats.

1½ pounds medium onions, sliced ¼ inch thick
1 cup water, dry white wine, or chicken broth, or more if needed
½ cup extra-virgin olive oil
2 to 3 tablespoons red wine vinegar, to taste
3 garlic cloves, peeled and crushed
Salt to taste
2 to 3 bay leaves, to taste
1 scant teaspoon sweet paprika
½ teaspoon cayenne pepper
3 scant tablespoons plain bread crumbs from stale rustic bread

1. Preheat the oven to 350°F. Bring a large pot of lightly salted water to a rolling boil and blanch the onions until the water comes to a boil again. Drain the onions.

2. Spread the onions in a medium ovenproof glass baking dish—the onions should come at least 1½ inches up the sides of the pan—and pour in the liquid. Toss the onions with the olive oil, vinegar, garlic, and salt. Disperse the bay leaves evenly throughout pan and sprinkle the surface of the onions with the paprika and cayenne, then the bread crumbs. Bake, covered, until the onions are golden, about 50 minutes. During baking, if needed, add more water, wine, or broth to keep the onions from burning.

Winter Squash Pilaf

KOLOKYTHORIZO

Makes 4 to 6 servings

Hard winter squashes slowly cooked with rice are popular in many parts of Greece. In the Aegean, this dish is usually made with pumpkin; elsewhere squashes similar to what Americans know as butternut are used. The dish goes well with boiled greens and good, sharp sheep's milk cheese.

4 pounds pumpkin or butternut squash
Salt
½ cup extra-virgin olive oil
2 large onions, coarsely chopped
2 tablespoons tomato paste diluted with
    2 tablespoons water
½ cup snipped fresh dill
1 cup long-grain rice
1 cup water
Freshly ground black pepper to taste

1. Trim and peel the squash, then scrape out the seeds. Cut into 1-inch cubes, place in a colander, and toss with salt. Let stand and drain for 2 hours.

2. Heat ¼ cup of the olive oil in a large, wide pot over medium heat and cook the onions, stirring, until translucent, 7 to 9 minutes. Add the diluted tomato paste and dill and stir for a few minutes to wilt. Add the squash and simmer over low heat until the squash is tender, about 20 minutes. Add the rice and water and toss to combine. Adjust the seasoning with additional salt and pepper if necessary. Cover and simmer until the rice is tender, another 15 minutes or so, adding more water if needed to cook the rice. As soon as the dish is ready, gently stir in the remaining ¼ cup olive oil. Let cool to room temperature and serve.

Baby Zucchini Simmered in Milk

KOLOKYTHAKIA STO GALA

Makes 4 servings

I was in Ano Pedina, a remote, almost isolated village in the Zagorohoria, when I was first told of this dish. My friend Vassilis Paparounas, a village native and the son of a shepherd's family, dismissed it as poor man's food, saying that no one eats it anymore. Then I found a similar recipe in a recently published book by a well-respected Greek author, Evy Voutsina, and I took a poet's license to alter my original recipe slightly to make it eminently palatable.

When this dish was in its heyday, it probably would have been the main course, together with some rough bread and local tsipouro *(grappa). It makes a lovely side dish for any simple meat recipe. I rather like it in combination with the* kimadopita *(ground meat pie) from Ioannina (page 159) and with the Epirus* kreatopita *(meat pie) (page 160).*

¼ cup (½ stick) unsalted butter or sheep's milk
    butter, or extra-virgin olive oil
6 scallions or spring onions, white and tender
    green parts, chopped
½ cup chopped fresh flat-leaf parsley
1½ pounds small zucchini, cut into 1-inch-thick
    rounds
Salt to taste
½ pound Greek feta cheese, preferably sheep's
    milk, crumbled
1½ cups milk
Freshly ground black pepper to taste

Heat 2 tablespoons of the butter or olive oil in a wide pot over medium heat and cook the scallions or spring onions and parsley together, stirring, until wilted, 7 to 9 minutes. Add the zucchini, season with salt, and toss gently to coat. Cook over medium-low heat until the juices exuded from the zucchini have boiled off, 6 to 8 minutes. Add the feta and toss gently. Pour in the milk and reduce the heat to low. Simmer until most of the milk has been absorbed and the mixture is thick and creamy, about 10 minutes. Season with pepper and serve.

⊙ Zucchini Simmered in Milk and Eggs (Kolokythaki sto Gala me Avgokopsi): Cook the zucchini exactly the same way, omitting the feta. Have the 2 large beaten eggs ready in a small, deep bowl. Pour a ladleful of the pot juices into the beaten eggs in a slow, steady stream, whisking the eggs all the while. Immediately pour the egg mixture into the pot and tilt the pot so that the egg mixture is evenly dispersed. Remove from the heat and serve. The dish should be thick but liquid, like a hearty soup.

Mixed Greens Cooked in Milk

LAHANIKA MAGEIREMENA STO GALA

 Makes 4 servings

Vlachs, Sarakatsans, and others in Epirus still make this simple dish. In fact, throughout the shepherds' communities of Roumeli and Thessaly greens cooked in milk are also common. It is an elegy to all the things these regions produce profusely, and it must have been a matter of simple logic to have married them a very long time ago. This would be a vegetarian main course for me, and I'd serve it with some good sourdough bread.

¼ cup (½ stick) unsalted butter or sheep's milk butter
4 scallions, white and tender green parts, chopped
1 cup chopped fresh flat-leaf parsley
2 pounds combined sorrel, chard, and flat-leaf spinach, trimmed, coarsely chopped, and washed well
Salt and freshly ground black pepper to taste
1 tablespoon all-purpose flour
¼ cup water
2 cups milk
1½ cups crumbled Greek feta cheese, preferably made from sheep's milk

1. Heat 2 tablespoons of the butter in a large, wide pot over medium heat and cook the scallions and parsley together, stirring, until wilted, 7 to 9 minutes. Add the greens, stir and toss to coat with the butter, and cook until they are wilted completely, 7 to 10 minutes. Season with salt and pepper.

2. Mix together the flour and water and pour it into the pot, tossing to combine. Pour in the milk. Reduce the heat to medium-low and simmer until the mixture is thick and creamy, 10 to 15 minutes.

3. Sprinkle the crumbled feta over the greens and continue cooking until the feta begins to melt, a few more minutes. Place the mixture in a serving bowl or platter. Melt the remaining 2 tablespoons butter and drizzle over the top. Serve hot.

SAVORY PIES

Pita—savory pie—is the lifeblood of the Epirote kitchen, a dish associated both with the daily and the festive table and so important to the local table that the local word for filling, *trofi,* means, simply, "food." There are pies made just for Christmas and New Year's; to this day sweet rice pies (rice was traditionally expensive and symbolically represents prosperity and fertility) celebrate a wedding engagement. Years ago, the parents of the newborn girl would leave bread, salt, and a rolling pin under the infant's pillow, symbolic wishes for a good marriage, since a girl's skill at making phyllo is commensurate with her ability to keep a good home.

Pita is especially suited to the shepherd's peripatetic life. But it is also a dish that crosses every socioeconomic and cultural boundary.

The range and variety of pies not only in Epirus but also in Macedonia, Thessaly, and Roumeli is enormous. In Epirus the vast majority are cheese pies or pies made with other dairy products. Greens pies, brimming with the stuff of a morning's foraging in the mountains or with reconstituted dried greens are made with almost equal frequency. There are also numerous meat pies, mainly reserved for holidays. There used to be a bevy of pies filled with legumes such as lentils or chickpeas, but these old, poverty-born dishes have virtually disappeared from the table.

It is the nuance in this simple dish that is its real beauty. Often not more than three or four ingredients are required to make a pie, but the same three or four ingredients are composed differently from village to village, cook to cook, so that the wealth of pies throughout Epirus is enormous.

There is a rhyme and reason for the existence of so many savory pies in this rugged mountain clime.

Economy and practicality are at the heart of it. For one, Epirus doesn't lend itself to much farming, so missing from the local traditional diet are many of the simple stove-top (or hearth-top) vegetable and legume stews that were the salvation of rural cooks elsewhere. Savory pies evolved in the local repertoire because they provided many things at once: Many are very easy to prepare—witness the gamut of batter pies and pies whose "crusts" are made just by sprinkling some cornmeal on top of the filling. These pies could be made in any environment, either in a permanent kitchen over the *masina,* or potbellied stove (nowadays replaced by the electric oven), or in the makeshift mobile stoves that were the realm of nomadic cooks—savory pies in Epirus are traditionally baked in a *gastra* or under a *sini,* essentially a portable, makeshift oven that was a dome-shaped lid fitted over a large round baking pan, which was, in turn, placed over and covered by embers. These pies could be made with ingredients that were usually part of the shepherd's larder—cheese, milk, and butter, and any one of the grain staples, from cornmeal to wheat flour, from rice to bulgur to *trahana.* Greens pies could be made with easily foraged ingredients, too. Most important, though, especially for a shepherding family, *pites* travel well and keep well, so they provide filling, nutritious food for long, strenuous journeys. All these reasons provided the impetus and the breeding ground for the development of one of the backbones of Greek and especially shepherds' cooking.

Three Phylloless Cheese Pies

EPIROTE CHEESE PIES

It would be impossible to document all the region's cheese pies, or *tyropites*. One should note that mostly they are made with feta, which is referred to generically as cheese *(tyri)* in the region, since, as the quintessential shepherds' cheese, it is so much a part of the local culinary traditions. Exceptions are specifically noted.

Some pies call for a filling of feta and eggs; others for feta, milk, and eggs; still others for feta, eggs, and *trahana* or feta, eggs, and rice. Some are batter pies, poured into a pan and baked; others require phyllo, anywhere from a few sheets to sandwich the filling to 15 to 20 sheets of handmade phyllo. Despite the nuances of each pie, common threads and rules apply to all. Eleni Skourti, a schoolteacher and local folklorist and my guide in the esoterics of northwestern Greek *tyropites,* says that although pies vary from place to place, they are never seasoned with herbs (despite the fact that the region is a veritable carpet of mountain herbs), and they always call for butter, not oil.

Traditional Greek and Epirote country cooks make pies in large, usually round pans. Many of the old pans still in use are made of copper, and many span 24 inches in diameter. It is easy to understand why: The pies were meant to feed a hungry family with lots of kids. They were time consuming to prepare so necessity forced the cook to make the pies big enough to make the fuss of their preparation worthwhile and also to make enough to go around.

Although it is easy to fit a 24-inch round pan inside an average American oven, you'll have difficulty finding one. You can come close by scouring the equipment shelves of Greek or Middle Eastern markets. There you'll find various sizes of heavy, round aluminum pans, usually about 2½ inches deep. Pizza pans work just as well, though, and they are a lot easier to find. The recipes that follow have been reworked to accommodate the needs of modern cooks.

Three Phylloless Cheese Pies

"Lazy" Cheese and Yogurt Pie

TEMBELOPITA APO TO ZAGORI

 Makes twenty-four 3-inch pieces

This easy pie gets its name because it doesn't require the hard task of rolling out phyllo.

2 cups thick Mediterranean-style or plain yogurt, drained (page 459), preferably made from sheep's milk
2 large eggs, lightly beaten
1½ to 2 cups water, as needed
2 tablespoons unsalted butter, melted
2½ cups crumbled Greek feta cheese
2 to 2½ cups all-purpose flour, as needed
¼ cup milk
3 tablespoons extra-virgin olive oil

1. Preheat the oven to 325°F. In a large bowl, combine the yogurt, eggs, and 1½ cups of the water. Mix in the melted butter. Add 1½ cups of the feta and then add about 2 cups of the flour. Stir well to combine. The mixture should have the consistency of a thick batter. Add more flour or water, if necessary, to achieve the proper consistency.

2. Rub a 12- by 18-inch baking pan with butter. Pour the batter into the pan and spread evenly with a spatula. In a small bowl, combine the remaining 1 cup feta with the milk and olive oil and pour this evenly over the surface of the pie. Place the pan on the center rack and bake until set and golden, about 1 hour and 10 minutes. Remove from the oven, let cool slightly, and cut into serving pieces.

Thin Batter Pie with Feta

ALEVROPITA AGINOTI

 Makes one 18-inch pie; 8 to 10 servings

I learned to make this and the next few batter pies one August a few summers ago after spending a couple of weeks in Ano Pedina, one of the most remote and most sparsely populated villages in the Zagorahoria. We stayed at a local inn, which also happened to be just about the only place in the village to eat. Reigning over the kitchen was a spry, seventyish lady named Kyria Stavroula. She wore a dark kerchief over her head and the typical dark, heavy, layered clothes of village women impervious to heat. Her face was wrinkleless from so many years spent in the cool, clean air of the Pindus Mountains, but her hands were another story. They were thick and strong like a man's hands, the manifestation of her energy. She made the butter and cheese at the inn herself, tended the garden, and every morning before most of us had taken our first sip of strong Greek coffee, she had gotten most of the day's cooking finished. Each day's menu always included a few of these batter pies. They seemed easy enough as I watched her make them, and they are. The trick is to keep them thin but to bake them properly so the bottom doesn't burn.

This and the next few pies are great as a fast supper together with a salad and also work well on buffet tables. These recipes may also be cut in half and baked in 8-inch round, preferably nonstick, pans.

2 cups all-purpose flour

1 scant teaspoon salt

2 large eggs

1½ cups plus 3 tablespoons water

1 pound Greek feta cheese, preferably made
    from sheep's milk, crumbled

5 tablespoons extra-virgin olive oil

1. Preheat the oven to 325°F. Brush a 15-inch round baking pan that is 2 inches deep with olive oil and sprinkle with a little flour, tapping the sides of the pan so that the flour coats the surface evenly.

2. Combine the 2 cups flour and the salt in a large bowl and make a well in the center. Add 1 egg to the well and pour in 1½ cups of the water. Mix with a fork to form a batter about as thick as pancake batter. Pour two thirds of the batter into the prepared pan and tilt the pan so that the batter spreads evenly all over the surface. Sprinkle the crumbled feta evenly over the batter.

3. Beat the remaining egg and mix it into the remaining batter. Add the olive oil and the remaining 3 tablespoons water, mix well, and spoon the mixture over the feta. There will not and should not be enough to cover the whole surface—some of the cheese will show through. Bake on the center rack until the pie peels away from the pan easily, about 40 minutes. The *alevropita* should be about ½-inch thick once baked. Remove from the oven, cool slightly, and serve hot or at room temperature.

⊙ **Thin Batter Pie with Grated Zucchini (Alevro-kolokythopita):** Trim and grate 1 large zucchini. Place in a colander and toss with salt. Work the zucchini with your hands, rubbing it against the holes of the colander and squeezing to rid it of as much liquid as possible. Add the grated zucchini to the batter in step 2. Continue as directed, spreading about two-thirds of the zucchini-studded batter over the bottom of the pan, sprinkling with feta, and covering with the remaining diluted batter. Bake until golden, remove from the oven, cool slightly, and serve, either warm or at room temperature.

PREBAKED PHYLLO

Many of the recipes that follow call for prebaking a number of phyllo sheets, especially for the middle layers of a pie, usually for pies with loose or heavy fillings—cheese and meat pies, in other words. It is an old technique that used to be done on the flat, round metal surface of a *masina,* or wood-burning stove, or on a makeshift griddle over hot embers. Prebaking is required to keep the pie from becoming soggy from a wet or dense filling, and it ensures that the middle layers bake completely. Nowadays home cooks in Epirus have transferred the practice to their modern electric kitchens and usually prebake the sheets over the bottom of a flat, round pan on top of the stove or in the oven. Directions follow in individual recipes. Greens pies almost never require this technique.

One last thing—you will note that several of the pies in this chapter call for them to be flipped and slid back into the pan to brown on the other side. This is also an old custom from the days before calibrated ovens, one that home cooks still cling to dearly.

Cheese Pie from the Villages of Zagori with Prebaked Phyllo

TYROPITA ZAGORIOU

Makes one 14- or 15-inch pie;
8 to 12 servings

Here is one of the many filling Epirote cheese pies that call for *trahana. The trahana absorbs excess moisture in the pie and also makes it a heartier, more substantial dish.*

1 recipe Epirote phyllo (page 453) or commercial
    phyllo, at room temperature
⅔ pound Greek feta cheese, preferably made
    from sheep's milk, crumbled

⅓ pound *anthotyro* or ricotta cheese
4 large eggs, lightly beaten
¾ cup milk
⅓ cup sweet *trahana* (see page 456) or coarse
    bulgur
Salt and freshly ground black pepper to taste

For the pan and for buttering the phyllo
Cornmeal
1 tablespoon unsalted butter
1 scant teaspoon salt
⅔ cup unsalted butter or sheep's milk butter,
    melted

1. On a lightly floured work surface, using your palms, roll the dough into a long rope about an inch thick. Divide into 10 equal pieces. Roll each piece into a ball and set aside for 15 minutes, covered, to rest.

2. Make the filling: Combine the feta, *anthotyro* or ricotta, eggs, and milk in a large bowl. Mix in the *trahana* and season with salt and pepper. Set aside, covered, until ready to use.

3. Prepare the phyllo. Preheat the oven to 400°F. Place a 14- or 15-inch-round aluminum or nonstick baking or pizza pan that is 2 inches deep upside down on the bottom of the oven so that it heats, almost like a makeshift griddle. Dust the bottom of a large round tray with cornmeal and have a bowlful of cornmeal handy.

4. Lightly dust a large work surface with flour. Flatten a ball of dough slightly on the flour with your palms. Sprinkle the surface lightly with flour. Using a rolling pin, roll the dough into a circle 14 inches in diameter. Place on the tray sprinkled with cornmeal and dust the top amply with cornmeal, too. Cover and set aside. Repeat this with 4 more balls of dough, rolling each out and setting it aside, stacked and dusted generously with cornmeal.

5. Take the tray over to the oven and have another, empty, tray handy. Open the oven, pull out the hot upside-down pan, and place a sheet of phyllo over it. Slide it immediately back into the oven and bake, turning, just long enough for the phyllo to stiffen and get some color, 3 to 4 minutes. Using kitchen tongs or a 2-pronged fork, flip the phyllo sheet over to bake the other side. Remove the phyllo and set aside on the other tray. Repeat with the other 4 sheets. When done, remove the pan from the oven and set aside to cool. You will need it again.

6. When the pan is cool, rub the inside of it with the tablespoon of butter. Sprinkle the salt over the surface and, with your fingertips, rub the salt into the cornmeal. This is an old Epirote cook's trick to keep the pie from sticking to the pan. Reduce the oven temperature to 375°F.

7. On a lightly floured work surface, roll out another ball of dough, this one into a circle about 18 inches in diameter. Place it in the pan with its edges hanging over the sides. Drizzle 1 tablespoon of the melted butter over its surface. Roll out 2 more balls of dough into circles 14 inches in diameter. Place them over the bottom sheet, drizzling each with 1 tablespoon butter. Spoon about ½ cup of the filling evenly over the phyllo. Next, layer in the 5 pre-baked phyllo sheets, one at a time, drizzling each generously with butter and spreading ½ cup of the filling over each. Roll out the remaining 2 balls of dough into 14-inch circles. Layer them over the filling, buttering them generously. Bring the excess phyllo that is hanging over the sides over the top layer and pour any remaining melted butter over the surface of the pie. Bake until golden, about 50 minutes. Remove from the oven. Using kitchen mitts, place a large plate over the pan and immediately flip the pie onto it. Slide the upside-down pie back into the pan so that the bottom layer is on top. Let cool slightly and serve.

Multilayered Cheese-and-Butter Pie Made with Homemade Phyllo

KASSATA

 Makes one 18-inch pie; 12 to 15 servings

This fascinating, difficult pie is a favorite among the Vlachs and takes its name from the Vlach word for cheese, kas *or* kash. *It is hard to prepare because of the number of gossamer, homemade phyllo sheets it requires. I learned to make it from a local Metsovo woman, one of that generation of women born with a dowel in their hands. You'll need a wooden dowel at least 24 inches long and ¾ inch in diameter in addition to the usual rolling pin.*

1 recipe Epirote phyllo (page 453), at room
    temperature

For the filling
2 pounds Greek feta cheese
1½ cups (3 sticks) unsalted butter

1. On a lightly floured work surface, using your palms, roll the dough into a long rope a little more than an inch thick, and cut into 12 to 14 equal pieces. Shape each into a ball and keep covered with a kitchen towel until needed.

2. Crumble the feta into a medium bowl. In a medium saucepan over medium heat, melt the butter. Remove from the heat. Set aside. Preheat the oven to 325°F.

3. Lightly dust your work surface with flour. Flatten one ball of dough onto the floured surface with your palm. Sprinkle a little flour on top of it. Using a rolling pin, roll the dough into a 6-inch circle. Place the dowel on the end of the pastry closest to you and roll the pastry around the dowel, pressing it gently, from the center toward its edges, with your hands. Unroll the pastry and lightly dust again with flour. Repeat the process several times, rolling out the dough from opposite sides and dusting a little each time, until a large circle (18 to 20 inches) forms.

4. Shake off as much excess flour as possible from the rolled-out pastry. Place it in an oiled 18-inch round baking or pizza pan that is 2 inches deep. Drizzle with melted butter. Roll out a second ball of dough in the same way and place it over the first sheet. Drizzle with melted butter and sprinkle with crumbled feta.

5. Repeat the process, buttering every sheet and sprinkling every second sheet with feta, until all the dough balls are used up. The last layer should have only butter, not butter and cheese.

6. Gently fold the top, bottom, and sides of the circle inward, toward the center, just enough to make a rounded square. Invert a large plate (large enough to fit the entire pastry) over the dough and flip, so that the folded sides are underneath. Slip the pie back into the baking pan. Using your fingertips, gently push the pastry out toward the periphery of the pan until the surface is covered.

7. Bake, uncovered, until light golden brown in color, about 1½ hours. Serve warm.

✳ **NOTE** You may reduce the ingredients by half and bake the pie in a 9-inch or 10-inch baking pan.

Zucchini Pie

KOLOKYTHOPITA

Makes one 18-inch pie;
12 to 15 servings

I watched my friend Elia's mother, Kyra Dimitra, to learn how to make this particular pie. The filling is rich, soft, and satisfying, and the pie just one of dozens, probably hundreds, that call for zucchini. Here semolina flour is used to help absorb the moisture from the zucchini.

5 pounds zucchini
1 tablespoon salt
¾ pound Greek feta cheese, crumbled
4 large eggs
¾ cup milk
½ cup fine semolina flour
¾ cup extra-virgin olive oil
Salt and freshly ground white pepper to taste
1 recipe Epirote phyllo (page 453), basic phyllo,
    or commercial phyllo at room temperature

1. Grate the zucchini coarsely. Place in a colander and toss with the salt. Let stand for 30 minutes, then wring with your hands a little at a time to rid it of excess liquid.

2. Combine the feta, eggs, milk, semolina, and ⅓ cup of the olive oil in a large bowl. Mix in the zucchini and stir to combine. Season with pepper, taste, and add more salt if needed.

3. Preheat the oven to 400°F. Divide the dough into 5 balls, with one slightly smaller than the others. Lightly oil an 18-inch-round baking or pizza pan that is 2 inches deep. On a lightly floured work surface, roll one of the large balls into a sheet about 22 inches in diameter and place in the pan with the excess hanging over the sides. Brush with some of the remaining olive oil. Repeat with the next 2 large dough balls so that the bottom of the pie has 3 layers of phyllo. Spread the filling over the phyllo. Roll out the last large ball of dough the same way, brushing the top with a little more olive oil. Finally, roll the small ball into a circle just 18 inches in diameter so that it sits snugly inside the pan without hanging over the sides. Brush with the remaining olive oil. Gently bring all the edges over the top sheet so that they form a kind of collar around the pan. Brush the top with olive oil. Score the pie vertically then diagonally to make 3-inch serving pieces. Sprinkle with a little water (by dipping your hand in a bowl and spritzing the top of the pie with your fingers). Bake until golden, about 50 minutes. Remove from the oven, let cool, and serve at room temperature.

✳ **NOTE** You may reduce the ingredients by half and bake the pie in a 9-inch or 10-inch baking pan.

The pie may also be made with commercial phyllo. For every sheet of homemade phyllo use 3 to 4 sheets of commercial phyllo. See directions (page 455) for more details on how to work with frozen phyllo.

Cabbage and Feta Pie from Zagori

TZAROUHOPITA

 Makes one 14- or 15-inch pie;
10 to 12 servings

1 recipe Epirote phyllo (page 453) or commercial phyllo, at room temperature

For the filling
1 large head green cabbage (about 4 pounds), cored and shredded
½ cup olive oil, or unsalted butter or sheep's milk butter, melted
1 pound Greek feta cheese, preferably made from sheep's milk, crumbled
Salt and freshly ground black pepper to taste

For brushing the phyllo
⅔ cup unsalted butter, melted, or extra-virgin olive oil

1. On a lightly floured work surface, using your palms, roll the dough into a long rope about 1½ inches in diameter. Divide into 7 equal pieces. Shape each into a ball and set aside, covered, for about 15 minutes.

2. Bring a large pot of salted water to a boil and blanch the shredded cabbage until wilted, about 3 minutes. Drain completely and let cool. Mix in the ½ cup olive oil and the crumbled feta and toss to combine. Season with salt and pepper. Set aside.

3. Preheat the oven to 375°F. Lightly oil a 14- or 15-inch round baking or pizza pan that is 2 inches deep. Dust your work surface with flour and, using a rolling pin or dowel, roll out a ball of dough to a circle about 18 inches in diameter. Place it in the pan, letting the excess hang over the edges. Drizzle

1 tablespoon of the melted butter or olive oil over the surface of the dough in a circular motion. Roll the next ball of dough into an 18-inch circle and place on top. Drizzle that, too, with 1 tablespoon melted butter or olive oil. Spread about one-third of the filling over the surface of the second sheet. Roll out a third ball of dough, this time to a circle just 14 inches in diameter. (It should not hang over the sides of the pan.) Place over the filling and drizzle with 1 tablespoon melted butter or olive oil. Repeat with 2 more sheets, each just 14 inches in diameter, and the remaining two-thirds of the filling, brushing each sheet of phyllo with 1 tablespoon butter or olive oil. Roll the next ball of dough into a 14-inch circle, place on top of the filling, and drizzle with 1 tablespoon butter or olive oil. Roll out the last ball, again into a 14-inch circle, and place on top. Drizzle 1 tablespoon butter or olive oil around the periphery and fold the excess dough over the surface so that it is flat, but rolled as for a thick rim. Drizzle the entire surface of the pie with the remaining melted butter or olive oil. Place in the center of the oven and bake until the phyllo is crisp and golden, about 1 hour and 10 minutes. Remove from the oven, let cool slightly, and serve.

The pie may also be made with commercial phyllo. For every sheet of homemade phyllo use 3 to 4 sheets of commercial phyllo. See directions (page 455) for more details on how to work with frozen phyllo.

Flatbread Baked with Caramelized Onions from Preveza

BROUST'LI

 Makes two 9- or 10-inch loaves

Another confusing and seemingly non-Greek name. A similar—but pan-fried, not baked—cheese bread is made in the opposite end of the country, in the southern Peloponnesos, and there it goes by the name broustoula. *My theory is that this pie made its way south with the various Balkan peoples who emigrated into Greece about half a millennium ago.*

3 to 3½ cups all-purpose flour, as needed
1 scant teaspoon salt
2 teaspoons active dry yeast
1¼ cups warm water
5 tablespoons olive oil
2 tablespoons unsalted butter or sheep's milk
    butter
2 medium onions, halved and thinly sliced

1. Prepare the dough. Combine 3 cups of the flour and the salt in a large bowl and set aside. Dissolve the yeast in the warm water in a small bowl and set aside, covered, until it begins to bubble up, about 15 minutes. Make a well in the center of the flour and add the yeast-and-water mixture. Mix the flour into the well with a fork until a dough mass begins to form. Using a little of the remaining flour, dust your work surface and knead the dough until smooth and pliant, 10 to 12 minutes. You can also do this in a stand mixer fitted with a dough hook. Rub a bowl with 2 tablespoons of the olive oil and place the dough inside. Roll to coat with the olive oil, cover the bowl with plastic wrap, and set aside until almost doubled in bulk, about 1 hour.

2. In a heavy, preferably cast-iron, skillet, heat the butter until it bubbles up. Add the onions, reduce the heat to medium-low, and cook slowly, stirring frequently, until the onions turn deep golden, about 25 minutes. Remove from the heat and set aside.

3. Preheat the oven to 375°F. Oil two 9- or 10-inch-round baking pans that are 2 inches deep with olive oil. Divide the dough into two balls of equal size, punch down lightly, and, using a rolling pin, roll each into a circle almost the size of one of the pans. Place the dough in the pans. Rub your palms with 1 tablespoon of the remaining olive oil and push out the dough in each pan toward the edges. Brush each with the remaining olive oil and place the caramelized onions and all their pan juices evenly on top of each. Bake the *broust'li* until the bread is golden, 35 to 40 minutes. Remove from the oven, let cool slightly, and serve.

⊙ Flatbread Baked with Leeks (Alevropita me Prassa): Prepare the dough as for Broust'li (page 154). Trim 2 large leeks, cut the white and tender green parts in half lengthwise, wash well, and thinly slice. Heat 3 tablespoons butter in a large skillet over medium heat and cook the leeks, stirring, until wilted and lightly browned, about 50 minutes. When the dough has risen, divide it in half, punch down lightly, and roll each ball into a 9-inch circle. Spread the leeks over the surface of each. Bring the edges of the dough toward the center of each pastry to cover the leeks, as though making a bundle, and shape into a ball, kneading slightly. Let them rest for another 30 minutes, then roll into two 9-inch circles again. Brush the surface with 2 tablespoons melted butter and let the leek bread rest and rise,

---

PHYLLOLESS GREENS PIES WITH CORNMEAL CRUSTS

All over the North of Greece, from western Macedonia to Epirus, then down the Pindus into Roumeli and Thessaly, crustless—or rather, phylloless—greens pies are part of the culinary traditions. Cooks avoid the time and expense of rolling out their own phyllo dough (remember, wheat flour was traditionally expensive among the shepherd communities of the North) by substituting a technique for making a grainy, toothsome, tasty crust with cornmeal. There are several techniques for working with it. In some pies the cornmeal is sprinkled on the bottom of an oiled pan, dampened with a little water or with some of the juices from the greens, then covered with another sprinkling of cornmeal. The result is a lovely, paper-thin, hard crust with a deep ocher or greenish color when baked. Other pies call for working the cornmeal first into either hot milk or water. These pies tend to have thicker, more cushiony crusts. In the recipes that follow, I have tried to offer a variety.

covered with a cloth, for another 30 minutes. Bake in two large oiled pans in the center of the oven until golden, about 40 minutes. Remove from the oven, let cool on a rack, and serve, warm or at room temperature.

Mixed Greens Pie with a Cornmeal Crust

BLATSARIA

 Makes 12 to 15 servings

The names of dishes can be a confusing business in Greek villages. Blatsaria *and pies similar to it are sometimes called* pispilita *(page 157) after the Greek word for "sprinkle" or* aradopita, *after the word for "line" or "row"—*arada. *This is a rustic pie and the Sarakatsan and other denizens of the mountainous Zagorohoria like to eat this with a glass of buttermilk.*

2 pounds mixed greens (spinach, chard, sorrel), trimmed, coarsely chopped, and washed well
1 bunch fresh flat-leaf parsley, coarsely chopped
1 bunch fresh dill, snipped
1 bunch fresh mint, finely chopped
8 to 10 scallions or spring onions, white and tender green parts, finely chopped
Salt to taste
2 medium onions, finely chopped
1½ cups extra-virgin olive oil
1 pound Greek feta cheese, crumbled (about 3 cups)
2½ cups milk
2 cups fine white or yellow cornmeal
1 to 1½ cups water, as needed
Thick Mediterranean-style yogurt, preferably made from sheep's milk, or plain yogurt, drained (see page 459), or buttermilk as an accompaniment

1. Combine the greens, herbs, and scallions or spring onions in a large colander and sprinkle with salt. Rub and knead the mixture, pressing it between your palm and the holes of the colander, until the greens and other vegetables exude their liquid. This will take 15 minutes. Squeeze the excess water out of the vegetables between your palms and place in a large bowl or basin. Mix in the onions.

2. Preheat the oven to 375°F. Drizzle 1 cup of the olive oil into the vegetable mixture and knead vigorously until the greens wilt, about 10 minutes or so. Add the feta and mix all together.

3. In a medium saucepan over medium heat, scald the milk. Add the cornmeal in a slow, steady stream, stirring all the while so that it doesn't lump. Season with a little salt. Keep stirring until the mixture thickens to the consistency of a heavy, almost solid batter. Remove from the heat.

4. Oil an 18-inch round baking or pizza pan or an 18- by 12-inch baking pan that is 2 inches deep with olive oil. Pour half of the milk-and-cornmeal mixture over the bottom of the pan, spreading it evenly. Spread the vegetable filling evenly over the batter and level the surface with a spatula. Dilute the remaining half of the batter with as much of the water as needed to obtain a thick but pourable batter. Pour this over the top, spreading it as evenly as possible. Don't worry if the batter doesn't cover the entire surface of the greens. Drizzle the remaining ½ cup olive oil over the surface. Place on the center rack in the oven and bake until the pie is dense and golden and the cornmeal crust set, about 1 hour.

To serve, let the pie cool for 20 to 30 minutes, then cut into wedges and serve topped with a little yogurt or with buttermilk on the side.

✳ **NOTE** The recipe may be halved. Bake the pie in a 10-inch round baking pan.

Cornmeal "Sprinkle" Pie with Nettles and Spinach

PISPILITA ME TSOUKNIDA

Makes one 18-inch pie;
12 to 15 servings

Pispilita *is one of the classic pies of Epirus. It means "sprinkle" pie—pispilizo in Greek is "to sprinkle"—for the way the cornmeal is dusted over the bottom of the baking pan and then over the greens themselves once the pie is assembled. Although almost any combination of greens or leeks and greens can go into the filling, I chose a* pispilita *with nettles because nettles are among the region's most esteemed greens. This and other, similar, pies also go by the name* babanatsa.

1 pound spinach or chard, trimmed, finely chopped, and washed well

1 pound nettles, trimmed, finely chopped, and washed well

1 cup chopped fresh mint

1 tablespoon salt

1 large leek, white and tender green parts, finely chopped and washed well

2 large onions, finely chopped

¾ pound Greek feta cheese, crumbled

Freshly ground black pepper to taste

3½ cups fine yellow cornmeal

2 cups extra-virgin olive oil

About 2½ cups water, as needed

1. Place the spinach or chard, nettles, and mint in a large colander. Sprinkle with 2 teaspoons of the salt and, using rubber gloves (raw nettles sting), mix the greens together, rubbing them between your fingers and against the holes in the colander so that they exude as much liquid as possible. This will take about 10 minutes. Let stand for 1 hour to drain further.

2. Using gloves, squeeze fistfuls at a time of the greens to rid them of any excess liquid, then place in a large bowl. Combine the greens with the leek, onions, and crumbled feta. Season with pepper.

3. Preheat the oven to 400°F. In a separate bowl, combine 2½ cups of the cornmeal with the remaining teaspoon salt, 1 cup of the olive oil, and 1 cup of the water, or enough to make a damp, mealy mixture. Oil an 18-inch-round baking or pizza pan that is 2 inches deep with olive oil. Spread the cornmeal mixture in the bottom of the pan, pressing it down gently and working it out a little toward the edges of the pan so that it comes about an inch up the side. Spread the greens mixture evenly over the cornmeal base. Pour ½ cup of the remaining olive oil evenly over the greens. Sprinkle the remaining 1 cup cornmeal over the greens and dampen by drizzling the remaining ½ cup olive oil over it. Also sprinkle with 1 cup water so that the cornmeal on top is moist. Bake, uncovered, until the pie is golden and the base set, about 1 hour.

✳ **NOTE** You may reduce the ingredients by half and bake the pie in a 10-inch round by 2-inch deep baking pan.

Chicken Pie with Graviera Cheese and Herbs

KOTOPITA ME GRAVIERA

 Makes one 14- or 15-inch pie;
8 to 10 servings

In Epirus general wisdom has it that almost anything can fill a savory pie. The region boasts a slew of savory meat pies, traditionally made with shredded or chopped leftover meats combined with cheese and herbs. Some of the best of these are the chicken pies, which local cooks turn into delicious, filling meals bursting with meat, cheese, eggs, and more.

3 tablespoons unsalted butter or olive oil

2 cups finely chopped red onion

2 garlic cloves, minced

2 cups cooked, shredded boneless chicken meat

½ cup chopped fresh flat-leaf parsley

¼ cup chopped fresh mint

Salt and freshly ground black pepper to taste

¼ pound *graviera* cheese, grated

¼ pound *kefalograviera* cheese, grated

1 recipe Epirote phyllo (page 453) or commercial phyllo, at room temperature

½ to ¾ cup (1 to 1½ sticks) unsalted butter, melted, for brushing the phyllo

2 tablespoons fine semolina flour

1 cup chicken broth

4 large eggs, lightly beaten

1. In a large, heavy skillet, heat the butter or olive oil and cook the onions and garlic, stirring, over medium heat until translucent, about 7 minutes. Add the chicken and herbs, season with salt and pepper, and cook together, stirring a few times, until the herbs wilt and the chicken browns lightly, 5 to 7 minutes. Remove from the heat. Toss the mix-ture with ¼ cup each of the *graviera* and *kefalo-graviera*. Set aside until ready to use.

2. Lightly oil a 14- or 15-inch-round baking or pizza pan that is 2 inches deep, and preheat the oven to 350°F.

3. On a lightly floured work surface, using your palms, roll the phyllo dough into a long rope about 1½ inches thick. Divide into 6 equal pieces. Roll each piece into a ball and set aside for 15 minutes, covered, to rest.

4. On a lightly floured work surface, roll out the first 2 balls of dough, one at a time, to circles about 18 inches in diameter. Place in the oiled pan, brushing each layer with melted butter, letting the edges of the phyllo hang over the sides. Roll the remaining 4 balls of dough into 14- or 15-inch cir-cles. Layer them, one at a time, in the pan, brushing each layer generously with butter and sprinkling each layer with 2 tablespoons of each of the cheeses.

5. Spread the chicken filling evenly over the last phyllo sheet and roll up the excess phyllo to form a thick rim all around the pie. Dissolve the semolina in the chicken broth and mix to remove any lumps. Whisk in the eggs. Season if desired with a little salt and pepper. Pour this mixture evenly over the sur-face of the pie and tilt the pan so that it goes all over. Place the pie in the oven and bake until the phyllo is golden and the top set and nicely browned, 50 min-utes to 1 hour. Remove from the oven, let cool slightly, and serve.

The pie may also be made with commercial phyllo. For every sheet of homemade phyllo use 2 to 3 sheets of commercial phyllo.

Ground Lamb Pie from Ioannina

KIMADOPITA IOANNINAS

 Makes one 14-inch pie; 8 to 10 hearty servings or about 16 *meze* servings

Several pies in the northern Greek repertoire call for meat or vegetables—usually zucchini—and a béchamel-like sauce in the filling. The meat pies are generally festive pies; in fact, meat pie is usually the food of good fortune at New Year's in Epirus, the dish into which a coin is inserted for good luck. There are similarities between this and the next recipe for Epirote Shepherd's Meat Pie (page 160). But there are differences, too. This recipe has a decidedly urban feel to it—the spice, the béchamel-like sauce, the construction all seem somehow elaborate and fancy. This pie isn't rustic like the others.

1½ pounds lamb shoulder, boned and ground (have your butcher do this), the bones reserved separately
Salt to taste
2 medium red onions, quartered
6 cups water
¾ cup (1½ sticks) unsalted butter
2 medium red onions, finely chopped
Freshly ground black pepper to taste
1 cinnamon stick
1 recipe Basic Homemade Phyllo Dough (page 453) or commercial phyllo, at room temperature
1 tablespoon fine semolina flour
1 cup milk, at room temperature
4 large eggs, lightly beaten

1. Place the lamb bones, quartered onions, and water in a large pot and bring to a boil. Season lightly with salt. Simmer for 1 hour, skimming and discarding the foam that forms on the surface. Strain the broth through a fine-mesh strainer, discarding the bones but reserving the onions and liquid separately.

2. In a large, heavy skillet or large, wide pot, heat 3 tablespoons of the butter over medium heat and cook the chopped onions, stirring, until translucent, 5 to 7 minutes. Increase the heat to medium-high, add the ground lamb, and cook until the meat is no longer pink. Add 2 cups of the lamb broth, season with salt and pepper, and add the cinnamon stick to the skillet. Cover and simmer over medium-low heat until all the liquid has been absorbed, about 15 to 20 minutes. Remove the cinnamon stick and let the mixture cool slightly.

3. Lightly oil a 14- or 15-inch round baking or pizza pan that is 2 inches deep. Preheat the oven to 350°F.

4. On a lightly floured work surface, using your palms, roll the dough into a long rope about 1½ inches thick. Divide into 8 equal pieces. Roll each piece into a ball and set aside for 15 minutes, covered, to rest. In a small saucepan, melt all but 1 tablespoon of the remaining butter.

5. On a lightly floured work surface, roll the first 3 balls of dough, one at a time, into circles about 18 inches in diameter. Place in the oiled pan, brushing each layer with melted butter and letting the edges of the phyllo hang over the side. Roll the next ball of dough into a circle about 14 or 15 inches in diameter and place in the pan. Spread the meat mixture evenly over it.

6. Place the onions reserved from the broth in a food processor fitted with a steel blade or in a blender and pulverize. Heat the remaining tablespoon butter in a saucepan over medium heat and stir in the semolina. Stir with a wooden spoon until lightly golden. Pour in the milk and ½ cup of the remaining lamb broth, season with salt and pepper, and stir over low heat until the sauce thickens, about 10 minutes. Remove from the heat, cool slightly, mix in the pulverized onions, and vigorously stir in the eggs. Spoon the sauce evenly over the meat in the pan.

7. Roll the remaining 3 balls of dough into 14- or 15-inch circles and layer them over the filling, brushing each sheet with melted butter. Gather up the edges of the phyllo and roll around the inner perimeter of the pan to form a rim. Take a sharp knife and make a few incisions in the surface of the phyllo. Place in the oven and bake until the phyllo is golden and crisp and the pie separates from the sides of the pan, 50 minutes to 1 hour. Remove from the oven, let cool for 30 minutes in the pan, and serve.

The pie may also be made with commercial phyllo. For every sheet of homemade phyllo use 3 to 4 sheets of commercial phyllo. See directions (page 455) for more details on how to work with frozen phyllo.

Shepherd's Meat Pie

EPIROTIKI KREATOPITA

Makes one 14- or 15-inch pie; 8 to 10 servings

This pita *is not dissimilar to the meat pie from Ioannina (page 159). It is a more rustic version, but then renditions of this dish are found all over Epirus, from Metsovo, the Vlach stronghold, to Zagori, where many Sarakatsans have settled. It is often made at New Year's and served like* vassilopita, *the traditional sweet New Year's bread with the coin inserted for good luck.*

2 pounds lamb shoulder, with bones, preferably
    from a year-old lamb
5 large onions, quartered
Salt to taste
1 recipe Epirote phyllo (page 453) or commercial
    phyllo, at room temperature
Cornmeal as needed
¾ cup (1½ sticks) unsalted butter, melted
6 to 8 large eggs, lightly beaten

1. Place the meat and onions in a large pot and pour in enough water to cover by about 2 inches. Bring to a boil, season with salt, and reduce the heat to low. Simmer for about 2 hours, skimming the foam off the surface, until the meat is so tender it falls off the bone. Remove the meat with a slotted spoon and set aside. Strain the broth, reserving both the liquid and the onions. Run the onions through a food processor fitted with a steel blade or a blender to pulverize. Pull the meat off the bones, shredding it into small pieces.

2. On a lightly floured work surface, using your palms, roll the dough into a long rope about 1½ inches thick. Divide into 7 equal pieces. Roll each piece into a ball and set aside for 15 minutes, covered, to rest.

3. Preheat the oven to 400°F. Place an aluminum or nonstick 14- or 15-inch round baking or pizza pan that is 2 inches deep upside down on the bottom of the oven so that it heats, almost like a makeshift griddle. Dust the bottom of a large round tray with cornmeal and have a bowlful of cornmeal handy.

4. Lightly dust a large work surface with flour. Flatten the first ball of dough slightly on the flour with your palms. Sprinkle the surface lightly with flour. Using a rolling pin, roll the ball into a circle 14 or 15 inches in diameter. Place on the tray sprinkled with cornmeal and dust the top amply with cornmeal, too. Cover and set aside. Repeat this with 2 more balls of dough.

5. Bring the tray over to the oven and have another empty tray handy. Open the oven, pull out the hot upside-down pan, and place a sheet of phyllo over it. Slide immediately back into the oven and bake just long enough for the phyllo to stiffen and get some color, 3 to 4 minutes. Using kitchen tongs or a 2-pronged fork, flip the phyllo sheet over to bake the other side. As soon as it turns a pale golden, remove from the pan and set aside on the other tray. Repeat with a second and third sheet. When done, remove the pan from the oven and set aside to cool. You will need it again. Reduce the oven temperature to 375°F. Let the pan cool and oil it.

6. On a lightly floured work surface, roll out another ball of dough, this one to a circle about 18 inches in diameter. Place it in the bottom of the pan, with its edges hanging over the sides. Drizzle 1 to 2 tablespoons of the melted butter over its surface. Roll out 3 more balls of dough to circles 18 inches in diameter. Place them over the bottom sheet, drizzling each with 1 to 2 tablespoons melted butter.

7. Break up the prebaked phyllo into irregular pieces about an inch or so wide and long. Sprinkle these on the bottom of the pie over the buttered phyllo and spread the meat filling over them. Drizzle the remaining melted butter over the meat. Gather up the excess phyllo and roll it up to form a rim around the inner perimeter of the pie.

8. Mix the onions with 1½ cups of the reserved lamb broth and stir in the beaten eggs. Season with a little salt. Pour this mixture over the lamb and place in the oven. Bake until the pastry is golden and the pie set, about 50 minutes. The egg-and-broth topping should also be golden when the pie is done. Remove from the oven, let cool slightly, and serve.

⊙ Chicken Pie from Zagori (Kotopita Zagorou): Follow the directions, replacing the lamb with a large, preferably free-range, chicken.

MEAT

Despite the hundreds of thousands of sheep, the goats, and the indigenous game, meat never figured prominently on the traditional shepherd's table in Epirus. Poverty and religion are the reasons why. For one, sheep were too dear to slaughter just for the sake of an ordinary meal. Alive, they provided much in the way of basic income, from their milk to their cheese to their wool. Second, the religious fasts were obeyed faithfully and occasions for eating meat were few and far between. In traditional shepherding communities, and especially among the Sarakatsans, the feasts occurred on Easter; on the feast day of Saint George, the traditional first day of their springtime migrations toward the summer pastures; on the Assumption on August 15; on the feast day of Saint Demetrios, in October, just at the time when shepherds were preparing to leave their summer abodes for lowland pastures; and, finally, at weddings and family name days.

Buttery Lamb with Sorrel and Onions

ARNI ME LAPATHA

 Makes 4 to 6 servings

A *delicious dish combining the region's 3 most prized ingredients—lamb, good butter, and sorrel, Epirus's national green.*

2½ pounds lamb shoulder, trimmed of fat and
    cut into stewing pieces
½ cup all-purpose flour
6 tablespoons unsalted butter or sheep's milk
    butter
1 cup chopped red onion
1 cup chopped spring onions or scallions
2 large garlic cloves, minced
2 pounds sorrel, trimmed, chopped, and washed
1 cup chopped fresh flat-leaf parsley
½ cup snipped fresh dill
Salt and freshly ground black pepper to taste

1. Dredge the lamb pieces in the flour and tap off the excess. Heat 3 tablespoons of the butter in a large, wide pot or Dutch oven over medium-low heat and cook the onion, spring onions or scallions, and garlic until wilted, about 10 minutes. Remove from the pot with a slotted spoon and set aside.

2. Add another 2 tablespoons of the butter, heat it over medium-high heat until it bubbles up and add the lamb. Brown the lamb, stirring to color on all sides. Add the onions and garlic back to the pot and stir to combine with the lamb. Add the sorrel, parsley, and dill and stir to combine. When the greens have cooked down, after 10 to 12 minutes, season with salt and pepper. Add enough water to come about two-thirds of the way up the contents of the pot. Cover and simmer over low heat until the lamb is fork-tender, about 1½ hours. Just before removing from the heat, swish in the remaining tablespoon butter and adjust the seasoning with salt and pepper if desired.

Meatballs Simmered with Leeks and Celery

KEFTEDES PRASSOSELINO

 Makes about 32 meatballs or
    6 to 8 servings

T*his recipe was given to me by the caretaker in the Monastery of Aghios Nikolaos in Metsovo. It is a northern Greek dish, found in Epirus and Thessaly but also in parts of Macedonia.*

For the meatballs
1 pound ground veal
1 pound ground lamb
1 large onion, finely chopped
3 tablespoons sweet *trahana* (see page 456)
2 tablespoons finely chopped fresh mint
½ cup finely chopped fresh flat-leaf parsley

2 teaspoons sweet paprika

Salt and freshly ground black pepper to taste

2 large eggs

For the vegetables

6 tablespoons unsalted butter

3 large leeks, white and tender green parts,
    washed well and cut into 2-inch pieces

2 to 3 celery stalks, to taste, cut into 2-inch
    pieces

1 to 2 teaspoons sweet or hot paprika, to taste

Salt and freshly ground black pepper to taste

1. Make the meatballs: Combine the veal, lamb, onion, *trahana,* mint, parsley, paprika, salt, pepper, and eggs in a large bowl and knead well. Let stand, covered, in the refrigerator, for 1 hour. Remove. Shape into golf ball–size meatballs. Set aside until ready to use.

2. Heat 4 tablespoons (½ stick) of the butter in a large skillet over low heat and cook the leeks and celery, stirring, until translucent, 7 to 10 minutes. Season with the paprika, salt, and pepper and toss to combine. Add the meatballs, toss everything together, and pour in enough water to come about two-thirds of the way up the meatballs. Cover and simmer over low heat until the meatballs are cooked and the vegetables very tender, about an hour. Check the liquid level and add more to the pot during cooking if necessary to prevent scorching. A few minutes before removing from the heat, add the remaining 2 tablespoons butter and tilt the pan back and forth to melt it and distribute it all over. Remove from the heat, let cool slightly, and serve.

Meatballs Baked with Yogurt

KEFTEDES ME YIAOURTI

 Makes 4 servings

A classic Epirote dish and again one that uses the region's ever-important dairy products in unexpected ways.

1½ pounds ground veal

2 large red onions, finely chopped

2 garlic cloves, finely chopped

½ cup finely chopped fresh flat-leaf parsley

1 teaspoon dried Greek oregano

Salt and freshly ground black pepper to taste

2 tablespoons red wine vinegar

1½ cups plain or Mediterranean-style yogurt,
    drained (see page 459)

2 large eggs, lightly beaten

1. Combine the meat, onions, garlic, parsley, oregano, salt, pepper, and 1 tablespoon of the vinegar in a large bowl and knead with your hands to combine well. Set aside, covered, in the refrigerator, for 1 hour. Preheat the oven to 375°F and oil a medium 2-inch-deep ovenproof glass or ceramic baking dish.

2. Shape a golf ball–size piece of the meat mixture into a 1½-inch meatball and place in the dish. Repeat with the remaining mixture. Bake, turning occasionally, until browned on all sides, about 30 minutes. Beat the yogurt, eggs, and remaining tablespoon vinegar together and pour over the meatballs, tilting the dish so that the mixture goes all over. Continue baking until the yogurt sets, another 15 to 20 minutes. Remove from the oven and serve hot.

Lamb's Liver Sautéed with Spinach and Croutons

SIKOTARIA ME SPANAKI KAI PSOMI

 Makes 4 *meze* servings or 2 main course servings

Another unusual dish and one that calls for the second-best-loved green in the region, spinach.

Salt to taste
1 lamb's liver, trimmed of membranes, washed, and patted dry
3 tablespoons unsalted butter
2 cups finely chopped scallions or spring onions
1 to 2 fresh green garlic stalks, to taste (see Note) or 2 large garlic cloves, minced
1 pound flat-leaf spinach, shredded and washed well
Freshly ground black pepper to taste
1½ cups plain croutons
2 tablespoons chopped fresh mint
½ cup chopped fresh flat-leaf parsley

1. Bring a medium pot of salted water to a boil and blanch the liver until it changes color, about 3 minutes. Remove from the water and cut into 1-inch cubes.

2. Heat the butter in a deep skillet over medium-low heat and cook the scallions or spring onions and garlic, stirring, until wilted, about 7 minutes. Add the cubed liver and cook until lightly browned, 5 to 7 minutes. Add the spinach, toss to combine, and cook down to half its volume, 5 to 7 minutes. Season with salt and pepper and add the croutons. Reduce the heat to low and simmer until the liver is tender and the pan juices absorbed, about 35 minutes. Five minutes before removing from the heat, add the herbs and stir to combine.

Adjust the seasoning with salt and pepper and serve hot.

✳ **NOTE** Fresh garlic is available in spring from some specialty greengrocers.

Aromatic Chicken Stewed with Sweet and Hot Peppers

PIKANTIKO KOTOPOULO ME PIPERIES

 Makes 4 to 6 servings

Another Balkan dish filled with sweet and hot peppers and the ubiquitous shepherds' butter.

6 tablespoons unsalted butter or sheep's milk butter
One 2½- to 3-pound chicken, cut into serving pieces
3 large onions, sliced
2 to 3 garlic cloves, to taste, minced
4 large green bell peppers, cut into ½-inch-wide rings
Salt and freshly ground black pepper to taste
¼ teaspoon ground allspice
½ teaspoon ground cloves
½ teaspoon ground cinnamon
1 to 2 small dried hot peppers, to taste
1½ cups peeled, seeded, and chopped tomatoes (canned are fine)

1. If desired, remove and discard the chicken skin. Rinse and pat the meat dry. Heat 3 tablespoons of the butter in a large, wide pot or Dutch oven over medium-high heat and sear the chicken pieces, in batches if necessary, until lightly browned on all sides, 7 to 8 minutes. Remove from the pot with a slotted spoon and set aside.

2. Add another tablespoon or two of the butter to the pot and cook the onions, garlic, and bell peppers, stirring, over medium heat until wilted, 7 to 8 minutes. Place the chicken back in the pot. Season with salt and black pepper, stir in the allspice, cloves, cinnamon, and hot peppers, and pour in the tomatoes. Add enough water to barely cover the chicken. Cover, reduce the heat to low, and simmer slowly until the chicken is very tender and the sauce thick, about 1½ hours. Just before removing from the heat, swirl in the remaining butter. Serve hot.

Rabbit with Garlicky Brown Butter Sauce and Walnuts

KOUNELI KAPAMAS

 Makes 4 to 6 servings

Thick, garlic-infused roux-based sauces are found all over the north of Greece and in parts of the Peloponnesos, too. Recipes similar to this one go by the name lagoto *in the Peloponnesos; in Kastoria, Macedonia, there is an unusual dish called* maskouli, *made with chicken and a very similar "white"* skordalia *but without the walnuts; and in Epirus two interesting dishes call for this rich, garlicky sauce—the* kouneli kapamas *here and a crayfish dish from the lake of Ioannina (see page 166).*

One 3½- to 4-pound rabbit, cut into serving
　　pieces
Salt to taste

5 tablespoons unsalted butter or sheep's milk
　　butter
Freshly ground black pepper to taste
6 garlic cloves, peeled
½ pound shelled walnuts, coarsely chopped
¼ to ½ cup red wine vinegar, to taste
2 tablespoons all-purpose flour

1. Rinse and pat the rabbit dry. Place the rabbit in a large pot and pour in enough water to cover the rabbit by 1 inch. Season with salt. Bring to a boil, reduce the heat to medium-low, cover, and simmer until tender, about 50 minutes. Remove the rabbit with a slotted spoon, strain the broth, and reserve.

2. Heat 3 tablespoons of the butter in a large, heavy skillet over medium-high heat. Season the cooked rabbit with salt and pepper and brown in the butter, 7 to 8 minutes. Set aside, covered, to keep it warm.

3. In either a large mortar or a food processor, pulsing on and off, pound or process the garlic and walnuts together until mealy. Add the vinegar by tablespoons, tasting as you go, until you reach the desired degree of sharpness. Transfer the mixture to a serving dish and set aside.

4. Heat the remaining 2 tablespoons of butter in a large saucepan over low heat. As soon as it melts, bubbles, and turns light golden brown, add the flour and stir vigorously with a whisk until the flour turns golden, 2 to 3 minutes. Pour in 2 cups of reserved rabbit broth in a slow, steady stream, whisking all the while. Keep stirring the sauce until it is thick and creamy. Season with salt and pepper.

5. To serve, pour a little of the sauce onto a large serving platter and place the rabbit pieces on top. Drizzle a little more sauce on top and sprinkle with a little of the walnut-garlic mixture. Serve the remaining sauce in a gravy boat or bowl and the remaining walnut-garlic mixture in a separate bowl.

FISH AND SEAFOOD

The rushing rivers and mountain lakes of Epirus provide lots of different fish and shellfish. The most prized are river trout and an indigenous salmon trout, both of which used to ply these mountain rivers in great quantities but now are increasingly scarce. In their place, farmed trout has taken over, for Epirus is one of the main regions in Greece where trout farming is a flourishing business. The trout is part and parcel of the fish lore up here, and to this day at the banks of rivers and in small villages bordering rivers, one is bound to find a taverna that serves it.

But there are other fish, too, worth noting. Eels, for one, which are another local specialty and which abound in the coastal waters along the Ambracian Gulf, in northwestern Greece. The gulf provides some other delicacies, too, most notably a large local species of blue-veined shrimp.

Besides the standard coastal fare of seafood *meze* and whole fresh fish grilled on a barbecue, some interesting cooked dishes call for fish, such as stewed eel or gray mullet, which also abounds in the Ambracian Gulf, baked with greens.

The next few recipes are among the mainstays of Epirote fish and seafood cookery.

Crayfish with Walnut–Garlic Sauce

KARAVITHES TOU GLYKOU NEROU ME SKORDALIA

 Makes 4 to 6 servings

16 crayfish or jumbo shrimp
1 large onion, peeled
2 celery stalks
½ cup white wine vinegar
3 to 4 fresh oregano sprigs, to taste
½ teaspoon black peppercorns
Salt to taste

For the sauce
4 large garlic cloves, peeled
Salt to taste
1 cup finely ground walnuts
3 tablespoons extra-virgin olive oil
2 to 3 tablespoons red wine vinegar, to taste

1. Wash the crayfish. Place the onion and celery in a large pot of water. Pour in the white wine vinegar and bring to a rolling boil. Add the oregano and peppercorns and season with salt. Add the crayfish and boil until bright red. Remove the crayfish with a slotted spoon and set aside. Reserve the crayfish stock.

2. Remove the crayfish meat from the tails and set aside. Place the shells in a food processor fitted with a steel blade and pulse to grind slightly. Place the ground shells in the crayfish stock and boil until the stock is reduced to about 3 cups. Strain through a fine-mesh sieve and set aside.

3. Make the sauce: Process the garlic, a little salt, and the walnuts together in a food processor fitted with a steel blade until ground. Add the olive oil and red wine vinegar in alternating spoonfuls, pulsing all the while, until the mixture is damp and mealy. Slowly add 1 cup of the hot stock in a stream, pulsing on and off to combine. Add more stock, again in a slow, steady stream, until the sauce drops off a spoon in big clumps; it should be pourable but thick, like loose oatmeal. Adjust the seasoning with additional salt or vinegar if desired.

4. Spoon a little of the sauce into a large, deep bowl or platter and place the crayfish on top. Spoon a generous amount of the remaining sauce over them and serve the rest separately in a gravy boat.

Fish Baked over Spinach

PSARI PSIMENO PANO SE SPANAKI

 Makes 4 to 6 servings

This dish appears in several variations throughout Epirus. In Ioannina it is commonly found with eels, while elsewhere, especially along the coast, grey mullet is the preferred fish.

2½ pounds grey mullet (4 to 6 fish) or other
　　medium fish suitable for baking, cleaned
Salt to taste
Juice of 2½ large lemons, or more to taste
2 pounds flat-leaf spinach, trimmed, chopped,
　　and washed well
4 to 6 scallions or spring onions, to taste, white
　　and tender green parts, finely chopped
2 to 3 fresh green garlic stalks, to taste (see
　　Note), finely chopped, or 2 garlic cloves,
　　minced
Freshly ground black pepper to taste
½ cup extra-virgin olive oil
1 teaspoon sweet paprika

1. Season the fish inside and out with salt and drizzle with the juice of 2 of the lemons. Cover and set aside in the refrigerator for 30 minutes.

2. Place the spinach, scallions or spring onions, and fresh garlic in a large colander and sprinkle with salt. "Knead" the mixture with the salt, rubbing it between the palm of one hand and the holes of the colander to wring out as much liquid as possible. Do this for about 10 minutes, until the mixture is wilted and macerated. Meanwhile, preheat the oven to 350°F. Lightly oil an ovenproof glass or ceramic baking dish. Spread the greens mixture on the bottom of the dish and season, if needed, with additional salt and the pepper. Place the fish on top of the greens. Pour the olive oil over the fish and greens and sprinkle the fish with the paprika. Bake, turning the fish once to cook evenly on both sides, until the fish is fork-tender and the greens cooked, about 25 minutes. Remove from the oven, sprinkle with the remaining lemon juice, and serve.

✳ **NOTE** Fresh garlic is available in spring from some specialty greengrocers.

Trout Pan-Fried with Butter and Wine from Arta

PESTROFA TINGA

 Makes 2 to 4 servings

2 pounds trout, cleaned
Salt and freshly ground black pepper to taste
5 tablespoons unsalted butter
2 medium onions, coarsely chopped
1 cup chopped fresh flat-leaf parsley
½ cup dry white wine
Juice of 1 large lemon

1. Season the trout with salt and pepper and set aside. Heat 3 tablespoons of the butter in a large, heavy skillet over medium-low heat and cook the onions, stirring, until translucent, about 7 minutes. Add half the parsley and stir until soft, another 2 to 4 minutes. Place the trout over the onions in the skillet. Cover and simmer over low heat for 8 to 10 minutes, then turn to cook on the other side. Six or 7 minutes before the trout is done, pour in the wine. When the fish is cooked, set aside, covered, to keep it warm and cook the pan juices down for a few more minutes.

2. In a small skillet, heat the remaining 2 tablespoons butter over medium heat and cook the remaining parsley, stirring until soft.

3. Place the trout on a serving platter with the onion mixture on top and pour on the hot butter and parsley. Sprinkle with the lemon juice and serve.

SWEETS

It isn't surprising that masters of phyllo, as Epirote cooks are, would also have devised numerous sweet pies that call for the ingredients most readily available. Epirote pastry chefs are famous for phyllo desserts such as baklava. Many of them spent years abroad as pastry makers in Constantinople, where they honed the art of making phyllo and syrup-soaked desserts even further.

To my mind, though, it is the more rustic, strictly regional sweets that are more interesting, sweets filled with milk-based custard, with other dairy products, and even with rice and nuts. It is these homey desserts I have concentrated on in the handful of recipes that follow.

Sweet Milk Pie from Ioannina

YIANNIOTIKI GALATOPITA

 Makes 8 servings

Galatopita, *milk pie, is one of the great surprises on the Greek dessert table. It is almost totally unknown outside Greece, rarely seen in restaurants, yet in a large swath of the country—namely, in Epirus, Roumeli, and Thessaly—it is probably one of the defining regional specialties. When made well it is a delicious, smooth, and creamy milk-custard pie with a beautiful caramelized top.*

6 large eggs
1½ cups granulated sugar
1 teaspoon pure vanilla extract
1 teaspoon ground cinnamon

5 cups whole milk

1 cup fine semolina flour

5 tablespoons unsalted butter

6 sheets commercial phyllo, defrosted and at
room temperature (see page 455)

4 to 6 tablespoons confectioners' sugar,
as needed

1. In a large bowl, using an electric mixer, beat together 4 of the eggs and 1¼ cups of the granulated sugar until the mixture is smooth. Add the vanilla and beat for a few seconds. In a small bowl, combine 2 tablespoons of the remaining granulated sugar and the cinnamon and set aside.

2. Lightly butter a 14-inch round or 14- by 11-inch baking pan that is 2 inches deep and set aside. Preheat the oven to 350°F.

3. Scald the milk in a large saucepan and remove from the heat. Pour the semolina into the hot milk in a slow, steady stream, stirring it vigorously all the while to keep it from clumping.

4. Place the milk-and-semolina mixture back on the burner over very low heat. Keep stirring and slowly pour the egg mixture into the milk. Stir until thick and creamy. Remove from the heat and stir in 2 tablespoons of the butter.

5. Melt the remaining 3 tablespoons butter in a small saucepan. Layer the first phyllo sheet on the bottom of the buttered pan so that the edges hang over the side. Brush with a little melted butter. Repeat with the next 2 sheets. Sprinkle the cinnamon sugar over the third layer. Top with the remaining 3 sheets phyllo, again so that they hang over the sides of the pan. Spread the semolina custard into the pie and pat it down with a spatula so that the surface is even. Roll the excess phyllo around the perimeter of the filling to form a rim. Beat the remaining 2 eggs and 2 tablespoons granulated sugar and pour this over the surface of the

pie. Bake until the filling is set and light golden, about 50 minutes. Remove from the oven, let cool slightly, and sprinkle with the confectioners' sugar just before serving.

"Strudel" Epirote Style

STROULLIA

 Makes 12 to 14 servings

This unusual dessert pie is an old recipe from the Zagori, given to me by a local folklorist named Eleni Skourti. She says that she remembers the pie from when she was a girl and that its name most likely is a transliteration of strudel, *a dessert many of the region's denizens came into contact with in their trade and travels through the greater Balkans. I have adjusted the recipe a little, calling for commercial phyllo over handmade because it is so very difficult to get the handmade variety sufficiently thin. This pie also traditionally calls for a local buttermilk cheese called* giza, *which is impossible to find outside farmhouses in the region. I have substituted unsalted Greek* anthotyro, *farmer's cheese, or ricotta and buttermilk together, which are available in specialty markets in America and which make for the closest substitute. You can also use the soft, slightly sour cheese called quark.*

3¼ cups unsalted fresh Greek *anthotyro*,
ricotta, or farmer's cheese

½ cup buttermilk

10 small eggs

10 sheets commercial phyllo, defrosted and at
    room temperature (see page 455)
10 teaspoons extra-virgin olive oil
2 cups sugar

1. Lightly oil an 18- by 12-inch baking pan. Cut a sheet of parchment paper to fit the bottom of the pan and place in the pan. Oil the parchment. Preheat the oven to 375°F.

2. In a large bowl, combine the cheese, buttermilk, and eggs and mix well. Have the phyllo sheets stacked and covered with a clean towel. Remove the first one and place it horizontally in front of you. Brush with 1 teaspoon of the olive oil and sprinkle with about 3 tablespoons of the sugar. Dot the surface of the phyllo with approximately 3 heaping tablespoons of the cheese-and-egg mixture and spread it out a little with a spatula. You don't have to worry about covering the whole surface since the filling will spread as it bakes. Roll up the phyllo to form a fairly tight cylinder and place it seam side down in the baking pan. Repeat with the remaining phyllo, olive oil, and filling, placing the cylinders snugly next to one another in the pan. Sprinkle the top of the *stroullia* with a little water to keep the phyllo from cracking during baking. Bake until the pastry is golden, 50 minutes to 1 hour. The sugar will caramelize and bubble up a bit. Remove from the oven, let cool slightly, and cut the cylinders on the bias like baklava. Serve either warm or at room temperature.

Sweet Rice and Raisin Pie

RIZOPITA

Makes one 18-inch pie;
10 to 12 servings

Versions of this dish appear throughout Epirus and Thessaly. The first time I had it was in Metsovo, where it is made with the addition of walnuts and is one of the classic sweets on the Lenten table. Elsewhere it is also eaten during Lent, but in parts of Epirus it is made in celebration of wedding engagements or as a gift to newlyweds. Sometimes the pie is sweetened with syrup, sometimes not. This particular recipe is from Ano Pedina in the Zagorohoria.

¼ cup extra-virgin olive oil
1 cup short-grain rice
Salt to taste
2 cups water
½ cup sugar
1 cup dark raisins
2 teaspoons ground cinnamon
1 recipe Epirote phyllo (page 453) or 1 pound
    commercial phyllo, at room temperature
    (see page 455)

1. Heat 2 tablespoons of the olive oil in a large skillet over medium heat and cook the rice, stirring, until it is coated and glistening, about 3 minutes. Season lightly with salt. Add the water, reduce the heat to low, and simmer the rice until all the liquid is absorbed and the rice is al dente, 8 to 10 minutes. Remove from the heat. Stir in the remaining 2 tablespoons olive oil, the sugar, raisins, and cinnamon. Set aside.

2. Lightly oil an 18- by 12-inch baking pan. Preheat the oven to 350°F.

3. If using homemade phyllo, divide the dough into 8 equal balls. Roll the first ball into a circle about 20 inches in diameter. Place in the pan and brush lightly with oil. Repeat with the second ball. Spread about ¾ cup of the filling over the second phyllo sheet. Roll out another 4 sheets. Layer in the pan, brushing each lightly with oil and spreading about ¾ cup of the filling over each of them. Pat the pie down a little with your palms. Roll out the remaining 2 sheets and place on top, brushing them, too, with olive oil. Score the pie into serving pieces. Sprinkle the top phyllo sheet with a little water and bake until golden, about 1 hour and 15 minutes. Remove from the oven, let cool for 25 to 30 minutes, and serve.

If working with commercial phyllo, layer 6 sheets on the bottom, brushing each with oil. Then, as directed, make 4 layers of phyllo, spreading each with ¾ cup filling. Place 3 sheets of phyllo on top to cover the pie, brushing each with oil. Bake as directed. Remove from the oven, let cool for 25 to 30 minutes, and serve.

⊙ Sweet Rice Pie from Metsovo (Rizopita apo to Metsovo): Reduce the amount of sugar in the filling to 2 tablespoons and add 1 cup chopped walnuts. Proceed as directed, but as the pie is baking, prepare a syrup: Combine 2 cups sugar with 2 cups water in a medium saucepan and bring to a boil. Reduce the heat to medium-low, add 2 teaspoons fresh lemon juice, and simmer for 12 to 15 minutes. Remove from the heat and let cool. Pour the cooled syrup over the hot pie when it comes out of the oven.

Prune Spoon Sweet

DAMASKINO GLYKO

 About 1 quart

Sweet and sour plums used to grow all over Epirus and western Macedonia, but many have been lost to more profitable crops. Nevertheless, there are many local recipes that still call for them. The Vlachs especially use both sweet and tart prunes in many of their dishes. This dessert is a specialty of Epirus, especially in the area around Zagori. It was given to me by my guide in the area, Eleni Skourti. Similar recipes for prunes in syrup can also be found farther south in Thessaly. Serve it as one would all spoon sweets—on a small plate accompanied by a tall glass of cold water.

6 cups sugar
3 cups water
2½ pounds pitted prunes
Juice of 1 lemon

1. In a large pot, bring the sugar and water to a rolling boil. Reduce the heat to medium-low and simmer until the syrup is thick, about 15 minutes. Add the prunes to the pot and bring back to a simmer. Cook the prunes in the syrup until the whole mixture is thick, about 10 minutes. Remove from the heat and let stand for 8 hours or overnight.

2. Later that day or the next day, reheat. Add the lemon juice and simmer over low heat until the mixture is very thick, 20 to 30 minutes. Remove from the heat and spoon the hot sweet into clean, hot jars. Cover tightly, let cool, and refrigerate.

Thessaly

A Sense of Place and Palate

Thessaly, the great plain of Greece, a soft, giant green-and-gold checkerboard of wheat, corn, and cotton, flanked by the massive, snow-capped peaks of the Pindus Mountains in the west and Mount Olympus in the north, has been forever intertwined with the culture, commerce, and life of all the north of Greece. The Thessaly plain, the center of Greece, with Larissa as its big urban heart (coastal Volos is the region's capital), essentially connects the isolated mountains of Epirus and western Macedonia with the rest of the country. Thessaly contains all the beauty of Greece in concentrated form—mountains, rivers, plains, and the sea all coincide here.

In the western part of Thessaly, the itinerant shepherds of Epirus traversed the Pindus every autumn to make their way to winter shelters in the villages along the plain. By 1960, many settled in the plain. Whole towns are still populated by Vlachs, Sarakatsans (see "Epirus," beginning on page 133), and other pastoral peoples, most of whom have long since forfeited their nomadic lifestyle for farming and commerce. The food in the region is a reflection of those pastoral roots; indeed, Thessaly's cuisine shares much with the cookery of Epirus. It is no accident, for example, that Thessaly's kitchen boasts as many savory pies as Greece's remote northwestern corner. Western Thessaly was traditionally poorer than the eastern, coastal part of the region. That is no longer the case, thanks to the agricultural wealth brought on by intensive grain farming. In western Thessaly, corn used to be the traditional staple crop; in the east it was wheat. Butter and lard—shepherds' products—were the traditional fats; in the east it was olive oil, from fertile Mount Pelion's groves.

There are, in other words, two fairly distinct cuisines in Thessaly: that of the inland plain and that of the coast and Pelion. You can sense the importance of meat just by walking around Larissa, smack in the heart of the plain, where the sharp, enticing aromas emanating from grills in action waft around every street corner. Skewered meats—beef, lamb, and pork—are a common sight in many local tavernas.

In the repertoire of home cooking, the recipes for stewed or roasted lamb and beef are endless. Many, in fact, such as meat stewed with prunes, with eggplants, with pickled cabbage, and more, are similar to dishes found in parts of Macedonia. The old recipes of Thessaly are mainly a litany of long-boiled mutton or barren ewes, specialties among the pastoral communities of Epirus and Roumeli, too.

Tradition has spawned a particular predilection for offal in Thessaly, and there are dozens of recipes for organ meats. Tripe, especially beef tripe, is a local delicacy. In Tyrnavos, as well as in other towns throughout the region, *skebetzidika,* or triperies—literally, "caul" houses—have long had an important place in the local dining scene. There are also many dishes for both beef and lamb liver, usually stewed with herbs and tomato. Offal is also an ingredient in some unusual savory pies, such as one from Tyrnavos that calls for a filling of sautéed sweetbreads, herbs, and cheese.

Nowadays, the prevalence of meat might have as much to do with tradition and geography (the plain provides one of the few large grazing grounds for cattle) as it does with economics, because as people become more affluent their diets change, usually for the worse. They forfeit the legumes and vegetables of their peasant past, disparaging them as the foods of sustenance, and embrace red meat instead.

Besides meat, though, animals have provided a rich variety of dairy products and cheese. Thessaly is one of the main cheese-making regions in Greece, home to excellent feta and center for the production of many traditional yellow cheeses. Cheese makes its way into myriad savory pies and is used to enrich a variety of stews and casseroles.

Grains also play their part in the cuisine here. Before wheat became the staple crop in Thessaly, corn was king. Up until the early 1960s, for example, most bread was made with cornmeal, while wheat flour was reserved for savory pies, the Sunday dish and the festive food, or *prosforon,* the bread offering for church. There was also a whole host of dishes based on cornmeal, many of which were part of the shepherds' repertoire, that used to belong to the traditional diet but have been lost over time. Among some of the most intriguing old recipes were certain pies, such as the *trahanoskepasti,* made with a cornmeal batter, *trahana,* and leftover pork. Another favorite old local dish is *bourani,* a kind of porridge made with cornmeal and nettles or, in some completely different versions, with rice and tomatoes.

Wheat was almost always used to make all the specialty and holiday breads, the decorative wedding bread rings, and more. It was also used to make *trahana,* the tiny pebblelike pasta kneaded with either buttermilk or regular milk and found throughout the Balkans. In Thessaly it was one of the most common foods, savored in both its sweet and sour versions with equal enthusiasm (see page 456 for more on *trahana*). Grains, especially semolina and corn were also used as the basis for the region's main sweet, halvah. There are several renditions of halvah throughout Thessaly—again, not all of them unique to the region. Some are strictly local specialties though. Among them is the famed *halva Farsalon,* or *sapoune* (lather), made with cornstarch, topped with a burned-sugar crust, and savored for its unctuous, smooth texture. I've read about old recipes for other halvah as well, such as one made with sesame seeds and one with chickpeas, but I have never been able to corroborate the information. There is one local sweet made with ground chickpeas that I have included here.

But there is more here besides grain and shepherds' customs. Mount Pelion and the coast have provided Thessaly with other, more Mediterranean fare. Pelion is carpeted with fruit orchards and olive groves, massive oaks and beech, and great, gnarled, water-sucking sycamore trees. Wild mushrooms and wild greens abound. Here one will find fiddle-head ferns in early spring, pickled and blanched and either eaten as a salad or pan-fried and tossed with a little vinegar. Here, too, in the local mountain tavernas and in the home kitchen, one of the best *mezethes* in Greece is made: *tsitsiravla,* the pickled tender buds of wild pistachio trees. Mount Pelion is famed for its apples, too, and is one of the country's premier orchards. One local variety, the *firiki,* small, firm, oblong, and extremely fragrant, is considered the best. One of the loveliest spoon sweets in the whole country is made with it.

Then there is Volos itself, the region's capital, a quaint but vital coastal city, where people take their evening constitutional along the lively seaside promenade, where daily life buzzes with all the activity of a port town, with its seafaring commerce and its large fishing boats that come to dock every morning selling their catch in an ad hoc market along the docks. The coast and the Pagasitic Gulf where Volos is perched teem with sea life. Most local fish recipes are pretty much what one finds all over the country—simply grilled or baked, in other words—but there is also a wealth of fish and seafood *mezethes* to be enjoyed.

Volos's claim to culinary fame is its *tsipouradika,* where local eau de vie and literally hundreds of different *mezethes* are served in a most unusual way. Most of the time, one doesn't exactly order (you can if you want to, but it isn't tradition); instead, with each round of firewater, the waiter brings out a different small plate of food, increasingly more interesting as the drinking progresses. Many of the

mezethes are based on seafood and vegetables, and might include things such as local shrimp grilled with garlic and tomato, or seafood *saganaki* in a small skillet with spices and cheese, grilled squid stuffed with local cheese, and more.

The Thessaly Pantry

CHEESE AND DAIRY PRODUCTS

Like Epirus, Thessaly has always had a strong dairy tradition, mainly, as mentioned earlier, because so many itinerant shepherds made their winter abodes here, and then finally settled. Larissa and Trikala are two of the major cheese-making centers of Greece, especially for yellow cheeses such as *kasseri, kefalo-graviera,* and *graviera.* In Trikala, one old local New Year's custom speaks tomes about the importance of dairy production in the local way of life: Local women would make their way to the nearest communal spring and endow it with gifts of butter, cheese, lard, milk, and wheat, a wish to the Powers That Be for the year ahead to be prosperous, that the milk might run like water, in other words, and assure the production of all the rest.

The shepherds, not only in Thessaly but all over the north, whether they were Vlachs, Sarakatsans, Koutsovlachs, or any other tribe, live among their own extended kin in a kind of familial hierarchy. It was not unusual for a clan to drive a flock of five to ten thousand sheep. But there was always one head *tselinga,* or shepherd, who arranged the trade and finances of the rest of the clan. Life centered around the production of milk, cheese, butter, wool, and meat, probably in that order. While the actual milking was taken care of en masse by each shepherd for his own flock, the cheese making wasn't. The shepherds would sell their milk to a cheese maker, and produce cheese only for their own immediate needs at the end of the summer, when there wasn't enough milk for it to be commercially important.

The basic cheese was feta (see page 139). With the whey that remained, they made one of several by-products: either *myzithra,* a fresh or dried cheese; butter; and from the residuals of that—from the buttermilk, in other words—a host of other soft, sour cheeses: *tsalafouti, xynotyri, galotyri,* and *xynogalo.* All are discussed in detail in the cheese section of Epirus.

There were and are still many other cheeses produced in Thessaly. Among them:

Boukouvala This is really a primitive cheese snack for kids, made by kneading fresh cheese and bits of crumbled leftover bread.

Graviera Agrafon *Graviera,* the mild yellow semihard sheep's milk cheese, is made in many parts of Greece. This is one of the best, made exclusively in the high altitude villages of the Agrafa Mountains, the extention, really, of the Pindus, which straddle Thessaly, Roumeli, and Epirus. Agrafa's *graviera* is a bit harder and whiter than that of Crete or Naxos, but is made in pretty much the same way. The flavor of this *graviera* is sweet, and aficionados say that all the aromas of the local mountain flora are captured within it.

Kasseri A relative of the pan-Balkan *kashkeval, kasseri,* a sheep's milk or combination sheep's and goat's milk cheese, is one of the best-known Greek yellow table cheeses, and one of the most commercial. It is not exclusive to Thessaly, but so much is produced here that the cheese has become closely

associated with the region. Although production has become sadly standardized, a few traditional *kasseri* meisters ply their trade in Thessaly and produce wonderfully supple, sweet cheeses. They say the best *kasseri* is produced from extremely fresh milk, about an hour old, and unpasteurized. It is this milk that gives the cheese its characteristic sweet taste.

Kasseri, like mozzarella, is a kneaded or pulled cheese, and therein lies the skill of the cheese maker. In brief, once the curds have been set and drained, they are cut again, fitted into baskets, and dipped in a hot water bath. The curds soften in the baskets, are salted and kneaded, drained, and kneaded again very well. Finally, the cheese is cut into twenty-two-pound pieces, and shaped and drained in large, wheel-shaped molds for about fifteen hours. It is then aged for at least three months.

Tsalafouti This is a soft, pungent, naturally fermented sheep's milk cheese made in August, when the milk is rich and the mercury high. The milk is boiled and then left to rest for a few days until it ferments and thickens naturally. *Tsalafouti* is often made over several months, with more and more milk added to the early batches. It is the shepherd's cream cheese, and eaten as such—spread on bread and savored as a snack.

TRAHANA

Trahana is made all over Greece, but in Thessaly (as well as in Roumeli and Epirus) its place on the local table is probably more important than anywhere else, save perhaps for Crete. *Trahana* is a tiny, pebblelike pasta made by combining milk and flour or milk and bulgur and shaping the mixture into small pieces, which are dried in the sun and then crumbled. It is always made in August, the hottest month of the year, to ensure that it dries as quickly as possible. There are two basic kinds of *trahana,* sour and sweet, and each, at least on Greece's mainland, has its own specific use. You will find a detailed discussion of *trahana* on page 456.

SAUSAGES

The original country sausages of Thessaly were a specialty of Mount Pelion. They were thin, short lamb sausages, about the size of a standard cigar, seasoned with cumin, paprika, and black pepper. Times have changed, and the country sausages are hard to come by now. The region has retained its sausage fame, nevertheless, even though most now come from proper manufacturers in Volos and are made with beef rather than lamb or, at best, with a combination of beef and lamb.

The Recipes

VEGETABLES

Since much of the cookery of Thessaly resembles what is also found in central Greece and in parts of the North, I have tried to isolate the few dishes that, in my own experience at least, seem strictly local. Some I've found by just eating around in Volos and elsewhere throughout Thessaly; others come from home cooks. Although the selection is small by comparison with vegetable entrees elsewhere, I think it is an interesting amalgam.

Warm Cauliflower Salad with Tuna and Olives

KOUNOUPIDI ME TONO KAI ELIES

 Makes 4 servings

I *was served this dish as a* meze, *after a few shots of* tsipouro *in a local Volos* tsipouradiko. *I can't say whether it is a real regional specialty or the creation of one local cook.*

1 medium head cauliflower, cut into very small florets
One 4-ounce can imported tuna packed in olive oil, rinsed and drained
1 small red onion, halved and sliced
1 cup Amfissa olives, not pitted, rinsed and drained
¼ cup extra-virgin olive oil
2 tablespoons red wine vinegar
Salt and freshly ground black pepper to taste

1. Steam the cauliflower until soft (Greeks like it very soft), 12 to 15 minutes. Drain.

2. Place the warm cauliflower, tuna, onion, and olives in a medium serving bowl and combine well. Mix together the olive oil and vinegar in a small bowl to emulsify. Pour over the salad. Season with salt and pepper, toss to coat well, and serve.

Eggplant Slices Rolled with Ground Beef

MELITZANES ROLA ME KIMA

 Makes 4 servings

One of the classics of Volos and a dish that probably came to the city in the early part of the twentieth century with the Asia Minor refugees. Similar dishes are found all over Macedonia.

½ cup extra-virgin olive oil

2 large onions, minced

½ pound ground beef

1 cup peeled, seeded, and finely chopped tomatoes (canned are fine)

4 to 5 allspice berries, to taste

1 cinnamon stick

Salt and freshly ground black pepper to taste

2 large eggplants (about 2 pounds total), cut lengthwise into ⅛-inch-thick slices

1 cup all-purpose flour

1 cup grated *kefalotyri* cheese or any hard yellow cheese

½ cup whole milk

1. Heat 3 tablespoons of the olive oil in a large, heavy skillet over medium heat and cook the onions, stirring, until wilted and translucent, 7 to 8 minutes. Add the ground beef and brown all over. Pour in the tomatoes, season with the spices, salt, and pepper, and simmer, covered, until the sauce is thick and the meat browned through, adding ½ to 1 cup water if necessary to prevent scorching. This will take about 20 minutes over low heat. Remove the cinnamon and allspice and set the mixture aside to cool.

2. Dredge the eggplant slices lightly in the flour, tapping off any excess. In another large, heavy non-stick skillet, heat 2 tablespoons of the remaining olive oil over medium heat and cook a few eggplant slices at a time, turning, until they are soft and pliant and very lightly browned but not overcooked, 1 to 2 minutes on each side. Set them aside on paper towels to drain. Repeat with the remaining eggplant slices and olive oil.

3. Preheat the oven to 350°F. Place a heaping teaspoon of the meat mixture in the center bottom of an eggplant slice. Roll it up carefully and place seam side down in a medium, ovenproof glass baking dish large enough to hold all the filled eggplants snugly in one layer. Repeat with remaining eggplants and filling, placing each roll next to the others so that they do not unfold.

4. Mix the grated cheese and milk together in a small bowl and spoon it over the rolled eggplant. Bake until the cheese is melted, bubbling, and golden, about 25 minutes. Remove from the oven, let cool slightly, and serve.

Oregano Fish Roe and Patties

RIGANOKEFTEDES PELIOU

 Makes about 30 patties

My friend Costas Skylas, a native of Volos and an expert forager in all things wild and edible, took me for a ride up Mount Pelion, which he knows like the back of his hand. It was a Sunday in early May, and we left his house in Ano Volos, in Pelion's foothills, and headed up a way past the tourists' main stop, Makrynitsa. We were going on a jaunt to pick wild spring oregano. The whole mountain was in full bloom. We pulled the car over to the side of the road, tramped for a few minutes over shin-high weeds and *wildflowers, and stopped in a place he knew of where wild oregano grew in abundant patches.*

The day's lesson was going to be about the making of riganokeftedes, *oregano patties, a strictly local, strictly regional dish and one of the few in all of Greek cuisine that calls for the use of fresh—not dried—oregano. Actually the name is a bit of a misnomer, since these little patties are really more like the* tarama *(carp roe) fritters that are common all over the country. The only exception and the whole key is the fresh oregano. "It has to be young oregano," Costas said. "And you always pick it before it flowers. It has the best flavor then."*

When we got back to his house, he made the little patties for me, doing something with the herb that I thought was odd. He blanched the sprigs before cleaning off the leaves. I liked them well enough when he finally served them, with a host of other mezethes *and his own* tsipouro, *but I thought the flavor had been diluted. So, when I went back to my own kitchen, I reworked the recipe a little bit, cleaning the oregano very well but not bothering to blanch it. The result, I think, is a much more flavorful patty. The herb balances very well with the strong taste of the roe. The result is a* meze *that is at once subtle but with a tangy undercurrent.*

1½ pounds waxy potatoes, peeled, washed, and
 cut into chunks

Salt to taste

30 large leafy fresh oregano sprigs, preferably
 Greek

¼ pound *tarama* (carp roe)

1 large red onion, finely chopped

Freshly ground black pepper to taste

1 large egg

⅔ to 1 cup bread crumbs from stale rustic bread
 or more as needed

All-purpose flour for dredging

Olive or other oil for frying

1. Bring the potatoes to a boil in ample salted water and simmer, uncovered, over medium heat until fork-tender, about 20 minutes.

2. Run your thumb and forefinger down along the oregano stems to strip off the leaves. Discard the stems. Wash the leaves in a colander and place on a kitchen towel to dry. Finely chop, either by hand or in a food processor.

3. When the potatoes are soft, drain them and let them cool slightly. Mash them by hand, while still hot, with a fork or potato masher. Add the *tarama,* oregano, and chopped onion. Season with salt and pepper and mix in the egg. Knead the mixture to combine well, adding a little bit of the bread crumbs at a time until the mixture is substantial enough to be formed into patties without falling apart. Adjust the seasoning with more salt and pepper if necessary.

4. Spread the flour over a large plate. Shape about 1 heaping tablespoon at a time of the mixture into a flat little patty about 1½ inches in diameter. Dust with flour on both sides. Heat 1 inch of oil to almost smoking in a large, heavy skillet over high heat. Fry the patties, in batches, until browned, about 2 minutes on each side. Remove with a slotted spoon and drain on paper towels. Serve hot, lukewarm, or at room temperature.

SAVORY PIES

The savory pie tradition is a formidable one in Thessaly, as important a part of the local cuisine as it is in Epirus, Roumeli, and parts of Macedonia, because the plains were the winter abodes of itinerant shepherds and, as I have said before, pies are shepherds' food. When many of these once nomadic peoples settled in Thessaly, their culinary customs took root here.

Crustless Buttermilk and Cornmeal Pie

XINOGALATOPITA

 Makes about 6 servings

Pies like this are made all over the northwestern part of Greece.

2 cups crumbled Greek feta cheese
2 cups buttermilk
2 cups coarse yellow cornmeal
1 teaspoon salt
½ cup (1 stick) unsalted butter, melted

1. Preheat the oven to 375°F and lightly oil a 13- by 9-inch ovenproof glass baking dish.

2. Combine the feta and buttermilk in a large bowl. Mix together the cornmeal and salt and stir them into the buttermilk mixture to form a dense but loose dough. Cover with plastic wrap and let rest for 15 minutes.

3. Spread the mixture in the baking pan and even it out with a spatula. Using the tips of your fingers, make indentations all over the dough like little potholes. Drizzle the melted butter all over the surface and bake the pie until the cornmeal is set and the pie comes away from the sides of the dish, 45 to 50 minutes. Remove from the oven, let cool slightly, and cut into squares to serve.

Meat Pie with Pork and Leeks

ΑΕΤΟΡΙΤΑ

 Makes 8 to 10 servings

Pork and leeks usually are cooked together in one of the most familiar stove-top dishes of Greece's North. Here the classic combination is prepared as a pie, mirroring the ingenious way home cooks can adapt almost anything.

2 pounds bone-in pork shoulder
Salt to taste
4 large leeks, white and most of the green parts, washed well and coarsely chopped
¾ pound Greek feta cheese, crumbled
2 large eggs plus a third if the filling is dry (depends on the texture of the feta)
Freshly ground black pepper to taste
1 pound commercial phyllo pastry, at room temperature (see page 455), or 1 recipe Basic Homemade Phyllo Dough (page 453), divided into 6 balls, each rolled out to 20-inch circles or 18- by 23-inch rectangles (depending on your pan), and stacked
½ to ¾ cup extra-virgin olive oil, as needed

1. In a large pot, bring the pork to a boil in enough water to cover it by 1 inch. Season with salt, reduce the heat to medium-low, and simmer until it is falling off the bone, 1½ to 2 hours. Skim the surface of the pot as the pork boils to remove any foam. Replenish the water during cooking if necessary. Remove the pork and set aside. Place the leeks in the same water, cover, and simmer until very soft, about 20 minutes. Drain.

2. While the leeks are simmering, bone the pork and shred the meat. Combine the pork and cooked leeks in a large bowl. Add the feta and eggs and mix well. Season with salt and pepper and set aside.

3. Preheat the oven to 375°F and lightly oil a 14- or 15-inch round or a 13- by 18-inch rectangular baking pan that is 2 inches deep.

If using commercial phyllo, open the package and place the sheets in front of you (see page 455). Keep them covered. Place 7 sheets, one at a time, on the bottom of the baking pan, brushing each with olive oil and letting the excess hang over the sides. Spread the filling evenly over them and top with another 4 to 6 sheets of pastry, brushing each with olive oil as well.

If using homemade phyllo, layer 3 sheets on the bottom of the pan, brushing each with oil, letting the excess hang over the sides. Spread on the filling and top the pie with 3 more sheets, brushing each with oil as well.

Gently press the pie down with your palms and join the excess bottom and top sheets of phyllo together to form a decorative rim around the perimeter of the pie. Sprinkle the top with a little water and score the pie into serving pieces without cutting all the way through from one end of the pan to the other. Place in the oven and bake until golden, 50 minutes to 1 hour. Remove from the oven, let cool slightly, and serve.

Sweet Chicken Pie with Raisins and Cinnamon

KOTOPITA GLYKIA

  Makes 8 to 10 servings

One 3-pound stewing chicken
Salt to taste
¾ to 1 cup extra-virgin olive oil
5 medium red onions, finely chopped
3 large eggs, lightly beaten
½ cup golden raisins
2 teaspoons ground cinnamon
Freshly ground black pepper to taste
1 pound commercial phyllo, defrosted and at
    room temperature (see page 455), or 1 recipe
    Basic Homemade Phyllo Dough (page 453),
    divided into 6 balls, rolled out to 20-inch
    circles or 18- by 23-inch rectangles
    (depending on your pan), and stacked

1. Bring the chicken to a boil in a large pot of salted water. Simmer, skimming the surface as needed to remove any foam, until the chicken is cooked, about 1 hour. Drain and set aside to cool. Remove and discard the skin. Bone the chicken and shred the meat; set the meat aside.

2. Heat ¼ cup of the olive oil in a large, heavy skillet or large, wide pot over medium heat and cook the onions, stirring, until translucent and wilted, about 7 minutes. Add the chicken meat to the skillet and cook all together over low heat for 10 to 12 minutes. Set aside to cool. Mix in the eggs and raisins and season with the cinnamon, salt, and pepper.

3. Preheat the oven to 375°F and lightly oil a 14- or 15-inch-round or 13- by 18-inch rectangular baking pan that is 2 inches deep.

If using commercial phyllo, open the package

and place the sheets in front of you (see page 455). Keep them covered. Place 7 sheets, one at a time, on the bottom of the baking pan, brushing each with some of the remaining olive oil and letting the excess hang over the sides. Spread the filling evenly over them and top with another 4 to 6 sheets of pastry, brushing each with olive oil as well.

If using homemade phyllo, layer 4 sheets on the bottom of the pan, brush each with olive oil, letting the excess hang over the sides. Spread the filling over them and top with 2 more sheets, brushing each with olive oil as well.

Gently press the pie down with your palms and join the bottom and top sheets of phyllo together to form a decorative rim around the perimeter of the pie. Sprinkle the top with a little water and score the pie into serving pieces without cutting all the way through from one end of the pan to the other. Place in the oven and bake until golden, 50 minutes to 1 hour. Remove from the oven, let cool slightly, and serve.

Trahana Pie

TRAHANOPITA

 Makes about 8 servings

Savory pies made with trahana *are a mainstay on the tables of central and northern Greece. It's not that* trahana *does not appear elsewhere in Greece, but here, and especially in Thessaly and Epirus, it is made and used the most. The rich dairy traditions ensured that there was always plenty of milk, and* trahana *was one way to preserve it for the winter. It also made for a quick, easy, and nutritious meal. In most of the rest of Greece,* trahana *is added to savory pie fillings in small amounts, the way one adds a little rice or bulgur, to help absorb the liquid from squash, pumpkin, or greens. But in Thessaly and Epirus* trahana *is the main ingredient. The number of* trahana *pies is endless in these two regions. The one that follows is one of my favorites.*

2 cups water

2 cups milk

2 cups sour *trahana* (see page 456)

¼ cup extra-virgin olive oil or unsalted butter, melted

Salt to taste

1½ pounds Greek feta cheese, crumbled

5 large eggs

1 recipe Basic Homemade Phyllo Dough (page 453), divided into 6 balls, or ½ pound commercial phyllo (see page 455), defrosted and at room temperature

½ cup (1 stick) unsalted butter, melted

1. Bring the water and milk to a boil in a large pot. Add the *trahana* and olive oil or melted butter and season with salt. Simmer over low heat until the *trahana* is soft and most of the liquid has been absorbed, 7 to 10 minutes. Add the crumbled feta, stir well, and continue to simmer for a few minutes, until the cheese begins to melt. Remove from the heat and let cool. Lightly beat 3 of the eggs together and stir them into the *trahana* mixture.

2. Lightly oil a 13- by 18-inch baking pan that is 2 inches deep and preheat the oven to 375°F.

If using commercial phyllo, open the package and place the sheets in front of you (see page 455). Keep them covered. Place 7 sheets, one at a time, on the bottom of the baking pan, brushing each with the melted butter and letting the excess hang over the sides. Spread the filling evenly over them and top with another 4 to 6 sheets of pastry, brushing each with the melted butter as well.

If using homemade phyllo dough, roll out the 6 balls, one at a time, on a lightly floured work surface to rectangular sheets 2 inches larger than the baking pan. Place the first 4 layers inside the baking pan, brushing each with the melted butter, and letting the excess hang over the sides.

Spread the *trahana* filling over the phyllo. Roll out the remaining 2 sheets and brush with butter. Roll the excess phyllo around the perimeter of the pan to form a decorative rim.

3. Beat the remaining 2 eggs together and pour them over the top of the pie. Pour the remaining melted butter over the entire surface and bake until golden, about 50 minutes. Remove from the oven, let cool slightly, and serve.

Scallion and Feta Pie

KREMMYDOPITA

 Makes 10 to 12 servings

Onions always provided a very economical way to fill a pie and hence a whole family's belly. In the North of Greece, the preferred varieties for pie fillings, stews, and roasts have always been scallions and leeks. There are lots of recipes, for example, for lamb or other meats cooked on a plump bed of scallions, spring onions, or leeks, and for leek pies. Here is a variation on the theme. It is essential to use as much of the upper greens as possible.

2 pounds scallions or spring onions
¼ cup (½ stick) unsalted butter
2 cups milk
Salt to taste
1 pound Greek feta cheese, crumbled
1 pound *myzithra* cheese, crumbled
4 large eggs, lightly beaten
Freshly ground black pepper to taste
1 pound commercial phyllo pastry (see page 455), defrosted and at room temperature
¾ cup extra-virgin olive oil

1. Trim away the root ends and the toughest part of the greens. Wash the scallions or spring onions thoroughly and chop. Heat 3 tablespoons of the butter in a wide pot or large, deep skillet over medium heat and cook the scallions or spring onions, stirring, until wilted, 7 to 9 minutes. Pour in the milk, season lightly with salt, reduce heat, and simmer, uncovered, for 6 to 8 minutes, stirring frequently to keep the milk from scorching the bottom of the pot.

2. Remove from the heat and let cool slightly. Mix in the cheeses and the eggs. Season with salt and a little pepper and combine well.

3. Preheat the oven to 375°F and lightly oil a 13-by 18-inch baking pan that is 2 inches deep. Open the phyllo and place on a work surface (see page 455). Cover with a cloth to keep it from drying out.

4. Place the first sheet of phyllo inside the baking pan, allowing it to hang over one edge. Brush with the olive oil. Repeat with the next sheet, aligning it so that it hangs over the opposite edge. Brush with olive oil. Repeat with 6 more sheets, allowing each to hang over one edge in alternating order so that there is enough excess phyllo to roll up and form a decorative rim once the pie is completely assembled. Spread the filling evenly over the phyllo. Cover with 6 more sheets, letting them hang over alternating edges and brushing each with olive oil. Roll up the bottom and top excess phyllo together around the perimeter of the pie to form a ring. Sprinkle the top lightly with water. Melt the remaining tablespoon of butter and pour it on top. Score the pie into serving pieces without cutting all the way to the bottom. Bake until golden, about 50 minutes. Remove from the oven, let cool for 30 to 40 minutes, and serve.

Creamy Eggplant Pie

MELITZANOPITA

 Makes 10 to 12 servings

My mother-in-law introduced me to the eggplant pies of Thessaly. There are many recipes for pies filled with eggplant, and the dish is something of a regional specialty, found very seldom in other parts of Greece. The filling is so substantial that, on first bite, most people think they are eating meat.

3 large eggplants (about 4 pounds total)
Salt to taste
½ cup extra-virgin olive oil
6 large onions, coarsely chopped
½ cup milk
4 large eggs
1 pound Greek feta cheese, crumbled
Freshly ground black pepper to taste
1 pound commercial phyllo (see page 455),
    defrosted and at room temperature
3 to 4 tablespoons extra-virgin olive oil for
    brushing phyllo

1. Peel the eggplants and cut into 1-inch cubes. Place in layers in a colander, sprinkling each layer with salt. Place a plate over the eggplants, place a weight on top of the plate, and leave the eggplants to drain over a bowl or the sink for 1 hour. Rinse with ample water and drain thoroughly. Pat the eggplant cubes dry.

2. Heat the olive oil in a large, wide pot over medium heat and cook the onions for a few minutes, stirring, to soften. Add the eggplant cubes, toss to coat with the oil, and cook, stirring, until the eggplant is tender, about 8 minutes. Remove from the heat and let cool.

3. Beat the milk and eggs together and add them to the eggplant mixture. Add the feta and toss everything together. Adjust the seasoning with additional salt and pepper.

4. Lightly oil a 13- by 18-inch baking pan that is 2 inches deep. Preheat oven to 375°F. Open the phyllo and place on a work surface (see page 455). Cover with a cloth to keep it from drying out. Place the first sheet of phyllo inside the baking pan, allowing the excess to hang over one edge. Brush with olive oil. Repeat with the next sheet, aligning it so that the excess hangs over the opposite edge. Brush with the olive oil. Repeat with 6 more sheets, letting the excess hang over alternating edges so that there is enough excess phyllo to roll up and form a decorative rim once the pie is completely assembled. Spread the filling evenly over the phyllo. Cover with 6 more sheets, letting the excess hang over alternating edges and brushing each with olive oil. Take the bottom and top excess phyllo and roll it up together around the perimeter of the pie to make a rim. Sprinkle the top lightly with water and score the pie into serving pieces without cutting all the way to the bottom. Bake until golden, about 1 hour. Remove from the oven, cool for at least a half hour, and serve.

MEAT

Sausage and Peppers

SPETSOFAI

 Makes 4 main-course servings or
6 *meze* servings

In the tavernas of Makrynitsa and other quaint, if touristed, parts of Mount Pelion, spetsofai *is served in every taverna, as much a part of the local traditions as paella is in Barcelona. The sausages are not what they used to be, though. The original dish calls for fresh, spicy lamb sausage, seasoned with cumin and pepper. Nowadays, most* spetsofai *is made with the commercially produced beef sausage. If you can find lamb sausages, by all means use them. If not, a good, spicy beef sausage will suffice.*

6 tablespoons extra-virgin olive oil
1½ pounds green bell peppers, cut into 1-inch-wide strips
2 pounds firm, ripe tomatoes, peeled, seeded, and coarsely chopped, or chopped canned tomatoes, drained
Salt and freshly ground black pepper to taste
½ teaspoon sugar
2 pounds fresh spicy lamb or beef sausage

1. Heat 4 tablespoons of the olive oil in a large, wide pot over medium heat. Cook the peppers, stirring, for about 5 minutes. Add the tomatoes, season with salt and pepper, add the sugar, and cook the mixture slowly over low heat until the sauce is thick and the peppers wilted and soft, 7 to 10 minutes more.

2. Meanwhile, heat the remaining 2 tablespoons olive oil in a large skillet over medium-high heat and cook the sausages until browned on all sides and cooked nearly all the way through. Remove from the skillet and cut into large chunks. Pour the sausages and their drippings into the pepper mixture, toss to combine, and cook all together for about 10 more minutes. Adjust the seasoning with salt, pepper, and additional sugar if necessary. Serve hot or at room temperature.

Chicken and Celeriac Stew with Egg-Lemon Sauce

KOTOPOULO AVGOLEMONO ME SELINORIZA

 Makes 4 to 6 servings

My friend Sophia Spyrou in Volos comes from a family of great cooks and avid small-scale farmers. Her mother, Kyria Stavroula, a thin, energetic woman in her sixties, prepared this dish for us on a Sunday a few winters ago, after a whole day spent skiing on the nearby slopes of Pelion. This is easy, hearty winter fare.

2 large celeriacs (celery roots)

Acidulated water (see page 458)

⅓ cup extra-virgin olive oil

One 2½- to 3-pound chicken, cut into serving
   pieces

2 large onions, finely chopped

Juice of 2 lemons

Salt and freshly ground black pepper to taste

2 medium eggs

1. Peel, halve vertically, and slice the celeriac, then place it in a bowl of acidulated water to keep it from discoloring.

2. Heat the olive oil in a large, wide pot over high heat and brown the chicken, in batches if necessary, until golden on all sides. Remove with a slotted spoon and set aside. Add the onions, reduce the heat to medium-low, and cook, stirring, until wilted, 5 to 7 minutes. Place the chicken back in the pot with the onions. Remove the celeriac from the acidulated water and add to the pot. Pour in half the lemon juice. Add enough water to come halfway up the contents of the pot. Season with salt and pepper, cover, and simmer the chicken and celeriac

until tender, about 50 minutes. Add more water to the pot if necessary to prevent scorching.

3. Just before removing from the heat, beat the eggs until frothy and add the remaining lemon juice. Take a ladleful of the pan juices and slowly drizzle them into the *avgolemono*, beating it vigorously with a wire whisk or a fork. Pour this into the pot and tilt the pot from side to side so that the sauce goes all over. Remove from the heat and serve.

One-Pot Chicken with Broth-Simmered Noodles and Ground Walnuts

KOTOPOULO ME HILOPITES KAI KARYDIA

 Makes 4 to 6 servings

I don't know if the practice of cooking pasta in broth or pot juices is something that evolved as a way to economize on water, which has generally been scarce in arid Greece, or if it is because the soft, glutinous texture that results—somewhere between a soup and a stew—has always been agreeable to the Greek palate. Versions of this dish are savored all over the north of Greece, as well as in other parts of country, proof enough that there is something to be said for its hearty, soul-warming consistency. This is Greek comfort food.

¼ cup extra-virgin olive oil

2 tablespoons unsalted butter

1 large 4- to 4½-pound chicken, preferably free-
   range, cut into serving pieces

6 large onions, coarsely chopped

Salt and freshly ground black pepper to taste

4 large ripe tomatoes, peeled, seeded, and coarsely chopped, or 1½ cups chopped canned tomatoes

2 tablespoons chopped fresh mint or ½ teaspoon dried

1¼ cups small egg pasta, preferably squares or tubetini

½ cup finely ground walnuts

1. In a large, wide pot, heat the olive oil and butter together over high heat and brown the chicken on all sides until golden, in batches if necessary. Remove with a slotted spoon and set aside. Reduce the heat to medium, add the onions to the pot, and cook, stirring, until wilted and translucent, about 7 minutes. Return the chicken to the pot, season with salt and pepper, and pour in the tomatoes. Add enough water to barely cover the chicken. Cover and simmer until the chicken is very tender, about 1 hour. Add the mint about 10 minutes before the chicken is cooked. Remove the chicken with a slotted spoon and set aside, covered, in a warm oven.

2. Add a cup or more of water to the pot—you'll have to use your own judgment; there should be enough for the pasta to be able to boil, but once done the mixture should be thick and souplike. Add the pasta and simmer until ready. Serve the pasta in a deep platter with the chicken on top, sprinkled with the walnuts.

Chicken Simmered with Roasted Eggplant

KOTOPOULO ME PSIMENES MELITZANES

  Makes 4 servings

Eggplant cooked with beef makes for a common stove-top specialty all over the country and a dish most likely brought to Greece with the waves of Asia Minor immigrants in the early 1920s. Here, chicken is the meat of choice. This dish is unusual because of the way the eggplant is used: first roasted, then added to the pot. When I came across this dish, it reminded me of an ersatz version of hunyar beyendi, *a classic beef-and-eggplant dish from Poli, where the eggplant is roasted and pureed with milk before being added to the pot. This is lighter, easier, and delicious.*

10 to 12 tablespoons extra-virgin olive oil, to taste

One 2½- to 3-pound chicken, cut into serving pieces

3 large, ripe tomatoes, peeled, seeded, and coarsely chopped, or 1 cup chopped canned tomatoes, drained

Salt and freshly ground black pepper to taste

3 large eggplants (about 3 pounds total)

1. Heat ½ cup of the olive oil in a large, wide pot over medium-high heat and cook the chicken until golden all over. Reduce the heat to medium and add the tomatoes. Season with salt and pepper and simmer, covered, for about 5 to 8 minutes, then add enough water to come halfway up the chicken. Keep the heat on low and simmer, covered, for about 30 minutes.

2. While the chicken is simmering, roast the eggplant: Puncture them in several places and place each of them over a low open flame on top of the stove or under the broiler on a sheet pan. Roast them, turning, until their skins are charred and the eggplants are soft on all sides. Remove from the heat and place on a large cutting board to cool until they can be handled. Cut away the stems of the eggplants, slit open the skins vertically, discard as many of the seeds as you can, and remove the pulp, keeping it as intact as possible. Chop the pulp into chunks. This whole process should take about 30 minutes.

3. As soon as you are done, place the eggplant chunks in the pot with the chicken, distributing the pieces evenly. The chicken should be about halfway done. Add the remaining 2 to 4 tablespoons olive oil and a little water if necessary to keep the contents moist. Adjust the seasoning. Simmer over low heat until most of the liquid has been absorbed, the sauce is thick and unctuous, and the chicken is tender, about another 30 minutes. Remove from the heat, let cool slightly, and serve.

Lamb's Liver Stewed with Dill, Butter, and Tomatoes

MAGEIRITSA STEGNI

 Makes 4 servings

Offal tops the list of carnivorous pleasures on Greece's Great Plains, and there are many unusual dishes attesting to the native predilection for organ meats. This is but one, a version of the otherwise traditional Greek Easter "soup" made with very little liquid, so that the end result is thick and sumptuous like a stew.

Salt to taste

1½ pounds lamb's liver, trimmed of membranes

¼ cup (½ stick) unsalted butter

1 bunch scallions, white and tender green parts, coarsely chopped

1½ cups peeled, seeded, and chopped tomatoes, preferably fresh

Freshly ground black pepper to taste

½ to ¾ cup snipped fresh dill to taste

1. Bring a large pot of salted water to a rolling boil and blanch the lamb's liver for 5 minutes. (This is a pretty common technique throughout Greece as a way to rid liver and other organ meats of their heavy aroma. It was also considered more hygienic to blanch it first as opposed to cooking it right away.) Drain and cut into 1½-inch chunks.

2. Heat 2 tablespoons of the butter in a large, wide pot or deep skillet over medium heat and cook the scallions and liver together, stirring, until the scallions wilt and the liver is nicely browned, 7 to 8 minutes. Add the tomatoes, season with salt and pepper, and add enough water to cover the contents of the pot. Cover and simmer slowly over low heat until the liver is very tender and the pan juices thick, about 1 hour. About 10 minutes before removing from the heat, stir in the remaining 2 tablespoons butter and the dill. Remove from the heat and serve.

Baked Beef and Vegetable Casserole with Cheese

KELAIDI

 Makes 4 to 6 servings

This dish, a specialty of Larissa, is great for a lazy weekend. It bakes slowly over several hours, so once it goes into the oven, the cook's work is pretty much finished.

3 pounds bone-in beef shoulder, trimmed of fat and cut into stewing pieces
5 tablespoons extra-virgin olive oil
Salt and freshly ground black pepper to taste
2 large onions, coarsely chopped
4 to 6 garlic cloves, to taste, chopped
6 large green bell peppers, cut into 2-inch-wide strips
4 large ripe tomatoes, peeled, seeded, and coarsely chopped, or chopped canned tomatoes, drained
¼ cup unsalted butter
1 pound Greek feta or kefalotyri cheese, cut into 1-inch cubes

1. Preheat the oven to 325°F. Lightly oil a large ovenproof glass or earthenware casserole dish and place the meat on the bottom. Toss with 2 tablespoons of the olive oil and season with salt and pepper. Place the onions and garlic over the meat, then the bell peppers and finally the tomatoes, seasoning each layer with a little salt and pepper and drizzling 1 tablespoon of olive oil over each. Cut the butter into small pieces and dab it on top.

2. Cover the dish with a sheet of aluminum foil and bake slowly until the meat is very tender, about 3 hours. Every half hour or so, pat the surface of the mixture down with a spatula. About 15 minutes

before the dish is ready—test the meat for doneness—add the cubed cheese, pushing some into the casserole with a fork or blunt knife and leaving about half the pieces scattered over the surface. Remove from the oven, let cool slightly, and serve.

Beef Smothered with Onions, Raisins, and Paprika

CAPAMAS VOLOU

 Makes 4 to 6 servings

Capamas is the name of a dish that claims dozens of different versions all over the country. It can be anything from a fragrant cinnamon-tinged lamb stew to a whole leg of lamb cooked in a large pot on top of the stove. Here capamas is a deliciously rich and sweet beef dish, perfect for cold winter nights.

1 to 2 tablespoons unsalted butter, as needed
1 to 2 tablespoons extra-virgin olive oil, as needed
3 pounds bone-in beef shoulder or any other cut suitable for stewing, trimmed of fat and cut into large pieces
6 medium onions, halved and thickly sliced
1 heaping teaspoon sweet paprika
Salt and freshly ground black pepper to taste
½ cup golden raisins
½ to 1 teaspoon sugar, to taste

1. Heat the butter and olive oil together in a large stewing pot or Dutch oven over medium-high heat and brown the meat on all sides. Add the onions, stir to coat with the butter and oil, then add the paprika and mix all together for a few minutes. Season with salt and pepper. Add enough water to barely cover the meat. Place the lid on the pot and simmer over low heat until most of the pan juices have been absorbed and the meat is very tender, about 1½ hours.

2. Meanwhile, plump the raisins for 15 minutes in a small bowl of warm water. About 10 minutes before removing the meat from the heat, add the raisins and their soaking water to the pot. Taste and adjust seasoning if necessary with sugar or additional salt and pepper. Serve hot.

Goat and Fennel Stew

KATSIKAKI ME MARATHO

 Makes 4 to 6 servings

I came across this recipe in a small book on the cooking of Mount Pelion. Wild fennel is not always easy to find in the United States, unless one has access to a specialty produce vendor, so I've given an alternative that approximates its flavor—fennel bulb, dill, and ouzo.

½ cup extra-virgin olive oil
One 3½-pound goat shoulder, trimmed of fat
    and cut into stewing pieces
5 fresh green garlic stalks (see Note), cut into
    2-inch pieces, or 4 scallions, white and most
    of the green parts, cut into 2-inch pieces,
    plus 3 large garlic cloves, thinly sliced
1 tablespoon tomato paste
Salt and freshly ground black pepper to taste

2 cups finely chopped fresh wild fennel leaves, or
    2 medium fennel bulbs, quartered and thinly
    sliced, plus 1 cup snipped fresh dill, and
    ⅓ cup ouzo

1. Heat the olive oil in a large, wide pot over medium-high heat and brown the goat meat on all sides, about 8 minutes. Remove with a slotted spoon and set aside.

2. Add the fresh garlic or the combination of scallions and garlic and toss to coat in the oil over medium heat. If using fennel bulbs, add them at this point and cook them together with the fresh garlic or scallions stirring, until wilted, 5 to 8 minutes.

3. Add the tomato paste to the pot and stir. Return the meat to the pot, season with salt and pepper, and pour in enough water to barely cover the contents of the pot. Whether using wild fennel or dill, add it now. Cover the pot and simmer the stew until the goat is very tender, about 1½ hours. About 15 minutes before removing from the heat, mix in the ouzo if using it. Remove from the heat, let cool slightly, and serve.

✳ **NOTE** Fresh garlic is available in spring from some specialty greengrocers.

FISH AND SEAFOOD

Many of the fish and seafood dishes of Thessaly belong to the region's *meze* traditions. Volos is famous for its ouzeries, and ouzo calls for strong-flavored, often salty dishes. I found these recipes by eating (and drinking) my way through the city's ouzo emporiums.

Cuttlefish Salad with Sweet Red Peppers, Capers, and Pickles

SOUPIA SALATA ME KOKKINES PIPERIES KAI TOURSI

 Makes 4 main-course servings or 6 *meze* servings

2½ pounds large cuttlefish, cleaned
   (see page 462)
Salt to taste
2 large red bell peppers, coarsely chopped
2 tablespoons small capers, rinsed and drained
½ cup pickled dill gherkins, rinsed and drained
½ cup chopped fresh flat-leaf parsley
¾ cup extra-virgin olive oil
4 to 6 tablespoons red wine vinegar, to taste
Freshly ground black pepper to taste

1. Cut the cuttlefish into 1½-inch-wide rings. Bring a medium pot of lightly salted water to a boil and blanch the cuttlefish until al dente, about 8 minutes. Remove from the water, rinse under cold water and drain well. Place in a large serving bowl.

2. Toss in the chopped peppers, capers, pickles, and parsley, reserving 1 tablespoon parsley for garnish. Mix together the olive oil and vinegar in a small bowl until emulsified and pour over the salad. Season with salt and black pepper and toss to combine well. Garnish with the remaining parsley and serve.

Whole Small Fish Cooked with Peppers

PSARI SPETSOFAI

 Makes 4 servings

A *variation on the classic sausage-and-pepper recipe from Pelion, without the sausage.*

Salt to taste
3 to 3½ pounds small red mullet or mackerel, gutted and cleaned
Olive oil or a combination of olive and other vegetable oil for frying
All-purpose flour for dredging
3 tablespoons extra-virgin olive oil
2½ pounds green bell peppers, cut into 1-inch-wide strips
2 to 3 garlic cloves, to taste, minced
4 large ripe tomatoes, grated (see page 459)
Freshly ground black pepper to taste

1. Salt the fish inside and out. Heat about ½ inch of oil in a large, heavy skillet. Dredge the fish lightly with flour, tapping off any excess. Fry the fish, in batches if necessary, turning once, until golden on both sides and cooked through. Remove with a slotted spoon and drain on paper towels. Pour off the oil, discard, and wipe the skillet clean.

2. Heat the extra-virgin olive oil in the skillet over medium heat and cook the peppers and garlic together, stirring, until the pepper strips are wilted, about 7 minutes. Add the grated tomatoes and season with salt and black pepper. Cover and cook until the sauce is thick and the peppers soft, 15 to 20 minutes. Uncover and add the fish to the skillet, spooning some of the sauce over the fish. Cook the fish and pepper sauce together for about 5 minutes, remove from the heat, let cool slightly, and serve.

Fish Stewed with Small Onions, Tomatoes, and Cinnamon

PSARI STIFATHO

 Makes 4 to 6 servings

Stifatho, *like* spetsofai, *usually refers to a meat-based dish. This is another favorite collected on recipe reconnaissance missions through the ouzo houses of* Volos.

4 pounds large bream or sea bass (about 2 fish), cleaned and gutted
Salt
¼ cup extra-virgin olive oil
3 cups small boiling onions, peeled
3 to 4 garlic cloves, to taste, chopped
1½ cups peeled, seeded, and chopped tomatoes (canned are fine)
2 bay leaves
1 small cinnamon stick
Freshly ground black pepper to taste

1. Cut the fish into 1½-inch wedges, reserving the heads, if desired, for soup. Salt lightly and set aside covered in the refrigerator. Heat the olive oil in a large, wide pot over medium-high heat and add the onions. Reduce the heat to low and cook the onions, turning a few times, until they begin to take on some color and soften, 20 to 25 minutes. Add the garlic and toss all together. Add the tomatoes, bay leaves, and cinnamon stick and season with salt and pepper. Cover and simmer for about 25 minutes, checking the pot occasionally and adding a little water if necessary to prevent scorching.

2. Add the fish to the pot and stir gently to combine with all the other ingredients. Cover and simmer until the fish is cooked through and all the flavors have melded, 10 to 15 minutes. Remove from the heat, let cool slightly, discard the cinnamon stick and bay leaves, and serve.

SWEETS

There isn't much of a dessert tradition in Thessaly. Few of the great Greek-Anatolian pastry masters brought their skills to the region as they did to Thessaloniki and Ioannina. Instead, most sweets are home grown; a vast array of spoon sweets is made in the region but, with a few exceptions, the same ones are made in the rest of Greece, too. If there is any difference in taste, it is less a matter of differences in recipes than of the exquisite quality of Mount Pelion fruits. Pelion's small apples, though, are the centerpiece of several regional sweets.

Halvah is something of a regional specialty, perhaps owing to the fact that Thessaly is Greece's granary; halvah is a sweet usually made with flour. A few versions are found specifically in Thessaly.

Cornstarch Halvah

HALVA FARSALON

 Makes 8 to 10 servings

On *roadsides all over Pelion, women set up tables to sell the amber-colored, burned-sugar-topped* halva Farsalon. *Of course, in Farsala, too, on the plain, one is more than likely to run into the sweet, hawked at local pastry and coffee shops.* Halva Farsalon *is unique in that it is made with cornstarch, not semolina. The result is a halvah that has a smooth, jellylike*

texture. The burned-sugar topping adds a nice contrast to the unctuousness of the halvah itself. Sometimes, halva Farsalon *is known as* sapoune—*or "lathered"—because of its smooth consistency.*

1 cup cornstarch
3 cups water
½ cup (1 stick) unsalted butter
2 cups plus 4 to 6 tablespoons sugar, to taste
1 cup blanched whole almonds
Ground cinnamon (optional)

1. Dilute the cornstarch in the water and mix it until it is completely smooth. In a large, wide pot over medium heat, melt the butter. As soon as it begins to bubble, add 2 cups of the sugar in a steady stream, stirring constantly with a wooden spoon. Stir until the sugar turns a light golden color, 8 to 10 minutes.

2. Slowly pour in the cornstarch-and-water mixture, stirring constantly. Keep the heat at medium and stir until the mixture peels away from the sides of the pot and is a deep amber color, another 10 to 15 minutes. Mix in the almonds.

3. Spread the halvah evenly into a large flame-proof serving dish and let it cool. Preheat the broiler. Sprinkle the top of the halvah with the remaining sugar and place the halvah under the broiler 4 to 6 inches from the heat. Broil until the sugar burns a little. Remove from the oven, let cool again, and serve, sprinkled, if desired, with cinnamon.

Grated Apples in Syrup

MILA TRIFTA

 Makes about 1½ pints

This is one of several spoon sweets calling for apples. To serve it, spoon a little into a small bowl and serve with cold water on the side. It is also excellent as a topping for plain, preferably drained (see page 459) yogurt.

The best apples for this recipe and the one that follows are no doubt the firikia *of Pelion, which are small, oblong, firm, and highly aromatic. Any apple may be substituted, but McIntosh comes closest to approximating the taste of* firikia.

3 pounds McIntosh apples
2½ cups water
2 cups sugar
1 teaspoon pure vanilla extract

1. Wash the apples very well. Peel and core them and set aside the skins. Coarsely grate the apples.

2. Place the apple skins in a pot with the water, cover, and bring to a boil. Reduce the heat to medium-low and simmer for 15 minutes. Remove from the heat and strain. Return the water to the pot and add the sugar. Simmer over low heat for 10 minutes. Add the grated apples and continue to simmer until the mixture is thick. Stir in the vanilla. Remove from the heat and place in a large, clean jar with the lid ajar. When the mixture is completely cooled, close the lid and refrigerate. Serve chilled. It will keep up to 3 months if properly stored.

Apple Spoon Sweet

MILO GLYKO TOU KOUTALIOU

 Makes about 2 quarts

Serve this as a spoon sweet, one or two pieces in a small bowl, with a glass of cold water.

6 cups sugar

2 cups water

5 pounds small McIntosh apples, peeled, cored, and halved

1 cinnamon stick

5 to 6 cloves, to taste

½-inch-wide strips of zest from 1 orange or mandarin

Place the sugar and water in a large, heavy pot over medium-low heat until the sugar melts, stirring while heating. Add the apples, spices, and zest. Simmer until the syrup is thick, about 30 minutes. Remove from the heat. Place the apples and syrup in 4 clean 2-pint jars. Let cool completely in the jars and close tightly. Serve chilled. Keep refrigerated for up to 3 months.

Ground Chickpea–and–Raisin Confection

REVITHATO

 Makes 10 to 12 servings

This interesting dish is very similar to another old recipe from Roumeli, where an ersatz baklava is filled with roasted chickpeas.

1 pound hulled dried chickpeas

3 cups dark raisins

2 large eggs

1 cup confectioners' sugar

1 cup extra-virgin olive oil

2 cups granulated sugar

2 cups water

1-inch strip of lemon zest

1. Soak the chickpeas overnight to soften. Drain well and grind to a coarse meal in a food processor fitted with a steel blade. Remove from the processor. Grind the raisins to a coarse meal and mix together with the chickpeas.

2. Preheat the oven to 350°F and lightly oil a 13- by 18-inch baking pan. Line the pan with parchment paper and lightly brush the parchment with oil.

3. Beat together the eggs, confectioners' sugar, and olive oil and add to the chickpea-and-raisin mixture. Mix well. Spread the mixture evenly in the pan, smoothing it out with a spatula. Bake until the chickpeas are set but not brittle, about 50 minutes.

4. While the confection is baking, make the syrup: Bring the granulated sugar and water to a boil in a small saucepan. Add the lemon zest, reduce the heat to low, and simmer for 10 minutes. Cool the syrup, either by placing it in the freezer or by placing the pot on top of an ice bath in a large bowl.

5. As soon as the chickpea confection is done, remove from the oven and score into bars or diamond-shaped wedges. Pour the cooled syrup over the hot dessert and let it set for at least 2 hours before serving.

Almond Confections from Skopelos

HAMALIA (SKOPELOS)

 Makes about 50 pieces

The islands of the Sporades were once a part of the prefecture of Thessaly. Culturally they share much in common with the coast of Pelion and Volos. I have included this recipe here, as part of the region, partly because it seemed like the best place for it and partly because it is such a classic that I didn't want to omit it.

4 cups blanched almonds
1 cup confectioners' sugar, plus more for dipping
1½ cups orange blossom water

1. Place the almonds in a food processor fitted with a steel blade and pulse until they are a fine meal. Place them in a medium bowl and knead together with the confectioners' sugar and ½ cup of the orange blossom water. The mixture should have the consistency of a dense dough.

2. Preheat the oven to 325°F. Line 2 sheet pans with parchment and lightly butter the parchment. Shape the almond confections into little mounded "fingers" and place in neat rows on the parchment. Bake until just barely golden, about 10 minutes. Remove from the oven and let cool on the sheet pans.

3. When the *hamalia* are completely cooled, dip them in a bowl of the remaining orange blossom water and then in confectioners' sugar to form a hard, packed crust. Store in cookie tins in a cool, dry place for up to 2 weeks.

Macedonia and Thrace

A Sense of Place and Palate

It all comes back now in a roller coaster of diverse images that I have tried to reference and cross-reference in my cook's mind. Macedonia. Vast, in terms of both space and culture. As I crisscrossed from Serres in the eastern reaches of the region to Prespes in the northwestern corner, I couldn't help thinking of the old anecdote about the blind man and the elephant. A blind man gropes his way along an elephant's body. As he touches the legs he asks, "What is it?" He moves farther, feeling parts of the animal's side. "What is it?" he wonders again. He gets to the trunk, another huge unknown. Able to touch only parts here and there, he finds that the whole eludes him, and in the end he never understands what the elephant is. To this itinerant cook, Macedonia is the elephant.

Complex, disparate, and whole all at once. A melting pot of flavors and culinary cultures that expresses itself constantly in all the different cuisines that have rooted themselves in Macedonia's fertile earth, in certain ways melding together yet retaining their individuality, too. The problem is where to begin dissecting them.

Macedonia is the largest single region in Greece, the great northern frontier, bordered by Bulgaria, the former Yugoslavia, and Albania. It is a land sculpted by mountains, valleys, sprawling plains, tiny inlets and coves, rivers, lakes, and the sea. It has always been the ultimate crossroads, "continental" Greece, the bridge between Europe and the East. Cultural—hence gastronomical—exchange has been part and parcel of the region since the time of Alexander the Great in the third century B.C. Thessaloniki, Greece's second-largest city, has thrived without interruption as an urban center and port for two thousand years.

Macedonia has been occupied throughout its history by many different people. Between the first and fourth centuries A.D., the ancient Romans literally linked the region between Europe and the Orient by building the famous Via Egnatia, or Apian Way, a vast overland trade route stretching from the Adriatic to Thessaloniki and

later to Constantinople. The region was frequently trafficked by Christian pilgrims en route to Jerusalem. The world's first hospice, in fact, was established to accommodate them, in the Macedonian town of Edessa at around the turn of the fourth century A.D.

Macedonia has absorbed tribes of neighboring Slavs and Bulgarians, whose mark is still visible in the propensity for certain foods and in the local dialects; of Vlachs, traditionally itinerant shepherds whose native tongue is not Greek but an old latinogenic language, who are the descendants of Roman guards, and who have been settled throughout the mountainous reaches of the region for centuries; and of Turks, whose occupying presence in Macedonia lasted until 1912, after the Balkan Wars returned the region to Greece. Macedonia also has been home to Jews, who, escaping the Spanish Inquisition in the fifteenth century, settled en masse in Thessaloniki—a predominantly Jewish city for much of its modern history—but disappeared in the tragedy of the Holocaust.

In our own times, the single most important historical event, and something that affected the region's table tremendously, was the influx, in 1922, of two million Greek refugees from Asia Minor. They flooded the country as a result of the political upheavals at the time between Greece and Turkey, forced to flee their homes and birthplaces in an exchange of populations that uprooted people all over the Balkans. They settled all over Greece, but the great majority of them settled in the North, in Macedonia and Thrace. The Mikrasiates, as these Asia Minor Greeks are called, changed the face of modern Greek culture and, by extension, of the country's until then simple, agrarian cuisine, bringing with them a blend of bourgeois European sensibilities and Anatolian exoticism.

The Asia Minor Greeks came from cosmopolitan urban centers such as Constantinople and Smyrna, from the depths of Anatolia, from the Black Sea, and from the hinterland tucked today between modern-day Greece, Turkey, and Bulgaria, a region known as Eastern Romylia. These "refugees" were, by and large, of a different socioeconomic class from their brethren in post-Ottoman Greece. Many were educated, well-to-do merchants or well-to-do farmers, and they were inured to the spice, variety, and heady flavors of the East, to the remnants of Byzantium of which they were the keepers and heirs—these were Greeks whose whole history was connected to the shores of present-day Turkey—to the vast wealth of fish from the Bosporus, to the cosmpolitan flavors and bourgeois cooking of Poli (Constaninople) and Smyrna. By now, nearly a century later, all their delicious food, a litany of rice-stuffed dishes, eggplant dishes, wrapped foods such as *dolmathes,* as well as a larder full of fragrant desserts and more, is entrenched in Macedonia's gastronomy—as well as in that of the whole of Greece.

Likewise, those Asia Minor Greeks who emigrated from the Black Sea, or Efxinos Pontos as it is called in Greek, added an equally powerful dimension to the cooking of the North. The Pontioi or Black Sea Greeks came in several waves, some in 1922 and some much more recently, for many back then had left the Turkish side of the Black Sea for its opposite shores in the old Soviet Union, across the Caucasus in Georgia, Azerbaijan, and other places. With the collapse of communism and the harsh economic realities that ensued, the Pontioi began emigrating again, also back to Greece. In the 1990s their numbers swelled. Tens of thousands arrived in Greece, mostly settling in Thessaloniki.

The Macedonian kitchen has embraced all these

different influences, which in turn have trickled down into the cooking of other urban centers. In one respect the region is a bit of a checkerboard. In some villages, for example, almost the entire population is comprised of Greeks who emigrated from the Black Sea—Pontioi—or of Smyrna Greeks, or Polites, Greeks from Constantinople. In some villages, especially in central Macedonia, the opposite is true: Almost no refugees settled in them, leaving the indigenous population and their foodways relatively cloistered.

It does seem to me, though, that there are some distinctions in the palette of flavors between eastern, central, and western Macedonia. In the eastern part of the region (as well as in Thrace), for example, so many dishes are redolent of Asia Minor and Pontian influences, simply because so many refugees settled here: the delicious *soutzoukakia,* spiced meatballs, of Drama; the *akhanes* of Serres, a butter-tinged *loukoumi* (confection) that is a specialty of the city and a legacy of the Turks; the penchant for eggplant, witnessed in at least two great Serres dishes, one a casserole with eggplant and chickpeas, the other eggplant cooked in a pungent walnut-garlic sauce.

In central Macedonia the one thing that seems to stand out more than any other is the distinction between the indigenous and the imported. For example, I was surprised to hear local cooks—really local, that is, in places that didn't see a large influx of immigrants from Asia Minor—declare that cabbage, celery, and chickpeas are never used in the indigenous kitchen; another that *dolmathes* (stuffed grape or cabbage leaves) are totally foreign. But overall such steadfastness is the exception rather than the rule, for the cuisine there has been anything but static.

Some of the most interesting recipes in central

Macedonia are to be found in Naoussa, among them dishes that have evolved out of the region's affinity for, and dependence on, grapes—Naoussa is one of the most important wine-producing regions in Greece. One local specialty is eggplant salad with *agourida,* the juice of sour, unripe grapes (verjuice), which is used in lieu of vinegar or lemon; and the local *meli* or ersatz honey, which is a kind of molasses made from the must of the native *xino-mavro* grape. It is used to preserve spoon sweets of eggplant and pumpkin.

In the western parts of the region, lake fish abound, as do roasted or pickled red peppers and a slew of other local ingredients. The food here seems somehow more Balkan, or Slavic, at least in name. Peppers, for example, are called *tsoutchka* in the local dialect, a word that also means "gossip"—as in caustic-tongued.

The irony, though, is that none of these distinctions is definitive. All over the region, similarities crop up regardless of who is doing the cooking or where. Macedonia is what its name has come to mean in the colloquial: a marriage of many different parts that form a fascinating whole.

THRACE

My trip through Thrace was an adventure into the isolated northeastern frontier of Greece. It was early spring when my friend Nenna Ismirnoglou and I drove the often harrowing coastal road from Thessaloniki to Alexandroupoli, the region's capital, then farther east and north, toward the calm, humid Evros delta, which divides Greece and Turkey. Young soldiers on their tour of duty are everywhere here. The unmistakable air of isolation—or maybe it is dislocation, since so much of

Thrace is populated by former Greek refugees from Asia Minor—permeates everything.

Many people told us that their families settled here to be near their homes in Poli (Constantinople) or in Eastern Romylia, a pocket even farther north and east where Greeks had lived for centuries. They had expected to see their homes again on the other side, but the tide of history was against them. Thrace, like Macedonia, absorbed hundreds of thousands of Asia Minor Greeks after the resetting of boundaries following the Balkan Wars (in 1912), the final demise of the Ottoman Empire, and the eventual political upheavals between Greece and Turkey that led to an exchange of populations in 1922. Thrace, although administratively separate from Macedonia, nonetheless shares many common cultural features.

One thing stands out here, though: Together with a small community on the island of Kos, Thrace is home to several communities of Muslims. Some are Turks who were exempted from the population exchange (as were the Greeks of Imvros and Tenedos), and others are Pomaki, a separate people who have lived in the area of the Rodopi Mountains, both in Greece and Bulgaria, for eons. Add to that sizable numbers of Sarakatsans (once itinerant shepherds, Vlachs, and others, and a picture emerges as complex and multifarious as anywhere else in Greece's north.

We ended up going full circle, up to the place that Greeks call the *trigono*—"triangle"—where Greece, Bulgaria, and Turkey meet. From there we swung around through the impoverished Pomaki villages of the Rodopi Mountains, through villages almost forgotten by time that see virtually no tourists. A few days on the back roads took us to Komotini, a sullen but fascinating provincial city where Greek Christians and Turkish Muslims live side by side, harmoniously; where the *cafeneia* are frequented by both; where the marketplace is a perfect representation of the two groups: on one side are the Turkish shops where women in veils do their daily shopping, while on the other side, miniskirts sway as young Greek housewives go about their daily chores. Finally, we ended our trip in the lovely, well-preserved university town of Xanthi and in the Pomaki villages just north of them.

Our trip was a feast through market bazaars more reminiscent of the East than of anything in Europe, through minaret-studded towns where the dawn and dusk wails of the imam blare over loudspeakers calling the pious to worship. We found entry into the living rooms of home cooks in remote villages, and into the humble abodes of Pomakis, in the poor villages nestled deep in the Rodopi Mountains but also in the wealthier ones outside Xanthi. Sunflowers and tobacco rippled along the roads. Whole towns in the northeast, especially around Vyssi, reeked of garlic—much of Greece's supply is grown here. Brightly kerchiefed Gypsy women sold fresh cow's milk cheese from tins on the edge of every bazaar. Pelicans sat perched in their incongruous nests, usually on the pinnacles of telephone poles.

In the homes of the Greeks we visited nostalgia seemed everywhere present. Not only were they filled with photographs from another life and time, but even today, eighty years after the emigrations, the decor still smacked of another era. Every surface, from the arms of upright old embroidered chairs to wooden commodes, was usually covered with hand-crocheted doilies. Vintage knickknacks from Poli and Smyrna shone on shelves and tabletops. This was one of my most memorable trips into the Greek countryside, and one that revealed much food lore.

There isn't exactly a definable "Thracean" kitchen. Instead, like that of Macedonia, the food in Greece's easternmost province is a checkerboard of the local and the imported. There are large communities of Pontian Greeks up here. Whole towns, just as in Macedonia, were settled by Greeks from specific places in Asia Minor. The cuisine is a potpourri of typical Balkan cooking, filled with paprika-scented recipes and dozens of pickled cabbage dishes, two telltale Balkan pantry items, but it also includes many different preparations calling for bulgur (one of the favorite grain products of Asia Minor Greeks), *trahana,* sesame seeds, tahini, and yogurt. There is even couscous, which locals call *kouskousi,* in Thrace—who knows, perhaps it arrived with the Ottomans, who disseminated it from the farthest western reaches of their empire. It is cooked with chicken and other sauce-laden meats.

Bulgur replaces rice in many dishes. For example, I came across recipes calling for "rice pudding" made with bulgur, and for *"tomatorizo"* or tomato pilaf made with bulgur. The *trahana* up here is nothing like that found in other parts of the country; it is made with the addition of sesame seeds and sweet and hot red peppers. One of the most unusual recipes is *trahana* simmered in grape must. There is a wealth of pies similar to those found in Macedonia, usually with different names, but that call for the same litany of ingredients, such as leeks or cheese. Charcuterie is one of the basics in the local larder, and offal is important on the festive tables. The national dish of Thrace is something called *babo,* a poached sausage filled with beef and pork, bulgur or rice, leeks, and oregano. It is standard fare on the Christmas table.

The desserts stand out as among the most distinct in Greece. Among them are the *soutzouk louk-oum,* a kind of sweet, sugar-dusted "sausage" with a core of shelled walnuts ensconced in a gel made of cornstarch or rice flour, although it is not the sort of sweet one usually makes at home. The *kaimaki* ice cream in Komotini, a luscious full-cream blend of vanilla and mastic (a specialty of Edin's sweet shop on the edge of town), is the best in Greece. There are some interesting Lenten pastries, too, among them the tahini-and-walnut-filled phyllo flutes we ran across in Xanthi.

I managed to get an inkling of the cooking of the Muslim minorities, especially the Pomaki. En route from Dadia, where there is a lovely nature preserve and a group of local women who run the canteen, producing some very authentic food, we went to the small village of Rousso, a Pomaki stronghold. There, we were able to visit the place where locals cook their feasts on holy days. It is called a *"deke,"* and was nothing more than a humble shack with no electricity. Blackened copper pots and cauldrons lay in one corner, together with large, long spoons and some other culinary accoutrements, for the preparation of various porridgelike dishes that make for the communal meals on holidays. We visited the home of one family in Smynthi, a village about eight miles north of Xanthi. The homes here are well kept and modern, nothing like the virtual encampment atmosphere that characterizes some of the villages burrowed deep in the dense Rodopi Mountains. We took our shoes off upon entering, abiding by Muslim custom. From outside their second-floor window, the tall silhouette of the minaret rose high against a warm, pink evening sky. Thin savory pies filled with leeks, rice or potatoes, and eggs, and seasoned with oregano, were among the dishes described to us by the woman of the house (the family did not want to give us their name). Other dishes seemed even more basic: bulgur porridges boiled in milk, *trahana* made with flour and yogurt and eaten as soup with grated cheese, and *arianni,* a refreshing drink made with strained yogurt mixed with cold water and flavored with mint and salt. This is not a Pomaki specialty; all of Thrace imbibes it.

TYPICAL FLAVOR COMBINATIONS

The Macedonian and Thracian palate has been honed by the tang of vinegar, brine, and yogurt, the crunch of walnuts, and the perfume of dozens of spices that local cooks use in loving profusion. Ground walnuts are used as a thickener and base for many sauces and, combined with garlic, appear in the local renditions of *skordalia* and *melitzano-salata:* (creamy eggplant salad).

Parsley is the Macedonian herb, said, in fact, to have originated here. In the Greek colloquial it is often referred to simply as *makedoniko.* In Thrace basil and *nanes*—Good King Henry—are preferred.

Red peppers—sweet, hot, fresh, dried—a Balkan staple that Macedonian and Thracian cooks embrace wholeheartedly, weave their way through indigenous, Vlach, Jewish, Armenian, Slav, and refugee cooking up here, appearing in dozens of different dishes. Sweet and hot paprika as well as dried pepper flakes, or *boukovo,* are favorites.

Fruit, too, is a common addition to savory dishes. There are lots of recipes for prunes and cherry plums mixed into vegetable and meat stews and even cherry plum mixed into fish soups. Sour apples, quinces, and grapes also appear in the savory cooking, in a whole bevy of meat and vegetable stews.

THESSALONIKI

They say you can leave Thessaloniki but that Thessaloniki never leaves you. Thessaloniki has a certain atmosphere unlike that of any other city in Greece. I can't say exactly what it is that draws one here—the water, perhaps, and the wide quays; the dozens of thousand-year-old churches, some regal, some stooped with time and dwarfed next to modern buildings; the old walls fraying on the city's original periphery. Maybe it's just the spell of being in a city that has thrived uninterrupted for two thousand years. Whatever it is, Thessaloniki beckons visitors to return.

I spent three weeks there, living in a top-floor apartment in the center of the city. I was within walking distance of all of its icons of culinary culture: the great Modiano Market, still owned by the original Jewish family on whose land the market sits; the tripieries; the *bougatsa* houses; the sweet shops; and all the small ouzeries and *mezedopoleia* where people from every walk of life gravitate to daily to see their friends and share a few bites over ouzo. Thessaloniki, even with a million inhabitants, is small enough to be familiar. That's one of its charms.

But Thessaloniki is also refreshingly cosmopolitan. At the beginning of the century, the influx of immigrants came from Asia Minor. The city was largely Jewish until the Second World War. It has always been a commercial center for people from all over the Balkans, and since the Iron Curtain came down, their presence in the city is even more pronounced. These days it isn't unusual to walk through the streets of Thessaloniki and hear Bulgarian, Albanian, and Russian—the last because of the most recent arrivals, Pontian Greeks, from Georgia, Tashkent, and other places in the former Soviet Union.

Its cosmopolitan heritage, its continuity as a city and a port, its place as the crossroads for the Balkans, Europe, and the East, all have played a part in the city's gastronomy. Thessaloniki isn't so much about a collection of recipes that are somehow representative of the way people enjoy food here—although there are a few of those, too—it is more about food as culture, entrenched in the way of life.

It is no surprise that Modiano and Kapsani, Thessaloniki's two adjoining central marketplaces, are the heartbeat of the city. All of Macedonia's formidable agriculture and fishing industry culminates here, in the mounds of deep red Florina peppers, Naoussa peaches, Edessa cherries, and more, depending on the time of year; in the freshwater carp and catfish, mussels, squid, and shrimp all culled from local waters, not to mention the myriad preserved fish that are so much a part of the local tradition. The dried fruit and nut emporiums sell things one can't find in Athens, from dried cherry plums, the cognac-colored pleasantly sour cousin to the prune, to walnut-and-chocolate halvah, a local specialty, to dried wild rosebuds, used to make infusions as well as an ersatz *petimezi* (molasses).

The market is also the center of political and social life. Its alleyways are crowded with ouzeries, open day and night. Places such as Myrobolou Smyrni, tucked right inside Modiano, are where the city's politicians, artists, and intelligentsia congregate to see and be seen. The dozens of small ouzeries around the market offer up a vast array of the *mezethes* for which Thessaloniki is famous: grilled butterflied sardines, stuffed squid, mussels *saganaki,* mussels pilaf, spicy feta, long hot peppers poached or fried and served with olive oil, and much more. Even the greasy spoons around the market are fun—places frequented mostly by men,

which serve up *doner kebab* (lamb grilled on a vertical rotisserie and sliced very thin) or *souvlaki* on small sheets of butcher's paper, with the requisite heap of *boukovo*—hot pepper flakes—nearby.

The market sets the pulse for the city's culinary life, but specialty foods are found all over town. For one, Thessaloniki is the only city in Greece where soup enjoys a certain exclusivity. There are restaurants, albeit dwindling in number, that serve almost nothing else but soup. Aptly called *soupatzithika,* these old tavernas used to cater mostly to men, and mostly to men of certain professions. They were almost always located near bus stations or near the port, for a clientele that worked odd hours, either all night, as in the case of the fishermen and fishmongers, or very early in the morning, as in the case of bus drivers. There are a few soup places still left in the city, but their glory days are past.

Triperies—*patsatsithika*—make for another of Thessaloniki's unique claims to culinary fame. The tripe houses came to the city with the Asia Minor refugees in the 1920s and, like the soup houses, catered to a mostly male, mostly working-class clientele.

The two other things that set this city apart as Greece's culinary capital are *bougatsa* and the plethora of sweet shops. *Bougatsa* is a large, thin, buttery phyllo pastry filled with cheese, meat, or sweet cream or served plain and sprinkled with sugar and cinnamon. It is the breakfast food of Thessaloniki, ordered almost exclusively to go. (Elsewhere in Greece, *bougatsa* refers only to the sweet cream–filled pastry). By far the most famous *bougatsa* is made by Dodoni on Egnatias, which has been in continuous operation since 1885. From the looks of the little shop, it seems like not very much has been done to its decor since then, but there is a tale about the time the owners tried to spruce the

THE JEWS OF THESSALONIKI

Jewish communities have existed in Greece from remote antiquity. Nikos Stavroulakis, in his book *The Cookbook of the Jews of Greece,* writes that there may have been individual Jews, if not Jewish communities, living in Greek cities as far back as the sixth century B.C., and by the first century B.C. there were Jewish communities all along the coast of Asia Minor and in many Aegean islands. By the fourth century A.D., when Christianity became the official religion of the Roman Empire, the Jewish communities became more isolated. When the empire split, the inhabitants in its eastern reaches remained proud of their Roman heritage, and thus the Jews of the Byzantine Empire called themselves Romaniotes. It was a name that was adapted by Jew and Christian alike, and to this day a rather poetic reference to the essence of Greekness is still called *romiosyni.*

The Romaniote Jews formed the majority of the Jews in Greece until 1492, when thousands of Sephardic Jews fleeing the persecutions of the Spanish Inquisition arrived. The Sephardic Jews settled in several cities, but mainly in Thessaloniki, the pearl of the Orient. They differed from their Romaniote brethren, mostly in being more cultured and educated. By 1613 they constituted 68 percent of the population of Thessaloniki. The city's lifeblood pulsed to the rhythms of Jewish mores and customs. Up until the beginning of the twentieth century, most of the city's commercial life stopped at dusk on Fridays. Ladino, a combination of Spanish, Greek, and Turkish, was spoken throughout the city. My own father-in-law, a Greek Christian who happened to have grown up in the Jewish quarter of Thessaloniki, still speaks a smattering of it.

Thriving Jewish life in Thessaloniki meant that the community was an integral part of the tapestry of what was then one of the most cosmopolitan cities in the world. Thessalonikan Jews had much contact with both Ottomans and Greeks, as well as with all the other peoples of the Balkans and Anatolia who made up the city's melting pot in its heyday. The foods of the Jews of Thessaloniki forged a kind of hybrid cuisine, mirroring their close ties not only with other ethnic and religious groups but with Jewish communities elsewhere in the Ottoman Empire. And, of course, running like an undercurrent in all their cooking was the Spanish influence from their past.

Claudia Rodin, in her essay on Thessaloniki in *The Book of Jewish Food,* points out that the Jewish cuisine in Thessaloniki was never grand. One of the favorite foods was the white bean. Typical Jewish dishes sound surprisingly like the food one still finds in Thessaloniki today. *Piaz,* for example, a white bean salad with olive oil, onions, and parsley, is still favorite taverna fare. Beef and chicken stews with cracked wheat hark back to the most ancient Greek foods, ones brimming, in fact, with ritual and religious significance. Stews that combine meat with nuts and pulses were also a favorite on Jewish tables, but they were—and still are—dishes found readily among Christian cooks, too, although names often would differ, with Spanish or Ladino names for many of the same dishes prepared by Christian cooks. Jewish cooks developed a plethora of savory pies, also mirroring the region's overall cuisine, for if there is one thing that is clearly Greek and entrenched in the Greek cook's psyche it is the wealth of *pites* (savory pies) that are made all over the country. Among the Jewish communities, though, one finds Passover renditions of the dish: While many Greek savory pies call for leavening in the pastry, Jewish cooks developed recipes with matzo, which they mixed with water to form a kind of dough.

The Spanish echoes in many of their traditional recipes can still be perceived. Among the most well-known such dishes are the *haminados,* eggs cooked over onion skins for many hours, and the many *frittadas* (baked omelets) still cooked among Thessaloniki's Jewish community.

In one of the greatest tragedies of the twentieth century, most of that community was deported to concentration camps in Poland in 1942 and 1943. Of the fifty-five thousand Jewish inhabitants of Thessaloniki before the war, there are only a few thousand left. Few of those who survived the camps returned to the pearl of the Orient, moving instead to America, to Israel, and elsewhere.

place up, modernize it by installing an electric oven. Its die-hard fans practically picketed outside, and to this day Dodoni is probably the only place left in Thessaloniki that bakes its *bougatsa* in a wood-burning oven.

As for the desserts—covered in the sweets section—I'll end by saying that Thessalonikans, whose love for their city is evinced in the fact that most locals are walking encyclopedias of urban history, call their city *glykomana*—sweet mother—for the vast number of pastry shops, many by now legendary within Greece, that are such a part of this city's food lore.

THE COOKING OF THE "POLI" GREEKS

Poli—City—refers to Constantinople, city of the world's desire, as one Byzantine had written. It was founded as a Greek colony, Byzantium, in the seventh century B.C., and was reestablished as the eastern capital of Christianity by Constantine the Great in A.D. 324. For a thousand years it was the spiritual heart of eastern Christendom and the spiritual and intellectual heart of Greece. Even the name by which it is known today, Istanbul, is a transliteration of the Greek *Eis stin Poli,* "In the City."

Greeks have emotional and historic ties to that famously rich city on the Dardanelles, the only city situated on two continents, and the Greek presence there lasted through two millennia, only to end abruptly in the twentieth century.

The influence of the million and a half Greek refugees who flooded continental Greece from Asia Minor, settling largely in the North, in Macedonia and Thrace (but also in Athens, the Eastern Aegean Islands, Crete, Roumeli, and other parts of the country), was far-reaching. Greek cuisine would not be what it is today were it not for these often well-to-do, educated Greeks whose cuisine was the culmination of Byzantine and even ancient legacies, of European and Anatolian aesthetics. In one example of such continuity, Soula Bozi, in her book *Politiki Kouzina, Paradosi Aionon (The Cuisine of the Constantinople Greeks),* writes about having found a recipe for the ancient garum, a sauce made with the salted, fermented entrails of mackerel and other oily fish, in the handwritten 1929 notebook of a home cook from Marmara, just oustide of Constantinople.

Greeks in Constantinople had at their disposal all the world's spices, since for so many centuries their city was a crucial crossroads on the silk and spice routes between China, Arabia, and the West and one of the world's most important natural ports. Many Greeks were wealthy merchants. In fact, after the Muslims, the Greeks were the main merchants in Constantinople and also controlled much of the trade in Smyrna (Izmir). The Ottomans' free trade policies and their frequent wars with Byzantium's former economic rival, Venice, allowed Greeks to attain powerful status as tradesmen and merchants. In 1477, two Greeks had managed even to outbid a Turk over the right to administer customs duties on all the wheat imports into the city of Constantinople. When history betrayed them and they were forced to flee Asia Minor in the 1920s, these Anatolian Greeks carried with them memories of grander days. It didn't take long before the aromas and spices of their rich culinary history insinuated themselves into the whole of Greek cooking. No other regional Greek cuisine is as complicated or varied as the food of Poli. None is as exotic.

The cuisine of Poli evolved from a combination of well-executed home cooking, palace cooking (the palace being Topkapi, where many of the chefs and pastry makers were Greek), the city's restaurant and taverna cuisine, much of which was controlled by Greeks, as well as from the many European influences, since Constantinople was such a cosmopolitan city. Cooking—at home, that is—was a serious pastime for the urbane Greek women of Poli, one of the few outlets for their creativity and independence.

Quinces, cinnamon, allspice, cloves, the pervasive sweetness of sautéed onions in dozens of stuffed vegetable dishes, of mint (thought to help digestion), eggplant glorified in dozens of different recipes, an almost frivolous—or at least profuse—use of pine nuts and raisins, and the copious use of olive oil in so many vegetable dishes—these and much more are the foundations of Politiki cooking. The Bosporus, which has been prized for the wealth and variety of its fish since antiquity, provided the seafood that plays such an important part in these Greeks' cooking: swordfish, mullet, bream, bass, mackerel, sardines, to name but a few. Fish was cooked fresh, in vine leaves and in stews, or preserved, either smoked, salted, or preserved in oil, for the *meze* table. It is no surprise that today Thessaloniki, thanks largely to the influence of the Asia Minor Greeks, boasts some of the best seafood dishes in Greece. Their legacy is evinced in other aspects of Thessalonikan life, too, for example, in the way the bread industry is organized. Like Poli, in Thessaloniki there are three different kinds of bakeries: those selling regular bread, those selling *bougatsa* (cream-filled phyllo pastry) and *loukoumathes* (honeyed dough puffs), and the one or two left that work all night making *kouloures*—sesame bread rings—which are hawked as snack food from stands all over the city.

The cooking of the Greeks of Poli is the marriage of East and West, of bourgeois, mostly French, techniques imported into their wealthy households, and of the pungent aesthetics of the East. As for their place in Macedonia, it's not that there are no Polites or Mikrasiates in the rest of Greece. There certainly are; just not as many. Their cuisine is entrenched in the North of Greece, which is my reason for including them here, as part of the tapestry of the North, rather than anywhere else.

THE BLACK SEA GREEKS AND THEIR CUISINE

The little specks of cracked corn shone like amber granules among the beans and flour at the farmer's market in Thessaloniki's Martiou, a Pontian neighborhood. I had never seen anything like them, hard as glass and with a strange, allusive name. *Korkota.*

"What's that?"

"If my wife were here, she'd tell you," said the vendor rather vaguely. "She's a Pontian. They use it. I think she mixes it in bean soups," he added. So, rather unceremoniously but not unpropitiously began my short foray into the cooking and lore of the Pontian Greeks. These are the Greeks who for centuries lived and flourished around the Black Sea, or Efxinos Pontos. The political upheavals in the early part of the twentieth century that culminated in an exchange of populations in 1922 and 1923 forced them to flee their ancient homeland en masse. Most emigrated to Greece, settling mainly in the North and in Athens. But many crossed the Caucasus and settled in the former Soviet Union. With the collapse of communism and the harsh economic conditions that ensued in the late 1980s and 1990s, they were forced to move yet again. So, in the

1990s Greece saw a fresh wave of Pontians from the likes of Georgia, Azerbaijan, Tashkent, and other places within the former Soviet Union. Their food culture combines the native dishes from their original birthplace with the foods of Russia. Pickled red cabbage, borscht, and more are among some of the specialties of the Rossopontioi, as the most recent wave of immigrants is called.

I wasn't a complete stranger to the cuisine of the Black Sea Greeks before immersing myself in Macedonia and Thrace. From friends and from a few good tavernas in Athens I knew several of the breads and stuffed pasta dishes—*varenika,* little pasta crescents filled with cheese or ground meat and served with butter; *manti,* not unlike ravioli but usually served with butter and crisped onions or with yogurt; *piroski,* a play on the Russian *piroshki*—the large array of delicious pickled vegetables, the red cabbage and bean dishes, and a few of the many soups that form the backbone of the cuisine.

Their cooking is quite varied, embracing seaside and mountain traditions, ancient Greek, nomadic, Georgian, Russian, Turkish, and other influences, but by and large Pontian cuisine is based on grains and dairy. Fermented milk products and a whole slew of grilled dough products form the foundation of the cookery. These are the goods on which the Greeks of Pontos have survived for so many centuries, raw ingredients that derive from their unique history, their peripatetic fate, their vast geography, and their difficult way of life.

The most basic dairy product in the Pontian larder is *tan,* which is essentially buttermilk. By boiling and straining *tan,* one gets to the next important dairy product, *paskitan,* which looks something like small-curd cottage cheese and is usually diluted with water to make a kind of thick yogurt. *Paskitan* is used in soups, which are also plentiful and basic

to the Pontian table, and as a sauce with certain traditional pastas. After *paskitan* comes *tsortan,* which is dried *paskitan* kept for use in the winter, in specific dishes made with wheat or barley. All are made almost exclusively with cow's milk.

Besides the formidable array of dairy products, pasta and grains provide an unusual glimpse into the continuity of cooking that characterizes much of what Pontians eat. The apparent antiquity of many of these preparations is impressive. Take, for example, *siron,* stout, cylindrical spirals—a kind of grilled pasta—that are dampened, then tossed with hot butter and *paskitan; evriste,* which are like very dry tagliatelle (without the eggs); and, finally, *yiohades,* very thin, dry, prebaked phyllo sheets that are used to make savory cheese pies. All these traditional pasta and dough products are made by grilling the pastry on a *satz,* a very hot iron surface, one of the world's earliest cooking tools.

As for the grain mentioned earlier, *korkota* is actually a little confusing. It refers to one of three granular-type ingredients, made either with dried or roasted cracked corn kernels, cracked barley, or cracked wheat kernels (not to be confused with bulgur, which is cracked boiled wheat). In the Pontian kitchen all three are used interchangeably in pilafs and as filler in certain soups.

All sorts of creamlike flour-based preparations, foods that recall earlier and certainly much poorer times, are still part of the Pontian tradition, as are a slew of great breads, many reminiscent of the flatbreads or quick grilled breads that are found throughout the Middle East.

Other things, such as a whole array of greens appear in cooked and raw salads, soups, and casseroles. Fish, especially fresh anchovies, or *hapsia* in the local dialect, are also very much a part of the cooking.

The Macedonian and Thracian Pantry

In Macedonia and Thrace, the repertoire of regional foods and flavors is vast because the land is so fertile. Some of Greece's most prized fruits and vegetables come from here: peaches from Naoussa; cherries from Edessa; peppers from Florina and Aridea; green plums from Halkidiki; beans from Prespes, and more. Following is a list of some of the basic items in the Macedonian and Thracian pantry.

CHEESE

Many of the well-known Greek table cheeses, such as *kefalograviera, kasseri,* feta, *myzithra, anthotyro,* and *manouri,* are produced in Macedonia and Thrace. A few cheeses are purely local specialties. Among them are:

Anevato This salmon-colored spreadable cheese belongs to the long list of soft, fiery, fermented Greek cheeses. *Anevato* is an appellation goat's milk cheese specifically from western Macedonia, around Grevena and Kozani. It is used in some local pies and is also eaten as a table cheese.

Batsos Basically, *batso,* a hard, pale yellow sheep's milk cheese with a porous texture, is a *kefalotyri* aged in brine for at least six months. It is an appellation-of-origin cheese unique to the central and western reaches of Macedonia, especially around Naoussa, and it takes its name from the Vlach word for the mountain hut in which the cheese was traditionally produced. It is generally pan-fried as for *saganaki.*

Telemes Essentially, this is a cow's milk brine cheese very similar to feta but always aged in tins.

SESAME AND TAHINI

Around the market of Komotini wafts the thick, delicious scent of ground sesame seeds. The perfume emanates from one of several old shops, called *tahinopoieia*—tahini processors—that specialize in sesame seeds ground to a paste, tahini, in other words.

Thrace used to produce the best sesame seeds and tahini in Greece, and the local variety is naturally dark. There is still some local cultivation, but it is very small, not more than about 500 pounds a year. Most is consumed locally, by connoisseurs in the know. (Now the majority of tahini in Greece is imported from Sudan, Pakistan, and China.)

The local seeds go to market unpeeled and are sold that way, as favored among northern Greeks. The local tahini is the color of peanut butter and has a delicious roasted scent. In Thrace, tahini is enjoyed alone, or mixed with *petimezi* (grape must molasses), honey, or sugar as a spread on bread. It is also used, as it is elsewhere in Greece, to replace olive oil during the holiest fast days of Lent and appears in some interesting local confections.

ROASTED CHICKPEAS

Called *stragalia* in Greek, roasted chickpeas are a traditional snack, usually served together with raisins and other nuts as a simple *meze.* Production of them has dwindled throughout Greece—only about 30 percent of those consumed are processed here, and Komotini is famed for them. There has even been an effort to garner an official appellation designation for them.

On the outskirts of the city several large producers busy themselves with the age-old task of roasting them in vast wood-burning ovens. They come sputtering out like popcorn from a special chute and then are either dampened with brine to make salted *stragalia* or flavored with hot pepper.

MACEDONIAN PEPPERS

Peppers are to Macedonia what corn is to Kansas—ubiquitous, a long agricultural tradition that has worked its way into every aspect of the local cookery, in the form of both vegetable and spice.

I visited Macedonia in late summer, when peppers flood the fields and markets. Dozens of different varieties are considered local, and each claims its own specific place in the kitchen. There is the small oblong pepper with four lobes on top, destined for stuffing; the "goat" pepper—*katsika*—a long, thin, usually green hornlike variety meant for the frying pan; the long, thin, diabolically hot pepper favored among the diehards; firm, short, and slim green peppers for pickling; others, almost the same size but somewhat plumper and picked both red and green, that are meant to be strung and dried for use in winter; and the *plakites,* or Florini pepper, long, fleshy, sweet, and very bright red, one of the best-known, most delicious, but newest, varieties in the region, having made its way across the former Yugoslav border in the middle of the twentieth century. The Florini is the pepper that Greeks roast and serve as a *meze* with olive oil, garlic, parsley, and vinegar.

Finally, though, and historically most important, are the peppers grown for spice. These are firm, medium-size sweet and hot peppers, varieties once identified with the central Macedonian area called Aridea or, as it is often still referred to, Karatzova, the name being a remnant of Ottoman rule, when the region reigned second only to Hungary as the pepper center of the Balkans. *Piperi karatzovas* was, in its heyday, akin to the best vanilla from Madagascar, a recognized, highly esteemed local product.

I followed the Macedonian pepper trail to the epicenter of Aridea, a small village called Piperia—pepper. Tellingly, there wasn't one pepper plant in sight. Five thousand hectares (about twenty thousand acres) of peppers used to be grown here for spice, and five huge pepper processors once operated here. Now only one has survived, that of Stavros Karageorgiades.

"Look, look at my hands. They're stained. They're slippery from all the oils. It doesn't even come off with soap," says Karageorgiades, lifting his hands to show me his orange-red palms. "Can you see the difference?" he asks, scooping up two handfuls of red pepper. The Aridea pepper was red, while the other variety was noticeably darker, browner.

It is not only color but also aroma that sets the Aridea variety apart. This area's sandy soil and humidity have always made it conducive to pepper production. The climate makes for spice peppers that are very thin skinned, the better for drying and pulverizing. It takes four kilos (about nine pounds) of local Aridea-grown peppers to make one kilo of spice; elsewhere, even in towns just twenty kilometers away, that ratio doubles, so that producers require eight kilos of peppers to get a kilo of spice.

Yet, despite the high quality of Aridea pepper, farmers have turned away from producing it in the last decade. Cheaper red pepper makes it difficult for the Aridea spice to compete.

Nevertheless, red pepper as a spice—whether sweet, hot, or in the form of the flakes known as *boukovo*—is an absolutely necessary seasoning in the Macedonian kitchen.

Making red pepper is an art. Once harvested—from the end of August through the middle to end of September—the peppers are left outside to dry like raisins. Then they are washed and dried in huge ovens for about eight hours, at 85°C (185°F). Once sufficiently dried, the peppers are ground between two millstones, either into flakes, seeds and all, for *boukovo,* or into a powder.

NORTHERN GREEK OLIVES

The olive finds its northernmost clime in Macedonia and parts of Thrace, namely in Chalkidiki and Maronia, on the coast between Komotini and Alexandroupolis. There are several local table olive varieties, among them:

Halkidiki Most people encounter this olive as the classic, large green Greek olive; however, it is cured in many different ways. When it is at later stages of maturity and eggplant-colored, it is salt-cured and makes for one of the great wrinkled Greek olives, fleshy, succulent, and thin-skinned.

Maronias These large mahogany-colored olives have a reputation for being the only olives in Greece one can eat straight off the tree because they are naturally sweet (as far as olives go, that is). Although they are not one of Greece's important commercial olives, locals adore them. Generally, they don't eat them raw, but cured in brine.

Thassos throumba This is the best-known northern Greek black wrinkled olive. It is matured on the tree and then cured in dry salt, and tends to have an oily, almost leathery texture.

PICKLED VEGETABLES

A crucial part of this region's pantry is the large array of pickled vegetables. Peppers, both hot and sweet, top the list, followed by cabbage, pickled either whole or in large wedges and then stewed with poultry and pork, stuffed in a local version of *dolmathes,* and sometimes baked into savory pies. There are some unusual pickles in the region as well, among them the brine-cured grapes that are a specialty of Naoussa and the pickled green tomatoes of Thrace.

DRIED GREENS

Because of the cold climate, drying has become one way to preserve wild greens for use in winter. Nettles, spinach, and sorrel are among the most commonly dried greens. Sometimes the greens are braided together fresh and hung to dry, or else dried and crumbled into large pieces. In winter local cooks reconstitute them in water and then cook them, in pies, stews, casseroles, and the like. They are found readily in markets all over Macedonia and Thrace as well as in the small agricultural cooperatives usually run by women in villages all over the region. In Thrace, basil and Good King Henry—*nanes* in Greek—are also favored herbs for drying.

DRIED FRUIT

Dried fruit is another important staple, used in lots of savory recipes. Prunes are especially revered. There are the dark prunes most of us are familiar with, as well as the *koromylla,* or cherry plums, which are tart and green and used, either fresh or dried, to lend an acidic balance to many meat, fish, and vegetable stews. They used to grow all over the region but were endemic to the western lake area and to Halkidiki. Now most of these sour plums have disappeared from the Macedonian landscape in favor of more lucrative crops. What one finds at markets both in the North and elsewhere are cultivated on the island of Skopelos.

CURED FISH

All over the region salted, air-dried, smoked, and pickled fish have been a longstanding tradition and standard fare on the *meze* table. In the western parts of Macedonia, especially in the lakes region of Prespes, most fish are salted and air-dried. In the eastern reaches, the tastes and traditions run more toward smoked fish or fish preserved in brine.

Here is a short list of some regional favorites:

Politiki lakerda This is the delicious fillet of bonito from the Bosporus and from the waters around Lesvos that has been cured in brine. *Lakerda* was the food of the poor during the Byzantine era, but nowadays it is one of the most revered *mezethes* for ouzo and a classic in the cuisine of the Poli Greeks. It is made with relatively large mackerel; the mastery lies in preparing it so that the fish is sweet, not salty. It is served plain or topped with raw red onion and, to cognoscenti, should never be served with either lemon juice or olive oil, a dictate most taverna owners do not abide by.

Tsiros These are the cured mackerel, another favorite *meze* among Poli Greeks. Traditionally the fish are tied whole in pairs and salted in large barrels, with about thirty pounds of salt per fifty pairs of fish, for ten hours. The fish exudes its own moisture (water and blood together), which, together with the salt, comprises the brine. They are then removed, cleaned, and steeped in sea water for another ten hours. Next they are hung to dry in the sun. Thus processed, the mackerel fillets last up to a year and a half stored in a cool, dry place. They are sold cured at the markets throughout Macedonia and Thrace (as well as in other parts of Greece). The fish is prepared for consumption in two ways: either as a salad, by running it whole over an open flame until its skin blisters, peeling it, and filleting it, then serving it with olive oil, vinegar, and dill; or, filleted, dipped in batter, fried, and served with garlic sauce.

Other cured fish Among the favorites are eels, which are smoked and considered a delicacy; *likourinos,* which is the male grey mullet, filleted and smoked or brine-cured; and smoked trout, which is now usually farmed but once was plentiful in local rivers and streams.

The lake fish of Prespes The lakes of Prespes, located in the northwestern corner of Macedonia, burgeon with fish, many indigenous, providing the local table with all sorts of specialties. Besides salmon trout, eel, and grey mullet, which are common enough in other parts of the country, Prespes also provides about fourteen species of carp, as well as catfish, bream, picarel, and sunfish. The favored way to preserve them is by drying. In spring, picarel's season, the fish is strung garlandlike, salted and dried, a sight to see outside of almost every home and taverna in the twelve villages around the two lakes. Carp, too, is dried: The fish is first filleted, then salted, then hung, in late summer or early fall, among the garlic braids, onion bunches, and red peppers that are the seasonal agrarian backyard decor in this beautiful backwater.

CHARCUTERIE

Macedonia and Thrace boast one of the greatest charcuterie traditions in Greece, and there are dozens of local recipes for the sausages, cured pork, and *pastourma* that are part of the local cuisine. Many of these preparations came to the region with the various waves of diaspora Greeks in the early part of this century and now, decades later, are inextricably woven into the local culinary tapestry.

Sausages The flavors of all cured meats in Macedonia run decidedly toward the spicy. In the western parts of the region, around Kozani, for example, there is a dark, air-dried sausage that became a local specialty via the Greeks from Caesarea in central Turkey, who settled here. It is made with a combination of ground pork and beef and seasoned generously with hot pepper flakes, black pepper, cumin, allspice, and paprika, and usually is eaten alone as a *meze* for *tsipouro* (eau de vie). Leeks are another favored addition to sausages all over Macedonia and Thrace, and there are dozens of sausages—thin, stout, fresh, dried—that combine pork, or more commonly pork and beef, with leeks, sweet and hot paprika, and black pepper. In some parts of Thrace, especially along the eastern edge in Songli, sausages are almost always fresh, not dried.

While most sausages call for either pork or pork and beef together, there are several, especially in the eastern parts of Thrace, where cattle have the space to graze, that call for all beef. Usually these are quite heavy and spicy, seasoned either with leeks or with garlic, cumin, and the omnipresent hot pepper flakes that run like wildfire through all of northern Greek cooking. The former are called *prasata,* after *praso,* the Greek word for leek, while the latter are called *skordista,* after the word for garlic, *skordo.*

There is at least one unusual recipe found among the Vlachs in Naoussa for sausage made with the minced meat of old female goats combined, for fat and flavor, with a little pork (the latter was usually bought or bartered for). The sausage is seasoned with leeks, oregano, black pepper, and allspice and air-dried.

One of the region's best known specialties is its *kavourma.* This is an old world preparation that is basically a kind of confit—pork, often together with onions and cumin, preserved in rendered fat and kept in clay jugs. Nowadays the homemade version is hard to come by, but *kavourma* can still be found in local butchers' shops throughout the region. A few of the larger charcuterie companies produce it, in the form of a loaf like any other cold cut. Traditionally, *kavourma* is added to omelets for a quick meal or served with bread as a *meze* for ouzo or wine.

Two unusual confitlike preparations can be found exclusively in Thrace. One is the *pousourti,* basically a fat sausage or loaf filled with chunks of pork, spices, and lard. The other is *osmanga,* a combination of pork bellies and thighs, finely chopped and boiled, then preserved in olive oil with a combination of leeks, hot peppers, and oregano. It is added, in small quantities, to local bean soups.

MACEDONIAN SAFFRON

It was five o'clock in the afternoon when we arrived in Kozani. The town was dull with inactivity, the way all provincial cities in Greece are in that no man's time between the end of the day's work and the evening's promenade. We had come here to witness the saffron harvest, for Kozani is one of the few producers of the world's most expensive spice.

By just walking around the city, we could gather no inkling of the work that consumes some two thousand farm families day and night for the length of the harvest in the forty or so villages around Kozani where saffron is produced. It was by sheer chance that we found Yiorgos Nenas and, ultimately, saffron, firsthand. The fiftyish cook was sitting alone by the window of his *mageirio* (an old-fashioned working-class restaurant), Ilyssia, just off the main square in town, when we walked in hungry. After sating our appetites, he led us to his village, Lefkopigi, and to his niece, who would be cleaning saffron that evening.

It was raining lightly, typical saffron harvest weather. The harvest usually lasts three weeks during mid-October and early November. At the height of it, the fields stretching left to right all around Kozani are covered with a purple robe of *Crocus sativus,* the delicate flowers with the three red threadlike stigmas that are saffron. The flowers grow no taller than three or four inches in neat rows so close together that they transform the otherwise muddy earth into a huge monochrome swath like some creation by the artist Christo.

Sultana Dougalis and her mother, Maria Nenou, were already busy at work in the dining room when we arrived. A mountain of the fragile mauve flowers was heaped over thick blue paper covering the table. The women's fingertips were stained deep yellow. Gossip and chatter punctuated their work. Soccer blared on the television above them, and Haris, Sultana's husband, kept the women company but didn't touch the flowers. Saffron is very much female work in Kozani, but it is hard, arduous work.

The women's hands moved in a blur of machinelike accuracy. With one hand they picked up the flower and slightly separated the petals. With the other they deftly pinched out the three red threads, carefully avoiding the other three yellow styles, which fetch considerably less per kilo. They tossed the threads into a small pan and dropped the spent flowers, which have no value except as compost, into a plastic wash basin.

Once the stigmas were all pinched off, Haris took them to the basement, where they were spread out and stacked on large screens to dry. Once dried, the stigmas are cleaned by hand again, to catch any of the yellow threads that are still mixed in.

The next morning Sultana and company would head to the fields and spend eight or nine hours stooped nearly to the ground to pluck the crocuses. This, too, is work that has to be done carefully. The flower has to be snapped right at its base, just above the stem. Getting part of the stem by accident doubles the workload because the flowers will have to be trimmed later to fit into the separation machine. "By the time you finish one row, more are cropping up behind you," explained Haris. A good picker can collect up to three baskets in one day.

The Dougalis family production is small—three kilos of dried saffron from about three-quarters of an acre of land, all of which fit perfectly into a large olive-oil tin. It takes about two hundred thousand flowers to produce a kilo of saffron. The county's larger producers turn out upward of twenty-five kilos or about fifty-five pounds of saffron a year. Kozani's total production is about six tons annually. Once the farmers finish drying their saffron, they are bound by law to sell their crop to the cooperative. Ironically, with the exception of coffee flavored with saffron and the local *tsipouro* (eau de vie), which is reddened with saffron, the spice appears nowhere in Macedonian cooking. Almost all of it is exported.

Psanorefi This is not to be confused with *psaronefri,* which in Greek is pork loin. This unusual air-dried "sausage" is made with a combination of ground pork and beef, seasoned with cumin, black pepper, and salt, stuffed into sausage casings, and pressed outdoors between planks of wood for about forty days so that its final shape is flat and wide. It is grilled, or cooked with eggs, and savored with the fiery local *tsipouro.*

Psanorefi is a specialty that came to Macedonia with the Greeks from Eastern Romylia, just across the Evros River in Turkey and Bulgaria.

Pastourma The last item on the shopping list of Macedonian charcuterie is the fenugreek-infused *pastourma,* and several of its less heavily spiced cousins. Connoisseurs say that the best *pastourma* is made with a kind of wild deer native to the Balkans, known as *zarkadi.* Camel meat is supposedly second. Both are extremely rare these days. Most *pastourma* is made from beef. There is no specific cut, although the loin is best. The meat is coated in coarse salt and left for about a week, after which it is rinsed and laid to dry for about another week outdoors, on planks covered with towels. It has to be completely dry before being coated with the spice rub. One end is tied as for prosciutto, to facilitate hanging it, then it is rubbed with a thick coat of spices that includes, first and foremost, fenugreek, which imparts the characteristic deep, incenselike aroma to the meat, combined with allspice, cumin, sweet and hot paprika, and black pepper. The meat has to be completely coated, with no part exposed, as the fenugreek acts not only to flavor the meat but to protect it from flies and insects. The *pastourma* is then left to hang for eight days or so, after which it is ready to eat. There are lots of recipes calling for it. Like all cured meats, *pastourma* is used readily in omelets, eaten on its own as a *meze,* and baked into a rich phyllo pie called *pita kaisarias,* together with *kasseri* cheese and tomato slices.

In some parts of Macedonia, as in some parts of the Aegean, there is a *pastourma* made with goat's meat. In the North it is a specialty of the Vlachs, who, as mentioned previously, were itinerant shepherds and therefore did not raise either cattle or hogs. Vlach *pastourma*—or *pastrama* as they call it—is seasoned with hot paprika and salt, not with fenugreek.

The Recipes

MEZETHES

Pepper Spread

PIPERIA ALESMENI

 Makes about 4½ cups

*M*acedonia offers many versions of this spicy relish, which is used as a condiment, especially with grilled meats and as a spread for bread. This recipe comes from a group of women at the Cooperative in Prespes, who make it and sell it at the hotel they run.

6 to 10 small thin hot peppers, such as serranos, to taste, seeded and finely chopped (see Note)

4 pounds red bell peppers, roasted and peeled (see page 460)

1 large eggplant, about 1 pound, roasted and peeled (see page 461)

2 pounds firm, ripe tomatoes, peeled, seeded,
  and chopped, or 2 cups canned crushed
  tomatoes
½ cup extra-virgin olive oil
6 garlic cloves, minced
½ cup finely chopped fresh flat-leaf parsley
Salt to taste

1. Puree the hot peppers in a food processor then add the roasted bell peppers and eggplant and continue processing until smooth.

2. Combine the puree and tomatoes in a large pot and bring to a simmer over medium heat, stirring constantly, until thickened slightly, about 10 to 15 minutes. Add ¼ cup of the olive oil. Simmer, stirring, until the sauce thickens and cooks down, about another hour. Add the remaining ¼ cup olive oil, the garlic, and the parsley, season with salt, and continue to cook, stirring, until all the liquid has cooked off, 15 minutes or so. Let cool slightly and spoon into a large, clean glass jar. Let it cool in the jar, cover tightly with the lid, and store in the refrigerator. The pepper spread will keep indefinitely.

✳ **NOTE** Wear rubber gloves when cleaning hot peppers.

Fried Hot Peppers with Yogurt

PIPERIES ME YIAOURTI

 Makes 4 to 6 servings

A classic meze *from the tables of Thessaloniki.*

1 pound long green hot peppers (or a combination
  of Italian green peppers and hot peppers)
  (see Note)
Olive oil for frying
Salt to taste
2 to 3 tablespoons red wine vinegar, to taste
2 cups thick Greek yogurt or 3 cups plain yogurt,
  drained (see page 459)
3 to 4 cloves garlic, to taste, peeled and crushed

1. Using a sharp knife, cut away the peppers' stems. Cut the peppers in half lengthwise and scrape out the seeds.

2. Heat about ½ inch olive oil in a large, heavy skillet and fry the peppers over medium heat until wilted, about 8 minutes. Remove with a slotted spoon and let cool. Peel the skins off the peppers.

3. Place the peppers on a serving platter, leaving a space in the center for the yogurt. Sprinkle the peppers with a little salt and vinegar. Cover and marinate for 1 hour.

4. Mix the strained yogurt with the garlic and 1 tablespoon olive oil. Place the yogurt in the center of the platter and serve.

✳ **NOTE** Wear rubber gloves when cleaning hot peppers.

Roasted Red Peppers in Olive Oil

At the end of summer, the sweet, almost fermented aroma of long, fleshy Florini peppers fills the markets of Thessaloniki, Athens, and other cities. These are one of the great treats of the season. Roasted, peeled, and stored under a bath of good Greek olive oil, these peppers make a wonderful snack, meze, *or accompaniment to almost any meal.*

There is no real recipe. But, since the long, thick variety that Greeks know as Florini peppers and hold in high esteem is unavailable in the United States, the next best thing are the big fleshy red bell peppers. Wash and dry them thoroughly. Roast them under the broiler, about 8 inches from the heat source, on sheet pans lined with aluminum foil, turning until charred on all sides. Remove from the oven, let cool slightly, cut off their crowns, and split the peppers in half lengthwise. Remove and discard the seeds. Peel the peppers carefully. Place in layers in a large clean glass jar and in between layers sprinkle a few pieces of thinly sliced garlic. Cover with extra-virgin olive oil, close, and keep stored in a cool, dark place or in the refrigerator. If refrigerated, bring to room temperature before serving.

Mixed Pickled Vegetables from Nymphaio

LAHANA TOURSIA APO TO NYMPHAIO

 Makes about 10 servings

1 cup shredded green cabbage
½ cup shredded carrots
½ cup coarsely chopped wild celery (see Note)
½ cup chopped green bell peppers
1½ cups chopped red bell peppers
⅓ cup seeded and chopped green hot peppers
2 tablespoons salt
Extra-virgin olive oil
White wine vinegar

Wash the chopped vegetables very well and allow to dry before pickling. Place in a large basin, sprinkle with the salt, and toss to combine. Place in two 3-cup mason jars, leaving about 3 inches of space on top. Pour olive oil halfway up the jars. Fill the rest of the way with vinegar. Close and turn upside down to combine inside the jars. Refrigerate for at least 3 weeks before serving. The vegetables will keep indefinitely.

✳ NOTE Wild celery is available at some specialty retailers or by mail order. If you can't find it, substitute ½ cup chopped regular celery plus ½ teaspoon celery seeds.

Pickled Cabbage

LAHANO TOURSI

 5 heads of pickled cabbage

Pickled cabbage is one of the great winter pantry staples of Macedonia, Thrace, and all the Balkans. Sometimes Greek specialty food shops pickle their own cabbage, and it is sold in pretty much the same way as it appears in Greek markets: quartered, brined, and bobbing in barrels.

I decided to include a recipe for it here, since it is so much a part of the traditional pantry and also because several recipes in this chapter call for it. Commercial sauerkraut doesn't come anywhere near the delicate, sweet-sour taste of homemade pickled cabbage and is far too harsh to use in any of the dishes that call for the pickled vegetable.

Northern Greek cooks wait until the weather just begins to turn cool, around late September, to start putting their cabbage up in brine. A lovely sight it is: In Thessaloniki, it isn't uncommon to see little old ladies, for whom traditional foodways die hard, navigating city streets while dragging behind them a whole shopping cart filled with cabbage heads. One cook in Didymotiho, at the far eastern edge of Thrace, let me in on a little secret: The cabbage heads should have rather loose leaves, not compact ones, to enable the softening brine to seep in.

I collected a few dozen recipes for pickled cabbage from every corner of northern Greece, from Kozani to the northeastern triangle of Thrace. Most cooks shared another little secret with me without being able to explain why: Whole dried chickpeas or whole dried corn or barley kernels should be added to the barrels. I asked my friend and colleague Evy Voutsina, who has probably spent more time than anyone else on the back roads of northern Greece

documenting this country's culinary heritage. She had the answer ready: The sugars in the corn and grain break down and help the brine ferment.

5 medium heads green cabbage, not too
    compact
Juice of 5 large lemons plus 3 of the juiced lemon
    halves
½ cup coarse sea salt
2 ounces whole barley kernels or dried chickpeas
2 ounces dried corn kernels (optional)

Remove and discard the tough outer leaves of the cabbage. Wash the heads thoroughly, then quarter them and cut out the cores. Place the cabbages in a large, deep plastic container or a small wooden barrel and toss with the lemon juice and lemon halves. Top with water and the salt, then add the barley or chickpeas and corn, mixing them in a little. Cover the cabbage with a large plate and place weights, such as cans, on top. Cover the container with a cloth. Let the cabbage stand for 3 weeks in a cool, dark place and during this time stir up the brine twice a day with a long, clean wooden spoon or spatula. The cabbage will be ready to eat by the end of 3 weeks, but it is best to keep it for longer. Local cooks say 3 months is the minimum. Remove as needed. It will keep for months, remaining in its brine.

You can serve the cabbage on its own, as a salad. Remove from the brine, rinse, and shred. Place in a bowl and drizzle with olive oil and a little *boukovo* (hot pepper flakes, see page 208) or hot Hungarian paprika.

Roasted Eggplant Salad with Unripe Grape Juice from Naoussa

NAOUSSA MELITZANOSALATA ME AGOURIDA

 Makes 6 to 8 servings

The juice of unripe grapes (verjuice) appears here and there in the country cooking of Greece as a replacement for fresh lemon juice when the fruit is out of season or unavailable. I've seen it used in fish soups in the Ionian Islands and here, in this unusual recipe for roasted eggplant salad. In the old country cooking of Macedonia, there was something called ardeni, *which was the boiled juice of sour grapes, something to keep on hand in the pantry in lieu of lemon juice. Lemon juice may, of course, be substituted in the likely event that unripe grapes are hard to come by.*

3 medium-large eggplants, roasted
   (see page 461)
½ cup extra-virgin olive oil
3 garlic cloves, peeled and crushed
3 to 5 tablespoons verjuice, to taste
Salt to taste

1. Place the eggplants over an open flame (stovetop or barbecue) and roast, turning, until their skins are charred on all sides.

2. Have the olive oil ready in a bowl. When the eggplants are done, cut open lengthwise and scoop out their flesh, removing and discarding as many of the seeds as possible. Place the eggplant pulp in a bowl and mix in the olive oil. Add the garlic and mix in. Mix and mash the eggplant mixture with a fork, adding a tablespoon at a time of the verjuice and seasoning with salt. Mix until all the liquid is absorbed.

⊙ Replace the verjuice with 2 to 3 tablespoons fresh lemon juice or red wine vinegar to taste.

⊙ You may also add 3 tablespoons Greek or Mediterranean-style yogurt or drained plain yogurt to the roasted eggplant dip.

Macedonian Garlic Sauce

MAKEDONITIKI SKORDALIA

 Makes 6 to 8 servings

The menu of one of my favorite meze *places in Thessaloniki, Aristotelous, in an arcade just above the main city square, lists ninety-five different items, all served up on small plates, to be consumed with something off the equally formidable wine and spirits list. Thessaloniki is a Mecca for* mezethes, *second only to Volos, whose traditions in distilling firewater and creating an unlimited number of dishes to down with it are unmatched anywhere in Greece. Dips and spreads, a whole slew of dried and salted fish, grilled and fried seafood, peppers, pickled vegetables, and more make up the* meze *selection in homes and tavernas all over the region.*

The regional love affair between garlic and walnuts plays itself out nowhere better than in this local skordalia *recipe. Serve as a dip or as an accompaniment to fresh or fried vegetables and fried fish.*

4 to 6 garlic cloves, to taste, peeled
Salt to taste
½ cup coarsely chopped walnuts (see Note)
Four 1-inch slices stale rustic bread, crusts
   removed

¾ cup extra-virgin olive oil

2 to 4 tablespoons red wine vinegar, to taste

Either in a mortar or in a food processor, pulverize the garlic and salt to a paste. Add the walnuts and pound or pulverize until the mixture is mealy. Dampen the bread under the tap, squeeze dry, and crumble. Add to the mortar or food processor and continue pulverizing. Drizzle in the olive oil and vinegar, alternating between them, and process together until the *skordalia* is creamy. If it is too thick, add a little water. Serve immediately.

✳ **NOTE** You can replace the walnuts with either pine nuts or almonds.

Garlicky Fish Roe Spread

SKORDOHAVIARO

 Makes about 2 cups; 6 to 8 servings

Another unusual dish from Naoussa, skordohaviaro is served as a dip for both fresh and fried vegetables as well as an accompaniment for fried fish.

2 to 3 large garlic cloves, to taste, peeled

⅓ to ½ cup extra-virgin olive oil, as needed

½ cup chopped fresh mint or 2 tablespoons dried

⅓ cup *tarama*, preferably white (see Box)

Four 1-inch slices stale rustic bread, crusts removed, dampened, squeezed dry, and crumbled, or 3 medium waxy potatoes, peeled and boiled in water to cover until tender

2 to 5 tablespoons water, as needed

Place the garlic with 1 or 2 tablespoons of the olive oil in a large mortar. Pound to a pulp with the pestle. Slowly add the mint, *tarama,* bread or potatoes, the remaining oil and water in small amounts, alternating between them and pounding well after each addition, until the mixture is smooth and creamy. Alternatively, place the garlic with 1 or 2 tablespoons of the olive oil in a food processor. Pulse on and off, then add the mint, *tarama,* and bread or potatoes. If using potatoes, mash slightly before adding to the food processor bowl. Pulse on and off for a minute or so, until the mixture is mealy. You don't want to do this too fast—the idea is to simulate the slower mortar-and-pestle method—otherwise the mixture will become too gummy as the starch breaks down. As you pulse on and off, slowly drizzle in the olive oil and water, alternating between them, until the mixture becomes smooth and creamy. Remove from the food processor and serve.

A WORD ON FISH ROE

*T*arama is the Greek word for fish roe; usually it comes from either carp, cod, or mullet, all of which have tiny, compact eggs. There are two types of *tarama,* differentiated by color. The first, which is pink or coral, has been dyed. This was a practice begun a few decades ago as a purely cosmetic addition. White *tarama* is the same thing, without added color. The stuff in jars is almost always dyed. You can sometimes find white *tarama* sold loose in Greek and Middle Eastern food shops, especially around February and March, when Lent occurs. Be careful to buy *tarama,* and not *taramosalata,* which is a processed food and spreadable salad, ready to eat as is.

Whipped Spicy Feta

HTIPITI

 Makes 4 to 6 servings

This spicy feta cheese dip calls for a combination of red and green hot peppers. It is one of the classics of the Thessaloniki meze repertoire and has many variations. The recipe that follows comes from one of the city's meze meccas, a small ouzerie in the Modiano Market called Myrovolou Smyrna. Here, only green hot peppers are used.

2 to 3 long green hot peppers, to taste, seeded
   and chopped
½ pound tin-aged hard Greek feta or *telemes*
   cheese, crumbled
⅓ cup extra-virgin olive oil
1 to 3 tablespoons fresh lemon juice, to taste

Pulse the peppers in a food processor until they are like a paste, then add the cheese a bit at a time, pulsing after each addition. Add the olive oil and pulse until smooth. Add the lemon juice, 1 tablespoon at a time, to adjust and balance the flavors. Refrigerate for 1 hour and serve, accompanied by bread or crudites.

✳ **NOTE** Wear rubber gloves when cleaning hot peppers.

Roasted Feta

FETA PSITI

 Makes 2 servings

No self-respecting taverna owner from Serres to Prespes would omit this classic from his menu. I like to serve this with an array of other mezethes, such as roasted red peppers (page 214), mussels sautéed with peppers (page 222), and the eggplant and caper salad from the Cyclades (page 314).

One 4- by 5- or 6-inch tin-aged slice Greek feta,
   about ½ inch thick (see Note)
2 to 3 thin slices ripe tomato, to taste
1 teaspoon *boukovo* or red pepper flakes
2 tablespoons extra-virgin olive oil

Preheat the oven to 375°F. Place the cheese on a large sheet of aluminum foil, with the tomato slices on top. Sprinkle with the *boukovo* or pepper flakes and drizzle with the olive oil. Fold the aluminum foil over to seal the feta and bake in a small pan until the cheese is slightly melted, about 15 minutes. Remove from the oven and serve immediately in the foil and on a plate.

✳ **NOTE** Simple as this recipe is, it is important to use tinned feta as opposed to barrel, because the tin-aged feta tends to be firmer. The feta should be intact, not melted.

Fried Cheese with Paprika Roux

KASH STO TIGANI

 Makes 4 servings

Vlach cooking is rich in cheese, butter, and all the other staples of a traditional, once itinerant shepherd culture. Kash is the Vlach word for "cheese," and this is a classic Vlach recipe from Nymphaio, a beautifully preserved Vlach village in central Macedonia. It is traditionally made with a hard local sheep's milk cheese called batsos *but it can be made with* kefalograviera, kefalotyri, *or with feta, too. This dish makes a lovely starter for a hearty winter meal.*

½ pound *batsos, kefalograviera, kefalotyri,* or hard Greek feta cheese
¼ cup all-purpose flour
½ cup (1 stick) unsalted butter
1 tablespoon sweet paprika
1½ cups water
Salt to taste

1. Cut the cheese into 2-inch squares. Dredge lightly in about 2 tablespoons of the flour, tapping off any excess.

2. Heat the butter in a large skillet over medium heat and when it bubbles, add the cheese and fry for a few minutes until it begins to color. Remove the cheese with a slotted spoon and set aside.

3. Place the skillet back on the heat and add 1 heaping tablespoon flour. Stir vigorously for a few minutes, until the mixture begins to thicken and brown. Add the paprika and stir. Slowly pour the water into the skillet, stirring until the sauce is thick. Season lightly with salt. Add the cheese back to the skillet and cook for another minute or so, just to warm it through. Serve immediately in a shallow bowl with good bread.

Roasted Potato Salad with Hot Pepper and Mint

PATATOSALATA PSITI ME BOUKOVO KAI DYOSMO

 Makes 4 to 6 servings

Yiorgos Haskos runs the kind of tiny taverna in the middle of nowhere that only locals know and love. I met him on my sojourns through the lake district of Prespes, and he shared several of his recipes with me. This is one of them.

5 to 7 medium baking potatoes
1 large red onion, halved and sliced
2 teaspoons *boukovo* or red pepper flakes
1 teaspoon dried mint
Salt to taste
½ cup extra-virgin olive oil, or more as needed

1. Preheat the oven to 400°F. Wash the potatoes very well, being sure to scrub the skins. Pat dry. Wrap each one in aluminum foil and roast until tender but still firm, about 1 hour. Remove from the oven, let cool slightly, and remove the skins. Cut into quarters or chunks.

2. Toss the potatoes with the onion, *boukovo* or red pepper flakes, mint, and salt. Just before serving, toss with the oil.

Fried Mussels

MYTHIA TIGANITA

Makes 6 to 8 servings

Northern Greek mussels tend to be the small, narrow variety and are extremely tasty. They are cultivated extensively in Halkidiki and, as a favorite among the Poli Greeks who had access to the vast fisheries of the Bosporus, have come to be one of the best-loved shellfish of Thessaloniki. Fried mussels, mussels saganaki *(sautéed with peppers and cheese), and mussel pilaf are the three classic northern Greek dishes calling for them.*

5 pounds mussels
Salt to taste
1½ cups all-purpose flour
Olive or vegetable oil for frying
1 recipe Garlic Sauce (page 216)

1. Wash the mussels, scrubbing their shells and pulling off their little "beards" with a sharp paring knife. Discard any mussels that will not close. Place the mussels in a steaming basket in a large, wide pot with about 2 inches of water. Cover, bring the water to a boil, and steam until the mussels open, 6 to 7 minutes. Drain, discarding any mussels that haven't opened.

2. Remove the mussels from their shells and place in a colander. Season lightly with salt and toss with the flour until all the mussels are coated. Tap the colander to rid them of excess flour.

3. Fill a large, heavy skillet with about 1½ inches oil and heat over medium-high heat until almost smoking. Add the mussels, in batches if necessary, and fry until crisp and golden, about 1 to 2 minutes. Remove, drain on paper towels, and serve hot, with the *skordalia* on the side.

A WORD ON KOUSKOUSI

I had first encountered this confusingly named pasta, which has nothing to do with Moroccan couscous, at the women's cooperative stores all over Thrace. The northern Greek *kouskousi* is an egg- and milk-infused pasta, made with either semolina flour or bulgur and a little wheat flour. Like *trahana*, it is prepared at the end of the summer. Eggs, milk, and a little salt are mixed together in a large basin. Bulgur or semolina is added to the liquid (the former is soaked in the liquid to soften it). Then regular flour is mixed in until a dense mass forms. This is then rubbed a little at a time between the palms to get the characteristic tiny ball-like shape. The little balls are left to dry on cotton sheets, turned over several days so that they don't stick together, and, finally, when rock hard, stored in cotton sacks.

Kouskousi is cooked like pasta, to accompany chicken or other meat swimming in rich, fragrant sauces. Sometimes it is added to soup or stew as a thickener, because, like *trahana,* its dry, milky heart breaks down and lends a creamy quality to whatever it is added to. Sometimes, too, it is used as a replacement for rice.

Mussel Pilaf with Tiny Pasta and Squid

MYTHOPILAFO ME KOUSKOUSI

 Makes 4 to 6 servings

My guide in Serres worked in the cultural affairs office of the town hall, and he knew everyone there was to know and everything there was to eat. As any Greek man is bound to do, he took me for a meal at what he promised was the best taverna in town. The meal turned into a four-hour event in the middle of the week in the middle of the workday, but Greece is like that.

The most interesting dish of the small plates that were paraded out before us was this rendition of a classic mythopilafo—*mussel pilaf—one of the definitive dishes in the cuisine of the Poli Greeks, as familiar to them as lasagne is to a Neapolitan. What was unusual in the plate before me was that here, in Serres, which is the heart of Greek rice growing, rice was nowhere to be found in the pilaf. In its place was a tiny, round local pasta called* kouskousi.

Some of the big Greek pasta manufacturers now produce it, and you can sometimes find it in Greek specialty food shops. In its place you can use the Sardinian tiny pasta called fregula *or Israeli couscous.*

3 pounds mussels

½ cup extra-virgin olive oil

3 garlic cloves, minced

1 large squid, about ⅓ pound, cleaned
   (see page 462), if necessary, body cut into
   ¼-inch rings and tentacles chopped fine

1 cup peeled, seeded, and chopped plum
   tomatoes (canned are fine)

½ cup chopped fresh flat-leaf parsley

Salt and freshly ground black pepper to taste

½ pound tiny spherical pasta, such as Sardinian
   fregula

1. Wash the mussels, scrubbing their shells and pulling off their "beards" with a sharp paring knife. Discard any mussels that will not close. Place the mussels in a large pot without any water, cover, and heat over low heat. Let them steam in their own juices until the shells open, about 5 minutes. Remove from the heat and discard any mussels that have not opened.

2. Heat the olive oil in a large skillet over medium heat and cook the garlic and squid tentacles until the tentacles are bright pink, about 3 minutes. Add the tomatoes and parsley, season with salt and pepper, and simmer the sauce for 20 minutes over low heat until thick. Bring a pot of salted water to a boil, add the pasta, and cook until tender but al dente, about 7 minutes.

3. Strain the mussels, reserving the liquid. Strain the liquid through a fine-mesh sieve. Shell half the mussels. Add the steaming mussel broth together with the mussels to the sauce. Drain the pasta, reserving 1 cup of the boiling liquid. Place the drained pasta back in the pot and toss with the sauce. Add enough of the liquid from the pasta to make the whole dish juicy. Serve hot.

Mussels Sautéed with Peppers

MYTHIA SAGANAKI

 Makes 4 servings

*S*aganaki *refers to a small two-handled skillet with a rounded perimeter that is used to make a whole slew of pan-fried dishes, from mussels to shrimp and feta to plain fried cheese. This is one of the all-time classics of the Macedonian* meze *table. I would venture to say that there isn't an ouzerie or taverna in Thessaloniki that doesn't include this dish, or some variation of it, on the menu. It usually is served sizzling hot in the pan.*

1½ pounds mussels

½ cup extra-virgin olive oil

1 scant tablespoon all-purpose flour

1 cup hot water

½ cup dry white wine

1 Italian green pepper, cut into ¼-inch-thick rings

1 or 2 red hot peppers, to taste, seeded and minced

1 teaspoon dried oregano

Salt and freshly ground black pepper to taste

1. Wash the mussels, scrubbing their shells and pulling off their small "beards" with a sharp paring knife. Discard any mussels that will not close. Steam the mussels by placing them in a steaming basket inside a large pot with about 2 inches of water. Cover the pot, heat until the water boils, and steam for about 5 minutes. Discard any mussels that haven't opened and remove the rest from their shells.

2. Heat the olive oil in a large skillet over medium heat and add the flour. Stir until very lightly browned, about 1 minute. Add the hot water, wine, peppers, oregano, and salt and pepper, and simmer until the peppers wilt, about 5 minutes. Add the mussels and simmer for just a minute or so, to warm through. Adjust the seasoning and serve immediately.

⊙ Add ⅔ cup cubed *telemes* or tinned feta cheese with the mussels and simmer for another minute or so, until the cheese begins to melt.

⊙ For Shrimp Saganaki: Clean 2½ pounds of shrimp but leave their heads and tails attached. Heat ½ cup of olive oil in a skillet and sauté 1 large, chopped onion and 1 seeded and chopped hot green pepper until wilted, about 5 minutes. Add 2 cups of grated fresh tomatoes or 2 cups of chopped canned tomatoes. Season with salt and pepper and simmer the sauce for 5 minutes, until it thickens slightly. Add the shrimp and half a pound of cubed feta cheese, and simmer over medium heat until the shrimp turn bright pink and the feta begins to melt, about 5 minutes. About 2 minutes before removing from heat add 3 tablespoons of ouzo if desired. Toss in 2 tablespoons of chopped flat-leaf parsley and serve.

Grilled Butterflied Sardines

SARDELES STIN SCHARA

 Makes 6 servings

The periphery of the market in Thessaloniki bustles with ouzeries, and people come here to eat and drink at all hours of the day and night. Mezethes are the fare of choice, and grilled local sardines one of the best of them, served with ouzo and topped with raw onions. Since most homes are not equipped with restaurant-quality grills, and the broiler is too difficult to control for this dish, I have added a variation to the original recipe that calls for the sardines to be "grilled" in a cast-iron or nonstick crêpe pan.

1 pound fresh sardines

Salt

3 to 4 tablespoons extra-virgin olive oil, as needed

1 teaspoon dried oregano (optional)

2 medium red onions, cut into thin rings

Lemon wedges for garnish

1. Clean the sardines: Remove and discard their heads and gut and wash the fish. Butterfly the sardines with a sharp paring knife. Rinse and pat dry with paper towels. Place in a large pan and season with salt.

2. Heat the grill. Brush the sardines lightly with the olive oil and sprinkle with the oregano if desired. Grill on both sides for a few minutes, until the flesh is lightly browned and tender and the fish are cooked.

3. Serve warm, spread on a large platter and topped with raw onion rings. Garnish with lemon wedges.

 This may also be done in a griddle on top of the stove: Use a heavy nonstick or cast-iron crêpe pan. Brush with 1 tablespoon olive oil and heat very well. Place the sardines in a single layer on the hot pan and press down with the back of a spatula to sear. You'll need to do this in batches. Grill on both sides. Remove from the pan, season with the oregano, and serve immediately with the raw onions and lemon.

SOUP

Yogurt Soup from Pontos

TANOMENON TSORVAS

 Makes 4 to 6 servings

On the periphery of the Kapani Market in Thessaloniki there is a small shop called Rayian that sells nothing but the raw ingredients necessary to cook the foods of the Pontian (Black Sea) Greeks. Incredible yogurt and all sorts of grains are among the repertory. I got this recipe from a Rossopontia—a Pontian Greek from Georgia. Yogurt soup is the absolute classic dish in all Pontian cookery. The egg and coriander in this recipe, so I was told at Rayian, makes this a variation on the classic. Nevertheless, when Maria Tsoubleklide cooked it for me, I loved it, and include it here.

1 cup bulgur

6 cups water

Salt to taste

6 tablespoons preferably Greek yogurt, drained
    (see page 459)
1 large egg
2 to 3 tablespoons unsalted butter, to taste
1 small onion, finely chopped
10 fresh coriander (cilantro) or mint sprigs,
    finely chopped

1. Bring the bulgur, water, and salt to a boil. Reduce the heat to medium-low and simmer until the bulgur is very tender, about 20 minutes. In a small bowl, beat together the yogurt and egg. Add a ladleful of the hot soup slowly to the yogurt-and-egg mixture, stirring with a whisk or fork all the while. Pour the mixture into the pot, stir, and remove the pot immediately from the heat.

2. Heat the butter in a small skillet over high heat and add the onion. Cook until golden and lightly crisped, 12 to 14 minutes. Add this to the hot soup, together with the coriander or mint, and serve.

PATSAS

Die-hard fans and a few armchair historians trace the origins of *patsa*, the pungent soup made with cow's stomachs and feet, to the mysterious and as yet unrevealed "black broth" that sustained the ancient Spartans and Dorians through all their military exploits. Local wisdom has it that some early form of the soup sustained Alexander the Great's troops, who supposedly introduced it to Persia and the depths of Anatolia.

Patsas—from the Turkish for "foot"—was long a tradition among Greeks and Turks alike in Constantinople. A Greek refugee from Poli named Lefteris Bafiadis opened the first *patsatzithiko* (*patsa* restaurant) in Thessaloniki in the early 1920s. It took but a few years for the number of *patsatzithika* to grow. By the 1950s there were dozens of *patsa* houses in the city. Although the number has dwindled to just a handful, these simple restaurants still play a part in Thessaloniki's daily life.

The *patsatzithiko* was and still is the restaurant of the working class. Open 7 days a week, 24 hours a day, it caters mostly to men, who stop in for a bowl on their way to or from work. Over the years, it has evolved into a nightowl's hangout, too, the last stop among late-night revelers who have had a bit too much to drink; the potent mix of simmered viscera, seasoned with garlic and vinegar (the basic recipe), is said to be both a preventive and a cure for hangovers. As one old saying goes, "For whatever ails you, take *patsa*."

The basic recipe calls for tying, then simmering the feet, large intestine, and stomachs together. The soup is skimmed, a process that takes about half an hour and determines its ultimate "whiteness"—the telltale sign of a master *patsa* chef. The fat is reserved separately, seasoned with pepper and added to the bowl upon serving.

Serving, too, has its ritual: The classic *patsa* is a concoction of broth and chopped feet; some people prefer just the stomachs, which in turn come in two versions: finely chopped or *douzlama,* which means "coarse." There is the red version, too, which is flavored with paprika and rendered fat. The seasoning accoutrements are on every table: salt and pepper, *boukovo*—hot pepper flakes—and a bottle of *skordostoumbi,* which is garlic steeped in vinegar.

Bean Soup in Four Versions

FASSOLATHA SE TESSEREIS EKDOSEIS

 Makes 8 to 10 servings

Until I traveled through Macedonia, I never really understood beans or appreciated bean soup, the making of which is something of a local art, born out of the cold-climate need for easy, nourishing dishes as well as the fact that Macedonia produces some of the best beans in Greece.

Prespes is the region to go to, in the early fall, to see the bean harvest at its height. The area, at more than a thousand meters (3,200 feet) above sea level, cold and damp to boot, is renowned for two types of beans: the local giant white bean, or gigantes as they're called in Greece, and the smaller, flat white bean. The former is meant strictly for baking, the latter for soups. They stretch to the horizon, cultivated tepee-fashion, in rows and rows of conical trellises. After the harvest, which starts in early October, one can find them for sale on roadsides and in grocery stores all over the immediate area. Even gas stations sell them. As for the soup itself, there are many variations throughout the whole of Macedonia.

When people still kept full country larders, one thing they always had on hand were pork bones (left after the winter slaughter and the making of sausages, smoked meats, lard, and kavourma, which is like confit), which they put up in brine and kept for the making of fassolatha. Nowadays they are hard to come by. Besides the various renditions that follow, made with celery, parsley, or the typically Macedonian duo of mint and hot pepper flakes, one of the most interesting variations comes from the Pontian Greeks, who make a simple bean soup and add to it what they call korkota fournisto, which can be either cracked wheat or cracked and roasted corn kernels.

The addition of either makes the soup extra creamy and hearty.

Pontian Greeks use a roasted nonsweet corn, a variety that isn't a hybrid. In the United States the closest equivalent and a fine substitute are toasted sweet corn kernels, available at specialty retailers.

1 pound dried small white beans or navy beans, picked over and rinsed
2 medium red onions
2 bay leaves
½ cup plus 2 tablespoons olive oil, or more if desired
1 scant tablespoon sweet paprika
2 large red bell peppers, roasted (see page 460), peeled, and cut into ½-inch strips
½ cup chopped fresh flat-leaf parsley
Salt to taste
2 to 3 tablespoons fresh lemon juice or red wine vinegar (optional), to taste

1. Soak the beans overnight or for at least 8 hours in ample water to cover. Drain and place in a pot with fresh water to cover, one of the onions, peeled and quartered, the bay leaves, and 2 tablespoons of the olive oil. Bring to a boil, reduce the heat to medium-low, and simmer slowly for about 1 hour.

2. Chop the remaining onion. Heat the remaining ½ cup olive oil in a skillet over medium heat and cook the onion, stirring, until wilted and translucent, 7 to 8 minutes. Add the paprika and stir for a few minutes to combine. Add the onion to the simmering beans, together with the peppers and parsley. Simmer until the beans are very tender and the soup is thick, another 50 minutes to 1 hour. Season with salt. Just before serving, adjust the flavor with lemon juice or vinegar and a little olive oil. Serve hot.

⊙ In lieu of parsley, add ½ cup chopped celery to the soup in step 1.

⊙ Simmer the soup with 2 medium whole peeled onions. Remove the onions with a slotted spoon about halfway through cooking, when they are soft and translucent. Chop and sauté in olive oil, seasoning them with paprika and 1 to 2 teaspoons *boukovo* or red pepper flakes. Add back to the soup. Instead of parsley or celery, add ½ cup chopped fresh mint to the soup.

⊙ Add a handful (about ½ cup) roasted sweet corn kernels or cracked wheat (bulgur) to the soup in step 1.

Chicken Soup with Trahana

KOTOSOUPA ME TRAHANA

 Makes 8 to 10 servings

Chicken soup with trahana, *the rustic, pebble-shaped, dairy-based Greek pasta, is found all over Macedonia and Thrace. In some recipes the final dish is more like a thick and hearty stew; in others just a handful of* trahana *is used as filler, the way cooks in the rest of the country use rice in their chicken soups. The use of paprika or preserved red peppers for both color and flavor is typical of northern Greek cooking, perhaps evincing one of the many Balkan influences on the cuisine up here. This dish falls somewhere in between. It's a homey, satisfying meal in itself, especially good on colder winter days.*

One 3- to 3½-pound chicken, cut into serving
   pieces
10 cups water
Salt to taste
⅓ cup extra-virgin olive oil
2 large red onions, chopped
1 heaping tablespoon sweet paprika or ⅓ cup
   Macedonian Pepper Spread (page 212)
½ cup sour *trahana* (see page 456)
Salt and freshly ground black pepper to taste

1. Place the chicken in a soup pot with the water. Bring to a boil and season with salt. Reduce the heat to medium-low and simmer the chicken until the meat falls off the bone, 1 to 1½ hours. While the chicken is simmering, skim and discard the foam off the top. Remove the chicken from the broth with a slotted spoon and set aside to cool slightly. Skin, bone, and shred the meat and set it aside.

2. Heat the olive oil in a medium skillet and cook the onions over low heat until wilted, 7 to 8 minutes. Add the paprika or red pepper spread and continue to cook for a few minutes. Add the onion mixture to the broth and stir in the shredded chicken.

3. Add the *trahana* to the soup, season with salt and pepper, and simmer over medium heat until it is cooked, 12 to 15 minutes. Serve.

Carp Soup with a Paprika and Walnut Sauce

PSARI SALTSISTO OR GAROUFA

 Makes 4 to 6 servings

There are variations of this dish all over central and western Macedonia. Fish with rich walnut-garlic sauces are a mainstay especially in the lake regions up there. This recipe comes from Kastoria.

1 cup extra-virgin olive oil

1 tablespoon all-purpose flour

1 tablespoon sweet paprika

1 medium-large carp or porgy, about 3 pounds, gutted and cleaned

2 quarts hot water

2 large carrots, cut into ¼-inch-thick rounds

3 wild or cultivated celery stalks, coarsely chopped

1 large red onion, chopped

Salt to taste

2 large firm, ripe tomatoes, peeled, seeded, and coarsely chopped, or ¾ cup canned crushed tomatoes

4 medium waxy potatoes, peeled and quartered

2 large garlic cloves, peeled

One 1-inch slice stale rustic bread, crusts removed

1 cup chopped walnuts

1. Heat ½ cup of the olive oil in a large soup pot over medium heat and add the flour and paprika. Stir for about 1 minute until thick, like a roux. Place the whole cleaned fish over this and turn it several times. Add the hot water, carrots, celery, and onion and bring to a boil. Season with salt. Reduce the heat to medium-low and simmer until the fish is very tender, 25 to 30 minutes. Remove the fish with a slotted spoon and set aside on a plate. Add the tomatoes and potatoes to the soup and continue to simmer until the potatoes are tender, another 25 to 30 minutes.

2. Bone the fish.

3. In a large mortar, crush the garlic cloves. Dampen the bread under the tap, squeeze dry between your palms, and crumble. Add the bread crumbs and walnuts to the garlic. Pound, adding the remaining ½ cup olive oil and 1 to 1½ cups of the hot fish broth, until the sauce is thick but liquid. Season with salt. Serve the soup in individual bowls and serve the fish on a platter with the walnut sauce on top.

VEGETABLES, BEANS, AND GRAINS

Peppers, leeks, nettles—these are the most beloved Macedonian vegetables. There are lots more, no doubt, since the great North of Greece is a farming belt, provider of plenty to tables not only within Greece but also to greater Europe.

The recipes that follow are some of my own favorites, culled from an otherwise vast repertoire of dishes that comprise local, Pontian, Asia Minor, and other influences. They are quite different, I think, from the kinds of pared-down vegetable dishes encountered in other parts of Greece. These seem more substantial, maybe a little richer, too, because, after all, the climate is cold.

As for grain dishes, tradition calls mostly for bulgur and *trahana,* together with a few local pasta preparations. Again, my own tastes have been my guide in choosing the dishes I think count as among the best or most interesting from the North.

Scrambled Eggs with Roasted Red Peppers

VLACHIKI STRAPATSATHA

 Makes 2 to 4 servings

Nerantza Boutari is a cook in one of the pensions of Nymphaio, a beautifully preserved Vlach village in the mountains of western Macedonia. I watched her prepare this simple dish for a group of tourists who had come to see the nature preserve and the bears that have made Nymphaio famous in recent years.

3 to 4 Florini or medium red bell peppers, to taste, roasted (see page 460) and peeled
½ cup peeled, seeded, and chopped tomatoes (canned are fine)
1 cup ¼-inch cubes *kefalotyri* or *batso* cheese
½ cup extra-virgin olive oil
2 tablespoons water
⅓ cup chopped *kasseri* cheese
3 large eggs, lightly beaten

1. Slice the peeled peppers into 1-inch rings and mix together with the tomatoes and *kefalotyri* in a medium bowl.

2. Transfer the mixture to a saucepan over medium heat. Add the olive oil and simmer until the cheese softens but does not melt, 5 to 8 minutes, stirring occasionally to keep the mixture from sticking to the bottom of the pan.

3. Add the water. By this point all the ingredients will begin to meld. Add the *kasseri*. When it melts, add the eggs. Cook for 3 to 5 minutes, remove from the heat, and serve. The dish should be almost liquid—the eggs are not supposed to set but be thick and moist, like very loose scrambled eggs.

Leek Fritters

PRASSOKEFTEDES

 Makes about 20 fritters

Leek fritters make either a delicious meze *or vegetarian main course. Serve with Macedonian Garlic Sauce (page 216).*

2 large waxy potatoes, peeled and sliced or cubed
Salt to taste
2 pounds leeks, white and tender green parts, halved lengthwise, washed well and thinly sliced
2 large eggs, lightly beaten
½ cup bread crumbs from stale bread
Freshly ground black pepper to taste
1 teaspoon dried Greek oregano
Olive or other vegetable oil for frying

1. Place the potatoes in a pot with enough water to cover by 2 inches. Salt the water lightly. Bring to a boil and simmer the potatoes until soft, 12 to 15 minutes. Drain and transfer to a large bowl.

2. Meanwhile, place the leeks in a steamer basket inside a pot with about 2 inches of boiling water. Cover and steam for 10 to 12 minutes. Remove and let cool slightly.

3. Preheat the oven to 200°F. Mash the potatoes until smooth and creamy. Mix in the leeks. Add the eggs, bread crumbs, 1 teaspoon salt, the pepper, and the oregano and mix well.

4. Heat about 1 inch of the olive or other oil in a large, heavy skillet over medium-high heat. Drop in about 2 tablespoons of the leek-potato mixture for each *kefte* and flatten each one with the back of the spoon to form a patty. Do this in batches. Fry on one side until golden, about 3 minutes, then flip to fry on the other side. Remove and drain on paper towels. Place the cooked leek fritters in the oven to keep them warm and continue with the remaining batter, replenishing the oil as needed. Serve warm.

Leeks Stewed with Prunes and Tomato

PRASO LATHERO ME DAMASKINO

 Makes 6 servings

This luscious winter dish is usually served alone and is a specialty of Lent, but it also makes a delicious accompaniment to roasted or grilled meats. The dried cherry plums that are optional in the recipe are a pretty standard pantry item in Macedonia. They are tart plums, and they counter the sweetness of the prunes and leeks nicely.

2 pounds medium leeks (not too thick), white
    parts only
⅔ cup extra-virgin olive oil
1 large firm, ripe tomato, grated (see page 459)
10 to 12 pitted prunes, to taste
6 dried cherry plums (optional)
Salt and freshly ground black pepper to taste
½ cup water or dry red wine, if necessary

1. Cut the leeks in half or in thirds, depending on how big they are, to get cylinders about 2½ inches long. Wash them well and pat dry.

2. Heat the olive oil in a Dutch oven or stewing pot. Add the leeks and cook over medium-low heat until they begin to caramelize, 20 to 25 minutes, turning several times. Add the tomato, prunes, and cherry plums. Season with salt and pepper. Cover

and simmer over very low heat until the leeks, prunes, and plums are tender, about 15 minutes more. Add a little water or wine to the pot if necessary to keep the leeks from burning. Serve hot.

⊙ Leeks Stewed with Quinces (Praso Lathero me Kydonia): Clean and cut 2 pounds leeks as directed. Peel and core 3 quinces and cut into wedges like an apple. As soon as you cut the wedges, place the leeks in a medium bowl of cold water into which you've squeezed the juice of 1 lemon. Cook the leeks over low heat in ½ cup olive oil for 20 to 25 minutes. Add the tomato, as directed, and the quince slices and season with salt and pepper. Add a little freshly grated nutmeg to the pot and ½ teaspoon allspice berries. Cover and simmer until the quince are soft, another 10 to 15 minutes. A few minutes before removing from the heat, add 2 tablespoons unsalted butter to the mixture and combine gently. Makes 4 to 6 side-dish servings and is an excellent accompaniment to roasted meat and poultry.

Beet Greens Cooked with Butter and Yogurt from Pontos

TA PORANIA

 Makes 4 to 6 servings

Beet greens and butter sound like a very un-Greek combination. The Pontian Greeks, like all pastoral peoples, use a lot of butter in their cooking, since that was the fat traditionally available to them. I love this dish, especially in the winter. It goes perfectly with Bulgur or cracked wheat and Walnut Pilaf (page 232).

Salt
2 pounds beet greens, trimmed and washed well
6 tablespoons unsalted butter
3 garlic cloves, pounded to a paste in a mortar
1 cup preferably Greek yogurt, drained
   (see page 459)
1 small red onion, coarsely chopped

1. Bring a large pot of lightly salted water to a boil and drop in the greens. Blanch for 5 minutes and drain very well in a colander.

2. Heat 3 tablespoons of the butter in a large skillet or flameproof casserole over medium heat and add the drained greens. Cook for about 5 minutes, stirring. Remove from the heat and place on a serving platter.

3. Combine the garlic and yogurt and spoon over the greens like a sauce. Heat the remaining 3 tablespoons butter in the skillet and cook the onion over high heat, stirring, until crisped, about 10 minutes. Sprinkle this over the yogurt and serve.

Giant Beans Baked the Way They Do Them in Prespes

GIGANTES STO FOURNO APO TIS PRESPES

 Makes 6 servings

The age of the beans is an important factor to ensure that they cook up well. Old beans never really soften up, and the success of this dish depends on getting that creamy texture at the end without disintegrating the beans. There's no way to tell what's in a bag, so try to buy the beans from a busy store where they move off the shelf fast and are replenished quickly.

As for the peppers, at the end of summer outside almost every house in Prespes, one can see the large, fleshy, sweet Florini variety of peppers strung up and drying. They are used in soups, stews, and casseroles in the winter and provide an excellent source of vitamin C in the cold, damp winter months up in Greece's pristine northern lake region. You might be able to find dried sweet Anaheim peppers, which approximate the taste of the dried Florini.

½ pound dried giant beans or butter beans,
   picked over and rinsed
1 large bay leaf
⅔ to 1 cup extra-virgin olive oil, to taste
2 large red onions, finely chopped
4 dried sweet red peppers, cut into ½-inch rings,
   or 4 red bell or Anaheim peppers, roasted
   (see page 460), peeled, and cut into strips
Salt and freshly ground black pepper to taste

1. Soak the beans in ample cold water for 8 hours or overnight. Drain. Place the beans in a large pot with enough fresh cold water to cover them by 2 inches. Add the bay leaf. Bring to a boil, reduce the heat to medium-low, and simmer for 1 hour, skimming the foam off the surface as the beans cook.

2. Preheat the oven to 350°F. Heat 3 tablespoons of the olive oil in a large nonstick skillet over medium heat and cook the onions, stirring, until soft, 7 to 8 minutes. Remove from the heat.

3. Drain the beans and reserve their liquid. Discard the bay leaf. Place in a medium baking pan, preferably one made of clay or ovenproof glass. Pour in the remaining olive oil, the onions, and the peppers and toss gently. Add enough of the cooking liquid from the beans to cover them. Bake the beans for 1 to 1½ hours, checking the liquid and adding more if necessary to keep them moist but not soupy. Season with salt and pepper and continue baking until the beans are very tender and creamy. Remove from the oven, adjust the seasoning, and serve, warm or at room temperature.

NETTLES

Nettles are one of the leitmotivs of northern Greek cooking, used readily from Thrace to Epirus. Nettles grow wild and also are a common sight at farmer's markets. The spiky, stinging green is a winter treat in Greece, in season from October to April. The tender top leaves of the plant are cut, then cooked in several ways. Mostly they are used in savory pies, together with cheese and/or leeks or other greens. The Greeks of the Black Sea make a nettle soup. The practice of cooking greens with milk is common in the pastoral communities all over the North of Greece.

As has been well documented, nettles are an excellent source of many vitamins and minerals, are rich in beta-carotene, and have been salutary, a cleanser for the whole body, from remotest antiquity. Make sure you wear rubber gloves when washing or cutting raw nettles because they sting.

Nettle Fritters from Edessa

TSOUKNIDOKEFTEDES

 Makes 6 to 8 servings

Greens fritters exist in the country cooking all over Greece. Like so much of the culinary repertoire in Greece, recipes evolved out of the need to make tasty, nourishing, filling food from sparse ingredients. Wild greens are available everywhere, although they vary from place to place. Nettles, as mentioned earlier, are especially esteemed all over the North.

1½ pounds nettle tops
1 cup finely chopped fresh flat-leaf parsley
½ cup finely chopped fresh mint
Two 1-inch-thick slices stale rustic bread, crusts
    removed
1 to 2 large eggs, as needed
Salt and freshly ground black pepper to taste
Olive oil for frying

1. Wear rubber gloves when handling raw nettles because they sting. Wash the nettles well and trim away any tough stems. Bring a pot of salted water to a boil and blanch the nettles for a minute or two, just until soft. Drain, squeeze dry between your palms, then finely chop.

2. Combine the nettles, parsley, and mint in a medium bowl. Crumble the bread by hand into the bowl. Add 1 egg and season with salt and pepper. If the mixture is too dry, add the second egg.

3. Heat about 1 inch of olive oil in a large, heavy skillet over medium-high heat. Shape heaping tablespoons of the nettle mixture (once blanched, they don't sting) into little patties. When the oil is very hot, fry until set and lightly golden, 2 to 3 minutes on each side. Remove from the pan, drain on paper towels, and serve.

Bulgur or Cracked Wheat and Walnut Pilaf from Pontos

PLIGOURI ME KARYDIA

 Makes 4 to 6 side-dish servings

I've added a bit of paprika and some chopped parsley to this otherwise hearty but plain dish. I serve this with an array of northern Greek specialties, such as roasted Florini peppers (page 214) or Macedonia Pepper Spread (page 214). It works well with Nettle Fritters from Edessa (page 231), too.

Salt to taste

2 cups water

2 tablespoons extra-virgin olive oil or unsalted butter

1 cup coarse bulgur

1 cup walnut halves

Freshly ground black pepper to taste

1 cup preferably Greek yogurt, drained (see page 459)

3 tablespoons chopped fresh flat-leaf parsley

½ teaspoon sweet paprika

½ teaspoon hot paprika

1. Salt the water and bring to a boil over medium heat in a medium saucepan. Add the oil or butter and stir in the bulgur. Bring back to a boil, reduce the heat, cover, and simmer until all the water is absorbed, about 10 minutes.

2. Meanwhile, pulverize the walnuts with a bit of salt in a food processor until completely ground. Add to the bulgur about 5 minutes before it is done. Season with pepper and additional salt if desired.

3. To serve: Place in a shallow ring mold and turn out on a large serving plate or simply spread out onto a serving plate. Place the strained yogurt in the center. Sprinkle the pilaf with parsley and paprika and serve.

Red Cabbage Wilted with Bulgur or Cracked Wheat and Onions from Pontos

GAPAMAS

 Makes 6 to 8 side-dish servings or about 4 main-course servings

Gapamas—or capamas, *as it is called in the rest of Greece—is one of the most confusing names in all Greek cookery because it refers to entirely different things from one place to another. The word derives from the Turkish for "cover," and the dish generally refers to some kind of meat stew, usually with tomato sauce. The Pontian rendition, meatless, defies all explanation, except for the fact that the pot is indeed covered while the meal cooks.*

⅓ cup extra-virgin olive oil

1 large onion, finely chopped

1 scant tablespoon sweet paprika or a combination of sweet and hot paprika, if desired

1 medium head red cabbage, cored and finely shredded

2 large firm, ripe tomatoes, grated (see page 459), or 1 cup peeled, seeded, and chopped plum tomatoes (canned are fine)

Salt to taste

2 cups water

1 cup coarse bulgur

2 to 3 tablespoons red wine vinegar, to taste

1. Heat the olive oil in a Dutch oven or flame-proof casserole over medium heat. Add the onion and cook, stirring, until wilted, 5 to 6 minutes. Add the paprika and stir until the onion is deep red, 4 to 5 minutes. Add the cabbage and tomatoes and season with salt. Stir with a wooden spoon to combine, cover the pot, and wilt the cabbage over low heat for about 15 minutes.

2. Pour in the water, increase the heat to high, and bring to a boil. Add the bulgur and stir to combine. Bring back to a boil, reduce the heat to low, cover, and simmer until the bulgur is tender and all of the water has been absorbed, about 10 minutes. Five minutes before removing from the heat, sprinkle in the vinegar and adjust the seasoning with salt.

SAVORY PIES

While savory pies are the stalwarts of the kitchen in Epirus and Thessaly, the food of sustenance for shepherds who until fairly recently lived a nomad's existence, in Macedonia they have a different place on the table. Up here savory pies tend to be special, almost festive dishes, made on Sundays or holidays or for other significant meals.

I think the one thing that attests most to the festive quality of Macedonian pies is the phyllo that envelops them. Macedonia claims a phyllo pastry all its own, most often made not with olive oil (which because of the cold climate, was never as endemic an element in the cuisine up here as it was elsewhere), but with butter. Perhaps that is a legacy, too, of the Constantinople Greeks, accustomed to the luscious, buttery pastries of Anatolia, who settled here in the first quarter of the twentieth century.

The technique for making Macedonian phyllo is unique. Unlike in the pies of Epirus and Thessaly, which usually call for at least four sheets (but often more) of paper-thin, homemade phyllo, Macedonian phyllo is made almost like puff pastry. A copious amount of melted butter is worked into the dough in layers, which are then folded over each other, rolled together, chilled, and finally rolled out again.

The traditional butter-brushed and folded dough makes for a final pastry that is flaky and layered, even though only two sheets per pie are called for.

Leek and Yogurt Pie with Variations

PRASOPITA ME YIAOURTI

 Makes 10 to 12 servings

Leek pie is one of the region's "national" dishes, a paean in all its variations to the affinity for leeks in this cold climate.

¼ cup (½ stick) unsalted butter
5 large leeks, white and tender green parts, washed well, drained well, and finely chopped
4 large eggs
1 cup plain, preferably Greek yogurt, drained (see page 459) or thick Mediterranean-style yogurt
Salt and freshly ground black pepper to taste
1 recipe Basic Homemade Phyllo Dough (page 453), Macedonian Phyllo (page 454), or commercial phyllo, at room temperature
Extra-virgin olive oil for brushing the phyllo

1. Heat the butter in a large skillet or wide, shallow pot over medium heat and cook the leeks, stirring, until wilted and translucent, about 7 minutes. Remove from the heat and let cool.

2. Beat the eggs and mix into the yogurt. Add the mixture to the leeks and mix well. Season with salt and pepper.

3. Preheat the oven to 375°F. Lightly oil an 18-inch round baking or pizza pan. On a lightly floured work surface, roll the ball of phyllo into a circle about 22 inches in diameter with a lightly floured rolling pin or dowel. Place on the bottom of the pan, letting the excess hang over the rim. Brush with oil. Spread the filling evenly over the phyllo. Roll the second dough ball into a 22-inch circle and place over the filling, leaving the edges hanging over the rim. Brush that with oil, too. Roll in the edges to form a crust and score the pie into serving pieces. Bake until the pastry is golden, about 50 minutes. Let cool in the pan and serve.

☉ Instead of yogurt, add 1 cup crumbled Greek feta cheese or soft *myzithra* cheese.

☉ There is a nettle pie with yogurt very similar to this one. Instead of leeks, chop and wash (with rubber gloves, because nettles sting) 2 pounds nettles. Cook in butter and combine, as directed, with either eggs and yogurt or eggs and feta.

✳ **NOTE** You may reduce the ingredients by half and bake the pie in a 10-inch round pan.

The pie may also be made with commercial phyllo. For every sheet of homemade phyllo use 3 to 4 sheets of commercial phyllo. See directions (page 455) for more details on how to work with frozen phyllo.

☉

Leek and Ground Meat Pie from Kozani

GIZLEMOPITA

 Makes 10 to 12 servings

This dish is found all over Macedonia and Thrace, to the east. The key is in using very-good-quality lean ground meat, lest the pie turn out unpleasantly greasy.

⅓ cup extra-virgin olive oil or unsalted butter, plus more oil for brushing the phyllo
4 large leeks, white and tender green parts, washed well and finely chopped
1 large onion, finely chopped
⅓ pound lean ground lamb
⅓ pound lean ground pork
Salt and freshly ground black pepper to taste
3 to 4 large eggs, lightly beaten
1 recipe Basic Homemade Phyllo Dough (page 453), Macedonian Phyllo (page 454), or commercial phyllo, at room temperature

1. Preheat the oven to 375°F. Lightly oil an 18-inch round baking or pizza pan.

2. Heat the olive oil or butter in a large, heavy skillet over medium heat and cook the leeks and onion until wilted and translucent, stirring, about 12 minutes. Add the ground meats, season with salt and pepper, and brown together with the leeks. Remove from the heat and set aside to cool for a few minutes. Mix in the eggs and adjust the seasoning.

3. Divide the dough into 2 equal balls. Keep the first ball covered with either a kitchen towel or an inverted bowl while you work with the second ball. On a lightly floured work surface roll the phyllo ball into a circle about 22 inches in diameter with a lightly floured rolling pin or dowel. Fit into the bottom of the pan, leaving the edges hanging over the rim, and brush with oil. Spread the filling evenly over the phyllo. Roll the reserved ball into a 22-inch circle and cover the filling. Brush that with oil, too. Roll in the edges to form a crust and score the pie into serving pieces. Bake until the pastry is golden, about 50 minutes. Let cool in the pan and serve.

✳ **NOTE** You may reduce the ingredients by half and bake the pie in a 10-inch or 12-inch round pan.

The pie may also be made with commercial phyllo. For every sheet of homemade phyllo use 3 to 4 sheets of commercial phyllo. See directions (page 455) for more details on how to work with frozen phyllo.

Savory Pie with Roasted Red Peppers and Onions

HORIATIKI PITA OR SELTSKA PITA TIS PRESPAS

 Makes 10 to 12 servings

In Prespes, I went to visit the local women's cooperative, which runs a hotel and a huge kitchen out of which the members make pickles, relishes, and other condiments for sale in their hotel. On the day I arrived one of the women was eating her lunch— this lovely Slavic-sounding pie filled with roasted red peppers and onions.

⅓ cup extra-virgin olive oil

2 large red onions, coarsely chopped

3 medium firm, ripe tomatoes, grated (see page 459), or 1⅓ cups peeled, seeded, and chopped plum tomatoes (canned are fine)

6 large red bell or Florina peppers, roasted (see page 460), peeled, and coarsely chopped

Salt to taste

1 recipe Macedonian Phyllo (page 454) or Basic Homemade Phyllo Dough (page 453), at room temperature

Olive oil for brushing the phyllo

1. Heat the olive oil and cook the onions over medium heat until soft, about 8 minutes. Add the tomatoes and peppers, season with salt, and simmer, until the mixture is thick and most of the liquid has evaporated, about 15 minutes.

2. Preheat the oven to 375°F. Brush an 18-inch round pizza or baking pan with olive oil. If using Macedonian phyllo, divide the dough into 2 equal balls. Keep one ball covered with a kitchen towel or under an inverted bowl while you work with the other dough ball. Place the ball on a lightly floured work surface and dust lightly with flour. Using a heavy, fat rolling pin, roll the dough into a circle 5 to 6 inches in diameter. Do this in sure, even strokes in every direction so that the circle is properly shaped from the start. Sprinkle the surface lightly with flour as you go, after every or every other stroke.

3. Next, place the dough in front of you and place a dowel or small broomstick at the bottom. Roll up the dough along the dowel, gently coaxing it out from the center to the edges as you go. Sprinkle after every or every other turn with a little flour. Turn the dough clockwise after every roll, too, to ensure that it rolls out evenly in all directions. Keep doing this until you get a circle that is about 22 inches in diameter. Place the dough inside the pan, letting the excess hang over the rim. Brush lightly with oil. Spread the filling evenly over the pastry, leaving the inch around the outer rim empty.

4. Roll the second piece of phyllo into a 22-inch circle and place this over the filling in such a way that it isn't pulled tight with the excess dough hanging over the edge, but wavy and undulating here and there all over the surface. Roll the bottom excess phyllo inward, in the shallow periphery, to form a thick crust.

If using basic phyllo dough, divide the dough into 5 equal balls. You'll need 3 sheets for the bottom and 2 for the top. Follow the same directions for rolling out Macedonian phyllo, but roll out and brush with oil 3 sheets for the bottom, spread the filling over them, and roll out 2 sheets for the top, maintaining the undulating surface and making the thick rim in the same way.

Bake until the phyllo is golden, about 50 minutes. Remove from the oven, let cool in the pan, and serve.

✳ **NOTE** You may reduce the ingredients by half and bake the pie in a 9-inch or 10-inch round pan.

Onion Pie with Tomatoes and Walnuts from Naoussa

KREMMYDOPITA ME TOMATES KAI KARYDIA

  Makes 10 to 12 servings

This dish is delicious and simple, and the ground walnuts give it a surprisingly substantial texture, as though the pie was filled with ground meat.

⅔ cup extra-virgin olive oil
5 large red onions, coarsely chopped
4 medium firm, ripe tomatoes, grated (see page 459)
Salt and freshly ground black pepper to taste
1½ cups coarsely chopped walnuts
1 recipe Macedonian Phyllo (page 454), Basic Homemade Phyllo Dough (page 453), or commercial phyllo, at room temperature

1. Heat ⅓ cup of the olive oil in a large skillet over medium heat and cook the onions, stirring, until wilted and translucent, 7 to 8 minutes. Add the tomatoes and simmer until most of the liquid has been absorbed. Season with salt and pepper and add the walnuts. Combine.

2. Preheat the oven to 375°F. Lightly oil an 18-inch round pizza or baking pan. If using Macedonian phyllo, divide the dough into 2 equal balls. Keep one ball covered with a kitchen towel or under an inverted bowl while you work with the other dough ball. Place the ball on a lightly floured work surface and dust lightly with flour. Using a heavy, fat rolling pin, roll the dough into a circle 5 to 6 inches in diameter. Do this in sure, even strokes in every direction so that the circle is properly shaped from the start. Sprinkle the surface lightly with flour as you go, after every or every other stroke.

3. Next, place the dough in front of you and place a dowel or small broomstick at the bottom. Roll up the dough along the dowel, gently coaxing it out from the center to the edges as you go. Sprinkle after every or every other turn with a little flour. Turn the dough clockwise after every roll, too, to ensure that it rolls out evenly in all directions. Keep doing this until you get a circle that is about 22 inches in diameter. Place the dough inside the pan, letting the excess hang over the rim. Brush lightly with oil. Spread the filling evenly over the pastry, leaving the inch around the outer rim empty.

4. Roll the second piece of phyllo into a 22-inch circle and place this over the filling in such a way that it isn't pulled tight with the excess dough hanging over the edge, but wavy and undulating here and there all over the surface. Roll the bottom excess phyllo inward, in the shallow periphery, to form a thick crust.

If using basic phyllo dough, divide the dough into 5 equal balls. You'll need 3 sheets for the bottom and 2 for the top. Follow the same directions for rolling out Macedonian phyllo, but roll out and brush with oil 3 sheets for the bottom, spread the filling over them, and roll out 2 sheets for the top, maintaining the undulating surface and making the thick rim in the same way.

Bake until the phyllo is golden, about 50 minutes. Remove from the oven, let cool in the pan, and serve.

✳ **NOTE** You may reduce the ingredients by half and bake the pie in a 9-inch or 10-inch round pan.

Mushroom Pie with Onions, Mint, and Paprika from Nymphaio

MANITAROPITA APO TO NYMPHAIO

Makes 12 to 14 servings

The woods around Nymphaio in central Macedonia burst with mushrooms several times a year. Locals here eat mostly portobellos. While almost any mushrooms—including plain old supermarket button mushrooms—will do for this dish, portobellos lend a meatiness to the filling unmatched by other varieties.

3 tablespoons unsalted butter
5 large onions, coarsely chopped
2 teaspoons sweet paprika
2½ pounds portobello mushrooms, brushed
    clean, stems removed, and caps coarsely
    chopped
Salt to taste
½ cup chopped fresh mint
1 recipe Macedonian Phyllo (page 454), Basic
    Homemade Phyllo Dough (page 453), or
    commercial phyllo, at room temperature
Olive oil for brushing the phyllo

1. Heat the butter in a large skillet, and cook the onions over medium-low heat, stirring, until wilted, about 10 minutes. Add the paprika and stir to mix. Add the mushrooms, season with salt, increase the heat a little, and cook until most of the liquid has evaporated, about 7 to 8 minutes. Remove from the heat and stir in the mint. Let the filling cool slightly.

2. Preheat the oven to 375°F. Lightly oil an 18-inch round pizza or baking pan. If using Macedonian phyllo, on a lightly floured work surface roll out half of the dough into a circle about 24 inches in diameter with a lightly floured rolling pin or dowel and fit into the bottom of the oiled pan.

If using basic phyllo, divide the dough into 6 to 8 balls. Roll each ball into a circle about 24 inches in diameter. Layer half the phyllo sheets into the bottom of the pan, leaving the excess to hang over the edge and brushing each with oil.

3. Spread the filling evenly over the phyllo and cover with the remaining sheet if using Macedonian phyllo or the remaining 3 or 4 sheets if using basic phyllo. Brush each with oil. Roll in the edges to form a crust and score the pie into serving pieces. Bake until the pastry is golden, about 50 minutes. Remove from the oven, let cool in the pan, and serve.

✳ **NOTE** You may reduce the ingredients by half and bake the pie in a 9-inch or 10-inch round pan.

The pie may also be made with commercial phyllo. For every sheet of homemade phyllo use 3 to 4 sheets of commercial phyllo. See directions (page 455) for more details on how to work with frozen phyllo.

Savory Kasseri Cheese Pie

KASSEROPITA

 Makes 10 to 12 servings

Kasseropita *is found all over Macedonia in various forms. Most common are the cheese-filled disks of puff pastry found at fast-food outlets and* tyropitadika—*cheese-pie emporiums. This version is considerably different. It is rich, Sunday afternoon food, the kind of dish made on special occasions and for big family feasts. Most likely it is a recipe that made its way to Greece via the immigrants from Constantinople. Pies like this are still made in Turkey today, delicious, rich, filled* yufkas, *and I also came across a very similar dish in Kos, which also has a large population of Asia Minor Greeks. What's unusual here is the pastry, which is essentially an egg-noodle dough, made without any water at all. Like pasta, the phyllo, oddly, is boiled before the pie is baked.*

For the pastry
8 large eggs
1 teaspoon salt
5 to 6 cups all-purpose flour, as needed
Cornmeal as needed

For the filling
3½ cups (7 sticks) unsalted butter, melted
1½ pounds hard *kasseri* cheese, grated

To serve
1 cup preferably Greek yogurt, drained
   (see page 459)

1. Make the dough: In a large bowl either by hand or with an electric mixer at medium speed, beat the eggs together with the salt. Add the flour, a little at a time, mixing it in with a wooden spoon until a dough mass begins to form. Knead the dough in the bowl, adding more flour if necessary, until it is pliant. It will be a little sticky. Let the dough rest for 30 minutes, covered, at room temperature.

2. Divide the dough into 10 to 12 small balls. On a lightly floured work surface, with a lightly floured rolling pin or dowel, roll each ball into a thin circle about 12 inches in diameter. Sprinkle a large tray with cornmeal. Place the phyllo in layers on the tray, sprinkling each layer with cornmeal to keep them from sticking together.

3. Preheat the oven to 375°F. Lightly oil a 12-inch by 2-inch deep baking pan.

4. Bring a large pot of salted water to a boil. Place one sheet of phyllo in the pot and boil for 2 minutes. Remove carefully and rinse under cold running water in a colander. Drain well. Place the first sheet in the oiled pan. Drizzle with 2 tablespoons of the melted butter and sprinkle with 3 to 4 tablespoons of the *kasseri*. Repeat with all the sheets, topping the pie with phyllo, not with a layer of cheese. Drizzle whatever butter remains over the top sheet. Score the pie into large diagonal wedges and bake until very lightly golden, about 1 hour. Remove from the oven, let cool slightly in the pan, and serve with yogurt on the side.

Savory Pickled Cabbage Pie with Prebaked Phyllo

PITA ME LAHANO TOURSI KAI PSIMENO PHYLLO

 Makes 8 to 10 servings

*T*his dish is found all over Macedonia and Thrace.

1 recipe Basic Homemade Phyllo Dough (page 453) or commercial phyllo, at room temperature
8 cups shredded Pickled Cabbage (page 215) or commercial sauerkraut
3 tablespoons extra-virgin olive oil
2 teaspoons sweet paprika
5 large eggs

1. Have the phyllo ready and at room temperature. Divide into 4 equal balls and keep covered with a kitchen towel.

2. Rinse and drain the cabbage thoroughly. If using sauerkraut, let it soak in several changes of cold water for at least 3 hours, then rinse and drain thoroughly.

3. Heat the olive oil over medium heat in a large heavy skillet and cook the shredded cabbage for about 5 minutes, until translucent. Toss with the paprika and remove from the heat.

4. Preheat the oven to 375°F. Oil a 15-inch-round by 2-inch-deep pizza or baking pan.

5. Turn upside down a 14-inch round by 2-inch deep aluminum or nonstick baking pan, and place it on the bottom of the oven, so that it heats almost like a makeshift griddle. On a lightly floured surface, roll out the first ball of dough to a circle about 14 inches in diameter. Open the oven, pull out the hot upside-down pan, and place the sheet of phyllo over it. Slide immediately back into the oven and bake, turning, for 3 or 4 minutes, just long enough for the phyllo to stiffen and get some color. Remove and set aside.

6. On a lightly floured surface, roll out the next piece of raw pastry to a circle about 18 inches in diameter. Place it on the bottom of the pan with its edges dangling over the sides of the pan. Brush with olive oil. Place the smaller, baked phyllo sheet over it. Beat 3 of the eggs lightly and add to the cabbage, mixing well. Add the filling to the pan, spreading it evenly over the phyllo. Roll out 2 more phyllo sheets to circles about 18 inches in diameter and place over the cabbage filling, brushing each with olive oil. Roll up the excess phyllo along the periphery of the pan. Beat the remaining 2 eggs and pour them over the top of the phyllo. Score the pie into large serving-size pieces, being careful not to draw the knife all the way through the length and width of the pan. Tilt from side to side so that the egg goes all over the surface. Bake for 45 to 50 minutes, until the phyllo is golden and the pie set. Remove from the oven, let cool slightly, and serve.

Sunday Squash Pie from Goumenissa

KYRIAKATIKI KOLOKYTHOPITA TIS GOUMENISSAS

  Makes 8 to 10 servings

I had gone up to Goumenissa, one of the wine appellation regions in Macedonia, a beautiful, lush place of gentle rolling hills about 55 miles northwest of Thessaloniki. It was early February, right around the season for pruning the vineyards, and our host was one of the town's talented young vintners, Christos Aidarinis. I learned a lot from him, about local specialties such as a cured pork loin called psaronefri (see page 333), which came to the region with immigrants from Eastern Romylia, a small pocket in the corner that adjoins Greece, Bulgaria, and Turkey and that now is part of Turkey. Christos took me to visit an aunt of his who is a wonderful cook. She showed me how to make this dish, one of Macedonia's most unusual pies. First, the rim of dough that crowns it is almost a rolled pie unto itself, something I hadn't encountered anywhere else. And second, the pie is open-faced, which is also something that makes it different from the majority of Macedonian pites. Kyria Sofia explained to me that the double filling was a "trick" she learned from her mother, grandmother, and aunts. It was a way to make the pie more substantial in the days when feeding a family meant feeding upward of 10 people.

For the pastry
3 to 3½ cups all-purpose flour, as needed
1 scant teaspoon salt
1 cup warm water
¼ cup extra-virgin olive oil
3 tablespoons red wine vinegar

4 to 6 tablespoons olive oil, as needed, for brushing the phyllo and the pan

For filling #1, for the center
1 large leek, washed well and finely chopped
One 2-pound pumpkin, seeded, peeled, and finely shredded (see page 461)
1 heaping tablespoon dried mint
½ cup crumbled Greek feta cheese
Salt and freshly ground black pepper to taste
1½ cups milk, scalded
3 large eggs

For filling #2, for the rim
1 cup crumbled Greek feta cheese

1. Prepare the phyllo: Combine 3 cups of the flour and salt in a medium bowl. Make a well in the center and add the water, olive oil, and vinegar. Work the flour into the liquid until a mass starts to form. Knead, adding a little more flour if necessary, until the dough is smooth and silky, about 10 minutes. Shape into a ball, cover with plastic wrap, and leave in the bowl to rest for 1 hour.

2. Prepare filling #1: Heat the olive oil in a large skillet over medium heat, and cook the leek, stirring, until wilted and translucent, 7 to 8 minutes. Remove with a slotted spoon and add the shredded pumpkin to the skillet. Cook until most of the liquid has evaporated. In a large bowl, combine the leek, pumpkin, mint, and feta and season with salt and pepper. Add the milk and eggs and mix well. Adjust the seasoning with additional salt if necessary.

3. Divide the dough into 6 equal balls. Preheat the oven to 325°F. Lightly oil a 12-inch cake pan with a removable bottom. Lightly flour your work surface and, with a lightly floured rolling pin or dowel, roll out the first 4 balls into 13-inch round phyllo sheets. Layer them inside the pan, brushing each layer with the olive oil. Bake until slightly crisp, 6 to 8 minutes. Remove the pan from the oven and increase the oven temperature to 375°F.

4. Roll the remaining 2 balls of dough into large, thin circles about 18 inches in diameter. Brush each with the olive oil and sprinkle with the crumbled feta. Roll up into tight cylinders. Fit the first one into half the pan, around the circumference, shirring it or twisting it slightly. Do the same with the second. Pour filling #1 into the center of the pie and bake at 375°F until the filling is set and the dough firm and golden, about 1 hour. Remove from the oven, and let cool in the pan. Remove the pie from the pan and serve, either warm or at room temperature.

MEAT

Meat cookery in Macedonia and Thrace doesn't differ tremendously from that in the rest of the country. Traditionally meat follows a season here: pork and some poultry and fowl in winter, lamb and goat in spring, and small game all year round, depending on the hunting seasons. What one does find up here, though, is a bevy of interesting meat stews that use strictly local ingredients such as red peppers and pickled cabbage. The traditions are cold-weather ones, and there are also lots of hearty meat and poultry dishes that fall somewhere between soups and stews and are cooked together with grain products such as *trahana,* bulgur, or the local couscous. There is a lot of pork as well as beef and veal in the region. Indeed, not too far from Thessaloniki, in the swamps near Serres, even buffalo are raised, and Soufli in Thrace is one of the biggest beef and pork centers.

Pork Loin Cooked with Chestnuts

HOIRINO ME KASTANA

Makes 4 to 6 servings

This recipe went through a few transformations. It is one of the classics in the northern Greek kitchen, but it is usually a stew. I never liked the texture of the cut-up pork and chestnuts together, and visually it wasn't that appealing either. So I reworked it with a whole rolled pork loin. It makes for lovely Sunday fare. Serve it with Savory Pie with Roasted Red Peppers and Onions (page 235).

1 pork loin (about 3 pounds), boned and rolled

Salt and freshly ground black pepper to taste

⅓ cup extra-virgin olive oil

1 cup dry red wine

4 medium onions, halved and sliced

1 cup peeled, seeded, and chopped plum
   tomatoes (canned are fine)

1½ pounds chestnuts, boiled and peeled
   (see page 458)

1. Season the pork with salt and pepper. In a large pot, heat the oil over high heat and sear the meat, turning to brown it on all sides. Pour in ½ cup of the wine and cook until about half of it evaporates, 5 to 6 minutes. Oil a 10-inch round clay or ovenproof glass baking dish that is 3 inches deep and place the seared meat in the dish. Preheat the oven to 375°F.

2. Place the pot back on the stove over low heat and add the onions. Cook in the oil and pork fat until wilted, about 10 minutes. Add the tomatoes, half the chestnuts, and the remaining ½ cup wine. Season with salt and pepper and simmer for about 10 minutes, until thickened a little. Pour the sauce over and around the meat. Cover the dish with a sheet of aluminum foil and bake until the meat is tender, about 1½ hours. About halfway through the baking, add the remaining chestnuts and a little water if necessary to keep the dish moist. Remove from the oven, let cool slightly, and serve.

Pork and Pickled Cabbage Stew

HOIRINO ME LAHANO TOURSI

Makes 6 servings

This is the classic Christmas dish in many parts of Macedonia and Thrace. Home cooks put cabbage up in late September and say that it has to steep for a full 3 months before it is ready. The flavor of local pickled cabbage is quite different from that of commercial sauerkraut. It is tangier, and the vegetable retains much of its crunchy texture. The closest one can find to the real thing is the cabbage sold in barrels at Greek and Middle Eastern food shops, but it pales in comparison, and its taste is often too sharp and overpowering. You can use it, but it needs to be soaked very well. You can also start about 3 weeks before preparing this dish and make your own pickled cabbage.

3 quarters of 1 head Pickled Cabbage
   (page 215), about 8 cups shredded

3 pounds boneless pork shoulder, trimmed of fat
   and cut into stewing pieces

½ cup all-purpose flour

⅓ to ½ cup extra-virgin olive oil, as needed

⅔ cup dry red wine

3 tablespoons unsalted butter

1 heaping tablespoon tomato paste or sweet
   paprika

1 heaping teaspoon *boukovo* or red pepper flakes (optional)

6 to 8 allspice berries, to taste

Freshly ground black pepper to taste

Juice of 1 lemon

1. If using commercial sauerkraut, soak it for 3 hours in several changes of water before using. Drain well. If using homemade pickled cabbage, remove from the brine and rinse under cold water. Shred finely.

2. Lightly dredge the pork in the flour. Heat ⅓ cup of the olive oil in a large, heavy skillet and sear the pork over medium-high heat, turning to brown on all sides. It will probably be necessary to do this in batches, and you may need to add more oil. Once browned, place all the pork pieces in the skillet and pour in the wine. Remove the pork from the heat as soon as the wine steams off.

3. In a large pot, melt the butter over medium heat and cook the drained cabbage, tossing it with the tomato paste or paprika, *boukovo* or pepper flakes, and allspice berries. Cook for about 5 minutes for the cabbage and spices to meld. Remove half the cabbage. Place the pork in the pot over half the cabbage, season with pepper, and cover with the remaining cabbage. Pour in the lemon juice, cover the pot, and simmer over very low heat until the meat is very tender, 1½ to 2 hours. Remove from the heat, let cool slightly, and serve.

⊙ Chicken Stewed with Pickled Cabbage (Kotopoulo me Lahano Toursi): In lieu of pork, use one 3-pound chicken, cut into serving-size pieces. Proceed as directed.

Pan-Fried Pork with Leeks, Hot Pepper, and Wine

TIGANIA

   Makes 4 to 6 servings

The word means, literally, "of the frying pan." There are lots of versions of this dish throughout the region, some plain, some fancy, like this one. Tigania is one of Macedonia's classic mezethes.

1½ pounds boneless pork shoulder, trimmed of fat and cut into 1½-inch cubes

Salt and freshly ground black pepper to taste

1 teaspoon sweet paprika

½ teaspoon *boukovo* or red pepper flakes, or more to taste

½ teaspoon dried mint

1 tablespoon grated orange zest

⅓ cup extra-virgin olive oil

1 large leek, white part only, washed well and chopped

1 large red onion, chopped

1 cup dry red wine

1. In a medium bowl, toss the pork with the salt, black pepper, paprika, *boukovo* or pepper flakes, mint, and orange zest. Cover and refrigerate for at least 1 hour.

2. Heat the olive oil in a large, heavy skillet over medium-high heat. Add the pork and cook, stirring, until browned on all sides. Remove with a slotted spoon. Lower the heat to medium, add the leek and onion, and cook, stirring, until translucent, 7 to 8 minutes. Add the pork back into the skillet, pour in the wine, and cover. Reduce the heat to low and continue to simmer until the pork is tender, 1 to 1½ hours. Add more water or wine to the skillet if necessary to keep the contents moist. Serve warm, as a *meze* or main course.

Veal with Eggplant Cream

HOUYIAR BEYIEDI

 Makes 4 to 6 servings

I know, I know, the name does not sound very Greek. Nevertheless, in the repertoire of delicious Sunday recipes, this classic of the Constantinople Greeks stands out.

3 tablespoons unsalted butter

2 pounds boneless veal shoulder, trimmed of fat and cut into stewing pieces

2 medium red onions, finely chopped

2 garlic cloves, minced

1½ cups peeled, seeded, and chopped plum tomatoes (canned are fine)

Salt and freshly ground black pepper to taste

1 teaspoon dried Greek oregano

½ cup dry red wine

2 large eggplants

For the béchamel

1 tablespoon unsalted butter

1 tablespoon all-purpose flour

½ cup milk

Salt and freshly ground black pepper to taste

A grating of nutmeg

½ cup grated *kasseri* cheese

1. Heat the butter in a large Dutch oven or wide pot over medium-high heat and brown the meat on all sides. Remove with a slotted spoon and add the onions and garlic. Cook over medium heat stirring, until wilted, about 8 minutes. Place the meat back in the pot. Pour in the tomatoes and season with salt, pepper, and oregano. Bring to a boil, reduce the heat to low, and simmer until the meat is tender, 1½ to 2 hours. About halfway through the cooking, add the wine.

2. Meanwhile, grill the eggplants over a gas or electric burner or grill set on low heat, turning, until the skins are charred and the eggplants are soft.

3. Make the béchamel: In a large saucepan, heat the butter until it bubbles; don't let it brown. Add the flour and stir with a whisk or wooden spoon over medium heat until it turns a light gold color. Add the milk and simmer, stirring all the while, until the sauce is thick. Season with salt, pepper, and nutmeg. When the sauce is thick, remove from the heat and stir in the cheese. Cover to keep warm.

4. Cut the eggplants open down the middle and remove the pulp. Place in a medium bowl, discarding as many of the seeds as possible. Mash the eggplant with a fork, then add it the hot béchamel, stirring gently but well to blend thoroughly. The eggplant and béchamel may also be combined in a blender or food processor.

5. To serve: Place the meat and pan juices on a serving platter and top with the eggplant cream or serve the eggplant cream on the side. Serve hot.

Veal Stewed with Tart Apples and Prunes

MOSCHARI STIFADO ME XINOMILA KAI DAMASKINA

Makes 4 to 6 servings

I *came across this dish in parts of western Macedonia.*

½ cup extra-virgin olive oil

2 pounds small stewing onions, peeled

1⅓ cups all-purpose flour

Salt and freshly ground black pepper to taste

2½ pounds boneless veal shoulder, trimmed of
fat and cut into stewing pieces

2 bay leaves

½ cup chopped fresh mint

8 to 10 pitted prunes, to taste

3 Granny Smith or other tart green apples,
peeled, cored, cut into 1½-inch cubes, and
held in acidulated water (see page 458)

1. Heat the olive oil in a large stewing pot or Dutch oven over medium heat and cook the onions, stirring, until golden and translucent, about 10 minutes. Remove with a slotted spoon and set aside. While the onions are cooking, season the flour with salt and pepper and dredge the veal lightly in it, tapping off any excess. Increase the heat under the pot to medium-high, add the veal, and brown.

2. Add the onions back to the pot, together with the bay leaves and mint. Season with salt and pepper. Add enough water to the pot to barely cover the meat. Reduce the heat to medium-low, cover, and simmer until the veal is tender, about 1½ hours. Add the prunes to the pot and continue to simmer for 15 minutes. Drain and add the apples and simmer, covered, for another 15 minutes. Remove from the heat, remove the bay leaves, cool slightly and serve.

Little Meatballs in Tomato Béchamel from Naoussa

KEFTEDES STIN ARMI

Makes 20 to 24 meatballs

M*any Macedonian sauces are thickened with roux. This dish comes from Naoussa and sometimes is made with fried cheese instead of little meatballs as in* Kash sto Tigani *(page 219) and sometimes with offal.*

1 large egg

1 medium red onion, finely chopped

1 tablespoon dried mint

1 tablespoon dried Greek oregano

1 teaspoon freshly ground black pepper

2 tablespoons extra-virgin olive oil

Two 1-inch-thick slices stale rustic bread, crusts
removed, dampened under the tap, and
squeezed dry

1 pound lean ground beef

¼ cup soda water

1 teaspoon salt

All-purpose flour for dredging

Olive or other vegetable oil for frying

For the tomato béchamel

3 tablespoons olive oil

2 tablespoons all-purpose flour

1 heaping tablespoon tomato paste

2 garlic cloves, minced

3 cups water

Salt to taste

2 bay leaves

1. In a medium bowl, combine the egg, onion, herbs, pepper, and olive oil. Crumble the dampened bread and add to the mixture. Add the ground beef and soda water, season with the salt and pepper, and knead well. Cover and refrigerate for 1 hour.

2. A heaping tablespoon at a time, shape the meat mixture into little balls. Dredge lightly in flour. Heat ½ inch of olive or other oil in a large, heavy skillet over medium-high heat. When the oil is very hot, fry the meatballs, in batches, until golden on all sides. Remove with a slotted spoon and drain on paper towels.

3. Make the tomato béchamel: Carefully discard the used oil and wipe the skillet clean. Heat the olive oil in the skillet over medium heat. Add the flour to the hot oil and stir with a wooden spoon until thick and lightly browned. Add the tomato paste and continue stirring. Add the garlic and stir, then pour in the water. Season with salt. Add the bay leaves. Stir the sauce constantly over medium heat until it is thick, about 5 minutes. Place the meatballs back in the skillet and cook together for about 5 minutes. Remove the bay leaves. Serve either warm or at room temperature.

KOURBANI

It was a most unusual introduction to the folkways of a small municipality once renowned only for its gentlemanly trades of silk and wine. At 7:00 A.M. we left our hotel and headed to the far side of Goumenissa, up a hill to the parish that belongs to the eastern Romyliote Greeks. It was February 1, the name day of Saint Tryphon, protector of the vine, which the eastern Romyliotes celebrate by upholding the ancient ritual of the *kourbani*, or offering.

Daylight cracked mauve over the hills beyond the church, prim with their rows of vines, and we hung around, apprehensive, sipping coffee and looking at old newspaper clippings, waiting for the event to begin. About 8:00 A.M., we heard the sound of trumpets and drums. We saw the bull, garlanded with flowers. Gypsy musicians trotted slightly ahead, beckoning the animal up the avenue. Two men, fighting its obstinance and strength, tugged the bull ahead with ropes that were tied around its horns.

Once at the top of the hill, the animal was secured to the wall on the left side of the church. Parishioners arrived. Some went directly inside the church for the Liturgy, others helped prepare for the fete. They washed the cauldrons and stoked the fire. They decorated the sides of the church and the icons of Saint Tryphon with grapes. They set up tables and made more coffee, and as we stood around drinking it, caught unawares, we suddenly heard the dull thump. There was no pomp. All we saw was the bull fall, killed skillfully and quickly with one shot to the skull from a silent revolver. The priest brought the Liturgy outside, to bless the uncooked meat. Then the bull was skinned and carved and boiled, blessed again, and distributed among parishioners and visitors during the feast which ensued. Its hide was pinned to the other side of the church, near the icons and the grapes.

The offering of a bull or other male animal is not unique to Goumenissa. In other parts of Macedonia, on different saints' days, male animals are also sacrificed. There is a well-known and well-organized *kourbani* at Petra in Mytillene on the name day of Saint Paraskevi in early summer, and a bull is also offered in Attica, in the town of Spata, a few kilometers outside Athens, each July 20, on the name days of Saints Peter and Paul. The word *kourbani* derives from the Turkish *kurban* and from the Hebrew *qorban*, which both mean offering.

What differentiates the *kourbani* at Goumenissa is its timeliness and its history. The tradition belongs only to the town's eastern Romyliotes, who brought the custom of the sacrifice with them when they emigrated from Bulgaria after the exchange of populations in 1924. At certain times over the last seventy years, either because of poverty or because the parish was not yet built, the offering was made with either a cock or a ram (bulls are expensive), and it took place at different intersections in the neighborhood of the eastern Romyliotes.

The ritual has come under scrutiny in the last few years, exposing the differences between the eastern Romyliote Greeks of Goumenissa and the town's other groups, which include the indigenous Greek population, the Pontians, and Gypsies, and casting light on the whole murky question of pagan ritual adapted to Christianity. The church takes a tepid stand, neither condoning outright nor forbidding it.

Festive Meat Stew from Thrace

KOURBANI

 Makes 6 to 8 servings

In parts of Thrace, especially among former pastoral communities, the kourbani *refers to the festive lamb and rice dish prepared on the feast day of Saint George, in early spring, just when local shepherds would begin their bi-annual migration to the highlands in the Rodopi Mountains. This recipe comes from a woman I met in Vyssa, a forgotten old town in the northernmost reaches of Thrace.*

I have taken some liberties with the original version of this dish, which calls for poaching the lamb and then cutting it up and adding it straightaway to the half-cooked rice. This dish would traditionally have been made in a wood-burning oven.

1 leg of lamb, bone in, about 5 pounds
Salt
Freshly ground black pepper to taste
⅔ cup butter
2 pounds scallions
2 tablespoons extra-virgin olive oil
2 teaspoons sweet paprika
½ teaspoon cayenne pepper (optional)
2 cups short-grain, polished rice, rinsed and
    drained
½ cup fresh lemon balm or lemon basil, coarsely
    chopped
½ cup fresh mint, coarsely chopped
½ cup golden raisins

1. Wash and pat dry the lamb, and season with salt and pepper. Heat half the butter in a flameproof casserole dish or roasting pan large enough to hold the lamb. Add the lamb, raise the heat to high, and sear on all sides until browned, about 10 minutes. Add enough water to cover the lamb. Bring to a boil, reduce heat to low, and poach the lamb for about 45 minutes. Remove the lamb from the pot, reserving the liquid, cool slightly, and cut into ½-inch slices. Cut each slice into smaller pieces, about 2 inches square. Preheat oven to 350°F.

2. While the lamb is simmering, bring a large pot of salted water to a boil. Cut the scallions into 2-inch pieces all the way up the green part (discarding only about an inch off the tops) and drop into the water. As soon as it begins to boil again, simmer the scallions for 3 minutes to soften. Drain, reserving the water.

3. In a large, wide skillet, heat the olive oil and add the scallions, paprika, cayenne, and salt. Stir all together for one minute, then add the rice. Stir for another minute. Add 2 cups of the lamb broth to the rice, season with salt and pepper, and simmer over low heat until the liquid is absorbed, 10 to 12 minutes. Remove from the heat.

4. Measure out the remaining lamb liquid and set aside. Toss the lamb, rice mixture, fresh herbs, and raisins all together in the roasting pan or casserole. Add 4 cups of lamb broth, or a combination of lamb broth and the liquid remaining from poaching the scallions, if there isn't enough left of the meat broth. Dot with the remaining butter. Cover the pan with aluminum foil and bake for about 1 hour, until the liquid is absorbed and the lamb and rice tender. Add more liquid if necessary during baking to keep the mixture moist.

Remove from the oven, let cool slightly, and serve.

Easter Goat Roasted on a Bed of Scallion Greens

PASCHALIATIKO KATSIKAKI TIS ORMAS

 Makes 6 to 8 servings

rma is a sleepy town in central Macedonia, not too far a drive from Aridea, where I had been to interview the last paprika producer in the region. The town square, like so many in Greece, is built around huge, centuries-old sycamore trees, and I parked under one and set off to find the person whose name I had gotten from my connection in Aridea, Kyria Yianna Zakou, owner of a small cafeneion.

It was a stifling hot late-summer day, and she sat me down and brought me a bottle of locally made lemonade. We went through the typical niceties, and then she started talking. Her daughter came over and sat down. Next came her husband and son-in-law, who had just snapped closed their backgammon board to join us, adding their own dose of knowledge about local food customs.

This dish could only belong to the North of Greece, and all the telltale signs of this region's cooking are to be found in it. For one, the use of nearly whole scallions. In many old recipes, scallion and onion greens were used in salads and in baked dishes such as this. It is common to bake lots of different meat and fish dishes over beds of vegetables, especially those in the onion family. As for the eggs, in the traditional cuisine that evolved out of the natural environment and the religious dictates after 40 days of fasting for Lent, lots of eggs were always on hand.

1 leg of goat, bone in (7 to 8 pounds) or 5 pounds
    stewing pieces with bone (see Note)
Salt and freshly ground black pepper to taste
⅔ cup extra-virgin olive oil, plus extra for
    rubbing if using leg

5 pounds scallions, tender greens only, washed
    and cut into 1-inch pieces (save the whites
    for another use)
2 to 3 tablespoons sweet paprika, to taste
2 cups chopped fresh mint
2 cups water
3 large eggs

1. Rinse and pat the meat dry with paper towels. If using a whole leg, season with salt and pepper and rub with olive oil, then heat ⅓ cup of the olive oil in a large flameproof baking pan over high heat. Add the meat and sear in the oil, turning to brown on all sides. If using stewing pieces, season with salt and pepper, then heat ⅓ cup of the olive oil in a Dutch oven or large stewing pot and brown the meat over high heat. Remove from the pan or pot. Preheat the oven to 375°F.

2. Meanwhile, heat ⅓ cup of the remaining olive oil in a large, wide pot over medium heat, add the scallion greens, reduce heat to low, and cook, stirring, until wilted, 7 to 8 minutes. Season with salt and pepper and add the paprika. Cook, stirring, until very soft and well blended with the paprika, another 10 to 12 minutes or so. Remove from the heat and mix in the mint.

3. Spread the scallions over the bottom of a large roasting pan. Place the meat (leg or stewing pieces) on top and place in the oven. Adjust the seasoning with salt and pepper, add the water, and roast, covered with aluminum foil, until the meat is very tender, about 1½ hours. About 15 minutes before the meat is ready, beat the eggs and pour over the scallions. Remove the foil and continue baking until the eggs form a crust. Remove from the oven, let cool slightly, and serve.

✳ NOTE You may substitute lamb for the goat.

Easter Lamb Cooked on a Bed of Spinach and Rice from Kozani

ARNAKI PSIMENO PANO SE SPANAKORIZO

 Makes 6 to 8 servings

¼ cup (½ stick) unsalted butter

1 leg of lamb, bone in (7 to 8 pounds)

Salt and freshly ground black pepper to taste

1 lamb's liver (optional), trimmed of membranes

½ cup extra-virgin olive oil

1 pound scallions or spring onions, white and
    tender green parts, coarsely chopped

1 tablespoon sweet paprika

4 pounds fresh flat-leaf spinach, trimmed,
    coarsely chopped and washed well

1 cup chopped fresh mint

1 cup short-grain rice

2 cups water

1. Melt the butter in a large roasting pan over high heat. Season the lamb with salt and pepper and sear in the butter. Set aside and preheat the oven to 400°F.

2. Meanwhile, simmer the liver in lightly salted water for 15 minutes. Drain and chop finely.

3. Heat the olive oil in a large, heavy skillet over medium heat and cook the scallions, stirring, until wilted, 7 minutes. Stir in the paprika and continue to cook for 2 to 3 minutes. Add the spinach, in batches, and cook until wilted, 7 to 10 minutes. Add the liver and mint and season with salt and pepper. Add the rice and cook for 5 minutes, stirring. Spread the mixture around the lamb in the pan, add the water, and roast until the lamb is tender or cooked to desired doneness and the rice soft, about 1½ hours. Remove from the oven, let rest for 15 minutes, and serve.

ROLLED LEAVES AND OTHER STUFFED DISHES

The range of rolled leaves and other stuffed dishes is large enough in Macedonia to have several different names. *Yiaprakia* is the local name given to cabbage *dolmathes,* of which there are many recipes; *sarmathes* are distinguished by their filling—rolled leaves (cabbage, vine leaves, lettuce, etc.) stuffed with meat; and *dolmathes* is a term used interchangeably with either. In the following recipes I have selected a few typical and not-so-typical Macedonian stuffed and rolled dishes.

Stuffed and Rolled Pickled Cabbage Leaves

YIAPRAKIA ME LAHANO TOURSI

 Makes 6 to 8 servings

You can find commercially pickled whole, half, or quartered heads of green cabbage in Greek specialty food stores. But commercially pickled cabbage is a far cry from the homemade kind. Usually it is extremely salty and stays that way no matter how long you soak it. I recommend starting at least 3 weeks before you prepare this recipe and making your own pickled cabbage (see page 215).

This dish is delicious served with roasted red peppers in oil.

2 pounds pickled green cabbage, core removed
    and leaves pulled away

¼ pound lean ground beef

¼ pound lean ground pork

¼ cup short-grain rice

3 large red onions, finely chopped or grated

⅓ cup plus ½ cup olive oil

1 teaspoon sweet paprika
½ teaspoon ground allspice
½ teaspoon ground cinnamon
1 tablespoon tomato paste diluted with
    1 tablespoon water
Freshly ground black pepper to taste
1 cinnamon stick
5 to 6 allspice berries, to taste

1. Rinse the pickled cabbage very well under cold tap water and drain well in a colander.

2. Combine the ground meats, rice, onions, ⅓ cup olive oil, the paprika, ground allspice, ground cinnamon, diluted tomato paste, and pepper in a large bowl and knead together well.

3. Separate the cabbage leaves. Cover the bottom of a large wide pot or Dutch oven with a layer of the torn cabbage leaves, or with those that are too small to roll.

4. Start to fill and roll the remainder: Place a leaf at a time in front of you and add a scant tablespoon of the meat-and-rice mixture to the bottom center of each leaf. Fold the bottom and sides over the filling and roll up, tucking in the sides as you go, to form a *dolma,* or small finger-size cylinder. Continue with the remaining filling and cabbage. Place the stuffed leaves seam side down, snugly next to one another in one or two layers, as necessary. Place the cinnamon stick and several whole allspice berries over the *yiaprakia.* Pour in the remaining ½ cup olive oil. Cover with a few more loose cabbage leaves and weigh down with a plate. Add enough water to the pan to cover the *yiaprakia* by 1 inch. Place the lid on the pan and bring the *yiaprakia* to a boil. Reduce the heat to low and simmer until the cabbage is tender and the meat and rice are cooked, about 1 hour.

Meat-Stuffed Carrots Constantinople Style

KAROTA GEMISTA TIS SOULAS BOZI

  Makes 4 to 6 servings

I was introduced to this dish by a friend and colleague named Soula Bozi, who includes a similar recipe in her book on the cooking of the Poli Greeks. Inspired by its very baroque and festive qualities, I have adapted it. It's an eye catcher and a great dish on buffet tables.

8 very large carrots, 1¼ to 1½ inches in diameter
3 tablespoons extra-virgin olive oil
2 medium onions, very finely chopped
½ pound lean ground beef
3 tablespoons short-grain rice
½ cup finely chopped fresh flat-leaf parsley
1 tablespoon dried mint
Salt and freshly ground black pepper to taste
2 tablespoons unsalted butter
½ cup dry white wine
Preferably Greek yogurt for serving, drained
    (see page 459) or *avgolemono:* 2 large eggs
    and juice of 1 large lemon

1. Peel and wash the carrots and trim them at both ends. Using a sharp boning knife or a vegetable corer, carefully bore a cavity into each of the carrots. This can be difficult. Start at the widest end and work slowly, being careful to bore the hole straight. Hold the carrot firmly in your palm while doing this to reduce the risk of its cracking apart. Discard the pulp or save it for another use in soups or dips, for example.

2. Heat the olive oil in a large skillet and cook the onions over low heat until wilted, about 7 minutes. Combine the meat, rice, onions, parsley, mint, salt, and pepper together in a medium bowl and knead well. Using your index finger or a chopstick or other similar tool, press the meat into the carrots.

3. Melt the butter in a large, deep skillet over low heat and add the carrots. Toss lightly in the butter to coat. Season with salt. Cook the carrots for 10 to 15 minutes, shaking them in the skillet. Add the wine and steam off. Pour in just enough water to cover the carrots and simmer, covered, over low heat until they are tender, about an hour, replenishing with additional water if necessary. Remove from the heat and let cool slightly.

4. To serve: Place on a serving platter, cut into large pieces, if desired, and dollop with yogurt, or make and serve with *avgolemono:* Using a wire whisk, beat the eggs and lemon juice together in a small bowl and add a ladleful of the pot juices to the mixture, stirring all the while. Pour the egg-and-lemon mixture back into the pot over the carrots and serve.

Quinces Stuffed with Ground Lamb

KYDONIA GEMISTA ME KIMA

   Makes 6 servings

Meat-stuffed quinces are yet another one of the great dishes of the Poli Greeks, those who emigrated from Constantinople in the early part of the twentieth century. This is a winter dish, when golden quinces are in season, and one that usually appears on festive tables.

6 large quinces
1 lemon, halved
6 tablespoons unsalted butter
2 large red onions, finely chopped
¾ pound ground lamb, preferably from the leg
1 large firm, ripe tomato, grated (see page 459) or ⅔ cup canned crushed tomatoes
Salt and freshly ground black pepper to taste
1 teaspoon ground cinnamon
½ teaspoon ground cloves
½ cup finely chopped fresh flat-leaf parsley
1 cup water

1. Preheat the oven to 375°F. Cut the tops off the quinces and reserve. Core the quinces with an apple corer, then, using a teaspoon, carefully scrape and scoop out the pulp without puncturing the fruit, until each quince shell is about ½ inch thick. Rub a cut lemon on the inside of each quince to keep them from discoloring. Finely chop the quince pulp.

2. Melt 2 tablespoons of the butter in a large skillet over low heat and cook the onions, covered, until pale and very lightly golden, about 15 minutes. Add the quince pulp and lamb, increase the heat to medium, and brown. Add the tomato, season with salt, pepper, cinnamon, and cloves, and simmer, uncovered, until most of the juices are cooked off. Remove from the heat, let cool, and stir in the parsley.

3. Take 1 tablespoon of the butter and dab a little inside each of the quinces. Fill with the meat mixture, mounding the mixture over the top of each quince slightly. Cover each quince with its cap.

4. Place in a buttered ovenproof glass or ceramic baking dish. Melt the remaining 3 tablespoons butter and pour over the quinces. Add the water to the pan, cover with aluminum foil, and bake until the quinces are fork-tender and the meat is cooked, 45 minutes to 1 hour. Serve warm.

⊙ In lieu of the tomato, add ⅓ cup raisins and 3 tablespoons toasted pine nuts (see page 458) to the filling.

FISH AND SEAFOOD

Where to begin on the subject of Macedonian fish and seafood? I mentioned in the introduction to the chapter that Macedonia is a land that has it all geographically: tiny coves that teem with fish and sea life, furious rivers, and calm mountain lakes. So it stands to reason that its fish and seafood traditions evolved out of the bounty of its marine environments—that, coupled, of course, with the complex ethno-social history of the North.

Several of the dishes in the Macedonian fish and seafood repertoire are *mezethes* and soups and appear within the chapter as such. In the handful of main course fish recipes that follow I have tried to provide a small but representative selection.

Carp and Red Pepper Stew

MANTZIA

 Makes 4 servings

This dish falls somewhere between a soup and a stew. The recipe is a specialty of the lake region of Prespes, bordering Albania and Skopia. There are several dishes that go by the same name, which basically means stew in the local dialect. Carp, one of the most common fish in the region, is almost always preferred for this dish, although grey mullet, which abounds in the beautiful lakes up here, is also sometimes called for.

2½ pounds carp or grey mullet, gutted and
    cleaned (bones and head intact), and cut
    into 1½-inch-thick wedges
Salt to taste
¼ cup olive oil
2 large onions, grated or finely chopped
1 large red bell pepper, seeded and chopped
1 large firm, ripe tomato, grated (see page 459)
Leaves from 1 small bunch fresh flat-leaf
    parsley, finely chopped
2 tablespoons all-purpose flour
2 tablespoons water

1. Season the fish with salt and set aside for a few minutes. Heat the olive oil in a large pot and cook the onions over medium heat, stirring, until soft and lightly golden. Add the bell pepper and cook for about 5 minutes, stirring, to soften. Add the tomato, parsley, and enough water to come about one-third of the way up the pot. Bring to a boil. Reduce the heat to low.

2. Stir the flour into the water and add it to the pot. Season with salt and stir. Place the fish over the vegetables and simmer, with the lid askew, for 35 to 45 minutes; the *mantzia* should be thick but liquid. Remove from the heat, cool slightly, and serve.

Red Mullet or Sea Bass Baked in Paper

BARBOUNI OR LAVRAKI STO LADOHARTO

 Makes about 4 servings

I ran across a few versions of this recipe in various Thessaloniki tavernas, so I include it here.

2½ pounds whole red mullet or small sea bass, cleaned and gutted, heads left on
Salt to taste
1 tablespoon extra-virgin olive oil per fish, plus extra for brushing parchment and oiling pan
1 tablespoon fresh lemon juice per fish
2 medium red onions, cut into rings ¼ inch thick
2 medium firm, ripe tomatoes, cut into thin rounds
2 garlic cloves, very thinly sliced
As many bay leaves as there are fish
Freshly ground black pepper to taste
½ cup chopped fresh flat-leaf parsley

1. Preheat the oven to 375°F. Sprinkle the fish with salt and set aside. Cut as many pieces of parchment as there are fish into 15-inch squares. Use 2 pieces of parchment per fish and place one on top of the other. Brush the surface with olive oil.

2. Place one fish on each square. Sprinkle each fish with 1 tablespoon lemon juice. Distribute the onion, tomato, and garlic slices evenly among the fish. Place a bay leaf on each fish. Sprinkle with pepper and parsley and drizzle each fish with 1 tablespoon olive oil. Fold the paper like a packet or an envelope over the fish. Tie each packet closed with a short string, the way you would ribbon on a gift. Place seam side up in a large, oiled baking pan. Sprinkle the outside of the parchment with a little water to keep it from burning. Bake until the fish are cooked through, 30 to 35 minutes. Remove from the oven, let cool for a few minutes, remove the bay leaves, and serve.

Sweet Water Fish Baked over Red Peppers

GRIVADI STIFADO

 Makes 6 servings

Throughout central and western Macedonia, I ran across many recipes that call for cooking either fish or meat on a bed of vegetables, which almost always includes onions, leeks, or scallions. It is a curious custom that isn't found in other parts of the country. In this and the next 2 recipes the ingredients vary slightly, but the basic idea remains the same.

6 carp fillets, cod fillets, or halibut steaks (2½ to 3 pounds total)
Salt to taste
⅓ cup extra-virgin olive oil
2 medium red onions, sliced
3 large red bell peppers, roasted (see page 460), peeled, and coarsely chopped
1 medium firm, ripe tomato, grated (see page 459)
2 teaspoons sweet paprika
¼ cup chopped fresh flat-leaf parsley
All-purpose flour for dredging the fish

1. Wash the fish and pat dry with paper towels. Season with salt and set aside. Preheat the oven to 350°F.

2. Heat the olive oil in a large skillet over medium heat and cook the onions, stirring, until wilted, 7 to 8 minutes. Add the roasted peppers, tomato, and paprika and simmer for 5 minutes. Remove from the heat and stir in the parsley.

3. Spread the mixture in the bottom of a medium oiled baking pan. Dredge the fish in flour, tapping off any excess, and place the fish side by side over the onions and peppers. Bake, turning once, until the fish are golden on both sides and the onion mixture soft, 25 to 35 minutes. Remove from the oven and serve.

☉ Replace the onions with 2 large leeks, white and as much of the green parts as possible, sliced, and omit the roasted red peppers.

Fresh Anchovies Baked with Onions

GAVROS STO FOURNO

 Makes 4 to 6 servings

2 pounds fresh anchovies
Salt to taste
⅓ cup plus ¼ cup extra-virgin olive oil
2½ cups halved and very thinly sliced red onions
2 garlic cloves, minced
1 fresh rosemary sprig
Freshly ground black pepper to taste
Juice of 1 to 2 lemons, to taste

1. Clean the fish: Wash, remove the heads and guts, and pull away the spines. Salt and refrigerate the fish for 1 hour.

2. Meanwhile, heat ⅓ cup of the olive oil in a large skillet over medium-low heat and cook the onions and garlic until wilted, 7 to 8 minutes.

3. Preheat the oven to 350°F. Layer the onions and garlic in a large shallow baking pan, preferably made of glass. Place the rosemary sprig in the center and the fish on top. Season generously with salt, pepper, and lemon juice and drizzle with the remaining ¼ cup olive oil. Bake until the fish are cooked through, about 35 minutes. Serve hot.

Cod Croquettes

BAKALIAROKEFTEDES

 Makes about 32 fritters

*B*atter-fried cod is no stranger to Greek tables since cod traveled inland with roving merchants and was often the only fish available to Greeks whose access to the sea was limited. This version, with parsley and onions added to the shredded cod, came to the local table via the Greeks who emigrated from Smyrna.

2 pounds salt cod fillets
1½ cups chopped fresh flat-leaf parsley
1 large onion, finely chopped
1 large egg, lightly beaten
¾ to 1 cup all-purpose flour, as needed
1 teaspoon baking soda
Salt and freshly ground black pepper to taste
Olive or vegetable oil for frying
1 recipe Macedonian Garlic Sauce (page 216) or
   any other *skordalia*

1. Soak the cod as directed on page 463. Drain and rinse. Place in a large pot, cover with water, and simmer until soft, about 7 minutes. Drain and let cool slightly. Remove any black skin and bones.

2. Crumble the cod by hand in a medium bowl. Combine with the parsley, onion, and egg. Combine ¾ cup of the flour and the baking soda and slowly add it to the cod, stirring, until the mixture is mealy and sticky. Season with salt and pepper. Test the consistency by shaping a small patty. It should hold together. Add more flour if necessary.

3. Heat about 2 inches of oil in a large, heavy skillet over medium-high heat. When the oil is very hot, drop a heaping tablespoon at a time of the cod mixture into the hot oil. Fry, turning once, until golden and crisp. Remove with a slotted spoon, drain on paper towels, and serve hot with the *skordalia*.

SWEETS

My favorite story in the annals of Macedonian patisserie is the one about the brothers Roumbos of Serres, renowned makers of the local specialty, *akhanes,* a kind of *loukoumi* (Turkish delight) in which the main flavor characteristic is butter. *Akhanes* traces its origins to the Turkish occupation, during which time the sweet was made high up in the mountain villages outside the city, where the local water is reputed to be of excellent quality. After the Turks departed, there wasn't enough year-round business in the mountain villages to sustain the *akhanes* makers, so they moved cityside to Serres. There are many makers of the buttery, button-shaped little *akhanes* today, but the best known are still the brothers Roumbos, whose father and grandfather had both been masters. Legend has it that the family secret was imparted to the present generation at the eleventh hour, when the brothers' father was on his death bed. Supposedly he whispered it to only one of his sons, worried that if they both knew it, they'd separate, become competitors, and destroy the family. His wisdom paid off . . . after all these years, they are still together. One brother makes the *akhanes*—in an old-fashioned workshop upstairs—and the other minds the till. The shop, on the city's main square, is just as the old man left it, a paean to 1950s aesthetics and good old-fashioned quality.

Sweets are taken very seriously in Greece's great North. There is a tradition for them unmatched anywhere else in the country, save perhaps for Crete, and the Roumbos brothers are just one of several legendary sugar masters in the region. Like everything else on this region's table, its desserts mostly owe their luster to the Asia Minor Greeks who brought with them a rich tradition in pastry making that has now become part of the region's culinary lore.

It is not an accident, for example, that the region is famous for its *siropiasta*—its syrup-soaked pastries and cakes; for a variety of nut-filled cookies and confections—nuts as raw ingredient are exquisite up here, especially in the northwestern part of Macedonia; for its share of sweets that take an unabashed cue from the East; and for a wide array of spoon sweets—fruits preserved in syrup. One of the most interesting of these comes from Naoussa. There, when the grape harvest begins and must is plentiful, locals make a delicious *petimezi* (grape syrup) from the indigenous *xinomavro* grape that they call *meli*—"honey." In this they preserve coin-sized chunks of eggplant and pumpkin, one of the most unusual spoon sweets in Greece.

In nearby Veria, another stalwart from the 1950s produces the one sweet for which this town is famous, at least locally: *revani.* Like the Roumboses of Serres, here it is Hohliouros's shop in the old part of the city where one is likely to find a line out the door. For some forty years he's sold nothing but trays and trays of the golden, syrup-soaked cake. Ever protective of his trade and slightly ornery, the sixty-something proprietor won't even talk about the *revani.* He just looks at you, asks how much you want, and goes on with the cutting of his precious cake into neat rectangular pieces.

Other strictly regional specialties include small rolls of baklava that are deep fried and favored in Kastoria; and the *saliara* of Kozani, which is something between a *kourambie* (shortbread cookie) and a *phoeniki* (syrup-soaked biscuit), filled with nuts and either submerged in syrup or dusted with sugar.

On the northern Greek sugar trail, though, all roads inevitably lead to Thessaloniki, the "sweet mother," as locals lovingly call their city. There is a roster of strictly local pastries and confections. *Bougatsa*—the warm flaky phyllo rectangles filled with cream, but also filled with savory cheese and meat—is in a whole other category, somewhere between sweet shops and bread bakeries. It is not the sort of dish one would make at home. Thessaloniki boasts an inordinate number of pastry shops and no dearth of legendary ones. Agapitos, in the heart of the city on Tsimiski Street, famous for the white marzipan cylinders filled with cream and known as *rodinia;* Hatzifotiou for *syropiasta;* and many more. My own favorite, and probably the city's best-known shop, is Hadzi, on Venizelou Street.

Nesmendin Hatzi, a Greek whose family came from Poli in 1922, is the third generation of pastry wizards to run the family business, and here the fare is decidedly exotic: *kazan tipi* (the name is Turkish and means "the burned bottom of the pot" for the way this rice-and-milk-based pie filling is literally burned on the bottom of the pot); *taouk gioutsouk* (another Turkish specialty, which is a delicate cream made by simmering chicken breasts and milk for several hours); *malembi* (a kind of rice pudding); a whole selection of miniature baklavas and other syrup-soaked sweets; *kaimaki* ice cream; and, finally, the pièce de résistance here—real *kaimaki* (buffalo milk cream that is as thick as butter) served atop the syrup-soaked bread called *ekmek* or as an accompaniment to *revani,* halvah, or the little finger-sized syrupy *touloumbes.*

Semolina and Ground Almond Cake

SAMALI

 Makes 24 pieces

One of the great sweets of Thessaloniki, made in pastry shops, at home, and hawked from small carts on the streets all around the Kapani market.

1 cup (2 sticks) plus 1 tablespoon unsalted butter, softened
1 cup confectioners' sugar
4 large eggs, separated
1 teaspoon pure vanilla extract
1½ cups coarse semolina
2 scant teaspoons baking powder
1 cup finely ground blanched almonds
1 teaspoon grated lemon zest
Pinch of salt
½ teaspoon fresh lemon juice

For the syrup
2½ cups granulated sugar
2 cups water
1 small cinnamon stick
4 to 5 whole cloves, to taste
One 1-inch strip lemon zest
2 tablespoons brandy

1. With an electric mixer in a large bowl, whip the cup of butter until soft. Add the confectioners' sugar a little at a time and whip until fluffy. Add the egg yolks, one at a time, beating after each addition. Add the vanilla and continue whipping for about 5 minutes.

2. Combine the semolina, baking powder, almonds, and lemon zest in a small bowl. Slowly add the semolina mixture to the butter and sugar, beating to combine thoroughly.

3. Preheat the oven to 375°F. Butter a 12- by 18-inch glass baking pan. In a medium metal bowl, place the egg whites, salt, and lemon juice and whip with an electric mixer until stiff peaks form. Fold the meringue into the semolina mixture, working fast to combine. Pour the batter into the prepared pan and bake until set, 35 to 40 minutes.

4. About 15 minutes before the *samali* is finished baking, prepare the syrup: Combine the granulated sugar and water in a medium saucepan and bring to a boil. As soon as the sugar dissolves, add the spices, zest, and brandy. Reduce the heat to medium-low and simmer until the syrup is viscous, about 10 minutes.

5. When the *samali* is baked, pull it out of the oven and reduce the oven temperature to 300°F. Score it into 3-inch square pieces with a sharp paring knife. Pour the warm syrup over the hot *samali* and place back in the oven. Bake until the syrup is absorbed, another 5 to 7 minutes, and remove from the oven. Let cool and serve.

Semolina Cake Doused in Aromatic Syrup

REVANI

 Makes about thirty 2-inch squares

This is another famed Macedonian dessert. The most renowned revani *is supposedly made in Veria, a large town in the central part of the region. Nowadays Veria has lost its edge on* revani, *although local sweet shops still carry it, and one in particular still draws a daily line of customers. There are many similar recipes for the syrup-soaked cake throughout the region, some calling for flour, others for flour and semolina, others still for a trinity of flour, semolina, and ground almonds. I like the flour-semolina combination best.*

For the syrup
2½ cups sugar
2½ cups water
One 1-inch strip lemon zest

For the semolina cake
2½ cups all-purpose flour
1½ cups fine semolina
2 teaspoons baking powder
1 cup (2 sticks) unsalted butter, softened
1¼ cups sugar
6 large eggs, separated
1 cup preferably Greek yogurt, drained
   (see page 459)
Grated zest of 1 lemon

1. Make the syrup: Combine the sugar, water, and zest in a medium saucepan and bring to a boil. Reduce the heat to medium-low and simmer for 10 minutes. Let cool completely.

2. Preheat the oven to 350°F and butter a large baking pan about 10 by 12 by 2 inches. In a large bowl, sift together the flour, semolina, and baking powder.

3. In another large bowl, with an electric mixer, beat together the butter and sugar until creamy. Add the egg yolks and continue beating until smooth and fluffy. Add the yogurt, beating constantly until combined.

4. In a medium bowl, whip the egg whites with an electric mixer until stiff peaks form. Using a rubber spatula, fold the whites into the butter-sugar mixture to combine well, then fold that into the flour mixture. Add the grated lemon zest. Pour the batter into the buttered baking dish and bake until golden, 40 to 45 minutes.

5. Pull the cake out of the oven, pour the cool syrup over the hot cake, and let it soak for at least 2 hours before serving.

Shepherd's Halvah with Cheese and Sugar

TSOPANIKOS HALVAS

 Makes 4 to 6 servings

This is an old shepherds' recipe that was given to me by a Vlach woman in Thessaloniki. It used to be the sweet of choice for special occasions and special guests, in spring and summer, when the shepherds return to their mountain villages and cheese making is at its height. It is similar to a dish called housmeri *found in several parts of northern Greece, in the eastern Aegean, and among the Greeks who trace their roots to Asia Minor, in which soft cheese is cooked with flour and either served immediately or kept, like* trahana, *for the winter larder.*

One caveat: This is a dish for the adventuresome and tireless cook. It's very labor intensive and decidedly rich and old-fashioned.

2½ pounds fresh unsalted whole-milk soft
   myzithra cheese or unsalted whole-milk
   ricotta cheese
3 large egg yolks
1 cup sugar
½ cup pastry flour
¼ cup (½ stick) unsalted butter

1. Crumble or grate the cheese coarsely. Place in a large bowl and mix in the egg yolks, either by hand or with a fork.

2. Place the cheese-and-egg mixture in a large pot and heat over low heat, stirring constantly with a wooden spoon, until the cheese melts. It will be like a thick, curdled cake batter in texture.

3. Add the sugar in a slow, steady stream, stirring constantly. Stir and simmer for 45 to 50 minutes, then add the flour. Continue stirring until the mixture starts to pull away from the bottom and sides of the pot and the flour is cooked, about 15 more minutes. Add the butter, stir until melted, and remove the pot from the heat. Place the halvah in a shallow bowl to set, cover it with a kitchen towel, and let stand for 30 minutes. Spoon into individual small plates and serve.

Baked Apples Stuffed with Halvah

MILO PSITO KAI GEMISTO ME HALVA

 Makes 6 servings

This is the *taverna dessert in Thessaloniki.*

6 Golden Delicious apples
6 generous teaspoons unsalted butter
¼ pound sesame halvah (sold in blocks)
Ground cinnamon and fresh mint leaves for
   garnish

1. Preheat the oven to 350°F. Cut off and reserve the apple crowns. Core the fruit and scoop out a hole about 1½ inches wide and deep.

2. Rub the inside of each apple with ½ teaspoon of the butter. Crumble the halvah with your fingertips and place equal amounts inside each of the apples, mounding the halvah decoratively. Place the tops back on the apples and place the apples in a baking dish. Melt the remaining butter and drizzle over the fruit. Bake, uncovered, until the apples are tender, 45 to 50 minutes. Remove from the oven, let cool slightly, and serve, sprinkled with a bit of cinnamon and garnished with a mint leaf.

Rice and Milk Pie from Kastoria

KASTORIANI RIZOPITA

 Makes about thirty-six 2-inch squares

In Kastoria, as well as in much of the rest of western Macedonia, the phyllo pastry used for sweet and savory pies is a kind of ersatz puff pastry. Very little liquid and very little fat go into the actual dough, but it is rolled out as for puff pastry—doused profusely with butter, folded up, and rolled out again—so that upon baking the pastry rises as if in layers.

For the pastry
4 to 5 cups all-purpose flour, as needed
1 teaspoon salt
1 cup water
1 tablespoon olive oil
1½ cups (3 sticks) unsalted butter, melted

For the filling
3 to 4 rose geranium leaves plus 1 cup water or
   1 teaspoon pure vanilla extract
1¼ cups long-grain rice
1¼ to 1½ cups water, as needed
½ teaspoon salt
¾ cup evaporated milk
2 tablespoons unsalted butter
1 cup granulated sugar
6 large eggs, lightly beaten

To serve
Confectioners' sugar and ground cinnamon for
   garnish

1. Make the pastry: Combine 4 cups of the flour and the salt in a large bowl. Make a well in center and add the water and olive oil. Mix in the flour, starting from the perimeter of the well, until it is completely combined. Knead well for about 10 minutes. The dough should be firm and smooth. Add more flour if necessary. Set aside to rest for 10 minutes.

2. Divide the dough into 2 equal balls. Using a lightly floured rolling pin or dowel on a lightly floured work surface, roll the dough into a circle about 18 inches in diameter. Brush the entire surface generously with melted butter. Fold in the 2 sides so that they meet in the center. Brush this surface generously with butter, too. Fold again so that the dough is now like a long panel 3 or 4 inches wide. Brush the surface with butter. Fold the top and bottom ends toward the center, brush the surface with butter, and fold again so that the dough looks like a block. Cover with plastic wrap and refrigerate until ready to use. Repeat with the second ball.

3. Make the filling: If using the scented geranium leaves, bring them to a boil in the 1 cup water. Remove from the heat and leave them to steep for 10 minutes. Remove the leaves and save the infusion.

4. In a medium saucepan, combine the rice, 1¼ cups water (use 1½ cups water if using vanilla instead of rose geranium leaves), and the salt and bring to a boil. Reduce the heat, cover, and simmer for 10 to 12 minutes. As soon as most of the water is absorbed, add the evaporated milk, butter, and granulated sugar. Simmer over very low heat for about 20 minutes, stirring frequently. You'll need to be on top of this toward the last 5 minutes of cooking, stirring the rice constantly to keep it from scorching. Remove from the heat and let cool. Add about ¼ cup of the geranium infusion or the vanilla and mix in the beaten eggs. The mixture will be fairly loose. Preheat the oven to 400°F.

5. Assemble the pie: Remove the phyllo from the refrigerator. Lightly oil a 15-inch round baking pan. On a lightly floured work surface, pat down the first block gently with your palm. Sprinkle the top with a little flour and roll into a circle about 20 inches in diameter. Fit into the pan, with the edges hanging over the side by about 2 inches. Spread the rice mixture on top, leaving a "gutter" of about an inch around the periphery. Roll out the second phyllo block in the same way, but to a circle 20 inches in diameter. Place it on top of the filling gently, pushing and pinching it a little so that the pastry seems "wrinkled" and wavy on top. Roll the excess phyllo inward, pressing it gently into the "gutter" to form a rim. Brush the top of the pie generously with the remaining melted butter. Bake until the phyllo is golden and crisp, 45 to 50 minutes. Remove from the oven, let cool slightly, sprinkle with confectioners' sugar and cinnamon, and cut into 2-inch squares to serve.

Phyllo Flutes Filled with Walnuts and Tahini

FLOGERES ME TAHINI KAI KARYDIA

 Makes about 30 pieces

I ran across this lovely dessert at a pastry shop in Komotini. It is a local Lenten specialty.

2 cups tahini

2 cups sugar

1 to 1½ cups water, as needed

3 cups finely ground walnuts

2 teaspoons cinnamon

1 pound commercial phyllo, thawed and at room temperature (see page 455)

½ cup extra-virgin olive oil

3 to 4 cups confectioners' sugar, as needed,
    for dusting

1. In the bowl of an electric mixer, whip together the tahini and sugar at high speed until smooth and creamy, about 5 minutes. As you whip the mixture, if it is too thick—it should be the consistency of peanut butter—drizzle in the water, in ¼-cup increments, until the proper consistency is achieved. Then, using a wooden spoon, mix in the walnuts and cinnamon, combining thoroughly. Set aside.

2. Preheat the oven to 350°F. Lightly oil 2 sheet pans.

3. Open the phyllo and place horizontally in front of you. Cut into three 6-inch strips. Stack the phyllo strips and keep them covered with a kitchen towel. Take one strip, place it vertically in front of you, and oil sparingly. Place a second strip on top. Place a tablespoon of the filling in the bottom center of the strip, fold in the sides, and then roll up to form a tight cylinder. Place seam side down on the baking pan. Continue with the remaining phyllo and filling until all the ingredients are used up. Bake until lightly golden, 8 to 12 minutes. Remove and cool slightly. While the pastry is still warm, sift confectioners' sugar over it generously. Store in tins in a cool, dry place. The pastry will keep for about 5 days.

The Islands of the Northeastern Aegean

A Sense of Place and Palate

I have a special affinity for the eastern reaches of the Aegean because the island of my ancestry is here, a wing-shaped parcel of land surrounded by choppy waters and named for the felled Ikaros of Greek myth. These islands are not like the Cyclades or the Dodecanese or the Ionian. Little links them. Their landscapes are different from one another, their histories individual, their dialects distinct. From the palest reaches of antiquity they each have had a separate identity. What defines them as a group, more than anything else, is their place on the map, a long way away from the rest of Greece, peering instead toward the East. Some are so close to the Turkish coastline that on a clear night you can see the streak of headlights across the water.

Ikaria, Samos, Chios, Lesvos, and Limnos make up the core of large islands here. Four small groups of satellite islands cluster around them: Fourni off the Ikarian coast, where some of the best fish and wildest *panigyria* (folk festivals) can be found; Inousses, just off Chios and home of some of Greece's most illustrious shipowners; Psara, a tiny island west of Chios, virtually untouched by tourism and home to some of the finest thyme honey in the Aegean; and, finally, Agios Efstratios, between Limnos, Lesvos, and Skyros. Thasos and Samothraki seem to belong, at least psychologically, to the North of Greece.

Greeks have lived in the islands of the northeastern Aegean since a thousand years before Christ. Some of the earliest urban centers were here, in Samos, in Chios, and on the coast of Asia Minor. Homer was born here, most likely in Chios. Pythagoras's birthplace was Samos. Limnos is home to the oldest city and maybe earliest democracy in Europe, Poliochni, which was the site of a bustling society as long ago as the third millennium B.C.

The Greeks of the northeastern Aegean, especially the people of Lesvos and Chios, have always had close ties with the Greek communities in Turkey, communities that had existed on the shores of Asia Minor for millennia but were forced to evacuate suddenly in 1922, after the political upheavals and war known as the Asia Minor catastrophe. The catastrophe culminated in an uprooting and relocation of populations, in which more than a million Greeks fled their homeland in Anatolia and moved westward into Greece proper. Before that, Lesvos, Samos, and Chios had enjoyed constant trade with Smyrna, Fokaia, Aivali, and so many other towns along the Anatolian Coast. In Lesvos it wasn't uncommon for one to cross the water into Smyrna just to shop. It stands to reason that when the political situation changed and masses of refugees swarmed into the nearby islands after 1922 (as well as into the North of Greece), they planted all the familiar tastes of the cuisine they knew in their new if hurriedly set up homes.

In some instances the dishes that made their way across the Dardanelles had to be adapted to the new landscape. Lesvos, for example, is one enormous olive grove blessed with a wealth of small coves that still teem with fish and shellfish. The island is famous for its sardines, and one local recipe for them stuffed with capers is virtually the same as an old Smyrna stuffed-fish dish, except that larger mackerels were the fish most likely to be eaten there. Limnos, with its gentle, undulating hills, was once the granary of the Aegean. The whole island is gold with wheat and barley, interrupted here and there by patches of vineyards where the famed local muscat and the ancient Limnio grapes are cultivated. Samos, a roller coaster of high mountains and fertile plains, seems like a textbook example of Mediterranean agriculture. In Ikaria the poverty of subsistence farmers is evident on every meager steppe: Narrow terraces are hewed out of sheer rock in some places, anything to provide room for a small garden that could sustain the family.

There are some common elements in these islands' kitchens. Fish has always been a staple food, and the meat of choice, by and large, is goat. There is a variety of fresh and aged goat's milk cheeses that resemble one another from place to place. The olives preferred here are the wrinkled black kind, called *hourmades* or, euphemistically, "prunes." Wild fennel is the herb of choice in all sorts of dishes, from stews to pies. Wheat-based dishes are common, especially in Chios, Samos, and Lesvos, but that is something found throughout the rest of the Aegean as well. Local pasta is a mainstay, especially in Limnos. Pureed fava beans, whole wheat kernels, and pumpkin are just some of the raw materials that play themselves out like a fugue in the cookery and traditions from island to island. But the fact remains that the islands in this part of Greece have always been islands in the truest sense—isolated and individual.

IKARIA

The journey to Ikaria begins before you even reach the island. It starts with the winds that rock you, winds that blow up to eight, nine, and ten on the Beaufort scale, or anywhere between 40 and 60 miles per hour, almost all year-round. The Ikarian Sea, which lies between Mykonos and Ikaros's island, is well known as some of the roughest waters in all the Aegean. But the wind, in a way, is like Ikaria's welcome. Even before you touch shore, you find yourself captive to its gossamer scents: Oregano and thyme and savory and pine honey glide on the sea breeze, enveloping you in an aroma that could be bottled as the perfume of Greece.

The gusts have kept people captive here in other ways, too. Because the island is surrounded by some of the roughest waters in the Aegean, from at least the time of the Byzantine Empire Ikaria has been a place of exile, a place to incarcerate political undesirables. The last exiles imprisoned here were from the Greek Civil War and left in 1962. Even one of Greece's most famous sons, the composer Mikis Theodorakis, was sent here for a time.

Because geography and poverty have imposed isolation on these islanders, Ikarians are independent and idiosyncratic. For example, the island is home to what all of Greece calls its "crazy" village—Christos, in Raches, some six hundred meters (2,000 feet) above the sea on the northern side of the island. Villages are organized differently here than elsewhere in the Aegean Islands, with most homes spread far apart, relatively isolated from one another instead of clustered all together in one large main area. It suited farmers to tend to their fields, which usually adjoin their homes, in the daytime and to save their chores, shopping, and socializing for the evening. So, in many villages a kind of upside-down schedule evolved over the years. In my father's village, Christos, for example, you won't find a soul in any of the shops at 9:30 A.M., but you will at 2:00 A.M., buying everything from sugar to shoes. The village baker, Kollia, who has a face as beautiful as ancient statuary, leaves his bakery open and cash drawer unlocked for people buying their daily loaf while he goes fishing.

Ikaria is among the poorest of the larger eastern Aegean Islands. Its landscape is rough and rocky, but its interior is a blanket of pine forests. The island's beauty is unpolished, and so is its food. Goats, superb fish, and wild greens define Ikarian cooking.

Few goats are penned here; most are left to roam the island's jagged mountains, chomping on whatever shrubbery they can find. At local *panigyria,* or village feasts celebrating various saints, goat is boiled or roasted and served to the crowds. At Easter, as elsewhere among the Aegean Islands, goat traditionally is stuffed and roasted at the local village oven. Even the local version of *pastourma,* which in the rest of Greece is a spicy, salt-cured beef loin, is made with goat. I saw it being prepared in my own village, Christos, at the home of one of the local goatherds named Yiangoula, a wild man who spent thirty years of his life running a pizzeria and fending off the Mob in south Philadelphia, then, like many Ikarians, returned to his native soil to farm and live in peace. It was late August, and the clothesline in his yard had been transformed into a virtual production line. Half-carcasses of goat hung covered with punctured plastic to dry, salted and rubbed with the Ikarian blend of savory and oregano. In a few weeks' time they would become the *meze* of choice among old-timers and diehards here. Goat meat *pastourma* is no prosciutto; it is tough, chewy, and stringy. The connoisseurs savor it in small shredded pieces with home-brewed *tsipouro* (eau de vie); the women, ever wiser, usually use it to add flavor to winter bean soups and stews. It is, by all accounts, an acquired taste. Yiangoula is one of the last of the goatherds to bother with its preparation, for refrigeration and modern ways have done away with the need to preserve meat, especially paltry goat meat, for the winter.

There are a few other specialties here. A few generations ago, when islanders survived on subsistence farming and work was scarce, the diet consisted largely of boiled Jerusalem artichokes, called *kolokassi,* corn, and greens. Corn was used whole in a dish that still survives, *mageirio* or *pampeion,* basically a vegetable stew with green beans, tomatoes, and onions. Corn, shelled, dried, and ground to coarse amberlike pebbles, used to replace the more expensive rice in the local version of *yiaprakia,* or stuffed cabbage leaves. The island's national dish though, is another vegetable medley called *soufiko,* which is a kind of skillet-made ratatouille, with sliced eggplant, zucchini, tomatoes, and onions, all cooked slowly in ample olive oil. On the south side of the island, around the capital, the *soufiko* changes; there it is a medley of pumpkin or calabaza squash, hot peppers, and tomatoes.

To this day, as in the rest of Greece, much of the food supply still comes from foraging, and in Ikaria that means seeking out wild mushrooms, snails (especially on the south side of the island, where they are pickled and preserved), and greens. Of the last there are many, but three stand out as favorites flavoring everything from savory pies to the stuffed Easter goat: lemon balm, wild fennel, and delicate, mild poppy leaves.

SAMOS

In contrast to the other islands in the eastern Aegean, Samos is rampant with tourism five to six months out of the year. When I visited, in the summer of 1994, raging fires had destroyed the forests and vineyards. A red haze shimmered over the whole sea, and for weeks afterward the deceptively pleasant smell of charcoal permeated everything. Fires raged again a few summers later and yet again in the summer of 2000.

It would seem that, between the whirl of thousands of rented motorbikes, the croissant shops that sully the quaint old port town and capital, and the scars of so much scorched earth, the inhabitants of Pythagoras's island couldn't possibly have held on to any of their culinary traditions. But Samos, implacable, surprised me.

For one, Samos is renowned for its delicious

dessert wines produced from the local muscat grape. I also found in Samos a rich culinary identity, some of it even visible to the average visitor, a virtual coup d'état in tourist-heavy Greece.

The best-known dish from Samos is stuffed goat's back, which is usually made on Easter and for very special occasions but can be found in restaurants year-round. At the marketplace in Vathy (Samos Town), you'll find regional cheeses, maybe the small local tomato known as *bournelo,* and the *petropepono,* or rock melon, which is grown here.

Most important, though, the crushed wheat used in two of the island's most distinct and festive dishes, *yiorti* and *kiskeki,* can be found in Samian emporiums. Of all the island cuisines in the northeastern Aegean, Samos's is the most enamored of wheat. These two dishes, both a kind of porridge made from goat's meat and wheat, are served at the *panigyria,* and also made at home. The two other traditional dishes from Samos that call for wheat or flour, *sitarozoumo* or "wheat juice," and *hilos* or, simply, "porridge," are important for their symbolic and religious value. Both are sweetened puddings. The first is a funerary dish, sweetened with sugar, flavored with sesame paste and nuts, and served after the memorial service for the dead. *Hilos,* made with the starchy water of boiled pasta mixed with a little flour, cinnamon, nutmeg, walnuts, and either sugar or grape must syrup, is eaten for breakfast on Clean Monday, the first day of the Lenten fast.

Samos is extremely well furnished in wild greens, which are mixed with all sorts of things, from snails to beans. Most are boiled, or braised with onion, but some, such as *fteres* (young fiddlehead ferns) and *ovries* (bryony, which looks like wild asparagus but isn't) are boiled, then fried.

From Samos also come some of the most interesting bean dishes in Greece. Broad beans, white beans, and chickpeas are braised with onions and sometimes served saladlike with chopped fresh tomato and arugula, if they are in season. Lentils are stewed with onions and chard. Bean purees, some that still call for the Neolithic vetch, a pulse that has always, it seems, been eaten in Greece but whose place on the modern table has faded elsewhere, are also found on the Samian table.

CHIOS

Chios, the richest of the eastern Aegean islands, is at first glance, a disappointment. The port is a rusty industrial little monster whose charms are clouded over by constant traffic, at least in summer, when I visited. But the port is also the first place where you get an inkling that Chios is somehow a world apart from its neighbors. In the summer, the lingua franca is American English. Chios, untrammeled by packaged-tour groups—the island has always been so wealthy that it never really had to support itself with tourism—nevertheless absorbs thousands of its children from abroad, mostly Greek Americans of Chiotiko descent who come to spend time with their kin. Still, you really have to move inland to discover this island's charm; it has plenty, perhaps more than anywhere else in the whole northeastern Aegean.

I stayed in Cambos, the island's large plain, about a half hour's drive from Chios Town. It was like staying in a medieval Italian city. The village was a vast labyrinth of stone-wall-lined roads and sequestered old estates, which you could barely see from outside. It was once the neighborhood of the long-ruling Genoese gentry, and it showed in the perfectly preserved architecture, in the insignia above so many doors, and in the general serpentine plan of the place. Even some of the very Italian-sounding family names of the present inhabitants—Argenti is the most renowned—speak tomes about the island's illustrious past.

In Chios, history is palpable. The island's past is the tale of an eight-hundred-year tug-of-war between foreign interests that either enjoyed or wanted a stake in Chios's rich mastic and silk production.

The continuum of wealth on the island—Chios also is home to many of Greece's oldest shipowning families—has afforded it a certain sense of propriety and order that's rare in the rest of Greece. The Chios Library is excellent. The island's architecture is well preserved, not only in Cambos but in many of the twenty-one mastic villages in the southern part of the island. Among them Mesta and Pyrgi are the best known, the former because it is an extremely well-maintained medieval fortressed town and the latter for its unique building decorations of gray and white geometric patterns. And there is even a quiet revival, or at least recognition, of the island's traditional foods.

The most unusual food find on Chios is very unusual, indeed. I was walking through the marketplace in town, eyeing the shop walls covered as if by stained glass—with shelf upon shelf of opalescent spoon sweets (Chios is famous for them); filled from floor to ceiling with pyramids of stout jars filled with *mastiha,* another confection, or with the myriad unusual liqueurs from bitter almond to bergamot, for which Chios is also reputed. Then something I had never seen before caught my attention: crates filled with a bluish green little berry, smaller than a dried pea. It was mid-August, the season for terebinth nuts, or *tsikoutha.* They are oilier than almonds and, until a few years ago, were pressed for their oil, which is sometimes still used in pastry making and for cooking during Lent. Every cook I spoke to on Chios reminisced about the Christmas biscuits kneaded with *tsikouthelaio* (terebinth nut oil) that they used to eat as children, but only one cook, in the town of Vrontados, had some of the oil on hand. It was light and smelled faintly of both pistachios and turpentine, which, it so happens, is also a product of the terebinth tree. The oil used to be pressed in March, when all the work with olive oil was finished. But the tiny terebinth berries clog the new automated presses, and so the oil is nearly impossible to find now. The dried nut is still considered a local delicacy and something that requires skill to eat. First, you peel the bluish skin with your front teeth, crack the berry in half with your back teeth, then swallow the soft green middle, which tastes a little like a pistachio.

The terebinth also came up when I was looking for some of Chios's other traditional foods, especially its pasta dishes. Pasta making is something of a custom on Chios, and in at least one old recipe hand-rolled pasta is cooked with a sauce of sun-dried local tomatoes and terebinth oil.

Most of the pasta comes from the mountain town of Pitious. I drove up there—it was a few hours on rough roads from the medieval town of Cambos, where I stayed. It was midmorning when I pulled into the sleepy town, one of those places where an unknown car elicits stares from everyone, where people open their windows and peer out through garden plants to see who the newcomer is. I went straight to an old *bakaliko,* or grocer's store. It was a great place, dark and cavernous, with an ancient potbellied stove in the center and everything from chewing gum to beach shoes to flour and beans out of sacks for sale. In a corner near the window an old man was hulling wheat. In the back his wife was rolling and cutting pencil-thin pieces of

pasta that looked something like ziti. Pitious is also the place where most of Chios's cheese is made, and there were little bundles of cheeses stocked and visible through the refrigerator glass.

Lots of local women up here, it turns out, make and sell pasta to supplement their farm incomes. There are three basic kinds, not that different from what one encounters elsewhere in Greece: handmade *fide* (vermicelli), *hilopites* (egg noodles, here shaped into tiny squares), and the hand-rolled ziti-like pasta just mentioned.

Chios was the first place I discovered in Greece where tomatoes are sun-dried and used regularly in the kitchen. The favored old variety on Chios is a small one that flourishes on very little water and, in fact, is called *anydra,* or "waterless." The first time I saw them on the island was in Mesta, the gray-and-white geometric gem of a mastic town. It was quite a sight, blood-red garlands of tomatoes strung by the hundreds and hanging outside the colorless local houses. It was like looking at a black-and-white photo that had been doctored. The dried tomatoes of Chios are not available outside the island, but they are delicious, with a concentrated sweet and tart tomato flavor that intensifies as the tomatoes shrivel up in the summer heat. Goat stewed with them is one local specialty.

Preserves of all sorts, sweet and savory, are another delicacy on the island. Chios was long known as one of Greece's major producers of rose water and orange blossom water, and the island's home cooks speak lovingly of the jams and preserves they make with rose petals and citrus blossoms, among other things. At the marketplace in town, every shop has jars piled high with Chios preserves and with sweet sugar paste scented with mastic, which is a traditional confection, dipped by the spoonful into cold water and served. At Yiorgos

Barias's shop in the heart of the market, a place distinguished by the tubs of pickled watercress, olives, and dried herbs that take up all of the sidewalk space outside, there is a selection of about nine different homemade savory preserves: whole pickled garlic, onions in their skins, broad beans, and pears, grapes, apples, apricots, plums, and melons. The shop is also a good source for local cheeses, including the difficult-to-find *Chiotiki kopanisti,* or soft, fermented goat's milk cheese.

LESVOS

Lesvos, aristocratic and urbane, somehow seems to belong to another era. The feel of the place is old, and its cuisine, too, harks to a time gone by. Walking through Lesvos's capital, Mytilini, is like stepping into old photographs of Greece circa 1920. When I went, in the mid-1990s, there were two enormous coffee shops on the main market street, cavernous places from another time, where every passerby falls under the scrutiny of proud, idle men. At the top of the market, a few rundown shops were bursting with antiques, especially old kitchen gear, everything from bread troughs to butter churners to fifty-year-old plates.

The memories of Asia Minor are still so vivid here that when I went in search of recipes I was often referred to a book called *The Notebook of Erato,* a compendium of old dishes from Smyrna by the late Greek writer Liza Miheli. "Whatever you find in there, that's our food, too," one woman told me.

In Lesvos, more than anywhere else, there was a constant exchange of peoples between both shores. The refugees of '22 brought with them a taste for stuffed fish and for quinces, a penchant for distilled spirits and customs that thread back to the most dis-

tant times. It is difficult, though, to define the island's cooking since it is the product of two distinct forces—the complicated cooking of Anatolia, imported with the refugees, and the stylized "European" cuisine enjoyed by the island's considerable bourgeois class at the beginning of the twentieth century. During the island's heyday many families employed French cooks, and they left their stamp on the island's cuisine. "Look at the way we cook lobster," one island cook and chronicler of Lesvos's culinary traditions, Dora Parisi, told me, "and you'll see it's almost exactly the same as what the French call *homard à l'américaine.*"

When researching this book, I was led to a 1915 handwritten notebook filled with recipes that belonged to a local teacher (passed down to her from her grandmother and mother). Next to the very Turkish-sounding *atzem pilaf* (meat baked with rice) and *mouhalembi* (rice pudding), for example, was a recipe for roast beef with cinnamon and tomato sauce served with *niok,* a kind of potato dumpling very much like gnocchi. The moussaka dishes were interesting, too—one with cauliflower and one with tomatoes, almost like gratins, in addition to the customary eggplant moussaka. Duck with olives and partridge *salmi,* a rich game stew here made with croutons and wine, were two other "traditional" recipes in the repertory of the island's well-to-do home cooks.

But older agrarian recipes still survive, too. One such dish is halvah (usually a puddinglike dish made with semolina) made here with fresh *myzithra* cheese. It is a specialty of Molyvos, a village on the north side of the island. It is traditionally made in the summer, and like the dairy-based pasta *trahana,* also a summer preparation, it was preserved for the winter and served with a little fresh sugar syrup poured over it, as an impromptu offering to guests.

Some local recipes bespeak their ties to a specific part of the island. For example, beef with yogurt is found only in Eresos and in eastern Lesvos, while there is a lovely stuffed chicken dish that comes from Mystegna, which is also in the eastern part of the island. At least in the case of the former dish, the influences seem clearly Anatolian—yogurt being one of the classic accompaniments for spicy or sauced meat dishes throughout Asia Minor. Traditions tied to specific holidays also remain intact. For instance, the standard fare for engagements and weddings is the white almond confection called *amygdalota*.

Lesvos is probably better known for its raw ingredients, though, than for the cuisine that derives from them. Anyone who visits the island is bound to notice the infinite olive trees and the flat tins of sardines on sale in nearly every shop. The olive oil, the ouzo, and the sardines of Lesvos are among the best in Greece, and the island is also famous for several of its cheeses.

THE SEA-WASHED CHEESE OF LIMNOS

The ride over the pebbles to the end of a beach near Kaminia in Petros Honas's Skoda was bumpy, to say the least. But this was a food reconnaissance mission, and Limnos's very able young wine maker took it upon himself to find the one thing that had eluded me here so far: the last stage in the making of *melipasto*, Limnos's sea-washed cheese.

I had been intrigued ever since I had first heard of the cheese several years earlier. Once on the island, I had chased the process from cheese maker to cheese maker, watching the beginning, when the curds are set, in Thanos, at the home of Kyria Foteini, who spends an intense month each summer making about five or six kilos of cheese a day in her kitchen so that her large family will have enough to last all winter long. Thanks to her, I also got to see and taste one of the oldest island dishes made with cheese, called *housmeri*. To make it, Kyria Foteini took slightly fermented day-old unsalted cheese, crumbled it, mixed it with half a plate of crumbled bread, and stirred the whole thing in a pot on the stove for about twenty minutes. The result was a delicious, if heavy, dish of melted cheese that once was a common winter snack. It tasted surprisingly like very good-quality mozzarella.

Back, though, to the *melipasto*. I had witnessed stage two of its making at a home-grown facility, that of a woman named Astera, in Karyolakas, near Kaspakas. There the little rounds of *melipasto*—or *melichloro,* as it is also called—were sitting in *kafasia* (screened wooden cupboards hung on a post outside), where they would stay to mature for about two weeks. The sea bath is the last stage before *melipasto* is ready to eat.

When I arrived there, Kyria Astera was already at the beach, tending to this last and crucial phase in the cheese's preparation. I saw her from a distance, kerchiefed against the sun and wet from the knees down, bending into the sea. Brush in one hand, cheese in the other, one by one she scrubbed the little disks of her *melipasto* that were afloat in an orange crate wedged between some rocks. Others, already brushed with seawater, were drying on a towel. This lovely local cheese, at once sweet and salty with nature's brine, is testament to how age-old ways persist even today.

LIMNOS

Much on Limnos in the way of food has remained surprisingly intact over the ages. Wine, for example, for which the island is well known, is often still fermented in huge amphorae. You can see them buried in the ground outside nearly every house. The local grape varieties are the Limnio, which Aristotle mentions and which is also now called by its Turkish name, Kalabaka, and the muscat of Alexandria, which first came to the island in 1910, probably via the many Limniotes who lived at the time in Egypt, and which now accounts for the vines found in the majority of vineyards. Limnos's dessert wines, produced exclusively by the island's cooperative, are as famous and revered as those of not-too-distant Samos.

The island also produces excellent fava, black-eyed peas, and sesame seeds and oil in ever-dwindling supply. Olives do not flourish here. But more than anything else on Limnos, what catches the eye and the palate are the endless, undulating, gentle slopes of honey-blond wheat and barley that stretch to the horizon in every direction. Since 3000 B.C. Limnos has been the granary of the Aegean. Today Limnos still contributes prominently to Greece's bread basket, cultivating about five thousand tons of wheat and barley annually. The wheat is an indigenous hard variety that produces some of the best, and most fragrant, flour in the country. "Oregano is the tallest tree here," says a local friend with characteristic humor.

It stands to reason then that the island should have a formidable pasta tradition. The height of summer is the right time to witness the making of many traditional local products, for even in this day and age home cooks here still make their *flomaria,* the short and thin-as-string or flat-like-linguine local egg noodles. They are cooked the way egg noodles are cooked all around Greece, with rooster and tomato sauce, or plain with butter and cheese. I did find one interesting recipe called *pseftopetino,* which translates as "pseudo rooster" and calls for eggplants and their stems (said to resemble a rooster's chin, hence the name) cooked in tomato sauce together with the noodles.

Trahana, the dairy-based, tiny pebblelike pasta, is also a local tradition. According to local journalist Ilias Kotsalis, the quality of the wheat made Limnos's *trahana* renowned since Byzantine times. There are two local varieties. The first is made with a mixture of *kourkouta,* which in island lingo refers to raw cracked wheat (not to be confused with bulgur, which is boiled cracked wheat), semolina, and milk. The second is a Lenten version, made with a combination of boiled chickpeas, tomatoes, onions, and flour. Both are used in soups and pilafs.

Fresh pasta is still made pretty regularly, too. There are several different shapes: *aftoudia,* little squares that are pinched together to look like ears; *makarounes* or *valanes,* which look like little curls; and *moustokoulika,* which look like miniature pretzels and are usually boiled in grape must.

As for other dishes made with grains, bulgur appears in several pilafs, most interestingly with octopus. Flour, of course, is used to make phyllo, too, but here the savory pie, or *pita,* tradition is limited. What there is, though, is unique. For one, savory pies are almost always made into either individual small coils or coiled figure-eight shapes. Rarely, if ever, are pies made to fit a large pan the way they are in most of the rest of the country. Greens pies made with wild fennel, mint, chervil, and chard abound, as do pies with local farmhouse cheeses, scallions, and mint.

Limnos is also known to have some of the best fishing grounds in the Aegean, and its myriad coves and inlets provide cover for a whole bevy of seafood that locals eat with alacrity. Efrosyni Ralli, a poet and general connoisseur in all things pertaining to her pocket of the world, but especially all things marine—her husband was a sailor and sponge diver—informed me of the long list of shelled and unshelled creatures that Limniotes love. Among them: octopus (which adores the scent of the local sea-washed *melipasto,* and reputedly comes calling when the cheese is being washed), *ahivades* and *krasahivades* (golden carp shells—clams—small and large respectively), *pinnes* (fan mussels), mussels, *kalognomes* (Noah's arks, a kind of clam), *streidia* (oysters), *htenia* (scallops), *fouskes* (sea skirts or violets in French, which Alan Davidson, in his classic *Mediterranean Seafood,* describes as "knobby creatures with leathery skin and a yellow inside that looks like scrambled eggs"), *kavouria* (crabs), *bebetsia* (tiny limpetlike shellfish), and *tsaganoi* (tiny lake crabs with a soft shell). Some are eaten raw with lemon, some are steamed, some served in pilafs. I was intrigued, too, by the prospects of finding a sun-dried lobster tail to grill, an old fisherman's specialty on Limnos, but had no such luck.

I did find, though, the most cherished sea creature of all, which turns out not to be a creature but a plant—the same rock-sucking anemone so beloved in Chios called *kolifathes.* In Efrosyni's kitchen, I watched the whole process of blanching the anemones, mashing them, and mixing them with onions, cumin, mint, and allspice. Flour, and more were readied for the skillet. It was close to noon, and here before us was a great wine *meze.* Petros was forthcoming with a bottle of his own. My cook's tour of Limnos came to an end. I spent the rest of my stay on Vulcan's island enjoying the wine, beaches, and those soothing, ubiquitous vistas of golden wheat swaying in every direction.

The Northeastern Aegean Islands Pantry

CHEESE

Every island in the northeastern Aegean produces fresh and dried goat's milk cheeses, usually made on a small scale by local shepherds as well as by local cooperatives. The cheeses differ, sometimes mildly, sometimes wildly, from place to place. When they are fresh, they can range in texture from being as soft as cream cheese to as pliant as mozzarella. When dried, they are quite salty, and oftentimes they are cured in brine. Here is a brief description.

Anthotyro Lesvou These are the hard or semihard, blue-rind, fez-shaped, aged whey cheeses made from sheep's milk and traditionally used for grating. Although found in many variations all over Greece, among the islands of the northeastern Aegean Lesvos produces the best known. Local custom dictates that the cheese, once air-dried, be dried even further in a low oven. The cheese ages for anywhere from two months to a year. When it is just a few months old, it is still soft enough to be eaten as a table cheese, and although this is not generally the tradition, it is delicious and buttery.

Chiotiko Tyri Otherwise translated simply as "Cheese from Chios," it is another white cheese made mostly from goat's milk with some sheep's milk added. It comes mostly from the northern villages of Vorissos and Pyrgi, but is easy to find at the bustling marketplace in Chios Town.

Kalathaki This is the goat's milk feta from Limnos, and one of the loveliest cheeses in Greece. Its name means "little basket" for the way it is shaped. This cheese is widely available, even in ethnic markets in the United States.

Kathoura The Ikarian goat's milk cheese. It is not made on a commercial scale, but is still very much the local household cheese, made by home cooks and cheese makers for personal consumption. *Kathoura,* when fresh, is reminiscent of mozzarella, but slightly saltier. It is also dried for use as a grating cheese and kept in brine, where it is eaten at various stages of its maturity.

Kryo Tyri The name simply means "cold cheese." Basically it is a kind of feta, made mostly with goat's milk, and is a specialty of Samos.

Lathotyri Literally, "oil cheese," lathotyri is a specialty of Lesvos, an island famous for its millions of olive trees and second, after Crete, in the production of sheep's milk. *Lathotyri* is a hard, yellow sheep's milk (or combination of sheep's and goat's milk) cheese that comes in one- to two-pound cylinders. The cheese is air-dried, and when it has lost about 40 percent of its moisture, it is stored in barrels of olive oil (about one-and-a-half quarts of oil per two pounds of cheese). The cheese can remain in the oil indefinitely; the longer it remains, the more peppery it becomes.

Mastello This is a relatively new cheese to the northeastern Aegean, found in the island of Chios. It is a pulled, white cow's milk cheese not unlike the Cypriote *haloumi*. It is made in small heads and usually consumed pan-fried, for *saganaki*.

Melipasto This is surely one of the most unique cheeses in Greece and hails from the island of Limnos. It is a combination sheep's and goat's milk

cheese which is lightly salted, then dried in the sun for 10 days or so, then brushed with seawater, which supposedly imparts a sweetness (see box on page 269).

Touloumotyri To the uninitiated, the sight of a 160-odd-pound old goat skin spread bellyside up and inside out, and burgeoning with chunks of soft white cheese, is startling at best. It is a sight one is likely to encounter in village shops in Lesvos and Samos, although the cheese is still made pretty much throughout the Aegean.

Soft, grainy, pungent *touloumotyri* is named for the goat skin *(touloumi)* in which it is stored. It is one of the oldest and rarest cheeses in Greece. It varies in color, from chalk white to pinkish, which is usually a sign that the cheese is exceptionally sharp.

The skin has to be cured before the cheese is stored in it. First, it is salted heavily, then folded and weighted down for about two weeks. Next, it is washed and shaven, the feet tied together, and the bag turned inside out, so that the hairy part is on the inside, which apparently keeps the skin from sweating, which would spoil the cheese by not allowing it to dry.

The secret to placing the feta-like chunks of cheese inside the bag is that they have to fill the skin without leaving any empty spaces between the pieces. Sometimes soft *myzithra* is added to the bag, to help fill in the spaces. A whole, filled skin weighs about 160 pounds. Most *touloumotyri* ages for at least three months.

Vrastotyri Literally, "boiled cheese," it is one of the local artisinal cheeses of Samos, made in somewhat large quantities since it can be found in local shops. It has a texture like Jell-O, at once solid and loose, light and sweet.

Xero The name translates as "dry." *Xero*, from Limnos, is basically the same cheese as *kalathaki*—a goat's milk feta—that is air-dried, then placed in brine.

The Recipes

MEZETHES

Bean Salad with Rocket (Arugula) and Onions from Samos

FASOULOSALATA ME ROKA KAI KREMMYDIA

 Makes 6 to 8 servings

Roka—rocket in English, or arugula—is one of the most intensely flavored greens that grow wild almost everywhere in Greece. Greek arugula is much more peppery than what one finds in American markets. Greeks sometimes cook with it, but it turns quite sharp and bitter then. Mostly they use it in salads, coarsely chopped or torn and mixed with other ingredients such as beans, tomatoes, and rusks.

This is an old Samian salad recipe. I have cut down on the olive oil and garlic in an effort to make it more palatable to modern cooks.

½ pound dried navy beans, picked over and rinsed

2 medium red onions, quartered and thinly sliced

1 garlic clove, peeled and crushed

A few olives or 1 tablespoon capers, rinsed and drained

Salt and cayenne pepper to taste

¼ cup olive oil

2 to 3 tablespoons red wine vinegar, to taste

1 pound arugula, trimmed, washed, dried, and leaves torn into 2-inch pieces

1. Soak the beans for at least 8 hours or overnight in water to cover. Drain. Bring the beans to a boil in a pot of unsalted water, reduce the heat to medium-low, and simmer, uncovered, until the beans are tender but not mushy, 30 to 45 minutes. Remove from the heat, drain in a colander, and rinse immediately under cold running water.

2. Place the beans in a large serving bowl and toss with the onions, garlic, olives or capers, salt, cayenne pepper, olive oil, and vinegar. Let stand for an hour at room temperature. Mix in the rocket a few minutes before serving.

Squash Blossoms Stuffed with Anchovies and Cheese from Lesvos

KOLOKYTHOKORFATHES YEMISTOI ME ANTZOUYIES KAI TYRI

 Makes 6 to 8 servings

The combination of cheese and fish is very rare in Greece. This recipe from Mytilini was given to me by an old doyen of Lesvos's capital.

12 salted anchovy fillets, rinsed well
1½ cups snipped fresh dill
2 cups fresh *anthotyro* or whole-milk ricotta cheese
1 cup grated *graviera* cheese
4 garlic cloves, minced
Freshly ground black pepper to taste
2 dozen large zucchini blossoms
3 large eggs, lightly beaten
1½ cups all-purpose flour
Vegetable or olive oil for frying

1. Finely chop the anchovy fillets and combine with the dill, cheeses, garlic, and pepper in a medium bowl.

2. Carefully fill each zucchini blossom with the cheese mixture, leaving a little room at the top so that the filling doesn't ooze out. Gently twist the tops closed.

3. Dip each zucchini blossom in the beaten egg, then the flour. Heat about 1½ inches of oil in a large, heavy skillet over medium-high heat. When the oil is very hot, fry the stuffed zucchini blossoms several at a time without crowding until golden and crisp, turning once, carefully, to brown on both sides, 2 to 3 minutes. Remove with a slotted spoon, drain on paper towels, and serve hot.

Onion Fritters from Mytilini

KREMMYDOTIGANITES MYTILLENES

 Makes about 15 fritters; 3 to 5 servings

A theme that runs through the cooking of the entire Aegean is the endless number of fritters made with greens and vegetables. Throughout this book there are many recipes for such simple dishes. They are a mirror of the easy but savory palate of island Greeks who, forced to contend with a constant dearth of raw ingredients, had to devise ways to keep their families from suffering from both hunger and boredom. These simple onion fritters make a great meze *and buffet dish for parties anywhere.*

1½ cups all-purpose flour
½ teaspoon salt, or more to taste
2 large eggs, lightly beaten
¼ to ½ cup water, as needed
⅓ cup grated *myzithra* or any hard cheese
1½ cups coarsely chopped white and tender green parts of spring onions or scallions
¼ cup finely chopped fresh mint
Salt and freshly ground black pepper to taste
Olive or vegetable oil for frying

1. In a large bowl, toss together the flour and salt and make a well in the center. Add the eggs and enough of the water to form a thick batter. Mix in the remaining ingredients, except the oil, combining everything well so that all the scallions, cheese, and mint are evenly distributed.

2. Heat about 2 inches of oil in a large, heavy skillet over medium-high heat. When the oil is very hot, almost smoking, drop a tablespoon at a time of the mixture into the hot oil. As soon as the bottom turns a light golden color, flip it with a metal spatula to cook until golden on the other side, about a minute or so on each side. Cook several at a time, without crowding them in the skillet. Remove with a slotted spoon, let drain on paper towels, and continue until all the batter is used. Serve warm.

Carp Roe and Fennel Patties from Chios

MALATHROPITES

Makes about 30 patties; 6 servings

The combination of tarama—*salted fish roe, usually from carp or grey mullet—and greens or herbs is not unusual in Chios. These small herb-and-*tarama *pies are adapted from a little book of traditional Chios recipes that were collected and published by the high school students in the town of Kallimasia. The word for fennel in Greek is* marathon, *but here it appears as* malathro, *which is fennel in the local island dialect.*

2 tablespoons *tarama* (carp roe)

¾ to 1 cup water, as needed

1 cup packed wild fennel leaves, finely chopped, or 1 cup packed snipped fresh dill and 1 heaping teaspoon ground fennel seeds

3 scallions, white and tender green parts, finely chopped

2 fresh plum tomatoes, peeled, seeded, and chopped

1½ cups all-purpose flour

Olive or other vegetable oil for frying

Lemon wedges

1. Dilute the *tarama* with ¼ cup of the water.

2. Combine the fennel, scallions, tomatoes, and diluted *tarama* in a medium bowl. Mix the flour sep-

arately with the remaining ½ to ¾ cup water to make a thick batter and combine it thoroughly with the other ingredients.

3. Heat 2 inches olive or other vegetable oil in a large, heavy skillet over medium-high heat. When the oil is very hot, almost smoking, drop 1 or 2 tablespoons of the batter at a time into the hot oil, frying it until a little fritter takes shape and becomes brown and crisp, 1 to 2 minutes on each side. Remove with a slotted spoon and let drain on paper towels. Serve hot, with lemon wedges.

WILD FENNEL

Wild fennel has been my nemesis throughout this book. So many dishes in the Greek kitchen are infused with its delicious aniselike aroma. The Greek countryside is carpeted with the feathery herb in spring, and cooks who don't pick their own can buy it, sold in bunches just like dill, at markets everywhere. But in the United States it's a different story. Most supermarkets and greengrocers carry fennel bulbs, and usually these have a few tough, stringy stalks protruding from them and a few tufts of leaves. You could conceivably use these, but you'd need to buy an awful lot of fennel bulbs to get a cup of chopped leaves. The texture of cultivated fennel is different, too. In Greece the stalks are long and thin and very full. They range in texture from exceedingly tender if the fennel is young to somewhat tough if it is late in the season. Cultivated fennel leaves—except for the tiniest, soft pieces closest to the bulb itself—tend to be tougher than the wild kind.

Usually, in the many recipes that call for wild fennel throughout this book, I have recommended a combination of fresh dill and ground fennel seeds or ouzo. Some specialty retailers do carry it.

Black-Eyed Peas Mashed with Garlic Sauce from Limnos

MAVROMATIKA ME SKORDALIA

 Makes 4 to 6 servings

Greeks adore mashed bean dishes. Usually they are made with either yellow split peas, as in the famed recipe from Santorini (see page 316), or with broad beans, which are popular in Crete and elsewhere. I like this Limnos dish because it calls for black-eyed peas, which are among my own favorite pulses, and it also calls for an unusual technique—mixing the beans with the garlicky dipping sauce skordalia.

Limnos produces excellent pulses, including yellow split peas, which could easily vie with the famously tasty ones from Santorini, and excellent, nutty black-eyed peas. Revered for having saved many people from starvation during World War II, these are still eaten widely on the island today. This recipe comes from Eleftheria Konstantou, an island cook from the village of Kaminia, with whom I spent a day learning many of the local dishes. I like to serve this dish with a few other northeastern Aegean specialties, such as either of the two stuffed sardine dishes (pages 289 and 290) and the skillet pie Kariotina *(page 282).*

1 cup dried black-eyed peas, picked over and
    rinsed

For the skordalia
1 medium garlic head (8 to 10 cloves)
Salt to taste
⅔ to 1 cup extra-virgin olive oil, as needed
¼ cup white wine vinegar, or more to taste

1. Place the beans and enough water to cover them by 2 inches in a medium pot and bring to a boil. Remove from the heat, drain, and place back in the pot with fresh water to cover by 2 inches. Bring to a boil, reduce the heat to medium-low, and simmer until the beans are soft and most of the water is absorbed, 40 minutes to an hour.

2. Meanwhile, make the *skordalia:* Using a large mortar and pestle, crush the garlic clove by clove, adding salt, ½ to ⅔ cup of the olive oil, and the vinegar in alternating doses until the whole mixture emulsifies into a smooth paste. You can do this in a food processor, too, but the texture will be looser.

3. When the beans are cooked, add the *skordalia*. Either with the pestle or with a wooden spoon or potato masher, stir and mash the mixture until it is a semipuree. You should be able to see whole beans in the dish, but the mixture should, by and large, resemble mashed potatoes. Adjust the seasoning with additional salt and more of the olive oil and vinegar if necessary. Serve warm.

VEGETABLES

One-Pot Vegetable Stew from Ikaria

TO SOUFIKO TIS DAPHNIS

 Makes 6 to 8 servings

Olive-oil-rich, one-pot vegetables stews—the easiest, most nutritious food in the world—are made all over Greece. In Ikaria there are two kinds of such medleys, soufiko *and* mageirio. *The first,* soufiko, *is unusual in that it is always made in a skillet and always includes squash. The second,* mageirio, *is exclusively a summer dish and always includes green beans and corn.*

4 long, thin eggplants, cut into ¼-inch-thick
   rounds
Salt to taste
⅔ cup extra-virgin olive oil
1 pound medium onions (about 4), halved and
   sliced
4 medium zucchini, cut into ¼-inch-thick
   rounds
2 garlic cloves, chopped
Freshly ground black pepper to taste
2 large firm, ripe tomatoes, cored and cubed

1. Place the eggplant slices in layers in a colander, lightly salting each layer. Place a plate or weight on top of the eggplant and let drain for 30 minutes. Rinse and pat dry.

2. Heat the oil in a large, deep skillet and cook the onions for 5 minutes over medium-low heat, stirring a few times, until wilted. Add the eggplant, zucchini, and garlic, and season with salt and pepper. Sprinkle the tomato cubes evenly over the top and season with salt and pepper. Cover the skillet and reduce the heat to low. Cook the *soufiko* until all the vegetables are very soft and have melded together, about 45 minutes. Serve warm or at room temperature.

Zucchini and Potatoes Cooked in a Skillet

SAMOS KOLOKITHAKIA MATISTA

  Makes 4 to 6 servings

Another skillet-made vegetable medley, this one from Samos.

5 to 6 tablespoons extra-virgin olive oil, to taste
4 medium waxy potatoes, peeled and diced
Salt to taste
4 garlic cloves, peeled and crushed
1 cup chopped fresh mint
2 medium firm, ripe tomatoes, peeled, seeded,
   and diced
3 to 4 medium zucchini, diced
Freshly ground black pepper to taste

1. In a skillet large enough to hold all the vegetables, heat 2 tablespoons of the olive oil. Add the potatoes and stir to coat with the oil. Sprinkle them with a little salt, a third of the garlic, and 3 tablespoons of the mint. Cover the skillet and cook over medium-low heat for about 8 minutes.

2. Next, spread half the diced tomatoes over the potatoes and add a little more of the mint, another third of the garlic, and salt. Layer the zucchini next, again sprinkling with mint, salt and pepper, and the remaining garlic, and top with the remaining tomatoes. Pour the remaining olive oil over everything, cover the skillet, and cook over very low heat until the vegetables are soft and all the flavors have melded together, 30 to 40 minutes. Serve warm or at room temperature.

Summer Vegetable Stew from Ikaria

MAGEIRIO OR PAMPEION

 Makes 6 to 8 servings

This old, simple dish is one of the classics of Ikaria's earthy island cuisine.

½ cup extra-virgin olive oil, plus more if desired

3 pounds green beans, trimmed and halved crosswise

2 medium red onions, coarsely chopped

3 ears corn, shucked and halved

4 medium waxy potatoes, peeled and cubed

3 large firm, ripe tomatoes, grated (see page 459)

2 large zucchini, cubed

Salt and freshly ground black pepper to taste

1. Heat the olive oil in a large pot over medium-high heat and add the beans and onions. Reduce the heat to medium-low, stir to coat, and cook for about 5 minutes. Add the corn and potatoes and stir to coat with the oil. Add enough water to barely cover the vegetables. Cover, increase the heat to medium, and bring to a boil. Reduce the heat to low and simmer for 25 minutes.

2. Add the tomatoes and zucchini. Season with salt and pepper. Stir gently to combine, cover, and simmer over low heat until all the vegetables are tender, another 25 minutes or so. Serve warm or at room temperature, drizzled, if desired, with additional oil.

Stewed Vegetables with Sausage from Limnos

ZARZAVATIKA ME KAVOURMA

 Makes 4 to 6 servings

This dish is inspired by the typical way cooks in Limnos prepare stewed vegetables, by adding a little kavourma—home-cured pork—to the pot. In its stead, I've subsituted mild pork sausage, removed from the casings.

½ pound mild pork sausage, removed from its casings

2 medium red onions, chopped

½ cup chopped fresh wild fennel leaves or 1 large fennel bulb, chopped, plus ⅓ cup snipped fresh dill

1½ pounds green beans, trimmed, or 1 medium zucchini, cut into quarters

2 large firm, ripe tomatoes, grated (see page 459)

⅓ cup chopped fresh mint

Salt and freshly ground black pepper to taste

3 to 4 tablespoons extra-virgin olive oil, to taste

1. In a large pot over medium heat, brown the sausage meat. Add the onions and cook together (in the fat exuded from the sausages) over medium heat until the onions are softened, about 5 minutes. If using fennel bulb, add it with the onions.

2. Add the beans or zucchini to the pot, together with the tomatoes and herbs (wild fennel or dill and mint). Season with salt and pepper and toss to coat in the fat. Add the olive oil as well as enough water to come about halfway up the vegetables. Reduce the heat to medium-low, cover the pot, and simmer until all the ingredients in the stew are soft, about an hour. Serve warm or at room temperature.

Batter-Fried Fava Beans with Garlic Sauce

KOUKIA TIGANITA ME SKORDALIA

 Makes 4 to 6 servings

Strolling through a small, nearly deserted mountain village in Samos one morning, I saw 2 old women cleaning fresh fava beans with their teeth. Dressed in black and minding grandchildren, they had a pile of fresh bean pods in a bag at their feet. They bit off the black "eye" of the fava bean between bits of conversation and placed each one in the bowl on their lap. I got one of my favorite recipes from them, for fresh broad beans fried crisp and served, like fried young fish, with skordalia, the Greek garlic dipping sauce. Fried favas are, in fact, a favorite meze in several of the eastern Aegean islands.

1 pound fresh large fava beans, shelled

For the skordalia
½ pound stale rustic bread
4 to 6 garlic cloves, to taste, peeled and crushed
½ cup extra-virgin olive oil
¼ cup red wine vinegar or fresh lemon juice
Salt to taste

For the batter and to fry
¾ cup all-purpose flour
½ teaspoon salt
¼ to ½ cup water, as needed
Olive or other vegetable oil for frying

1. Bring a pot of unsalted water to a rolling boil and blanch the favas for 5 minutes. Transfer to a colander and rinse immediately under cold running water.

2. Make the *skordalia:* Cut the crust off the bread and discard. Dampen the remaining bread with a little water and squeeze. Break it up into large chunks and place it in a food processor. Process to crumbs. Add the garlic, then the olive oil and vinegar or lemon juice in increments, pulsing on and off until the *skordalia* is creamy but still textured. Season with salt. Don't overprocess it, or it will become too starchy.

3. Combine the flour and salt in a medium bowl. Add just enough of the water to make a thick batter.

4. Fill a large, heavy saucepan or deep-fryer with 3 inches of oil and heat over medium-high heat until very hot, almost smoking. Meanwhile, quickly toss the beans in the batter. Fry them over high heat for a few seconds in batches, without crowding them, until they are crisp and golden. Remove with a slotted spoon, let drain on paper towels, and serve on a platter with the *skordalia* in a bowl in the center.

⊙ Instead of batter, you can dredge the fava beans lightly in a little salted flour and fry.

Egg Noodles Cooked with Eggplant from Limnos

PSEFTOPETINO

 Makes 4 to 6 servings

The name of this dish means "false cock's comb," because the eggplant in the sauce traditionally is cooked whole with its stem, which supposedly resembles a rooster's comb. I love the name, but no one seemed to know why the eggplant stems were cooked into this dish to begin with. "It's just the way it's done" was the standard answer. Although I've kept the authentic spirit of the dish by opting to cook the noodles in the sauce the way Greeks traditionally do, I've exercised a touch of cook's license, too, by cutting the eggplants into rounds.

⅓ cup extra-virgin olive oil

2 medium onions, chopped

1 pound long, thin eggplant, each cut into 4 thick
    rounds

3 large firm, ripe tomatoes, grated
   (see page 459)

2 garlic cloves, minced

Salt and freshly ground black pepper to taste

3 or 4 allspice berries, to taste

1 cup dry Limnos white wine or any dry white wine

1 teaspoon sugar (optional)

1 quart water

1 pound thin linguinelike egg noodles

1. In a large pasta pot, heat the olive oil over medium heat and cook the onions, stirring, until soft, about 7 minutes. Add the eggplant and cook until they begin to soften and the skins start to brown, stirring occasionally, about 10 minutes. Add the tomatoes, garlic, salt, pepper, and allspice and bring to a simmer. Add the wine, then taste and add sugar if necessary. Bring to a simmer and cook, covered, over low heat until thickened, about 30 minutes.

2. Add the water to the pot, increase the heat to high, and bring to a boil. Add the egg noodles to cook in the sauce and simmer until they are tender. Serve hot.

SAVORY PIES

There isn't a great savory pie tradition in these islands, but what does exist is tasty and often in the form of a *meze*—small pies, in other words, or skillet pies. There is also a medley of different aromatic herbs that appears again and again, first among which are the feathery leaves of wild fennel. As for the fillings themselves, pumpkin and other squashes, cheese, and wild greens such as poppy leaves and chervil make up many of them.

Pumpkin Coils from Samos

SAMIOTIKO BOUREKI

 Makes 8 to 10 servings

Unlike most of the rest of Greece, and rather ironically given the availability of both wheat and wild greens on the island, the Samian kitchen never developed a savory pie culture. There are only two pies indigenous to the island. The first is the individual coil- or S-shaped boureki *made with pumpkin, and the second is an interesting version of a greens pie or spinach pie.*

3 pounds pumpkin, peeled, seeded, and cut into
    1-inch chunks
2 tablespoons extra-virgin olive oil, plus more
    for brushing
3 large red onions, finely chopped
1½ cups crumbled Greek feta cheese
    (about ¾ pound)
2 heaping tablespoons dried mint
2 large eggs, lightly beaten
2 tablespoons short-grain rice or fine bulgur
Salt and freshly ground black pepper to taste
1 pound commercial phyllo, defrosted and at
    room temperature (see page 455)

1. Bring about 1½ inches of water to a rolling boil. Place the pumpkin chunks in a steaming basket inside the pot, cover, and steam until soft, about 15 to 20 minutes. Remove and place in cheesecloth or a colander to drain. Let it cool, then squeeze out all the excess moisture.

2. Heat 2 tablespoons olive oil in a large skillet and cook the onions over medium-low heat, stirring constantly with a wooden spoon, until wilted, about 8 minutes.

3. Combine the pumpkin and onions in a medium bowl and mash with a fork. Mix in the feta, mint, and eggs. Add the rice or bulgur and combine thoroughly. Season with salt and pepper.

4. Preheat the oven to 375°F. Oil an 18-inch round nonstick pan that is 2 inches deep. Open the phyllo and keep it covered with a cloth. Place one sheet at a time on your work surface with a long side facing you. Brush the surface with olive oil. Fold it in half from the bottom up so that the fold is nearest you. Spread about 2½ tablespoons of filling in a straight line across the bottom of the folded phyllo, leaving about ¾ inch on both ends and the same on the bottom. Fold in the edges and gently roll up the phyllo so that you have a cylinder about 1¼ inches

in diameter. Place it seam side down in the center of the pan, coiling it like a snake. Continue with the remaining phyllo and filling, coiling from where the last one left off, working outward toward the rim.

5. Bake the pie until it is golden and crisp, about 50 minutes. Remove from the oven, let cool for about 30 minutes, and serve warm or at room temperature.

✳ **NOTE** You may reduce the ingredients by half and bake the pie in a 12-inch round pan.

Savory Pumpkin Skillet Pie from Chios

TABOURAS ME KREMMYDIA STO TYGANI

 Makes 8 servings

I love this dish—it reminds me of a savory tarte Tatin or a peasant-style potatoes Anna—and it is one of several interesting crustless pies made in a skillet that are part of the cooking traditions in this part of Greece.

3 pounds pumpkin
Salt to taste
2 large onions, thinly sliced
2 cups all-purpose flour
Freshly ground black pepper to taste
3 tablespoons extra-virgin olive oil
½ pound soft goat cheese, crumbled

1. Try to find a small oval pumpkin, about 5 inches in diameter. Leave it whole. Cut off the stem end and the bottom, stand it up on a cutting board, and, using a sharp boning knife, cut away its rind. Scrape the seeds out with a knife or with a long corer. Cut the pumpkin into round slices about ¼ inch thick. (If you can't find such a small pumpkin, peel and core a larger one the same way. Cut it in half and from that cut thin crescent-shaped slices.)

2. Lightly salt the pumpkin slices. Layer them in a colander. Place a plate, then a weight on top and leave them to drain for an hour.

3. Open a doubled newspaper page and spread the flour on it. Toss with salt and pepper. Turn the pumpkin slices in the flour on both sides, tapping off any excess. Heat the olive oil in a large nonstick or well-seasoned cast-iron skillet. Place the floured pumpkin rounds in the skillet over medium-low heat. Layer the onion slices on top and sprinkle with salt and pepper. Then make a layer of the crumbled cheese and finally one more with the remaining flour-dusted pumpkin rounds. Cover the skillet and let the skillet pie cook for about 15 minutes. Jerk it back and forth by the handle to keep it from sticking. Remove the cover. Place a plate over the skillet and—be sure to wear an oven mitt to do this—flip the pie over onto the plate. Then slip it back into the skillet to brown on the other side. Remove from the heat when cooked through and golden, about another 15 minutes, and serve immediately.

Batter Pie with Wild Greens from Samos

KARIOTINA

  Makes 4 to 6 servings

Only someone aware of the rivalry between Samos and its poor neighbor, Ikaria, would really appreciate the name of this simple but tasty dish. Kariotina means "a woman from Ikaria." This pie was so named because it was the dish people ate when they had little else—poor man's food, Ikarian's food. On the island for which it is named, though, the filling changes slightly, and for the better. Ikarians who make a version of this batter pie fill it with sweet spring greens such as chard and spinach, wild fennel, dill, fresh oregano, poppy leaves, lemon balm, and fresh mint.

1 pound mixed greens and herbs
¼ cup olive oil
2 medium red onions, chopped
Salt and freshly ground black pepper to taste
A grating of nutmeg (optional)
1 cup all-purpose flour
½ teaspoon baking powder
1 large egg
¾ cup water

1. Remove the stems and coarsely chop the greens. Wash thoroughly, squeeze dry, and set aside. Wash and finely chop the herbs.

2. Heat 2 tablespoons of the olive oil in a large skillet and cook the onions over medium-low heat, stirring constantly, until wilted, 7 to 8 minutes. Transfer the onions to a large bowl, add the greens to the skillet, and cook them for a few minutes, until wilted. Mix the greens with the onions in the bowl and add the fresh herbs. Season with salt, pepper, and a grating of nutmeg, if desired.

3. Combine the flour, baking powder, and 1 teaspoon salt in a medium bowl. Make a well in the center and add the egg and water. Using a fork, slowly mix the flour into the liquid, fairly vigorously, until a thick batter forms.

4. Heat the remaining 2 tablespoons olive oil in a well-seasoned 8- or 10-inch cast-iron or nonstick skillet over medium heat. Pour ⅓ cup of the batter into the skillet. When it begins to bubble on top like a pancake, spread about a third of the filling over it, covering the surface of the batter. Pour another ⅓ cup batter over the top of the filling to cover it evenly. Place a lid on the skillet, reduce the heat to low, and cook until the bottom is completely golden and crisp, about 15 minutes. Turn it over carefully to cook on the other side: If you are dexterous enough, flip it with a large flat spatula; otherwise place a plate over the skillet and, using an oven mitt, flip the whole thing, the way you would a cake coming out of the pan. Slide the pie back into the skillet to cook on the other side for 8 to 10 minutes, until golden. Remove from the skillet, keep covered in a warm oven, and repeat with the remaining ingredients. Serve hot, warm, or at room temperature.

Small Cheese Pies from Limnos
LIMNIOTIKES TYROPITES

 Makes about 16 small pies

Savory pies on Iphestos's (Vulcan's) island— Limnos—have one particular characteristic: they are almost always made into small, individual pies. The large pans of savory pies cut up into squares or diamonds are unknown here. Usually individual pies are shaped into coils or figure eights.

For the phyllo
1½ cups fine semolina
1½ cups all-purpose flour
1 teaspoon salt
1 cup water, or more if necessary

For the filling
1 pound Limnos *kalathaki* cheese or other Greek feta cheese
1 bunch scallions, white and tender green parts, finely chopped
¼ cup finely chopped fresh mint
⅓ cup finely chopped wild fennel or dill leaves
4 large eggs
Freshly ground black pepper to taste

To bake
Olive oil for brushing phyllo

1. Make the dough: Combine the semolina, flour, and salt in a large bowl. Pour in the water a little at a time and turn and mix until a mass begins to form. The amount of water is somewhat inexact, depending on the weather, the condition of the flour, etc. The dough, however, must be firm. Knead until it is tight and doesn't stick, 10 to 12 minutes. Set aside, covered, for at least half an hour to rest.

2. Meanwhile, make the filling: Crumble the cheese into a medium bowl and combine with the remaining filling ingredients.

3. Brush a large shallow baking pan or sheet pan with olive oil and preheat the oven to 375°F. Divide the dough into quarters and cut each quarter in half. Sprinkle your work surface with a little flour and roll each piece of dough into a thin, flat rectangle, about 12 by 14 inches. Spread 2 tablespoons of the filling along the bottom of the pastry, about ½ inch from the edge. Fold the edge over the filling and roll over twice, forming a fairly tight cylinder, using up about half the sheet. Cut it. Shape the filled cylinder into a coil. Place on the oiled baking dish or sheet pan. Fill the other half of phyllo the same way. Continue with the remaining pastry and filling until both are used up.

4. Place the coils seam side down in the oiled pan about 2 inches apart. Bake until golden, 20 to 25 minutes. Remove from the oven, let cool in the pan and serve, either warm or at room temperature.

Cheese-and-Spice New Year's Pie from Agiasos in Lesvos

VASSILOPITA AGIASOU

 Makes 12 to 15 servings

For the phyllo
2½ cups water
2 tablespoons fennel seeds
8 to 10 cups all-purpose flour, as needed
2 teaspoons baking powder
½ teaspoon salt
1 tablespoon sugar
⅔ cup extra-virgin olive oil
1½ cups (3 sticks) unsalted butter, melted, to taste

For the filling
3 cups grated aged *myzithra* cheese
1 cup grated *kefalotyri* cheese
½ teaspoon peeled and grated fresh ginger
½ teaspoon ground cloves
½ teaspoon ground cinnamon
½ teaspoon freshly grated nutmeg
½ teaspoon ground allspice

1 coin, wrapped in aluminum foil, to be inserted into the pie for good luck

For garnish
1 large egg, lightly beaten
1 cup sesame seeds

1. Make the phyllo: In a small saucepan, bring the water and fennel seeds to a boil, then reduce the heat and simmer for 5 minutes. Remove from the heat, let the seeds steep for another 5 minutes, and pour the infused water through a strainer into a bowl to cool. Discard the seeds.

2. Place 8 cups of the flour in a large bowl or basin and make a well in the center. Stir the baking powder, salt, and sugar into the infused water and pour the mixture into the well. Add the olive oil to the well. Using a wooden spoon, combine the liquid and flour until a dough mass begins to form. Knead it in the bowl, adding more flour if necessary to make a soft, pliant but smooth dough. (This may also be done in a stand mixer fitted with a dough hook, but in batches.) Cover the dough and let it rest for an hour.

3. Meanwhile, make the filling: Combine the cheeses and spices in a medium bowl and mix thoroughly.

4. Cut off 2 pieces of dough slightly smaller than the size of your fist and shape them into balls. Divide the remaining dough into 12 equal balls. Butter the bottom and side of a 15-inch round baking pan that is 3 inches deep and preheat the oven to 350°F. On a lightly floured work surface, roll the first of the 2 larger balls into a circle 22 to 24 inches in diameter and place it in the buttered pan so that it comes up the sides and hangs over the edge by about 2 inches. Brush it generously with melted butter and dot it with ⅓ cup of the filling. One by one, roll out the 12 smaller balls of phyllo into circles 14 to 15 inches in diameter (just big enough to fit snugly inside the pan). Layer them, one at a time, brushing each with ample melted butter and dotting each with ⅓ cup of the filling. The last layer should be phyllo, not cheese. Place the good luck coin within one of the layers.

5. Bring the edge of the bottom sheet of phyllo over the last layer to close up the sides. Brush the periphery with ample melted butter. Roll the second of the 2 larger balls into a circle 13 to 14 inches in diameter. Carefully place it over the top sheet of phyllo and press it against the rim so that the excess phyllo stands up against the wall of the pan. Press the whole pie down gently with your palms. Brush this last sheet with the beaten egg and sprinkle it with all the sesame seeds. Bake the *vassilopita* until golden and baked through, 1½ to 2 hours. The pie has to bake slowly to ensure that all the cheese-filled layers cook. Remove from the oven, let cool completely in the pan, cut, and serve.

MEAT

In the local cuisine of the northeastern Aegean, as just about everywhere else in Greece, meat does not figure very prominently. It was always scarce, hence reserved for special occasions and holidays. Two of the three meat dishes that follow are part of this repertoire of festive dishes. In the northeastern Aegean, Easter is not synonymous with skewered whole lamb.

Instead, most home cooks stuff baby goat or lamb with rice and all sorts of herbs or nuts. Generally the ingredients depend on what is available locally.

Stuffed Easter Lamb or Goat from Samos

YEMISTO ARNI TIS SAMOU

 Makes 6 to 8 servings

I saw this being done in the kitchen of a mother of a friend, and I felt as though I were witnessing some delicate and tricky surgery. This dish is complicated, and everything depends on the cut of meat. Butchering follows its own logic in Greece, and meat is cut quite differently there. To adapt this to the American table, order a whole lamb or goat shoulder. It must be trimmed of fat, but the thin membrane over it has to be left intact, for this is what is opened like a pocket and then stuffed.

Extra-virgin olive oil
15 scallions, white parts only, finely chopped
1¼ cups long-grain rice
½ cup water
2 bunches fresh wild fennel leaves or dill, trimmed and finely chopped
1 bunch fresh flat-leaf parsley, trimmed and finely chopped
1 lamb's liver, trimmed of membranes and chopped
Salt and freshly ground black pepper to taste
1 lamb or goat shoulder, fatty outer membrane intact
Juice of 1 to 2 lemons, as needed

1. Heat 2 to 3 tablespoons olive oil in a large skillet and cook the scallion whites over medium heat, stirring, until wilted, about 7 minutes. Add the rice and stir for a few minutes. Pour in the water and cook until the rice absorbs all the liquid. Transfer to a large bowl.

2. Combine the rice and scallions with the chopped herbs. Heat 1 to 2 tablespoons more olive oil in the same skillet and cook the chopped liver over medium heat, stirring, until browned, about 5 minutes. Mix it in with the rice. Season with salt and pepper.

3. Preheat the oven to 400°F. Using a sharp boning knife, trim the excess fat from the meat, leaving the membrane intact. With the same knife, carefully separate the bottom of the thin membrane that stretches over the surface of the lamb's shoulder. Push your hand gently and slowly through it to open a pocket between the membrane and the meat. Try not to tear it. Place the lamb in a large oiled baking pan.

4. Slowly spoon the filling into the pocket, pushing it into every nook and cranny but leaving about 1½ inches at the open end—room, in other words, for the rice to expand during cooking. Pat the membrane down a little to close securely. Rub the lamb with olive oil and ample salt and pepper and pour the lemon juice all over it. Place any leftover filling around the lamb. Pour enough water into the pan to come about halfway up the side of the pan and drizzle in about ⅓ cup olive oil. Place the lamb in the oven and bake for 10 minutes. Reduce the oven temperature to 375°F and continue baking for another 20 minutes per pound, basting the lamb every 15 to 20 minutes with the pan juices. Add more water to the pan if necessary to keep the rice moist and enough basting liquids in the pan. An average stuffed shoulder will take about

2 hours to cook the way Greeks like it—well done and crisp on the outside. Remove from the oven and let rest for about 20 minutes before serving. To serve, place on a large platter, carefully loosen the membrane, and spoon out the rice filling and any rice that was cooked in the pan all around the meat.

⊙ Stuffed Easter Lamb or Goat from Lesvos (Yemisto Arni/Katsiki apo tin Lesvou): In Lesvos the stuffing for the Easter lamb or goat is a little different. For the filling, use ¼ cup of butter, 2 cups of long-grain rice, 1 lamb's liver, 1 tablespoon ground cinnamon, ¼ cup sugar, 1 cup blanched chopped almonds, 1½ cups cooked, shelled chestnuts, crumbled, 1 cup of chopped flat-leaf parsley, and olive oil as needed. Follow the directions above for cooking the liver and rice and then stuff the shoulder as directed for the Samos stuffed lamb.

Christmas Pork with Chickpeas, Chestnuts, and Spices from Lesvos

CHRISTOUGENIATIKO HOIRINO APO TIN LESVOU

 Makes 8 to 10 servings

Meat cooked with legumes is a theme one finds frequently on the Greek table. Meat was scarce until a few decades ago, so home cooks needed to be inventive about ways to stretch it. Mixing it with another source of protein—usually either chickpeas or dried white beans—is common. With pork being one of the traditional Christmas mainstays, it stands to reason that a dish such as this holiday special from Lesvos would evolve and flourish. A similar dish, but made with beef, makes for the island's standard wedding food, usually cooked in huge batches for the hundreds of guests who attend village marriage ceremonies. The pork and chestnuts here make wonderful and hearty fare, perfect for any winter table.

½ cup dried chickpeas, picked over, rinsed, and
    soaked overnight in water to cover
⅓ to ⅔ cup extra-virgin olive oil
3 pounds boneless pork shoulder, trimmed of fat
    and cut into stewing pieces
4 cups chopped red onion
Salt and freshly ground black pepper to taste
2 cups peeled, seeded, and chopped tomatoes
    (canned are fine)
1 heaping teaspoon ground cumin
1 teaspoon allspice berries
2 bay leaves
8 new red potatoes, peeled and quartered
1 cup cooked and peeled chestnuts

1. Drain the chickpeas. Place them in a large pot with cold water to cover and bring to a boil, skimming the foam off the surface. Simmer over low heat until slightly softened, 35 to 40 minutes. Remove from the heat and drain.

2. Meanwhile, heat ⅓ cup of the olive oil in a large flameproof casserole dish or Dutch oven over high heat and brown the meat on all sides, stirring frequently. Transfer the meat with a slotted spoon to a plate, heat another ⅓ cup oil if none is left in the pot, then add the onions to the pot. Cook over medium heat, stirring, until softened and lightly browned, about 8 minutes.

3. Place the meat back in the pot, season with salt and pepper, pour in the tomatoes and enough water to cover the meat, and stir in the cumin, allspice, and bay leaves. Cover, bring to a boil, and reduce the heat to low. Simmer for about 40 minutes, then add the drained chickpeas, stir, and pour in additional water if necessary to keep the mixture covered. Simmer, covered, until the chickpeas are almost cooked, about an hour. Add the potatoes and chestnuts and continue cooking until the meat and chickpeas are very tender, another 30 to 40 minutes. Add water if necessary as the stew simmers. Adjust the seasoning with salt and pepper. Remove from the heat, remove and discard the bay leaves and allspice berries, and serve hot.

Meat-Filled Mini Omelets

CHIOS AVGOKALAMARA

 Makes 12 small omelets; 4 servings

This recipe was inspired by a dish I found in a brochure on local cookery from Chios. It is quite unusual, mainly because its name, avgokalamara, *generally refers to a kind of sweet dough fritter made with an egg-rich pastry. But in Chios, as well as in Crete, savory* avgokalamara *make their way into the kitchen repertoire. On Chios these little omelets, for that is essentially what they are, are filled with ground meat. On Crete ground walnuts go into the filling (see page 401).*

For the filling

¼ cup olive oil

1 small onion, minced

⅓ pound lean ground beef

1 firm, ripe tomato, grated (see page 459), or ⅓ cup chopped canned tomatoes

1 small cinnamon stick

4 to 5 allspice berries, to taste, ground

Salt and freshly ground black pepper to taste

For the omelets

3 large eggs

6 tablespoons water

3 tablespoons all-purpose flour

Salt to taste

1 tablespoon olive oil or unsalted butter, or as needed

1. Make the ground meat filling: Heat the olive oil in a medium skillet over medium heat and cook the onion, stirring, until softened, 7 to 8 minutes. Add the meat, increase the heat a little, and stir until browned. Add the tomato and spices, season with salt and pepper, and cook the mixture over low heat, covered, until the meat has absorbed all the pan juices, about 7 minutes. Remove and let cool slightly. This can be done a day or two in advance and kept refrigerated. Warm slightly before using.

2. Beat the eggs well in a small bowl. Combine the water with the flour and stir until smooth. Stir into the eggs. Season with salt.

3. Have the ground meat mixture ready and nearby. Heat the olive oil or butter over medium heat in a large nonstick or cast-iron skillet. Pour in 2 tablespoons of the egg mixture and let it spread to a neat circle.

4. As soon as the egg begins to set (the top should still be a little wet), place 1 heaping teaspoon of the meat filling in the center and, using a fork and spoon, roll up the omelet so that it forms a cylinder. As soon as the egg browns a little on the outside, remove from the skillet and repeat with the remaining egg mixture and filling until it is used up. As you do this, keep the prepared omelets covered and in a warm oven. Serve immediately.

FISH AND SEAFOOD

Sardines Stuffed with Parsley, Garlic, and Tomatoes

SARTHELES GEMISTES ME MAINTANO, SKORDO KAI TOMATES

 Makes 4 to 6 servings

2 pounds large fresh sardines

Fresh lemon juice to taste

Salt to taste

2½ cups finely chopped fresh flat-leaf parsley

6 garlic cloves, minced

3 to 4 tablespoons plain dried bread crumbs, to taste

3 cups finely chopped firm, ripe plum tomatoes

Freshly ground black pepper to taste

4 to 5 tablespoons extra-virgin olive oil, as needed

1. Preheat the oven to 350°F. Clean, gut, and bone the sardines. Cut away the heads and cut open so that the fish are just partially attached in the center. Sprinkle with a little lemon juice and salt.

2. Combine 2 cups of the parsley, the garlic, bread crumbs, and 1 cup of the tomatoes. Season with salt and pepper. Spread a spoonful of stuffing evenly inside each sardine. Close each fish like a sandwich and place side by side in a large, shallow lightly oiled baking dish. Pour the olive oil and remaining tomatoes and parsley over the sardines and bake until the fish are tender and the sauce thick, 45 minutes to an hour, and serve.

THE SARDINES OF LESVOS

Υou want to see our salted sardines?" asked the taverna owner, somewhat amused. "Anthi, go and get the tupper," he ordered his wife. I had driven all the way from Mytilene, the capital, to Kalloni, a small fishing port that over the last decade has reinvented itself as a tourist resort, to see the one thing for which Lesvos is most famous—sweet, oilier than most sardines called *papalina,* fished from the Gulf of Kalloni. When I arrived, the sardine boats were already gone and the late-morning fishermen were pulling mackerel from their nets instead. But a red-penned poster advertised the sardines just outside a local tavern, so I stopped to taste them.

Sardines in the style of Kalloni are salted for only a day, at most two, which keeps them sweet, juicy, and virtually raw, an oddity indeed in Greece, where fish is usually preferred extremely well cooked. Anthi came back a minute later with two containers, one a small shallow plastic container and the other a small clay dish, both layered with silvery fish that had been sprinkled heavily with rock salt. Everything I'd heard about the sardines of Kalloni was true. They are sweet, and the little time they spend under coarse salt makes them more succulent than other tinned sardines.

About one hundred tons of the sardines are fished annually from the Gulf of Kalloni, but many more from the surrounding Greek waters are processed on the island. The canning industry is vibrant here, and the flat, wide tins of locally cured sardines and mackerel are stacked in every shop on Lesvos, usually next to a pyramid of equally famed ouzo, their natural partner at table.

Although the salted sardines of Lesvos are the most famous in the northeastern Aegean, the tradition of cured fish is shared with other places. In Samos, for example, small bream and grey mullet are the fish most prized in the salt barrel. They are processed differently—placed upright in a wooden barrel and sprinkled liberally with coarse salt, then left for five or six days. Unless you stumble into a very hospitable fisherman, these are not easy to find nowadays.

In Chios the cured sardine is also a specialty, but local tastes dictate that the fish spend a little more time under salt—five or six days at the least.

Stuffed Sardines Breaded and Fried

SARTHELES GEMISTES KAI TIGANITES

 Makes 4 to 6 servings

2 pounds large fresh sardines
1 cup finely chopped fresh flat-leaf parsley
⅔ cup finely grated *graviera* or Lesvos *lathotyri* cheese
4 garlic cloves, minced
Salt and freshly ground black pepper to taste
1 cup plain dried bread crumbs from stale bread
1 cup all-purpose flour
3 large eggs
Olive oil for frying

1. Clean, gut, and bone the sardines. Cut away the heads and cut open so that the fish are just partially attached in the center.

2. Combine the parsley, cheese, garlic, salt, and pepper in a medium bowl. Fill each sardine with a little of the mixture and close securely with a toothpick.

3. Spread the bread crumbs and flour on 2 separate plates. Crack the eggs into a bowl and beat lightly. Dip the sardines in the flour first, then in the beaten eggs, then in the bread crumbs. Heat about 1 inch of oil in a large, heavy skillet over medium-high heat. When the oil is very hot, fry the sardines several at a time until the coating is golden brown on both sides and the fish are tender, about 5 minutes. Drain on paper towels and serve hot.

Little Fish and Flour Skillet Pie

GONES

 Makes 4 servings

*O*n Samos and Chios, there is a recipe for a kind of skillet "cake" made with small whole fish and a little flour. It has survived intact from antiquity and was quite popular during the time of the Byzantine Empire. In Samos it is called *gones* (or baby fish), but it is outlawed now since the catch it calls for is too small to be legal. The penalty is stiff for being caught with a boatload of tiny new fish, so locals have adapted their recipes slightly, calling now for tiny but fully grown fish such as smelts. In Samos, as well as in the Dodecanese, the fish are fried together with tomatoes and onions, but in Chios the recipe is simpler— just fish and flour. This dish goes well with boiled horta—greens—(page 404), with the *Santorini* fava (page 316), or *Limnos Black-Eyed Peas Mashed with Garlic Sauce* (page 276).

About 1½ cups all-purpose flour
Salt to taste
Olive or other vegetable oil for frying
1½ pounds whole tiny fish, such as smelts

Season the flour with salt. Heat about 2 tablespoons of oil in an 8-inch cast-iron or nonstick skillet over medium-high heat until very hot. Toss a handful of the fish with some of the flour and quickly place in the skillet. Reduce the heat to medium. Using a spatula, pat the fish down so that the fish take up all the space in the pan. When one side is browned, after about 5 minutes, place a plate over the skillet and turn the fish over. Return to the skillet and fry on the other side until browned. Remove. Continue until all the fish are fried, pouring out the used oil and replenishing it if necessary. Serve immediately.

Mackerel Stuffed with Raisins and Walnuts from Lesvos

SKOUMBRI GEMISTO ME STAFIDES KAI KARYTHIA

 Makes 4 to 6 servings

I remember coming across a very similar dish twelve years ago after meeting a deli owner from Smyrna who waxed poetic about the ornate stuffed mackerel his father used to make at their shop in what is now Izmir.

3 pounds mackerel (about 6 medium whole fish, gutted and boned)

Salt to taste

1½ cups peeled, seeded, and chopped firm, ripe plum tomatoes

6 scallions, whites parts only, thinly sliced

4 garlic cloves, chopped

½ cup golden raisins

1 cup shelled walnuts, coarsely chopped

Freshly ground black pepper to taste

Several fresh oregano sprigs, finely chopped

4 to 5 tablespoons extra-virgin olive oil, to taste

1. Salt the fish lightly inside and out, cover, and refrigerate.

2. Preheat the oven to 350° F. In a large bowl, combine ½ cup of the tomatoes, the scallions, garlic, ⅓ cup of the raisins, ½ cup of the walnuts, salt and pepper, and the oregano.

3. Remove the fish from the refrigerator and fill each cavity lightly with the stuffing. Either press closed or secure closed with a toothpick.

4. Lightly oil a shallow baking pan and place the fish in it snugly, side by side. Combine the remaining walnuts and raisins and sprinkle them over the fish in the pan. Pour on the olive oil and the remaining tomatoes. Bake until the fish are tender, 30 to 40 minutes. Serve immediately.

Spiny Lobster Cooked with Spring Onions and Herbs from Lesvos

ASTAKOS MAGIATIKOS

 Makes 6 servings

In the cold, deep waters of the northern and eastern Aegean, and especially around rocky isolated coastlines, spiny lobster—what Americans also call crawfish, prawn, or langoste—abounds. This is the lobster that Greeks generally know. (Atlantic lobster, while sometimes found in the Mediterranean, is generally not common. Greeks call it astakokaravida—*crab lobster—because of its large claws, but disparage it as bland compared to their beloved indigenous spiny lobster.)*

Spiny lobster is red or reddish brown and grows to a maximum length of about 15 inches. Besides its spiny shell, the other characteristic that distinguishes it from the Atlantic lobster is that it doesn't have claws. There is yet another lobster that Greeks hold in great esteem, the kolohtypa, *which literally means "butt hitter" for the way it swims. This is the flat lobster known as* cigale *in French.*

Most Greek cooks prepare lobster by simply boiling it and serving it with olive oil and lemon juice. Fishermen in the eastern Aegean sun-dry then grill the spiny crustacean. The recipe below, from Lesvos, is another favorite.

5 pounds live spiny lobster, or 4 pounds frozen spiny lobster tails (about 5 ounces each), or 2 pounds jumbo shrimp

2 quarts water

2 tablespoons red wine vinegar

½ cup extra-virgin olive oil

4 cups coarsely chopped white and tender green parts of scallions

1 cup peeled, seeded, and chopped plum
   tomatoes (canned are fine)
½ cup snipped fresh dill
1 cup finely chopped fresh flat-leaf parsley
Salt and freshly ground black pepper to taste
1 large lemon, cut into wedges, for garnish

1. If using frozen spiny lobster tails, first defrost in the refrigerator. Place the water and vinegar in a large pot and bring to a rolling boil. Drop the lobsters into the boiling water. The temperature will drop, causing the water to stop boiling. When it resumes, boil for about 6 minutes. Remove from the water with a slotted spoon and rinse under cold running water. Using kitchen shears, cut the underside of the lobster's shell, splitting it lengthwise from its tail to its head. Remove and discard the thin, dark intestine that runs along the length, just beneath the surface. Remove the meat from the tail and as much of the contents of the head as possible. Discard the gritty pouch at the far end of the head—the gastric mill, as Alan Davidson poignantly calls it in his classic book *Mediterranean Seafood.* Set the lobster meat aside.

2. In a wide, flat pan, heat the olive oil over medium-low heat and cook the scallions, stirring, until translucent, about 8 minutes. Add the tomatoes and bring to a simmer. Add the herbs, season with salt and pepper, cover the pan, and simmer for 20 minutes over very low heat. You may need to add up to ½ cup water to the mixture to keep it moist during cooking. Add the lobster meat and toss gently to combine. Continue cooking over low heat until the lobster meat is warmed through. Serve immediately, garnished with lemon wedges.

Clams (Noah's Arks) with Pasta

KALOGNOMES ME KOFTO MAKARONAKI

 Makes 4 to 6 servings

*S*hort pasta *(ditalini) is most often cooked with octopus in Greece. Not in Limnos. Here at least one old recipe calls for cooking short pasta with one of the Mediterranean's indigenous bivalves, Noah's Arks. It is hard to say how these clams got their name. Not even Alan Davidson, author of the classic* Mediterranean Seafood, *seemed to know. In Greek they're called* kalognomes, *which means "of good opinion," another etymological puzzle. These bivalves grow to about 3 inches in length and have ridged, undulating shells. They are cooked with pasta in other parts of the Mediterranean, too, especially in Liguria. You can substitute any fresh North American clam.*

3 dozen Noah's Arks or other clams
3 tablespoons olive oil
2 medium onions, finely chopped
2 large firm, ripe tomatoes, grated
   (see page 459)
½ cup dry white muscat wine
Salt and freshly ground black pepper to taste
2 teaspoons dried mint
1 pound short pasta such as ditalini

1. Prepare the mollusks: Soak them in cold water for several hours, changing the water 4 or 5 times. Using a sharp, strong knife, shuck them, then cut away the tough membrane with scissors.

2. Prepare the sauce: Heat the olive oil over medium heat, then cook the onions, stirring, until soft, 7 to 8 minutes. Add the tomatoes, wine, salt, pepper, and mint and simmer over low heat for 20 minutes.

3. Bring a large pot of salted water to a boil and cook the pasta until al dente.

4. Place the Noah's Arks in a steaming basket in a large pot over about 1½ inches of water or wine. Cover and steam until opened. Discard any that do not open. Add them to the sauce and toss. Drain the pasta and toss with the sauce.

BREAD

The bread traditions of Greece are so rife with symbolism and haunted with shadows of the ancient world that it would be presumptuous to say that one region's breads are more important than another's. There are differences, to be sure, from place to place, but by and large, throughout the Aegean Islands, the bread culture shares many of the same attributes and characteristics.

A number of related anthropomorphic breads, for example, are found all over the islands. One of these is the Lazarus breads made on the Saturday before Easter, the day that commemorates Jesus's raising Lazarus from the dead. The bread is always shaped like a small child, with arms folded, corpselike, over its chest. It is decorated with spices, such as peppercorns and cloves, or with dried chickpeas, for the eyes. In most of the islands of the Aegean a slew of small, individual Easter breads are also made for children, sometimes nothing more than a rope of sweet dough left over from the main batch and twisted around a red-dyed egg.

Among the islands in this chapter, Samos probably has the richest bread culture. Three specific breads are made as offerings for church on the island. The first, called *prosforon,* which means, simply, "offering," is a perfectly round and plain loaf, made with finely sifted flour, not unlike the holy bread—also called *prosforon*—made all over Greece. What's unusual about the Samos version is the way home bakers place a thin piece of dough on top of it when it first goes into the oven, which they say keeps it from burning or from baking unevenly. The other sacrificial bread is *artos* (the proper name for holy bread), made in Samos with the same dough but flavored with cinnamon and mastic, which are worked in after the kneading and which give the bread a subtle sweetness. *Artos* is baked only a few times a year, as a kind of personal offering to a favorite saint. Sometimes it is sprinkled with nigella seeds (what the Greeks call black sesame), and it is always pressed with a wooden stamp carved with the figure of the saint in whose honor the bread has been made. A smaller loaf of the *artos* no longer found now was a prayer bread that mothers used to make for their children.

Perhaps the most important bread anywhere, is Saint Basil's bread, or *vassilopita,* made specifically for New Year's. It is the bread into which Greeks insert a coin; whoever gets the piece with the coin is said to have good luck for the ensuing year. *Vassilopita* is de rigueur on the holiday tables all over Greece and by no means limited to the tables of the northeastern Aegean.

In most parts of Greece nowadays, *vassilopita* has been gentrified. The recipes found in bakeries and made by most urban cooks are the ones either from Smyrna or from the Peloponnesos for sweet, egg-laden bread, not unlike the Jewish challah and seasoned respectively with either mastic or *mahlepi* (the kernel of a species of cherry tree) or orange and lemon rind. But the regional variations on *vassilopita* are vast, and in many parts of Greece, including some of the islands of the northeastern Aegean, the bread isn't sweet at all.

In some islands, such as Samos, *vassilopita* is traditionally shaped into a round loaf and decorated with one unshelled walnut, symbol of longevity, and with dough strips rolled into the trapezoidal shape of a Byzantine cross. One of the most distinctive recipes for *vassilopita* is that of the town of Agiasos in Lesvos. Here the *vassilopita* isn't a bread at all, but a rich and spicy layered cheese pie, redolent of ginger, cloves, nutmeg, and more, and covered with a blanket of sesame seeds. A recipe for it is included in the savory pie section on page 284.

Raisin-Stuffed Lazarus Bread from Lesvos

LAZARAKIA APO TIN MYTILINI

 Makes 6 small breads

One of the many symbolic decorative breads in the Greek kitchen, these are usually made for children on the Saturday of Lazarus, just before Easter Sunday.

For the bread dough
7 cups water
2 cinnamon sticks
Three ¼-ounce envelopes active dry yeast
1 cup sugar
2 to 2½ pounds all-purpose flour
    (16 to 20 cups), as needed
½ teaspoon salt
¾ cup extra-virgin olive oil

For the filling
3 cups dark raisins
1 tablespoon ground cinnamon
2 teaspoons ground cloves

For garnish
Whole cloves as needed
1½ cups sesame seeds mixed with 3 tablespoons
    sugar

1. Combine the water and cinnamon sticks in a medium saucepan and bring to a boil. Reduce the heat and simmer, covered, for 5 minutes. Remove from the heat and let the cinnamon steep for another 5 minutes. Remove the sticks and let the infused water cool to tepid.

2. Dissolve the yeast and sugar in the tepid water. Combine 2 pounds (16 cups) of the flour with the salt in a large bowl or basin. Pour in the olive oil and rub the mixture between your fingers until the texture becomes mealy. Make a well in the center. Pour in the yeast mixture. Mix the flour into the liquid with a wooden spoon until a mass begins to form. Knead, either in the bowl or in batches on a work surface or in a stand mixer, adding more flour if necessary, until a smooth, silky dough forms. This will take 15 to 20 minutes. Cover the dough and let it rise in a warm, draft-free place until doubled in bulk, about 2 hours.

3. Make the filling: Chop the raisins to a pulp in a food processor. Combine thoroughly with the spices and set aside.

4. Remove one fist-size ball of dough from the mass, punch it down, and set aside. This will be used to shape the arms. Divide the remaining dough into six equal balls. On a lightly floured work surface, roll the first one into a thick oval about 10 inches long and 6 inches wide. Cover most of the dough's surface (leave about an inch around the edge clear) with about ½ cup of the chopped raisins. Fold one side of the dough over the raisins, and the other side of the dough over the fold to secure closed. Shape into a fat, stout loaf, making sure that the filling doesn't spill out anywhere. Take a walnut-size piece off the extra ball of dough and roll it into a strip about an inch wide. Cut and shape like an X in the center of the loaf, to simulate folded arms. Place 2 cloves where the eyes should be, one for the mouth, and one in the center of the X. Continue with the remaining dough and raisins to make a total of 6 breads. Line 2 large sheet pans with parchment paper and oil the parchment. Place 3 loaves on each sheet pan, spaced as far apart as possible. Cover with a dishcloth and let rise for about an hour in a warm, draft-free place.

5. Preheat the oven to 375°F. Just before baking the breads, brush with a little water and sprinkle with the sugared sesame seeds. Bake until golden, about an hour. Remove from the oven, let cool, and serve. These can be eaten individually or cut into slices.

✳ **NOTE** The recipe may be halved to make 3 breads.

⊙

SWEETS

Besides the typical gamut of Greek sweets—*kourambiethes* (shortbread cookies), *melomakarona* (honey-doused biscuits), baklava, etc., in the northeastern Aegean, local specialties include delicious pastry filled with pumpkin and spices and oddest of all, a grain-based dish cooked in grape must syrup.

Sweet Pumpkin Ravioli from Chios

RAVIOLIA ME KOLOKYTHA

 Makes about 40 pieces

The word ravioli *appears in many areas of Greece, a ghost of the Venetians'—or, in the case of Chios, Genoese—formidable presence in this country between the 15th and 19th centuries. Ironically,* ravioli *on Greek soil usually refers to something sweet; in Monemvassia, for example, in the Peloponnesos, the pastry known as* rafioli *is a luscious, nut-filled crescent encrusted with confectioners' sugar; in Chios, the name refers to the following dish, lovely pumpkin-filled pastries drizzled with syrup. Many, many pumpkin-filled sweets are found in every corner of Greece.*

For the pastry
3 cups all-purpose flour
½ teaspoon salt
¼ cup extra-virgin olive oil
1 cup water

For the filling
1½ pounds pumpkin, peeled, seeded, and cut into chunks
¼ cup long-grain rice
½ cup water
2 teaspoons olive oil or unsalted butter
1 teaspoon ground cinnamon
½ teaspoon freshly grated nutmeg

For the syrup
1 cup honey
1 cup water

To make the crescents and fry
1 large egg white mixed with ¼ cup water, for brushing pastry
Vegetable oil for frying

1. Make the pastry: In a large bowl, sift together the flour and salt. Drizzle the olive oil over the flour and rub it in with your fingers until the flour is mealy. Pour in the water and knead, adding more flour if necessary, until a soft, smooth dough forms. Set aside, covered with plastic wrap, for at least an hour. (At this point the dough can be refrigerated for up to 3 days and brought back to room temperature 2 hours before being used).

2. Prepare the filling: Place the pumpkin in a medium pot with just enough water to cover it. Cover and bring to a boil. Reduce the heat to medium-low and simmer, covered, until the pumpkin is soft, 20 to 25 minutes. Meanwhile, place the rice and water in a small pot or skillet, bring to a boil, reduce the heat to low, and simmer, covered, until soft and all the water has been absorbed, 6 to 8 minutes. Toss with the oil or butter and set aside.

3. Remove the pumpkin from the heat and place in a large double thickness of cheesecloth. Tie the cheesecloth around the pumpkin like a little satchel and leave it hanging from the kitchen faucet for at least 2 hours to drain completely. (You can also do this in a strainer or in a colander with small holes.)

4. Make the syrup: Combine the honey and water in a small saucepan and heat slowly until the mixture begins to boil. Let it simmer, uncovered, for 10 minutes. Remove from the heat and set aside.

5. Place the drained pumpkin in a large bowl and mash it by hand or with a potato masher, adding the cinnamon and nutmeg. Mix in the buttered rice.

6. Lightly dust your work surface with flour. Divide the pastry dough into 6 equal balls. Roll each ball into a circle about 14 inches in diameter and about as thick as a dime. Using a round cookie cutter or a glass 3 or 4 inches in diameter, cut circles

out of the dough. Place a teaspoon of the filling on each, then fold over each circle to form a crescent. Dip a fork into the egg white wash and pat down the edge of the dough, pressing it together with the prongs of the fork.

7. In a large, heavy skillet, heat about 2 inches of vegetable oil over medium-high heat until a small piece of bread crust tossed into it immediately rises to the surface. Place a handful of the ravioli in the skillet and fry until golden, turning once to brown on both sides. Remove with a slotted spoon and let drain on paper towels. Place the ravioli on a serving platter and drizzle with the sugar syrup. Serve warm or at room temperature.

⊙ There is another, more interesting, way to prepare these pumpkin crescents. Until the 1950s they were called "tile cakes," *keramidopites,* in Chios because they were baked on hot stone. A similar method can be found in Samos, not in the same recipe but in a pancakelike dish called *mamarites,* which gets its name from the the slabs of marble heated over an open flame that acted as a kind of makeshift griddle. If you have a baker's stone for bread baking, try baking the little pumpkin crescents directly on top of it instead of frying them. You can make the filling savory by replacing the cinnamon and nutmeg with a little crumbled feta cheese and some chopped herbs such as dill or parsley.

Pancakes with Yogurt and Currants

TIGANITES ME YIAOURTI KAI STAFITHES

 Makes about fifteen 3-inch pancakes

Pancakelike dishes abound in Greece, usually served as snack food or breakfast for young children. This version, with yogurt and currants, was inspired by an old dish from Chios.

2 cups all-purpose flour
½ teaspoon baking soda
½ teaspoon salt
2 tablespoons sugar
1 cup plain yogurt, drained (see page 459)
2 large eggs, lightly beaten
½ to 1 cup water, as needed
½ cup dried currants
Unsalted butter
Orange marmalade or honey

1. Sift the flour, baking soda, and salt together in a medium bowl. Mix in the sugar. Make a well in the center and add the yogurt, beaten eggs, ½ cup of the water, and the currants. Mix the batter with a fork, working the flour into the liquid little by little. The batter should have the consistency of a thick pancake batter. Add a little or all of the remaining water if it is too thick.

2. Heat 1 tablespoon butter in a large, nonstick or cast-iron skillet over medium heat and drop 2 tablespoons batter into it for each pancake. When the bottom has browned lightly and small bubbles form on the surface, flip each pancake over to cook on the other side. Continue, adding more butter to the skillet as necessary, until all the batter is used up. Remove from the skillet and spread with marmalade or drizzle with honey.

Muscat-Scented Sugar Cookies

SAMOS KOURKOUBINIA

 Makes about 100 cookies

10 cups all-purpose flour
2 teaspoons baking soda
2 cups extra-virgin olive oil
1 cup Samos muscat or any sweet muscat wine
1 cup granulated sugar
1 cup rose water or Samos muscat wine
Confectioners' sugar for dusting

1. Preheat the oven to 375°F. Combine the flour and baking soda in a large bowl.

2. In another large bowl, whisk the olive oil and wine together to emulsify. Slowly add the granulated sugar in a steady stream, beating all the while.

3. Slowly add the flour to the liquid, mixing vigorously with a wooden spoon until a soft dough forms. Knead it by hand in the bowl until it is silky smooth.

4. Break off a small knob of dough at a time, about the size of an unshelled walnut, and shape into a small mounded cigar, about 2 inches long. Place the *kourkoubinia* 1 inch apart on an ungreased cookie sheet lined with parchment or wax paper and bake until light golden, 10 to 15 minutes. As soon as you remove them from the oven, sprinkle with rose water or muscat, and a few minutes later dust them liberally with confectioners' sugar. Store in a cookie tin in a cool, dry place.

Homemade Pasta Simmered in Grape Must Syrup from Limnos

MOUSTOKOULIKA

 Makes about 24 *moustokoulika*

I have long been intrigued by the bevy of sweet pasta dishes found throughout Greece and sought a full explanation for their existence. I know that in Crete certain kinds of pasta are often boiled in milk and sprinkled with sugar and served to new mothers. Folk wisdom dictates that the dish helps them produce milk. One of the oddest such dishes is surely the one that follows, for homemade pasta boiled in grape must from the island known as the granary of the Aegean, Limnos.

Petros Honas, one of the most important winemakers on Limnos, took me to see an aunt of his one early morning so that I could spend the day cooking with her. He promised that she was one of the island's best cooks. We drove from the capital to the northeastern side of Limnos, to a small village called Kaminia, where his aunt, a portly, smiling woman, Eleftheria Konstantinou, was waiting for us in her front yard. I learned to make the majority of the Limnos recipes in this book from her, but the most memorable by far was the lesson she taught me about what must surely be one of the most unusual dishes in the whole Aegean, indeed in all of Greece: moustokoulika.

It's hard to describe what these are like—something between a pretzel, a dumpling, and a doughnut cooked in grape must syrup. They were dense and filling, the kind of dish I could see being savored after the harvest and during the week or so that farmers spend pressing their grapes each fall.

It is always amazing to me to observe the dexterity with which experienced Greek home cooks work with dough. Eleftheria certainly had a facility for it, rolling out long ropes of firm dough, breaking off a small piece at a time, and twisting it around the tines of a fork in such a way that within a second or two she had achieved the shape, which was a little like a pretzel. As she did this, Petros plied us with wine. I touched the dough, and Eleftheria immediately parted with her pearl of wisdom concerning the proper consistency for it. "It has to be tight," she kept reminding me each time she rolled out, cut, and twisted another dough rope. About a half hour later, she began poaching the dough twists in the grape must syrup, and here, too, maybe with a little help from the wine, she shared another piece of advice: "These have to be just like sisters-in-law," she said. "They should never stick!"

2 to 2¼ cups hard wheat flour and 1 to 1¼ cups fine semolina
Pinch of salt
1¼ cups warm water
1 quart grape must syrup (*petimezi*)
2 cups water

1. Combine 2 cups of the flour, 1 cup of the semolina, and the salt in a large bowl or basin. Make a well in the center and slowly add the warm water. Using your fingertips, slowly incorporate the flour from the inner rim of the well, working it into the water until a mass begins to form. Continue doing this until the dough is more or less formed. It will be sticky and dense. Knead the pasta dough until it is smooth and firm, adding the remaining flour in increments. Knead for 7 to 10 minutes. Let it rest for a few minutes.

2. Divide the dough into 6 equal balls. Dust a large work surface with flour. With your fingertips and palms, roll each ball into a rope about 1 inch in diameter. Working from one end, roll this rope a little at a time into a thinner strand, about ½ inch in diameter. Break the dough off at 4-inch intervals. Bring the end around so that it forms 2 loops like a figure 8. Continue until all the dough is used.

3. Bring the *petimezi* and 2 cups water to a boil in a medium saucepan and add the pasta, a little at a time. Simmer for 8 to 10 minutes. To test for doneness, remove one *moustokouliko* and taste it. The dough should be cooked through. Remove with a slotted spoon, and cook the rest, in batches, and place in a bowl or on a platter. Serve warm.

MASTIC, THE SPICE FROM THE TREE THAT CRIES

Of all the unusual foods, spices, and herbs that Greece is known for, none is quite as illustrious as mastic, the crystallized resin from the tree *Pistacia lentiscus*. Mastic has been known for its healing properties since classical antiquity. Recent research has revealed that mastic is very effective in curing certain kinds of stomach ulcers.

Chios is the world's sole producer of what is otherwise known as gum arabic. No one knows for sure why mastic is produced only here and only in the twenty-one mastic towns on the southern cape of the island. Some say the subterranean volcanoes off Chios provide the clue; others relish the legend of Saint Isidore, tortured by the Romans and left bleeding to death under a mastic tree. In sympathy for the martyr, the tree began to cry, and its tears became the crystal mastic.

In a way the trees still have to "cry" for mastic to be harvested. Every June the ground is cleared under the hardwood mastic trees that dominate the landscape on the southern tip of Chios. Then they are "wounded"—their trunks slashed—so that the thick crystal sap within can trickle out and drop onto clean earth. It takes five years for a tree to start producing its resinous diamonds, and on average one tree provides only about 100 grams of mastic gum a year.

In cooking, the rock-hard, somewhat sticky crystals have to be pounded to a fine dust, usually with a bit of sugar to keep them from sticking to the mortar and pestle or spice grinder. Mastic is a natural chewing gum. It also goes into a local liqueur that is like ouzo and flavors a kind of sugar paste. It is used in pastry, breads, and confections. Its great claim to fame, though, is in *kaimaki* ice cream, a luscious, almost gooey ice cream that pulls away from the dish when you put a spoon to it.

In the United States, mastic is easy to find in Greek and Middle Eastern food shops and at some gourmet markets. It has a wonderful, deep aroma and flavor, at once woody, earthy, and musky like incense. It lends a kind of gustatory resonance to the pastries and dried fruits to which it is added.

Mastic-Scented Baked Figs

PASTELARIES

 Makes 50 pieces

These wonderful mastic-scented figs are made at the end of the summer on Chios, when figs are ripe and mastic is ready to be harvested. They are one of many different ways to season dried figs.

100 dried Greek figs
¼ cup blanched almonds
¼ cup walnuts
2 teaspoons ground cinnamon
1½ tablespoons sesame seeds
10 bay leaves
1 teaspoon mastic crystals ground in a mortar
    with 1 teaspoon sugar

1. Preheat the oven to 300°F. Place the figs in a large shallow ovenproof glass baking dish and set in the oven just long enough to warm through. You may have to do this in batches. Meanwhile, coarsely chop the almonds and walnuts.

2. Combine the nuts with the cinnamon and sesame seeds. Remove the figs from the oven and, using a sharp paring knife, fill the figs with a pinch of the nut mixture. Taking two stuffed figs at a time, press them together or pound them together lightly with a mallet. Place back in the dish. When all the figs are filled, sandwiched, and placed side by side in the dish, reheat, at a slightly higher temperature—350°F—just until they begin to brown. Remove from the oven and let cool.

3. Place the cooled figs in layers in a tin or jar and between layers place several bay leaves and a dusting of mastic sugar. Store for at least 1 week before serving. The figs will keep indefinitely.

The Cyclades

A Sense of Place and Palate

If Greece is her islands, then the Cyclades are her heart. These islands are the stuff of travel posters: white-washed houses, narrow, winding village streets, brilliant sun, deep blue sea. Their collective name means "circle," for the way the island group is situated—starting with Andros, the northernmost island, and ending with Sifnos, the circle closes. In between, are legendary places—Santorini, Syros, Mykonos, Delos, Paros, Naxos, Tinos, and more that make up the thirty inhabited islands of the Cyclades and the dozens of uninhabited ones, mere parcels of rock and shrub afloat in the turquoise Aegean.

The Cyclades never ceased to be a center, or bridge, for the whole eastern Mediterranean. Because the climate in most of these islands is arid, inhabitants never relied on agriculture as the basis of local economies. Instead they turned to what was all around them: the sea. From prehistoric times they were avid sailors, and trade bustled in their busy ports. The islands were also endowed with a wealth of minerals: obsidian and chalk in Kimolos, emery in Naxos, gold in Sifnos, bronze in Serifos, and clay almost everywhere with which to shape the pottery that also became characteristically sophisticated so early on.

Naxos, the largest island in the group, and Paros, were renowned for the quality of their marble. They gave Athens many of the artisans who built the Parthenon and chiseled her statuary. In classical times, Paros was the economic center of the Cyclades. The island was esteemed for the high quality of its olive oil and wine. Paros, Serifos, Sikinos, and Milos were also well known for their wine, while Naxos was famed for its vegetables. And throughout these islands, despite a relative dearth of grazing lands and the arid climate, thousands of sheep and goat roamed freely, giving islanders meat and milk from which to make the cheeses that are still famous and almost unchanged today.

In 1207, three years after the Byzantine Empire fell to the Ottoman Turks, the

Cyclades fell to Venice, which established the Duchy of Naxos as its center of operation, until 1566, when the Turks conquered all the islands except Tinos, which fell in 1715. The 351 years that the Venetians ruled these islands left a stamp that remains to the present day. In Syros, almost half the population is Catholic, and there are large Catholic communities in Naxos and Tinos as well. In terms of local food, such things as blood pudding, *rafiolia*, Christmas Eve feasts of fish and seafood, and a host of other local specialties owe their provenance to the Venetians and to the Catholic population.

Like the austere and barren landscape that marks most of the Cyclades, so, too, is the cooking of these thirty-odd islands marked by an exquisite simplicity. The Cyclades have waged an eternal struggle for water, have always had little in the way of fruitful earth. Writers who made their way through these parts millennia later, notably the English and French on the grand tours between the sixteenth and nineteenth centuries, were mostly disparaging about the islands' food, describing the majority of things the peasants ate as horrid.

Impressions change. In our own time, most people associate the Cyclades with vacation paradise. The native dishes go largely unnoticed by the masses who swarm here each summer. But every island in the Cyclades is a world unto itself, with its own local culture and customs, its own local food. There are many common threads, in the way of flavors, raw ingredients, and finished dishes, from place to place. In the tapestry of Cycladic cooking, capers, a whole bevy of beans and pulses, small game birds and rabbit—the birds often put up in brine—pork and all its products, delicious goat's and sheep's milk cheeses, tomatoes, and rusks are the motifs.

The sweets constitute a long list of small pas-tries, usually filled with nuts or cheese. Many are magnificent in their simplicity. I love, for example, the *kopania* of Santorini, a sweet made by pounding the traditional barley rusk together with raisins in a mortar and pestle, shaping the mass into small balls, and rolling each in toasted sesame seeds. Another minimalistic sweet comes from Kea and is made by kneading stale bread with local raisin wine and sprinkling it with sugar and cinnamon. There are still some delicious strictly local spoon sweets to be found, notably lemon blossom (in Andros) and apricot (in Tinos). Bread puddings survive from the times of the Venetians, especially in Santorini. Sesame-seed brittle, *pastelli,* is made in Andros and Tinos and served individually on lemon leaves as the sweet for special occasions, especially weddings. Syros supplies the whole country with *loukoumi—* Turkish delight—as well as with *halvadopites,* thin wafers filled with a nougatlike meringue.

SANTORINI

It was early spring the first time I visited Santorini. We landed at dawn, by ship. The island rose out of the water pitch black, darker than a shadow.

Crescent-shaped Santorini, at the southernmost tip of the Cyclades, is the paradigm Greek island, both ethereal and orgiastic. In summer the foreigners run amok among the seasonal bars, restaurants, clubs, and shops. In winter, though, the villages shrink back to their timeless rhythms, dampened by the island's heavy fogs and wind. Somewhere between the two extremes, local traditions miraculously have stayed intact. Santorini has a culture and a cuisine all its own.

The island is quite different from the rest of the Cyclades. For one, it has an active volcano, sculpted by some thirty feet of pumice stone that blanket its surface. Its cliffs rise high and forbidding. Water has always been scarce. Little grows wild here besides shrubs, dandelions, poppies, herbs, nettles, capers, and weeds, but the island's volcanic soil has always been conducive to grape growing—some of Greece's best white and sweet wines are from Santorini—and wine production has thrived here since Minoan times. Rabbits and birds make up the island's wildlife.

From the Ventian presence onward and largely up until World War II, the island's economy was feudal, with the population divided between the extremely rich controlling families and the peasants. As in Corfu, the class differences are mirrored in the local table. The wealthy feasted on dishes culled from a clearly Western tradition—roast beef, stews simmered with tomatoes and cognac, and *poutinga,* a kind of pudding served with a sauce similar to the Italian zabaglione except that it is made with Santorini's own sweet wine, *vin santo,* and not Marsala.

The yellow split pea, the caper, and the tomato are the raw materials of Santorini's peasant cookery which has remained by and large unchanged. The split pea is as basic as bread, and it appears in dozens of recipes. It is the basis of several soups, it is cooked with eggplants and tomatoes, pureed and topped with stewed capers, "married," as the locals say, with sautéed onions, turned into patties and fried, and baked into timbales. In some of the island's more remote villages, old women still grind whole split peas by hand, working them between the stone slabs of their ancient hand mills.

The caper, a kind of leitmotiv in the cooking of many of the Cycladic islands, also appears on tables of Santorini. Here the buds are either pickled or dried, so as to be had all winter long, and the leaves

are eaten, too, either steamed in salad or preserved in brine.

The island is also known for the quality of its small, waterless tomatoes, which were probably brought here by the Italians who occupied Santorini before World War II. Until the 1950s, in fact, tomato cultivation—and canning—was the mainstay of Santorini's economy. One of the island's signature dishes is its mock *keftedes,* patties made with tomatoes and herbs that are battered then fried.

Another vegetable unique to Santorini is its small white eggplant, which was probably brought to the island from Egypt with the wealthy families of Alexandrian Greeks who dominated Santorini's near-feudal economy in the early part of this century. Santorini is one of the only places in Greece where saffron—cultivated locally for eons— appears in some local dishes, namely an Easter biscuit. In the traditional cookery, seaweed was also commonly eaten, especially in the form of salads and batter-fried patties. One of Santorini's most unusual dishes, still to be found in some villages, is a variety of *skordalia*—the Greek garlic puree—made not with potato or bread as it is throughout the rest of the country, but with yellow squash as its base.

Meat was always rare, and when cooked was almost never roasted, mostly because there were too few trees on the island to produce a supply of wood. Vinewood was the most prevalent fuel. Many of the traditional dishes were cooked in a skillet or saucepan. Various wild fowl appear in the old cooking of Santorini, and traditionally such game was preserved in salt to be savored throughout the winter.

Because of the rough and extremely deep waters around the island, fishing was never much of an occupation here either, and most recipes for fish call for salt cod, which was a cheap import until overfishing depleted much of the world's supply. Small fish such as whitebait were also common and, like the wild fowl, were usually preserved in salt or turned into *keftedes.*

Small barley rusks, called *kritharoboukies,* were and still are a traditional island bread, and there are several local cheeses (see page 307).

Syros

Many travelers to Greece come in contact with Syros, the capital of the Cyclades, even if they never step foot on the island. Actually, Syros comes to them, in the form of old-fashioned boxes of *loukoumi,* Turkish delight, that are hawked on passenger ships and ferries all over Greece in the summer.

I came to Syros on a brilliant late October day when the tourists were all gone, the *loukoumi* workshops well stocked and quiet, and the season's first *louzes* (air-cured pork) dangled like lanterns from the local butcher shops. I had come looking, as always, for food and lore, but food traditions need a long past, and that seems to be the one thing missing from this most unusual island. Syros's capital, Ermoupolis, 176 years old, is a new city by Greek standards. It was born during the Greek Revolution and was not, as one tourist brochure wryly notes, "founded on past tradition."

It stands to reason, then, that the food here is also "not founded on past tradition." The two dishes for which Syros is most famous—*loukoumi* and the local cheese *San Mihali*—are, indeed, relatively new. The former, Turkish in origin, was imported with the Greek refugees from Asia Minor in the 1920s. The latter was brought to the island in 1963 when a cheese maker from Gastouni in the Peloponnesos landed a job at the newly founded

factory, Biosyr, and taught his colleagues how to make the cheese. It was named arbitrarily after the Catholic church in Upper Syros.

Syros has absorbed waves of Greek refugees from Asia Minor, and also has a formidable Catholic population with a five-hundred-year history on the island. They all have left some traces on the local table, but in subtle ways.

For one, the well-to-do and well-educated refugees of the last century were responsible for the high level of culture that Syros enjoyed in the nineteenth and early twentieth centuries. It was here that the first cookbook was published in modern Greece, a translation of an Italian cookbook, called *H Mageiriki Ek tou Italikou (Cooking in the Italian Manner).* At least one recipe that is very popular on the island today, for batter-fried cauliflower, is made almost exactly the same way as described in that book.

In Syros, though, there isn't a "style" of cooking; rather there are dishes and other specialties unique to the island. As the epicenter of the Cyclades, Syros's cuisine is a combination of the urbane, bourgeois food that is the legacy of the island's mercantile and refugee past and the sparse, stark cookery typical of the rest of the Cyclades.

For example, capers—a staple throughout the Cyclades—are significant in Syros, too. They are both sun-dried and pickled. Dried capers cooked in tomato sauce and served with fried fish such as *kolios* (chub mackerel), *safridi* (scad), and *gopes* (bogue) is probably the best known dish on the island.

Another Cycladic specialty—sun-dried tomatoes—also plays a role in the island's cookery. As in neighboring Tinos, they are soaked, then dipped in batter and fried as a *meze.* Here they are also combined with scallions, dill, and cheese and made into ersatz *keftedes,* something that locals seem to like a lot. Purslane and potatoes are also mashed together, dredged in flour, and fried into mock *keftedes.*

Snails and all sorts of seafood are enjoyed on Syros. Fan mussels *(pinnes),* which the nineteenth-century English traveler Theodore Bent noted as forming a major part of the local diet, are still the favorite food on Clean Monday, the first day of Lent, when they are grilled and eaten with the traditional Lenten flatbread, *lagana.*

As for sweets, besides *loukoumi,* there are the *halvadopites,* thin wafers with nougatlike filling and hawked on ships, as well as one local specialty called *sfoliata,* which is a phyllo pastry filled with semolina and blanched almonds, seasoned with orange blossom water, and drenched with syrup.

Syros claims about a dozen recipes all its own but also boasts a respectable list of local food products that add to its repertoire of specialties.

TINOS

The farmer's market on the edge of Hora, the capital, in Tinos at first glance seemed like an unpropitious way to begin a foray into this island's food and cooking: A few vans were lined up in a row, a few cases of vegetables were spread out before them, and the vendors were standing lazily about. But it didn't take long to get beyond the usual fare of eggplants, onions, potatoes, and cabbage and to find the real treasures here: Garlands of home-dried tomatoes, ready after spending all summer in the sun; disks and rounded pyramids of local cheeses—*vollakia, petroma, petrotiri;* wild greens, mostly chard this time of year (it was too early for the *skalfa,* a local green not unlike spinach). A few steps away, on a back street off the port, the butcher

shops were filled with local fennel-flavored sausages and wine-soaked *louzas* (cured pork loin), so different from the *louzas* in neighboring Syros and Mykonos.

I had come to Tinos in late October, a kind of no-man's time. The weather teeters between summer heat and early winter rains, too late to witness the caper harvest or the drying of tomatoes, too soon for the island's famed pork slaughters to be under way or to see other rituals surrounding the holiday table. Nevertheless, locals were happily back in their own routines. The place was theirs again after the onslaught of the summer throngs. I spent several days touring the island's dainty, manicured villages and talking to women about the way they cooked, farmed, lived. In the backdrop, amid conversations and memories of foods long gone, two things were ever present: the thousand-odd dovecotes that dot Tinos's landscape, many still providing shelter for her pigeons, which in turn provide food for their keepers; and the cows, beautiful insolent cows slumbering along the rocky walls at dusk, on their way back from pasture.

At one time, bovine and bird made up the mainstay of people's diets here, and both owe their existence on the island to the Venetians, who ruled Tinos from 1207 to 1715. (The island was the last of the Cyclades to fall to the Turks.) The pigeons provided an accessible delicacy for local cooks. Traditionally, only fledglings were savored, usually in soups. But the birds played a second, though equally important, role in the local ecosystem, providing extremely fertile manure for the island's fields and gardens.

Until recently there was a breed of local cattle, big boned and tall (actually the Tinos cow was the biggest Greek species), that first arrived on the island in the sixteenth century with the Venetians who had the insight to import a breed that could survive in Tinos's dry climate, one that needed little care and pastured easily. In the last twenty years the local species has been lost through crossbreeding with more productive Dutch cows that provide up to three times more milk than the Tinos breed.

It is that milk, much more than meat, that provides Tinos with what is perhaps the most important staple on the local table: cheese—lots of it and all of it delicious. Meals in Tinos are almost always accompanied by cheese. Besides *graviera,* which is the most important cheese commercially, although it has been produced on the island only since the 1980s, there are about half a dozen traditional cheeses, almost all made with cow's milk. Cheese appears in many cooked dishes as well. There are cheese-stuffed tomatoes and small sweet cheesecakes for sale at local pastry shops. There are crustless cheese pies, cheese pies seasoned with fennel or with *petimezi* (boiled grape must syrup), and Easter cheese pies. Best of all, though, is the way locals savor plain cheese, served in the true connoisseur's way, with fresh fruit such as grapes and figs.

Probably the best-known dish on the island, though, has nothing to do with cheese. It is *froutalia,* also found in neighboring Andros. Basically it is a big, thick omelet, traditionally cooked in lard and filled most often with potatoes and local sausage, although greens and legumes figure prominently in other versions of the dish, too. I was introduced by a local cook named Nicoletta Delatolla to the Catholic specialties on Tinos and was especially intrigued by the foods of Christmas, which seem so different from those in the rest of Greece. On Christmas Eve, among the Catholic population, seafood and fish provide the basis for a very festive, albeit fasting, meal. One of the most unusual specialties is jellied eel. Other dishes, shared through-

out the island, include the sweet chard pastries filled with raisins, walnuts, and the green; beef stew; cabbage *dolmathes;* roast beef; and beef soup *avgolemono.*

Tinos's cuisine, like that of all her sister islands, is simple, pared down. The palette of flavors is characterized mostly by fennel and its seeds, collected in the fall and dried for use as a spice in everything from breads to cheese pies. The local flora is rich in mushrooms, which are either stewed or fried; in olive trees, which are called *agrelia* locally; and in greens. Figs once were very important in the local pantry, and at least seven varieties are indigenous to the island. Only one, the *kavouraki,* is traditionally used to make the delicious local *pastellaries,* a kind of baked fig sandwich layered and patted with sesame seeds, walnuts, and cinnamon, something found all over Greece in endless variations.

ANDROS

Andros is not a place renowned for the breadth of its table. But, like nearly everywhere in Greece, it reveals its culinary riches slowly and only to those willing to wield the metaphoric magnifying glass.

Andros is legendary for the shipowning families who hail from it, among them the Goulandris and Embeirikos families. But the island's seafaring traditions have intersected little with its culinary heritage. Riches trickled into the kitchen via another, unlikely, route—through the generations of poor women who worked as wet nurses in Constantinople. "The influences from Asia Minor are strong," says Maria Kore, who works at the Goulandris museum, is a walking and vocal encyclopedia of local lore, and who was my guide through Andros's foodways. "Don't forget, these women were working in the wealthiest households, and because of their duties they had to eat the finest, richest, best foods. They saw many new things and took much of what they saw back with them to Andros," she explained. Hence dishes such as *soutzoukakia* (spicy ground meat sausages), *giouverlakia* (rice-studded meatballs), *imam bayaldi* (stuffed eggplant), and a plethora of *bourekakia* (little pies)—sweet and savory—which are, indeed, reminiscent of the cooking of the Poli Greeks (as the Greeks from Constantinople—the "city," or "poli"—are called), are common in Andros.

The island is also no stranger to local regional differences, however minute, from place to place, village to village. Within its thirty-eight square kilometers, there are the villages settled hundreds of years ago by Christianized Albanians in the northwestern part of the island, where the cuisine tends to be simpler, more rustic; there are also the areas in the Southwest, around Korthion, which were settled by Greeks from the Thessalian plain. Here, characteristically, one finds something that does not appear anywhere else in the island's cooking traditions—savory pies, especially those made with sorrel and spinach, as well as yeast-leavened biscuits.

The table in Andros is also a reflection of the one thing that probably differentiates it from every other island in the Cyclades—water, and plenty of it. "Because we always had water, we always had very good gardens," explains Mrs. Kore. Vegetables are the most prominent foodstuff on the island's table. Obscure agrarian delicacies, though, like the old world Andros salad made with raw pea shoots and seasoned with olive oil and vinegar, have, unfortunately, been lost. But vegetables cooked with eggs, with meat, with fish, and in the form of one-pot stews remain hallmarks of the local fare. Islanders enjoy vegetables with leeks and celery

avgolemono, and vegetables (especially potatoes) *yiahni* (in tomato sauce) cooked together with the local sausage or with *louza,* the salted, air-cured pork fillet also common in Tinos, Syros, and Mykonos. Local specialties such as cauliflower stewed with sausages, batter-fried leafy greens such as sorrel and chard, and chard stuffed as for *dolmathes* are all pan-Cycladic dishes that find a home in Andros, too.

The Cyclades Pantry

CHEESE

Nowhere else in Greece has one particular food enjoyed the kind of unbroken continuity that cheese making has in the Cyclades. There is a host of simple curd cheeses made with sheep's and goat's milk, some fresh, others strained, pressed, and/or dried; the yellow cheeses of the Cyclades are also among the finest in Greece, and one unique aspect of these is that many are made with cow's milk. Other cheeses in the Cyclades include various pungent and soft fermented cheeses and a host of hard cheeses preserved in lees or in the pastelike dregs at the bottom of the olive oil barrel. Here is at look at the cheeses of the Cyclades, organized alphabetically.

Arseniko Its name literally translates as "masculine," because—at least this is the local lore—the cheese is hard and tastes very good! *Arseniko* is essentially a hard yellow table or grating cheese, what most of the rest of Greece would classify as a *kefalograviera,* hence one of the oldest, most traditional Greek cheeses. On Naxos, it is made from a combination of raw sheep's and goat's milk (the best is said to be made from milk from the first, morning milking), which is heated, then set with rennet. The mass is then cut, the curds collected, then left to drain in 2- to 4-kilo basket molds, from which it takes its final shape. Once it has drained sufficiently and the curds hold together, the cheese is dipped in whey again, rubbed with salt, and left to mature (outside the baskets) for at least 60 days, although the best is at least six months old. *Arseniko* is both a wonderful table cheese and grating cheese and it is easy to cook with, too, especially good as an ingredient in savory pies.

Chloro This is the most traditional local cheese from Santorini. It is usually eaten as a fresh cheese, hence its name, which means "fresh." *Chloro* is traditionally made with goat's milk, and produced in winter and spring when there are plenty of fresh greens to graze on. In summer, to accommodate tourist demand, cow's milk is sometimes used to produce it. Locals also preserve fresh *Chloro* in salt brine, in which case it becomes very hard and is used as a grating cheese. It is difficult to find outside the island, and often difficult to find on Santorini itself, since production is almost exclusively limited to the home and consumption almost exclusively personal.

Ghilomeno or Manoura Without doubt, this is one of the most unusual cheeses in all of Greece, if not in all the Mediterranean. *Ghilomeno* is essentially a traditional, hard cheese, made almost exclusively with raw goat's milk. It takes its name from the local name for the lees—the dregs of the wine barrel—which in Sifnos and elsewhere are called *ghilomeno*. Once set, the cheese is preserved and matured in the lees at the bottom of the wine barrel.

Wine-soaked cheeses are found in several parts of Greece, namely the islands, and in the Cyclades they are a regional specialty in Sifnos and Folegandros. The cheese is usually made into small heads. The exterior is dark, almost muddy, but aromatic. *Ghilomeno* is a pungent, very hard cheese. It is excellent as a *meze,* especially with *tsipouro* or ouzo. Locals usually use it as a grating cheese, and it is exquisite over fresh steaming pasta with a little olive oil and pepper.

Graviera *Graviera* is one of the most beloved table cheeses in all of Greece. It is a relative newcomer to the repertoire of Greek regional cheeses, made for the first time in this century, and first in the Peloponnesos. Knowledge of production quickly spread. Today the mainland and Crete are both well known for their sheep's milk *gravieras*. The Cyclades, however, hold the distinction of being the only place in Greece where cow's milk *graviera* is produced.

Graviera in the Cyclades is associated with two specific islands, Naxos and Tinos. Since 1996, Naxos has been granted an appellation-of-origin distinction. Typical Naxos *graviera* is dense and pleasantly pale, its texture marked by tiny irregular holes. It is made from pasteurized cow's milk. Unlike the *gravieras* of Crete or even of nearby Tinos, Naxos cheese makers salt the cheese in brine, not dry salt, once it is set. It is then left to mature on wooden shelves in special temperature-controlled rooms or cellars for at least two months, during which time it develops a hard, natural rind. It is usually made into 10-kilo wheels. The cheese is nutty and sweet, with a full, round, buttery flavor. It is one of the best table cheeses in Greece and is also an excellent cooking cheese.

The *graviera* from Tinos, while not a designated appellation-of-origin product is nonetheless extremely good cheese. It is made much the same as its neighbors', from pasteurized cow's milk. Because of slight differences in the flora on which animals feed from island to island, the *graviera* from Tinos tends to be slightly yellower than that from Naxos. It makes a superb table cheese.

Kalathata or **Tyri Vrasto** This is a boiled cow's milk curd cheese, made both in Tinos and Andros, that is drained in baskets, salted, then left outdoors for several weeks, until it becomes hard enough to use as for grating.

Kefalysio Spilias Milou This is another of the many artisinal cheeses produced for eons by small cheese makers throughout the Cyclades. It is essentially a *kefalotyri*—a hard yellow cheese—that is rubbed with the mashed pulp left over after pressing olives for oil and then kept in clay jugs. The cheese takes on a dark, almost sticky exterior as a result, which is generally cleaned before eating. It is excellent as both a hard table cheese and a delicious grating cheese. The cheese is almost always aged for at least six months, and sometimes for upward of a year.

Kopanisti *Kopanisti,* the name of which is the source of much confusion, is found in almost every island of the Cyclades, although the places best known for it are Syros, Tinos, and Mykonos. It is also in these islands where commercial production is most advanced.

Essentially, *Kopanisti* is a soft, fermented cheese with a very pronounced sour, peppery, piquante taste. The techniques for making it vary both from island to island, and vary, too, depending on whether the cheese is homemade or commercially produced. Biosyr, the cheese cooperative is Syros, for example, produces it, and *kopanisti mykonou* is also produced commercially and widely available in supermarkets all over Greece.

Generally, *kopanisti* is made from unpasteurized milk (either goat's, sheep's, or cow's) set with natural rennet, and strained in cheesecloths. Traditionally, it is placed in clay jugs or small barrels, and more and more cheese is added to the batch over the course of several months. The growth of certain desired bacteria gives it its characteristic pinkish or blue color, a distinct pepperiness, and a strong aroma to match.

Malahto Literally, "soft" cheese. It is a specialty of Andros, and is nothing more than fresh, rock-pressed cheese (see Petroti) that has been crumbled and kneaded with some salt. It has the consistency of good ricotta but a much tangier taste.

Myzithra Although in much of the rest of Greece, the term *myzithra* refers to a whey cheese, in the Cyclades *myzithra* is a fresh curd cheese made with whole milk.

Niotiko This is the traditional cheese of Ios. It is a hard yellow sheep's milk cheese, not unlike the *arseniko* of Naxos or like a more traditional *kefalotyri*. It is left to mature for at least three months.

Petroti or **Petrota Tyria** or **Petrotyria** These delicious, homespun cheeses with the unusual name—roughly translated they mean "rock" cheeses—are specialties of Andros and Tinos. They take their name from the way the fresh cheese is pressed and drained, usually between two marble slabs so that the weight forces out as much liquid as possible. In Tinos, there is even a special marble bowl with a spout and close fitting cover that has evolved to facilitate the task. The final shape of these cheeses is usually disklike, a result, obviously, of the way they have been pressed.

In Andros the cheese is made either with goat's

or cow's milk, but in Tinos it is made almost exclusively from cow's milk, since that is what prevails on the island. These cheeses are basically fresh; once they have been set and strained in cheesecloths, the mass is pressed for a few hours and then eaten as table cheese. But the *petroma* or *petroti* can also be used as the foundation for making other, more mature, local cheeses (see Malahto, Vollaki, and Sklavotyri).

San Mihali A hard, pale yellow, pecorinolike cheese, which is produced exclusively in Syros by the local cheese cooperative, Biosyr. Like many cheeses in the Cyclades, *San Mihali* is made with cow's milk, in this case pasteurized. Since 1996 it has been recognized as an appellation-of-origin product. Despite its status as an officially recognized regional specialty, it is a relative newcomer to the pantheon of Greek "traditional" cheeses, having been first made just a few decades ago.

Nevertheless, there is a long history of cow's milk cheeses in the Cyclades that dates back to the Venetian occupation of the islands. *San Mihali* is named for a mountain on the island which is also the locale of the main Catholic Church. *San Mihali* has a fat content of 2.8 to 2.9 percent. It is aged for at least three but usually four months, and is quite sharp. Usually it is eaten as a table or grating cheese, although it is also a good cheese to cook with and easy to use in savory pies, or grilled, as for *saganaki.*

Sklavotyri or **Malathouni** These little cheeses, also a specialty of Tinos, are much like the *vollaki* mentioned except that instead of being round and mounded in shape they are formed in individual baskets. The baskets still go by their ancient name, *tyroboli.*

Skotiri From the word *asko,* for skin. This is the traditional, soft goat's milk cheese from Ios, which is aged in goatskins. Although there are many such artisinal cheeses throughought Greece, what sets this one apart is that the curds are kneaded with the herb savory before being placed in the skins to ferment.

Vollaki Another byproduct of the original rock-pressed cheese, this one from Tinos. The word means "ball," and the cheese is so named because of its round, almost breastlike shape. Once the original, fresh, disk-shaped cheese is ready, it is crumbled and salted, then reshaped into small balls about the size of a man's fist. Most local artisinal cheese makers then hang the cheese in cheesecloth, outdoors in a cool, shady place, which helps the cheese drain and dry even further. The final result is a delicious, creamy, irrestistible table cheese. *Vollaki* is dense, buttery, and mild.

Xynomyzithra This is similar to many of the sour curd cheeses found among shepherd communities all over Greece. In the Cyclades, one finds *xynomyzithra* made from sheep's and goat's milk, or, as in Naxos and Tinos, from cow's milk. The Naxos variety is especially good, as thick and creamy as Chantilly but tangy like yogurt. It is made the same way almost everywhere: as soon as the animal is milked (either sheep, goat, or cow in Naxos), the milk is strained and placed in the same vessel that the cheese is always made in. A little natural rennet is added to it—it is not heated; this is a raw milk cheese by tradition—and the cheese sets for 24 hours. It ferments, becoming thick and tart like yogurt. It then is strained in a cheesecloth for several hours and eaten. It is sometimes lightly salted. Generally, though, the cheese has to be eaten within a few days because it doesn't last.

Xynotyri This is essentially the same cheese as *xynomyzithra* except that it is allowed to dry for several weeks until it is rock hard. In this form, it is used as a grating cheese.

CHARCUTERIE

The food life of the Cyclades, as elsewhere in the Greek countryside, is still marked by seasonal preparations. One of the most important, especially in Andros and Tinos, is the winter pork slaughter, which takes place between November and January. The event is reason for a feast.

It goes without saying that every part of the animal is used and consumed. It takes about three days to complete all the work surrounding the slaughter, and over that time the foods eaten by those participating follow a certain order. Usually the first treat is the liver, fried for the afternoon meal on the first day of the slaughter. At night, dinner might be pasta with ground pork sauce or, especially in Tinos, a soup made with the neck, carrots, celery, potatoes, and tomatoes.

It takes days to finish making all the sausages, which in the Cyclades are often seasoned with fennel seeds; to make the head cheese, *pihti;* the wine-soaked pork loin called *louza;* the rendered lard. The intestines are put to several uses, as are the bones and tongue.

It takes all the family women to prepare the different cured and cooked pork dishes. Many of these preparations can be found commercially, both in the islands and in Athens. Here is a look at some of them:

Pork loin, *Louza* The name comes from the cut of the animal, *louza* for "loin." In Syros, the meat is salted for twenty-four hours, washed, then seasoned with peppercorns, allspice, cloves, and cinnamon. Next it is enveloped in the intestine, wrapped in towels, and weighted down overnight so that it takes on its characteristic flat, wide shape. The next day it is sprinkled with black pepper and hung to dry for about two months.

In Tinos and Andros, the loin is salted for three days, then marinated in sweet red wine for several more days. Once removed from the wine, it is rubbed or studded with fennel seeds, black pepper, and allspice, enveloped in the intestine, towel-wrapped, and pressed as in Syros, then smoked for four hours over vinewood. The wine and the smoking give it a deep purplish red color. After it is smoked, it is hung to air-dry for about two months. To eat, the *louza* is thinly sliced and the intestine cut away.

Santorini's local cured pork, *Apokti* It is similar to the *louza* found elsewhere in the Cyclades, in that it is made with the loin, but it is seasoned differently, never encased in intestine, and never smoked. Once the loin is trimmed, it is salted for a day, then steeped in vinegar for three days. It is removed from the vinegar, then patted dry and rubbed with cinnamon. It is left for five or six hours with the cinnamon rub, so that the spice adheres to the meat. Then it is rubbed with ground black pepper, dried savory, and more cinnamon and hung to dry for several weeks.

Sausages in the Cyclades They are made almost exclusively with pork. A favorite seasoning, especially in Syros and Tinos, is fennel seed. Fennel-flavored sausages are often cooked with rice in *pilafi.* Syros and Tinos are also known for their *skordoloukanika,* or garlic sausages, in which the meat is kneaded with garlic and sweet wine and left to marinate for several hours before the sausages are stuffed. It is a preparation found almost exclusively in homes. Some of the most renowned sausages come from Mykonos; they are seasoned with savory and air-dried and generally contain more lean meat than fat, which is why they are said to be among the best.

Sissira is an old local specialty made in Syros and Tinos. In Syros, it is made from what remains of the pig after almost everything else has been prepared. The leftover meat and bits of *gleena* (lard) are stuffed into the stomach, often together with sautéed onion, which is then boiled, weighed down, and kept for several months. It is usually eaten in spring, around Easter, cut into thin slices. In Tinos, *sissira* refers to a dish more akin to *confit,* in which small pieces of pork left over after the slaughter are cooked and their fat rendered. They are then stored in the fat, which turns white and solidifies like butter.

CURED FISH

Throughout the Cyclades, small fish and small game birds traditionally were cured to last the winter. The cured fish, called *psarolia* (*psari* in Greek means "fish"), are usually made with either picarel or bogue. The fish are cleaned, then salted and sun-dried, usually in August and September. They are eaten plain—as a very salty *meze* for ouzo or *tsipouro* (eau de vie)—and sometimes soaked, chopped, and kneaded into fish *keftedes* (patties).

CAPERS

The rocky, dry climate of most of the Cyclades is friendly toward wild capers, which sprout out of rocks and are there for the picking from about May to the end of June. They are prepared in several ways. The buds are picked and put up in brine or in coarse salt or sun-dried and rehydrated for use in winter. The leaves are boiled for salad or pickled and eaten throughout the year for salad. Capers appear in all sorts of dishes—cooked with fish, especially salt cod; made into fritters and used as a filling for omelets, both specialties of Kimolos; used to season eggplant salad; and stewed in their own right. The caper doesn't flourish on all the islands, though. In Naxos, for example, they are almost completely absent from the local flora and hence the local table. But in Santorini, Sifnos, Serifos, Syros, Tinos, Andros, and Kimolos they are staples. No home on these islands is without its own cured capers.

The Recipes

MEZETHES

a smooth, creamy consistency. Season with salt and pepper and pulse to combine. Remove from the food processor and serve.

✳ **NOTE** Dishes containing raw eggs carry the risk of salmonella. Use only the freshest eggs and eat this dip on the day it is made.

Parsley-and-Onion Dip from Syros

MAINTANOSALATA TIS SYROU

 Makes about 12 servings

*T*his is a classic Syros meze, *served as a spread for bread or a dip for crudités or as an accompaniment to grilled fish.*

Leaves from 1 large bunch fresh flat-leaf parsley
    (about 1½ cups packed)
½ pound loaf stale rustic bread, crusts removed
1 medium red onion, chopped
1 large egg yolk (see Note)
½ to ¾ cup extra-virgin olive oil, as needed
Juice of 1 lemon
1 to 2 tablespoons red wine vinegar, to taste
Salt and freshly ground black pepper to taste

1. Coarsely chop the parsley and set aside. Run the bread under the tap to dampen and squeeze dry in your palms. Crumble the bread.

2. Place the parsley and onion in a food processor fitted with the steel blade and pulse until pulverized, as for pesto. Add the bread and continue pulsing until the mixture is like a paste. Add the egg yolk and pulse on and off to combine. Add ½ cup of the olive oil in a thin, steady stream, alternating with the lemon juice and vinegar and pulsing on and off to combine. Drizzle in part or all of the remaining olive oil, pulsing to combine, if necessary to achieve

Tomato Paste Spread with Capers

BERTES ME KAPARI

 Makes 6 to 8 servings

*T*his exceedingly simple recipe and the one that follows are from the tiny island of Kimolos. Many cooks still make their own tomato paste in Greece. In the islands, the hot, dry summers help to produce extremely sweet vine-ripened tomatoes. Homemade tomato paste made with such fruit tastes completely different from the typical canned tomato paste on the supermarket shelf. The flavor is vibrant, full, and deep. Seek out great, preferably organic tomato paste.*

½ cup good-quality, preferably organic tomato
    paste
2 to 4 tablespoons extra-virgin olive oil, as
    needed
¼ cup Greek capers, rinsed, drained, and
    chopped
Six to eight 1-inch-thick slices stale rustic
    bread, grilled or toasted

In a small bowl, mix together the tomato paste, 2 tablespoons of the olive oil, and the capers. If the mixture is too thick, add the remaining oil. Spread on the bread and serve as an hors d'oeuvre.

☉ Tomato Paste Spread with Onions (Bertes me Kremmydi): Replace the capers with 1 small red onion, finely chopped, and proceed as directed above.

Roasted Eggplant Salad with Capers and Onions

MELITZANOSALATA ME KAPARI KAI KREMMYDIA

 Makes 6 to 8 servings

Roasted eggplant spreads and salads come in many variations throughout Greece and are usually embell-ished with local flavor. In the North, yogurt is often added to the eggplants, for example; throughout the Cyclades, it is the ubiquitous caper and tomato that season this delicious dish.

3 large eggplants, roasted (see page 461)

½ cup extra-virgin olive oil

Salt to taste

1 medium onion, finely chopped

3 garlic cloves, pressed or minced

¼ cup small, preferably Greek capers, rinsed and drained

1 large firm, ripe tomato, peeled, seeded, and finely chopped

¼ cup finely chopped fresh flat-leaf parsley

2 tablespoons red wine vinegar, or more to taste

Freshly ground black pepper to taste

1. Wash and pat dry the eggplants. Roast them whole over an open flame on top of the stove or under the broiler, turning, until the skins are charred on all sides. (This may also be done on a grill.) Remove and let cool slightly.

2. Have a large bowl with the olive oil ready. Cut the eggplants open lengthwise and remove as many of the seeds as possible. Scoop out the roasted eggplant pulp and place it in a bowl with the olive oil. Salt lightly. With a fork and knife, cut the egg-plant so that it is chunky. Add the onion, garlic, capers, tomato, and parsley and mix with a fork to combine well. Add the vinegar and adjust the sea-soning with additional salt, pepper, and vinegar if desired.

Cheese- and Bread-Filled Tomatoes

TOMATAKIA GEMISTA ME TYRI

 Makes 10 servings

I sought out Nikoleta Foskolou when I went to Tinos in search of the island's foods. She had written a small book on the island's cuisine and was still brimming with the pride of having done it. She is a rare breed for a woman in her thirties, what we call in Greek a noikokyra, a word whose every translation falls short. The closest expression we have in English is housewife or lady of the house, *but in Greek the word implies much more: she is the staff-of-life kind of person, a loving mother of three kids who keeps an impeccable home and manages to pursue her own passions as a cook without forsaking house and family. She lives in a typical Greek apartment house in Tinos's capital, with members of the immediate family occupying every flat in the building, kids and cousins, aunts and uncles coming in and out at will. She had prepared a feast for me, made up of dishes she had collected and tested herself in the course of writing her book. This was one of them. We spent a few days together roaming the island and visiting villages and homes, and I have her to thank for almost all the information on Tinos's food that appears in these pages.*

This dish is light and easy. You could serve it as one of several mezethes. *I like it the way it is presented in Tinos, with some grilled fennel-seed-studded fresh sausages and a tangy green salad.*

10 small firm, ripe tomatoes

3 tablespoons unsalted butter

1 tablespoon extra-virgin olive oil

1 large yellow onion, very finely chopped

1 cup grated *kefalotyri* cheese or any hard yellow cheese, or more if necessary

1 cup plain bread crumbs from stale rustic bread, or more if necessary

½ cup very finely chopped fresh flat-leaf parsley

2 large eggs, lightly beaten

1 to 2 teaspoons sugar, to taste

Salt and freshly ground black pepper to taste

1. Using a sharp knife, cut the caps off the tomatoes and discard or save for another use. With a small spoon, carefully scoop out the seeds and pulp, discarding the seeds but reserving the pulp and the scooped-out tomatoes. Finely chop the pulp or puree it in a food processor and set aside until ready to use.

2. Heat 1 tablespoon of the butter and the olive oil in a skillet and cook the onion over medium heat, stirring, until translucent, 7 to 8 minutes. Add the tomato pulp and simmer with the onion over low heat for about 15 minutes, until the tomato pulp is cooked and most liquid evaporated.

3. In a small bowl, combine the grated cheese and bread crumbs together with the sautéed onion and tomato, parsley, and eggs. Taste and adjust the seasoning with the sugar, salt, and pepper. The filling must be dense. Adjust the texture, if needed, with additional grated cheese or bread crumbs. Preheat the oven to 350°F and butter an ovenproof glass baking dish large enough to hold all the tomatoes with the remaining 2 tablespoons butter.

4. Using a teaspoon, fill the tomatoes carefully, mounding the filling slightly over the top. Bake, uncovered, until the filling is set and golden and the tomatoes are slightly blistered, 50 minutes to an hour. Remove from the oven, let cool slightly, and serve warm or at room temperature.

"Married" Yellow Split Peas from Santorini

FAVA PANTREMENI TIS SANTORINIS

 Makes 4 servings

*F*ava *is what Greeks call yellow split pea puree, a popular* meze *and a national dish in bone-dry Santorini, where little besides pulses and grapes flourishes on the island's volcanic soil. Tourism has obliterated much that this island knew as traditional, but even today in some of Santorini's villages one might stumble across an old woman grinding the pebblelike pulses manually between two round stones to shell them. The island's* fava *cooks up to a beautiful yellow color and is renowned throughout Greece for its delicate flavor and quality. The split-pea puree acts as a base for many different dishes, some of them included here. As for the "married"* fava, *it is so called because the puree isn't served alone but "joined" with sautéed onions and tomatoes. You can also top* fava *with stewed capers (see page 317).*

⅓ to ⅔ cup extra-virgin olive oil, to taste

1 medium red onion, finely chopped

1 cup dried yellow split peas, picked over, rinsed, and drained

5 to 7 cups water, as needed

Salt and freshly ground black pepper to taste

1 teaspoon dried Greek oregano

2 to 3 tablespoons red wine vinegar, to taste

For the sauce

½ cup olive oil

3 large red onions, halved and sliced

2 medium firm, ripe tomatoes, grated (see page 459), or 2 tablespoons tomato paste diluted with 3 tablespoons water

½ teaspoon ground cinnamon

1 bay leaf

Salt and freshly ground black pepper to taste

1. Heat ⅓ cup of the olive oil in a large pot over medium heat. Add the onion and cook, stirring, until soft, 6 to 8 minutes. Add the split peas and toss to coat with the oil, stirring for 1 to 2 minutes. Add enough of the water to cover the peas by 2 inches. Cover and bring to a boil over medium heat. Reduce the heat, uncover, and cook over very low heat, stirring occasionally to prevent sticking, until the split peas are completely disintegrated, 1½ to 2 hours. During the course of cooking, add water as needed to keep the peas covered. When the split peas have reached the consistency of loose mashed potatoes, remove from the heat, season with salt and pepper, and stir in the oregano and vinegar. Cover with a cloth and let sit for 1 to 2 hours.

2. Meanwhile, prepare the sauce: Heat half the olive oil in a large skillet and cook the onions over medium heat until translucent, about 10 minutes. Add the tomatoes, cinnamon, and bay leaf and season with salt and pepper. Simmer, covered, over low heat until the sauce is fairly thick and the onions are very soft, about 20 minutes.

3. To serve, spread the set *fava* on a platter and spoon the sauce on top. Serve at room temperature. Drizzle with the remaining olive oil.

✳ **NOTE** I have always cooked *fava* in this slow, time-consuming way, letting the split peas disintegrate at their own pace in the pot. It's the way island cooks do it, too, and I think you achieve the fullest flavor that way. But, for expedience's sake—after all, this is a very easy dish to make—you can cook the split peas over higher heat and, once softened, puree them in a food processor fitted with a metal blade. *Fava* made this way will be grittier.

⊙ Fava with Stewed Capers (Fava me Kapari Yiahni): This dish traditionally calls for dried capers. They impart a completely different flavor from the pickled buds, but they are impossible to find outside the Cyclades. You can use the pickled buds as a substitute, but soak them overnight and wash in several rinses of cold water to rid them of their briny taste as much as possible. To make the recipe, follow the directions for making *fava*. Instead of the onion-and-tomato garnish, top with the stewed capers:

1½ cups small salted Greek capers
½ cup extra-virgin olive oil
2 large red onions, coarsely chopped
2 tablespoons tomato paste or 2 large firm, ripe
     tomatoes, grated (see page 459)
Freshly ground black pepper to taste
½ teaspoon ground cinnamon (optional)

1. Soak the capers overnight in water to cover and rinse thoroughly.

2. Heat the olive oil in a large skillet and cook the onions over medium heat, stirring, until lightly golden, about 15 minutes. Add the tomato paste and stir into the oil and onions to bind for about 5 minutes (or add the grated tomatoes and simmer for 10 minutes over low heat). Stir in the capers. Season with pepper and cinnamon, if desired, cover, and simmer for about 15 minutes over very low heat, adding a little water if necessary to keep the stew from burning. Remove from the heat and let cool to room temperature. Serve as garnish over the *fava* or as an accompaniment in a separate bowl.

SOUP

Greece, with its temperate clime and nearly eight months a year of perfect weather, is not a country that boasts a large repertory of soups. The main Greek soups are those based on fish or chicken and thickened with *avgolemono;* a few bean and vegetable soups; and a few more simple meat soups.

There are some unusual regional recipes, however, and as it turns out, many of them are found in the Cyclades. For one, the best Greek fisherman's soup comes from the Cyclades. Chickpeas, a staple in several of the Cyclades, are the main ingredient in a famed soup from Sifnos. Finally, there are some soup recipes that seem very un-Greek. One is for a sour apple soup, which I have not included here. Another is the Cyclades rendition of vichyssoise—in this case made with potatoes and onions, not leeks, in which whole eggs are added and poached.

Clay-Baked Chickpea Soup from Sifnos

SIFNOS REVITHADA

 Makes 6 to 8 servings

This soup is one of the simplest, most delicious dishes in all of Greece. In Sifnos, it is the mainstay of the Sunday meal. We were staying in the village of Artemona when I first saw how the local revithada *is made and all the rituals surrounding it. Local cooks use juglike clay vessels to bake it in. They prepare the soup on Saturday evening and take it to the wood-burning oven of the village baker. There it simmers*

all night—the oven is not ignited, but it is always warm. On Sunday the baker lines up the vessels on the old tiled floor of the bakery. Some have names marked on them; some are new. Most, though, are charred from use and somehow easily recognizable by their owners, who pick them up after church.

The secret to making this properly is in the clay vessel and in the extremely slow cooking, so you will also need a deep earthenware dish with a lid. You will need to start this soup the day before.

1 pound dried chickpeas, preferably organic, picked over and rinsed
1 teaspoon baking soda
2 medium onions, finely chopped
½ cup extra-virgin olive oil
1 bay leaf
Salt and freshly ground black pepper to taste

1. Soak the chickpeas overnight in ample water to which you have added the baking soda. Drain, rinse, and drain again.

2. Place the chickpeas, onions, olive oil, bay leaf, salt, and pepper in a large pot. Add enough water to cover everything by 3½ inches. Bring to a boil, reduce the heat to medium-low and simmer until the chickpeas have softened slightly, 45 to 50 minutes.

3. Preheat the oven to 350°F. Empty the contents of the pot into a large earthenware dish. Cover the dish and bake until the chickpeas are tender, about 2 hours. The timing on this dish is never exact, because much depends on the age of the chickpeas—if they've been on the shelf for a while, they will take a long time to cook. In any event, the chickpeas should remain whole and not disintegrate, but the soup should be thick. While the chickpeas are baking, check the water content occasionally and add more water if necessary to keep everything from sticking. Remove the bay leaf. Serve hot.

Christmas Beef Soup with Egg-Lemon Sauce from Tinos

CHRISTOUGENIATIKI MOSCHAROSOUPA TIS TINOU

 Makes 8 servings

In the Catholic villages of Tinos, of which there are many, tradition has it that the Christmas table is a communal one and that the meal takes place in several stages. The first seating is for the men of the village only. They take along their own fork, knife, glass, and wine, tied up knapsacklike in a large napkin. Beef stew, cabbage dolmathes, roast beef or pot roast with tomato sauce, and arugula and radish salad make up the traditional fare. After they are done, the women and children join them, and at this point the soup is served, a simple beef soup with celery and onions, enriched with avgolemono sauce.

2 pounds stewing beef with bones, preferably shoulder
3 celery stalks, cut into pieces about 1½ inches long
2 large carrots, cut into pieces about 1½ inches long
1 large onion, quartered
10 cups water
Salt to taste
⅔ cup short-grain rice
2 large eggs
Juice of 1 lemon, or more to taste
Freshly ground black pepper to taste

1. Place the beef, vegetables, and water in a large pot, salt lightly, and bring to a boil. Reduce the heat to low and simmer for 2 hours, skimming any foam off the top of the soup. The meat should be very tender and falling off the bone. Remove the meat and vegetables with a slotted spoon, set aside on a serving platter, and keep warm.

2. Add the rice to the soup and bring to a boil. Reduce the heat to medium-low and simmer until the rice is very tender, about 15 minutes.

3. Prepare the egg-lemon sauce: With a wire whisk, beat the eggs and lemon juice together lightly in a small bowl. Add a ladleful of the hot broth to the egg mixture, in a slow, steady stream, whisking all the while. Repeat with a second ladleful. Turn off the heat, then pour the *avgolemono* into the soup and tilt the pan back and forth so that it spreads all over. Adjust the seasoning with additional salt or lemon juice and season with pepper.

4. To serve: Serve the vegetables and meat separately on the platter and serve the soup in individual bowls.

Winter Pork Soup from Tinos

HEIMONIATIKI HOIRINOSOUPA APO TIN TINO

 Makes 8 to 10 servings

From November through March in Tinos and elsewhere throughout Greece, village denizens look forward to the rituals of the pork slaughter. Although this is a dying tradition as young people leave the villages and farmers are fewer and fewer with each passing year, there are still places all over Greece in which to witness the feast. It is something people do at home over several days, and the meals usually follow a certain pattern with specific preparations reserved for specific meals. In Tinos, the evening meal on the first

day of the slaughter consists of this hearty soup, which is always made with the neck of the animal (substituted for here, as it is a hard cut to come by in American butcher shops).

2 pounds stewing pork with bones, preferably
   shoulder
5 medium onions, quartered
10 cups water
Salt to taste
3 medium waxy potatoes, peeled and cut into
   1½-inch cubes
2 cultivated celery stalks or 2 to 3 wild celery
   stalks with leaves (see Note, page 214), cut
   into ½-inch pieces
1 bay leaf
2 large eggs
Juice of 1 lemon
Freshly ground black pepper to taste

1. Place the pork, onions, and water in a large pot, salt lightly, and bring to a boil. Reduce the heat to medium-low and simmer, skimming the foam off the surface of the soup with a large spoon, for 1 hour. Add the potatoes, celery, and bay leaf and continue to simmer for an hour. Remove the meat and clean it off the bones. Shred the meat and return it to the soup; discard the bones.

2. Prepare the egg-lemon sauce: Using a wire whisk, beat together the eggs and lemon juice in a small bowl. Add a ladleful of the hot broth to the egg mixture, in a slow, steady stream, whisking all the while. Repeat with a second ladleful. Pour the *avgolemono* into the soup, stir, and turn off the heat. Adjust the seasoning with additional salt or lemon juice and season with pepper. Remove the bay leaf. Serve hot.

Eggs Poached in Potato Soup from Kimolos

AVGA BOULERI

Makes 4 to 6 servings

This is an elegant, very simple country soup. It's an excellent winter dish. I like to serve this with the Kimolos Pork Loin Stuffed with Myzithra Cheese and Carrots (page 333) and a simple salad of raw or boiled greens.

4 large waxy potatoes, peeled and cut into
    chunks
2 large onions, coarsely chopped
⅔ cup extra-virgin olive oil
Salt and freshly ground black pepper to taste
4 large eggs
Juice of ½ to 1 lemon, to taste

Place the potatoes and onions in a large pot and pour in enough water to cover them by 2 inches. Bring to a boil. Add the olive oil and season with salt and pepper. Reduce the heat to medium and simmer until the potatoes are very tender and almost disintegrating, about 40 minutes. With the soup simmering, carefully crack each of the eggs into it, trying to keep the yolks from breaking. Simmer the soup over low heat until the eggs set, another 5 to 7 minutes. Stir in the lemon juice and serve hot with good toasted bread.

FISHERMAN'S SOUPS: KAKAVIA

Kakavia is the fisherman's soup of Greece, the meal prepared on board or on shore from the day's catch. The name, like that of bouillabaisse, derives from the pot in which the soup is prepared, called a *kakavi.*

Kakavia is the meal fishermen cook from whatever fish is not fit for market, fish that have been torn or scarred by other fish and therefore are not comely enough to sell. Nevertheless, the fish is always incredibly fresh. Fishermen also prefer their *kakavia* made with a few spoonfuls of the Aegean in it and so add seawater. Authentic *kakavia* requires a variety of fish, high heat, an unsparing amount of olive oil, and fresh lemon juice.

The kinds of fish vary, depending on what waters one is working in and what the catch provides. Considered de rigueur are those fish whose feeding ground is in fairly deep water around rocky coasts. In Greek they are referred to as *petropsara,* or rock fish. The best are considered scorpionfish, although smaller "rock" fish such as perch also often make their way into *kakavia.* If these are not available, sometimes mullet is used instead, or grouper, which is very rich in gelatin and makes for a thick, hearty *kakavia.*

Kakavia inevitably includes some vegetables, among them almost always onions and often potatoes, which disintegrate and help to thicken the soup. Celery is another favorite. The vegetables, always go in first, cooked—almost steamed—in ample olive oil. Then the fish is added. Water, olive oil, and lemon juice are added, the pot is sealed with its lid, and the whole thing boils for however long it takes to cook the fish. The fish are served either separately or in the bowl with the broth, and bread or *paximathia,* thick dried rusks (especially if the soup is prepared at sea), are always on hand. In the Cyclades the traditional *kakavia* includes onions, vinegar, and the fish on hand.

There is another, more complicated version of *kakavia,* found mainly in the Dodecanese, which requires certain specific fish and vegetables, among them one select species such as bass, a variety of smaller rock-grazing fish, picarel, and shrimp or crabs. The vegetables called for are onions, tomatoes, celery, and carrots, together with bay leaf, salt, pepper, olive oil, and lemon juice.

Fisherman's Soup

CYCLADITIKI KAKAVIA

 Makes 6 servings

2 cups extra-virgin olive oil
4 large onions, finely chopped
⅓ cup red wine vinegar
2 pounds fish suitable for soup (scorpionfish, perch, grouper, bream, and/or bogue), whole, cleaned, and gutted
Salt to taste
Fresh lemon juice (optional)

1. In a large pot, heat the olive oil over medium heat then add the onions. Cover the pot, reduce the heat to low, and steam the onions in the oil until wilted and very soft, about 15 minutes. Pour in the vinegar. After a minute or so, when the vinegar steams off, add the fish, building the soup so that the larger ones are on the bottom, the smaller ones on top. Season each layer with a little salt. Add enough water to cover the fish by about 1 inch. Cover the pot and cook the *kakavia* over medium heat until the fish is fork-tender, about 20 minutes.

2. To serve, remove the fish and place it on a serving platter, drizzled, if desired, with additional olive oil and lemon juice. Serve the broth in individual bowls, with plenty of bread. Or serve the fish and broth together in individual bowls.

VEGETABLES

In the simple diet that marks much of the Cyclades, vegetable fritters have always played a very important role. Made with all manner of garden and wild greens and vegetables—from tomatoes to cauliflower to wild fennel—they are an easy way to make a filling meal out of two or three ingredients. Basically they consist of cooked greens or other vegetables mixed with batter and fried in olive oil. They can be served either hot or at room temperature. Here are several local specialties.

Sun-Dried Tomato Fritters as They Are Made in Syros, Tinos, and Kimolos

TOMATOKEFTEDES APO TIN SYROU, TIN TINO KAI TIN KIMOLO

 Makes 15 to 20 fritters

The best-known tomato fritters in Greece are those made on the island of Santorini, famous mainly because Santorini is one of the major tourist destinations in the Cyclades, indeed in all of Greece; it stands to reason that its food is better known that that of other, quieter islands. But tomato fritters are very common in many of the Cyclades, especially in Syros, Tinos, and Kimolos. This recipe with sun-dried tomatoes is a composite of recipes from those three islands. These tomato fritters, called pseftokeftedes—*false* keftedes—*are made with the island's indigenous small tomato, scallions, spices, and batter.*

10 sun-dried tomatoes

2 cups warm water

2 scallions, white and tender green parts, finely
    chopped

⅓ cup grated *kefalograviera* or *kefalotyri* cheese

½ cup snipped fresh dill

Salt and freshly ground black pepper to taste

⅔ cup self-rising flour

2 large eggs, lightly beaten

Olive oil or a combination of olive and vegetable
    oil for frying

1. Soak the tomatoes until they are plump and soft, about 1 hour. Drain, reserving the water.

2. Chop the tomatoes coarsely. In a small bowl, combine them with the scallions, cheese, and dill. Season lightly with salt and pepper.

3. In a medium bowl, combine the flour and about ⅔ cup of the reserved soaking liquid to form a thick batter. Add the eggs and stir to combine. Mix in the tomato mixture. Add more liquid or flour if necessary to give the mixture the consistency of a thick pancake batter.

4. Heat about 1 inch olive oil in a large, heavy skillet over medium-high heat. When the oil is very hot, almost smoking, drop a tablespoon at a time of the tomato mixture into the hot oil. You should be able to fry 3 or 4 fritters at a time. Fry, turning once, until golden on both sides. Remove with a slotted spoon and drain on paper towels. Serve warm.

⊙ Replace the dill with a little chopped wild fennel and flat-leaf parsely, the herbs preferred for this dish in Tinos.

⊙ Replace the dill with a little chopped fresh mint and 2 minced garlic cloves, which is how the fritters are seasoned in Kimolos.

Fresh Tomato Fritters from Santorini

PSEFTOKEFTEDES SANTORINIS

 Makes about 20 fritters

On Santorini this dish is made with the island's local tomato, which is small and oval in shape and possesses relatively little moisture. Locals refer to it, in fact, as "waterless." Although these little tomatoes aren't succulent, their flavor is intense and sweet. Good plum tomatoes, preferably organic, are the closest substitute.

1½ pounds firm, ripe plum tomatoes, grated
    (see page 459)

3 scallions, white and tender green parts, finely
    chopped

2 tablespoons finely chopped fresh flat-leaf
    parsley

2 tablespoons chopped fresh mint

Salt and freshly ground black pepper to taste

1¼ to 1½ cups all-purpose flour, as needed

½ teaspoon baking powder

Olive or vegetable oil for frying

1. In a large bowl, mix together the grated tomatoes, scallions, herbs, salt, and pepper. Combine 1¼ cups of the flour and the baking powder in a small bowl and add it to the tomatoes, mixing well. Add flour if necessary to give the mixture the consistency of a thick batter. Taste and adjust the seasoning with salt and pepper.

2. Heat about 1½ inches of oil in a large, heavy skillet over medium-high heat. When the oil is very hot, drop a tablespoon of the batter at a time into the skillet and fry the tomato fritters on both sides until golden. Remove with a slotted spoon and let drain on paper towels. Serve hot.

Cauliflower Fritters with Grated Cheese and Tomato Sauce from Kimolos

TIGANITES KOUNOUPIDIOU APO TIN KIMOLO

 Makes 2 to 3 main-course servings (for a light meal) or 6 side-dish servings

Tiny, untraveled Kimolos has some surprisingly good food. These cauliflower fritters differ markedly from those made in Syros. Here the florets are kept whole, dipped in batter and cheese, and fried. The tomato sauce that accompanies them is an excellent foil to the fritters. With a salad or some boiled horta *(page 404), these could stand on their own as a meal.*

Salt to taste
1 large head cauliflower (1½ to 2 pounds), cut into florets and stems discarded
3 tablespoons olive oil, plus more for frying
2 medium onions, finely chopped
2 garlic cloves, finely chopped
2 cups grated firm, ripe tomatoes (see page 459) or crushed canned tomatoes
½ teaspoon sugar
Freshly ground black pepper to taste
½ cup shredded fresh basil
5 to 8 tablespoons all-purpose flour, as needed
2 large eggs, lightly beaten
1 cup plain bread crumbs from stale bread
¼ cup grated hard *myzithra* cheese or any hard, aged sheep's milk cheese

1. Bring a medium pot of salted water to a boil and blanch the cauliflower florets for 5 minutes. Drain in a colander.

2. Prepare the sauce: Heat the 3 tablespoons olive oil in a large skillet over medium heat and cook the onions and garlic, stirring, until softened, about 7 minutes. Add the tomatoes and bring to a boil. Reduce the heat to very low, add the sugar, and season with salt and pepper. Add the basil and simmer, covered, for 15 minutes.

3. Combine 5 tablespoons of the flour and the eggs in a medium bowl to create a thick batter, adding more of the flour if needed. Combine the bread crumbs and cheese in a shallow bowl.

4. Heat about 1 inch of olive oil in a large, heavy skillet over medium-high heat. When the oil is very hot, dip the cauliflower florets one by one first in the batter, then in the cheese and bread crumb mixture and fry on all sides in the hot oil until golden, about 3 minutes. Remove with a slotted spoon and drain briefly on paper towels.

5. To serve: Spoon a little of the sauce onto a serving platter, place the cauliflower on top, spoon the remaining sauce over the vegetables, and serve.

Purslane and Potato Fritters from Syros

HORTOKEFTEDES TIS SYROU

 Makes about 24 fritters

The variety of vegetable fritters in the Greek island kitchen is vast. These simple foods helped stretch an otherwise sparse larder. Purslane is enormously popular in Greece, it grows everywhere, and it is eaten both raw in salads and cooked. When it is cooked, though, it is usually stewed. I came across this unusual recipe in my travels through Syros. You could serve these fritters with some olives and a simple tomato salad to make a light summer meal.

3 large waxy potatoes

1 pound purslane

1 cup grated *kefalograviera* or any hard cheese

2 large eggs

Salt and freshly ground black pepper to taste

1 cup all-purpose flour, or more if necessary

Olive or other vegetable oil for frying

1. Wash the potatoes. Put them in a medium pot full of water, bring to a boil, and boil until the skins crack open and the potatoes are soft, about 20 minutes. Drain and let cool slightly.

2. While the potatoes are boiling, trim the tough bottoms off the purslane. Bring a separate pot of salted water to a boil and blanch the purslane until wilted, 5 to 7 minutes. Drain in a colander, rinse under cold running water, and drain again.

3. Peel the potatoes and place in a large bowl. Chop the cooked purslane, add it to the potatoes, and mash them together using a fork or a potato masher. Mix in the cheese and eggs and season with salt and pepper.

4. Place the flour on a plate. Heat about 1½ inches of oil in a large, heavy skillet over medium-high heat. When the oil is very hot, shape spoonfuls of the purslane-and-potato mixture into small patties. Dredge lightly in the flour, tapping off any excess, and fry in the hot oil, in batches, turning until golden on all sides, about 3 minutes. Remove from the oil with a slotted spoon, drain on paper towels, and serve.

Classic Omelet with Potatoes and Sausage from Andros

FROUTALIA ME PATATES KAI LOUKANIKA

 Makes 4 to 6 servings

This is a vegetable-and-egg medley, slowly cooked in a skillet. "Froutalia is not an omelet," says Mrs. Kore, my guide in Andros, emphatically. It isn't thin or folded like an omelet but rather resembles a thick, crustless pie. The most common version and the one visitors will find most readily in a few tavernas (often only by special request) is potato froutalia. But the real delicacies are Andros's fresh fava bean froutalia cooked in spring and froutalia made with fresh black-eyed peas. Onion froutalia, seasoned heavily with mint, is another great dish. For all versions of froutalia, the vegetables are traditionally sautéed in a little pork fat (called singlina) before the eggs are added. The whole thing is served with the islands' chunky anise-and savory-scented sausages whole on top.

3 tablespoons unsalted butter or lard

3 tablespoons extra-virgin olive oil

4 large waxy potatoes, peeled and cut into
    ¼-inch-thick rounds

⅔ pound fennel-flavored pork sausage, cut into
    2-inch pieces

Salt and freshly ground black pepper to taste

4 jumbo eggs

2 tablespoons grated *kefalograviera* cheese

3 tablespoons milk

1. Heat the butter or lard and olive oil together in a heavy 12-inch skillet over high heat. Add the potatoes and sausage and season with salt and pepper. Reduce the heat to medium and cover the skillet. Let the potatoes and sausage cook slowly for 20 to 25 minutes, shaking the pan occasionally to keep them from sticking. The potatoes should be cooked through, crisp and lightly browned.

2. In a small bowl, beat together the eggs, cheese, and milk. Season with a little pepper and salt if desired. Pour the eggs over the potatoes and sausages, tilting the skillet so that the eggs are distributed evenly. Cover and cook slowly over low heat, tilting the pan a few times until the eggs are set on the bottom, 4 to 5 minutes. Have a large plate ready. Remove the skillet from the heat and place the plate over it (use an oven mitt). Flip the *froutalia* onto the plate and slide it back in the skillet to cook until set on the other side, about 3 minutes. Slide onto a serving platter and serve hot.

Omelet with Fresh Fava Beans from Andros

KOUKOFROUTALIA

 Makes 4 to 6 servings

Dimitris Bliziotis, a chef in Athens who was born in Andros, gave me this recipe.

1½ pounds fresh young tender fava beans,
    unshelled, or 1 pound frozen shelled fava
    beans, defrosted
2 tablespoons unsalted butter
2 tablespoons lard or extra-virgin olive oil
5 large eggs
1 to 2 teaspoons dried mint or marjoram,
    to taste
Salt and freshly ground black pepper to taste

1. Wash the fava beans and drain well. Blanch for 5 to 7 minutes in ample boiling water and drain. In a heavy 12-inch skillet, melt the butter and lard or olive oil together over medium heat. Add the fava beans, reduce the heat to low, cover, and cook until the beans are very tender, 8 to 10 minutes.

2. Beat the eggs lightly with the mint, salt, and pepper in a small bowl. Pour into the skillet, tilting the pan to cover the fava beans and so that the egg spreads evenly throughout the skillet. Cook over low heat, covered. As soon as the bottom sets, 4 to 5 minutes, place a large plate over the skillet (use an oven mitt) and flip the omelet onto it. Slide the omelet back into the skillet and cook on the other side until set, about 3 to 4 minutes. Slide onto a serving plate and serve.

⊙ This dish is also made with fresh borlotti, or cranberry beans—*barbounofasoula* to the Greeks. Use the beans whole, trimming away the stringy fiber along their seam. Follow the directions for the recipe, blanching and sautéing the whole fresh beans, adding the eggs, flipping, etc. It is not all that different from the green bean omelet cooked in Crete.

Zucchini Omelet from Syros

TIRITIM

 Makes 4 to 5 servings

This recipe was inspired by one that I found in a small leaflet of traditional recipes from Syros compiled by students at the local technical high school, the Technical-Professional Lyceum of Syros.

1 pound small zucchini, cut into ¼-inch-thick
   rounds
Salt and freshly ground black pepper to taste
⅓ cup extra-virgin olive oil
3 spring onions or scallions, white and tender
   green parts, finely chopped
1 tablespoon shredded fresh mint or 1 teaspoon
   dried
⅓ cup snipped fresh dill
4 jumbo eggs
3 tablespoons milk

1. Place the sliced zucchini in a heavy nonstick 12-inch skillet, season generously with salt and pepper, and cook, covered, over low heat until the juices from the zucchini boil off, about 5 minutes. Add the olive oil to the skillet and increase the heat to medium. Add the spring onions or scallions and cook, stirring, until wilted, another 5 to 7 minutes. Add the mint and dill and cook for another minute or so.

2. Beat the eggs lightly with the milk in a small bowl. Pour them over the contents of the skillet, tilting the pan so that they are spread evenly. Cover and cook slowly over low heat until the bottom is set, 4 to 5 minutes. Have a large plate ready. Remove the skillet from the heat and place the plate over it (use an oven mitt). Flip the omelet onto the plate and slide it back into the skillet to cook until set on the other side, about 3 minutes. Slide onto a serving platter and serve hot or warm.

Chard-Filled Ravioli from Tinos

RAVIOLIA ME SESKOULA APO TIN TINO

 Makes 8 hearty servings

The name and nature of this dish makes me assume that it came to the island with the Venetians hundreds of years ago. This is one of my favorite recipes in the whole book, a dish that is at once elegant and homey, that I learned in the kitchen of an expert cook.

For the pasta
4 to 4½ cups all-purpose flour, as needed
¼ teaspoon salt
3 large eggs, lightly beaten
½ cup warm water
Cornmeal as needed

For the filling
3 pounds chard
2 tablespoons extra-virgin olive oil
2 large onions, very finely chopped
2 large eggs
1 cup grated *kefalograviera* or any hard yellow
   cheese
Salt and freshly ground black pepper to taste

For the sauce
6 tablespoons olive oil, plus more for drizzling
3 large firm, ripe tomatoes, grated
   (see page 459)
Salt to taste
½ to 1 teaspoon sugar, to taste
Grated *kefalotyri,* hard *myzithra* cheese, or other
   hard grating cheese for garnish

1. Prepare the pasta dough: Combine 4 cups of the flour and the salt in a large bowl and make a well in the center. Add the eggs and water to the well. Using a fork, incorporate the flour from the inner rim first into the liquid. Stir with the fork, working in more and more flour as you go. When a dough mass begins to form, start kneading by hand. Knead the dough for 8 to 10 minutes, adding flour if necessary to make a smooth dough that is no longer sticky. Shape into a ball, place in a clean bowl, and cover with a cloth. Let rest for 30 minutes. Or wrap the dough tightly in plastic wrap and refrigerate for up to 2 days. Bring back to room temperature before using.

2. Prepare the filling: Trim and chop the chard, discarding the toughest parts of the stems. Wash thoroughly. Blanch in lightly salted water for 5 minutes and drain very well in a colander.

3. Heat the olive oil in a medium skillet over medium heat and cook the onions, stirring, until wilted, about 7 minutes. In a large bowl, mix the chard, onions, eggs, and *kefalograviera* together. Season with salt and pepper.

4. Divide the dough into 6 equal balls. With your palm, flatten the first dough ball to a disk about ½ inch thick. Pass it through a pasta maker at the widest setting. Fold both ends of the dough toward the center—into thirds, in other words. Press down lightly with your fingers, then pass it through the pasta maker again. Fold and pass the dough through the pasta maker 6 or 7 times, until it is smooth and elastic. Move the setting on the pasta maker one notch to a narrower gauge and pass the dough strip through it. Sprinkle the strip with a little flour. Pass the dough strip through the machine again, on the next, narrower setting. Repeat several times, working your way down to #3 or #2 on the gauge. The strip should be thin but not so gossamer that it won't hold up to the filling.

5. Place the dough strip in front of you vertically. Place 8 scant teaspoonfuls of filling in 2 rows of 4 each from the bottom to the center of the dough. Fold the strip over so that the 2 narrow ends

meet, in other words, covering the bottom half of the dough with the top half. Press down the edges along the horizontal sides to squeeze out the air. Using a round serrated pasta cutter or a scalloped pizza cutter, cut the ravioli into either squares or rectangles. Repeat until all the dough and filling are used up. There will be scraps of dough left over after cutting; form these into a ball and pass through the pasta maker as well. Place the *raviolia* on kitchen towels sprinkled with cornmeal so that they don't stick. Do not layer them. The filling is very moist, and the pasta has to dry for about 30 minutes before being boiled.

6. Prepare the sauce: Heat the olive oil in a skillet over medium heat and add the grated tomatoes. Season with salt and cook just long enough for the pan juices to cook off, about 7 minutes. Adjust the seasoning with sugar and additional salt if desired.

7. Bring a large pot of salted water to a boil. Add the *raviolia,* in batches, and simmer until cooked but still al dente, 4 to 5 minutes. Remove with a slotted spoon and drain. Serve, drizzled with olive oil and the fresh tomato sauce. Sprinkle with grated *kefalotyri* or *myzithra* cheese.

SAVORY PIES

Savory pies were never a great tradition in the arid Cyclades, where garden vegetables, wild greens, and ample wood to light ovens on a whim were in short supply, but a few interesting pies calling for potatoes do exist, and I have recorded them here. Ditto for small skillet pies—most greens and vegetables are mixed with a little flour and fried into mock *keftedes,* as opposed to being stuffed into phyllo parcels and cooked.

Mashed Potato Pie from Tinos

PATATOPITA TINOU

 Makes 4 to 6 servings

This is yet another recipe from my preeminent guide in Tinos, Nikoleta Foskolou.

2 pounds waxy new potatoes
Salt to taste
2 tablespoons unsalted butter
1 large onion, finely chopped
4 large eggs, slightly beaten
1 cup grated *kefalotyri* cheese
½ cup milk
2 teaspoons dried mint or Greek oregano
½ cup chopped fresh flat-leaf parsley
Freshly ground black pepper to taste
3 tablespoons extra-virgin olive oil
½ cup plain bread crumbs from stale bread

1. Bring the potatoes to a boil in a large pot of salted water. When the skins begin to crack open and the potatoes are fork-tender, after about 12 minutes, remove and drain in a colander, rinsing immediately with cold running water. Peel, pass through a ricer, and place in a large bowl or peel and mash with a potato masher in a large bowl.

2. Heat the butter in a large skillet over medium heat and cook the onion, stirring, until soft, about 7 minutes. Add the onion to the bowl with the potatoes. Add the eggs, cheese, and milk and stir. Mix in the oregano and parsley and season with salt and pepper.

3. Preheat the oven to 400°F. Oil a 9- by 13-inch baking pan. Spread the mixture evenly in the pan and score into diamonds. Sprinkle with the bread crumbs. Drizzle the olive oil on top and bake until the pie is set and a golden crust has formed on top, 50 minutes to an hour. Remove from the oven and serve, either warm or at room temperature.

Savory Easter Cheese Pies from Kimolos

TYRENIES

 Makes about 30 pieces

Variation on a theme: These Kimolos cheese pies are one kind of dozens of similar cheese pies found throughout the Cyclades.

For the pastry
4 cups bread flour
½ teaspoon salt
1 large egg
½ cup extra-virgin olive oil
½ to 1 cup warm water, or more if necessary
Olive oil for brushing pan
1 large egg yolk, lightly beaten, for brushing
    pastry

For the filling
½ pound fresh *manouri* or *anthotyro* cheese
2 medium eggs
Freshly ground black pepper to taste

1. Make the dough: Combine the flour and salt in a large bowl. Break the egg into the dough and mix by hand until the dough is mealy. While working the egg into the dough, slowly add the olive oil, kneading until the mixture is coarse and mealy. Add the water in a slow, steady stream, kneading vigorously, until you have a smooth but firm dough. Cover and let rest for 20 minutes.

2. While the dough is resting, prepare the filling: Combine the cheese, eggs, and pepper in a medium bowl and mix well. Lightly oil several baking sheets. Preheat the oven to 400°F.

3. Divide the dough into 6 balls. Flatten each ball and pass it through a pasta maker several times, starting at the widest gauge and working up to about the third one, until the pastry is about as thick as a quarter. Place the strip in front of you and cut into 2½-inch squares.

4. Place a heaping teaspoon of filling in the center of each square. Fold the points of the square inward so that they all meet in the center, over the filling. Brush lightly with the beaten egg yolk. Place on the baking sheets and bake until golden and puffed, 20 to 25 minutes. Remove from the oven, cool slightly on racks, and serve either warm or at room temperature. To store, keep covered in the refrigerator.

☉ For a slightly differently version, add 1 bunch chopped wild fennel to the cheese mixture.

Savory Pastries Filled with Pumpkin, Fennel, and Cheese

KOLOKYTHENIES

 Makes about 72 pieces

For the filling
1½ pounds pumpkin, peeled and seeded
Salt
¾ cup grated *myzithra* or any hard, aged
    sheep's milk cheese
½ cup chopped wild fennel leaves or ½ cup
    chopped dill and 1 scant teaspoon ground
    fennel seeds
Freshly ground white pepper to taste

For the pastry
4 cups bread flour
½ teaspoon salt

1 large egg
½ cup extra-virgin olive oil
1 cup warm water, or more if necessary
1 large egg yolk, lightly beaten, for brushing
    pastry

1. Make the filling: Finely chop the pumpkin. Place in a colander with a little salt and knead together. Let the pumpkin drain in the colander for 1 hour. Squeeze between your palms to rid it of as much liquid as possible. Place in a medium bowl and combine with the *myzithra,* fennel, and pepper.

2. Lightly oil several baking sheets. Preheat the oven to 400°F.

3. Make the dough: Combine the flour and salt in a large bowl. Break the egg into the dough and mix by hand until the dough is mealy. While working the egg into the dough, slowly add the olive oil, kneading until the mixture is coarse and mealy. Add the water in a slow, steady stream, kneading vigorously, until you have a dough that is smooth but firm. Cover and let rest for 20 minutes.

4. Divide the dough into 6 equal balls. Flatten each ball and pass through a pasta maker several times, starting at the widest gauge and working up to a middle one, until the dough is about as thick as a quarter. Place each strip in front of you. Using a glass or a cookie cutter, cut into 3-inch circles. Place a teaspoon of filling in the center of each circle and fold over to form a half-moon. Press the edges closed with a fork or your fingertips and brush with the beaten egg. Bake until golden, about 25 minutes. Remove from the oven and serve warm.

MEAT

Game has always been an important part of the impoverished diet of the Cyclades. Even now in Santorini, preserved quail still sometimes make up a staple in the winter larder, although the custom is dying fast. In Tinos, pigeon was the bird of choice, domesticated and fed by almost every island family, who kept pigeon coops for that purpose. Game was a significant component in the local diet because it was a cheap—free—source of protein. But pork, too, was the traditional meat all over the Cyclades.

Meat traditions are fairly limited here as a result, with most old recipes centering around ways to preserve a luxury item that was savored only a few times a year. But there are several delicious specialties, from the stuffed turkey that some island cooks prepare at Christmas to herb- and rice-stuffed goat for Easter.

Chard-Stuffed Turkey from Naxos

PATOUDO NAXOU

 Makes about 8 servings

*P*atoudo *is the name of several stuffed meat dishes in the Cyclades. We find the term in Naxos, where it refers to both the Christmas-stuffed bird, usually turkey, and the Paschal stuffed lamb or goat, which is an island specialty all over the Aegean. Depending on the flora in individual places, the stuffings change accordingly. In Naxos,* seskoula—chard—*is the green of choice for both the Christmas turkey and the*

Easter lamb or goat, combined with wild fennel and rice.

1 cup extra-virgin olive oil
2 large onions, coarsely chopped
2 pounds green chard or spinach, trimmed, washed, drained, and coarsely chopped
1 cup chopped wild fennel leaves or 1 cup finely chopped fresh dill plus ⅓ cup ouzo
½ cup short-grain rice
Salt and freshly ground black pepper to taste
½ cup (1 stick) unsalted butter
Turkey gizzards, finely chopped
One 8- to 10-pound fresh turkey
2 to 3 pounds waxy new potatoes, to taste, peeled
4 garlic cloves, minced
2 teaspoons dried Greek oregano

1. Heat ½ cup of the olive oil in a large pot over medium heat and cook the onions, stirring, until wilted, 5 to 7 minutes. Add the chard or spinach and fennel or dill. Toss and stir until wilted, a few minutes longer. Add the rice, cover, and cook slowly over medium-low heat until the pot juices have been absorbed and the rice is plump and tender but not completely cooked, about 10 minutes. If using ouzo, add it to the rice 5 minutes before removing from the heat. Season with salt and pepper. Preheat the oven to 400°F.

2. In a small skillet, heat 1 tablespoon of the butter over medium heat and cook the gizzards, stirring until browned. Add them to the chard stuffing.

3. Stuff the turkey loosely with the chard-and-rice mixture and sew closed or secure with skewers. Rub the bird with some of the remaining butter and season with salt and pepper. Place on a rack in a large roasting pan. In a large bowl, toss the potatoes with the garlic and season with oregano, salt and pepper, then place them in the pan around the turkey. Dot them with the remaining butter and drizzle with the remaining ½ cup olive oil. Roast the turkey for 20 minutes, then reduce the oven temperature to 325°F and roast until an instant-read thermometer inserted into the thickest part of the thigh reads 175°F to 180°F (or the pop-out thermometer pops out) and the thigh juices run clear, 2 to 3 hours, or 12 to 15 minutes per pound. Baste every 10 to 15 minutes with the pan juices while roasting. Remove from the oven and let rest for 15 minutes. Remove the thread or skewers and place the stuffing in a bowl. Serve the stuffing separately and the turkey on a large serving platter, surrounded by the roasted potatoes.

Stuffed Easter Lamb or Goat from Andros

LAMBRIATIS

 Makes about 8 servings

Salt to taste
Liver from the goat or lamb, membranes
    removed
1 cup (2 sticks) unsalted butter
1 pound scallions, white and tender green parts,
    chopped
1 cup snipped fresh dill
1 cup finely chopped wild fennel leaves (see
    Note) or 1 teaspoon ground fennel seeds
1 cup chopped fresh mint leaves
1 pound each Greek feta cheese, fresh *myzithra,*
    or whole-milk ricotta cheese, and
    kefalograviera or any hard yellow cheese
10 large eggs, lightly beaten
Freshly ground black pepper to taste

1 milk-fed lamb or goat (10 to 12 pounds),
    innards removed
5 to 8 lemons, to taste
3 pounds Idaho potatoes, peeled and quartered

1. Bring a small pot of lightly salted water to a boil and poach the liver in barely simmering water for about 8 minutes. Drain, cool slightly, and chop.

2. Heat 2 to 3 tablespoons of the butter in a large skillet over medium heat and cook the scallions, stirring, until wilted, about 6 minutes. Add the herbs and liver and stir together for a few minutes.

3. Combine the cheeses and liver-and-herb mixture in a large bowl and toss together. Add the eggs and mix until well distributed. Season generously with salt and pepper.

4. Preheat the oven to 450°F. Place the lamb or goat in a large baking pan. Cut the lemons and rub them all over the animal on the inside and out, squeezing as you go. Season generously with salt and pepper. Fill the cavity of the lamb loosely with the stuffing and either sew closed or secure with skewers. Place the potatoes all around the lamb and season with salt, pepper, and more lemon juice. Melt the remaining 13 to 14 tablespoons butter and pour over the lamb. Roast for 30 minutes, then reduce the oven temperature to 400°F and continue roasting until crisp on the outside and tender inside, about 2 to 2½ hours. If necessary, add a little water to the potatoes as they bake. Remove from the oven and let cool slightly.

5. Remove the thread or skewers and place the stuffing in a bowl. Serve the lamb or goat on a large serving platter, carved, with the potatoes and stuffing on the side.

✳ **NOTE** If you can't find wild fennel, increase the dill to 1½ cups and mix the fennel seeds in with the filling.

Clay-Pot Lamb Cooked over Vinewood from Sifnos

MASTELLO

 Makes 8 to 10 servings

*M*astello—*after the name of the wide, stout clay vessel in which this dish is baked—is the Easter specialty on Sifnos. It is also a dish that has crossed holiday lines and made its way more recently into some of the island's village tavernas. Like the clay-baked chickpeas that are also a long-standing tradition on Sifnos, the* mastello *usually is brought to the village bread baker's wood-burning oven, where it roasts slowly for several hours. The dish is a great example of island ingenuity: the lamb is roasted over a bed of potatoes, which in turn sit on a kind of "rack" made with several vinewood branches. The vinewood not only imparts flavor but acts as a filter for all the lamb drippings, which are later collected and used to flavor pilaf, also served on Easter Sunday. I've modified the recipe a little, using leg or shoulder of lamb, to make it easy to prepare in a home kitchen. You'll need a very large and deep baking dish, preferably, but not necessarily, made of clay. (A large oval enamel one will work fine.) Gourmet shops and garden stores all over the country carry vinewood.*

6 to 8 pounds lamb with bones, either shoulder or
    leg, trimmed of fat and cut into 2- to 2½-
    inch cubes
Freshly ground black pepper to taste
6 cups dry red wine
Salt to taste
2 cups snipped fresh dill
1 cup extra-virgin olive oil
3 pounds Idaho potatoes, peeled and cut into
    2-inch cubes

4 to 5 branches vinewood, cut to fit into the
    baking pan

1. Place the lamb in a large bowl. Toss with pepper and pour in about 5 cups of the wine or enough to cover the meat. Leave the lamb to marinate in the refrigerator for at least 2 hours or overnight.

2. Remove the lamb from the marinade with a slotted spoon and place in another bowl. Season generously with salt and toss with the dill, ⅓ cup of the olive oil, and additional pepper.

3. Preheat the oven to 375°F. In a large bowl, toss the cubed potatoes with salt, pepper, and the remaining ⅔ cup olive oil.

4. Place the vinewood in a single layer on the bottom of the baking dish. The branches need to be snug and even. Place the potatoes over the vinewood and the lamb over the potatoes. Pour in the remaining cup wine. Place a sheet of butcher's or wax paper over the lamb and cover the baking dish with its lid. Place in the oven and bake for 30 minutes, then reduce the oven temperature to 350°F and bake the *mastello* until the lamb and potatoes are fork-tender, 2½ to 3 hours. Check occasionally, adding water or wine to the dish if necessary to keep it from burning. Remove from the oven, let cool slightly, and serve.

✳ **NOTE** You can measure out the drippings and use them to make pilaf. Greeks use a 3:1 ratio of liquid to rice. Once you measure out the drippings, add enough water to cook the rice properly. Although not traditional, my favorite rice for pilaf is basmati.

Rabbit with a Rich Egg-and-Cheese Sauce

KOUNELI TYRAVGOULOS

Makes 4 to 6 servings

This savory and unusual dish is a specialty of Santorini. I got the recipe from a friend and restaurateur named Yiorgos Hatziyiannakis, who is a kind of local bard of the table, recounting endless bits of information about the island's cuisine. Tyravgoulo, he says, is a variation on the avgolemono *theme that resonates throughout the Greek kitchen. On Santorini, though, lemons were scarce, so the sauce is thickened with what was on hand—farmhouse cheese, which is sharp and tart.*

¼ cup (½ stick) unsalted butter
1 rabbit (about 2½ pounds), cut into stewing
    pieces
Salt and freshly ground black pepper to taste
1 large onion, finely chopped
1 scant tablespoon all-purpose flour
2 garlic cloves, minced
1 cup dry red wine
2 bay leaves
2 large eggs, lightly beaten
¾ cup grated *kefalotyri* or any hard yellow
    cheese

1. Heat 3 tablespoons of the butter in a flameproof casserole or Dutch oven over medium-high heat. Season the rabbit with salt and pepper and sear in the hot butter, turning to brown on all sides. Remove from the pot and set aside. Add the remaining tablespoon butter to the pot and cook the onion, stirring, until translucent and light golden, about 10 minutes. Sprinkle with the flour and stir over medium heat until the flour darkens a little and turns a golden color, about a minute or two.

2. Add the rabbit back to the pot. Add the garlic and stir for a minute. Pour in the wine and enough water to barely cover the rabbit. Add the bay leaves, season with salt and pepper, cover, and bring to a boil. Reduce the heat to low and simmer the rabbit until fork-tender, about an hour.

3. In a small bowl, lightly beat the eggs. Pour a ladleful of the pan juices into the eggs in a slow, steady stream, stirring with a wire whisk. Stir in the cheese and pour the mixture back into the pot. Simmer, stirring, for 1 to 2 minutes over very low heat. Remove the bay leaves. Serve hot.

Pork Loin Stuffed with Myzithra Cheese and Carrots from Kimolos

PSARONEFRI GEMISTO ME MYZITHRA KAI KAROTA

Makes 6 to 8 servings

This is one of those dishes that gets eaten down to the last morsel. It's not exactly "traditional," in the sense that it isn't rustic but urbane, and is a good example of Greek "Sunday" cooking.

One 3-pound boneless center-cut pork loin
1 cup dry white wine
¼ cup fresh lemon juice
½ pound fresh *myzithra* or ricotta cheese
½ pound Greek feta cheese, crumbled
3 garlic cloves, pressed or finely chopped
Salt and freshly ground black pepper to taste
2 teaspoons dried Greek oregano
1 large carrot, peeled
6 tablespoons extra-virgin olive oil

1. Marinate the pork in the wine and lemon juice for 2 hours in the refrigerator, turning it several times.

2. Preheat the oven to 350°F. Combine the cheeses and garlic in a medium bowl and set aside.

3. Remove the pork from the marinade and season on both sides with salt and pepper. Sprinkle half the oregano on one side. Spread the cheese evenly over the same surface of the pork and place the carrot on top so that it is aligned vertically in the center. Drizzle 2 tablespoons of the olive oil over the filling. Tuck in the ends of the pork and roll the meat up along its length.

4. Truss the pork to secure it closed. To do this, wrap cotton string around one end of the pork loin, then tie with a double knot. Continue tying the loin with the string at 2-inch intervals until it is all securely closed. Turn the meat over and cut the string, leaving enough to wrap lengthwise around the roast to the original knot. Turn the meat over again, wrap the string around the front end and secure it to the first knot that you tied.

5. Heat the remaining ¼ cup olive oil in a large, wide pan over high heat and cook the rolled pork, turning to brown it on all sides. Remove from the pan. Season the outside of the meat with the remaining oregano, place in a lightly oiled baking pan, and roast until done, 55 to 60 minutes, or until an instant-read thermometer inserted in the thickest part of the loin reads 155°F. Remove from the oven and let cool slightly.

6. To serve, cut away the string and cut into ¾-inch-thick slices. If desired, pour the pan drippings over the meat before serving.

FISH AND SEAFOOD

The Greek islands conjure up images of sparkling sapphire seas and all that goes with them, from the small, brightly painted fishing boats to the tawny, leather-skinned fishermen who ply the Aegean for their livelihood. In some islands fishing is more of a traditional profession than in others, a fact that has much to do with the fecundity of the land (it's easier and less dangerous to till than to fish), the local economy, and the way villages evolved (for example, in many islands, the earliest villages were always inland, camouflaged, and safe). But, on the islands, fish naturally have always played a major role, both economically and practically.

Greeks prefer their fish exceedingly simple. For sure, the best Greek fish dish is one most of us know, in which the freshest catch is simply grilled over hot coals and seasoned with a little olive oil and lemon juice.

In many of the Cyclades there are preparations for small sun-dried fish. Picarel (*marithes*) and scad are among the favored fish for drying. In Santorini, they are served with *fava* (puree of yellow split pea), the island's national dish. In Tinos, salted, sun-dried small fish is smoked over oregano. In Syros and Paros one encounters salted, sun-dried mackerel, seasoned with pepper and oregano. It was hard for me to include these preparations here, because they are virtually impossible to make in an American kitchen.

Red Mullet with a Caper-Scented Tomato Sauce from Kimolos

BARBOUNIA ME KAPARI

 Makes 4 to 6 servings

Red mullet usually finds its way into frying pans in Greece. There are, though, several island recipes, from both the Cyclades and the northeastern Aegean, that call for poaching the fish with various vegetables.

Salt to taste
2 pounds red mullet, cleaned, gutted, and heads left on
⅓ cup extra-virgin olive oil
2 large Spanish onions, halved and sliced
3 garlic cloves, minced
2 cups grated firm, ripe tomatoes (see page 459) or good-quality chopped canned plum tomatoes, with juice
1 bay leaf
1 cup small Greek salted capers, soaked in warm water for 1 hour and drained
Freshly ground black pepper to taste

1. Lightly salt the fish and set aside, covered, in the refrigerator until ready to use.

2. Heat the olive oil in a large skillet and cook the onions over medium heat, stirring, until translucent, about 10 minutes. Add the garlic and stir for a minute. Add the tomatoes and bay leaf, bring to a boil, reduce the heat to medium-low, and simmer for 10 minutes. Add the drained capers and simmer for a minute. Add the fish, season with pepper and additional salt, if desired, cover, and simmer until the fish is fork-tender, 15 to 20 minutes. Serve hot.

Smelt-and-Onion Skillet Pie

ATHERINOPITA

 Makes 4 to 6 servings

Small fish fried pielike in a skillet is something Greeks have been savoring since time immemorial. There are many recipes for dishes like this one all over the Aegean. I like to serve this with plain boiled greens, horta *(page 404), or with the stewed greens dish from Corfu,* tsigarelli *(page 79).*

1 pound smelts, washed and gutted
⅔ to 1 cup all-purpose flour, as needed
Salt to taste
3 medium yellow onions, halved and thinly sliced
Vegetable oil for frying
Juice of 1 lemon

1. Drain the fish very well in a colander. Place ⅔ cup of the flour in a large bowl, mix with a little salt, then add the fish and onions and gently toss all together to combine. (All the fish and onions should be generously dusted with flour. Add more if necessary. The mixture will be dense; as you pick up handfuls of it to fry, shake off any excess.)

2. In a medium, heavy skillet, heat about ½ inch oil. When the oil is very hot, take 2 small handfuls of the fish and onions together and place them in the skillet (the mixture should be in one layer and should fill the skillet). Fry on one side over medium heat until golden, 6 to 7 minutes total. Remove the skillet from the heat for a second. Take a plate, place it over the skillet, and, using oven mitts, flip the fish onto the plate, then slide it back in to fry on the other side. When golden, slide onto a serving plate and serve with a sprinkling of lemon juice. Repeat with the remaining fish and onions.

Salt Cod Cooked in a Creamy Garlic Sauce

BRANDADA SANTORINIS

 Makes 4 servings

The Santorini brandade *is similar to its Provençal cousin in that both call for salt cod to be cooked with a creamy garlic sauce. While the Provençal dish calls for a thick sauce of garlic, milk, and olive oil, the Santorini version depends on ingredients from the local larder—tomatoes, potatoes, and garlic combined to form a thick sauce. It is a classic in the island's kitchen repertoire, usually served at room temperature.*

The flavors here are strong. I think this dish is best accompanied by simple boiled greens (page 404).

1 pound salt cod fillets

½ pound (2 medium) waxy potatoes, scrubbed

3 to 4 garlic cloves, to taste, minced

Salt to taste

½ to ¾ cup extra-virgin olive oil, as needed, plus 2 tablespoons for the sauce

¼ cup red wine vinegar

6 to 8 tablespoons olive oil, as needed, for pan-frying the cod

2 tablespoons tomato paste diluted with ¾ cup water

1 scant teaspoon sugar

1. Rehydrate the cod as on page 463.

2. Bring the potatoes to a boil with water to cover in a medium pot. Simmer until fork-tender, about 30 minutes. Remove and let cool slightly.

3. Peel the potatoes and have the garlic ready. Either in a large mortar or in a mixer fitted with a paddle or wire whisk, place the peeled hot potatoes one or two at a time and some of the minced garlic and pound, adding a little salt and the extra-virgin olive oil and vinegar in slow, steady, alternating streams until a loose, thick sauce forms. (I give a range in the amount of olive oil because potatoes vary in their ability to absorb liquid. Use as much as needed to achieve the consistency of a thick but pourable batter.)

4. Drain and trim the cod of any remaining black skin, and remove any bones. Cut into serving pieces. Heat 2 tablespoons at a time of olive oil and cook the cod in batches over medium-high heat until golden and crisp, 5 to 6 minutes on each side. Preheat the oven to 350°F and lightly oil a large ovenproof glass baking pan, big enough to fit all the fish pieces in one layer.

5. In a large skillet, heat the 2 tablespoons extra-virgin olive oil. Stir the diluted tomato paste into the hot oil over medium-low heat until thick, 1 to 2 minutes. Add the potato-garlic mixture to this and stir to combine. Taste and adjust seasoning if necessary with a little sugar or salt.

6. Spoon a little sauce over the bottom of the baking pan and place the fried cod on top. Spoon the remaining sauce over the fish and bake until heated through, 8 to 10 minutes. Remove from the oven and serve hot.

☉

Squid Stuffed with Rice and Olives

KALAMARAKIA GEMISTA ME ELIES KAI RIZI

 Makes 6 servings

I don't know if this dish is really traditional in the Cyclades. I ran across it at a taverna in Syros and loved it, so I have tried to replicate it here.

2½ pounds medium squid, preferably fresh

For the stuffing
5 tablespoons extra-virgin olive oil
2 small garlic cloves, chopped
½ cup basmati rice
½ cup water
⅓ cup rinsed and coarsely chopped Kalamata olives
1 cup finely chopped fresh flat-leaf parsley
1 large egg, lightly beaten
Juice of 1 lemon
Salt and freshly ground black pepper to taste

To cook the squid
3 tablespoons olive oil
2 garlic cloves, chopped
1½ cups peeled, seeded, and diced tomatoes, preferably fresh
1 cup dry white wine

To serve
2 tablespoons finely chopped fresh flat-leaf parsley
1 lemon, sliced

1. Clean the squid, if necessary: Remove the head and tentacles. Pull out the head from the body of the squid. Cut away and discard the intestines and push out and discard the mouth and eyes. What should be left are the tentacles attached to a chunky bit of the head. Set aside. Remove the soft bone from inside the body of the squid and discard. If desired, remove the purple membrane. Wash the squid body and the tentacles well. Finely chop the tentacles and set aside.

2. Heat 2 tablespoons of the olive oil in a skillet and cook the chopped tentacles over high heat, stirring, until they turn bright pink, about 2 minutes. Add the garlic and stir for a minute over medium heat. Add the rice, then pour in the water. Cook over very low heat, stirring, until all the water is absorbed, about 5 minutes.

3. Combine the rice mixture with the olives and parsley in a medium bowl and mix well. Add the egg, lemon juice, and the remaining 3 tablespoons olive oil and mix well. Season with salt and pepper. Using a teaspoon, gently stuff the squid body with the rice-and-olive mixture, leaving a little room at the top for the rice to expand. Either sew the squid closed with a needle and thread or secure closed with a toothpick.

4. Heat the olive oil in a skillet. Add the garlic and cook stirring, over medium heat, until golden. Remove and discard. Add the squid to the skillet, fit one snugly next to the other. Cover and cook for 6 to 8 minutes, turning once. Add the diced tomatoes and wine and enough water just to cover the squid. Cover the skillet and cook over low heat until the squid are tender and the rice is cooked, 35 to 40 minutes. Remove from the skillet, place on a platter, sprinkle with parsley, garnish with the lemon slices, and serve hot.

BREAD

European travelers to the Cyclades in the seventeenth, eighteenth, and nineteenth centuries sometimes remarked on the paucity of the local diet, and in so doing never failed to mention the hard black bread—barley rusks, in other words—that sustained most islanders. With the exception of Syros, which was the capital of Greece in the early nineteenth century, when the nation was young, most of the Cyclades were marked by dire poverty, and barley bread was still the staple food of many islanders right up until the onslaught of tourism, and hence affluence, in the 1960s.

Hard barley tacks notwithstanding, the bread traditions throughout the Cyclades are relatively simple. One still finds some interesting holiday breads, such as the dove-shaped little loaves turned out on Pentecost in Sifnos and the anthropomorphic loaves made in several islands during Lent and Easter. In Tinos, for example, small Easter breads called *vlahoules,* which means "little country girl," are, in fact, made specifically for little girls; little boys get the *axiomatikia,* or "officers," little breads shaped to resemble soldiers. But what is most interesting is the use of local ingredients in ways not found anywhere else in Greece. For example, with the exception of Astypalaia in the Dodecanese, only in the Cyclades do we find saffron bread and rusks, Easter specialties usually. In Kimolos, local bakeries sell a slew of pizzalike pies made with bread dough and simple toppings, something, again, not encountered anywhere else.

Easter Saffron Rusks from Santorini

PAXIMATHIA ME ZAFORA APO TIN SANTORINI

  Makes about 48 *paximathia*

I *visited Santorini once just a few days after Easter and found these golden rusks on the table of a local grape farmer just a few yards down from the Boutari winery. Saffron is indigenous to the island as evidenced in one of the most starkly beautiful works of art from prehistoric Greece, the wall fresco unearthed at Akrotiri in Santorini depicting a young woman harvesting the saffron crocus.*

12 to 14 cups bread flour, as needed
Two ¼-ounce envelopes active dry yeast
4¼ cups warm water
½ to 1 teaspoon saffron threads, to taste
½ teaspoon salt
¾ cup (1½ sticks) unsalted butter, softened
1½ cups sugar
5 large eggs
1 tablespoon ground fennel
1 large egg yolk mixed with 2 tablespoons milk
    and 1 tablespoon water
Sesame seeds for garnish

1. Combine 2 cups of the flour with the yeast in a medium bowl and add ¾ cup of the warm water. Mix until a dough mass begins to form. Knead, adding a bit more flour if necessary, until the dough is soft and silky. Cover with a cloth and let sit in a warm, draft-free spot for 8 hours or overnight.

2. Place the saffron in a cup and pour in 1 cup of the warm water. Cover with a cloth and let the saffron steep for several hours.

3. Combine 10 cups of the remaining flour and the salt in a large bowl and make a well in the center. Break the starter up into small pieces and place in the well. Pour in the saffron water and threads. Cream the butter and sugar together until smooth, then add the eggs, one a time, until the mixture is creamy. Pour this into the well, too.

4. Have the remaining 2½ cups warm water on hand. Begin kneading the dough by hand, adding the water slowly as you go, until a dough mass begins to form. Add the ground fennel. (The mixing and kneading may also be done in a large stand mixer fitted with a dough hook, in 2 or 3 batches if necessary.) Knead until smooth, adding flour if necessary to make the dough silky.

5. Lightly oil four 12-inch loaf pans. Divide the dough into 4 equal balls and shape each into an oblong loaf. Place in the oiled pans. Using a pastry cutter or knife, cut through each of the loaves at 1-inch intervals to mark slices, but do not cut all the way to the bottom of the loaves. Cover and let rise in a warm, draft-free place until doubled in bulk, about 2 hours.

6. Preheat the oven to 400°F. Brush each loaf with the egg wash and sprinkle with sesame seeds. Bake until lightly golden but not completely done, about 45 minutes. The loaves will sound dense, not hollow, when tapped. Remove the loaves and let cool on wire racks. Cut into slices where marked and place flat side down on unoiled sheet pans. Reduce the oven temperature to about 200°F (or to the "warm" setting), and bake the *paximathia* until rock hard, about 3 hours. Let cool completely and store in cookie tins indefinitely.

Saffron Cheese Bread from Anafi

TYROPSOMO ME ZAFORA APO TIN ANAFI

 Makes two 10- to 12-inch round loaves

½ teaspoon saffron threads
¼ cup warm water
2 cups whole milk
Two ¼-ounce envelopes active dry yeast
6 large eggs, lightly beaten
½ cup extra-virgin olive oil
1 scant teaspoon freshly grated nutmeg
3 cups coarsely grated aged *myzithra* or any
     hard, aged sheep's milk cheese
2 teaspoons salt
4 to 5 cups all-purpose flour, as needed, plus
     more for dusting
4 to 5 cups bread flour, as needed

1. Dissolve the saffron in the warm water and set aside for 15 minutes. Meanwhile, warm the milk (do not scald) and place in a large bowl. Dissolve the yeast in the warm milk and let rest until it starts to bubble, about 15 minutes. Pour in the saffron and saffron water, eggs, and olive oil, then stir in the nutmeg, cheese, and salt and mix well.

2. Add 4 cups each of the all-purpose and bread flours to the liquid in alternating ½ cup increments and stir with a wooden spoon to combine. Mix until a dough mass forms. Remove and knead on a floured work surface until the dough is dense but smooth, 10 to 15 minutes, adding more flour if needed. Place in an oiled bowl, turn to coat with oil on all sides, and cover with a cloth. Let rest in a warm, draft-free place until doubled in bulk, about 2 hours.

3. Lightly oil a large baking sheet. Divide the dough into 2 equal balls and shape each into a round loaf, 8 to 10 inches in diameter. Place on opposite sides of the sheet pan or in two separate sheet pans. Cover with a cloth and let rise for another 45 minutes. Meanwhile, preheat the oven to 375°F. Bake the cheese breads until golden, about 50 minutes. Remove from the oven, let cool, and serve.

Bread Topped with Tomatoes and Onions from Kimolos

LATHENIA

 Makes 4 to 6 servings

Kimolos, one of the smallest and most remote of the Cyclades, has a few specialties. Among them is this savory pizzalike bread. The dish was born, like so much in Greece, out of the need to make use of a leftover, in this case bread dough after the weekly or bimonthly bread baking. Now most home cooks just go down to the local baker to buy some dough. The pies are also sold at the bakeries themselves.

One ¼-ounce envelope active dry yeast
1½ to 1¾ cups warm water, as needed
4 to 4½ cups bread flour, as needed
½ teaspoon salt
3 to 4 medium-large firm, ripe tomatoes, peeled and chopped
3 medium red onions, thinly sliced
3 tablespoons extra-virgin olive oil
Salt and freshly ground black pepper to taste

1. Dissolve the yeast in 1½ cups of the warm water and let sit until bubbly. Combine 4 cups of the flour with the salt in a large bowl and make a well in the center. Add the yeast mixture and begin to knead the dough by hand. Knead for about 10 minutes, adding more water or more flour if necessary to make a smooth, elastic dough that doesn't stick.

2. Oil an 18-inch round pizza pan or a 12- by 18-inch baking pan. Shape the dough into a ball and flatten it with your palm. Roll out the dough to fit the pan and place inside. Cover with a cloth and let the dough stand in a warm, draft-free place until almost doubled in bulk, about 1½ hours.

3. Preheat the oven to 400°F. Combine the tomatoes and sliced onions with the extra-virgin olive oil, salt, and pepper in a large bowl. Using the tips of your fingers, press the dough down in the pan, docking it to make indentations. Spread the onion-and-tomato mixture evenly over the dough. Bake the *lathenia* until the bread is golden, about 50 minutes. Remove from the oven, let cool slightly, cut into wedges, and serve, either hot or at room temperature.

SWEETS

Outside of Thessaloniki, with its myriad sweet shops, the best, most fragrant, and delicate sweets in Greece are found in the Cyclades.

The Cyclades share one type of sweet with almost all the rest of the Aegean islands: the cheese-filled pastries that are usually an Easter specialty and that abound in many variations from north to south in the Aegean. But in the Cyclades one also finds some truly unique stuffed pastries, such as several from Tinos that are filled with sweetened chard and with sweet potato.

Some islands, such as Andros, are renowned for particular confections, such as lemon-blossom spoon sweet and a whole array of almond-based sweets that one usually buys rather than makes at home.

The following recipes represent just a handful of the many pastries, confections, and desserts that belong specifically to Greece's most famous islands.

SWEET CHEESE PASTRIES

Sweet cheesecakes are among the oldest pastries in Greece, made and savored with unbroken continuity from Homeric times. They are found in various versions all over the Cyclades at Easter.

The cheese used is often fresh white sheep's or goat's milk cheese—except in Tinos, Syros, and Naxos, where cow's milk is more prevalent. It is similar in texture to ricotta but sweeter and richer and made especially in spring, when the animals have plenty of fresh grasses and greens to feed on and their milk is tasty. The sweets come in various shapes, from the cupcakelike tartlets of Tinos with their pleated pastry, to the star-shaped *melitinia* of Santorini, which I have omitted here because the recipe appears in my first book, *The Food and Wine of Greece.* Some are open faced; in others the cheese is enclosed as though in a pocket of homemade pastry. The flavorings change, too, from orange blossom and rose water to mastic, cinnamon, and local thyme honey. I have set down to record two of these island pastries.

Easter Honey-and-Fresh-Cheese Tartlets from Sifnos

MELOPITA SIFNOU

   Makes 24 pieces

This is probably Sifnos's most famous dish, the island's culinary claim to fame. What sets it apart from other sweet Easter cheese pies of the Aegean is the fact that it is made into a whole pie and not into individual dainty pastries.

For the pastry
2½ cups all-purpose flour
½ cup confectioners' sugar
½ teaspoon baking powder
1 cup (2 sticks) chilled unsalted butter
2 large eggs, lightly beaten
¼ cup brandy
2 to 3 tablespoons cold water, as needed

For the filling
1½ pounds fresh *myzithra*, fresh *anthotyro*, or whole-milk ricotta cheese
1 cup honey
5 large eggs, lightly beaten
4 to 5 tablespoons all-purpose flour, or more as needed
1 tablespoon ground cinnamon, plus more for sprinkling

1. Prepare the pastry: Sift the flour, sugar, and baking powder together in the bowl of a food processor and pulse to mix. Cut the butter into small pieces and add to the dry ingredients. Pulse on and off for about a minute, until the mixture is mealy. Add the eggs and brandy and pulse until a dough mass forms. If it is too dense, add the water, 1 tablespoon at a time, until the dough is pliant but still firm.

Alternatively, if you don't have a food processor, you can mix the dough by hand: In a large bowl, sift together the flour, sugar, and baking powder. Cut the butter into small pieces and, using a pastry cutter or a fork and knife, cut it into the flour quickly until the flour is mealy. Make a well in the center, add the eggs and brandy, and mix quickly by hand until a dough mass forms. If it is too dense, add the water, 1 tablespoon at a time, until the dough is pliant but firm. By hand, the whole process shouldn't take longer than about 5 minutes.

Remove from the food processor or mixing bowl, divide in half, and shape into 2 large disks. Wrap each in plastic wrap and let rest in the refrigerator for 30 minutes. (The pastry may be made a day ahead.)

2. Prepare the filling: In a large bowl, mix together the cheese and honey. Add the eggs and combine. Add ¼ cup of the flour and the cinnamon and mix. The filling should be as loose as Jell-O. If it is too loose, add the remaining tablespoon flour and even more, if necessary.

3. Preheat the oven to 350°F. Line an 8- by 12-inch baking pan with parchment paper. On a lightly floured work surface, roll the first piece of dough into a rectangle 10 by 14 inches. If it cracks, just pinch it together. Fit it into the pan, leaving the excess to hang over the edge, then spread the filling on top. Roll out the second sheet to the same size and place over the filling, turning the edges in to form a rim. Bake until golden, about 40 minutes. While still warm, sprinkle with cinnamon. Let cool and cut into 2-inch squares.

Crustless Cheesecake

MYZITHROPITA HYTI

 Makes about twelve 3-inch squares

*T*his recipe appears in various renditions thoughout several of the Cyclades. In Syros, it is baked without the addition of flour. Elsewhere, as in Tinos, for example, where the cake is called tyropita hyti— "poured"—semolina is added to help bind the cheese and the pie is garnished with sesame seeds.

2 pounds unsalted fresh *anthotyro*, fresh
   myzithra, or whole-milk ricotta cheese
5 cups sugar
12 large eggs, lightly beaten
Grated zest of 1 orange
2 scant tablespoons ground cinnamon
1 teaspoon pure vanilla extract (optional)
¼ to ⅓ cup fine semolina, as needed
½ cup sesame seeds

1. Preheat the oven to 375°F. Mash the cheese with a fork in a large bowl. Add the sugar and combine well. Add the eggs, orange zest, cinnamon, and vanilla (if desired) and mix with a wire whisk until smooth. Add ¼ cup of the semolina and stir. The mixture should be dense like a porridge. If it seems too loose, mix in the remaining semolina.

2. Butter a 9- by 13-inch baking pan. Sprinkle half the sesame seeds over the bottom of the pan and pour in the cheese mixture. Sprinkle the remaining sesame seeds over the top. Bake until set, 1 to 1½ hours. Test for doneness by inserting a knife in the center. It should come out clean. The pie should be dense. Remove from the oven and let cool slightly. While still warm, cut into 3-inch squares and serve.

Semolina Pudding from Santorini

SANTORINIA POUTINGA

 Makes 8 servings

Like Corfu's poutinga, Santorini's dessert springs from the island's bourgeois past. This was a dish only the rich could afford, with its generous use of butter, sugar, and eggs. Desserts that were part of the island's peasant traditions are decidedly more rustic and simpler.

For the pudding
3 cups milk
3 cups sugar
2 tablespoons unsalted butter
½ cup plus 2 teaspoons fine semolina
1 tablespoon ground cinnamon
4 large eggs, lightly beaten

For the sauce
6 large egg yolks
6 tablespoons sugar
¾ cup Santorini or Italian *vin santo* wine

1. In a large pot over low heat, cook the milk, sugar, and butter, stirring, until the sugar is dissolved, 5 to 7 minutes. Add ½ cup of the semolina, pouring it in a slow, steady stream and stirring constantly so that it doesn't clump. Stir until the mixture is the consistency of thick cream, about 8 minutes. Stir in the cinnamon. Remove from the heat and let cool completely. Stir in the eggs, mixing thoroughly.

2. Preheat the oven to 375°F. Butter an 8- by 12-inch ovenproof glass baking dish and sprinkle the remaining 2 teaspoons semolina over the bottom. Pour in the semolina cream and spread evenly with a spatula. Bake the pudding for 1 hour, then reduce the oven temperature to 250°F and continue to bake until the pudding is completely set, dense and firm, and lightly golden on top, about another 1½ hours. Remove from the oven and score into serving pieces.

3. Make the sauce: Place the egg yolks in a metal bowl or the top of a double boiler over boiling water and whip with a wire whisk until the yolks are liquid. Add the sugar in a slow stream, whisking all the while. Add the wine and continue whisking vigorously until the sauce is thick, about 5 minutes.

4. To serve: Place a piece of hot or warm pudding on a plate and pour a little of the sauce over it.

Honeyed Pastry Crescents Filled with Sweet Potato and Walnuts from Tinos

MOURTADELLA

 Make about 36 pieces

This is a very old recipe from Tinos probably with roots in the island's Venetian past and in its Catholic population. I could find no clues as to the odd name, reminiscent of the Italian cold cut, with which this dish has nothing in common. There is another old dish, apparently also called mourtadella, *which was a kind of blood sausage and also part of the Catholic tradition here. The following recipe used to be made around Christmastime. A similar sweet potato pie is also made in Paros, but there ouzo flavors the filling and the pie is sprinkled with sesame seeds. As for sweet potatoes themselves—not yams—they are*

rather popular on the island and elsewhere, in both the Cyclades and the Ionian Islands, where, in both instances, they were introduced by the Venetians.

For the pastry
2 to 2¼ cups all-purpose flour, as needed
½ teaspoon salt
¼ cup extra-virgin olive oil
2 large eggs
2 tablespoons fresh orange juice

For the filling
2½ pounds sweet potatoes
½ pound shelled walnuts, finely ground
½ cup honey or *petimezi*
1 teaspoon ground cinnamon

To fry and serve
Vegetable oil
1½ cups honey for drizzling or confectioners'
    sugar for sprinkling

1. Make the pastry: Combine 2 cups of the flour and the salt in a large bowl. Make a well in the center and add the olive oil, eggs, and orange juice. Knead by hand until a firm, smooth dough forms, about 10 minutes, adding more of the flour as needed. Let the dough rest, covered, at room temperature for 30 minutes. (The dough may be prepared a day ahead, wrapped in plastic wrap, and refrigerated. Bring to room temperature before using.)

2. Meanwhile, make the filling: Peel the sweet potatoes and cut them into chunks. Place in a large saucepan with enough water to cover by 2 inches and bring to a boil. Reduce the heat to medium and simmer until fork-tender, about 25 minutes. Drain and mash, either with a potato masher or by passing through a ricer. Place in a large bowl and mix with the walnuts and honey or *petimezi*. Stir in the cinnamon.

3. Divide the dough into 6 small balls. Pat down the first ball to form a rectangle. Using a pasta maker, pass the dough through, starting on the widest gauge and working up to #3, to get a long strip about 3 inches wide. Cut circles out of the dough strip using a 3-inch glass or round cookie cutter. Place a scant teaspoon of filling in each circle and fold over to form a half-moon. Press the edges together with a fork to close. Continue until the dough and filling are used up. Place on a platter in single layers, with a kitchen towel between layers to keep the pastries from sticking together.

4. Heat about 1½ inches of vegetable oil in a large, heavy skillet over medium-high heat. When the oil is very hot, fry the *mourtadelles* a few at a time, turning once, until lightly golden on both sides. Remove with a slotted spoon, drain on paper towels, let cool slightly, and drizzle with a little honey or dust with confectioners' sugar.

✳ **NOTE** You may also roll the dough open by hand. Follow directions in step 3 of Sweet Chard Crescents, page 345.

Sweet Chard Crescents with Rice, Walnuts, and Raisins from Tinos

FESKLOPITA TINOU

 Makes 40 to 50 crescents

Greeks generally do not relish the notion of combining sweet and savory ingredients. There are a few instances though, in pies found in Macedonia and the Peloponnesos and in this one from Tinos, where greens are mixed with raisins and sweetened. This is yet another Tinos dessert I learned to make from Nikoleta Foskolou. These little fried crescents are a Lenten sweet usually prepared during the traditional fasting days before Easter on Tinos. They can be made in two different ways, either shaped into crescents, deep-fried, and dusted generously with confectioners' sugar or baked as a whole pie and sometimes sprinkled with sesame seeds.

For the pastry
2 to 2¼ cups all-purpose flour, as needed
½ teaspoon salt
2 to 4 tablespoons water, as needed
1 tablespoon fresh strained orange juice
1 tablespoon fresh strained lemon juice
2 tablespoons olive oil
1 small egg, lightly beaten

1 pound green chard
¼ cup short-grain rice
½ cup honey or *petimezi*
½ cup finely chopped walnuts
1 teaspoon ground cinnamon
½ teaspoon ground cloves
⅓ cup dark raisins or grated zest of 1 orange
Vegetable oil and 1½ cups confectioners' sugar
    if frying or ¼ cup olive oil and ¾ cup sesame
    seeds if baking

1. Make the pastry: Combine 2 cups of flour and salt in a large bowl and make a well in the center. Add the remaining ingredients and work the flour into the liquid by hand. Mix until a dough mass starts to form. Knead in the bowl, adding additional flour if necessary to make a firm, smooth dough. The dough may also be prepared in a mixer with a dough hook. Shape into a ball, place in a lightly oiled bowl, and cover with plastic wrap. Let rest for 30 minutes.

2. Trim the tough stems off the chard and discard. Chop the greens and wash thoroughly. Drain. Place about 1 inch of water in a large pot and add the greens. Cover and simmer until the chard is wilted, about 8 minutes. Stir in the rice and continue simmering until the rice is tender and all the liquid is absorbed, about 15 minutes. Remove from the heat and let cool. Mix in the honey, nuts, cinnamon, and cloves, as well as either the raisins or the zest.

3. Divide the dough into 2 balls and flatten each of them into a rectangle. On a lightly floured work surface, roll the dough into a large rectangle (about 12 by 16 inches). Cut the rectangle into 3-inch-wide strips. Place one strip at a time on your work surface with a long edge facing you. Place a teaspoon of filling along the center of the dough strip at 2-inch intervals. Fold one edge of the dough over the filling so that it meets the other edge. Cut around each mound of filling with a serrated pastry cutter to form a crescent or half-moon. You can do this with a round cookie cutter, too. Set aside on a lint-free kitchen towel. Repeat with the remaining dough and filling, reusing the dough scraps until the dough and filling are used up. Pat the edges down with your fingertips or with a fork to secure closed.

4. To fry: Heat 2 inches of vegetable oil in a large, heavy skillet over medium-high heat. When the oil is very hot, fry the crescents, turning once, until golden and crisp on both sides, about 1½ minutes. Remove with a slotted spoon, drain on paper towels, and let cool. Place in layers on a serving platter. The pastries may be eaten plain or with confectioners' sugar sifted on top.

To bake: Preheat the oven to 375°F. Lightly oil a 9- by 13-inch baking pan. Divide the dough into 2 equal balls. On a lightly floured work surface, roll the first ball into a rectangle slightly larger than the baking pan. Fit into the pan and brush with a little of the olive oil. Spread the filling evenly over the phyllo. Roll the next ball of dough into a rectangle and place on top of the filling. Trim the edges to remove excess dough and pinch the top and bottom phyllo sheets together, turning them in to form a decorative rim. Brush the top sheet with olive oil and score into squares or diamonds. Sprinkle generously with the sesame seeds. Bake until the phyllo and sesame seeds are golden, about 1 hour. Remove from the oven and let cool. These will keep for about 5 days.

 NOTE You may use a pasta maker to work the dough into strips. Divide it into 4 small balls and follow directions in step 3 of Honeyed Pastry Crescents, page 343.

Sesame Brittle Flavored with Ouzo from Kimolos

PASTELLI APO TIN KIMOLO

 Makes about forty 1-inch pieces

In the Cyclades, pastelli *is often made for weddings and served individually atop the lovely elliptical leaves of lemon trees. This is a slightly different* pastelli *recipe from that found in Andros and Tinos, first because it is made with sesame seeds, hot rusks, and nuts, and second because it is flavored with ouzo, not orange blossom water.*

3 cups honey
1 pound sesame seeds
2 cups all-purpose flour, sifted
¼ cup ouzo
¼ cup water
Ground cinnamon

1. In a large stainless-steel saucepan, heat the honey over medium-low heat until it reaches the firm-ball stage on a candy thermometer (244°F to 248°F).

2. Add the sesame seeds and stir vigorously with a wooden spoon. Slowly add the flour, stirring as you go to prevent clumping. Keep stirring until the mixture pulls away from the sides of the pot.

3. Remove the mixture and let cool slightly, just enough to be able to handle. Flatten the mixture with your palms, then work it with a rolling pin until it is flattened and about ¼ inch thick. As you knead, sprinkle it with the ouzo and water. Cut into diamond-shaped pieces, place on a serving platter, and sprinkle with a little cinnamon. To store, place between layers of wax or parchment paper in tins and keep in a cool, dry place. Keeps indefinitely.

Almond Confections from Andros

AMYGDALOTA ANDROU

 Makes about 115 pieces

Ground *almond confections are made all over Greece. The Aegean Islands boast numerous ones. They vary in shape and size—some are formed into little pears, others into buttons or fingers, for example—and they are flavored differently from place to place. In Hora, the capital of Andros, local sweet shops vie for first place when it comes to the making of* amygdalota.

2 pounds blanched almonds
6 large egg whites
3 cups confectioners' sugar
1 cup fine semolina

To finish
½ cup orange blossom water
2 to 3 cups confectioners' sugar, as needed

1. Grind the almonds to a fine, almost pastelike consistency in a food processor fitted with the steel blade.

2. In a large metal bowl, whip the egg whites with an electric mixer, adding the sugar in a slow, steady stream as you go, until a stiff meringue forms. Fold in the ground almonds and semolina.

3. Preheat the oven to 350°F. Line several baking sheets with parchment paper. A tablespoon at a time, shape the mixture into small "pears." Place on the parchment and bake until the confections just start to turn pale yellow or pale gold, about 20 minutes. Remove from the oven.

4. Dip your hand in the orange blossom water and sprinkle over the warm almond confections.

Let cool. Sift the confectioners' sugar over the *amygdalota* and serve or store in a tin in a cool, dry place. *Amygdalota* will keep for up to 2 weeks.

Pounded Barley-Rusk-and-Raisin Confection from Santorini

KOPANIA TIS SANTORINIS

 Makes about 2 dozen pieces

An *old, very simple, yet surprisingly elegant confection from Santorini that came to me via a friend and restaurateur named Yiorgos Hatziyiannakis, who owns Selini, one of the best bistros on the island.* Kopania *comes from the Greek* kopanizo, *"to pound," for the way the rusks are pulverized. This is a perfect example of a rustic sweet that is still enjoyed today.*

2 cups sesame seeds
2 Cretan barley rusks (see Note)
2 cups golden raisins, preferably from the local Assyrtico grape of Santorini
2 to 6 tablespoons water, as needed

1. In a large dry skillet over low heat, toast the seeds, stirring constantly to prevent burning, until they are light golden, 2 to 4 minutes. Remove from the skillet and set aside.

2. Place half the sesame seeds in a large mortar and pound to a fine crumb with the pestle. Break up the barley rusks and add them, little by little, to the mortar, pounding them until ground. Add the raisins and continue pounding until the mixture is a damp pulp. You may have to add a few tablespoons of water to get the right consistency.

Or you can do this in a food processor fitted with the steel blade. First, pulverize half the toasted sesame seeds, then break up the barley rusks and add them, little by little, until ground to a coarse powder. Remove the mixture from the processor. Place the raisins in the bowl of the processor and pulse until they are a dense, damp mass. Slowly add the ground-up sesame seeds and barley rusks and

process, pulsing on and off, until the whole mixture is mealy and adheres together. You may have to add a little water to get the right consistency.

3. A heaping tablespoon at a time, shape the mixture into small balls or little logs. Roll lightly in the remaining sesame seeds and serve. Store between layers of parchment or wax paper in tins and keep in a cool, dry place.

✳ **NOTE** Cretan barley rusks, called *Krithina paximathia* in Greek, can be found in Greek food shops.

The Dodecanese

A Sense of Place and Palate

We left the small harbor of Agios Kirikos in Ikaria and headed south toward the Dodecanese on a hot, late-August day. My traveling companion was my five-year-old daughter, and we spent a few weeks on the road together, island-hopping through the southeastern Aegean. It was one of the last journeys for this book, and I had saved it for a summer's end, because sailing from island to island is the quintessential Greek experience. I didn't visit every one of the Dodecanese islands. I couldn't. But I knew enough about their history, as complicated and contorted as anywhere else in this ancient country, to choose the islands that held the most interest gastronomically. These islands, in the far southeastern corner of the Aegean, are, like their neighbor Crete, at a crossroads between three continents. Unlike other islands in the Aegean, though, especially those in the northeastern corner, the Dodecanese are not disjointed from one another; in fact, from remotest history they seemed to form a group.

The Dodecanese—literally, the "Twelve Islands"—is a bit of a misnomer because they actually number fourteen: Astypalea, Halki, Kalymnos, Karpathos, Kassos, Kastellorizo, Kos, Leros, Lipsi, Nisyros, Patmos, Rhodes, Symi, and Tilos. There are dozens of smaller isles and islets that dot the southeastern parts of the Aegean, but many of them are sparsely populated or uninhabited or used only as grazing ground.

The northernmost of the Dodecanese is Patmos, the holy island, for here, banished by the Romans from Ephesus in A.D. 95, Saint John the Divine wrote the Apocalypse. Each Easter, twelve monks from the island's famed monastery reenact the Last Supper. It stands to reason that Patmos is the soberest of the Dodecanese. Agriculturally, it is also one of the poorest. The island is dry and produces little beyond a meager supply of wheat and barley, a few vegetables, and wine grapes. As a result, island natives have had to turn to the sea and to the rearing of a few goats and chickens for sustenance. There are a few island specialties here, but no cuisine to speak of. A

cheese pie shaped like a small pouch and a beggar's purse filled with almonds and doused with syrup (not unlike other such confections found throughout the Dodecanese) are the two local specialties.

Near Patmos are the two tiny islands of Lipsi and Leros. The former, known for its dark sweet wine and Dionysian religious feasts, is of little interest gastronomically. It is one of the smallest and quietest of the Dodecanese. Leros, though, has a bit more to recommend it. In ancient times the island was known for its honey and its licentiousness.

Leros is sculpted by beautiful, deep bays. Its mountains are barren, but the interior of the island is lush with olive, fig, and carob trees. Today it is a popular Carnival destination, known for its pre-Lenten festivities, where children masquerade as monks, perhaps a throwback to an incident that occurred on the island in the eleventh century, when the Byzantine emperor ceded much of the island to the blessed monk Christodoulos (who built the monastery of Saint John in nearby Patmos). Locals protested and threw the monk into the sea, whereupon he spread his robe across its surface and floated to Patmos. Or so legend has it.

While there is nothing tremendously unique in the way of cuisine here, there are a few local specialties. The most interesting foodstuff that Leros produces is the local *myzithra* cheese. Although not unique to the island, the best-loved local recipes are for octopus grilled over hot embers, small fish marinated with rosemary, and *fouskes*—a yellow-fleshed shellfish a little bit like the Italian scungilli, which has a pronounced iodine flavor. The English translation, at least according to Alan Davidson in his classic book *Mediterranean Fish and Seafood,* is sea-skirt. Local cooks also make a drink called *dasogalo*—literally, forest milk—with almond syrup,

and various phyllo confections filled with almonds and soaked in syrup.

My travels in the Dodecanese took me to Kalymnos, Kos, Nisyros, Symi, Rhodes, and then on to Karpathos and Kassos to the southwest, in the direction of Crete. Sailing between these islands in this remote corner of the Aegean, one can't help being struck by the looming presence of the Turkish coast. These islands have always had a connection to Asia Minor. From remotest antiquity until the political upheavals of the early 1920s, many islanders, for want of arable land, kept their flocks on the Asia Minor side and traveled back and forth regularly to tend to them.

Another presence lies to the south. The inhabitants of many of these Dodecanese islands have always had a connection with the coast of North Africa, one that goes back to the Rhodian presence in the commercial center of Naucratis on the Nile Delta about a thousand years before Christ. Rhodes figures peripherally but importantly in the culinary history of western Europe, too. After the fall of Rome, the continent was bereft of the wealth of spices that the Romans had long imported from Asia and Arabia. When the Knights of Saint John conquered Rhodes in the fourteenth century, they established a powerful fleet to protect both the island and its commercial interests, among which was a hefty trade in spices, procured mainly from nearby Egypt. Rhodes exported cardamom and many other aromatics to western Europe. In our own times, the ties to Egypt have been equally strong—many of these islanders emigrated to Alexandria or moved back and forth between their island homes and work, mainly in Alexandria.

Among these southern Dodecanese islands there is a certain homogeneity in the cuisine. One of my own favorite stops was Kalymnos, the sponge-fishers' island, with its beautiful churches and its brightly painted houses. Kalymnians have the reputation for being among the most independent-minded of the Dodecanese. When the Italians forbade the teaching of the Greek language and religion during their reign over all the Dodecanese between 1912 and 1948, locals brazenly painted their houses blue and white so that from afar the amphitheatrical port looked like an enormous Greek flag. The sponge fishermen gave the island many local delicacies culled from the sea, which I detail further on.

In contrast to small and tranquil Kalymnos is nearby Kos, birthplace of Hippocrates, the third largest Dodecanese island after Rhodes and Karpathos, and one of the most heavily touristed and therefore liveliest. Kos Town, despite its impressive fortress built by the Knights of Saint John and its lovely old quarter, is a strip mall of tourist shops with few of the quiet charms of other Greek islands. The landscape here is different from that of many other islands. Kos is relatively flat and, of all the Dodecanese, has the most available ground water. Kos produces a large quantity of grapes, grains, tomatoes, and honey. The tomato business used to be big here, and the island is known for a small local variety that is used mainly in the production of tomato spoon sweet, a local specialty found in many island shops. Another local specialty is *kokkinotyri*, or "red cheese" (see page 357), which is preserved in the lees of wine.

There are some interesting pies and pasta dishes unique to the island. One favorite is an old dish called *passa makarouna*, a kind of *pastitsio* made with homemade phyllo that is blanched and then layered and baked. The filling is made with ground pork and local fresh *myzithra* cheese, and the whole thing is drenched in meat broth and milk before being baked. The dish seems Anatolian, and, in fact, I have found very similar recipes among the Asia Minor Greeks of Macedonia. In Kos the dish is made on the last Sunday of the pre-Lenten Carnival, when Greek custom dictates that people indulge in rich cheese- and milk-laden dishes before the onset of Lent.

Most of Kos's culinary traditions, though, have been abandoned as the island has succumbed to tourism. One has to go to small isolated villages inland and on the far southern tip of the island to find anything akin to old country ways.

Nisyros, however, is another story. This tiny volcanic island has retained much in the way of local food customs. Farmers' ways are still alive in the wealth of bean and legume dishes, in the penchant for vegetable and bean fritters, and in the relative dearth of meat on the traditional table. Easter here, as on every one of the Dodecanese, is still marked by a clay-baked stuffed baby goat or lamb. The cooking here reflects that of Rhodes and the other islands greatly, except that mass tourism hasn't decimated many of these traditions. Nisyros also produces an interesting cheese, like that of Kos, which is preserved in wine lees.

The cuisine of Dodecanese islands culminates—as do their histories—in that of Rhodes, always the heart and pulse of the Dodecanese. While some islands, such as Symi, Halki, and Kalymnos, have traditionally had strong links to the sea, Rhodes hasn't. The island's coastal area had long been abandoned as people sought inland shelter and protection from pirates. Not until the tourist boom began to turn that around in the 1950s and 1960s did locals take once more to the sea.

Rhodes is a rich and fertile island with a glorious past. Even now, obscured by the hordes of visitors—a few million—who descend on the island each year, Rhodes's former self is still a wonder. The old town on the island's capital is one of the best-preserved medieval cities in Europe, marked by beautiful old, winding streets, the Castle of the Grand Masters, which was completely renovated by the Italians, and dozens more fourteenth- and fifteenth-century edifices. People actually live within the walls of the old city.

Rhodes's cuisine is mostly a reflection of the island's ties to the land. Most locals occupied themselves with farming before hotel after hotel began going up and to this day the vast, forested interior of the island is an idyllic paradise. Tourism has left its mark, though. It is very difficult to find anything authentic beyond one or two of the island's signature dishes, and at the hands of taverna owners even those pale compared to how they would be made at home.

The most memorable meal I had in Rhodes was after a day of traversing its back roads, hours from the capital. I had gone in search of a local priest in the village of Agios Isidoros who runs a small taverna with his wife and daughter and serves traditional cuisine. I wanted to try the *pitaroudia* and stewed purslane and other Rhodian specialties. I sat my daughter down between the oil tins spilling over with flowers and the cats, and the proprietor made his appearance at our table. The priest was portly and jolly. Under a dark, worn frock, he had donned blue jeans and a plaid shirt, and he was wearing a pair of electric blue eyeglasses. I had found paradise. His wife did the cooking, and he did the talking, about his years in Canada as a barber, his adventures with "the ladies," as he said, and how his amorous interests forced him to learn to cook. He spoke perfect English and, detecting a kindred North American spirit, he brought us out plate after plate of delicious country food. Simple stuff—moist, plump, cumin-scented chickpea patties,

greens fritters, my sought-after stewed purslane, fish cakes made with small fry, chicken with tomato and sage sauce, his wife's own cheese, and, finally, to wash it all down, a carafe of his own wine, made from one of Rhodes's indigenous grape varietals, Amorghiano.

That, in a nutshell, is what the cooking of Rhodes and of the greater Dodecanese is all about. The cuisine from the north to the south of the Aegean is relatively uniform. Hence, many dishes found in the Dodecanese are also found in the rest of the Aegean. Things such as the stuffed Paschal lamb—almost every Aegean island has its own rendition of this dish—festive wheat and meat dishes (found especially in the eastern Aegean islands, from Lesvos to Rhodes), skillet fish "pies" made with small fry and flour, and a wealth of beans and legumes, as well as simply prepared fish, are leitmotivs in the cuisine throughout the whole region and are not specific to the Dodecanese.

What is perhaps different here is the frequent use of certain spices, such as cumin, which one also finds readily in the cuisine of nearby eastern Crete. Another shared characteristic with the Cretan kitchen—there are many—is the plethora of barley rusks that are a basic part of the table. Sesame seeds and sesame paste (tahini) play a greater role in the Dodecanese than elsewhere in the Aegean, perhaps owing to these islanders' continual contact with Egypt. Some sesame is still cultivated on the islands, especially on Rhodes, and you can see little golden pyramid-shaped bundles of it drying at the end of summer. Tahini breads and pies, like those found in Cyprus, are made on Rhodes during Lent. There are also tahini soups and sauces for fish and some very unusual dishes for sweetened tahini and pasta. There are also a number of dishes found in the Dodecanese that are almost identical to those found in Cyprus, which is close and with which there has always been frequent contact.

Dodecanese cooking, like all Greek cooking, is a combination of influences. Whether an island's livelihood was dependent on the sea, as in Kalymnos, Symi, and Halki, or turned inland to the mountains, as in Rhodes and Karpathos—combined with the inevitable stamp that proximity to Asia Minor and Africa and also to Crete and Cyprus was bound to impress on the local populations—strictly local needs and landscapes have forged the characteristics of the Dodecanese kitchen.

THE SEA

The people of Symi, a tiny, arid island not too far from Rhodes, have a nickname. Their big neighbors across the way sometimes call them, jokingly, *sardelotzoumia*—sardine juice—because of the large amounts of salted fish these veteran fishermen are known to consume.

In Symi and Kalymnos, both famous for their sponge fishermen, one encounters some of the most unusual preserved seafood in all of Greece. The sponge fishermen would leave their homes just after Easter and not return again until the fall. They needed a supply of food for their long months at sea and, as a result, perfected the art of preserving fish and seafood. Although the sponge industry has all but died among these islanders, their eating habits have remained intact. Fishermen in Symi, for example, have a special hankering for the tiny sun-dried picarel, which they string and hang to dry for several days. The parrotfish, *skaros* in Greek, especially esteemed throughout all the Dodecanese, is also salted and dried in Symi. This fish has an unusual reputation among Greek gourmets—because it is

strictly herbivorous, it is best savored together with its intestines. In Symi, the fish as well as the intestines are dried, separately, and enjoyed as *mezethes.*

The sponge fishermen are known to have been avid lobstermen, too, and one local delicacy, in both Symi and Kalymnos, is sun-dried lobster tail, which was eaten during Lent. In fact, this is a delicacy savored among many Aegean fishermen—I found the dish in Limnos, too. Sun-dried octopus is another local specialty, savored in these parts during the pre-Easter fast. One odd but esteemed *meze* is a local version of *botargo,* but made with octopus roe. The fishermen prefer the eggs of large octopus, which can weigh up to two pounds. They air-dry them slowly, over about a month, then savor the dried eggs either raw or grilled over charcoal. They also make a delicacy out of octopus ink, frying the ink sacs with olive oil, salt, and pepper, and eating them with bread.

Surely the most unusual of the fishermen's preserved-seafood larder is the array of various shellfish put up in seawater. The best known (locally, that is), is the *spinialo,* made with either fan mussels, sea urchins, or sea-skirts (in Alan Davidson's words, "a knobbly creature with a leathery skin which lives anchored to rocks and is so constructed as to permit the sea water to pass through it. Its yellow flesh, like scrambled eggs, is considered a delicacy in Provence"). Symi fishermen add snails to their list of seawater-brined creatures, too. Once cleaned and salted, they are preserved in seawater and usually kept, for economy's sake, in old retsina bottles. Sponge fishermen would take along a supply of *spinialo* with them to sea and eat them together with one or another type of barley rusk and some olive oil and lemon. The *spinialo* is an acquired taste, to be sure, redolent of iodine but delicious.

THE LAND

By and large the fruits of the land are the same from island to island, not only among the Dodecanese but among most of the Aegean islands. The traditional diet here boasts a host of dishes based on bread and grains, with bulgur and cracked wheat claiming a prominent place. Islanders throughout most of the Dodecanese make a delicious dish of homemade pasta with caramelized onions. It is so much a part of the local palate that even tavernas serve it. There are also many old dishes, both sweet and savory, based on flour—creamlike dishes akin to polenta that were simple, cheap, and filling and could satisfy the hunger of hardworking shepherds and their families. Most of these dishes—things such as the stale crusts of country bread cooked in milk, pasta or bulgur wheat cooked in milk, and much more—were abandoned long ago, for these dishes came to be associated with the dire poverty that marked most of these islands before tourists discovered them.

Staples like the yellow chickpea—in some places, such as Nisyros, so much a food of sustenance that the word for them in the local dialect, *maerema,* is synonymous with cooking itself; fresh and dried black-eyed peas; wild greens not unlike those found in Crete; and myriad dry barley rusks—in these parts most often spiced—still make up the typical Dodecanese larder. The chickpea, in fact, is something of a national dish and appears most frequently in the form of fried patties, especially in Rhodes, Kos, and Nisyros. Meat in the traditional diet was always rare. Local farmhouse preparations include the typical array of preserved and salted meats that one finds all over Greece, although there is no substantial charcuterie tradition to speak of, as there is in the Cyclades.

BREAD CUSTOMS

In the Dodecanese, one of the most endearing customs was that of bread proffered as a wedding invitation. It is something families used to do in villages all over Greece. In Rhodes the bride's family would send small, usually sweet buns or other breads to the closest friends and relatives on the Friday before the wedding, which almost always took place on Sunday. These little breads were made from regular bread dough, shaped into round loaves. As soon as they came out of the oven, they were split open by hand, spread with fresh butter and honey, and sent throughout the village to the intended guests. The custom has faded into obscurity, but others are still flourishing.

The bread preparations begin long before the actual wedding and last well after it. The engagement bread, still baked on many islands, is usually a beautifully sculpted round loaf laden with ornate and highly symbolic dough ornaments. In Kos the engagement bread is always decorated with two birds, symbolic of a married couple in Greek folklore, holding the wedding bands in their beaks.

The actual wedding, of course, is another occasion celebrated with myriad breads. In Kos, there used to be a fascinating wedding bread called *lazaros tou gambrou*—the groom's Lazarus—which was an oblong, somewhat anthropomorphic loaf decorated with dough snakes and studded with cloves. One of the most beautiful wedding breads, made by the bride for the groom, is still found in some of the interior villages of Rhodes. Called *gamokouloura,* or, simply, "wedding bread," it is a huge round loaf (the circle representing eternity), decorated with dozens of red- and green-dyed eggs, walnuts, almonds, and sculpted dough motifs.

After the wedding, naturally, comes birth, and

throughout the Dodecanese a slew of breads and pastries are made specifically to celebrate the new-born child. In Karpathos a *psilokouloura* similar to the wedding bread is made, served with *sisamomeli,* a very soft version of sesame brittle, made with honey and eaten with a spoon, and *alevria,* a polenta-like dish prepared with cooked flour and butter or tahini. It still is the custom for visitors to come and see a new baby on the seventh day after its birth, and these three dishes are almost always prepared for them.

At Easter the custom of giving bread as gifts, of fulfilling one's wifely or motherly duties by preparing specific breads for in-laws and godparents, and of making highly decorative loaves continues. The braided Greek Easter bread, *tsoureki,* is widely known outside of Greece and easy to find in Greek pastry shops across the United States. But there are dozens of regional versions. In Kassos, for example, the local *tsoureki,* called *harkhaes,* is a sweet, large, plump, ornate bread ring that is made specifically by the daughter-in-law and given to her mother-in-law at Easter as well as at Christmas. If it is the young woman's first year of marriage, she decorates the loaf with red ribbons. It is presented and accepted with much ceremony and placed on a white embroidered doily for all to see.

At Easter Greeks bake profusely. Home cooks in the Dodecanese, as well as in many other of the Aegean islands, prepare special Easter breads called *avgoules,* after the Greek word for egg, *avgo,* because they are invariably decorated with dyed, hard-boiled eggs. These are made in different shapes—to resemble snakes, a common motif, birds, baskets, and more.

In Nisyros, in addition to the typical array of Easter breads, local cooks make the difficult *eptazymo*—chickpea bread. They call it *afros* here,

which means "foam," for the way the crushed chickpeas bubble up as they ferment to make the starter. This unusual bread is found all over Greece, but it has come to be associated, more than anywhere else, with the Cretan kitchen, where it is seldom eaten fresh and is usually made into a rusk. In the Dodecanese, though, *eptazymo* is often encountered fresh. In Kos, where it is prepared not for Easter but in honor of the Virgin Mary on August 15, the Assumption, the loaves are always round, with the surface scored horizontally and vertically into squares. Each square is pressed with the brittle, starlike top of a dried poppy, which leaves a stamp-like impression.

The Christmas season is another time of constant baking in Greece. Some of the most fascinating holiday breads are made to this day in Karpathos, unique among the Dodecanese because of its relative isolation. On January 6, one of the most important religious holidays, Ta Fota, or the Holy Light, which commemorates Jesus's baptism in the Jordan River, it is custom in Karpathos to prepare a variety of breads. One is the *zimbilli,* a bread ring stuffed with raisins and given especially to children as gifts. Another custom is that of the *vouopita* or, odd as it may seem, "bovine bread," a large round loaf made especially for shepherds, blacksmiths, and midwives. After the evening church service—after the bread has been blessed, in other words—it is custom to cut a small piece off for the farm animals, especially cows, to eat, a kind of wish for good health and fertility for the animals on which most families depended heavily.

Other Christmas breads in the Dodecanese are sometimes decorated like Easter bread, with dyed eggs. In some islands the snake motif (symbol of fertility) is prevalent, with a green-dyed egg stuffed between the snake's jaws. Turtles, fish, and other animal shapes are also popular. These breads are almost always spiced with cloves, mastic, and cinnamon, and it was believed that they provided a great source of strength, especially in the cold winter months.

By and large, the breads of the Dodecanese and the customs surrounding them share much with the bread lore of Crete. In both places, for example, barley has always been the predominant bread grain. Pure wheat flour was too dear to fritter away on the daily loaf. So rusks made with barley flour have always been the farmer's mainstay in the fields. In the Dodecanese, these rusks are often shaped like rings and spiced.

I came across many old and extant recipes for breads and rusks, ritualistic and not, throughout these islands. In the few bread recipes that follow, I have tried to cull those that an American cook will actually want to make.

The Dodecanese Pantry

Like everywhere else in Greece, there is a bevy of local goods, some completely unique to the Dodecanese, others shared with the rest of the Aegean. The larder isn't as big here as it is elsewhere, because in these islands mass tourism has done all it can to obliterate local foodways. Generally, though, the Dodecanese larder shares much with that of Crete. What follows is a short list of what you might find on a culinary peregrination through the southeastern Aegean islands.

OLIVES

The typical array of brine-cured green and black olives exists here, but there are some distinctly regional variations.

Elies neratzates are olives that, once cured, are steeped in the juice of bitter oranges. It is a favorite flavoring in several islands of the southeastern Aegean, especially in Cyprus and Crete (see page 452), but there small green olives are the usual candidates. In Rhodes, many different kinds of olives are perfumed with bitter-orange juice: early-harvest green olives, ripe black olives, and slit greens, to which hot peppers and wild fennel leaves are also added.

Zoupes is the local name of wrinkled black olives in Rhodes. *Zoupes* are basically an end-of-the-harvest black olive—hence mature and shriveled—that is salted with coarse salt and thus processed/cured until the olives' own mahogany juices are completely exuded and the olives begin to exude their oils. At this point they are seasoned, here with dried savory and with the strong, musky, incenselike leaves and berries of the *schinos* bush (*Pistachio lentiscus*). If you've tasted mastic, then you know more or less what *schinos* is like, because the two are closely related. It's a flavor most Greeks know from childhood—chewing on the gummy berries of the *schinos* is a kid's countryside game, like whistling through acorns in America. The leaves and nuts are a favorite seasoning for olives in Crete, too, but there they are put in the barrel with plump, brine-cured olives. *Schinos* has been exploited for its unusual taste since antiquity, when both its nuts and tender shoots were themselves pickled in brine.

CHEESE AND OTHER DAIRY PRODUCTS

I wound my way through the Dodecanese, looking for the real thing, the small shacks where local shepherds boil their daily supply of sheep's milk and turn it into cheese. Throughout the Aegean, there is both a wealth of regional cheeses and a huge spectrum of flavors even when it comes to similar cheeses. The typical very simple fresh and dried whey and whole-milk cheeses are made by home producers in the Dodecanese as elsewhere. But the Dodecanese islands generally do not produce any of the yellow cheeses—*graviera, kefalograviera,* etc.—made in Crete, in several of the Cyclades, and, of course, on the mainland. While there is some cow's milk cheese, most dairy products come from either sheep's or goat's milk. And, surprisingly, in many islands, especially the southernmost—Rhodes, Karpathos, Kassos—cheese making was traditionally secondary in commercial importance to the making of butter and butter by-products. Here is a look at the local larder of dairy-based foods. Most are still made today, and many are commercially available.

Butter and butter products Several traditional butter products are found in the Dodecanese, mainly made from sheep's and/or goat's milk. Basically the evening's milk, left to sit overnight, is then heated and cooled for 12 to 24 hours. The cream—*kaimaki* to the Greeks of the north, *drillos* or *gria* to the Greeks of the southeastern Aegean—that rises to the top is skimmed and collected over a period of days or weeks. When there is enough of it, the process of turning it into butter begins.

Traditionally there are two ways of doing this. The first involves heating the cream slowly while simultaneously churning it to separate the butter from liquid, which is buttermilk. The second, older method, involves pouring the cream into a goatskin and shaking it vigorously to separate it. The resulting "raw" butter was often savored fresh but rarely sold, because it had very little shelf life.

Kokkinotyri or **Krassotyri** The name translates as "red cheese" or "wine cheese" respectively, because the cheese, like the *ghilomeno* and *manoura* of the Cyclades, is steeped in the lees as a way to preserve it. In the Dodecanese, *krassotyri* is a specialty of Kos, Nisyros, and Leros. It is usually drained in long, cylindrical baskets, which give it its characteristic loaflike shape. Traditionally, *krassotyri* is almost always a goat's milk cheese, but in Kos, where it is also made and sold commercially by several large local producers, cow's milk is also used. Once set and drained, the cheese is sun-dried, then placed in brine for about a week. After that, the cheese is sun-dried again for several days and, finally, steeped in another, unusual, brine: boiled vinegar and salt, or a combination of boiled wine (or the lees), vinegar, and salt. It acquires a deep brick-colored exterior as it steeps, but the color doesn't exactly come from the boiled wine or wine and vinegar mix. It comes from a handful of sea-washed pieces of pine bark that are boiled along with the wine mixture and impart a deep red color.

The cheese is delicious, and of all the wine-steeped cheeses in Greece the *krassotyri* has the most pronounced winey flavor. The commercial variety tends to be uniform and semihard, but if you stumble upon the artisinally made cheese it will be quite different, smaller and harder and more strongly flavored. In Kos, the village of Kefalos on the far end of the island, away from the capital, is the place to go looking for the real thing.

Myzithra Ko This is a typical Greek *myzithra*—whey cheese—made from sheep's and/or goat's milk to which whole milk is added. The only difference in this version from Kos is that a little seawater is added for flavor to the whey as it boils.

Myzithra Lerou One of the most unusual cheeses in all of Greece. This cheese, from the island of Leros, is also called simply *Leriko tyri* (Leros cheese). It is a hard, dried *myzithra* also preserved in wine lees, but here the technique for preserving it differs from that of other islands. For one, the milk itself used to make the *mizithra* is mixed with a little seawater for flavor before the cheese is set. Then, once salted and drained in the requisite baskets, and air-dried to the proper consistency, Leros's cheese is rubbed with a salve of wine dregs, savory, pepper, and oil. The cheese, thus swaddled, is left to mature and then used almost exclusively as a grating cheese over fresh pasta and accentuated by a sprinkling of dried mint.

Sitaka This surely accounts for one of the most unique—and confusing—dairy products in the southeast Aegean islands. Sitaka can be essentially one of two things: the first, like the Cretan *staka*, a kind of clarified butter. The cream is collected from fresh sheep's milk over several days or weeks, then heated so that the milk proteins separate from the liquids. The solid proteins are then skimmed and reheated until they become pale golden. Called *stakovoutyro*, this is used as a flavoring—melted and browned—over pasta or wedding pilafs in Karpathos and other parts of the Dodecanese, and in Crete, where it goes by the name *staka*. The residual liquids are then mixed with a little flour (about a tablespoon per three cups) and heated until they, too, coagulate. What results is *sitaka*, which is also used as a flavoring, but also as a cooking fat in foods such as pies, pastries, and sunnyside-up eggs.

The second is the somewhat different *sitaka* of

Kassos: a tart, creamy yet slightly grainy spread, not unlike yogurt cheese or the sour *kopanisti* found throughout the Greek islands. To make it, whole-fat sheep's milk or a combination of sheep's milk and goat's milk are left to stand for several days in order to ferment slightly. The milk is then salted generously and stirred over a very low wood fire for hours until it is reduced considerably and set. As a result of the slow reduction, the milk takes on an ivory color. Sitaka is eaten as a kind of cream cheese, but it is also savored together with pasta and caramelized onions, one of the most delicious dishes of all the Dodecanese. Both renditions probably take their name from the Italian *staccare*, to separate.

DRIED GRAPE LEAVES AND CYCLAMEN LEAVES

I was perusing the marketplace in Kalymnos when I saw gray-green bunches of dried grape leaves dangling from the rafters of grocery store after grocery store. In the rest of Greece fresh grape leaves, plucked in the spring when they are at their most tender, are usually preserved either in brine or, nowadays, frozen. Throughout the Dodecanese, though, the preferred method is to dry them. The leaves are strung laurel-like and hung for a few weeks until they are brittle. They are very fragile, but local cooks claim that once reconstituted they retain all their flavor and delicacy. There is a plethora of interesting recipes for *dolmathes* throughout these islands.

Cyclamen leaves are used as *dolma* wrappers in Rhodes and Nisyros, and the bulbs are cooked in syrup and made into a spoon sweet in Rhodes. In all my travels through Greece, I had never encountered the cyclamen flower in the kitchen. In ancient texts it is rarely mentioned, especially as a food, so I am still at a loss to explain this very local custom.

FIGS

As everywhere in Greece, figs have always been an important source of nourishment, especially on the tables of the poor. After they were dried, in the late summer, they provided an easy and portable snack for farmers in the field, as basic as bread and olives. Dried figs are also considered a *meze* for ouzo and the grappalike drink called *tsipouro* that prevails all over Greece. Unfortunately, in the last few years many of the native varieties have either diminished or been lost altogether. In the island of Nisyros alone, the local varieties once numbered fifteen and ranged from red figs to black figs to thin-skinned white ones (which were prized and reserved for guests) to white ones with red flesh and more. Each variety was dried and kept separately.

In the Dodecanese, as all over Greece, dried figs are often flavored with herbs and nuts. Here the preferred seasonings include sage in Rhodes; bay leaf or basil in Nisyros; and myrtle, cloves, and/or cinnamon in Kassos. Plates of dried figs were sent as a good wish to couples upon their engagement, and in many islands, dried figs, almonds, bread, and ouzo are still offered as funerary foods, together with *kolyva* (boiled sweetened wheat kernels) and other things.

APRICOTS AND MEDLARS

In Rhodes it is still tradition to make both apricot spoon sweets with the whole fruit and apricot paste, which is similar to quince paste and served as a confection. Another specialty of Rhodes, like apricots, medlars are also cooked into a paste. The sweet is rare nowadays, found only in some remote villages.

CURED MEATS

One finds the usual array of cured pork products found throughout much of the rest of Greece— sausages, smoked meats, headcheese, etc.—but there isn't any unique charcuterie tradition to speak of in this part of Greece. The most unusual cured meat is the *pastourma* of Karpathos and a few other places, made not with beef but with local wild goat. The meat is air-dried in large pieces—often entire goat sides—and then rehydrated before being consumed, either alone, as a *meze* for *raki* (eau de vie), or shredded and added to bean and vegetable stews. Goat meat *pastourma*—an acquired taste to be sure, and one not accessible to most travelers—is also found on the island of Ikaria.

Another strictly local cured meat is the beef *kavourma* of Kalymnos. *Kavourma,* akin to *confit,* is found all over Greece, but most often it is made with pork. In Kalymnos the preparation used to be made specifically for the sponge fishermen's larder. The preferred cut was beef thigh, which was boned, cubed, fried, and then salted. Usually it was prepared just before Easter (it was forbidden during Lent) and ready just after Easter, when the fishermen set sail for their six-month journeys. Once the salting process was completed, the meat was placed in seventeen-kilo tins and preserved in butter. "We would use only Dutch butter," one old fisherman's wife told me, naming a specific brand. They would melt the butter, brown it lightly, and pour this over the meat. Then they would sprinkle a generous amount of salt on top and close the tin. The meat was a staple on board the vessels, usually added to bean soups and stews, to sauces for pasta, especially orzo, or cooked with eggs and lemon. There was another, lesser *kavourma,* called *istiko,* which was made the same way but with the boned meat of sterile ewes.

The Recipes

MEZETHES

Thin Garlic Sauce from Rhodes

RHODITIKI SKORDALIA

 Makes about 1 cup, or enough dipping sauce for about 4 people

The skordalia (*garlic sauce*) *in Rhodes tends to be thinner than that in the rest of Greece. This recipe is really an instant* skordalia, *easy to make and a nice accompaniment to mezethes.*

4 to 5 garlic cloves, to taste, peeled
Salt to taste
2 tablespoons all-purpose flour
½ cup extra-virgin olive oil
¼ to ½ cup warm water, as needed
Juice of 1 to 2 lemons, to taste

Using a large mortar and pestle, pound the garlic and salt together into a paste. Add the flour and pound until it is one pasty mass with the garlic. Add the olive oil, water, and lemon juice in a slow stream, alternating between them and working each in so that they bind and become a smooth paste, a little looser than mayonnaise. When all the oil has been used up, adjust the seasoning with salt and add water if necessary to make the *skordalia* as loose as a thick sauce.

Chickpea Fritters from Rhodes

PITAROUDIA

 Makes about 12 large patties

Pitaroudia, *literally "little pies," is the generic name for fritters or patties all over Rhodes. (They are made in many other of the Dodecanese islands but go by slightly different names, depending on the local dialect.) Rhodes's most renowned recipe is for chickpea patties, which are served on many restaurant and taverna menus, especially in the island's capital and in its other major city, Lindos. But off the tourist trail, in the backwaters and mountain villages of this beautiful, lush island, home cooks make fritters from onions, grated potatoes, zucchini, and/or ground meat. All have one thing in common—the use of cumin, by far this island's best-loved spice. Unlike small, meatball-size chickpea fritters elsewhere in Greece and certainly a distant cry from the Egyptian falafel, the Rhodian version calls for big, plump, filling patties.*

½ pound dried chickpeas, picked over and rinsed
1 cup finely chopped onions
1 medium firm, ripe tomato, grated
   (see page 459)
¼ cup finely chopped fresh mint
1 heaping teaspoon ground cumin (optional)
Salt and freshly ground black pepper to taste
2 to 3 tablespoons all-purpose flour, plus
   ¾ to 1 cup for dredging the patties
Olive or other vegetable oil for frying

1. Soak the chickpeas for 8 hours or overnight in ample water to soften them. Drain, place in a pot with ample fresh water, and bring to a boil. Reduce the heat to medium-low and simmer the chickpeas until soft, about 1½ hours. Remove from the heat, drain, and rinse.

2. Place the chickpeas in a food processor fitted with the metal blade and pulse on and off until they are coarse and mealy.

3. Combine the ground chickpeas with the onions, tomato, mint, and cumin, and season with salt and pepper. Add enough flour to make a dense mass that can be shaped into individual patties.

4. Spread the remaining flour on a large plate. Take about 2 tablespoons at a time of the chickpea mixture and shape into large, flat patties. Heat about ¼ inch of olive oil in a large, heavy skillet over medium-high heat. When the oil is very hot, dredge the patties lightly in flour, tapping off any excess, and fry until golden, flipping once to cook both sides, 2 to 4 minutes. Remove with a slotted spoon and let drain on paper towels. Continue until all the chickpea patties are fried, replenishing the oil if necessary. Serve hot, warm, or at room temperature.

⊙ In Nisyros, legume fritters are most often made with yellow split peas. Replace the chickpeas with yellow split peas, which don't need soaking and should be simmered slowly in just enough water to cover them by about 2 inches. Simmer until the split peas are so soft they have disintegrated and the liquid has been absorbed, about 1½ hours. They do not need to be ground. Add enough flour to form a shapable mass and continue as directed, from step 3, seasoning them with fresh mint or fresh oregano. Yellow split-pea patties are also made in Santorini.

Wild Mushroom Fritters Seasoned with Cumin from Masari in Rhodes

PITAROUDIA APO TO MASARI ME AGRIOMANITES KAI KYMINO

   Makes about 15 fritters

My trip to Rhodes was an amalgam of several odd experiences. For one, I had my little daughter with me, so every recipe hunt was punctuated by afternoon stops at big hotel pools, playgrounds, puppet shows, and anything else I could dig up in the roster of local entertainment to keep a five-year-old happily bribed so that she'd be a good girl for Mommy on the next recipe jaunt. Then there were the strange meetings with local women, so many of whom work at menial jobs in the island's huge hotels. So it was that I met Stavroula, a jolly, fiftyish woman clad in a frock and kerchief from a small mountain village called Masari in the center of Rhodes.

She worked in the laundry room of one of the big hotels, and we met there, surrounded by towels and sheets drying on dozens of very long lines. My daughter kept herself busy snaking through the maze of clean hotel laundry, and Stavroula and I talked incongruously of food. "There are lots of pitaroudia,*" she said, "not just the stuff they serve to tourists." Then she got up, disappeared for about five minutes, and came back with a small plastic container with her lunch. "We make these in Masari," she said, showing me small, flat, dark fritters. I asked her where she found wild mushrooms in the middle of summer— not their season—and she explained that she dried them herself. Almost any combination of mushrooms will do, although I think that mild-tasting mushrooms work best with the cumin.*

2 tablespoons olive oil, plus more for frying

4 cups chopped combined portobellos, field
    mushrooms, wood ears, and oyster
    mushrooms, or any combination of cultivated
    and/or wild mushrooms

1 cup all-purpose flour

½ teaspoon salt

1 teaspoon baking powder

½ cup water

2 large eggs, lightly beaten

⅔ cup grated *myzithra* or any hard, aged sheep's
    milk cheese

1 teaspoon ground cumin

1. Heat the 2 tablespoons olive oil in a large skillet over medium heat and cook the mushrooms, stirring, until wilted, about 4 minutes. Remove from the heat and let cool.

2. Combine the flour, salt, and baking powder in a medium bowl. Make a well in the center and add the water and beaten eggs. Mix to make a thick batter. Stir in the cheese, cumin, and mushrooms.

3. Heat about ½ inch of olive oil in a large, heavy skillet over medium-high heat. When the oil is very hot, drop 2 tablespoons of the batter at a time into the hot oil. Fry on one side until golden and then flip to fry on the other side until lightly browned and golden, about 3 minutes. Remove with a slotted spoon, let drain on paper towels, and continue with the remaining batter, replenishing the oil if necessary. Serve hot.

Onions Caramelized in Olive Oil

SYVRASI

 Makes 4 to 6 garnish portions

I was intrigued by this practice, simple as it is, as soon as I encountered it. Onions are caramelized—and then usually served over pasta, flour-based creams, greens, legumes, and even cheese pies—throughout the Dodecanese, on nearly every one of the islands. Oddly, this caramelized-onion topping is encountered rarely anywhere else in Greece. It goes by slightly different names from island to island, depending on the local dialect.

4 to 6 tablespoons extra-virgin olive oil or
    unsalted butter, to taste

6 cups coarsely chopped onion

Heat the olive oil or butter in a large, heavy non-stick skillet over medium-high heat and add the onion. Reduce the heat to medium-low and cook, stirring frequently, until the onions are soft and golden brown, 20 to 30 minutes. Remove from the skillet and set aside as a relish for boiled greens or for lentils and orzo (page 371) or other bean dishes.

✳ **NOTE** Throughout the Dodecanese, especially in Kassos, Kalymnos, and Rhodes, a favorite dish is pasta served with a *ghee*like butter product called *sitaka* (*staka* in Crete) and with *syvrasi,* or caramelized onions, on top (see page 371). If preparing that dish, cook the onions in butter, not olive oil.

☉ *Syvrasi,* caramelized onions, can also be made with the addition of tomatoes. Peel and seed 1 or 2 large firm, ripe tomatoes and grate them (see page 459). When the onions are golden brown, add the tomatoes to the skillet and continue simmering until most of the liquid has boiled off.

Tomato, Onion, and Sea Urchin Salad from Kalymnos

TOMATOSALATA ME AHINOUS

 Makes 4 servings

I was served this delicious salad on my first day in Kalymnos. We settled in at a small seaside taverna with a local acquaintance. The sea smacked against the rocks just below the taverna, and suddenly I caught a whiff of iodine. The waiter had just brought us a variation on the general theme of Greek villager's salad, this one with fresh sea urchins.

2 to 3 large, ripe tomatoes, to taste

1 large red onion, halved and sliced

6 to 8 raw sea urchins, to taste, cleaned
   (see page 463)

4 to 6 tablespoons extra-virgin olive oil, to taste

Coarse sea salt

1 or 2 barley rusks, broken up

1. Core and cut the tomatoes into 6 to 8 wedges each. Toss in a salad bowl with the onion. Add the sea urchins. Drizzle with the olive oil and season with sea salt.

2. To eat properly, use broken-up barley rusk, dipping the rusks into the salad and eating them together with the tomatoes, onions, and sea urchins.

SOUP

Tahini Soup with Tomatoes, Orzo, and Lemon from Rhodes

TAHINOSOUPA ME TOMATA KAI LEMONI

 Makes 4 servings

This is very simple, very old Lenten fare.

6 cups water

Salt to taste

2 cups peeled, seeded, and chopped firm, ripe
   tomatoes and their juices

1¼ cups orzo

½ cup tahini (sesame paste)

Juice of 2 lemons

1. Bring the water, salt, and tomatoes to a boil in a wide pot. Add the orzo and simmer until al dente, about 8 minutes.

2. Place the tahini in a medium bowl. Add a ladleful or two of the hot broth (try not to get pasta in the ladle) to the tahini and mix it vigorously with a fork or whisk, then add the lemon juice. Pour back into the pasta, stir to mix, and simmer for another minute or so. Remove from the heat and serve.

Sweet Sprouted-Wheat Soup with Raisins and Spices from Kastellorizo

CHRYSAFI

 Makes 8 to 10 dessert servings

The name means "gold" in Greek, referring to the color of the wheat. Chrysafi *is one of the most unusual preparations in all of Greece. Whole wheat kernels have long been cooked for the ritualistic funerary dish called* kolyva, *wheat being symbolic of the cycle of nature, of rebirth. But I have never encountered such a festive dish as this one from the remote island of Kastellorizo, where* chrysafi *is made on Christmas, New Year's, and January 6, the Epiphany. Locals say the sprouts resemble Saint Basil's beard (in Greece it is Saint Basil, not Saint Nick or Santa Claus, who bears gifts). Traditionally this dish is made as a festive offering from daughter-in-law to mother-in-law.*

Unsprayed lemon, orange, myrtle, or carob
   leaves (from the tree) or sterilized cotton
½ pound whole wheat kernels
One 3- or 4-inch cinnamon stick
4 to 6 cloves, to taste
1 cup sugar
2 cups dark raisins
1 to 2 tablespoons ground cinnamon, to taste,
   plus more for garnish

1. Line a basket with the fresh leaves or line a large tray with the cotton and spread the wheat kernels on top. Sprinkle the kernels with water. Leave them for a day and sprinkle with water daily or several times a day for 3 to 5 days, until the wheat kernels sprout.

2. Carefully separate the wheat from the leaves or cotton. If using cotton as a base, removing the wheat will be more time-consuming since it will have taken root in the soft cotton. To remove them expediently, pluck a few kernels at a time off the cotton until they are all removed. Pick off any excess cotton from the kernels, rinse gently, and drain.

3. Place the sprouted wheat in a large pot and pour in enough water to cover by 3 inches. Bring to a boil and add the cinnamon stick and cloves. Reduce the heat to medium-low and simmer until the wheat is soft enough to eat, about 3 hours or more. About 45 minutes before removing from the heat, add the sugar and raisins. During the course of simmering the wheat, add more water if necessary to keep the mixture moist and the liquid like a very thick porridge. When the wheat is cooked, remove from the heat and let cool.

4. Remove the cinnamon stick. To serve, ladle the sweet soup into serving bowls and sprinkle with cinnamon.

During the summer, when the heat bleaches the color out of the Greek countryside, few wild greens flourish. By summer's end, even the *vlita* (amaranth)—about the only green that grows in the arid Greek clime then—have toughened and gone bitter. But purslane flourishes, and Greeks eat a lot of it.

Purslane, a thick-stemmed, juicy-leafed crawler, grows wild all over the country. It is a green Americans are just coming to know. It has a mild, refreshing, almost lime-tinged flavor and a succulent, crisp texture. The whole plant—stems, buds, juicy leaves—is eaten. Although it grows wild in many common suburban backyards, it is still fairly difficult to find at market. If you can't find it, you can grow it from seed. Paula Wolfert, in her classic *The Cooking of the Eastern Mediterranean,* suggests looking for it at Mexican markets, where it goes by the name *verdolaga.*

When young, it is delicious raw in a salad. Larger purslane is usually stewed in Greece, a dish we find in several areas of Greece, but especially in the Dodecanese.

VEGETABLES AND BEANS

Some of the loveliest bean dishes come from this part of Greece, and some of the most luscious, shamelessly rich pasta dishes.

Amaranth and Purslane Stew from Rhodes

BLITA KAI GLISTRIDA YIAHNI

Makes 4 to 6 servings

Stewed greens are common in many of the Greek islands, especially Crete, parts of the Ionian Islands, and parts of the Peloponnesos. This is a strictly seasonal dish, made in the summer, when both purslane and amaranth grow profusely all over the countryside.

½ to 1 cup extra-virgin olive oil, to taste
2 large onions, finely chopped
3 to 4 garlic cloves, to taste, peeled and crushed
1½ pounds amaranth, trimmed and washed well
1½ pounds purslane, trimmed and washed well
Salt to taste
2 large ripe tomatoes, grated (see page 459)
½ cup water
5 to 6 small zucchini
Juice of 1 lemon
Freshly ground black pepper to taste

1. Heat the olive oil in a large, heavy pot and cook the onions over low heat, stirring, until wilted and translucent, about 10 minutes. Add the garlic and stir for another minute or so. Add the amaranth and purslane and toss to coat with the oil. Season with a little salt, cover the pot, and let the greens wilt, 5 to 7 minutes. Add the tomatoes and water. Cover and simmer until most of the pot liquids have cooked off, about 20 minutes.

2. Add the zucchini and continue cooking, covered, until the greens and zucchini are very tender, about 15 minutes. Add the lemon juice. Toss to combine and continue simmering for 5 minutes. Adjust the seasoning with salt and pepper. Remove from the heat, let cool, and serve warm or at room temperature.

Eggs Cooked Loosely in Tomatoes from Kalymnos

KALYMNIOTIKO AVGOZOUMO

 Makes 2 servings

One pleasant afternoon my guide on Kalymnos, Giorgos Giannikouris, dispatched me to his mother in the small village of Argos. I sat with the whole family under a huge fig tree in the garden. My daughter was occupied with Giorgos's two kids, playing an old game with dice made from the kneecap of a goat. Giorgos's father-in-law, a priest who happened once to have done a stint as a cook in Pennsylvania, disagreed with Giorgios's mother on nearly every recipe she recounted to me. The whole afternoon was great fun. Kyria Giannikouri brought out plate after plate of local specialties, from the island's famed clay-baked goat-and-cracked-wheat stew to tiny stuffed grape leaves to this simple, common island dish whose name loosely translates as "egg broth." "It should be runnier," the priest said, starting off another round of verbal sparring and explaining that the dish may be eaten on its own or as a sauce for pasta.

2 tablespoons extra-virgin olive oil
1 large red onion, finely chopped
4 large ripe tomatoes, grated (see page 459)
Salt and freshly ground black pepper to taste
3 large eggs
⅓ cup water

1. Heat the olive oil in a large, heavy, preferably nonstick skillet over medium-low heat and cook the onion, stirring a few times, until wilted and translucent, 7 to 8 minutes. Add the tomatoes and simmer until about half the juices have cooked off, 5 to 10 minutes, depending on the juiciness of the tomatoes. Season with salt and pepper.

2. Beat the eggs lightly with the water and pour them into the skillet. Cover the skillet, reduce heat to low, and cook about 3 minutes, or until the eggs are set but loose. Remove from the heat and serve with plenty of hearty bread.

Grape Leaves Stuffed with Eggplant from Kalymnos

KALYMNIOTIKA FILLA GEMISTA ME MELITZANES

 Makes 8 to 10 servings; about 70 *dolmathes*

I had never encountered eggplant as a stuffing for dolmathes, *but apparently it is fairly traditional Lenten fare on Kalymnos.*

One 10-ounce jar grape leaves in brine
½ cup extra-virgin olive oil
5 large onions, coarsely chopped
2½ pounds (about 4 medium-large) eggplants, cut into ½-inch cubes
½ cup short-grain rice
1½ cups peeled, seeded, and chopped plum tomatoes (canned are fine)
Salt and freshly ground black pepper to taste
1 cup chopped fresh flat-leaf parsley
2 large ripe tomatoes, halved, cored, and thinly sliced
Juice of 2 lemons

1. Drain the grape leaves and rinse them well in a colander. Bring a large pot of water to a rolling boil and blanch the grape leaves, in batches if necessary, for 3 to 5 minutes to soften. Drain and immediately rinse under cold running water. Trim the tough stems off the leaves and set aside the ones that are either very small or torn.

2. Heat 2 to 3 tablespoons of the olive oil in a large skillet and cook the onions, stirring a few times, over medium-low heat until translucent, about 7 minutes. Add the eggplant cubes and cook until soft, about 7 minutes, adding a little more oil to the skillet if the eggplant absorbs it. Add the rice, toss to combine with the eggplant, and pour in the chopped tomatoes. Season with salt and pepper, reduce the heat to low, and simmer until the liquid is absorbed, about 5 minutes. Remove from the heat and let cool slightly. Mix in the parsley.

3. Place the grape leaves, shiny side down, in rows on a large table. Place the ripped or very small ones on the bottom of a large pot. Place a heaping teaspoon of filling in the bottom center of each leaf on the table. Fold the sides over the filling, then fold the bottom over it and roll up, tucking the sides in as you go (see page 465). Place the grape leaves seam side down in the pot, snugly next to each other, in layers. Place the sliced tomatoes over the *dolmathes* and pour in the remaining olive oil and the lemon juice. Add enough water to barely cover the surface of the *dolmathes.* Cover with a plate to keep the grape leaves in place and place the lid on the pot. Simmer until the leaves and rice are tender and the pot juices absorbed, about 50 minutes. Remove from the heat and serve, either hot or at room temperature.

GRAPE LEAVES

"It just isn't Sunday without leaves," Kyria Giannikouri said as we sat in her garden and as she recounted several recipes to me for stuffed grape leaves. *Dolmathes* vary greatly in shape and size around Greece. In many Aegean islands, for example, they tend to be tiny. Usually, however, the fillings are pretty consistent—rice and herbs, sometimes with nuts and raisins, or ground meat and rice, in both cases with lots of onions. In Kalymnos there are several distinctions when it comes to *dolmathes* and many unusual fillings. The main thing that distinguishes stuffed grape leaves in Kalymnos are the leaves themselves. If not used fresh, they are usually dried as opposed to being put up in brine to preserve them. I've adapted the recipes with brined leaves since this is what is available in the United States.

Grape Leaves Stuffed with Pumpkin and Rice from Kalymnos

FILLA GEMISTA ME KOLOKYTHA

Makes 8 to 10 servings;
about 70 *dolmathes*

I have had some of the best meals of my life in Greek monasteries. Greek monks and sisters do not eat meat, so the food served at monasteries is often some of the best vegetarian fare to be found anywhere in the country. Most of what they do eat is culled from the well-tended gardens and groves that are part of each monastery's land. It is custom, upon entering a monastery as a visitor, to be offered something, usually a spoon sweet and homemade lemonade or almond water (soumatha). I was with my know-everything-and-everyone-there-is-to-know guide to *the island, Giorgos Giannikouris, when we visited the serene Evangelismos Monastery, a beautiful Byzantine refuge run by a handful of sisters. It was a late summer day, and the first early-harvest pumpkins had just been picked. Giorgos explained that I was collecting lost and obscure traditional recipes. His mother had told me about this dish, and I had come here in search of it. One of the sisters nodded her head, disappeared for a few minutes, and came back to the drawing room with a plate full of these delicious, nugget-sized dolmathes. Another sister, the monastery cook, followed her and gave me the recipe.*

One 10-ounce jar grape leaves in brine
½ cup extra-virgin olive oil
5 large red onions, finely chopped
2½ pounds pumpkin, peeled, seeded, and
    coarsely shredded (see page 461)
⅔ cup short-grain rice
Salt and freshly ground black pepper to taste
½ cup chopped fresh mint
½ cup chopped fresh flat-leaf parsley
Juice of 2 to 3 lemons, to taste

1. Drain the grape leaves and rinse well in a colander. Bring a large pot of water to a rolling boil and blanch the grape leaves, in batches if necessary, for 3 to 5 minutes to soften. Drain and immediately rinse under cold running water. Trim the tough stems off the leaves and set aside the ones that are either very small or torn.

2. Heat 3 to 4 tablespoons of the olive oil in a large, heavy skillet over medium heat and cook the onions, stirring frequently, until translucent, 7 to 8 minutes. Add the shredded pumpkin, in batches if necessary, cooking it until most of its liquid has cooked off, 10 to 15 minutes. Add the rice and simmer, stirring, just to soften a little, 6 to 7 minutes. Season with salt and pepper, remove from the heat,

and let cool slightly. Mix in the mint and parsley and toss with the remaining olive oil.

3. Place the grape leaves, shiny side down, in rows on a large table. Place the ripped or very small ones on the bottom of a large pot. Place a heaping teaspoon of filling in the bottom center of each leaf on the table. Fold the bottom over the filling, then fold the sides over it and roll up, tucking the sides in as you go (see page 465). Place the grape leaves seam side down in the pot, snugly next to each other, in layers. Pour in the lemon juice and add enough water to barely cover the surface of the *dolmathes.* Cut a piece of parchment to the circumference of the pot and fit it over the leaves. Cover with a plate to keep the grape leaves in place and place the lid on the pot. Simmer until the leaves and rice are tender and the pot juices absorbed, about 50 minutes. Remove from the heat and serve, either hot or at room temperature.

⊙ Instead of pumpkin, use the same amount of grated zucchini. Add 1 or 2 grated firm, ripe tomatoes to the filling as well.

Grape Leaves Stuffed with Bulgur or Cracked Wheat and Cumin from Rhodes

DOLMATHES ME HONDRO KAI KYMINO

Makes 8 to 10 servings;

about 70 *dolmathes*

Dolmathes *in Rhodes resemble those made in eastern Crete, where bulgur is often used instead of rice and where cumin pervades so many dishes. It is also the key spice in Rhodian cuisine.*

1½ cups cracked wheat

4 cups finely chopped red onion

3 large ripe tomatoes, grated (see page 459)

½ cup extra-virgin olive oil

Salt and freshly ground black pepper to taste

2 heaping teaspoons ground cumin

1 cup snipped fresh dill

½ cup chopped fresh mint

One 10-ounce jar grape leaves in brine

Juice of 1 large lemon, plus more to taste

1. Combine the cracked wheat, onion, tomatoes, and olive oil in a large bowl. Season with salt, pepper, and the cumin. Cover and let rest for 2 hours, then mix in the dill and mint.

2. While the wheat mixture is resting, drain the grape leaves and rinse well in a colander. Bring a large pot of water to a rolling boil and blanch the grape leaves, in batches if necessary, for 4 to 5 minutes. Drain and immediately rinse under cold running water. Trim the tough stems off the leaves and set aside the ones that are either very small or torn.

3. Place the grape leaves, shiny side down, in rows on a large table. Place the ripped or very small ones on the bottom of a large pot. Place a heaping teaspoon of filling in the bottom center of each leaf

on the table. Fold the bottom over the filling, then fold the sides over it and roll up, tucking the sides in as you go (see page 465). Place the grape leaves seam side down in the pot, snugly next to each other, in layers. Pour the lemon juice over them, then pour in enough water to barely cover the surface of the *dolmathes.* Cut a piece of parchment to the circumference of the pot and fit it over the leaves. Cover with a plate to keep the grape leaves in place and place the lid on the pot. Simmer until the leaves and cracked wheat are tender and the pot juices absorbed, about 50 minutes. Remove from the heat and serve.

Black-Eyed Peas Topped with Caramelized Onions from Nisyros

TA PAPFOUTHIA TIS NYSSIROU

Makes 4 to 6 servings

Black-eyed peas, *either fresh or dried, have long been the food of sustenance on tiny Nisyros. This simple recipe is reminiscent of other legume dishes topped with caramelized onion, a trademark throughout the Dodecanese.*

½ pound dried black-eyed peas, picked over and rinsed

Salt to taste

½ cup extra-virgin olive oil

2 to 4 tablespoons red wine vinegar, to taste

⅓ cup chopped fresh flat-leaf parsley

2 medium onions, very finely chopped

1 recipe Onions Caramelized in Olive Oil (page 362)

1. Place the black-eyed peas in a pot with enough water to cover by 3 inches. Bring to a boil. Drain and place back in the pot with fresh water to cover. Bring to a boil, reduce the heat to medium-low, and simmer until tender but still intact, about 45 minutes. Five minutes before removing from the heat, season with salt. Remove from the heat and drain.

2. Place the black-eyed peas in a serving bowl and toss with the olive oil, vinegar, parsley, and chopped onions. Top with the caramelized onions. Serve immediately.

PASTA

There are numerous dishes combining pasta and beans in the Dodecanese. Throughout the rest of Greece, with the exception of at least one old Jewish recipe I know of from Corfu, pasta is generally not cooked with pulses. But in the southeastern Aegean, all the way down to Cyprus, the combination is a common one and the dishes are often spiced with the likes of cinnamon, allspice, or cumin.

Chickpeas Baked with Tagliatelle and Spices from Rhodes

MATSI ME REVITHIA

 Makes 6 to 8 servings

1½ cups dried chickpeas, picked over, rinsed, and soaked for 8 hours in ample water
1 large red onion, coarsely chopped
1 cinnamon stick
4 to 5 allspice berries, to taste
1 bay leaf
Salt to taste
1 pound tagliatelle
1½ cups peeled, seeded, and chopped plum tomatoes (canned are fine) or 1½ cups grated firm, ripe tomatoes (see page 459)
⅓ to ½ cup extra-virgin olive oil, to taste
Freshly ground black pepper to taste

1. Rinse and drain the soaked chickpeas. Place in a pot with the onion and pour in enough water to cover by about 2 inches. Bring to a boil. Reduce the heat to medium-low, add the spices and bay leaf, and simmer until the chickpeas are almost completely cooked, about 1½ hours. Skim the foam off the surface as the chickpeas simmer. They will be al dente when done. Do not drain. Preheat the oven to 375°F.

2. Bring a large pot of salted water to a boil and add the pasta about 5 minutes before the chickpeas are done. Simmer until half cooked, about 5 minutes. Drain and rinse immediately with cold water.

3. Place the pasta, chickpeas, pot liquid, and spices in a large baking pan. Pour in the tomatoes, toss with olive oil, and season generously with salt and pepper. Add more water if necessary to keep the mixture moist. Bake until the chickpeas and pasta are both tender, about 20 minutes. Remove from the oven, discard the spices, and serve.

Lentils Cooked with Orzo and Topped with Caramelized Onions from Rhodes

FAKES ME KRITHARAKI KAI SYVRASI APO TIN RODO

 Makes about 4 servings

I want to believe that the practice of cooking beans and pasta together somehow came to the Dodecanese via the Italians who occupied the islands for 50 years, starting from the end of the nineteenth century. But the Italians were so disdained that it seems unlikely islanders anywhere would adopt their oppressors' food habits, and anyway a very similar dish to this one is also found in Cyprus. The combination of pasta and beans is found in one other part of the country—the Ionian Islands—where the Venetian presence was strong for more than 400 years.

You'll notice that for the main part of the dish the onion is not cooked in oil first, but rather boiled directly with the lentils. Although I think you get a better, sweeter taste out of the onion when it has been softened in oil, I decided to stay true to the local technique here, because cooks in these parts, as elsewhere in Greece, sometimes will tell you that a dish becomes exceedingly heavy with the addition of oil-cooked onions.

½ pound dried lentils, picked over and rinsed

1 large onion, minced

1 large bay leaf

2 to 3 dried Greek oregano sprigs or 1 teaspoon ground

Salt to taste

¼ pound orzo

Freshly ground black pepper to taste

¼ cup extra-virgin olive oil

1 recipe Onions Caramelized in Olive Oil (page 362)

1. Place the lentils in a pot with enough water to cover by 3 inches and bring to a boil. Add the onion, bay leaf, and oregano, reduce the heat to medium-low, and simmer until the lentils are almost cooked through, 20 to 25 minutes.

2. Season with salt and add the orzo. Increase the heat and bring to a boil. Reduce the heat to medium-low and simmer until the orzo is tender and most of the liquid is absorbed. Adjust the seasoning with additional salt, if necessary, and pepper. Pour in the olive oil. Serve the lentils and orzo in a deep plate, topped with the caramelized onions. Serve hot.

Pasta with Yogurt and Caramelized Onions from Kassos

MAKAROUNES TIS KASSOU

 Makes 4 to 6 servings

I lived on this dish, despite the summer heat, when I visited Kassos. Virtually the same dish is prepared in Karpathos and many other of the Dodecanese Islands. There is something so sating about the combination of good drained yogurt, fresh pasta, and caramelized onions. The sweetness of the onions is balanced by the tartness of the yogurt, and the whole thing makes for one of the best—and easiest—dishes in all of Greek cooking. One caveat: The yogurt must be good-quality, Mediterranean-style thick or drained yogurt. If you can find sheep's milk yogurt, all the better.

There are several variations of the dish. Often it is

doused not with yogurt but with browned sitaka *(page 358), akin to clarified butter or* ghee.

Salt

1 pound tagliatelle or penne (preferably fresh)

2 cups preferably sheep's milk yogurt, drained (see page 459), or 1½ cups sour cream mixed with 1 cup plain yogurt

½ to 1 cup coarsely grated *kefalotyri* cheese or any sharp, hard grating cheese to taste

1 recipe Onions Caramelized in Olive Oil (page 362)

1. Bring a pot of salted water to a boil and cook the pasta to desired doneness. Combine the drained yogurt or sour cream and yogurt with ½ cup of the pasta cooking water and mix well. Drain the pasta and toss with the yogurt or sour cream mixture.

2. Serve on individual plates or on a serving platter, sprinkled generously with the grated cheese and topped with the caramelized onions and their juices.

⊙

Sweetened Noodles Cooked with Tahini

MATSI ME TAHINI APO TIN AFANTOU

 Makes 8 to 10 servings

This recipe comes from a village in the interior of Rhodes called Afandou. During Lent, when butter and, on certain days, oil, were forbidden, tahini (sesame paste) assumed an important place in local kitchens all over Greece. This odd dish for pasta, cooked with tahini, is a sweet made almost exclusively on Good Friday, when the strictest abstentions are in order. There are other, similar dishes for sweetened pasta found not only in Rhodes but elsewhere in the Dodecanese and in Crete. In Rhodes, another dish calls for boiling noodles (usually homemade) in milk and serving them with sugar, cinnamon, and sesame seeds. In nearby Crete, sweet pasta was served to new mothers in the belief that rich, calorie-filled foods helped them produce more milk.

I am not sure how appealing noodles cooked with tahini will be to modern tastebuds. It's an interesting dish, however, and an odd one, little known even in Greece these days. Nevertheless, I list it here if for nothing else than posterity. Matsi, a traditional Rhodian pasta, are flat and wide like tagliatelle but short. One local cook gave me her trick for simulating the original dish with store-bought noodles—just break them into pieces.

1 pound tagliatelle or other noodlelike pasta, preferably made without eggs

Salt to taste

6 tablespoons sesame seeds, toasted (see page 458)

1 teaspoon ground cinnamon

1 cup tahini (sesame paste)

½ cup sugar

1. Break the pasta into pieces about 1½ inches long. Bring a pot of lightly salted water to a boil and add the pasta. (There should be just enough water to cover the pasta by 2 inches. Remove any excess with a ladle.) Simmer the pasta until soft. Meanwhile, grind the sesame seeds and cinnamon together with a mortar and pestle.

2. Place the tahini and sugar in a small bowl and beat with an electric mixer. Add a ladleful of the hot pasta liquid to the bowl and beat the tahini mixture until smooth and creamy. As soon as the pasta is cooked, remove from the heat and pour the tahini mixture into the pot. Stir to combine.

3. To serve: Place the hot noodles and their liquid in individual bowls and top with 1 tablespoon of the ground sesame seeds and cinnamon.

MEAT

The meat and poultry dishes included here are a combination of ordinary, everyday dishes and more festive fare. As I mention in the general introduction to the region, some of the culinary habits in this part of Greece closely resemble those in the Near East and Cyprus, such as the use of bulgur and meat together, in patties or meatballs, which are similar to the *kibbe* of Lebanese, Israeli, and other Middle Eastern cuisines. But there are dishes that bespeak the commonest Greek island traditions, too, such as the ones for stuffed lamb, a preparation found in endless variety all over the Aegean.

Chicken Stewed with Tomatoes and Sage

KOTOPOULO ME ALESFAKIA

 Makes 4 to 6 servings

This otherwise common stew takes on another note when it is prepared in the mountain village of Koskinou, not too far from Rhodes's capital. There home cooks flavor the dish with sage, which is otherwise usually reserved for teas and infusions in Greece.

4 to 6 tablespoons extra-virgin olive oil, as needed
One 3- to 3½-pound chicken, cut into serving pieces
2 large onions, coarsely chopped
Salt and freshly ground black pepper to taste
1½ cups peeled, seeded, and chopped plum tomatoes (canned are fine)
1 to 2 dried sage sprigs, to taste
½ cup dry white wine (optional)

1. Heat the olive oil in a large, wide pot or Dutch oven over medium-high heat and sear the chicken, turning, until golden brown on all sides, about 6 minutes. Remove with a slotted spoon and set aside. Add the onions to the pot and cook, stirring, until translucent and lightly colored, about 6 minutes.

2. Place the chicken pieces back in the pot and season with salt and pepper. Pour in the tomatoes and add enough water just to come about two-thirds of the way up the chicken. Add the sage sprigs to the pot. Reduce the heat to medium-low, cover, and simmer until the chicken is tender and cooked through, about 1 hour. Five minutes before removing from the heat, add the wine, if using. Remove from the heat and serve.

Bulgur or Cracked Wheat and Meatballs Cooked on a Bed of Onions

VOLOI ME PYRGOURI

 Makes 25 to 30 meatballs;
6 to 8 servings

Bulgur and ground meat are the two ingredients in that masterpiece of eastern Mediterranean cooking, kibbe, *in which the ground meat is encased in a bulgur shell and usually fried. Greeks (with the exception of those living in Cyprus, where a local dish called* koupes *is pretty much the same thing as* kibbe*) generally do not make wheat-encrusted meatballs, but they do cook meat and wheat together in several old dishes. I liked this classic Rhodian dish because it is a rendition of the traditional Greek* yuverlakia, *which are meatballs studded with rice, cooked in broth, and served with either yogurt or* avgolemono. *Here rice, an expensive ingredient on the tables of yore, is replaced by bulgur, and* avgolemono *is supplanted by tomato sauce. It is a lovely dish in cool weather. It goes nicely with a side of plain drained Greek yogurt or with some boiled or stewed greens.*

This recipe is adapted from Roditikes Syntages (Rhodian Recipes) *by the Lyceio Ellinidon of Rhodes.*

1 pound lean ground beef
1 large onion, finely chopped
1 cup fine bulgur
2 garlic cloves, minced
Salt and freshly ground black pepper to taste
3 tablespoons extra-virgin olive oil
3 large onions, thinly sliced and separated into rings
2 large ripe tomatoes, grated (see page 459)
1 cup water

1. Combine the ground beef, chopped onion, bulgur, and half the garlic in a medium bowl, season with salt and pepper, and knead until a dense mass forms. Set aside, covered, for 1 hour.

2. Take a golf ball–size piece at a time, shape the mixture into oblong little sausages or into meatballs. Set aside.

3. Heat the olive oil in a medium pot over medium heat and cook the onion rings, stirring, until wilted, about 7 minutes. Add the remaining garlic and cook together for 1 minute. Add the tomatoes and water. Season with salt and pepper and bring to a simmer.

4. Place the little meat-and-bulgur balls in the pot on top of the onions mixture. Add enough water to come about two-thirds of the way up the contents of the pot. Cover, reduce the heat to low, and simmer until tender, about 50 minutes. Remove from the heat and serve hot.

Leg of Lamb or Goat Roasted with Bulgur or Cracked Wheat and Cumin

PASCHATI

 Makes 6 to 8 servings

*It would have been redundant to recount all the Easter lamb dishes of the Dodecanese. Most share one overriding characteristic: They call for stuffing a baby lamb (or goat) and cooking it in a clay vessel in a low oven for hours. These stuffed dishes go by myriad names—*vyzanti *in Karpathos,* kapamas *or* lakani *(which means "cavity" or "basin") or* lapas *(the word for soft rice in Greek) in Rhodes; and* mououri *in Kalymnos, where the dish is named after the stout clay vase in which it is cooked. The list goes on. These dishes don't vary greatly from the stuffed lamb dishes that are traditional in other Aegean islands and for which several recipes also appear in other chapters. In the Dodecanese most call for either bulgur or rice as the mainstay of the stuffing, together with sautéed chopped liver, raisins, and herbs. Cumin is the preferred spice, something not found readily in islands outside the Dodecanese.*

I've opted to include just one Easter lamb recipe, Paschati *(after the word for Easter in Greek), from the mountain village of Agios Isidoros in Rhodes, which calls for roasting the lamb together with bulgur instead of stuffing it.*

1 leg of lamb or goat, bone in (about 6 pounds)
3 tablespoons extra-virgin olive oil
Salt and freshly ground black pepper to taste
1 tablespoon dried thyme
½ cup (1 stick) unsalted butter
4 large onions, finely chopped
1 tablespoon ground cumin
¼ cup tomato paste
1 cup bulgur
½ cup water
2½ cups boiling water

1. Preheat the oven to 425°F. Trim the fat off the meat and discard. Rub the leg with the olive oil, and then with salt, pepper, and the thyme. Place in the center of a large roasting pan and place in the oven. Roast until the surface of the meat is browned, about 1 hour.

2. Meanwhile, melt the butter in a large skillet over medium heat and cook the onions until wilted. Add the cumin and stir. Add the tomato paste, season with salt and pepper, and stir together. Add the bulgur, cook for about a minute, then pour in the ½ cup water. Reduce the heat to medium-low and cook until the water is absorbed, 3 to 4 minutes. Remove from the heat and fluff with a fork.

3. Place the bulgur mixture in the roasting pan around the lamb. Pour the boiling water into the pan, stirring it into the bulgur. Place the pan back in the oven. Roast until the meat is tender and the bulgur cooked, another 35 to 40 minutes. Remove from the oven, let cool slightly, and serve on a platter, with the leg of lamb or goat in the center and the bulgur fluffed and spooned around it.

FISH AND SEAFOOD

The best Dodecanese fish dishes are the simplest: fresh fish brought in daily from the legions of local fishermen who make their livelihood at sea, simply grilled. It's the Greek island classic, one for which there is no recipe beyond procuring the best possible catch, grilling it skillfully, preferably over a wood or coal fire, and dressing it with olive oil, lemon juice, and salt.

But there are a few unusual preparations to contend with from these parts, too. I love the octopus recipe from Kalymnos. To my mind and palate, it has only those from Ithaca as competition, where the cephalopod is also counted highly among local cooks. I love the unusual fish dish from Rhodes with tahini sauce, one more in a long litany of dishes from the island that call for what apparently is one of its most revered ingredients.

I think you will find these recipes delicious and easy, foods that can be cooked up as both festive and common fare.

GRILLED OCTOPUS DIPPED IN OUZO

OUZOHTAPOTHO

▼

"This isn't really a recipe," my acquaintance and guide Giorgos explained. "You just kind of do it, casually, as you sit around enjoying a little grilled octopus." The combination—grilled octopus and ouzo—is divine.

There are two schools of thought when it comes to grilling octopus. Some cooks believe the octopus should be boiled first to soften it, then grilled. Some even go so far as to say the octopus should be skinned so that only its pinkish white flesh shows. I am of the latter school, among those cooks who believe that octopus should be grilled without boiling. Grilled octopus, like great steak, is not something that should melt in your mouth but something you need to work at, chew well, and force the flavor out of. Boiling makes it insipid.

Have a grill ready. Cut an octopus of 3 to 4 pounds into pieces, each with a tentacle. Brush each tentacle with a little olive oil and grill until dark purple-black and leathery. Remove from the grill. Dip each grilled tentacle into the ouzo (about 2 ounces) and serve. It's as simple as that.

Octopus Patties from Kalymnos

HTAPOTHOKEFTEDES APO TIN KALYMNO

 Makes sixteen to twenty 2-inch patties; 4 to 6 servings

This is Kalymnos's major contribution to the Greek meze *table. It's an island classic and a great dish.*

1 octopus (2½ to 3 pounds), cleaned
  (see page 462)
2 to 3 barley or whole wheat rusks (see Note)
1 large onion, finely chopped
2 to 3 garlic cloves, to taste, minced
1 teaspoon dried savory
2 large eggs, lightly beaten
Salt and freshly ground black pepper to taste
1 cup all-purpose flour for dredging
Olive or other vegetable oil for frying

1. Place the cleaned octopus in a medium pot, cover, and cook over very low heat with no liquid until the octopus is bright pink and tender, 45 to 50 minutes. Remove from the heat and let cool slightly.

2. Break up the barley rusks and grind them to a fine crumb either with a mortar and pestle or in a food processor.

3. Using a large, sharp knife or meat grinder, mince the octopus so that it is more or less the consistency of ground meat.

4. Combine the octopus, two thirds of the ground rusks, the onion, garlic, savory, and eggs in a large bowl. The mixture should be dense and mealy. If it is too loose, add a little more rusk. Season if necessary with salt and pepper. Cover and refrigerate for 1 hour to firm the mixture up.

5. Spread the flour on a large plate. Shape the octopus mixture into small patties. Heat about ¼ inch of oil in a large, heavy skillet over medium-high heat. When the oil is very hot, dredge the patties lightly in the flour, tapping off any excess. Fry several patties at a time until golden, turning to cook on both sides, 4 to 5 minutes. Remove with a slotted spoon, let drain on paper towels, and serve hot.

✳ **NOTE** Barley or whole wheat rusks, *paximathia* in Greek, can be found in Greek or Middle Eastern specialty food shops.

Whole Fish Baked with Tahini Sauce

PSARI PSIMENO ME SALTSA TAHINI

Makes 2 to 4 servings

Tahini is rarely used as a sauce in Greek cuisine. I like to serve this with the tomato and sea urchin salad (page 363) as a starter.

Salt to taste
2 large whole groupers, snappers, or other white
    fish suitable for baking (2 to 2½ pounds
    each), cleaned and gutted
Juice of 1 lemon
2 large onions, halved and thinly sliced
2 garlic cloves, very thinly sliced
2 large ripe tomatoes, grated (see page 459)
2 tablespoons tahini (sesame paste)
¼ cup water
⅔ cup dry white wine
Freshly ground black pepper to taste
3 tablespoons finely chopped fresh flat-leaf
    parsley

1. Salt the fish inside and out and sprinkle with the lemon juice. Cover with plastic wrap and set aside until ready to use.

2. Preheat the oven to 350°F. Lightly oil a glass baking dish large enough to hold the fish. Place the onions, garlic, and half the tomatoes on the bottom of the baking dish. Place the fish on top and set in the oven. Bake until the onions begin to soften, about 10 minutes.

3. Meanwhile, whisk together the tahini and water. Pour over the fish and add the remaining tomatoes as well as the wine. Season with pepper and additional salt if desired. Bake until the fish is fork-tender and the vegetables are cooked, about 30 minutes. Remove from the oven, sprinkle with the parsley, and serve hot.

Stuffed Red Mullet from Lipsi

BARBOUNIA GEMISTA ME GALETA

Makes 4 to 6 servings

Red mullet is one of the quintessential Greek fish. It is also one of those fish people tend either to love or hate because of its distinct "muddy" taste. The most common way to prepare it is just to flour and fry it, but throughout the Aegean islands the fish also appears in several "cooked" recipes, with sauces or stuffings. This one, from the tiny island of Lipsi, is unusual in that the fish is stuffed with and surrounded by a bread crumb–thickened sauce.

2½ pounds medium red mullet, cleaned and
    gutted
Salt to taste

Juice of 2 lemons

1½ cups fresh bread crumbs or ground barley rusks

3 to 4 garlic cloves, to taste, minced

½ cup plus 2 tablespoons chopped fresh flat-leaf parsley

Freshly ground black pepper to taste

1 cup warm water

½ cup extra-virgin olive oil

½ cup dry white wine

1. Sprinkle the mullet with salt inside and out and then with the lemon juice. Cover with plastic wrap and refrigerate until ready to use.

2. In a bowl, combine the bread crumbs, garlic, ½ cup of the parsley, and a little salt and pepper. Toss with the warm water. Heat 2 tablespoons of the olive oil in a medium nonstick skillet over medium heat and add the bread crumb mixture, stirring, until golden, about 3 minutes. Remove from the skillet, set aside, and wipe the skillet clean.

3. Fill each mullet with 1 or 2 tablespoons of the bread crumb mixture and press down to secure closed. Heat the remaining 6 tablespoons olive oil in a large, heavy nonstick skillet over medium-high heat and fry the stuffed mullets, in batches if necessary. Turn once to brown on both sides. Remove from the skillet and place, covered, in a low oven to keep warm.

4. Heat the remaining stuffing in the skillet over medium heat. Place the browned fish on top, add the wine, and heat until the liquid has been absorbed, 2 to 3 minutes. Remove from the heat and serve, sprinkled, if desired, with the remaining 2 tablespoons chopped parsley.

BREAD

Olive Bread from Rhodes

ELIOPSOMO RODOU

 Makes one 12-inch round loaf

I've seen this bread prepared in two ways in Rhodes, in the form of small buns covered with sesame and nigella seeds or as a larger, round bread made by sandwiching the olives between two layers of dough.

Traditional cooks also make traditional sourdough starter with a fistful of leftover dough from their previous bread baking, which they leave to ferment in a bowl of warm water, covered, all day. Then, at night, they take a certain amount of flour (about one-fifth of the total) from the quantity to be used for the fresh batch of bread and mix this into the thick sourdough-water mixture to make a small ball of dough, which they cover and leave to rise overnight. This ball becomes the starter for the fresh batch of bread. They place it in a large, usually clay bowl or in a wooden bread trough and add the remaining flour and lightly salted water, enough to make a dense, malleable bread dough. Sometimes they also add olive oil.

Rhodian olive bread traditionally is made this way. The onions are worked into the dough, but the olives are added last, once the dough is formed and as it is being kneaded. It is similar to the onion-flavored olive bread from Cyprus, with one exception: In the Cypriote version mint is used, whereas in Rhodes no herbs go into the bread.

For the sake of time and convenience I have modified the recipe to begin with yeast.

For the starter
One ¼-ounce envelope active dry yeast
¾ cup warm water
2 cups bread flour, or more as needed

For the dough
2 teaspoons salt
2 to 2½ cups warm water, as needed
⅓ cup extra-virgin olive oil
1 medium onion, minced or grated
6 to 7 cups bread flour, as needed
1½ cups wrinkled black olives, pitted
2 teaspoons sesame seeds
2 teaspoons nigella seeds

1. Start the night before: Dissolve the yeast in the ¾ cup warm water. Add the 2 cups flour to the mixture and stir until a small dough mass begins to form. Knead it, adding a little more flour if necessary to make the dough smooth. You should have about a fist-size piece of dough. Place it in an oiled bowl, cover it with plastic wrap, and leave it to rise overnight in a warm, draft-free place.

2. The next morning, place the starter in a large bowl. Mix the salt into 2 cups of the warm water and pour into the bowl. Stir the starter and water together. Add the olive oil and onion and mix. Slowly add 6 cups of the flour, mixing with a wooden spoon until a dough mass begins to form. Knead, adding more flour or water if necessary to form a firm, smooth dough. This may be done in a stand mixer fitted with a dough hook. Knead until smooth, 10 to 12 minutes by hand, slightly less in a mixer.

3. Divide the dough into 4 equal balls. Shape each into a round disk about 10 inches in diameter. Spread half the olives over the first disk. Cover with another disk. Knead lightly together to join the 2 halves. Repeat with the remaining two disks and olives. Set aside in 2 lightly oiled shallow 12-inch

round pans. Cover and let rise in a warm, draft-free place until doubled in bulk, about 2 hours.

4. While the dough is rising, preheat the oven to 375°F. Sprinkle 1 teaspoon each of the sesame and nigella seeds over each of the breads. Bake until golden and set, about 50 minutes. To tell whether the bread is baked, remove from the pan and tap the bottom; it should sound hollow. Remove from the pans and let cool on wire racks before slicing.

Sweet Tahini Bread from Rhodes

TAHINOPSOMO

 Makes two 12-inch round loaves

All over Greece on the first day of Lent, called Clean or Pure Monday, people eat a special flatbread known as lagana. *In Rhodes the start of Lent was usually marked by tahini bread, not* lagana. *In many villages, especially in the untouristed, mountainous interior, home cooks still make it.*

For the starter
One ¼-ounce envelope active dry yeast
¾ cup warm water
2 cups bread flour, or more as needed

For the dough
½ teaspoon mastic crystals
½ cup plus 1 teaspoon sugar
1 cup tahini (sesame paste)
1 teaspoon salt
1 teaspoon ground cinnamon
6 to 7 cups bread flour, as needed

½ teaspoon ground cloves

2½ cups warm water

½ cup sesame seeds

1. Prepare the starter the night before: Dissolve the yeast in the ¾ cup warm water. Add the 2 cups flour to the mixture and stir until a small dough mass begins to form. Knead it, adding a little more flour if necessary to make the dough smooth. You should have about a fist-size piece of dough. Place it in an oiled bowl, cover it with plastic wrap, and leave it to rise overnight in a warm, draft-free place.

2. The next morning, place the starter in a large bowl. Using a mortar and pestle or spice mill, pulverize the mastic crystals together with 1 teaspoon of the sugar.

3. Using an electric mixer, whip the tahini together with the remaining ½ cup sugar and the salt until smooth. Beat in 1 cup of the warm water and whip until the mixture is thick.

4. Add the remaining 1½ cups warm water to the bowl with the dough starter. Add the tahini mixture and spices and mix thoroughly. Slowly add 6 cups of the flour, mixing with a wooden spoon until a dough mass begins to form. Knead, adding more flour if necessary to form a firm, smooth dough. This may be done in a stand mixer fitted with a dough hook. Knead until smooth, 10 to 12 minutes by hand, slightly less in a mixer.

5. Divide the dough into 2 equal balls. Shape each into a large, round loaf, about 10 inches in diameter. Spread ¼ cup of the sesame seeds on a large flat plate. Flip a loaf over so that the top is sitting in the sesame seeds and gently pat it down so that the sesame seeds adhere to the surface. Place the loaf in an oiled shallow 12-inch round baking pan. Repeat with the second loaf and the remaining ¼ cup sesame seeds. Cover the loaves with kitchen towels and let rest in a warm, draft-free place until doubled in bulk, about 2 hours.

6. While the dough is rising, preheat the oven to 375°F. Bake until golden, about 50 minutes. Remove from the pans and let cool on a wire rack before slicing.

RUSKS FROM KARPATHOS AND KALYMNOS

Crete has cornered the market as well as the imagination when it comes to Greek barley rusks, laying claim to these twice-baked breads and rightfully calling them one of the foundations of the healthful Cretan diet. Granted, bakers on Crete produce many different rusks, in all shapes and sizes, spiced, plain, sesame-covered, etc. But the humble, exceedingly hard bread that was long the stuff of agrarian and seafaring salvation throughout the Greek islands is also a cornerstone in the cooking of several Dodecanese islands.

One of my most memorable experiences in Kalymnos, the sponge fishermen's island, was sitting with a local acquaintance at a seaside taverna and having him order a delicious *mirmizelli*—a beautiful *café au lait*–colored, tough-as-nails barley rusk that had been softened under the local tap and drizzled with local oil and then served up smothered with onions and sea urchins. In Kalymnos these rusks both sated the hunger and soothed the homesickness of fleet after fleet of sponge divers who spent months at sea, usually off the Libyan coast, where they dove for their livelihood.

Elsewhere in these islands, twice-baked bread is also a veritable culinary tradition. Two more delicious rusks come from the remote island of Karpathos, where islanders show a penchant for a variety of heady spices. In the bakeries in the island's main town, cumin-spiced rusks as well as rusks flavored with onions are common. As elsewhere in Greece, they are dampened and softened and then eaten, usually with olive oil, cheese, olives, and tomato, or simply as a substitute for fresh bread.

Spiced Barley Rusks from Karpathos

KRITHINES KOULOURES

 Makes 20 to 25 rusks

Two ¼-ounce envelopes active dry yeast
2¼ to 2¾ cups warm water, as needed
4 cups barley flour
4 cups all-purpose unbleached flour
2 teaspoons salt
1 tablespoon ground cumin
2 teaspoons ground cinnamon
1 teaspoon freshly grated nutmeg
1 teaspoon ground cloves
2 cups sesame seeds mixed with 1 cup nigella
    seeds

1. Dissolve the yeast in 2¼ cups of the warm water, cover, and let stand for 30 minutes in a warm, draft-free place. In a large bowl, combine 3 cups of the barley flour, 3 cups of the all-purpose flour, the salt, and spices. Make a well in the center and add the yeast-and-water mixture. Work the flour into the liquid with a wooden spoon from the walls of the well until a dough mass begins to form. Knead, either in the bowl or on a lightly floured work surface, adding more of each of the flours or the water as you go until a smooth, firm dough forms. By hand this will take 10 to 15 minutes.

You may also do this in batches in a stand mixer fitted with a dough hook; first mix the yeast mixture with the 6 cups of the flour, salt, and spices until a dough mass forms. Divide it into 4 equal pieces and knead each one separately in the mixer, adding more flour to make a smooth dough. When all the dough has been kneaded, work the separate pieces together to form one large mass. Let the dough rest for 30 minutes, covered with a kitchen towel.

2. Lightly oil 2 sheet pans. Take a small piece (about the size of a lemon) at a time, roll out the dough on a lightly floured work surface to make a dough snake 8 to 10 inches long and a little thicker than a pencil. Shape each strip into a ring, overlapping the ends by about an inch and a half. Have the sesame and nigella seeds spread on a platter and dip the rusks in them to coat. Place on the prepared sheet pans, leaving about 1½ inches between rings. Cover with kitchen towels and leave to rise in a warm, draft-free place until almost doubled in bulk, about 1½ hours.

3. While the *kouloures* are rising, preheat the oven to 375°F. Bake the *kouloures* until light golden and set, about 40 minutes. You may have to do this in batches, depending on how many sheet pans fit into your oven. Rotate them as the bread rings bake. Remove from the oven and let cool completely.

4. Heat the oven to the lowest possible temperature, about 200°F or 250°F. Place the rings on racks in the oven and bake slowly until they are very hard, about 2 hours. Remove from the oven, let cool completely, and store in large tins. They will keep for months in a cool, dry place.

Rusks with Onions and Fennel Seeds from Karpathos

KOULOURES ME KREMMYDI KAI GLYKANISO

 Makes 20 to 25 rusks

Two ¼-ounce envelopes active dry yeast

2½ to 2¾ cups warm water, as needed

4 to 4½ cups barley flour, as needed

4 to 4½ cups all-purpose flour, as needed

2 teaspoons salt

⅓ cup extra-virgin olive oil

1 large onion, finely chopped

3 tablespoons fennel seeds

1. Dissolve the yeast in 2¼ cups of the warm water, cover, and let stand for 30 minutes in a warm, draft-free place. In a large bowl, combine 3 cups of the barley flour, 3 cups of the all-purpose flour, and the salt. Make a well in the center and add the yeast-and-water mixture, olive oil, onion, and fennel seeds. Work the flour into the liquid with a wooden spoon from the wall of the well until a dough mass begins to form. Knead, either in the bowl or on a lightly floured work surface, adding more of each of the flours or the water as you go until a smooth, firm dough forms. By hand this will take 10 to 15 minutes.

You may also do this in batches in a stand mixer fitted with a dough hook; first, mix the yeast mixture with the 6 cups of flour, the salt, oil, onion, and fennel seeds until a dough mass forms. Divide it into 4 equal pieces and knead each one separately in the mixer, adding more flour to make a smooth dough. When all the dough has been kneaded, work the separate pieces together to form one large mass. Place it in a lightly oiled bowl, cover, and let it rest in a warm, draft-free place until doubled in bulk, about 2½ hours.

2. Punch the dough down and knead lightly. Break off golf ball–size pieces of dough. Shape into balls and roll with your palms into long ropes about as thick as a thumb. Shape each rope into a ring, overlapping the ends by about 1½ inches. Press the teeth of a serrated knife lightly into the surface of each rusk. Place on oiled baking sheets, cover, and let rise again in a warm, draft-free place for about 1 hour, until about 1½ times the original size.

3. While the *kouloures* are rising, preheat the oven to 375°F. Bake the *kouloures* until light golden and half baked through, about 20 minutes. You may have to do this in batches, depending on how many sheet pans fit into your oven. Rotate them as the bread rings bake. Remove from the oven and let cool completely.

4. Heat the oven to the lowest possible temperature, 200°F or 250°F. Place the rings on racks in the oven and bake slowly until they are very hard, about 2 hours. Remove from the oven, let cool completely, and store in large tins.

SWEETS

The sweets of the Dodecanese are among the most unusual in Greece. The use of tahini in pies, the taste for sweetened pasta dishes of yore, the highly unusual, almost ancient in its spirit, sweet wheat soup called *chrysafi* (see page 364) all attest to the unique characteristics of these islands' local specialties. Of course, all the other Greek sweets are made here, too, from spoon sweets to baklavas to honey-drenched biscuits and sugar-dusted shortbread cookies, but I have opted to omit them all throughout the book just because they are not place specific. (You can find these classics in my first book, *The Food and Wine of Greece.*)

All those interested in trying their hand at some of the sweets that follow should be prepared for a taste of the unusual and the exotic.

Lenten Tahini Pies from the Village of Arhangelos in Rhodes

TAHINOPITES APO TON ARHANGELOS

 Makes 10 small pies

These flattened, coiled sesame-paste pies are similar to a recipe found in Cyprus and attest to the many similarities between Cypriote and Dodecanese cuisine. Tahini pies were traditionally grilled on the bottom of a wood-burning oven but nowadays are more likely to be "grilled" in a nonstick skillet. They are the traditional sweet on Clean Monday, the first day of Lent, but they also make great breakfast food.

4 to 4½ cups all-purpose flour, as needed

½ teaspoon salt

1 tablespoon active dry yeast

1½ cups plus ⅓ cup warm water

⅔ cup tahini (sesame paste)

⅔ cup sugar

1 scant teaspoon ground cinnamon

1 scant teaspoon ground cloves

1 scant teaspoon freshly grated nutmeg

1 cup sesame seeds

1. Combine 4 cups of the flour and the salt in a medium bowl and make a well in the center. Dissolve the yeast in 1½ cups of the warm water and pour the mixture into the well. Work the flour from the wall of the well into the liquid with a wooden spoon until a dough mass begins to form. Knead in the bowl until smooth, adding a little more flour if necessary. Shape into a ball, cover the bowl, and let stand in a warm, draft-free place for 30 minutes.

2. Using an electric mixer, whip together the tahini and the remaining ⅓ cup warm water, slowly adding the sugar and working it in with the mixer. In a small bowl, combine the cinnamon, cloves, and nutmeg.

3. On a lightly floured work surface, using a rolling pin, roll an egg-size piece of the dough into a circle about 10 inches in diameter. Spread 1½ to 2 tablespoons of the tahini mixture over the surface of the dough. Sprinkle with a little of the spice mixture and then with a tablespoon or so of the sesame seeds. Roll up the dough tightly to form a cylinder and shape this into a coil. Flatten it gently with your palms or with the rolling pin. The seams of the coil should still show once the bread is flattened. Repeat with the remaining dough, filling, and sesame seeds.

4. Heat a nonstick skillet over high heat. Place the first *tahinopita* in the skillet, reduce the heat to medium-low, and cook until golden on one side, about 6 minutes. Flip and brown on the other side, 3 to 5 minutes. The key is to do this over relatively low heat so that the inside cooks through. Remove from the skillet and serve, either warm or at room temperature. Repeat with the remaining *tahinopites.*

Fried Baklava from Rhodes

TAKAKIA

 Makes 25 to 30 pieces

Fried baklava is found all over the Dodecanese, but especially in Kastellorizo, where it is called strava, and in Karpathos, and in Rhodes, where the dessert is known as takakia. It is a classic on the Christmas table. You will need a long ⅛-inch-diameter dowel for this.

For the pastry
4 to 4½ cups all-purpose flour, as needed
½ teaspoon salt
1½ to 1¾ cups water, as needed

For the filling
2½ cups blanched almonds
2 cups walnuts
2 heaping teaspoons ground cinnamon
¼ cup sugar

For the syrup
2½ cups honey
1¼ cups water

To fry
Vegetable oil for frying

1. Make the pastry: Combine 4 cups of the flour and the salt in a large bowl and make a well in the center. Add 1½ cups of the water and work the flour into the water from the wall of the well with a fork or wooden spoon until a dough mass forms. If it is too dense, add a little more water; if it is too loose, add more flour. Knead on a lightly floured work surface until silky and smooth. The dough should be relatively firm. Cover and let rest for 30 minutes.

2. Make the filling: Pulverize the nuts in a food processor until ground and mealy. Transfer to a bowl and mix in the cinnamon and sugar. Set aside.

3. Make the syrup: Bring the honey and water to a boil in a medium saucepan, reduce the heat to medium-low, and simmer for 10 minutes. Remove from the heat and let cool.

4. Divide the dough into 3 equal pieces and shape each into a ball. On a lightly floured work surface, using a rolling pin, roll the first ball into a circle about 18 inches in diameter. Sprinkle the surface with one-third of the nut mixture. Fold the bottom edge of the pastry over the nuts, making a "lip" that is about 1½ inches wide. Place the dowel in the center and roll up the nut-covered pastry circle tightly along the dowel. Push the two ends of the pastry toward the center, to shirr or gather, as for curtains. Slip the dowel out and place the shirred roll seam side down on the work surface. Repeat with the remaining pastry and filling. Cut the rolls diagonally into 1½-inch pieces.

5. Heat 4 inches of vegetable oil in a large, heavy pot over medium-high heat. When the oil is very hot, deep-fry the *takakia* until golden and cooked through, 3 to 4 minutes. The key here is that the oil needs to be hot but not exceedingly so, lest the pastries brown on the outside but remain uncooked in the center. Remove with a slotted spoon and let drain on paper towels. Dip each piece in the honey syrup and place on a serving platter. Serve. To store, place in pleated paper pastry cups and keep in tins in a cool, dry place. They will keep for several weeks.

Carnival Cheese Crescents with Pepper and Honey from Karpathos

APOKRIATIKA POUNGIA TIS KARPATHOU

 Makes about 8 servings

For the pastry
2 to 2¼ cups all-purpose flour, as needed
½ teaspoon salt
1 teaspoon active dry yeast
¾ cup warm water
¼ cup extra-virgin olive oil

For the filling
1½ cups fresh *myzithra* or whole-milk ricotta
    cheese
⅓ cup sugar
1 heaping teaspoon ground cinnamon
Freshly ground black pepper to taste
1 large egg, lightly beaten

To serve
Greek (preferably thyme) honey for drizzling or
    1 recipe Onions Caramelized in Olive Oil
    (page 362)

1. Make the pastry: Combine 2 cups of the flour and the salt in a large bowl. Dissolve the yeast in the warm water, cover, and leave for 5 minutes. Make a well in the center of the flour and add the water-and-yeast mixture and the olive oil. Work the flour from the wall of the well into the liquid with a fork or wooden spoon until a dough mass forms. Knead in the bowl or on a lightly floured work surface, adding more flour if necessary, to form a smooth, pliant dough. Shape into a ball. Brush a clean bowl with olive oil and turn the dough in the bowl to coat with oil. Cover and let rise in a warm, draft-free place for 1 hour.

2. Make the filling: In a large bowl, combine the cheese, sugar, cinnamon, and pepper. Add the egg and mix thoroughly.

3. Cover 2 sheet pans with parchment paper and butter lightly. Preheat the oven to 350°F. Divide the dough into 4 equal balls. Using a rolling pin on a lightly floured work surface, roll the first ball into a large sheet. Cut circles out of the dough using a glass or circular cookie cutter with a diameter of 4 inches. Keep covered. Reknead and reroll any scraps and cut out more circles. Place a scant tablespoon of the filling in the center of each pastry circle and fold over to form a crescent. Press the edges closed, either with the tips of your fingers or with the tines of a fork. Repeat with the remaining dough balls and filling. Place the crescents in neat rows 1 inch apart on the sheet pans and bake until golden, about 35 minutes. Remove from the oven. To serve, drizzle with honey or top with the caramelized onions. They will keep, covered and refrigerated, for up to 5 days.

✳ **NOTE** The pastry may also be rolled open using a pasta maker. Follow the directions for rolling and filling as indicated in steps 4 and 5 of Chard-Filled Ravioli (page 326).

Crete

A Sense of Place and Palate

It was early December the first time I visited Crete. I had arrived mid-morning, and by late afternoon I had made it up to Amari, a village in the mountains above the old Venetian port of Rethymno on the central-western part of the island. It was dark. A slow rain sank into everything. It had been drizzling for days, and the water had finally taxed the local power supply into temporary oblivion. The only sources of light were our headlights and the wood fire flickering through a crack in the door of a small barn at the far end of the village. Inside, the *kazani,* or still, purred, and from its spout came dripping out a potent brew: *raki* or *tsikouthia,* as it is called in Crete, aka eau de vie, distilled from the residuals of the local wine grapes.

I had come to witness this yearly winter ritual, as well as other things in Crete, from the island's mythic, heart-saving diet, exemplar of simplicity and variety, to its seemingly limitless flora—over half the twelve thousand indigenous plants in Europe are found on Minos's island.

Around the still stood a handful of village men, cups in hand, stooping every so often to catch some of the warm liquid spirit as it came sputtering out. Whether it's had straight and warm or, later, from the bottle, *raki* is the stuff of machismo posturing. But even in Crete, where men sport pistols and mustaches with equal ease, and where blood feuds are a matter of everyday justice, no man dares drink *raki* without simultaneously settling his stomach with some food. On the few chairs around the old copper still, *mezethes* were spread haphazardly over butcher's paper and small plates. The array was typical of this island's startlingly simple cuisine: green olives steeped in bitter orange juice, dried and toasted fava beans that tasted like a cross between chestnuts and popcorn, baked dried figs dipped in grape must, heavily salted sardines, a *meze* that is de rigueur during the ritual of the firing up of the still, and a local sheep's milk cheese called *tis tripas,* which literally means "from the hole" for the way it is aged in mountain caves. A grill in the corner sizzled with some pork chops. Someone tossed a few foil-wrapped potatoes under the embers, and when they emerged, soft and wrinkled like elephant's skin, I was shown the savoir vivre of savoring them—placing one on the table, pounding it lightly with my fist until it burst, then dousing it with olive oil and salt and eating it, steaming hot, straight from the skin. On hand, too, was another Cretan staple: the thick, rock-hard, twice-baked bread rusks called *eptazymo,* which are made with chickpea flour. Depending on whom you ask, the word is said to mean either "kneaded seven times" or "self-rising." But it is also known as the devil's bread, derided by old local priests because it requires no leavening to swell, leaving room for the folk belief that magic makes it rise. In Crete there is a tale for almost everything on the table.

I was later to go back to Crete several times in search of food and lore, awed by the island's sullen vastness, by its imposing mountains, its history, seduced by the hospitality of its inhabitants. Crete is really like nowhere else in Greece; self-sufficient and self-contained, steeped in its own strong traditions, the island is separated from the rest of the nation by more than just geography. Some people go as far as to say that Crete is almost like another country.

The island is at the crossroads of Europe, Africa, and Asia, the real and mythic cradle of the Mediterranean. But it is on the island's interior that one starts to feel the pulse of the land and to sense that despite its place as the Mediterranean's fifth largest island (after Sicily, Sardinia, Cyprus, and Corsica), Crete, at least today, is really more about mountains than the sea.

The entire spine of the 160-mile-long island rises with some of the highest peaks in Greece: the low-lying Sitia Mountains in the east; the snow-capped Dikti Massif farther west, on whose fertile plateau (Lasithi) some of the best pulses and potatoes in all of Greece are cultivated, Mount Ida Psiloritis in the center, which hovers over the vast and olive-rich Messara plain; and finally, the White Mountains, *Ta Lefka Ori* to the Cretans, which rise up in sheer rock from the Libyan Sea and whose intractable terrain has spawned the most fiercely independent Cretan shepherds and no small number of revolutionaries. In a way, Crete's mountains gave rise to the whole of Western civilization, when, as legend has it, Zeus was born in a cave on Psiloritis and nursed from a goat's horn by the nymph Amaltheia. Our own English word, *cornucopia*—the horn of plenty—derives from that myth.

Today the island is an amalgam of past and present. The whole northern coast, with its vast hotel complexes and tourist towns, overflowing in summer but ghostly still in winter, is one source of Crete's considerable wealth. On the southeastern side, especially in Ierapetra, stand the monuments of its other source of income: row after row of greenhouses that supply the rest of Greece and much of northern Europe with tomatoes, cucumbers, eggplants, peppers, and more year-round. Farming is big business here. Juxtaposed against this present-day scenario are the black-clad old women collecting bagsful of *horta* (wild greens) every morning or selling their hand-crafted wares—everything from rugs to doilies—in mountain villages. Old men stubbornly dressed in sixteenth-century garb, in the *vrakes,* the black and dark blue pantaloons worn with sturdy high black boots and dark headdress, still sit at the local *cafeneia, raki* and coffee in one hand, cell phone in the other, making for an equally anachronistic and incongruous image. Like its uncanny and often incomprehensible facade, so is Crete's food a representation of the strange tug of war between past and present.

More than almost anywhere else in the country, the most remote past is still palpable on the table. Archaeology has revealed that the earliest Cretans—the Minoans—survived and flourished on the Mediterranean triad of grains, olives, and the vine. The Minoans ate broad beans, peas, and lentils. They enjoyed the vast array of wild herbs and greens that grow more profusely in Crete than anywhere else. For meat they relied on a few cows, goats, sheep, and a great number of pigs. They hunted wild ibex—*agrimi,* as it is known locally (still a delicacy although almost extinct now)—as well as red deer, hare, and rabbit. They knew cheese—Bronze Age cheese strainers have been found in archaeological remains on the island. For a sweetener, as everywhere in the Old World, they relied on honey (sugarcane was to come to the island much later, with the Moors, around the tenth century), and their fruit gardens were laden with figs, apples, pears, and the quince, a Cretan native. Barley, the staple grain of the Minoans as well as of the ancient Greeks, appears on the Cretan table to this day, in the form of breads and myriad rusks. Nowhere else in Greece is it used with such frequency. The *paximathi,* Cretan bread, which is nothing more than a rock-hard, twice-baked rusk and so prepared to facilitate its long keeping, is often made of barley. (Barley, which has less gluten than wheat, dries faster and keeps longer.) Until a generation ago, breakfast was often the same as it would have been thousands of years ago—barley rusks dipped in wine. And today, a visit to any bakery on the island will reveal that the *paximathia* are still basic to the local table; dozens of types are made all over Crete.

The subject of bread in Crete could comfortably support a whole book. Food rites lost to the mist of time crop up in uncanny places on the island. For example, one of the most enduring and endearing food customs is the ornate decoration of certain festive breads. On some we still find dough-sculpted trees, a motif that might hark back to the prehistoric worship of trees. Likewise many Cretan cheeses produced today have remained surprisingly unchanged since time immemorial. One of the oldest, *kouroupiasto,* a goat's milk cheese preserved in salt brine, is one of the forerunners of present-day feta.

The Byzantines, probably more than anyone else, affected the local table in ways too numerous to count. For example, the Byzantines had a great penchant for salt-curing and drying meat. In Crete's mountain reaches—as well as in other parts of Greece, especially the Peloponnesos and the Cyclades—one still encounters the *apokti,* salted, sun-dried meat made almost the same way as the synonymous charcuterie mentioned in Byzantine Cretan poetry, comedy, and drama. The islanders preferred to salt-cure their beloved *agrimi* (or ibex), and up until a generation ago people still did, perhaps with a little too much zeal, for the animal has all but disappeared nowadays. Now *apokti,* as well as its cousin, *apaki* (which is smoked), are for the most part made with pork and not wild mountain goat.

Likewise the Byzantine penchant for honey- or raisin-sweetened meats manifests itself in at least one unusual dish on the island, the local rendition of *omaties* (stuffed caul), here filled with rice, offal, and raisins. Its ancestor is a dish by the same name, again mentioned frequently in Byzantine literature and predating it in fact; *omaties* originally were a kind of blood sausage. According to some conjecture, the dish's precursor is the black broth, or *melanos zomos,* the dish of sustenance for the ancient Spartan soldiers. During the Byzantine era, the Church forbade the eating of blood, believing it represented the soul. But the dish evolved and still survives. It is a specialty at Christmas and, in Sitia on the eastern side of the island, at weddings.

The Byzantines also liked to use honey in savory dishes, especially for huge roasts, particularly for pork. I have run across recipes and dishes in Crete that call for marinating meat in honey for days before roasting it. One of the great drinker's *mezethes* on the island, something savored during the making of *raki* in the winter, is grilled pork dipped in honey. All the Byzantine spices were readily appropriated, too. Black pepper, cinnamon, cloves, and nutmeg came from the markets of Alexandria and still flavor the Cretan pot, although not in great quantity, as one of the hallmarks of the Cretan table is its integrity. Food is not embellished here, but rather kept as pure and unadorned as possible.

The larder began to change again when the Venetians took control in the thirteenth century. On one hand, new spices and herbs appeared, namely cumin, dill, and—surprisingly because it is such a Mediterranean staple—garlic, imported from Apulia, Naples, and Ravenna respectively. Likewise, vinegar, wild celery, and leeks, among other foodstuffs, were exported. The Venetians plied an active trade in dozens of local agricultural products but they concentrated mainly on the olive and the vine, to the detriment of most other crops. Under Venetian rule, in fact, the cultivation of the olive was greatly intensified—something they fostered in Corfu as well. They also exploited the island's highly esteemed wine (Malmsey, or Malvasia as it was known to the Cretans), as well as raisins and honey, the latter of which has been renowned since antiquity. Wheat, however, had to be imported.

It is extremely difficult to single out Venetian influences on the Cretan table. Many dishes have

names that bear an Italian stamp, though etymology doesn't always reflect the provenance of a dish or ingredient. For example, there are the sweet and/or savory little cheese pies called *kallitsounia,* which sounds like the Italian *calzone* but are remarkably similar to recipes dating all the way back to Homer. Some parts of the island claim a dish called *kanelonia.* In Crete, these aren't exactly pasta but more like stuffed crêpes; the dough is soft, and the *kanelonia* are usually fried. In Crete (as in the Ionian Islands) we also find the Italian-sounding *polpetes,* little meatballs or vegetable fritters, known elsewhere in Greece as *keftedes.* There used to be an old, clearly Venetian dish called *skatzeto,* a kind of beef and onion soup (by some accounts, strangely, made with seawater). (In Venice, *squazzetto* can be a soup or stew, made with lamb, beef, or pork and sometimes served with polenta.) Another interesting and clearly Italian custom is that of the afternoon snack of yore, called *marenda* in Crete, an etymological stone's throw to the Italian *merende,* which is almost exactly the same thing. The list goes on and on.

The Turkish influences—the Ottomans occupied the island for more than two hundred years—present an even greater problem. Depending on whose view of history one abides by, the general picture of Crete, indeed of Greece, under the Ottomans differs.

There is very little in the way of written accounts of daily life, although the foreign travelers to Crete in the seventeenth and eighteenth centuries often give a picture of what and how people ate. If their accounts are any guide (these highly educated Western travelers on their grand tour of Greece, although infatuated with antiquity, often disparaged both Greeks and Turks alike, as well as their customs, culinary or otherwise, as somehow less civilized than those in their native England, France, or Germany), then it seems the Turkish influences on the Cretan table are generally subdued.

Most of the foreign travelers' descriptions of local meals shared with villagers or in monasteries sound remarkably similar to the kinds of things Cretans have always eaten, dishes shaped mainly by what the land provides. Robert Pashley, who visited the island in the early 1830s, writes of artichokes boiled and swimming in olive oil, among other things. About fifty years later, when the English traveler Charles Edwards visited Crete, he described barley bread, snails in olive oil, *myzithra,* small cheese pies from Sfakia, and vegetable snippings and roots squeezed with lemon juice. The same foods can pretty much be found on any modern Cretan menu.

Hints of Ottoman influence in the local cuisine, however limited or difficult to define, are evinced in some interesting techniques that still survive on the island. For example, Cretan cooks show less of a penchant for the typical Greek egg-and-lemon sauce (*avgolemono*) but a liking for *derbiye,* lemon juice and flour used as a thickener in myriad dishes, a technique that came to the island most likely via the Turks. At least one dish, one of Crete's most unusual at that, was also introduced by the Ottomans. It is the *tzoulama, cirlama* in Turkish, which traditionally is a pie made with chicken livers and cinnamon. The same dish still appears in both Turkey and Tunisia, suggesting, perhaps, that the Ottomans disseminated it. In Crete today it is still made with chicken livers but more often can be found in its Christianized version, made with either pork liver or lamb liver. A recipe for it appears in my first book.

Added to this mix of Byzantine, Venetian, and Ottoman influences is the unique place that the island's Jews played in its commercial, agricultural,

and, by extension, culinary life. The Jews never numbered more than a few thousand out of a population of several hundred thousand on the island, yet they played a pivotal and often intermediary role between the native population and the foreign usurpers. According to Zvi Ankori in his essay "Jews in the History of Medieval Crete," "Agricultural production became geared to the tastes and the religious scruples of the Jewish merchant in Candia and of his customers in Alexandria, Constantinople, or Thessaloniki. . . . Wine and cheese production, for example, often followed kosher dictates."

In our own century, again as the outcome of Greco-Turkish upheavals, thousands of Greek refugees from Asia Minor settled in Crete in the 1920s, and their stamp on the local cookery has been felt deeply, as it was all over the country. In Herakleion for example, around the Leondario Fountain, some of the best *bogatsa* (custard in phyllo) in all of Greece is to be found in the two shops run by Armenians and Asia Minor Greeks who have called this spot home since the 1920s. Dishes such as lamb with quince, purslane with yogurt, even moussaka probably all found their way into the local cookery via the Asia Minor Greeks.

Despite the seemingly endless litany of "foreign" inroads into the local palate, the land itself has played the most important role in shaping the island's table. For one, meat traditionally is much more prevalent on the western and southwestern sides of the island, especially in the environs of Hania and Sfakia, than it is in the east. Because the local population in the west were avid shepherds, butter, too, is much more common here than in the east. Fish and seafood are eaten more readily on the southeastern coast, in Sitia, than elsewhere. And in eastern Crete handmade pasta is traditionally more common than it is on the western part of the island, where rice is often the preferred grain. In the east, bulgur commonly replaces rice in pilafs and stuffings. There are many regional variations of the same dish as well. Small cheese pies, for example, vary a fair amount from Sfakia in the southwest to Sitia in the east. The flora, although always rich, changes, too, so that some of the wild greens that prevail in the east might be little known on the other side of the island.

Crete's diet has indeed remained uncannily intact since the earliest days of the island's history. In the last twenty-five years, Crete has transformed itself into one of the world's tourist meccas and in the process has co-opted such foods as croissants, schnitzel, and mass-produced hamburgers to appeal to the summer visitors. Affluence has manifested itself in some frightening statistics, too. Since 1974, for example, the consumption of meat has jumped tremendously. Today Cretans devour somewhere in the vicinity of 114 pounds each per year, but in keeping with time-honored tastes, most of it is in the form of lamb, goat, poultry, game (rabbit), and pork. Beef is all but anathema, even today.

Although Cretans today eat much more cheese than they did traditionally and fewer fruits, much of what has nourished them for eons—bestowing on them the longest life spans in the West—is prepared in the modern kitchen. The home cooking here is refreshingly simple. One-pot meals and myriad vegetable and legume stews form the backbone of Cretan cuisine. Spices, with the exception of cumin and cinnamon, are generally absent from the Cretan pot, replaced instead with the countless aromas of Crete's formidable wild herbs. Greens and olive oil are consumed in mind-boggling quantities. Snails are as loved today as they were thousands of years ago, as a nourishing and important source of pro-

tein. The land is blessed here and so is the cuisine, a rich tapestry of the ancient and the new. Modern life may have bruised the line of continuity connecting Crete's table to its long, illustrious past, but it hasn't by any means broken it. The island still boasts one of the most fascinating and comprehensive cuisines in all of Greece, one in which the cooking and foodways of the entire Aegean seem to be distilled.

In Crete the cuisine moves like a fugue; the same ingredients play off each other in endless combination, and the same, typically simple techniques apply to many dishes. It is always fascinating to see how Cretan home cooks "build" on a certain theme. The basic ingredients—artichokes, wild greens, lemon-flour sauce, snails, bulgur wheat—are used again and again in myriad combinations. Most vegetable stews can stand perfectly well on their own in Crete, but home cooks will nevertheless add snails or bulgur to them to make them more substantial. The combinations of greens or vegetables and protein in a pot are endless here, too, but the basic idea, regardless of specific ingredients, remains the same. For instance, an island favorite is lamb simmered with artichokes, but one also finds rabbit cooked the same way, chicken combined with artichokes, beans with artichokes, and so on.

In other words, simplicity is taken to the nth degree in Crete, and ingredients are appreciated for what they are, without much need of embellishment.

The Cretan Pantry

OLIVES AND OLIVE OIL

The olive has been the unrivaled foundation of Crete's cuisine and commercial wealth for ages. Indeed, Crete was the first home of the olive tree in Greece. The Minoans used to crush olives by hand in stone bowls: From archaeological remains, especially at Phaestos, it is known that the pulp was placed in vases so that the oil could rise to the top—the first oil, like the prized cold-pressed oil of today. The pulp was then pressed again on mats made of animal hair to make oil of lesser quality, again like that known today.

Until a few centuries ago olive oil played a role beyond that of mere nourishment. Olive oil was as good as cash, a currency in its own right that enabled people to buy property and pay laborers, among other things. Today Cretans still consume almost twice as much oil as their already copiously consuming fellow Greeks: Per capita consumption on Minos's island is somewhere in the vicinity of thirty-eight quarts annually.

Although the island always relied on the olive as a staple, it was the Venetians who implemented its intense cultivation and for whom it had become one of the most important agricultural exports. Its commercial value would be exploited by the Ottomans as well and continues well into our own time. About a hundred years ago, according to British diplomatic and consular reports of trade with the island, Crete boasted ten million olive trees. That number today stands at thirty-five million. The island produces more extra-virgin oil than anywhere else in Greece, and total production is about a hundred thousand tons annually. Most groves are planted with a local variety of the Coroneiki olive, the fore-most oil olive in Greece (about 60 percent of Greek olive oil is pressed from it), which here often goes by the name *psiloelia.*

The use of olive oil in the Cretan kitchen is profuse. Together with wild greens and bread, olives and their oil have helped stave off starvation in Crete for generations, providing islanders with a constant supply of nutrients, enough certainly so that their independent spirits were never compromised. As one old saying, attesting to just that, goes, "Every Cretan has an olive tree, even if just to hang himself by."

There are several indigenous olives on the island. One of the best is the tiny *psirolia,* another oil olive and in the same family as the *psiloelia,* which is also cured in salt brine for use as table olives and still known by the ancient name *kolimbades,* or "swimmers." The *psirolia* is found most readily in central Crete.

Other varieties include the *mourati,* in southwestern Crete, and there are also plantings of the Spanish *mantzalias,* as well as of Kalamata olives.

By far, though, the most delicious and interesting Cretan table olives are the *neratzoelies* or *neratzates.* These are small slit green olives that, once soaked for the requisite month or so (so that their bitterness leaches out), then steeped in salt brine for another few days, and finally in bitter orange juice, are preserved in olive oil. The result is an olive with a faint orange aroma and one of the most delicious in Greece. (See page 452 for how to make them.)

CHEESE

Cheese, like oil, greens, and bread, has always been a staple food in Crete. The island's formidable mountains make husbandry and shepherding natural occupations; the variety of grasses and wild herbs and greens provides excellent nourishment for sheep and goats and also makes their milk particulary tasty.

At least one early cheese, made around the area of Herakleion from full-cream sheep's milk, formed in baskets and aged in huge amphorae filled with brine, seems to have been a precursor to present-day feta or to a regional Cretan cheese still made and known locally as *kouroupiasto*. It was known from at least the first few hundred years of Byzantine rule. Cheese has also been of considerable commercial value to the island, exported to Constantinople when the Byzantines ruled Crete, to Egypt and other Muslim countries from as early as the tenth century, and then, under the Venetians in the fifteenth and sixteenth centuries, to Corfu (a Venetian Duchy), Apulia, and Naples.

Following is a list and description of Crete's cheeses:

Anthotyro and **Myzithra** These are confusing names in Crete because they mean completely different things in different parts of the island. In Hania—as in the rest of Greece—*anthotyro* is a soft, fresh whey cheese, usually made from sheep's milk, and usually a by-product of making *graviera*. The same (soft) cheese in Herakleion is called *myzithra*. On the contrary, *anthotyro* in Herakleion refers to the hard version of the same whey cheese, and usually comes in small fez-shaped parcels, covered with a blue-molded rind. It is considered excellent for grating. In Hania, it is the opposite: *myzithra* refers

to the hard, aged version. Nevertheless, this cheese, whether fresh or aged, is some of the oldest made in Greece.

Graviera Cretan *graviera* is possibly Greece's most delicious table cheese, despite the fact that it is relatively new. It was first made in 1914 by one of the fathers of modern Greek cheese making, Swiss-educated Nikos Zigouris, while he was working on the royal estate in the Peloponessos. Zigouris had studied cheese making in Switzerland. As the story goes, there was such a surplus of sheep's milk on the king's estate that Zigouris decided to experiment a bit, and thus made a sheep's milk cheese in the method of Gruyère, which he had learned to make as a student. Greek *graviera* indeed takes its name from a transliteration of the Swiss gruyère, and the two are cooked, pressed cheeses. But the technique for making the Greek cheese has evolved over the years so that today Greek *graviera* is nothing like its Swiss cousin.

Cretan *graviera* comes in wheels that weigh anywhere from twelve to fifty pounds. It has a lovely, full, sweet aroma and its taste is rich and round and full with the buttery flavor of sheep's milk. It can also be quite nutty, reminiscent of hazelnuts or almonds. In Crete, it is often eaten as a dessert cheese, cut into wedges and drizzled with the island's distinctive thyme honey. Since 1996 it has been legally recognized as an appellation-of-origin cheese. The cheese is aged for at least three months, but the best are older, from six months to a year.

Kefalograviera Another popular hard, yellow cheese, some of the best of which comes from Crete. The cheese falls somewhere between *kefalotyri* and *graviera* in terms of texture. It is a new cheese in Greece, barely thirty years old, yet it has become one of the most important commercially, with some 3,000 tons produced around the country annually. *Kefalograviera* is distinguished by its firm texture and by the air holes spread throughout its body. In flavor, it ranges from mild to medium. While elsewhere in Greece it is made with a combination of cow's milk and sheep's milk (or cow's, sheep's, and goat's milk) in Crete it is almost exclusively made with sheep's milk.

Kefalotyri This is the oldest hard Greek cheese, some of the best of which is produced on Crete, almost exclusively from sheep's milk, like the majority of Cretan cheese. The first such cheeses were made high in the mountains of Psiloritis, Kryoneritis, and Kendros, where they were aged at first in caves, as a way to keep them cool and well preserved in the warm summer months when itinerant shepherds moved into the higher altitudes with their flocks. Later they were aged in stone edifices called *mitata,* which still exist. One still finds such cheese traditionally produced in Crete; it is known as *"tis tripas,"* literally "of the hole."

Malaka Another old Cretan cheese, dating at least to the Byzantine era. Its name comes from *malako,* for soft. The cheese is an exclusive specialty of Hania. It resembles mozzarella in taste and texture, except that it is made with sheep's milk. Traditionally, *malaka* is a seasonal cheese available only around Easter time, and it is the preferred cheese for use in at least one local specialty, *haniotiki tourta,* a savory lamb and cheese pie (see page 421).

Piktogalo Hanion Literally, "thick milk from Hania," *piktogalo* is a very soft, spreadable cheese made with unpasteurized sheep's or a combination of sheep's and goat's milk, which is heated, set with rennet,

and left to ferment for about twenty-four hours. The curds aren't cut but salted and drained in cheesecloth until it acquires the consistency of thick yogurt, at which point it is ready to eat. It is one of many soft, sour, naturally fermented cheeses made in shepherds' communities all over Greece.

Tyrozouli A primitive goat's or sheep's milk cheese still made in the mountain villages above Rethymno, especially in the vicinity of Milopotamo. The milk is boiled, then curdled with vinegar, lemon juice, or fig sap. Once the curds are formed, they are drained in baskets, then lightly salted, and the cheese is subsequently air-dried. It is eaten young—locals consider it ready after about two weeks. Sometimes the cheese is stored in either milk or oil, or rubbed with olive oil to keep the dust off as it dries.

Xynomyzithra This is a spreadable, sharp whey cheese made with either goat's whey or a combination of goat's and sheep's whey. Fresh whole milk is often added as the whey heats. As the curds rise to the top, they are collected, cut, and strained to rid them of as much moisture as possible. Then they are salted, kneaded a little, and pressed very well for about a week, during which time the cheese begins to ferment. It then is left to ferment in barrels for another two months. The result is a soft cheese with a pleasantly sour, sharp, and acidic taste. In fact, *xyno* in Greek means sour. *Xynomyzithra* is eaten as a table cheese but is also much liked as the filling for the island's myriad small cheese pies.

GREENS

Crete boasts more than eighteen hundred indigenous plant species, one sixth of which are edible. Everything from absinthe (not edible) to tender wild carrots, to asphodels and thistles (the artichoke's ancient, native ancestor) grows here. To this day the foraging of wild greens is a kind of national obsession in Crete. There is even a word in the local dialect for the act of picking greens—*vrouvologo*—as well as special gear: Local women don a kangaroolike apron with a huge front pocket for storing their daily harvest.

I was lucky to find the best guide, the most knowledgeable person on the island, if not in Greece, when it comes to greens: Zaharias Kypriotakis, a slight man with professorial gray hair and beard and serene blue eyes, who happened to have just completed his Ph.D. on the flora of Crete's rocky mountain crevices when I met him.

We had arranged to meet early one morning and go foraging so that I might garner more than just vicarious knowledge of the milieu of Cretan botany. Time was limited, so we settled on combing through the campus grounds of the Technical Institute where Dr. Kypriotakis teaches, a mere two kilometers from downtown Herakleion. It seemed an inauspicious start. Little could I ever have guessed, though, that in the fifty-meter walk around the grounds, he would identify more than twenty edible wild greens. As we plodded on through the muddy earth, Dr. Kypriotakis bent down every few steps to show me something else. We crunched frail fresh asparagus between our teeth, rubbed wild fennel leaves, savored the delicate taste of a green known locally as "the rabbit's rusks." He pointed out bitter greens and sweet greens, not to mention the native Cretan celery, which has a keen, astringent taste, so

much more interesting than the ubiquitous, insipid supermarket celery that has become the commercial favorite. "Look over here. This is the weed of the future," he said, pointing to thin sheaths of grass jutting from the damp earth. *Skordouli.* Its name means "little garlic" in Greek, and indeed its aroma resembled that of garlic. "Excellent in salads," he added, "and goats' favorite, although you have to keep them away from it because it makes their milk smell."

Cretans use greens in three different ways: in their cooking, as teas and tisanes, and medicinally.

All of Greece enjoys the ad hoc, nutritious pleasures of foraging for wild greens. *Horta,* as we call our edible weeds, have kept us healthy in times of both want and excess. But Crete stands apart for several reasons. First, because, unlike most other Greeks for whom *horta* is something to be boiled until limpid, Cretans savor many greens raw. The island differs, too, in the enormous variety of greens that people recognize and eat here. There are at least three hundred edible greens on Crete, but most people who are knowledgeable recognize about a hundred, says Kypriotakis.

The local palate dictates that specific categories of greens be used for specific dishes. Bitter greens, for example, such as the whole range of wild chicories (*rathikia*), including the famed *stamnangathi* (literally "the water-jug thorn"), a spiny chicory that was used as a stopper in clay vessels (for water or otherwise) and today makes for one of the greatest Cretan salads; the ancient thistle, *askrolymbros*; bitter dandelion, *picrosirida*; mustard greens; watercress; even the leaves of the deadly nightshade (it is the tiny white flowers from which strychnine is derived, that are poisonous) appear in boiled salads, usually with vinegar, or raw especially when they are young and tender. Sometimes they are mixed with sweet greens for balance.

Sweet greens—everything from sweet dandelion (*taraxo*) to purslane (*anthrakla or glistritha*), salsify (*tragopogon*), and mâche (*galatsida*)—claim a wider range of cooking methods. They are eaten both raw and boiled in salads (sometimes mixed with bitter greens to give balance), baked in pies, or stewed in the famed *yiahnera*, cooked in a pot that is, with copious amounts of the island's other staple, olive oil, and sometimes with onion or tomato. For stews, one of the most beloved wild greens is the asphodel, *dryllos*, which in Crete is collected in Lasithi and above Rethymno in Milopotamo in spring and cooked with potatoes or meat. Elsewhere in Greece, asphodels have been long forgotten.

Buds form another whole category of wild things Cretans love to eat, from tomato and potato buds to the tender tops of fresh favas and the wild ancient vetch, to female asparagus shoots, wild chicory buds, and, for a taste of the prosaic, the shoots of tender spring grapevines or fresh young chickpeas.

There is a lengthy list of dishes where greens are combined in hearty stews with other vegetables or with snails (a Cretan favorite), seafood, and certain meats—rabbit, fowl, lamb, or goat but almost never beef. I had some delicious food in Crete—hare cooked with wild cardoons and lemon sauce; lamb cooked with wild artichoke leaves and *avgolemono*; octopus stewed with wild leeks and asparagus, and on another occasion with bryony, which looks like wild asparagus but has a sharp, rather than sweet, taste; cuttlefish simmered with wild fennel, to name but a few. Small pies filled with upward of a dozen leafy greens make their way into almost every kitchen, usually in the form of crescent-shaped parcels of dough, fried unabashedly in olive oil. I even came across *moloha*—mallow—heroic mallow, as Kypriotakis calls it, because it saved Cretans from starvation during the German Occupation—turned into tiny, delicate *dolmathes*. The list of wild greens is endless.

In Crete, as the good doctor said to me again and again, if you know how to forage for wild greens, you will never go hungry. Sound advice for venues far beyond the island's shores.

VINEGAR SAUSAGES AND OTHER CHARCUTERIE

Cretan charcuterie saw its heyday in centuries long gone, when the Byzantines and Venetians both introduced various cured meats to the island. In medieval Crete there were sausages known as *saltitsounia* and blood sausage, which was called *bouldouni*. *Mortadelles* and *saloumia* also existed, probably not unlike what we still call by similar names.

Today there are two island specialties. The first is the *apokti*, relatively rare but nevertheless still made in some villages. It is salted pork that has been sun-dried. A similar preparation is the *apaki*, salted, air-dried pork, usually cut from the thigh, which one can find at most island butchers. To make *apaki*, the meat is salted, then marinated in vinegar for twelve hours. Then the meat is smoked over aromatic woods such as cypress and over herbs such as oregano, sage, or savory. It is hung about three feet from the heat source and smoked over two or three days, for about an hour each day, which helps to dry it. Then it is rubbed with a mixture of black pepper, cumin, oregano, and savory and air-dried for two to four months, depending on the weather. To serve, *apaki* is sliced thinly and sometimes heated in a skillet, with or without olive oil.

Sausages in Crete nowadays are limited to the thin, vinegar-flavored pork sausage that is traditionally made at Christmas (when the pork slaughters customarily took place in village homes) and savored throughout the year. It is either eaten plain and uncooked as a *meze* or added to omelets and other cooked dishes to enhance them. Beef, anathema to most Cretans even today, never was cured for charcuterie.

SOMETHING LIKE CLOTTED CREAM, STAKA

In all the Cretan pantry, nothing is quite as unusual as *staka.* It is a preparation sure to burst the bubble of anyone who romanticizes the olive-oil-rich, butter-poor Mediterranean Diet! Its saving grace in light of healthful traditions is that it is savored sparingly, whereas olive oil was and is the daily salve.

So, what is it? *Staka*, from the Italian *staccare,* to separate, is essentially a kind of clotted cream. It is almost always made from fresh, raw sheep's milk, which is left in a vessel to stand for several hours until the cream rises to the top. This cream, called *tsipa,* is collected over several days or weeks and stored. When enough has been gathered—at least about two cups—it is mixed with a little salt and, traditionally, a little barley flour or, more commonly nowadays, wheat flour. The mixture is then heated over a low flame until the butter separates and rises to the top. The butter, *stakoboutyro,* is collected, stored, and used to flavor certain dishes, such as pilaf and some savory pies, and sweets. What remains, the *staka* itself in other words, is used as a fat in cooking. Cretans love to fry their eggs in it.

The Recipes

MEZETHES

As in all of Greece, in the villages and small towns of Crete the *cafeneia* are a male-dominated forum for discussion and often for just whiling away the time. In Crete, though, the *cafeneia* are still the best place to sample local fare and to experience the sense of ritual that imbues even the simplest snack. Here an old custom prevails: the *tezaki,* which is essentially the counter where the coffee master prepares his brew. Customers sit around him, on three sides like the Greek *pi* of mathematics but facing out. When friends and acquaintances pass by, the men already inside try to lure them in for a drink. Usually they succumb; it is an afternoon ritual before men go home for lunch and a siesta.

What is fascinating is the array of *mezethes* on hand as the drinking of local eau de vie (*raki*) progresses. While at night there might be a cooked dish or two, things like octopus cooked with wild asparagus or ember-roasted eggs, in the day the repertoire is decidedly simple: raw quinces, small apples, wild pears, dried figs or dates, hazelnuts and walnuts, ember-roasted potatoes, skewered and quick-roasted olives, raw artichokes with olive oil and salt, raw fava beans done up in the same dressing, roasted chestnuts, and the ubiquitous rusks. In the small village in Rethymno where I experienced this (accompanied by a male friend), the favored brew is *raki* mixed with honey. The locals call it *rakomelo.*

Barley Rusks with Grated Tomato

DAKOS ME TOMATA

 Makes 4 to 8 servings

4 large Cretan barley rusks (see Note)
½ cup extra-virgin olive oil
2 large firm, ripe tomatoes, grated
    (see page 459) or peeled, seeded, and
chopped
Salt to taste
2 teaspoons dried Greek oregano

Fill a bowl with water and submerge each of the rusks for a few seconds, until soaked through. Hold up and drain off all the water or wring dry in a lint-free kitchen towel. Place the rusks on a serving platter. Drizzle each with 1 tablespoon of the olive oil and spoon the grated tomatoes evenly over them. Sprinkle with the salt and oregano and pour on the remaining ¼ cup olive oil. Serve.

✳ NOTE Cretan barley rusks are available in Greek food shops.

Grilled Wrinkled Olives

ELIES OFTES

 Makes 4 to 6 servings

This is from a tiny cafeneion in an equally tiny village called Mixorouma, just outside Rethymno, where the cooks and owners, Pericles and Evangelia Seiragadakis, serve them up to their legion of regulars. I've had to adapt this otherwise primitive recipe, since Kyria Evangelia usually throws the olives on top of her potbellied stove. Here a cast-iron griddle stands in. You might also want to try Olives Flavored with Bitter Orange Juice on page 452.

1 cup wrinkled black Greek olives
2 to 3 tablespoons coarse sea salt

Skewer 5 olives at a time on small wooden skewers and sprinkle them very lightly with sea salt. Heat the griddle over medium heat, then grill the olives for 3 to 4 minutes, turning to grill all sides. Remove from the heat and serve.

Raw Artichoke and Lettuce Salad

ANGINARES KAI MAROULI SALATA

 Makes 4 servings

My friend Chris Veneris, a Cretan chef, is a poet of the artichoke, as are most good Cretan cooks. This salad is an island favorite that I first learned from him.

1 head romaine lettuce, washed and shredded
3 large artichoke hearts, quartered
   (see page 459)
3 scallions or spring onions, white and tender
   green parts, thinly sliced
1 small bunch fresh dill, snipped
⅓ to ½ cup extra-virgin olive oil, to taste
3 to 4 tablespoons fresh lemon juice or red wine
   vinegar, to taste
Salt and freshly ground black pepper to taste

Combine all the salad ingredients in a serving bowl. Whisk together the olive oil, lemon juice or vinegar, salt, and pepper and toss with the salad. Serve immediately.

Stewed Parsley

MAINTANO YIAHNI

 Makes about 4 to 6 servings

This is really more of a relish, eaten with bread, cheese, and olives, than a proper stew. It is also excellent as an accompaniment to grilled meats. The dish is a specialty of Rethymno.

½ cup extra-virgin olive oil
2 medium onions, chopped
8 cups coarsely chopped fresh flat-leaf parsley
1½ cups chopped plum tomatoes (canned are
   fine)
Salt and freshly ground black pepper to taste

Heat the olive oil in a wide, heavy pot and cook the onions over medium-low heat, stirring a few times, until wilted and translucent, about 8 minutes. Add the parsley and toss to coat. Cook, covered, until wilted completely, about 7 minutes. Add the tomatoes, season with salt and pepper, and stir. Simmer until most of the liquid has been absorbed, about 20 minutes. Serve warm or at room temperature, accompanied by bread, olives, and Greek feta cheese or any Cretan table cheese.

EGGS

Eggs are usually considered a light summer meal in Crete. Mostly, though, they are cooked as omelets, and almost anything can become an omelet, fom leftover greens and green beans to okra, asparagus, zucchini, cauliflower, and more. All it takes is to cook the vegetables a little first, so that they are tender by the time they are added to the skillet with the eggs. The term *omelet* is a loose one in Greece. Generally it refers to beaten eggs cooked in a pan until set. Rarely are omelets folded or flipped.

There are also a few unusual egg dishes, such as ember-roasted whole eggs and a very unusual omelet filled with nuts, which I have detailed here.

Eggplant Omelet

MELITZANES OMELETA

 Makes 2 to 3 servings

1 small eggplant, sliced into ¼-inch-thick
   rounds
Salt as needed
Extra-virgin olive oil as needed
⅔ cup crumbled Greek feta cheese
3 to 4 large eggs, to taste, lightly beaten

1. Place the eggplant slices in layers in a colander and salt each layer. Cover the eggplant with a plate and a weight on top and leave to drain for 40 minutes to an hour. Rinse and pat dry.

2. Pour enough olive oil into a large, heavy, nonstick skillet to cover the entire surface by about ⅛ inch and heat over medium heat. Cook the eggplant until golden and soft on both sides, 7 to 10 minutes. Cover the surface of the eggplant with the crumbled feta and cover the skillet. Cook over low heat until the feta has almost melted, 5 to 8 minutes. Pour in the eggs, shake the skillet a little from time to time, cook until the eggs are set to the desired consistency, and serve.

Artichoke Omelet

ANGINARES SFOUGGATO

 Makes 4 to 6 servings

Another paean to the island's favorite vegetable, the artichoke.

⅔ cup extra-virgin olive oil
4 large artichoke hearts, quartered
   (see page 459) and kept in acidulated water
   (see page 458)
Salt and freshly ground white pepper to taste
½ cup snipped fresh dill
4 to 6 eggs, to taste, lightly beaten

1. Heat ½ cup of the olive oil in a wide pot or skillet over medium heat. Remove the artichokes from the acidulated water. Place in the pot with the oil, stir, and add just enough water to barely cover the artichokes. Season with salt and pepper. Cover and simmer until the artichokes are tender, about 15 minutes. Drain well.

2. In a large, heavy skillet, heat the remaining oil. Spread the artichokes evenly in the skillet. Pour the eggs evenly around the skillet and season with salt and pepper. Reduce the heat to low and cook until the bottom is golden, about 5 minutes. Remove the skillet from the heat, place a plate over it, and flip the omelet. Slide the omelet back into the skillet and cook until golden brown on the other side. Serve.

Walnut–Filled Omelet

AVGOKALAMOURA MALEVIZIOTIKA

Makes 6 servings

The name avgokalamoura *or* avgokalamara *appears throughout Greece and refers to one of two things, either thin, almost crêpelike omelets or egg-laden dough fritters drizzled with honey and nuts. We find the crêpelike omelets in Crete and in Chios, where the filling is usually ground meat. In Crete, both renditions exist. When I first read of this recipe in Nikos and Maria Psillakis's book on traditional Cretan cuisine, something nagged at me. I had seen it before, and sure enough, in searching through books on ancient cuisine, I found a recipe for a nut-filled omelet in* The Classical Cookbook *by Andrew Dalby and Sally Grainger, which is an interpretation of a dish by the ancient Roman gastronome Apicius. One*

more proof that in Crete so much food has its roots in the most ancient past.

3 tablespoons unsalted butter
½ pound walnuts or almonds, coarsely ground
Salt and freshly ground black pepper to taste
6 large eggs, beaten with a little salt

1. Heat ½ tablespoon of the butter in a medium nonstick skillet over medium heat and toast the nuts for about 5 minutes, stirring or shaking constantly in the pan. Transfer to a bowl and mix with a little salt and pepper.

2. Heat half the remaining butter in a small nonstick skillet over medium heat. When the butter sizzles, add half a ladleful of the eggs, spreading it to a thin circle in the skillet, about 5 inches in diameter. As soon as it begins to cook on the bottom, add a tablespoon of the nuts to the center. Fold over so that the omelet looks like a half-moon. Cook until one side is lightly golden, then flip carefully with a large spatula to brown lightly on the other side. Remove from the skillet and keep covered and warm in a warm oven. Repeat with the remaining butter, eggs, and nuts until done. Serve warm.

SOUP

Bean Soup with Vegetables and Orange Zest from Hania

HANIOTIKI FASOLATHA

 Makes about 6 servings

Oranges figure subtlely but prominently in some of the dishes on Minos's island. Cretans flavor their tiny green olives with the juice of bitter Seville oranges; they layer sliced oranges in fragrant rabbit stews; and they season soups such as this otherwise simple peasant bean soup with orange zest. I first tasted this in Kolimvari, outside Hania, at an unforgettable lunch as part of a conference sponsored by the International Olive Oil Council.

½ pound dried navy beans, picked over and
    rinsed
1 cup extra-virgin olive oil
1½ cups finely chopped red onion
1 cup finely chopped cultivated celery with leaves
    or ¾ cup chopped wild celery with leaves
1 large carrot, chopped
¾ cup peeled, seeded, and chopped tomatoes
    (canned are fine)
1 large strip orange zest
Salt to taste

1. Soak the navy beans for 6 to 8 hours or overnight. Drain and rinse. Place in a pot with enough fresh water to cover them by 3 inches. Bring to a boil, remove from the heat, and drain. Place the beans back in the pot with enough water to cover them by 3 inches, bring to a boil, reduce the heat to medium-low, and simmer for 30 minutes.

2. Meanwhile, heat ⅓ cup of the olive oil in a large, heavy skillet over medium-low heat. Cook the onion, celery, and carrot, stirring with a wooden spoon, until softened, about 10 minutes.

3. Add the sautéed vegetables to the beans, together with the tomatoes and another ⅓ cup of the olive oil. Simmer slowly until the beans are very tender and the soup is thick and creamy, 2 to 2½ hours, depending on the age and condition of the beans. About 20 minutes before removing from the heat, add the orange zest and season with salt. Just before removing from the heat, pour in the remaining olive oil.

⊙ Beans and grains are often cooked together in Crete. One can easily add sour *trahana* (see page 456), called *xinohondro* in Crete (see page 457), to this soup. Add ½ cup halfway through cooking.

Pork and Sour Trahana Soup with Egg and Lemon

HOIRINOSOUPA ME XINOHONDRO KAI AVGOLEMONO

 Makes 6 to 8 servings

This is filling winter fare, Cretan style.

½ cup extra-virgin olive oil
3 pounds bone-in pork shoulder, cut into large
    cubes
2 large onions, finely chopped
Salt and freshly ground black pepper to taste

2 quarts water

1⅓ cups Cretan *xinohondros* (see page 457) or
  sour *trahana* (see page 456)

2 large eggs

Juice of 2 large lemons

1. Heat the olive oil in a large soup pot over high heat and brown the meat on all sides. Remove the meat with a slotted spoon and add the onions the pot. Reduce the heat to medium and cook the onions, stirring, until wilted, 7 to 8 minutes. Add the pork back to the pot, season with salt and pepper, and add the water. Bring to a boil. Reduce the heat to medium-low and simmer, skimming any foam off the surface of the broth as it simmers, until the pork is very tender and falling off the bone, 1½ to 2 hours.

2. Remove the meat and onions with a slotted spoon and set aside. Add the *xinohondro* or *trahana* to the pot. Season with salt and pepper. Simmer until soft, about 15 minutes.

3. Make the egg-lemon sauce: Whisk the eggs and lemon juice together in a medium bowl. Add a ladleful of the hot soup to the egg-and-lemon mixture in a slow, steady stream, whisking all the while. Pour the *avgolemono* into the pot. Turn off the heat and shake the pot a little from side to side to combine.

4. Serve the soup, with the meat and onions on the side.

Pork in Broth with Bulgur or Cracked Wheat Patties

HOIRINO ME VOLOUS APO HONDROS

 Makes 6 to 8 servings

*When I ran across this recipe in a collection that my friend and fellow cooking teacher Giorgos Anastasiades asked his students to research, I realized it was one more to add to the already considerable variety of dumpling-like dishes—*kofte, kibbe, koupia, *and the like—that are part of the cooking traditions of the eastern Mediterranean. Not surprisingly, this recipe hails from the eastern part of Crete, where the cooking shares much with that of the Dodecanese Islands and Cyprus, both places where wheat balls and patties are readily found. Unlike* kibbe, *though, the Cretan bulgur balls are not stuffed. I've changed the original recipe a little, enriching the pork broth with some vegetables for flavor's sake.*

2 pounds bone-in pork shoulder, cut into large
  cubes

⅔ cup plus 3 to 4 tablespoons olive oil, as
  needed

8 to 10 cups water, as needed

1 medium onion

2 large carrots

1 bay leaf

Salt and freshly ground black pepper to taste

1 cup finely chopped red onion

2 cups fine bulgur

½ to 1 cup all-purpose flour, as needed

2 teaspoons dried Greek oregano

2 large eggs

1. Rinse and pat the meat dry. Heat ⅓ cup of the olive oil in a large soup pot over high heat and brown the meat on all sides. Remove from the pot and pour off the burned oil. Place the pork back in the pot, add 8 to 10 cups of the water as needed, the unpeeled onion, carrots, and bay leaf. Bring to a boil, season with salt and pepper, and reduce the heat to low. Simmer, partially covered, until the meat is falling off the bone, 1½ to 2 hours. Skim the foam off the surface of the broth as it simmers.

2. Meanwhile, heat the remaining ⅓ cup olive oil in a small skillet over medium heat and cook the chopped red onion, stirring, until wilted, 7 to 8 minutes. Combine the chopped onion and bulgur in a medium bowl. Toss with ½ cup of the flour and the oregano. Add 2 tablespoons of the remaining olive oil, the eggs, salt, and pepper, and knead until the mass holds its shape when formed into golf ball–size balls. Add more oil if necessary, or, if it is loose, add a little more flour to bind. Take one piece at a time and shape the mixture into balls. Set aside for a few minutes.

3. Strain the soup, reserving the broth. Remove and discard the onion, carrots, and bay leaf. Remove the meat and set aside to cool. Shred the meat into small pieces and discard the bones.

4. Bring the broth to a boil. Reduce the heat to medium-low, add the bulgur patties, and add remaining water if necessary to cover them. Poach until tender, 20 to 25 minutes. Place the shredded meat back in the pot and simmer all together for 5 minutes or so, just to warm through. Season with salt and pepper. Serve in soup bowls.

VEGETABLES

Minos's island provides everything from tomatoes to obscure wild greens to legions of Greeks across the country as well as to Europeans, as the island is one of the most important farming belts in the entire Mediterranean. It makes sense, then, that fertile Crete should claim so many native vegetables and greens and so many dishes made from them. One whole category could easily be stewed greens and other vegetables. One-pot cookery is something that defines much of Greek country cooking as a whole; in Crete, though, vegetables are simmered in the stewing pot in infinite variety and with skill unmatched anywhere else in the country. I don't really know if there's a reason Cretan cooks seem to have such a good hand at making one-pot vegetable dishes. Certainly one reason that these dishes have evolved on the island is that Crete is both blessedly fecund and rich in the Mediterranean's liquid gold, olive oil, which is the fat always used in these dishes and always used unstintingly.

There are so many vegetable stews in Crete that selecting a few to fit into the pages of a book is a daunting task at best. You'll see that throughout the Cretan chapter vegetables appear in almost every recipe, married with beans, meat, fish, and snails in many, many different ways. In the following handful of dishes, I have chosen my own favorites from the stewing pot.

BOILED GREENS FOR SALADS OR *HORTA*

Almost any green can be boiled for salad. Chicory and amaranth make two of the most common, but rarer greens, such as thistles, stinging nettles, and bryony, are also boiled for salad. After trimming and washing the greens very well, boil in ample salted water in a pot with the cover ajar, until tender. Drain well. *Horta* can be eaten warm (not hot) but is usually preferred at room temperature. Dress with olive oil, fresh lemon juice or vinegar, and salt just before serving.

Slow-Cooked Vegetable Stew

SOFEGADA OR SYMPETHERIO

 Makes 6 to 8 servings

The etymology of sofegada, *and hence its provenance, is the subject of some debate on Crete. The dish is essentially a slow-simmered vegetable stew. By some accounts the dish is Venetian. Certainly its name is neither Greek nor Turkish. Nikos Psillakis, in his detailed book on Cretan food, says that it was mentioned in medieval Cretan manuscripts and that it referred to some kind of meat dish "smothered" in steam, which would indeed suggest a long, slow cooking process. He says the word comes from the Italian* sofocazione, *"to suffocate." However, there is a remarkably similar-sounding dish that comes from Catalonia called* sofregita *that indeed is a very slowly cooked medley of vegetables, most often onions, that are then used as a basis for sauce. There is also a Spanish dish called* favas ofregadas, *which literally means "smothered," as in cooking the beans, or any vegetables for that matter, in little moisture for a long time. Perhaps the dish arrived with the Sephardic refugees in the fifteenth century, or perhaps it came to Crete via Venice; the Catalan kingdom reached various parts of Italy, and certainly by the sixteenth century, according to the historian Fernand Braudel, trade between Catalonia and Venice was common.*

Some sources assert that the dish arrived in Crete as sofegada *but then, over time, became utterly Cretanized under the name* sympetherio, *which means "fellow in-laws," the logic being that ingredients unknown to one another before their marriage in this pot now must learn to survive together and complement one another.*

For all the fuss over its name and provenance, sofegada/sympetherio *is a fairly simple medley of vegetables stewed in a generous amount of Cretan olive oil.*

1 cup olive oil, or more to taste
2 large onions, chopped
3 garlic cloves, minced
1 pound fresh green beans, trimmed
1 pound small, thin okra, trimmed
1 pound waxy potatoes, peeled and quartered or cut into chunks if large
Salt to taste
2 to 3 green bell peppers, coarsely chopped
1 pound long, thin eggplants, cut into 2-inch thick rounds
2 pounds firm, ripe tomatoes, grated (see page 459)
Freshly ground black pepper to taste
1 pound medium zucchini, cut into 2-inch-thick rounds
10 zucchini blossoms (optional)

1. Heat the olive oil in a large pot and cook the onions over medium heat until wilted, 7 to 8 minutes. Add the garlic and stir for another minute or two.

2. Add the green beans, okra, and potatoes to the pot. Season with salt and toss to coat. Pour in enough water just to cover the vegetables. Cover the pot, bring to a boil, reduce the heat to medium-low, and simmer for 20 minutes. Add the peppers and eggplants and toss to coat. Add the tomatoes and additional water if necessary to cover, adjust the seasoning with salt and pepper, and simmer, covered, for about 40 minutes. Add the zucchini and zucchini blossoms, toss gently, cover, and continue simmering until all the vegetables are very tender and the dish is rich and unctuous. Serve warm or at room temperature with plenty of bread.

Artichoke and Fava Bean Stew with Lemon Sauce

ANGINAROKOUKIA ME DERBIYE

 Makes 4 to 6 servings

Artichokes must have a special place in the hearts of Cretan cooks, because there are so many local ways of preparing them. The island favorite is without doubt the thorny wild artichoke, which Cretans love to eat raw, sprinkled with salt and lemon and a little olive oil. It makes for one of the best early-spring mezethes. Cretans also savor the artichoke's ancient wild ancestor, the thistle, which they boil for salad, cook with avgolemono, *or combine with meat and game. Although this dish is prepared elsewhere in Greece, it is such standard fare on the springtime table in Crete that it is considered an island classic.*

⅔ cup extra-virgin olive oil

2 scallions, white and tender green parts, chopped

1 garlic clove, minced

2 pounds fresh fava beans, shelled (see Note)

6 to 8 large artichokes, cleaned (see page 459)

Salt to taste

1 scant tablespoon all-purpose flour

Juice of 2 lemons

1. Heat the olive oil in a large, wide pot over medium heat and add the scallions and garlic. Toss to coat in the oil, reduce the heat to low, and simmer, covered, for 5 minutes. Add the fava beans, toss to coat, and add enough water to cover by 1 inch. Cover, bring to a boil, reduce the heat to medium-low, and simmer for 10 minutes. Place the artichoke hearts, tops down, in the pot. Season with salt. Add enough water to come about halfway up the artichokes. Cover and simmer over low heat until the artichokes are very tender, 35 to 40 minutes.

2. Whisk the flour and lemon juice together. Add a ladleful of the pan juices to the flour-and-lemon mixture in a slow, steady stream, whisking all the while. Pour this mixture into the pot, tilt the pot back and forth so that the mixture spreads evenly throughout, and simmer until the sauce thickens, 3 to 4 minutes. Remove from the heat and serve.

✳ **NOTE** If the fava beans are young and tender, there is no need to shell them. Simply trim the shells as for green beans.

⊙ Artichoke, Fava Beans, and Snails with Dill and Vinegar (Anginarokoukia me Hohlious): You can prepare this dish with the addition of snails and dill. Five minutes after placing the artichokes in the pot, add 1 pound snails (cleaned according to the directions on page 463) and ½ cup snipped fresh dill. In lieu of lemon juice, add red wine vinegar.

Artichokes Cooked with Yogurt

ANGINARES ME YIAOURTI

 Makes 4 servings

½ to ⅔ cup extra-virgin olive oil, to taste
1 medium onion, finely chopped
6 to 8 artichokes, cleaned (see page 459)
Salt and freshly ground white pepper to taste
2½ cups Greek yogurt (see page 459), drained,
   or thick Mediterranean-style yogurt

1. Heat the olive oil in a large, wide pot and cook the onion over medium heat until wilted and translucent, 7 to 8 minutes. Add the artichokes, stems down, and season with salt and pepper. Add enough water to barely cover the artichokes. Place the lid on the pot slightly ajar and simmer over medium-low heat until the artichokes are fork-tender and about half the liquid in the pot has been absorbed, about 25 minutes.

2. In a medium bowl whisk the yogurt together with about ½ cup of the warm pot juices and add to the pot, tilting back and forth to spread evenly. Remove from the heat and serve immediately.

Baked Layered Vegetables with Feta and Tomato Sauce

MERABELIOTIKA

 Makes 8 servings

Good friend and great cook Christoforos Veneris first showed me this dish, named after the region in east-central Crete from which it comes.

½ cup olive oil
3 garlic cloves, minced
3 pounds firm, ripe tomatoes, grated
   (see page 459)
Salt and freshly ground black pepper to taste
½ teaspoon sugar (optional)
1½ pounds large Russet potatoes, peeled and
   sliced ⅛ inch thick
3 medium zucchini, sliced ¼ inch thick
3 medium eggplants, sliced ¼ inch thick
Olive oil for frying
2 cups crumbled Greek feta cheese

1. Make the sauce: Heat the olive oil in a pot and cook the garlic over medium heat for a minute or so. Add the grated tomatoes. Season with salt and pepper and simmer for 15 minutes. Adjust the seasoning with salt, pepper, and a little sugar if desired. Remove from the heat and set aside.

2. Pat the sliced vegetables dry. Heat about an ⅛ inch olive oil in a large, heavy skillet over medium-high heat. Pan-fry the potatoes in batches until softened and very light golden, turning once to cook on both sides, about 10 minutes. Remove from the skillet and drain on paper towels. Repeat with the zucchini and eggplant slices, adding olive oil as necessary.

3. Preheat the oven to 350°F. Lightly oil a 12- by 18-inch baking pan. Place the potatoes on the bottom in one overlapping layer. Spread one third of the sauce on top and sprinkle with about ½ cup of the feta. Continue with the eggplant, adding sauce and ½ cup feta. Finish with a layer of the zucchini slices. Pour the remaining sauce and remaining 1 cup feta on top. Bake until the vegetables are set and the cheese is melted and light golden on top, about 50 minutes. Serve hot or at room temperature.

BEANS AND PULSES

In the traditional diet all over Greece, beans have always been the key source of protein as well as the food savored during the long periods of fasting dictated by the Orthodox calendar. In Crete, their place in the local kitchen is equally, if not more, long-standing and vital. Beans, of course, form one of the cornerstones of the Cretan diet, which has been singled out among scientists and nutritionists as the model for the entire Mediterranean diet.

In addition, though, to their practical place in the kitchen, in Crete many bean and pulse dishes seem the direct heirs of ancient food customs. Lupines, for example, were a staple in the diet of the ancient Cynic philosophers and the main meal at the end of each month in antiquity, made as a kind of offering to the gods but also meant to be shared with and served communally to the poor. Until a generation ago in Crete, lupines, which are in season in February and March, were one of the mainstays of the Lenten table. On the island they are prepared in the same way as that of the Mani, due north as the crow flies, across the Mediterranean from Crete, with which the island shares many food customs. Once they are boiled (to soften them), they are left to soak in seawater for two or three days. This rids them of bitterness. Then they are savored, usually as a *meze,* together with olives and bread rusks, with strong *raki,* which is sipped all year round, through feasts and fasting periods alike.

One of the most fascinating of all bean dishes in Crete is called *palikaria,* a medley of different beans and pulses cooked together, whose roots lay in the remotest past, when offerings of beans and grains were made to the gods around harvest time. It is a custom that survived all over Greece until as recently as the 1960s, when, on certain saints' days, bowls of cooked pulses, often sweetened, were left as votives in church. In Crete, until a generation ago, on January 5, a day before the Epiphany (Christ's baptism), *palikaria* were cooked and eaten not only by the whole family but shared with the farm animals, too. Nikos Psillakis, in his book on traditional island food, relates that the custom survives in some parts of the island, as old village women will sometimes throw a plate of *palikaria* on the rooftop to be had by the birds.

Baby Fava Bean and Raw Artichoke Salad

KOUKIA SALATA ME ANGINARES

Makes 4 servings

4 large fresh artichoke hearts (see page 459), thinly sliced or quartered
1 pound fresh baby fava beans, shelled, washed, and drained
2 to 3 scallions or spring onions, to taste, white and green parts, thinly sliced
2/3 cup slit green Greek olives
1 small bunch fresh dill, snipped
1/2 cup extra-virgin olive oil
Juice of 1 large lemon
Salt and freshly ground black pepper to taste

1. Combine the artichokes, fava beans, scallions or spring onions, olives, and dill in a serving bowl.

2. Whisk together the olive oil, lemon juice, salt, and pepper and toss well with the salad. Serve immediately.

Fresh Favas Stewed with Leeks and Potatoes

HLOROKOUKIA ME PRASA KAI PATATES

 Makes 4 to 6 servings

This is Lenten fare, from the environs of southeastern Crete.

1/2 to 2/3 cup extra-virgin olive oil, to taste
3 medium leeks, white and tender green parts, cut into 2-inch-long cylinders, washed well, and drained
4 large all-purpose potatoes, peeled and quartered or cut into 1 1/2-inch cubes
2 pounds fresh fava beans, shelled and "eye" removed (see Note)
Salt and freshly ground black pepper to taste
1 cup finely chopped fresh wild fennel leaves (see Note)

1. Heat 1/2 cup of the olive oil in a large, wide pot over medium heat. Add the leeks and cook, stirring, until translucent, about 8 minutes. Add the potatoes and favas to the pot, season with salt and pepper, and pour in enough water to cover. Cover the pot and simmer until the potatoes are fork-tender and the favas soft, about 25 minutes.

2. Stir in the fennel and cook for 10 minutes. Adjust the seasoning with salt, pepper, or more olive oil. Remove from the heat and serve, either warm or at room temperature.

✳ **NOTE** If the fava beans are very young and tender, simply remove the ribbonlike seam and cook whole. If fresh wild fennel is not available, substitute dill and pour in 3 tablespoons of ouzo together with the dill.

Mashed Dried Fava Beans with Olive Oil

KOUKOFAVA

 Makes 6 servings

There is a certain ritual to making and eating this exquisite and simple dish. The mashed favas are never mixed with lemon juice or vinegar, as is done, say, with puree of yellow split peas (also called fava). The acid comes on the side, in the form of various accompaniments, since koukofava *is almost never eaten on its own in Crete. It is served alongside smoked herring, salted sardines, or olives; with raw onions and a little parsley on top; or accompanied by snails* boubourista *(page 433), deep-fried salt cod, or pickled peppers.*

½ pound dried favas beans, picked over and rinsed
Salt to taste
1 cup extra-virgin olive oil, or more if desired

1. Soak the fava beans in ample water for 8 hours or overnight. Using a sharp paring knife, remove their shells and black "eye."

2. Place the favas in a large, wide pot with enough water to cover by about 2 inches. Bring to a boil, reduce the heat to medium-low, and simmer until most of the liquid has been absorbed and the fava beans have nearly disintegrated, about 1 to 1½ hours. With a wooden spoon, mash them further, pressing them against the sides and bottom of the pot. This dish should not be smooth but chock-full of chunky, mashed beans. Season with salt while still warm. Mix in the olive oil and serve as described above.

⊙ You can add a peeled and diced potato or two to the favas as they cook and mash the whole thing together. The addition of potato makes the overall consistency of this dish creamier, but since potatoes absorb a goodly amount of olive oil, you might need more than 1 cup to achieve the proper texture.

FEASTING ON FAVAS

If there is one legume that Cretans favor over all others, it is the fava or broad bean, one of the foods of sustenance, especially among the island's rural population. Cretan cooks transform this most ancient pulse into sheer poetry in countless dishes that use the fava both fresh and dried. There are two main types: the small *misiriotika* fava beans, essentially the same as the *foulia* of Egypt, whence they came; and the larger indigenous favas, called by their generic Greek name, *koukia.* There used to be a third, tiny, wild fava called *meratzounia,* but it disappeared from the culinary repertoire sometime around 1940.

Fresh fava beans come into season in early spring in Greece, from March to the middle or end of April. In Crete the season is a little earlier. When they are young and the pods tender, fresh favas are generally not shelled in the Greek kitchen; instead, using a small knife, cooks remove the ribbonlike spine, which can be stringy and tough. In Crete, and generally in Greece, if the favas are large they are shelled but not peeled. If very large, sometimes their hard little "eye," which turns black as the beans age, is removed.

Dried Favas Stewed with Onions and Cumin

FAVA YIAHNI

 Makes 6 to 8 servings

This recipe was given to me by Eleni Daouraki, the wife of the local high school principal in Sitia, on the eastern side of Crete. Although one of the standard-bearers of the Cretan kitchen, this dish changes slightly from one side of the island to the next. In Sitia, cumin is the telltale seasoning; in Hania, the dish comes smothered with mint.

1 pound dried fava beans, picked over and rinsed
¾ to 1 cup extra-virgin olive oil, to taste
2 large onions, finely chopped
1 teaspoon ground cumin
2 to 3 large firm, ripe tomatoes, to taste, peeled, seeded, and chopped, or 1½ cups chopped canned plum tomatoes
1 cup chopped fresh flat-leaf parsley
2 to 3 bay leaves, to taste
Salt and freshly ground black pepper to taste

1. Soak the fava beans in ample water for 8 hours or overnight. Drain. Using a sharp paring knife, remove their black "eye." If desired, peel about 1 cup of the soaked favas. These will disintegrate during cooking and make for a creamier stew. Place all the favas in a large, wide pot with enough water to cover by 2 inches. Bring to a boil. Reduce the heat to medium-low and simmer, partially covered, until the beans soften but are still al dente, 30 to 40 minutes. Remove from the heat and drain.

2. Rinse and dry the same pot. Heat half the olive oil over medium-low heat and cook the onions for a few minutes to soften. Add the cumin and stir. Add the tomatoes, parsley, and bay leaves and sea-son with salt and pepper. Simmer, covered, over low heat for about 10 minutes. Add the beans to the pot, together with enough water to barely cover. Partially cover the pot and simmer over low heat until the beans are tender and almost all the liquid is absorbed, about 1 hour. Remove from the heat, pour in the remaining oil, let cool to room temperature, remove the bay leaves, and serve.

⊚ In lieu of parsley and cumin, add 1 cup chopped fresh mint leaves.

⊚ Add 1 cup red wine to the beans as they stew with the tomatoes.

Dried Favas with Wild Greens

XERA KOUKIA ME HORTARIKA

 Makes 4 to 6 servings

Cretan cooks often combine dried favas with greens. Some prefer obscure greens such as vine shoots and wild carrot tops, but commonly found leafy greens such as spinach, chard, dill, and fennel leaves work equally well.

½ pound dried favas beans, picked over and rinsed
⅔ to 1 cup extra-virgin olive oil, to taste
2 large onions, coarsely chopped
1 pound leafy greens, such as a combination of spinach, chard, and dill coarsely chopped and washed well
Salt and freshly ground black pepper to taste
Juice of 1 to 2 lemons, to taste

1. Soak the beans in ample water for 8 hours or overnight. Drain and, using a sharp paring knife, remove the shells and black "eye." Place the favas in a large, wide pot with enough water to cover by 2 inches. Bring to a boil, reduce the heat to medium-low, and simmer for 15 minutes. Drain the beans and place back in the pot with fresh water to cover by 2 inches. Bring to a boil, reduce the heat to medium-low, and simmer for about 1 hour.

2. In a large, heavy skillet, heat ⅓ cup of the olive oil over medium-low heat and cook the onions until softened, 7 to 8 minutes. Add to the beans and toss. Add the greens to the pot and continue to simmer until most of the liquid has been absorbed and the beans are tender, about 35 minutes. Season with salt and pepper. About 5 minutes before removing from the heat, pour in the remaining olive oil and the lemon juice. Remove from the heat, let cool to room temperature, and serve.

⊙ Dried Favas with Leeks (Xera Koukia me Prasa): Omit the onions and replace the greens with 3 cups leek whites cut into thin rounds. Cook the beans as in step 1. Cook the leeks in olive oil to soften and add to the beans together with 2 chopped tomatoes. Simmer all together for about 35 minutes. Season with salt and pepper. About 5 minutes before removing from the heat, pour in the remaining olive oil and the lemon juice. Remove from the heat, let cool to room temperature, and serve.

Roasted Dried Fava Beans
SOUFROUS

The idea of throwing dried beans in the fire, then soaking them in a little salted water to soften seems almost archaic. It might well be, if one considers how long the fava bean has been linked to the diet of the Cretans. Nevertheless, this "recipe" was given to me by Mihalis Koutakis, a retired schoolteacher from the village of Kastamonitsa outside Herakleion whose family participated in the by-now famous Seven-Country Study. This odd but tasty snack can still be found in village *cafeneia,* where it is served as a Lenten *meze* for *raki.* The name comes from the word *soufrono,* to wrinkle, for the way the favas shrivel up when roasted. This unusual snack is delicious, something between popcorn and roasted chestnuts.

Place dried favas on a rack or grill over hot embers and roast on both sides until lightly charred and wrinkled. Remove and place in a bowl with salted water for several hours to soften. Drain, dry, and serve.

SOAKED DRIED FAVAS

VREHTOKOUKIA

The simplest of dishes yet one of the mainstays of the Easter fast and de rigueur on Clean Monday, the start of Lent. The word literally means "wet favas," and essentially that is all it is: Soak dried fava beans in ample salted water for 8 hours or overnight in a large pot. In the morning, drain them and place back in the pot with ample salted water. By afternoon, they should be ready: Drain and peel them. Serve the *vrehtokoukia* sprinkled with a little sea salt. They make for an excellent *meze,* especially for *raki* or *tsikouthia* (Cretan eau de vie), and are usually served with a few wrinkled olives and Cretan barley rusks.

PASTA AND RICE

In Crete, grains and pasta appear in several basic forms. On the eastern side of Crete pasta prevails, whereas on the western side of the island rice is favored. There are, nevertheless, nearly a dozen traditional handmade pastas found throughout the island. Pasta was always the farmer's fast food, usually made the same day it was cooked, but sometimes air-dried and stored for later use. Pasta was quick and easy to cook, filling, and usually savored at the evening meal after a hard day's work in the fields, simply boiled—often served as a kind of broth—with a little homemade cheese, butter, olive oil, and sometimes tomato. Sometimes pasta was simmered in milk; sometimes it was fried.

Nowadays, the making of homemade pasta is almost exclusively the domain of old women in Crete. The younger generation satisfies itself with the packaged store-bought stuff, although a few enterprising artisans have opened little workshops that prepare the traditional shapes and sell them fresh, dried, and sometimes frozen.

But all over Greece, the tiny pebble-shaped sun-dried pasta made with flour and buttermilk or yogurt called *trahana* is a mainstay of the table. Although fewer and fewer people make their own at the end of each summer, some excellent *trahana* can be found both packaged and prepared, especially in small cities and large towns by artisans in their own workshops.

Cretans don't exactly have *trahana.* Instead they have something called *hondros* and *xinohondros.* The former is nothing more than cracked wheat, used profusely in pilafs, stuffings, soups and casseroles. The latter, literally "sour" *hondro,* is like *trahana,* in that buttermilk or yogurt is mixed with the cracked wheat, which is then sun-dried. (See

page 457 for a more detailed description.) Since the latter is hard to find in the States—some health food stores and specialty food emporiums might carry it—I have taken the cook's license to replace cracked wheat in traditional Cretan recipes with more accessible bulgur.

Sour Trahana with Fresh Green Beans

XINOHONDRO ME FRESKA FASOLIA

 Makes 4 servings

½ cup extra-virgin olive oil, or more if desired
2 large onions, finely chopped
2 pounds fresh green beans, ends trimmed
1½ cups chopped plum tomatoes (canned are fine)
Salt and freshly ground black pepper to taste
⅔ cup Cretan *xinohondro* (see page 457) or sour *trahana* (see page 456) or bulgur

1. Heat the olive oil in a large, wide pot over medium-low heat and cook the onions until wilted, 7 to 8 minutes. Add the beans and toss to coat. Add the tomatoes, season with salt and pepper, and add enough water to cover the beans by 1 inch. Cover and simmer over low heat until the beans are very soft, 1 to 1½ hours. Add water to the pot if necessary to keep the beans moist.

2. About 15 minutes before removing from the heat, check the liquid contents of the pot. Add enough water to cover the beans by ½ inch and, as soon as it starts to simmer, add the *xinohondro* or *trahana* and stir to combine. Simmer until the *xino-*

hondro or *trahana* is tender, about 15 minutes. Remove from the heat, let cool, and serve. If desired, pour in more olive oil.

☉ Sour Trahana with Okra (Xinohondros me Bamyies): Follow the directions, replacing the green beans with trimmed, washed small okra. To trim okra, cut around the rim of the stem with a paring knife. Sprinkle the okra with ¼ cup red wine vinegar, let steep for 30 minutes, and rinse.

☉ Sour Trahana with Eggplant (Xinohondros me Melitzanes): Another great Cretan dish is stewed eggplants with sour *trahana*. Replace the beans with 3 long, thin eggplants, cut into three-inch cylinders. Add 2 chopped garlic cloves to the onions in step 1, and proceed with the recipe as directed, using the eggplant instead of the beans. Cook for about 30 minutes, add the *xinohondro,* and continue cooking another 15 minutes or so, until tender.

RICE DISHES

The relative dearth of rice dishes in Crete, and the special place it plays in the cuisine—in certain festive dishes, in sweets, or as a curative for the sick—attests to the fact that it was traditionally considered a luxury item and used with economy. Generally, too, rice is more prevalent on the western side of the island than on the eastern side, where bulgur was often used to replace it in fillings and pilafs. However, foreign travelers to the island, especially in the nineteenth century, often mention simple rice dishes that they were fed in households and monasteries, but again, even these accounts recall rice eaten mostly in and around Hania, Crete's first capital and its western jewel.

Pilaf Simmered in Chicken or Beef Broth from Sfakia

SFAKIANO PILAFI

 Makes 4 servings

You can find Sfakiano pilafi *in tavernas all over western Crete, from the small place perched intrepidly over the Samarina Gorge to the tourist traps of Hania. The tourist versions pale by comparison to the real thing, which is redolent of the delicious aroma of local sheep's milk butter. The dish is traditionally festive. Cooked in huge cauldrons, it becomes the food of wedding feasts and baptisms. Cooked at home, it is the stuff of Sunday meals and holidays. On the eastern side of the island, where, as mentioned earlier, rice is rare, a similar meal is prepared with local pasta, both at home and at big festive communal meals.*

3 cups good chicken or beef stock, preferably homemade
1 cup long-grain rice
Salt to taste
2 to 4 tablespoons fresh lemon juice, to taste
3 to 4 tablespoons unsalted butter or sheep's milk butter

1. Bring the stock to a boil in a medium saucepan and add the rice. Season with salt. Simmer over low heat, stirring occasionally, until the rice is tender and all the liquid has been absorbed, about 20 minutes. About halfway through cooking, season with lemon juice.

2. When the rice is nearly done, heat the butter in a skillet and brown lightly. Pour into the rice and stir. Spread the rice over a serving platter and serve, accompanied by meat or by Slow-Simmered Lamb with Onions and Lemon (*Sfakiano Yiahni*) (page 424).

SAVORY PIES

One of the characteristic elements of the Cretan table is the seemingly limitless array of small savory pastries, usually called *bourekia* or *kallitsounia,* filled with greens, cheese, meat, and other ingredients. Unlike in the North, where many pies were born of the nomadic shepherds' need to prepare transportable meals that could be baked in make-shift ovens, in Crete the frying pan is the place to find most of the island's pies. In fact, nowhere else in Greece lays claim to such a variety of small fried pies. This particularly Cretan idiosyncrasy probably evolved from sheer economics: Wood was scarce; hence lighting the oven often was not a practical option. That's also the reason for the existence of so many types of rusks. Olive oil, though, was always plentiful, so frying was an expedient way to cook. Overall, in fact, most Cretan cooking is stovetop.

In certain parts of the island, however, namely in and around Hania, full-pan pies are more common than elsewhere. It is here that one encounters the *tourta,* a delicious blend of lamb and soft, sweet sheep's milk cheese. It is in the environs of Hania that one will also find the local *boureki,* not a skillet pie but a full-pan pie filled with zucchini and soft, sour sheep's milk cheese (in some parts of the province, thinly sliced potatoes replace the dough).

Small Summer Pies with Amaranth and Scallions

HORTOPITAKIA ME VLITA

 Makes 35 to 40 crescents

Summer is the poorest time for greens all over Greece; there is virtually no rain and therefore few wild greens besides the common amaranth, which grows unchecked in most people's vegetable gardens. Nevertheless, with its green-gray and sometimes mauve-tinged, ribbed leaves and pleasant, subtle flavor, it is a lovely green and one that works very well as a filling in pies but also stewed.

½ cup extra-virgin olive oil
8 to 10 scallions, to taste, white and tender green parts, or 2 large onions, finely chopped
2 garlic cloves, minced
1¾ pounds amaranth, tough stems discarded, leaves washed well, drained, and finely chopped
1 cup finely chopped fresh flat-leaf parsley
Salt and freshly ground black pepper to taste
1 recipe Cretan phyllo (page 454) or commercial phyllo, defrosted and at room temperature
Olive oil for frying

1. Heat the olive oil in a large skillet over medium heat and cook the scallions or onions, stirring, until wilted, 7 to 8 minutes. Add the garlic and amaranth and cook, stirring, until the greens are wilted and all the liquid has evaporated. Remove from the heat and let cool for 10 minutes.

2. Add the parsley to the amaranth and season with salt and pepper. Set aside.

3. Divide the dough into 3 equal balls. On a lightly floured work surface, roll the first ball into a large sheet about as thick as a dime. Using a round cookie cutter or glass about 3 inches in diameter, press and cut circles out of the dough. Gather up the remaining dough, reroll, and cut again into circles. Place a scant tablespoon of the greens mixture in the center of each circle, fold to form a half-moon, and press the edges closed with the tines of a fork. Set aside. Continue with the remaining dough and greens until both are used up.

4. In a large heavy skillet, heat about 1 inch of olive oil to just below the smoking point. Place about 4 or 5 crescents in the skillet, or as many as will fit loosely, and fry until lightly golden on both sides, about 5 minutes. Remove with a slotted spoon and drain on paper towels. Continue until all the *hortopitakia* are fried. Serve warm or at room temperature.

Small Onion Pies from Hania

KREMMYDOKALITSOUNES HANIOTIKES

 Makes about 30 pieces

Small onion pies are traditionally a Lenten dish on Crete. Onions replace cheese, which is forbidden during fasting. In Hania they can be fried or baked. Elsewhere on the island, they are almost always fried.

This particular recipe comes from Mrs. Victoria Athanasiadov, the sister of the archbishop of Hania. Together with a group of local home cooks, she has organized a kind of ad hoc recipe group. When I visited her in the cavernous kitchens of the archdiocese, she showed me how to make these tasty little pies.

¼ cup extra-virgin olive oil, plus more for frying
2 pounds onions, coarsely chopped
1 cup chopped fresh wild fennel leaves or 1 cup snipped fresh dill plus 1 tablespoon ground fennel seeds
½ cup chopped fresh mint
Salt and freshly ground black pepper to taste
1 recipe Cretan phyllo (page 454) or commercial phyllo, defrosted and at room temperature

1. Heat the ¼ cup olive oil in a large, heavy skillet over medium-low heat and cook the onions until very soft, translucent, and light golden, about 20 minutes. Transfer the onions to a large bowl. Mix in the fennel or the dill plus fennel seeds and the mint and season with salt and pepper.

2. Divide the dough into 2 equal balls. On a lightly floured work surface, roll the first ball into a large sheet about as thick as a quarter. Using a round cookie cutter or glass about 4 inches in diameter, press and cut circles out of the dough. Gather up the remaining dough, reroll, and cut again into circles. Place a heaping tablespoon of onion mixture in the center of each circle, fold to form a half-moon, and press the edges closed. Set aside. Continue with the remaining dough and onions until used up.

3. In a large, heavy skillet, heat about 1 inch olive oil to just below the smoking point over medium-high heat. Place a few crescents at a time in the skillet and fry until light golden on both sides. Remove with a slotted spoon and drain on paper towels. Continue until all the *kremmydokalitsounes* are fried. Serve warm or at room temperature.

⊙ To bake: Preheat the oven to 350°F. Line several sheet pans with parchment paper and oil. Place the *kremmydokalitsounes* in rows, brush the surface with olive oil, and bake until golden, about 15 minutes. Serve either warm or at room temperature.

SKILLET CHEESE PIES

This is a genre the Cretans show a particular affinity for. There are dozens of small cheese pies—some savory, some sweet, and many that go both ways—which are made all over the island. To my mind the sheer array of them mirrors the need of simple country cooks to make the most out of a limited number of ingredients. The pies vary by shape from place to place and season to season: some are folded like small square parcels, while others are formed into half-moons, coils, or star-shaped tartlets. The pastry can be flavored with ouzo or local *tsipouro,* with orange juice, or with vinegar, among other things. As for the filling, in the savory pies it is almost always just cheese (sometimes with the addition of mint or eggs) and usually one of the local soft white cheeses, *myzithra* or *xynomyzithra.* The seasonings change. Mint, mastic, cinnamon, rose water, and more find their way into the sweet cheese pies.

Most of the cheese pies in Crete call for *xyno-myzithra* or for other, strictly local cheeses that are all but impossible to find outside the island. I still have not settled on the combination of cheeses available in America that might approximate the pleasant, sour taste and creamy texture of Cretan *xyno-myzithra.* The cheese isn't pungent and peppery the way some other naturally fermented soft Greek cheeses are. Instead, *xynomyzithra* has a subtle sourness about it.

In these recipes, I use several combinations of cheese or cheese and yogurt in an attempt to come up with a flavor and texture that best reminds me of the Cretan specialty. The combinations aren't always the same from recipe to recipe, a fact that reflects my own indecisiveness and nothing more. It's just that various combinations of soft Greek *anthotyro* or ricotta (which approximates the texture), feta, chèvre, yogurt, even quark, all come close but none really hits the mark.

"Wet" Cheese Pies from Sitia

NERATES MYZITHROPITES

  Makes 8 to 10 small pies

An elderly woman named Maria Peraki in the village of Kroustas, south of Agios Nikolaos on the eastern side of Crete, taught me to make these unusual pies. The technique is fascinating and unlike anything I've ever encountered in the realm of pita *making, sweet or savory, anywhere in Greece.*

The dough is very wet and yeasty almost like doughnut dough. She had made it earlier in the day, and it had risen to become loose, spongelike, and rather sticky. Getting that texture right is the first part of mastering this recipe. Then comes the hard part: handling it! The secret is to keep your hands moist by wetting them with water. The pies are always shaped in the palm of your hand and near the faucet. When I tested this recipe, I was afraid that I would never master it, but it turned out to be a lot less daunting than I had anticipated. Even on the first try you'll get results that are pretty close to the original. A similar skillet pie is made on the western side of Crete, too, in and around Hania. There the technique for handling the dough is a little different: Olive oil is used to moisten the hands, and the dough, once made and risen, is not dampened with water again.

For the dough
1 tablespoon active dry yeast
3 tablespoons warm water
½ cup strained fresh orange juice
1½ cups water
⅔ cup extra-virgin olive oil
4 to 5 cups all-purpose flour, as needed
½ teaspoon salt

For the filling
3 cups Cretan *xynomyzithra* cheese or 2 cups soft
chèvre combined with 1 cup fresh whole-milk
ricotta or fresh Greek *myzithra* or *anthotyro*
cheese
3 to 4 tablespoons water, as needed

To cook and serve
2 teaspoons olive oil
Honey (optional), for drizzling
Ground cinnamon (optional), for sprinkling

1. To make the dough: In a small cup, dissolve
the yeast in the warm water and set aside for 5 minutes. Place the orange juice, water, and ⅓ cup of the
olive oil in a large bowl. Add 1 cup of the flour and
the salt. Slowly add as much of the remaining flour
as is needed to form a very soft, sticky dough.
Knead, adding the remaining ⅓ cup olive oil as you
work the dough. Cover with plastic wrap and set the
dough aside in a warm, draft-free place and let rise
for 2 hours. It will be very spongy.

2. Prepare the filling: Mash the cheese(s) with
the water and set aside.

3. To make the pies: You'll need to be near the
sink, with the faucet running in a slow, steady
stream. Heat 2 teaspoons olive oil in an 8-inch nonstick skillet over medium heat. Wet your hands and
scoop up a handful of dough about the size of a
small orange. Flatten the dough in your palms, wetting them a little more and patting the dough
between both palms to flatten to a disk about 4
inches in diameter. Place a heaping tablespoon of
the filling in the center of the dough.

4. With wet hands, pull up the outer edges of
the dough and pull them over the cheese to make a
bundle. With always wet hands, flatten the
myzithropita by patting it gently between both
palms and pat it back and forth between both palms

to flatten. It should be about 1½ inches thick. Place
the *pita,* seam side down, in the hot skillet. Wet the
back of your hand and, using the back side of your
fist, press the dough down and spread it in the skillet so that it takes up the entire pan. Fry over
medium heat until the bottom is golden, 3 to 4 minutes. Flip the *pita* onto a plate and slip it back in the
skillet to fry on the other side. Remove when the
bottom is golden. The whole process shouldn't take
more than 5 minutes for each *pita.* Continue with
the remaining dough and cheese. Serve hot, either
plain or drizzled with honey and sprinkled with cinnamon if desired.

Pancakes Filled with Cheese and Mint from Rethymnon

RETHYMNIOTIKA KALITSOUNIA ME MAGIA

 Makes about 30 pancakes

It was fun to spend time with Victoria Athanasiadov and the church ladies of Hania. They weren't all from Hania proper but rather from different parts of western Crete, and they bickered playfully over the proper way to prepare all sorts of small skillet pies as well as over the provenance of each pie. Differences, sometimes so minute as to be practically undetectable, sometimes quite obvious, exist in the way local cooks prepare so many similar recipes from village to village. This recipe, from the beautifully preserved port town of Rethymnon, is not unlike the previous skillet cheese pie from eastern Crete. The dough and fillings differ slightly, but the results are nearly the same.

For the dough
2 cups warm milk
One ¼-ounce envelope active dry yeast
4 to 5 cups all-purpose flour, as needed
½ teaspoon salt
1 cup strained fresh orange juice
2 large eggs, lightly beaten

For the filling
1 pound fresh ricotta or *anthotyro* cheese
⅓ pound Greek feta cheese, crumbled
1 large egg, lightly beaten
2 teaspoons dried mint

To fry
2 to 6 tablespoons olive oil for frying, as needed
1 cup olive oil to moisten hands

1. Place the warm milk in a medium bowl and dissolve the yeast in it. Cover and let rest for 10 minutes in a warm, draft-free place. Stir in 1 cup of the flour and the salt and combine. Add the orange juice, eggs, and another cup of flour and stir to combine. Keep adding the flour, in ½-cup increments, stirring with a wooden spoon, until a soft, loose dough mass begins forms. Knead for 10 minutes. The dough will be sticky. Cover and let rest in a warm, draft-free place for 1 hour. The dough will rise and be spongy.

2. Make the filling: Combine the cheeses, egg, and mint in a medium bowl.

3. To construct the pies: Heat 1 tablespoon olive oil over medium heat in a large nonstick skillet. Have the cup of olive oil nearby. Spread some oil on the palm of one hand and dip the fingertips of the other hand into the oil as well. With your fingertips, take a golf ball–size piece of dough and press it gently into your oiled palm, spreading it with your fingertips to form a small, thick circle. Place a heaping tablespoon of the cheese mixture into the center and close up to form a ball, covering the filling. With the pancake in your oiled palm, pat it down with your other hand to flatten into a circle about 4 inches in diameter and an inch thick. Place in the hot oil and fry until the bottom is golden, 3 to 4 minutes. Flip with a spatula and fry on the other side until golden. Remove from the oil with a slotted spoon and drain on paper towels. Continue with the remaining dough and cheese filling, replenishing the oil after 5 or 6 pancakes, as needed. Serve warm.

✳ **NOTE** You may reduce the ingredients by half.

Cheese-and-Squash Pie from Hania

BOUREKI HANIOTIKO

  Makes 8 to 10 servings

Traditionally this dish is made with a local cheese called xynomyzithra, *which is sour like feta but much creamier. The cheese is difficult, if not impossible, to find in America, but a good simulation comes from combining crumbled feta and fresh ricotta or fresh Greek* myzithra, *which is available at specialty shops.*

2 pounds zucchini, cut into ¼-inch-thick rounds
Salt
½ pound *anthotyro* or ricotta cheese
½ pound Greek feta cheese, crumbled
¼ cup plain thick, Mediterranean-style yogurt
    (see page 459)
1 recipe Cretan phyllo (page 454)
¼ cup olive oil
¼ cup all-purpose flour
1 heaping teaspoon dried mint
Freshly ground black pepper to taste

1. Layer the zucchini in a colander and salt each layer lightly. Press the zucchini down in the colander with the cover of a pot and let it drain for 30 minutes. Rinse and pat dry with a lint-free towel. In a large bowl, mix together the *anthotyro* or ricotta, feta, and yogurt.

2. Divide the phyllo in half. Oil a 15-inch round pan that is 2 inches deep or a 12 by 15 by 2-inch rectangular pan with 1 tablespoon of the olive oil. Preheat the oven to 375°F. Lightly dust your work surface with flour and roll out the first ball of dough to a circle slightly larger than the pan. Place the phyllo in the pan and brush with another tablespoon of the olive oil.

3. Pour the ¼ cup flour into a large, shallow dish and mix with a little salt. Toss a handful of the zucchini in it to dredge, tapping off any excess. Place the zucchini neatly on the bottom of the pan, starting from the rim and working toward the center, overlapping the slices a little, dredging and adding more zucchini until the bottom dough is covered completely. Dot generously with half the cheese and yogurt mixture, season with pepper, and sprinkle with ½ teaspoon of the mint. Dredge the remaining zucchini, adding a little more flour if necessary, and repeat the layering and seasoning.

4. Roll out the second dough ball, place over the filling, and neatly turn in the edges to form a decorative rim. Brush the top with remaining 2 tablespoons olive oil and bake until the pastry is golden, about 50 minutes. Remove from the heat and let cool for at least 15 minutes before serving.

⊙ Substitute the homemade phyllo with 12 sheets of commercial phyllo, thawed and at room temperature, using 7 sheets on the bottom, brushing each with ½ teaspoon olive oil, and 5 sheets on top, each also brushed with ½ teaspoon olive oil.

⊙ You can use potatoes instead of phyllo for this dish, as they do in some parts of westernmost Crete. Peel and cut 5 large potatoes into ¼-inch rounds. Oil the bottom of the baking pan, cover with a single layer of potatoes, and season lightly with salt and pepper. Strew a layer of flour-tossed zucchini on top, add a layer of the cheese mixture, and continue until all ingredients are used up. Drizzle about ¼ cup of olive oil over the top and bake as directed above.

✳ NOTE You may reduce the ingredients by half and bake the pie in a 9-inch round or small rectangular pan.

Lamb and Cheese Pie from Hania

HANIOTIKI TOURTA

 Makes 8 servings

My source for some of the best food on the western side of Crete was a woman named Nena Kondoulaki. She and her husband, Manoli, own a beautiful old farm and estate just outside Hania. The first time we met, a few years back, she cooked up a Lucullan feast of regional specialties, from dried favas stewed with mint and onions to eggs cooked in the famed Cretan staka *to this fabulously rich pie, a specialty of Easter. It reminded me a lot of a* pizza rustica, *and in both name and concept the pie does not resemble the typical Greek savory* pita. *For one, it is thick and tall, chock-full of rich ingredients. The original recipe calls for the meat to be on the bone when it goes into the pie, which makes it unwieldy to eat. I've called for boneless lamb, choosing to make the dish suitable for an urban palate.*

For the dough

One ¼-ounce envelope active dry yeast

1¼ cups warm water

4 to 4½ cups all-purpose flour, as needed

1 teaspoon salt

¼ cup extra-virgin olive oil plus more for greasing bowl

2 large eggs, very well beaten

For the fillings

2 tablespoons olive oil

4 scallions, finely chopped

2 pounds lean boneless lamb, diced

2 teaspoons ground cinnamon

Salt and freshly ground black pepper to taste

1 pound fresh *myzithra* cheese

½ pound Cretan *graviera* cheese, grated

1 large egg

To finish

1 large egg

Sesame seeds

1. Dissolve the yeast in the warm water in a small bowl and set aside for 5 minutes. In a medium bowl, combine 4 cups of the flour and the salt. Make a well in the center. Add the yeast mixture, ¼ cup of the olive oil, and the eggs to the well. Stir with a fork from the center outward until a dough begins to form. Lightly dust your work surface with flour. Knead the dough until silky to the touch, 10 to 12 minutes, adding more flour if necessary. Grease a bowl with olive oil. Place the dough in the bowl, cover, and allow to rise in a warm, draft-free place until doubled in bulk, about 1 hour.

2. In a large heavy skillet, heat 2 tablespoons olive oil. Add the scallions and cook over medium heat, stirring until wilted, about 7 minutes. Add the lamb, season with the cinnamon, salt, and pepper, and brown on all sides, stirring frequently, about 10 minutes.

3. Combine *myzithra* with the grated *graviera* cheese. Stir in one egg until well combined.

4. Lightly oil a 9- or 10-inch springform pan. Divide the dough in half. On a lightly floured work surface, roll the first half into a circle about 14 inches in diameter. Place on the bottom of the pan and lightly press around the sides. There should be at least an inch of dough hanging over the pan's top rim. Spread half the lamb mixture over the bottom of the pan. Spread half the cheese mixture over the lamb. Repeat with remaining lamb and cheese mixtures. Roll out the second half of the dough and place over the filling. Trim the edges, leaving 1 to

1½ inches of dough hanging over the edges of the pan. Roll up the dough edges to form a rim of crust around the top of the pan.

5. Preheat the oven to 350°F. Beat the egg. With a sharp knife, make 4 slits in the surface of the dough. Brush the dough with the beaten egg and sprinkle the sesame seeds on top. Bake until the pastry is golden and begins to separate from the sides of the pan, about 50 minutes. Let cool slightly on a rack. Remove the sides of the pan just before serving.

MEAT

Crete, as the embodiment of the Mediterranean Diet, doesn't capture the mind as a place where meat is savored regularly. Traditionally, it wasn't (likewise for the rest of the country). Meat appeared as a special meal, reserved for Sundays and festive occasions, with some preparations unique to specific holidays. At Easter, for example, lamb stewed with artichokes is the classic Cretan dish; at Christmas, *omaties,* a kind of offal sausage, is the favorite food.

One of the hallmarks of the traditional Greek diet is the combination of greens and meat in slowly simmered stews. All over the country one encounters dishes such as lamb fricassee—with lettuce, spinach, or other greens and *avgolemono*—lamb with artichokes, pork with celery, and more. In Crete the tradition continues, but because of the island's vast array of wild greens, the variety of such dishes is endless. Here are a few classics from the island's traditional meat cookery.

One-Pot Chicken with Parsley and Egg-Lemon Sauce

KOTOPOULO ME MAINTANO

 Makes 4 to 6 servings

When I first sampled this dish, I was surprised at the copious amount of parsley it calls for. Crete is not the only place where such parsley-laden stews are made, however. In Thrace and parts of Macedonia, parsley is coupled with either beef or lamb in much the same way.

½ cup extra-virgin olive oil
One 3- to 3½-pound chicken, cut into serving
  pieces
1½ pounds fresh flat-leaf parsley, stems
  removed and leaves finely chopped
Salt and freshly ground black pepper to taste
1 large egg, separated
Juice of 2 large lemons

1. Heat the olive oil in a large pot over medium-high heat and brown the chicken. Stir in the parsley and reduce the heat to low. Season with salt and pepper. Add enough water to come about halfway up the contents of the pot. Cover and simmer until the chicken is very tender, about 1½ hours, adding water if necessary to prevent sticking. There should always be liquid in the pot.

2. When the chicken is cooked, prepare the egg-lemon sauce: Beat the white until foamy and almost stiff. Whisk the yolk and lemon juice together. Fold the yolk-and-lemon mixture into the beaten white. Add a ladleful of the pot juices to the egg mixture in a slow, steady stream, whisking all the while. Pour the *avgolemono* into the pot, remove the pot from the heat, and tilt the pot so that the sauce is distributed evenly. Serve immediately.

Lamb Stewed with Wild Greens and Egg-Lemon Sauce

ARNI ME HORTA AVGOLEMONO

 Makes 6 servings

Christoforos Veneris first showed me how to make this dish with the Cretan technique for avgolemono, *a technique he learned from his mother, who learned it from her own mother. In this version, as in most of the recipes from Crete where* avgolemono *is used, the eggs are separated and the whites beaten to a meringue before the* avgolemono *is constructed. The result is a sauce that is thick and creamy.*

½ cup extra-virgin olive oil
2½ pounds lamb shoulder, trimmed of fat and
    cut into stewing pieces
2 cups coarsely chopped onion
Salt and freshly ground black pepper to taste
2½ pounds trimmed greens (spinach, chard,
    chicory, sorrel, wild fennel, vine shoots,
    chard, bryony, or sow thistles), washed well
    and drained
2 large eggs
Juice of 2 lemons

1. Heat the olive oil in a large, wide stewing pot over medium-high heat and add the lamb. Brown on all sides, then remove from the pot and set aside. Add the onion to the pot and cook, stirring, over medium heat until translucent, about 8 minutes. Return the meat to the pot and stir together with the onions. Season with salt and pepper. Add enough water just to cover the lamb. Cover the pot and simmer over medium-low heat until the meat is very tender, about 1½ hours.

2. Meanwhile, wash and drain the greens. Bring a large pot of lightly salted water to a boil and blanch the greens for a few minutes to wilt. Drain and rinse under cold running water in a colander. Add the greens to the lamb and continue cooking for another half hour. Add more water during cooking if necessary to prevent sticking. There should always be liquid in the pot.

3. Make the egg-lemon sauce: Separate the yolks from the whites. Beat the whites until foamy and almost stiff. Whisk the yolks and lemon juice together. Fold the yolk-and-lemon mixture into the beaten whites. Add a ladleful of pot juices to the egg mixture in a slow, steady stream, whisking all the while. Pour the *avgolemono* into the pot, remove from the heat, and tilt the pot so that the sauce is distributed evenly. Serve immediately.

Lamb and Artichoke Stew with Egg-Lemon Sauce

ARNI ME ANGINARES

 Makes 6 to 8 servings

In some parts of Crete, as in some parts of the Mani, lamb cooked with artichokes is the traditional Easter dish. Whereas in the Mani, however, the meat and artichokes are roasted, in Crete the dish is prepared on top of the stove and topped with egg-lemon sauce.

⅔ cup extra-virgin olive oil
10 scallions, white and tender green parts,
    coarsely chopped
3 pounds bone-in lamb shoulder, trimmed of fat
    and cut into 2- or 3-inch chunks
Salt and freshly ground black pepper to taste

8 artichokes, cleaned (see page 459) and kept in
　　acidulated water (page 458)
1 cup snipped fresh dill or wild fennel leaves
2 large eggs
Juice of 2 large lemons

1. Heat the olive oil in a large pot over medium heat and cook the scallions until wilted, stirring, about 6 minutes. Remove with a slotted spoon and set aside. Increase the heat slightly, add the lamb, and brown on all sides. Return the scallions to the pot. Season with salt and pepper and add enough water to cover the lamb. Cover, bring to a boil, reduce the heat to low, and simmer for about 1½ hours, until the lamb is tender and almost falling off the bone.

2. Add the artichokes and dill or fennel to the pot and toss gently to combine. Adjust the seasoning with salt and pepper and add more water if necessary. Cover the pot and simmer until the artichokes are tender, 25 to 30 minutes.

3. Make the egg-lemon sauce: Separate the yolks from the whites. Beat the whites until foamy and almost stiff. Whisk the yolks and lemon juice together, then fold the yolk-and-lemon mixture into the beaten whites. Add a ladleful of the pot juices to the egg mixture in a slow, steady stream, whisking all the while. Pour the *avgolemono* into the pot, remove the pot from the heat, and tilt it so that the sauce is distributed evenly. Serve immediately.

⊙ Chicken with Artichokes (Kotopoulo me Anginares): Follow the directions for lamb with artichokes, replacing the lamb with a 3- to 3½-pound chicken, cut into serving pieces. The chicken will need about 1½ hours of total cooking time, so add the artichokes after about an hour.

Slow-Simmered Lamb with Onions and Lemon

SFAKIANO YIAHNI

 Makes 4 to 6 servings

*S*fakia, *the wild southwestern half of Crete, birthplace of some of the island's fiercest revolutionaries, home to sheep marauders and blood feuds, is an isolated, rugged no-man's-land looking at the Libyan Sea. I drove there, up and down Crete's monumental mountains, around precipitous bends, and over harrowing gorges to look for the three dishes this part of the island is known for: its buttery rice pilaf made with the famed sheep's milk butter* staka, *its skillet cheese pies laced with either thyme or sage honey (the name Sfakia actually comes from a transliteration of* faskomilo, *Greek for sage), and, finally, its simple lamb stew. The secret of this dish is in the quality of the meat. How can one reproduce the flavor of a lithe Greek-island lamb nourished on mountain herbs? New Zealand lambs pale in comparison, as does much of the meat available in the United States. Opt then for organically fed lamb, the best one can do unless there is a pantaloon-clad, black-kerchiefed Cretan mountain man in the family who happens to be a shepherd.*

½ cup extra-virgin olive oil, or more if desired
2 large red onions, chopped
2½ to 3 pounds bone-in lamb shoulder or other
　　stewing cut, trimmed of fat and cut into
　　2-inch cubes
Salt and freshly ground black pepper to taste
Juice of 2 large lemons
1 cup water, or more as needed

1. In a Dutch oven or large, wide flameproof casserole, heat the olive oil over medium heat and cook the onions, stirring, for about 5 minutes to soften. Remove with a slotted spoon. Add the lamb and brown on all sides over medium-high heat. Season with salt and pepper.

2. Return the onions to the pot. Add the lemon juice and water. Cover and simmer over very low heat until the meat is tender, about 2 hours. Check it occasionally for its moisture content. The trick to this dish is to let the lamb cook in as dry a pot as possible without burning it. Add water incrementally if necessary but with caution. By the end of cooking, the pot juices should be thick and almost emulsified.

Rabbit Stew

KOUNELI STIFADO

 Makes about 4 to 6 servings

I realize that time and again the name of my friend and mentor in all matters Cretan, Christoforos Veneris, crops up. More than anyone else, he has shown me the ropes when it comes to the food of his native island. The recipes exist in written form in various books in Greek, documented in women's handwritten heirloom recipe books, and passed down by word of mouth. But unless one stands next to the cook, carefully eyeing what he or she does, the intangibles remain just that. This recipe, like many more in this chapter, is an amalgam of experiences, first of hearing of a dish, sometimes of reading about it, and almost always of watching it in practice. That last bit I owe to Christoforos. He's let me into his kitchen countless times, to watch, to ask, to savor; this dish is one of his all-time greats.

One 3-pound rabbit, cut into serving pieces

For the marinade
2 cups dry red wine
2 bay leaves
6 to 10 allspice berries, to taste
1 cinnamon stick

For the stew
1 cup extra-virgin olive oil
Salt and freshly ground black pepper to taste
2 pounds small boiling onions, peeled
All-purpose flour for dredging
1 orange, washed and cut into 8 wedges
2 cups dry red wine
1 cup chopped tomatoes (canned are fine)
2 bay leaves
1 cinnamon stick

1. Wash the rabbit and pat dry. Place in a large bowl with the wine, bay leaves, allspice berries, and cinnamon stick. Marinate the rabbit overnight, covered, in the refrigerator, turning several times.

2. In a wide, heavy stewing pot, heat ½ cup of the olive oil over medium-high heat. Add the onions, reduce the heat to very low, and cook until lightly browned and translucent, about 20 minutes.

3. Meanwhile, remove the rabbit from the marinade, pat dry, and dredge lightly in flour, tapping off any excess. Discard the marinade. Remove the onions from the pot with a slotted spoon and set aside. Add the remaining ½ cup olive oil to the pot and heat over medium-high heat. Place the rabbit pieces in the pot and sear to brown on all sides. Place the orange wedges over the rabbit. Pour in the wine and tomatoes and add the bay leaves, cinnamon stick, and salt and pepper. Reduce the heat to low and cover. Simmer the rabbit until tender, about 1½ hours. Remove from the heat, let cool slightly, remove the bay leaves, and serve.

Rabbit Stewed with Artichokes

KOUNELI ME ANGINARES

 Makes 4 to 6 servings

A *variation on the general theme of meat and vegetables cooked together.*

One 3-pound rabbit, cut into serving pieces

For the marinade
Juice of 3 lemons
2 cups dry white wine

For the stew
⅔ cup extra-virgin olive oil
10 scallions, white and green parts,
   coarsely chopped
1 cup all-purpose flour
Salt and freshly ground white pepper to taste
6 artichokes, cleaned (see page 459) and halved
   and kept in acidulated water
   (see page 458)
1 bunch fresh dill or wild fennel, snipped

For the lemon sauce
2 scant teaspoons all-purpose flour
Juice of 2 large lemons

1. Wash the rabbit well and pat dry with paper towels. Place in a large bowl and toss with the lemon juice and wine. Cover and refrigerate overnight, turning occasionally. The next day, remove the rabbit from the marinade and pat dry. Discard the marinade.

2. Heat the olive oil in a large pot over medium heat and cook the scallions, stirring, until wilted, about 8 minutes. Meanwhile, dredge the rabbit pieces lightly in flour, tapping off any excess. Remove the scallions from the pot with a slotted spoon and increase the heat slightly. Add the rabbit to the pot and brown, turning on all sides. Reduce the heat to medium and add the scallions back to the pot. Season with salt and pepper and add enough water to cover the rabbit. Place the lid on the pot, bring to a boil, reduce the heat to low, and simmer until the rabbit is nearly cooked, about 1 hour.

3. Add the artichokes to the pot, fitting them in between the rabbit pieces. Add the dill or fennel, adjust the seasoning with salt and pepper, and add more water if necessary to prevent sticking. Cover the pot and simmer until the artichokes are tender, about 25 minutes.

4. Make the lemon sauce: Whisk the flour and lemon juice together. Add a ladleful of the pot juices to the lemon mixture in a slow, steady stream, whisking all the while. Pour the lemon sauce into the pot and tilt the pot so that the sauce is distributed evenly. Simmer for another 5 minutes to thicken slightly. Remove from the heat and serve immediately.

RABBIT IN CRETE

Rabbit—and hare—like snails, fava beans, and the copious use of olive oil, is a motif that appears and reappears in the island's cookery. Few other Greeks love rabbit and hare as much as the Cretans do, and few are as adept at cooking them. There is a decided difference between the two, hare being the wild critter and requiring special care and attention, rabbit being the urban cook's alternative.

FISH AND SEAFOOD

"Flames for meat, embers for fish," goes an old Cretan saying about the heat needed for each and the simple cooking method—grilling—that defines how most Cretans still like their fish.

There is a fascinating wealth of fish and seafood dishes that are indigenous to the island and many that seem clearly to derive from Byzantine practices. Several, such as fish cooked with leeks or with wild fennel, and several old fish pies, are mentioned by the Byzantine chronicler and historian Phaedon Koukoules, and they remain surprisingly unchanged to this day in Crete. Cooks here treat fish in the same way they treat meat: as a dear source of protein that is often mixed with greens, vegetables, or grains to make a substantial and filling meal. Nowhere else in Greece does one encounter as many fish stews as in Crete, and islanders show a special affinity for octopus and cuttlefish, the latter often dried as a way to preserve it for the winter. In mountain villages, where fresh fish was and still is relatively scarce, salt cod reigned supreme, and there, too, many recipes call for cooking it together with greens or pulses.

Fish Baked with Okra

PSARI ME BAMIES

 Makes 4 servings

This dish is an old summertime specialty from the northern coast of Crete, especially around Herakleion and Malia, and it was traditionally made with local fish called sarpa, *or salema in English, a fish with golden-yellow skin, which is native to the Mediterranean. It's a relatively small but beautiful fish. They say it's herbivorous, which accounts for its rather large intestine, but once cleaned the flesh is very tasty. Local fisherman even used to sun-dry the* sarpa *so as to have it in winter, and local gardeners often would sun-dry okra, so the entire recipe could be reconstituted when the ingredients were not in season. Now one is more likely to find okra prepared with red snapper or various kinds of bream.*

1½ pounds fresh small okra

1¼ cups red wine vinegar

One 2½- to 3-pound sea bream, sea bass, or
    snapper, cleaned, gutted, and scaled

Juice of 1 lemon

Salt and freshly ground black pepper to taste

½ cup extra-virgin olive oil

2 medium onions, quartered and thinly sliced

2 garlic cloves, finely chopped

8 to 10 plum tomatoes, to taste, peeled, seeded,
    and coarsely chopped (canned are fine)

½ cup dry white wine

1 bunch fresh dill, snipped

1. Trim the okra: Remove the tough upper rims and a bit of the stems. Rinse, drain, and marinate in the vinegar in a large bowl for 30 minutes.

2. Season the fish inside and out with the lemon juice, salt, and pepper. Cover with plastic wrap and refrigerate for 1 hour.

3. In a large pot, heat the olive oil over medium heat and cook the onions, stirring, until wilted, 7 to 8 minutes. Add the garlic, then the okra, stirring gently to combine. Pour in the tomatoes and wine, cover the pot, and simmer over medium-low heat until the okra is tender but al dente, 35 to 40 minutes. About 5 minutes before removing from the heat, add the dill.

4. Spread half the okra evenly on the bottom of a baking pan large enough to hold the okra and fish. Place the fish over it and spread the remaining okra around and over the fish. Bake, covered, until the fish is flaky, about 25 minutes. Serve hot.

⊙ A similar dish, which is another classic summer preparation, may be prepared as a stovetop casserole with salt cod. Soak a 2-pound fillet of salt cod for 36 to 48 hours in ample cold water, changing the water frequently. Remove any remaining dark skin or bones. Prepare the okra as directed. About 20 minutes before the okra is cooked, add the salt cod, cut into 3-inch pieces.

Fish Stewed with Leeks

PSARI ME PRASSA

 Makes 4 to 6 servings

Here is another example of vegetables and fish cooked together, a custom found in the cuisines of various parts of Greece but that, in Crete, through the sheer variety of greens and vegetables, evolved into an art.

One 3-pound red snapper, sea bream, or sea
    bass, cleaned, gutted, and scaled
Salt and freshly ground black pepper to taste
Juice of 3 lemons
⅔ cup extra-virgin olive oil
2½ pounds leeks, white and tender green parts,
    washed well and cut into 2-inch lengths
2 cups water
2 large eggs, at room temperature

1. Place the fish on a platter and sprinkle with salt, pepper and one third of the lemon juice. Cover with plastic wrap and refrigerate until ready to use.

2. Heat ½ cup of the olive oil in a large, wide pot and place the leeks in the pot. Cover and steam in the oil over low heat, turning them occasionally, until lightly caramelized, about 25 minutes.

3. Place the fish over the leeks, add the water, cover, and simmer over low heat until the fish is fork-tender, 20 to 25 minutes.

4. Make the egg-lemon sauce: Separate the egg yolks and whites. Beat the whites vigorously until foamy and nearly stiff. Beat the egg yolks with the remaining lemon juice and then whisk into the whites. Add a ladleful of the pot juices to the *avgolemono* in a slow, steady stream, whisking all the while. Pour the sauce into the pot and tilt the pot to distribute it evenly. Pour in the remaining olive oil and serve.

⊙ Fish Stewed with Leeks and Fennel (Psari Psimeno me Prassa kai Maratho): Add 1 cup chopped fennel leaves to the leeks and cook together.

⊙ Fish Baked with Leeks (Psari Psimeno me Prassa): Omit the water and eggs. Follow the directions for caramelizing the leeks in the olive oil, then add 2 firm, ripe large tomatoes that have been grated (see page 459). Simmer the leeks and tomatoes for 25 minutes. Preheat the oven to 350°F. Pour the remaining olive oil into a large ovenproof glass baking dish and spread half the leek mixture on the bottom. Place the fish over the leeks and cover with the remaining leek mixture. Pour in the remaining lemon juice. Bake until the fish is fork-tender, 20 to 25 minutes. Serve immediately.

Grouper Stewed with Purslane

SFIRIDA MAGEIREFTI ME ANTRAKLA

 Makes 4 servings

2½ pounds grouper, cleaned, gutted, and cut
    into 1-inch-thick steaks
Salt and freshly ground black pepper to taste
Juice of 2 lemons
⅓ to ⅔ cup extra-virgin olive oil
1 large onion, finely chopped
1 clove garlic, minced
2 pounds purslane, trimmed, washed well, and
    drained
2 cups chopped plum tomatoes, preferably fresh

1. On a platter, season the fish with salt, pepper, and the lemon juice. Cover with plastic wrap and refrigerate until ready to use.

2. Heat ½ cup of the olive oil in a large, wide pan and cook the onion and garlic over medium heat, stirring, until wilted, 7 to 8 minutes. Add the purslane, toss to coat, and add the tomatoes. Cover and simmer over low heat for 20 minutes. Place the fish over the greens, cover the pot, and cook until the fish is fork-tender, another 20 to 25 minutes.

3. To serve, spread the cooked greens on a serving platter, with the fish on top. Drizzle, if desired, with remaining olive oil.

Chickpeas Stewed with Salt Cod

REVITHIA YIAHNI ME BAKALIARO

 Makes 6 to 8 servings

1½ pounds salt cod fillets
1 pound dried chickpeas, picked over and rinsed
⅔ to 1 cup extra-virgin olive oil, to taste
2 medium onions, halved and sliced
4 to 5 large, firm, ripe tomatoes, to taste,
    peeled, seeded, and chopped
Salt to taste
Juice of 2 lemons

1. Rehydrate the salt cod as directed on page 463. Place the chickpeas in a large pot of water to soak overnight. Drain, rinse, and drain again. Cut the salt cod into strips about 2 by 4 inches. Set aside.

2. Place the drained chickpeas in a large pot with enough water to cover by 2 inches and bring to a boil. Reduce the heat to low and simmer, skimming the foam off the top, for 50 minutes to 1 hour.

3. Meanwhile, heat ⅓ cup of the olive oil in a medium skillet over medium heat and cook the onions, stirring, until wilted, 7 to 8 minutes. Add the onions and tomatoes to the chickpeas. Season with a little salt and simmer until the chickpeas are very tender, 1 to 1½ hours. About 20 minutes before removing the chickpeas from the heat, add the salt cod and stir gently. About 5 minutes before removing from the heat, season with salt again, if necessary, and add the remaining ⅓ to ⅔ cup olive oil and the lemon juice.

⊙ Chickpeas Stewed with Buttermilk Pasta or Trahana (Revithia Yiahni me Xinohondro): Follow the directions for stewing the chickpeas (without the cod). About 15 minutes before removing from the heat, add ⅔ cup sour *trahana* or Cretan *xino-hondro* to the pot. Add enough water, if necessary, to keep the contents of the pot covered by about 1½ inches. The *trahana* absorbs 3 to 4 times its volume of liquid. Simmer until the *trahana* is soft and the mixture thick but slightly soupy, about 15 minutes.

Cuttlefish Stewed with Fennel and Green Olives

SOUPIES ME MARATHO KAI ELIES

  Makes 4 to 6 servings

I was in Rethymnon with my friend Nikos Plessas, who was doing his 2-year-long rural duty as a physician in a small outpost about 10 miles from the city. He'd befriended the local cafeneion owners, Pericles and Evangelia Seiragakis, whose old shop in the village of Mixorouma was the central station for the village men. It was a damp winter afternoon, and Kyria Evangelia served us up the bone-warming raki that her husband distills. On the meze plate were a few spoonfuls of this dish, one of the real classics of the Cretan kitchen. Fennel, olives, and all manner of cephalopods crop up on the table all over Crete.

2½ pounds cuttlefish (see Note)
⅔ cup extra-virgin olive oil
2 cups chopped onion
4 cups chopped fresh wild fennel leaves or 2 large
    fennel bulbs, quartered and sliced, plus ½
    cup snipped fresh dill and 1 tablespoon ouzo
Salt and freshly ground black pepper to taste
1 cup water
1 cup cracked green olives, pitted and rinsed

1 scant teaspoon all-purpose flour
Juice of 2 lemons

1. Clean, gut, and wash the cuttlefish thoroughly, as described on page 462, discarding the ink sacs and rinsing all the ink away. Cut the cuttlefish into 1½-inch-wide rings and coarsely chop the tentacles.

2. Heat the olive oil in a large, wide pot over medium heat and cook the onions and, if using, sliced fennel bulbs until translucent and soft, about 8 minutes. Add the cuttlefish. If using, add the wild fennel leaves. Season lightly with salt and pepper. Add the water to the pot, cover, and simmer over low heat until the cuttlefish are tender, about 1 hour.

3. Add the olives and, if using, dill and ouzo and simmer for another 10 minutes so that the flavors meld.

4. Whisk together the flour and lemon juice in a small bowl. Add a ladleful of pot juices to the lemon-flour mixture in a slow, steady stream, whisking all the while. Pour the sauce into the pot and stir for about 3 minutes with a wooden spoon to combine and thicken. Remove from the heat. Serve either warm or at room temperature.

✳ **NOTE** You may substitute large squid for the cuttlefish.

Cuttlefish Stewed with Fresh Fava Beans

SOUPIES ME FRESKA KOUKIA

 Makes 4 to 6 servings

This dish comes from the southern part of eastern Crete, from the village of Zakros, where it appears on the traditional Lenten table.

3 pounds cuttlefish (see Note)
½ cup extra-virgin olive oil
10 scallions, white and tender green parts, cut into 2-inch lengths
Salt and freshly ground black pepper to taste
½ cup finely chopped fennel leaves or ½ cup snipped fresh dill plus ½ teaspoon ground fennel seeds
1 cup dry white wine
2 pounds fresh fava beans, pods trimmed, shelled if large (see Note)

1. Clean, gut, and wash the cuttlefish completely, as described on page 462, discarding the ink sacs and rinsing all the ink away. Cut into 1½-inch-wide rings and chop the tentacles coarsely.

2. Heat the olive oil in a large pot over medium-high heat. Add the scallions, season with salt and pepper, reduce the heat to medium-low, and cook until the scallion whites are pearly and translucent, 7 to 8 minutes. Add the cuttlefish and cook, turning it frequently, for about 5 minutes. If using fennel seeds, toss them in and stir for another minute. Add the wine. As soon as it boils off, add the fava beans and fennel or dill. Cover and simmer over low heat until most of the pot juices have evaporated, about 1 hour. Adjust the seasoning with additional salt and pepper. Remove from the heat and serve warm or at room temperature.

✳ **NOTE** You can substitute shelled frozen favas for fresh ones, in which case the cooking time needs to be reduced. If using frozen favas, defrost completely and add them to the pot after the cuttlefish has been simmering for about 1 hour. Continue cooking for another 25 to 30 minutes and remove from the heat.

You can substitute large squid for the cuttlefish.

Octopus Cooked in Wine with Fennel and Potatoes

HTAPOTHI KRASATO ME MARATHO KAI PATATES

 Makes 4 to 6 servings

As I mentioned earlier, fennel coupled with cephalopods is one of the classic combinations of the Cretan table.

1 medium octopus (about 2½ pounds)
¾ cup extra-virgin olive oil
1 cup dry red wine
1 cup chopped red onions
1 cup chopped wild fennel leaves or ½ cup snipped dill plus 1 scant teaspoon ground fennel seeds
3 large firm, ripe tomatoes, grated (see page 459)
2 to 3 large waxy potatoes, to taste, peeled and cut into 1½-inch cubes

1. Rinse and clean the octopus, if necessary, removing and discarding its beak and sac (see page 462). Place in a large pot, cover, and cook over very low heat until the octopus is bright pink and has exuded much of its liquid, 20 to 30 minutes. Remove the octopus, cut it into 8 pieces (separating the tentacles), and place back in the pot. Add 6 tablespoons of the olive oil to the pot and stir. Add the wine, cover, and simmer the octopus for another 15 minutes.

2. In a small skillet, heat the remaining 6 tablespoons olive oil over medium heat and cook the onions, stirring, until wilted and translucent, about 10 minutes. Add the ground fennel if using, and cook for another minute. Add the onions to the octopus, together with the tomatoes and fennel, and stir. Cover and simmer for another 10 minutes. Add the potatoes, toss gently to combine, cover, and simmer until the octopus and potatoes are tender, about 30 more minutes. If using dill, add it to the pot about 15 minutes before the octopus is done. Add a little water if necessary to keep the contents of the pot moist. Remove, cool slightly, and serve.

SNAILS

In Crete, snails—*hohlioi* in the regional dialect, after the ancient Greek word for helix—have always played an extremely important part in the local diet, supplementing vegetables and grains during the long periods of fasting. There are probably as many recipes for snails in Crete as there are for greens. Often they are added to stews and casseroles that could easily stand on their own, hence the plethora of dishes such as snails with okra, with potatoes and tomatoes, with artichokes and fava beans, with all sorts of wild greens, with pumpkin, with cracked wheat or *xinohondro,* Cretan *trahana.* Cretan snails even find their way into *dolmathes* and moussaka.

There are three basic varieties of snails on the island. There are the small white or beige snails called *lianohohlioi,* which are collected during their period of hibernation, in summer, whose shells are sealed with a tough white membrane. These are usually poached or boiled. Next are the *hondroi hohlioi,* or fat snails, which are brown and large. Connoisseurs collect these meaty snails from February through June, as they have had all winter to wake on and off with the rains, forage for food, and fatten up. They are found usually under rocks, inside the cavities of trees, at the roots of vines, and in other hidden places. These snails are also collected in fall, after the first rains, but they are at their weakest and thinnest then, having just awakened from their summer hibernation, and need to be fed for ten days before they can be eaten. *Hondroi hohlioi* usually are cooked as stews or casseroles or in the skillet with salt and olive oil in one of the island's best-known dishes, *boubourista.*

The third variety of snails are the *bouboures,* which are small, with a thin shell but a fair amount of meat. They are found in the soil, usually around just-tilled vineyards, and are collected in spring when locals go out to pick fresh grape leaves. *Bouboures* are considered by many to be the superior variety, and are stewed simply with tomato and onion.

For the recipes that follow, look for large land snails, which can be found in Greek and Middle Eastern as well as in Chinese markets. For more on how to clean snails, see page 463.

Snails in a Skillet with Olive Oil, Vinegar, and Rosemary

HOHLIOI BOUBOURISTOI

 Makes 4 *meze* servings

This is probably the best-known snail dish in Crete and a wonderful meze *for either wine or* tsikouthia *(eau de vie). It is also the only recipe that does not call for blanching the snails before cooking them. There are two stories regarding the provenance of the name. According to some Cretan cooks, it is onomotopoeia for the crackling sound the snails make upon contact with the hot salt. Others, however, say it comes from the Cretan word* abouboura, *which means "face-down."*

1 tablespoon kosher salt
1½ pounds large snails, membrane removed and washed well (see page 463)
⅔ cup extra-virgin olive oil
⅓ cup strong red wine vinegar
2 fresh rosemary sprigs

Spread 1 tablespoon salt evenly over the surface of a large, heavy nonstick skillet set over medium heat. Place the snails, open side down, over the salt. As soon as the snails stop sizzling, add the olive oil and stir for 3 to 5 minutes. Pour in the vinegar and add the rosemary sprigs. Cover the skillet and cook another 3 to 4 minutes over low heat. Remove from the heat and serve piping hot in a deep bowl with all the pan juices.

Snails Stewed with Chard

HOHLIOI ME SESKOULA

 Makes 6 servings

There are dozens of recipes for snails cooked with various wild greens in Crete, including vine shoots, sow thistles, amaranth, wild leeks, chard, fennel, and more, depending on seasonal availability and regional varieties. Taking into account that many such obscure greens are not readily available to Americans, I've opted for the most accessible.

⅔ cup extra-virgin olive oil
2 medium onions, finely chopped
1½ pounds green chard, trimmed, washed well, and chopped
Salt and freshly ground black pepper to taste
2 cups chopped, strained tomatoes (canned are fine)
2 pounds large snails, cleaned and blanched (see page 463)

1. Heat ⅓ cup of the olive oil in a large, wide pot and cook the onions over medium-low heat until wilted, 7 to 8 minutes.

2. Add the chard, season with salt and pepper, and toss to coat in the oil. Cook, uncovered, over medium heat until the greens are wilted and most, but not all, of their liquid has boiled off, about 15 minutes. Pour in the tomatoes, adjust the seasoning with salt and pepper, and cover the pot. Simmer over low heat for about 15 minutes, until the greens are tender. There should be some liquid in the pot, but its contents should not be soupy.

3. Add the blanched snails and toss to coat. Cook all together for another 15 minutes over medium-low heat. Remove from the heat, pour in the remaining ⅓ cup olive oil, and serve.

Snails Cooked with Bulgur

HOHLIOI ME HONDRO

 Makes 6 servings

There are many renditions of this dish in Crete, some with the addition of zucchini or even potatoes. Others, such as this, are simpler. This particular version comes from Kritsa near Agios Nikolaos in the eastern part of the island. The cumin that flavors it is the characteristic spice in many dishes from the eastern part of Crete. I've also taken a cook's liberty with the bulgur; Greeks tend to like their pasta, rice, bulgur, and the like cooked until very soft. I don't, and I've adjusted the recipe accordingly.

½ cup extra-virgin olive oil
1 large red onion, finely chopped
3 large firm, ripe tomatoes
1 scant teaspoon ground cumin, or more to taste
2 pounds large snails, cleaned and blanched
    (see page 463)
1 cup dry red wine
1 bay leaf
Salt and freshly ground black pepper to taste
3 cups water
1½ cups coarse bulgur

1. Heat the olive oil in a large pot or flameproof casserole. Add the onion and simmer over medium-low heat, covered, until wilted, about 8 minutes.

2. Meanwhile, grate the tomatoes (see page 459). Set aside.

3. Add the cumin to the onion and stir for a minute or so. Add the snails to the pot, keep covered, and simmer in the oil over low heat for about 5 minutes. Add the wine, bay leaf, and tomato. Season with salt and pepper. Cover and simmer for another 15 minutes.

4. Remove the snails with a slotted spoon and set aside. Add the water to the pot, together with a little more salt. Increase the heat slightly. As soon as it comes to a boil, slowly pour in the bulgur, stirring all the while with a wooden spoon. Keep stirring until the bulgur is almost cooked, about 8 minutes. The consistency should be fairly compact, somewhat like that of a pilaf, but wetter. Add the snails back to the pot and continue to stir for another few minutes to warm through. Remove from the heat, toss well, remove the bay leaf, and serve.

⊙ One of my favorite versions of this dish comes from Hania, where wild fennel and scallions accompany the bulgur: Wilt 10 chopped scallions in ½ cup olive oil over medium-low heat. Add 2 cups chopped fresh wild fennel leaves (or 1½ cups snipped fresh dill and 1 teaspoon crushed fennel seeds if wild fennel is unavailable), and 2 large grated or pulverized tomatoes. Add 2 pounds blanched snails. Season with salt and pepper and pour in 1 cup water. Simmer, covered, over low heat for 25 minutes. Remove the snails with a slotted spoon and set aside. Pour in another 2 cups water or chicken broth, bring to a boil, and add 1¼ cups bulgur in a slow, steady stream, stirring all the while. Simmer, stirring, until the bulgur is tender and most of the liquid has been absorbed, 10 to 12 minutes. Add the snails back to the pot. Toss gently and cook for another 5 minutes. Add 1 tablespoon olive oil or butter to the pot just before removing from the heat, toss, and serve.

⊙

BREADS AND RUSKS

Barley has been the lifeblood of Crete from time immemorial. Because of barley, farmers in Herakleion a hundred years ago became livid over the proposed plans to excavate Knossos, where the Minoan Palace lay buried. The digging would have destroyed their fields of the precious grain. They lost, of course, but as a result Knossos, revealed, stands as proof of Crete's great past. Today the number of breads and rusks still made with it make for a uniquely Cretan staple.

Bread, either fresh or twice-baked as for *paximathia* (rusks), is the single most important food in Crete. Even today, an invitation to lunch is often literally an invitation "to come and eat some bread." There are breads kneaded with water, with milk (which was also a custom in Byzantine Crete), with *raki*; there are breads made with chickpea flour, with whole wheat, even with oats. There are anthropomorphic breads and the intricately decorated ornamental breads that are made for engagements, weddings, births, and baptisms and that can be found, lacquered and hooked and sold as wall decorations, in the markets of Herakleion and Hania.

There is a sense of the sacred about bread. I remember walking into a small general store in a village outside Agios Nikolaos on the eastern side of Crete, where we had gone to visit a few local women who were to be making hand-rolled pasta that day. I spent the afternoon with them, and by the end of it, after much thought on the part of one, I was honored with a rare gift: a fist-size ball of local starter. She told me that it was almost unheard of to share the starter with someone outside the family, because if that person was in some way unworthy of it, the whole lot could be jinxed. Bread is never thrown away in Crete and never wasted. Even if a piece has

fallen to the ground, some good soul will move it to the side for an animal or bird to find.

Most daily bread and *paximathia* are made with either wheat or barley flour or with a combination of the two. The specialty breads are mostly made with more expensive white flour or with *eptazymo,* a difficult dough made with a starter from chickpea flour, and many of the customs surrounding them are uncannily similar to bread customs dating all the way back to the Minoan civilization. For example, Minoans offered breads from the first wheat harvest of the year as a kind of bloodless sacrifice to their gods. In some villages in Crete, breads made with new wheat are still offered in church.

The decorative breads are an art unto themselves. At Christmas, bread is traditionally more important on the table than meat, which is almost always a dish of boiled pork and wheat. Cretan Christmas breads, *Christopsomo,* come in many versions. Sometimes it is nothing more than a simple round loaf, spiced and highly aromatic with coriander seeds, black pepper, aniseed, cinnamon, cloves, and, sometimes, sugar; in some villages it is decorated with an elaborate carved cross in the center. Elsewhere on the island, the *Christopsomo* is covered with delicately sculpted designs: small ploughs, yokes, goats' bells, the Cretan lyre, among other things. In the southern part of central Crete, the Christmas bread is decorated with a dough-sculpted tree embellished with walnuts and almonds, a custom, according to one local folklorist, that might trace its roots to the ancient worship of trees, which was widespread in Crete in prehistoric times. In the villages above Rethymnon, where one finds the most ornate ornamental breads, the round Christmas loaves are often made to look like the sculpted wooden templates found in Greek churches. One thing remains constant, however, no matter how the bread is decorated: In Crete, as elsewhere, only the master of the house has the right to cut the first slice of Christmas bread, a custom usually upheld for all the specialty holiday breads.

Other decorative breads include the *koukounares* or *kikines,* shaped like turtles, birds, crabs, rabbits, fish, and octopuses (the latter two especially in seaside villages) and made before Easter on the Saturday of Lazarus.

The craftsmanship of ornately sculpted bread wreaths for Cretan wedding rings is most impressive. Once, in Amari, a small village in the mountains above Rethymnon, I was witness to a group of women busy with the making of Cretan wedding rings. There were about eight women gathered in the home of the one whose daughter was getting married. As the custom goes, the bride's family and friends gather to help with the bread, and the women in the groom's family do the same. Then the families give each other the breads as gifts. Each of the breads is laden with beautifully designed motifs, most symbolizing fertility and prosperity.

When I arrived there, the group of women were all sitting around a table. Sheets were spread out on the couch and chairs to hold the dough shapes as they were made. One woman was good at making the flowers—lemon blossoms, roses, etc. Another coiled the dough snakes and made worry beads and birds. Others made small beads with the dough to resemble pomegranate seeds (a symbol of fertility), grapes, and pine nuts. Similar ornate breads are also made for baptisms.

Cretan Cross–Shaped Christmas Bread

CHRISTOPSOMO

  Makes 4 large loaves

¼ ounce compressed yeast
3 to 4 cups warm water, as needed
5 pounds bread flour (about 20 cups)
3 cups plus 1 teaspoon sugar
1 cup extra-virgin olive oil
1 cup fresh orange juice
1 teaspoon mastic crystals
1 tablespoon ground cinnamon
1 tablespoon ground coriander
1 tablespoon ground fennel seeds
4 walnuts in their shells
1 large egg, beaten lightly with 2 tablespoons
    water
1½ cups sesame seeds mixed with ¼ cup sugar

1. In a large bowl, dissolve the yeast in 1 cup of the warm water and mix in 1 cup of the flour. Stir well, cover, and let stand to proof for 1 hour. Mix in 1 cup of the sugar, ½ cup of the olive oil, the orange juice, and 1 cup of the flour. Mix with a wooden spoon, adding more flour if necessary, to form a soft dough. Knead until smooth. Set this aside, covered, in a warm, draft-free place until it doubles in bulk, about 2 hours.

2. Using a mortar and pestle or a spice grinder, pulverize the mastic crystals with 1 teaspoon of the sugar. In another bowl, one large enough to hold all the remaining ingredients, combine the remaining flour and 2 cups sugar and the spices. Make a well in the center and place the first batch of dough in the middle. Start kneading the flour into it, working it in little by little and adding the remaining water in increments, until a firm but smooth dough forms.

Turn out onto a lightly floured work surface and knead until silky, about 20 minutes by hand, less if using a dough hook and stand mixer. Shape into a large ball, place in a clean, oiled bowl, cover, and let rise in a warm, draft-free place for 2 to 3 hours, until doubled in bulk.

3. Divide the dough into 8 equal balls and roll each one into a thick rope about 8 inches long. To make individual loaves of *Christopsomo,* take 2 of the ropes and place one on top of the other to form a cross, pressing the center together to keep the two pieces from separating. Set aside on oiled baking sheets until almost doubled in bulk, about 1½ hours.

4. Preheat the oven to 400°F. Place a whole, unshelled walnut in the center of each cross and brush the dough with the egg wash. Sprinkle the sesame seeds on top and bake until golden, about 40 minutes. Remove from the oven, let cool on racks, and serve. Store, wrapped in plastic and refrigerated for up to a week.

✳ **NOTE** You may reduce the ingredients by half.

Easter Bread Ring Kneaded with Milk and Cream

GALATERA KOULOURIA

 Makes six 10-inch coiled loaves

Adapted from Eleni Bitsikaki's recipe in Kritiki Paradosiaki Kouzina *(Traditional Cretan Cuisine by Nikos and Maria Psilakis). You'll need to start this the day before.*

2 quarts milk

¼ ounce compressed yeast

4 cups sugar

5 to 6 pounds (20 to 24 cups) bread flour, as needed

½ cup heavy cream

1 heaping tablespoon ground cinnamon

1 heaping tablespoon ground cloves

1 large egg, lightly beaten with 2 tablespoons water

1. Start the night before: Warm 2 cups of the milk (do not boil). In a large bowl, crumble and dilute the yeast in the warm milk, together with ½ cup sugar and 1½ to 2 cups flour, just enough to form a thick batter. Cover and let stand overnight.

2. The next morning, warm the remaining 6 cups milk and the heavy cream together in a medium saucepan over medium-low heat until tepid. Place in a large bowl. Mix in the remaining 3½ cups sugar and the spices. Mix in the starter with a wooden spoon. Slowly add as much of the remaining flour to the liquid, stirring with a wooden spoon, as needed to form a dough mass. Transfer the dough to a lightly floured work surface and knead, adding flour if necessary, until the dough is smooth and silky but firm. Place the dough in an oiled bowl, cover, and let rise in a warm, draft-free place for 2 to 3 hours, until doubled in bulk.

3. Divide the dough into 6 equal-size balls. Roll each ball into a thick rope about 15 inches long. Form each rope into a ring or loose coil. Place on oiled baking sheets, cover, and let rise again, until almost doubled in bulk, about 1 to 1½ hours. Preheat the oven to 350°F.

4. Brush each loaf with the egg wash and bake until golden, 50 minutes to 1 hour. Remove from the oven, let cool on racks, and serve. Store wrapped in plastic and refrigerated for up to 10 days.

CHICKPEA BREAD

I had gone to Krousta in eastern Crete to see *schiou-fichta* (a handmade twisted pasta) and *eptazymo* being prepared. I walked into the local *cafeneion* where a group of village women were waiting for me. They had already started on the pasta, rolling and curling each piece with the graceful dexterity characteristic of that generation of women for whom the making of such time-consuming pantry staples is second nature, just another seasonal chore learned so long ago, from mothers, aunts, and grandmothers, that it has become almost innate.

The bread was another story. They giggled when I asked about it, a little nervous and a little surprised that I had expected to be witness to its making, for *eptazymo* is no ordinary bread. It is learned (and made) in secrecy and never talked about, lest its difficult preparation be jinxed with the "evil eye." "*Eptazymo*, little one? You want to see *eptazymo*?" one of them asked, laughing at me kindly. "You know, we never talk when we make it," she said. "Well, almost," another one shot in. "The starter, you know, has to foam, to expand, and it takes time. All night. So if I know that Katerini here is making it, I might ask her if she did it, the thing. You know, sex. That you can ask," she said, and they all started howling with laughter. It was quite an exchange, I in my jeans and pullover, they, sixtyish all of them, clad in black or dusty blue and draped with their aprons, laughing about sex. "Sometimes," one of them added, "I throw a pair of man's pants over the dough." "Why?" I asked. More giggling. "So that the bread will rise like what's inside a man's pants," she said, and we all cracked up.

Spiced Chickpea Bread

ΕΠΤΑΖΥΜΟ

Makes five 12-inch loaves or about 40 *paximathia*

*T*his unusual Cretan bread, found elsewhere in Greece but not with anywhere near the same frequency, is made with chickpea flour, which is fermented and used to make the starter. Eptazymo *is sometimes eaten fresh, but mostly it is made into* paximathia. *The word is a transliteration of* autozymo, *or self-rising. The bread calls for no yeast or other leavening. In times gone by, it was also known as the devil's bread, derided by old local priests who believed that, without leavening, only magic could make the* eptazymo *swell. Traditionally, because it is a difficult bread to make, it was prepared at night, when no one could hear the cook going about her business. That way, at least she could avoid the evil eye. The starter, or* kounenos *as it is called in Crete, is fragile, and if it doesn't turn out properly, the bread won't rise.*

For the starter

½ pound dried organic chickpeas, picked over and rinsed

2 to 3 dried hot peppers, to taste

1 teaspoon salt

1 teaspoon cracked black peppercorns

5 to 6 bay leaves, to taste

1 cinnamon stick

5 cups water

For the remaining bread

4 to 6 cups bread flour, as needed

4 to 6 cups durum flour, as needed

1 teaspoon salt

1 teaspoon ground cinnamon

2 teaspoons ground cumin

1½ cups extra-virgin olive oil, plus 5 teaspoons
1 cup sesame seeds or nigella seeds, or both

To finish
¼ cup honey, preferably Greek thyme honey
¼ cup dry red wine

1. Prepare the starter late in the afternoon so it will be ready the next morning. Either with a large, deep mortar and pestle, a meat grinder, or a sturdy food processor, pound the chickpeas to a coarse meal about the size of coarse bulgur. Seed and chop the hot peppers. In a large, preferably earthenware pitcher or a large mason jar, place the ground chickpeas, salt, chopped hot peppers, and peppercorns and stir to combine.

2. Place the bay leaves and cinnamon stick in a pot with the water and bring to a boil. Simmer for 5 minutes. Strain out the spices and discard. Let the spiced water cool to a little warmer than lukewarm and pour it into the pitcher or mason jar. Stir with a wooden spoon. The mixture should be loose and liquid. Cover with plastic wrap, then wrap the entire pitcher or jar in an old woolen blanket, or as Paula Wolfert suggests in *Mediterranean Grains and Greens,* with an electric blanket heated to low. The starter is ready when it foams, which can take anywhere from 7 to 24 hours, depending on the temperature and the freshness of the chickpeas. The telltale sign is its aroma: The starter should smell pleasant and yeasty; if it smells foul or extremely sour, it has failed. Start over with fresh chickpeas.

3. Pour the starter into a very large, preferably earthenware bowl. Combine 2 cups of the bread flour and 2 cups of the durum flour with the salt. Add this to the starter, stirring slowly, until a dough mass forms. (If the mixture is too dense, add a little hot water; if it is too loose, add a little more flour.)

Knead lightly and leave in the bowl. Cover with plastic wrap and then wrap the whole bowl in a woolen or electric blanket. Let stand for about 2 hours to rise in a warm, draft-free place. Don't be dismayed. It won't double in bulk but will swell to about a third more than its original size.

4. Mix the cinnamon and cumin with 4 more cups of the mixed flours and slowly add this to the starter, alternating with the olive oil. Knead in the bowl, adding more of the flours as you go, until the dough is smooth and silky. Knead well for about 10 minutes. Divide the dough into 5 equal-size balls and let them rest for 10 minutes.

5. Oil five 12-inch bread pans. Shape each dough into a long loaf large enough to fit inside the pans. Spread the sesame or nigella seeds on a work surface and roll each loaf in the seeds so that it is completely covered. Using a sharp paring knife, score each loaf lengthwise, not on top but along the sides, just below the top. Place each loaf in an oiled bread pan. Using a pastry cutter, push the cutter to the bottom of the loaf at 1½-inch intervals, to form thick slices. Cover and let rise for about 1½ hours in a warm, draft-free place. Preheat the oven to 400°F. Bake the bread until lightly golden, about 50 minutes.

6. Meanwhile, heat the honey and wine together in a small saucepan over low heat until the honey is dissolved. Set aside. Remove from the oven and immediately brush each loaf with a little of the honey-and-wine mixture. Let cool on racks and serve, breaking off each slice.

To make rusks (*paximathia*):

Remove the bread from the oven after it is three-quarters baked. Carefully break apart the slices and set on large sheet pans, face down. Let them cool. Turn the oven temperature down to the lowest setting possible and place the sheet pans in the oven.

Leave the *paximathia* to dry out this way for several hours, turning them occasionally. Every oven, obviously, will be slightly different, so it is difficult to gauge the amount of time needed, but count on anywhere between 3 and 8 hours. Let the *paximathia* cool completely and store in cloth bags or tins.

The rusks are eaten for breakfast or as a snack, dipped into wine or coffee or savored with a little cheese and olives.

Rusks with Raisins and Spices

PAXIMATHIA ME STAFITHES KAI BAHARIKA

 Makes about 3 dozen

One more in the long litany of Cretan rusks. This recipe comes from Andonis Veneris, a well known baker in Herakleion.

3 pounds bread flour (about 12 cups), or more if
  necessary
1 cup sugar
1 heaping teaspoon ground cinnamon
1 heaping teaspoon ground cloves
1 envelope active dry yeast
2 cups warm water, or more if necessary
1½ cups extra-virgin olive oil
1 cup strained fresh orange juice
½ cup brandy
Juice and grated zest of 1 large lemon
4 cups golden raisins
1 cup chopped walnuts

1. Mix the flour, sugar, cinnamon, and cloves together in a large bowl and sprinkle with the yeast.

Make a well in the center. Add the warm water, olive oil, orange juice, brandy, and lemon juice and, using a wooden spoon, fork, or your hand, work the flour into the liquid from the periphery of the well inward, until most of it has been incorporated. (The dough may also be mixed in a large stand mixer fitted with a dough hook.) Knead in the bowl (or mixer) until smooth, adding more flour or water if necessary to make a pliant but silky dough. Add the lemon zest, raisins, and walnuts and knead into the already formed dough until they are distributed evenly. Form into a large ball, place in an oiled bowl, cover, and set aside to rise in a warm, draft-free place for 2 to 3 hours, until doubled.

2. Divide the dough into 4 equal balls and shape each into a loaf about 4 inches wide. Oil 2 baking sheets and place 2 loaves on each. Cover and let rise for another hour or two, until nearly doubled in bulk. Preheat the oven to 400°F. Using a pastry cutter, score the loaves into 1-inch-thick slices, being careful not to go all the way down to the bottom of the loaf; the pieces should not separate. Bake until golden, about 45 minutes. Remove from the oven and let cool slightly on racks.

3. Turn the oven temperature down to the lowest setting. Cover the baking sheets with parchment and place the slices on the parchment. Place in the oven and bake until the *paximathia* are completely dry and rock-hard, 3 to 12 hours, depending on your oven. Turn during the baking so that both sides get some color. Remove from the oven, let cool, and store, either in cookie tins or in lint-free cotton sacks in a cool, dry place.

4. To serve: These are usually eaten for breakfast or as a midafternoon snack with a little cheese and coffee.

SWEETS

Sweets in Crete follow the gamut of sweets in most of the rest of Greece: spoon sweets made with almost every imaginable fruit, usually cooked whole in a thick sugar syrup; a few cakes; myriad sweet biscuits and rusks; various fritters made with dough or batter and drizzled with honey or grape must syrup. A few things stand out, though, as uniquely Cretan.

For example, among the spoon sweets, the most typically Cretan is made with either grapes or raisins, since there is much production of the two on the island. One of my earliest memories of Crete, in fact, was driving past a raisin farm outside Herakleion and seeing kilos of raisin grapes drying in whole clusters in the sun, dangling like laundry from specially outfitted frames. But without doubt, the Cretan sweet par excellence is *kallitsounia*, small packets of delicate pastry filled with sweetened cheese. These come in dozens of slightly different versions all over the island.

Some of the ubiquitous small sweet cheese pies enjoyed in Crete are shaped like little packets or parcels; others like makeshift tartlets; still others like half-moons. It is a little difficult to reproduce the exact taste of most of these pies because the cheese available in the United States is so different. In Crete, the kind of soft white cheese used in many of these pies varies with the season. Some call for full-fat, unsalted *myzithra*, a soft white sheep's milk cheese. Others call for the salted version of the same cheese and still others for a sour version of it, which is delicious. Other than these minor differences, the fillings are more or less the same: in some parts of the island cinnamon, mint, or mastic is preferred; elsewhere bitter almonds are mixed in with the cheese filling. The dough, too, can vary quite a bit from place to place and from season to season.

Some pastries are flavored with orange or lemon juice, others with ouzo, brandy, or *tsikouthia* (Cretan *raki,* or firewater). Some use only milk and never water. As for leavening, this, too, is a point of considerable difference from recipe to recipe. Most traditional home cooks prefer to use their own sourdough starter, while others opt for compressed yeast; still others use baking powder. It is clearly impossible to detail the minutiae from recipe to recipe.

What follows are a few of my own favorites.

Little Easter Parcels Filled with Sweetened Cheese

PASCHALINA KALLITSOUNIA

 Makes about 60 *kallitsounia*

Andonis Veneris is a baker in Herakleion. His brother, Christoforos, is a chef and good friend. After much coaxing, they let me spend time in the Veneris family bakery and glean as much as possible regarding the details of many of the island's breads and pastries. Andonis turns out breads, rusks, biscuits, and a whole slew of kallitsounia—*little parcels—daily. These next few recipes come from him. A note on the name:* Kallitsounia, *despite the word's Italian etymology (it sounds uncannily like* calzone*), have existed in Crete for eons, possibly since the Minoans first strained cheese in punctured bronze baskets. There are many different shapes. Generally, those that call for baking powder as a leavener are shaped into little free-form tartlets and those that call for starter or yeast are shaped into parcels.* Kallitsounia *used to be strictly an Easter specialty, although nowadays,*

thanks to the likes of pro bakers like the Venerises, they are made all year round.

For the pastry
5 to 6 cups all-purpose flour, as needed
1 cup sugar
2 teaspoons baking powder
¼ cup fresh lemon or orange juice
1½ cups (3 sticks) unsalted butter, melted
1 cup milk

For the filling
1½ pounds soft sweet, Cretan *myzithra* or whole-milk ricotta cheese
2 medium eggs
¾ cup sugar
1 scant teaspoon ground cinnamon
2 tablespoons chopped fresh mint

For the garnish
Ground cinnamon

1. Make the pastry: Sift 5 cups of the flour into a large bowl. Add the sugar and stir lightly. Make a well in the center. Dissolve the baking powder in the citrus juice, stirring to smooth it out. Add the melted butter, milk, and baking powder mixture to the well and work the flour into the liquid from the periphery of the well inward, using a wooden spoon or fork. When a dough mass begins to form, knead it in the bowl, adding the remaining flour, sifted, as needed, to form a pliant, silky dough. Let the dough rest, covered, for 1 hour.

2. Make the filling: Combine the cheese, eggs, sugar, cinnamon, and mint in a large bowl and mix well.

3. Divide the dough into 3 or 4 equal balls. Preheat the oven to 350°F and butter several baking sheets.

4. On a lightly floured work surface, roll the first dough ball into a thin rectangular sheet about as thick as a quarter. Using a round cookie cutter or glass about 4 inches in diameter, cut circles out of the dough. Fill the center of each circle with a scant tablespoon of the cheese mixture. Shape the excess dough around the cheese, pinching it decoratively between your thumb and forefinger, to form a kind of mini tartlet with the cheese showing like a button in the center. Place on the baking sheet. Knead the remaining cut-out dough into a ball, let rest, reroll, and cut more circles. Repeat with the remaining dough and filling until both are used up. Bake until golden, about 12 minutes. Remove from the oven, let cool on racks, and sprinkle with cinnamon. Serve at room temperature. These will keep up to a week, refrigerated.

Wafer-Thin Skillet Cheese Pie from Sfakia

SFAKIANI PITA

 Makes 8 *pitas*

I *drove the hairpin turns from Herakleion to Sfakia, over some of the most precipitous and imposing terrain in Greece, just to see isolated Sfakia, to get a feel for the intractable Sfakians, and to taste these crêpe-like cheese-filled pies, as famous on the island as the irascible locals. This part of Crete is known more for its blood feuds (usually over stolen animals) and its revolutionaries than for its cuisine, which is based mostly on dairy and meat, with little olive oil, since most of the local population has historically made a*

living raising sheep. I had gone there with a great sense of adventure and anticipation. On my way there, crossing the mountains and looking out over the Libyan Sea, I had been filled with that strange, almost eerie, feeling one gets when being close to a frontier. Then I was shocked. Even in this no-man's land, tourism had reared its ugly, tradition-obliterating head. Every cafeneion, *indeed every shop, had signs in German and French, and the rare treat I had been anticipating all morning suddenly became everywhere available, for every shop advertised the Sfakiani* pita. *To make matters worse, the tourist-trapping* cafeneion *owners had piles of their village pie stacked in the freezer, ready to throw into the skillet as soon as the first foreigner walked through the door. Nevertheless, the trek was worth it. Even the freezer-to-skillet version was delicious.*

I stopped at what looked like the most authentic place, a small café where an old woman was holding court behind the counter. There were only two customers, locals, and both were facing a plate of this flat little pita *and a cup of thick Greek coffee. It took a while for the woman, Kyria Maro, to warm up to me—I was traveling alone and was not a foreigner, which made me something even worse. Then I mentioned* Ta Nea—*the paper I worked for—and the ice broke. Journalists, even females, command a certain respect, especially in small towns. We got to talking, Maro came around from her counter to sit with me, and, after a little while, she shared with me her recipe for the town's famous cheese-filled pancakes.*

For the dough
4 to 5 cups all-purpose flour, as needed
½ teaspoon salt
1¼ cups water
¼ cup extra-virgin olive oil
2 tablespoons ouzo or *raki*

For the filling
1 pound fresh *myzithra* cheese or ½ pound cream cheese mixed with ½ pound ricotta salata cheese, crumbled

To serve
Honey

1. Combine 4 cups of the flour and the salt in a medium bowl and make a well in the center. Add the water, olive oil, and ouzo or *raki* to the well. Using a fork, mix the flour into the liquid until a dough mass forms. Sprinkle ½ cup of the remaining flour on your work surface and knead the dough until firm and smooth, adding more flour if necessary. Cover and set aside to rest for 30 minutes.

2. Divide the dough into 8 equal balls. Divide the *myzithra* into 8 egg-size mounds.

3. Using a rolling pin, roll each dough ball into a circle about 6 inches in diameter. Place a mound of cheese in the center. Pull the dough up and over the cheese, almost pouchlike, overlapping as you go so that the cheese is completely covered. Form this into a ball, dust the rolling pin with flour, and roll out the pastry again, to a circle 6 inches in diameter. Do this with all the dough and cheese.

4. Heat a nonstick skillet. These skillet pies require no oil. Place the first *pita* in the skillet and heat over medium-low heat until the bottom is lightly golden, about 3 minutes. Flip and cook on the other side until it, too, is golden, another minute or two. Remove from the skillet and serve warm, drizzled, if desired, with ample honey.

Turban Pies

SARIKOPITES

 Makes 10 *pitas*

It's the shape that sets these lovely pies apart: filled with cheese and coiled, they are nicknamed sariko-pites *after* sariki, *the word for turban in Turkish.*

For the dough
4 to 4½ cups all-purpose flour, as needed
½ teaspoon salt
1 cup water
3 tablespoons extra-virgin olive oil
3 tablespoons red wine vinegar

For the filling
2 cups Cretan *xynomyzithra* cheese or 1⅓ cups
    crumbled chèvre combined with ⅔ cup ricotta
    cheese

To fry and serve
Olive oil
Honey, *petimezi* (grape must syrup), or
    confectioners' sugar for garnish

1. Combine 4 cups of the flour and the salt in a medium bowl and make a well in the center. Add the water, olive oil, and vinegar to the well. Using a fork, mix the flour into the liquid until a dough mass forms. Sprinkle a little more flour on your work surface and knead the dough until firm and smooth, adding more flour if necessary. Cover and set aside to rest for 30 minutes.

2. Have the filling ready in a bowl.

3. Divide the dough into 2 equal balls. Lightly flour your work surface and roll the first ball into a large square, about 15 by 15 inches. Cut the dough into 3-inch-wide strips. Spread about 3 tablespoons

of the filling along the center length of each strip. Fold over to close and roll up each strip to form a coil. Flatten a bit with your palms. Repeat with the remaining dough and filling.

4. In a large, heavy skillet (preferably 15 inches in diameter), heat about 1 inch of olive oil over medium-high heat. When the oil is very hot, fry the *sarikopites* a few at a time, flipping them over carefully with a spatula, until lightly golden on both sides, about 5 minutes total. Remove from the oil with a slotted spoon and drain on paper towels. Drizzle with honey or *petimezi* or sprinkle with confectioners' sugar. Serve warm.

✳ **NOTE** *Petimezi* is available in Greek, Middle Eastern, and specialty food shops.

Spiced Cake with Grape Must Molasses

PETIMEZOPITA

 Makes 12 to 16 pieces

The grape harvest, which in Crete begins in the middle of August, is a happy, celebratory time, one that has spawned at least three very traditional sweets. Moustalevria, *which literally translates as "grape-must-and-flour," is a kind of pudding, and a recipe for it appears in my first book,* The Food and Wine of Greece. *Ditto for* moustokouloura, *or grape must biscuits.* Petimezopita, *or grape must cake, is not exactly unique to Crete, but it is made there frequently enough during the end of summer and later*

as well that it seems, somehow, to belong to the island. It is a pretty common cake and one that probably harks back to a time before sugar was the predominant sweetener.

1 cup water

1 cinnamon stick

1 teaspoon whole cloves

2 cups extra-virgin olive oil

½ cup sugar

2 cups *petimezi* (see Note)

¼ cup ouzo or *raki*

Grated zest and juice of 2 large oranges

1 teaspoon baking soda

5 to 6 cups all-purpose flour, as needed, sifted

½ cup sesame seeds mixed with 2 tablespoons
    sugar

1. Preheat the oven to 350°F. Bring the water, cinnamon stick, and cloves to a boil in a small saucepan. Remove from the heat, let cool, and strain, discarding the spices. Using an electric mixer, beat together the olive oil and sugar in a large bowl until creamy. Add the spiced water and *petimezi* and beat for a minute or so until combined. Add the ouzo or *raki* and grated zest and mix to combine. Dissolve the baking soda in the orange juice and add it to the bowl, mixing. Slowly add the sifted flour until a thick batter forms, mixing well.

2. Lightly oil a 12-inch round springform pan. Pour the batter into the pan and sprinkle the sugared sesame seeds on top. Bake until set and until a toothpick inserted inside the center of the cake comes out clean, about 1 hour. Remove from the oven, let cool in the pan, and unmold. Serve. Store in a cool, dry place for up to several weeks.

✳ **NOTE** *Petimezi* is available in Greek, Middle Eastern, and specialty food shops.

Sweet Barley Biscuits with Olive Oil, Cinnamon, and Cloves

KRITHINA KOULOURAKIA

 Makes about 13 dozen biscuits

These are one of many small sweet biscuits savored in Crete for breakfast or as a snack with afternoon coffee.

1 cup water

1 cinnamon stick

5 or 6 whole cloves, to taste

1½ cups extra-virgin olive oil

1½ cups sugar

1 cup brandy or ouzo

2 teaspoons baking soda

4 to 4½ cups barley flour, as needed

3 to 3½ cups unbleached all-purpose flour,
    as needed

½ teaspoon of salt

1. Bring the water, cinnamon stick, and cloves to a boil in a small saucepan and set aside. When ready to use, strain out the spices.

2. In a large bowl, using an electric mixer, beat together the olive oil and sugar until creamy. Add the brandy or ouzo and the spiced water. Stir in the baking soda.

3. Combine 4 cups of the barley flour with 3 cups of the all-purpose flour in a large bowl. Mix in the salt. Slowly add the flour to the oil-sugar mixture, stirring with a wooden spoon until a dough mass begins to form. When you can't stir any longer, begin kneading the mixture by hand, adding more of both flours if necessary, until a heavy, stiff dough forms. It should be dense but not sticky. Cover and let rest for 30 minutes.

4. Line several baking sheets with parchment paper and preheat the oven to 375°F. Break off a walnut-size chunk of dough at a time and roll the piece into a strip as thin as either a pencil or a woman's finger. Shape into twists, coils, or rings as desired. Place on the baking sheet and continue until all the dough is used up. Bake until lightly colored and firm, 12 to 15 minutes. Remove from the oven, let cool, and store either in tins or in lint-free cotton bags in a cool, dry place.

Grape Spoon Sweet

STAFYLI GLYKO

 Makes about 10 cups

Spoon sweets are made and savored all over Greece. Cherries, orange or bergamot rind, figs, and more are found everywhere, without a connection to any one place. Some spoon sweets, though, are strictly a regional specialty. Andros boasts its lemon blossoms in syrup, Aegina its young pistachios. In Crete, grapes and raisins both are considered local specialty spoon sweets. I include a recipe for the former here because it is my own personal favorite.

3 pounds seedless yellow grapes
1½ pounds sugar (3 cups)
Juice of 2 lemons
1½ cups water
3 to 4 scented geranium leaves, to taste (optional)
1 tablespoon pure vanilla extract

1. Pick through the grapes, discarding any that are bruised. Remove and discard the stems. Wash and drain.

2. In a large sauce pot, layer the grapes and sugar, alternating between each. Pour in the lemon juice and let the mixture stand for 12 hours.

3. Add water and bring to a boil over medium heat. Reduce the heat and simmer for 10 minutes. Remove the pot from the heat and let cool and rest for a minimum of 12 and a maximum of 24 hours. Bring back to a boil over medium heat, add the geranium leaves and the vanilla. Reduce the heat to low and simmer the sweet for about 25 minutes, or until the syrup is thick and viscous.

4. Let cool completely then store in sterilized mason jars. Seal and store in a cool, dry place. Refrigerate once opened.

Athens

It will seem odd that there is such a small section in this book—and the last one at that—on Athens or Attica, the province in which it is located. The reason is simple—Greece's capital and its environs don't really have a regional cuisine, for here the entire country is represented.

What Athens does have, though, is a vibrant restaurant scene, and its place on Greece's culinary landscape is important because the city is host to all the recent efforts to create a new culinary vernacular. Restaurants that boast "new," "creative" Greek cuisine abound. Athens is also a fun place to catch a first glimpse of the country's garden bounty. For a tourist, a stroll through one of the neighborhood farmer's markets or through the Central Market is one of the most interesting things to do in the city.

The Changing Greek Food Scene

Athens used to be a city of casual, neighborhood tavernas where the food was as good as home cooking and affordable for every pocket. In the last decade, though, tavernas have lost their luster among the throngs of restaurant-goers. Nowadays, many people want fine dining places to go to eat and socialize. The city has seen a major restaurant boom. Greek fusion is the mantra of the moment, and countless places boast a cuisine loosely defined as "creative Greek cooking."

The fusion craze was probably unavoidable. In the last ten years in Greece the number of new food products to reach the Greek supermarket from abroad has soared. Everything from Asian wrappers to English farmhouse cheeses is now readily available in Athens (and elsewhere), and chefs have had a field day experimenting with them all. The profession itself has also seen a turnaround in its fortunes; whereas most of the old-school cooks became cooks because there was little else open to them—many, in fact, came from the galleys of Greece's formidable merchant marine—now chefs enjoy star status, reigning over the stoves in restaurants whose prices compete with those of any major European or American city.

At the same time, though, there has also been a renaissance in regional Greek cuisine. Distribution networks are much better than they used to be, and it is now much easier to find artisanal, regional products in various shops around the city. Some food emporiums even specialize in the products of specific areas, such as Crete, the Pelopennesos, or the Cyclades. These, too, are fodder for chefs, and many once-obscure regional foods, everything from preserves to small-production cheeses to wild greens such as nettles and Cretan chicories, are everywhere evident on modern Athenian menus.

I have been reviewing restaurants for Athens's largest daily newspaper, *Ta Nea,* for nearly a decade now, and in that time have amassed a collection of menus that are the standardbearers of Greece's new cooking. The cuisine has gone in a decidedly more pan-Mediterranean direction. As of this writing, Athenian menus include dishes such as eggplant salad *(melitzanosalata)* with tomato sorbet; *fava* (puree of yellow split pea) with truffle oil; rack of lamb with dried fig sauce; venison with pears in ouzo; fresh cod with beet and garlic coulis; shredded wheat patties *(kataifi)* topped with strained sheep's milk yogurt and *botargo;* grilled feta in phyllo seasoned with thyme honey and sesame seeds; rooster with candied kumquats; smoked swordfish and leek napoleon; and twisted phyllo pastries filled with Greek goat's milk cheese and sun-dried tomatoes and much more. Some of the new stuff is totally over the top. One of the city's more dynamic chefs, for example, recently set forth a plate of "Greek" sushi, not over elegant vinegared

rice but over small mounds of traditional Greek rice dishes such as spinach-rice pilaf and tomato rice.

I have said throughout this book that Greece is the ultimate crossroads. In the case of Athens and its food scene, the tug-of-war is between the all-too-well-known foods that have become clichés on Greek menus across the world and those which are struggling to represent a new, modern Greek sensibility.

The Central Market

No talk of Athens would be complete without a foray into its bustling Central Market. Every city and large town in Greece has a large, usually enclosed market area. Among the most vivid are the one in Hania, Crete, and the Modiano Market in Thessaloniki. But these are gentrified compared to the raw energy of Athens's Central Market.

The Central Market is on Athinas Street, in the heart of what is euphemistically called *palaia Athina,* old Athens—what used to be the city limits before the city began to sprawl unchecked in every direction. The fish and meat markets are bordered on the back side by Aiolou Street and flanked on the sides by Evripidou and Sophocleous streets. The building that houses the fish and meat markets is over a century old and, rare among Athenian landmarks, its purpose has remained unchanged. It was built to be a market and still is.

Construction began on the market in 1878, and its official birthday is 1886. It was originally to be open-air, and to this day there are interior lanes with street names—the original boundaries of the market. The intent, back when Athens was a young city of a mere 250,000 inhabitants, was that it should accommodate twice that number, since the city was growing. (There are over four million people in Athens now, and the market is overwhelmed by throngs daily.) In 1902 the fruit and vegetable market opened across the street.

The market is a raucous symphony of unabashed huckstering. The carnal, almost salacious, odors of the meat market and its 45-odd stalls (replete with pigs' heads and cows' tongues dangling on hooks, tripe, and just about everything else displayed without much heed to the heat or to more puritanical issues such as hygiene) segue to the unmistakable scents of salt and iodine next door, where almost twice as many fishmongers hawk the catch from ice-filled stands. Here and there, between the bounty of land and sea, the sharp briny smells of pickles and olives pierce the air, emanating from the few stalls that sell such "delicatessen" items along the market's three internal alleyways.

Outside, on stools jutting from the market's porticoes, heavy-set old women—part mendicants, part beggars, part shrewd merchants—station themselves and wail out the glories of the garlic they have tied up in bunches, or the greens and herbs they collect to sell on these streets. Later in the day, when the market is on the verge of closing, whole families of gypsy hawkers enjoy lunch alfresco, hovered in the nooks and crannies off Athinas Street, cardboard matting their only tableware.

The streets flanking the market are really just an extention of the mercantile havoc within it. Evripidou and Sophocleous streets are thick with the smells of cheese and other dairy products, for here are clustered most of the shops selling such things. Their immediate neighbors are the shops that sell dried goods—dried fruits and nuts, pastas and grains loose in large sacks, olives, dried fish, sausages, and more. Across Athinas, also on Evripidou, is Athens's spice bazaar, where one can find everything from medicinal teas to vanilla pods. Other shops on the periphery of the market specialize in one product only: oils, olives, eggs (stacked tenuously from floor to ceiling), garlic, or—it's the last such shop left—dried lamb's intestines for making sausages. Quite a sight! Still others evince the changing cultural makeup of the city, for in the streets below the markets are all the shops catering to Athens's Filippino, Sri Lankan, Pakistani, and African communities, something that even five years before this writing did not exist.

The few inner-city blocks around the market are alive twenty-four hours a day. At dawn, all the market's deliveries arrive. By mid-morning and through about three P.M. (later on certain days), what seems like half the city has descended to do its daily shopping. The cycle lulls to a near halt by late afternoon, when only the cleanup crews occupy the aisles. But there is yet another shift readying for evening. The market comes back to life in the wee hours after midnight as the place where denizens of Athens's late-night scene, from hookers and their beaux to ordinary citizens out on the town, come to reap the salutary benefits of *patsa,* tripe soup, said to be the best remedy in the world for a bit too much drink.

Athens's Central Market is like a big, old, churning machine. Although modern, neon-lit supermarkets with their pristine aisles and neat rows of packaged foods have helped to chip away at the market's importance, it is still, as its original intent, the raw, real heart of the city.

The Basics of Greek Cooking

Egg-and-Lemon Sauce
Avgolemono

This is probably the best-known sauce/liaison in all of Greek cooking, used to thicken and flavor soups and stews. There are two basic techniques:

The first is simpler and calls for beating the whole eggs together with a little lemon juice (see individual recipes for amounts). Using a wire whisk, beat the eggs and lemon together until frothy and then add one to two ladlefuls of hot pot juices in a slow, steady stream, beating all the while. The *avgolemono* should be thick and frothy. Make sure the food to be sauced is off the heat (so that the eggs don't cook) but very hot. Pour the *avgolemono* into the pot, tilt from side to side, and serve. Dishes that call for *avgolemono* need to be eaten immediately.

The second method calls for whipping the egg whites, which makes for a thicker sauce. Separate the yolks from the whites. Whisk the whites until foamy and almost stiff. Whisk the yolk and lemon juice together until frothy. Fold the yolk and lemon mixture into the whites. Take a ladleful of pot juices and add them to the egg mixture in a slow steady stream, whisking all the while. Pour the *avgolemono* into the pot, turn off the heat, and tilt the pan so that the sauce is evenly distributed.

To reheat: Always do this in a double boiler, stirring, so that the eggs do not cook.

Olives and Olive Oil

EXTRA-VIRGIN OLIVE OIL

Most Greek olive oil is extra-virgin. Greeks use it profusely in their cooking, but also use it raw in salads and as a condiment in vegetable and bean stews. The recipes in this book call almost exclusively for extra-virgin olive oil, and I highly recommend the Greek oils for two reasons: first, because of their very good quality, and second, because they are still some of the best buys on the market. Often a better quality Greek oil will be a fraction of the cost of an Italian or Spanish oil. The main difference is in the packaging. Most Greek oils tend to look prosaic. Don't let that fool you.

CURING OLIVES

Inspired by the sheer number of ways to cure and season olives all over Greece, I have reworked some of the preferred methods in the Peloponnesos so that an urban cook could cure a few beads of this most sacred fruit.

Olives are usually cured in an 8 to 10 percent salt-brine solution, which is a weight to volume ratio; in other words, 2.85 to 3.5 ounces of salt (approximately) per quart of water. One can do this empirically: Dissolve the salt (coarse salt is preferred) into the water (which should be cold) and then place a raw egg in the brine. It should float in such a way that about a quarter-size area of its tip rises to the top.

CURING BLACK (KALAMATA) OLIVES

Wash and slit 4½ pounds of black olives in two places, making sure not to hit the pit. Place the olives in a bucket of clean water. Let them soak for 2 days, changing the water 4 times. Then place in a 1-gallon plastic or clay container that closes tightly. Make an 8 to 10 percent salt brine—for 4½ pounds of olives, that would come to 5.7 to 7 ounces of coarse salt dissolved into 2 quarts of water. Leave them to steep for 3 months. The olives then may be removed from the brine and marinated in red wine vinegar. When marinating, add enough olive oil on top to cover by 2 inches. Leave the olives to steep in a cool, dark place for 2 weeks in the marinade before consuming.

CURING GREEN OLIVES

Wash and drain 4½ pounds of large, firm green olives. Slit them horizontally in the center, in one spot only, making sure not to cut all the way down to the pit. Place the olives in a container large enough to hold them and cover with cold water. Seal the container tightly and leave the olives undisturbed in a cool, dry place for 4 to 6 weeks. Taste one after the fourth week to gauge its bitterness. The degree of desired bitterness is subjective. Once they are debittered, rinse the olives and place them back in the container in an 8 to 10 percent salt-brine solution: 4½ pounds of olives require 5.7 to 7 ounces of coarse salt dissolved in 2 quarts of water. At this point, they may be flavored to taste with sliced fresh lemons and the juice of several lemons, garlic cloves, herbs such as whole sprigs of dried Greek oregano or thyme, fresh wild fennel, black peppercorns, hot pepper flakes, or whole chile peppers. Pour in enough olive oil to cover the top of the container by 2 inches and leave the olives to steep for at least 6 weeks, but preferably up to 3 months, before consuming. Always keep them in a cool, dry place away from direct sunlight.

Olives Flavored with Bitter Orange Juice

ELIES NERATZATES

My first taste of these olives was an epiphany. We were sitting in the garden of Manolis and Nena Kondoulakis in Perivoli, a village a few kilometers from Hania in Crete, under the shade of a towering eucalyptus. Kyrio Manoli had just finished giving us a tour of his beautiful farm and a walk around a few of the thousand-year-old olive trees that twist out of the earth behind his house. His wife, Nena, brought us a raki *and these tiny, dark green olives steeped in the bitter juice of Seville oranges, one of Crete's greatest contributions to the foods of Greece.*

Method 1

4½ pounds olives

9 to 10 ounces coarse salt, as needed

1½ to 2 quarts fresh bitter Seville orange juice or a 3:1 ratio of fresh orange juice and fresh lemon juice

Extra-virgin olive oil to store the olives

1. Slit the olives in 2 places, being careful not to cut all the way to the pit. Place the olives in ample cold water and keep covered in a cool, dark place for about a month, changing the water every day.

2. When the bitterness of the olives has been leached out, make a 12 to 14 percent salt brine: Dissolve the coarse salt in water (approximately 2 quarts water to 10 ounces salt) and steep the olives for 2 days.

3. Remove the olives and place in a container with the bitter orange juice or with a combination of regular orange juice and lemon juice. Leave them to marinate for 48 hours. Remove and place in a jar, and pour in enough extra-virgin olive oil over them

to cover by 1 inch. The olives are ready to be consumed at this stage.

Method 2

1. Follow the above directions. Instead of preserving the olives olive in extra-virgin olive oil, preserve them in a 1:1 ratio of bitter orange juice and an 8 percent salt brine. That means that once the olives have been debittered, brined for 48 hours, and marinated in bitter orange or orange-lemon juice, you need to make a new, weaker brine, combining 1 quart of water and 2.8 ounces of coarse salt.

2. Prepare an equal amount of freshly squeezed, strained bitter orange or orange-lemon juice and pour both the brine and the juice over the olives. Pour in enough olive oil to cover the surface of the jar by about 1 inch. Marinate for at least 2 weeks before consuming.

Phyllo

There are about as many recipes for homemade phyllo as there are regional cooks in Greece. The recipe below for homemade phyllo is my basic, all-purpose recipe. It makes for a malleable dough that is easy to work with and easy to roll. It may be used to prepare any of the pies in this book, and will be enough for either a 15-inch or 18-inch savory pie. You may halve the recipe (and, by extention, individual pie and filling proportions) to make smaller pies in 8-inch or 10-inch round baking pans.

Of course, I could not in good conscience omit

the regional variations, which appear after the basic phyllo recipe. I have also included a recipe for Macedonian phyllo, which is quite different because it is so similar to puff pastry.

BASIC HOMEMADE PHYLLO DOUGH

 Enough pastry for a 15-inch or 18-inch round pan

4 to 4½ cups all purpose flour, as needed
1 scant teaspoon salt
1½ cups warm water, or more if needed
¼ cup extra-virgin olive oil
2 tablespoons red wine vinegar or fresh lemon juice, as needed

Combine 4 cups of the flour and the salt in a large mixing bowl and make a well in the center. Add the water, the olive oil, and the vinegar or lemon juice. Work the flour into the liquid with a fork, until a dough begins to form, then knead it in the bowl, adding a little more flour or water if necessary, for about 10 minutes. The dough should be silky, pliant, and smooth. Cover and let rest at room temperature at least one hour before using.

Follow the directions for making the individual savory pies.

All homemade phyllo may be stored in the refrigerator in an airtight bag for up to three days. Bring it to room temperature before using.

✳ NOTE Phyllo dough may also be made in a kitchen mixer fitted with a dough hook.

⊙ **Phyllo Afrato, Phyllo in the Ionian Islands** Follow the same directions as for basic phyllo, but reduce the water to 1 cup and add ½ cup of strained plain yogurt together with the remaining liquids. The yogurt produces a springy pastry, sometimes referred to as *afrato,* or light.

⊙ **Phyllo in Roumeli** Follow the directions for basic phyllo, reducing the amount of water to 1 cup, increasing the amount of olive oil to 1 cup, and reducing the vinegar or lemon juice to 1 tablespoon. The additional olive oil makes for a slightly flakier final result. They also add shortening for an even flakier crust. To do this, work ½ cup vegetable shortening into the flour with your fingers until it is mealy. Reduce the amount of olive oil to ¾ cup and add it to the well together with the other liquids.

⊙ **Phyllo in Epirus** Reduce the amount of water to 1¼ cups and add one large egg, beaten.

Epirote cooks traditionally use a slightly different technique than the one prescribed above for mixing the dough. In step 1, mix together 4 cups of the flour and the salt in a large basin and make a well in the center. Add the egg to the well. With one hand, sprinkle in the water, a little at a time, and, as you do this, knead the dough by pressing it as it dampens with the back of the other fist, as though "punching" the dough. Keep sprinkling and kneading until a dough mass forms that is smooth and firm and doesn't stick. Sprinkle in a little more flour if necessary to achieve the proper consistency.

Roll out the dough immediately into a rope about an inch thick and divide it into as many individual pieces as the individual recipe specifies. Rub each ball with 1 teaspoon of olive oil and set aside, covered with a kitchen towel, to rest for about 10 minutes. Roll out following the directions in the individual recipes.

⊙ **Phyllo in Crete** Most cooks add yeast and a little eau de vie to the basic phyllo dough recipe. Combine 1 teaspoon of active dry yeast in step 1 of the basic recipe, together with the flour and salt. Follow the same directions for mixing and kneading, but use warm water and reduce the amount to 1 cup while increasing the olive oil to ½ cup and the lemon juice or eau de vie (not vinegar) to 3 tablespoons. This is the basic phyllo used for making the gamut of Crete's small skillet pies. It will provide enough dough for 30 to 40 pastries.

Macedonian Phyllo

MAKEDONITIKO PHYLLO

Throughout Macedonia, most phyllo is made almost like puff pastry, except that instead of cold butter, melted butter is used to fold into the dough. There are two methods for opening and buttering the dough. Both are traditional and both result in a flaky, almost layered, final pastry.

 Enough pastry for a 15-inch or 18-inch round pan

Method 1
4 to 4½ cups all-purpose flour
½ teaspoon salt
1½ to 1¾ cups water
1 tablespoon olive oil
1½ cups melted, clarified, unsalted butter
   (see page 459)

1. Combine the flour and salt in a large bowl. Make a well in the center and add the water and oil. Mix in the flour, starting from the perimeter of the well, until it is completely combined. Knead well for about 10 minutes. The dough should be firm and smooth. Divide into 2 equal-size balls and set aside to rest, covered with plastic wrap.

2. Using a rolling pin or thin dowel and working on a lightly floured surface, roll open the first ball of dough to a large circle about 20 inches in diameter. Brush the entire surface generously with melted butter. Fold in the two sides so that they meet in the center. Brush this surface generously with butter, too. Fold again, so that the dough is now like a long panel, 3 to 4 inches wide. Brush the surface with butter. Fold the top and bottom ends toward the center, brush the surface with butter, and fold again, so that the dough becomes like a block. Cover with plastic and refrigerate for 1 hour or up to one day. Repeat with the second ball. Leave the phyllo at room temperature for about 30 minutes before using.

Method 2

1. Follow the directions for mixing the dough in step 1 of Method 1. Once the dough has rested, flatten the first ball with the palm of your hand and shape it into a square. Roll it open on a lightly floured surface, using either a rolling pin or dowel, to a large square, 20 to 22 inches on all sides.

2. Place a dessert plate in the center of the square. Brush the entire surface of the dough with melted butter. Then, using a sharp paring knife, slit the dough in 8 places, working at equal distances around the rim of the plate outward toward the rim of the pastry like radii.

3. Remove the plate and fold one of the wedges over the center like a flap. Brush the exposed surface of the folded wedge with butter. Repeat with the remaining wedges, working clockwise, folding and brushing each "flap." The end result will be almost like a stack of phyllo flaps, the tips of which stick out. Pat around the edges with your hands to shape into a rectangle or circle. Cover the dough with a clean cloth and let it rest for 10 minutes at room temperature, or wrap it in plastic and store it in the refrigerator for up to a day. Make sure it is at room temperature when you are ready to make the pie. Repeat with the remaining piece of dough.

Follow the individual savory pie recipes for rolling out the phyllo and assembling the pie.

COMMERCIAL FROZEN PHYLLO

Almost all the pies in this book, save for some of the Cretan ones, may be made with commercial phyllo. Figure three sheets of commercial phyllo as a replacement for one sheet of homemade. For a heavy filling, place six or seven sheets on the bottom of the pan.

To fit commercial phyllo into pie pans: If using large round pans, as indicated in many of the recipes in this book, you will need about six sheets for the bottom of the pan. Begin by placing the first one in the center. Brush with olive oil or melted butter. Place the remaining five sheets fanlike from the center outward, so that they hang over the edge. Brush each with oil or melted butter before placing the next one on top. Fill the pie as indicated in the individual recipe and cover with about five more sheets, spreading them fanlike from the center as well and brushing each with oil or butter.

BUYING FROZEN PHYLLO

Buying a package of frozen phyllo is a little like buying a pig in a blanket—you never know what condition the pastry will be in, whether it was stored properly at the market, or whether air somehow got inside, causing the pastry to be brittle.

To reduce the possibilities of opening a useless package, the pastry should be at room temperature when you use it, and it has to be defrosted properly. Remove it from the freezer to the refrigerator to defrost overnight, then leave the unopened box out at room temperature for two hours. If you thaw phyllo too quickly and if the sheets are still cold when you open them, they will crack along the folds or stick together in the corners.

The pastry will dry out very quickly, especially if the kitchen is hot, so it has to be kept covered. Place two towels over the open pastry. The first should be dry and the second, on top, damp. For me, the most reliable brands are Apollo and Athena, and both are widely available in ethnic markets and supermarkets.

BUTTERING THE PHYLLO

Phyllo sheets always have to brushed with a little fat—about a teaspoon per sheet—before baking. Butter makes the phyllo crisp, but it should be melted and preferably clarified (see page 459) before brushing. Olive oil is delicious in savory dishes.

Trahana

In the tiny pebble-shaped pasta that is *trahana* lie all the reasons I am still, after all these years, completely in awe of Greece. Here, where nothing is ever what it first appears to be, where every wall, every word, every speck of earth hides an old story, history permeates even the most mundane things, even a plate of *trahana.* Behind a food so trivial lies a complex history that throws light on the past of the whole region, from the Balkans to Persia.

Trahana, one of the eastern Mediterranean's oldest processed foods, is a granular grain product made with semolina or wheat flour, or bulgur or cracked wheat, mixed with milk, yogurt, buttermilk, or vegetable pulp. The mass is broken up into smaller pieces that are dried outdoors at the end of summer in the scorching, arid Greek heat.

Throughout the Balkans and parts of eastern Europe it is known by several different but similar names, and it can be found from Hungary to Persia. Trying to track down both the etymological and culinary roots of *trahana,* though, is probably futile. *Trahana* claims a range of interconnected meanings.

Whatever its origins, the ancient version and the modern *trahana* seem to have evolved most likely out of a pastoral tradition. Shepherds needed food that was quick to prepare and easy to carry between their lowland abodes in the winter and their highland homes in the summer. The granular little pasta could be boiled with plain water to produce a filling and nourishing meal.

It is definitely Greece, though, that lays claim to the widest variety of dishes employing this ancient shepherd's food and also to the widest range of *trahana;* following is a short list and description of each. There are two basic kinds of *trahana,* sweet and sour.

SOUR TRAHANA

This is essentially wheat flour kneaded with either tart buttermilk, yogurt, or rich, buttery August milk and a little salt. If fresh August milk is used, the dough is left to rest in the heat for about a day so that it sours a little, and then it is broken into small pieces and dried on a sheet in the sun. When the pieces are almost dried but not yet completely brittle, they are passed through a special sieve, rubbed along the grates, so that the *trahana* takes on its characteristic pebbly texture. It is left to dry a little more and, when it is ready, is stored in muslin bags in the cellar or pantry or any other cool, dry place. Sour *trahana* is cooked up on its own as a soup, in water or broth, sometimes with a little tomato or meat, or sometimes in milk. It is also used in stuffed and rolled vegetable dishes and in hearty stews and other soups.

Until a generation ago, sour *trahana* was the shepherd's and farmer's breakfast. Cooked, sour *trahana* is one of the classic savory pie fillings in Thessaly, Epirus, Roumeli, and parts of Macedonia.

SWEET TRAHANA

This is made with cracked wheat simmered in fresh milk. When the cracked wheat has softened and absorbed all the milk, the mass is broken into small pieces, left to dry in the sun, and then grated or passed through a sieve, as with sour *trahana,* to get the characteristic pebblelike consistency.

Its uses in the kitchen are slightly different than that of sour *trahana.* Sweet *trahana* is cooked into hearty stews with chicken or other meat and sometimes used as a filling for stuffed vegetables, especially tomatoes and peppers. It is also used to make some sweets, combined with grape must to make a kind of pudding, or with milk and sugar as filler in sweet pies.

LENTEN TRAHANA

There are many versions of *trahana* made with flour and vegetable pulp all over Greece. In the Aegean Islands, tomato pulp is used most often. One of the most interesting versions of dairy-free *trahana,* though, comes from Thrace, where flour is mixed with a pulp made from hot and sweet peppers and combined with sesame seeds. You can find this in markets all over eastern Macedonia and Thrace.

CRETAN XINOHONDROS

This is essentially a kind of *trahana,* made exclusively in Crete. Its name means "sour cracked wheat" (*hondros* being the Cretan word for cracked wheat). It is made like sour *trahana,* with either buttermilk or yogurt, but instead of flour it is prepared with cracked wheat, which is steeped in the milk until it has absorbed it and forms a dense mass. Then it is formed into large chunks and dried. Cretan *xinohondros* is larger than typical Greek *trahana,* not pebble-shaped but rather like small, amorphous pieces about 1½ inches in size. A very similar grain product is also made in Lesvos, called *koupes,* which means "cups," because of the way it is shaped—into flat oval little saucers.

A Word on Greek Rice

Most of the recipes in the book that call for rice—whether they are for soups, pilafs, or stuffings—reflect my own predilection for basmati. Greeks, however, traditionally use two basic kinds of rice. For pilafs, they prefer long-grain, usually polished rice, and for stuffings and soups a medium-grained, polished rice is preferred. The latter is known in Greek as *nihaki*—little nail—and can be found in Greek and Middle Eastern food shops.

Greek Cheese

One of my main purposes in this book is to introduce American cooks to previously unknown Greek regional foods and food products. By extension, I hope that retailers will be spurred to seek out more interesting, artisanal products from Greece. You will find detailed information on Greek regional cheeses in each chapter. I am fully aware that many of them are still difficult to find in America, but I hope that won't be the case for long. Already, some of the most obscure cheeses are being imported by a few gourmet-minded companies. In many instances, though, I have had to revert to suggesting substitutes. In the case of *myzithra,* the hard whey cheese used in Greece mainly as a grating cheese, there is nothing similar. The closest would be a good pecorino from the south of Italy.

Some Useful Techniques

WORKING WITH A MORTAR AND PESTLE

Anyone with even a perfunctory interest in Mediterranean cooking should count a mortar and pestle among the most basic cooking tools. In Greece cooks typically use either large wooden mortars or old, heavy marble ones. Wooden mortars need to be cleaned carefully. I usually wipe mine with a damp, hot cloth, avoiding direct contact with running water, which would eventually damage and split the wood. The accumulated flavors of garlic and spices will permeate the wood over time and add an unexpected flavor dimension to many diverse dishes. I have a different, smaller marble mortar and pestle for pounding mastic and certain spices that are used in making some Greek sweets.

There is no special technique for pounding garlic, bread, potatoes, and other things in a mortar. Start with a small amount, either crushing it in a round, hard rotating motion against the bottom and bottom rim of the mortar or pounding directly in quick, hard, sure movements. Add ingredients incrementally to ensure that everything gets pulverized to the proper consistency. You have to teach yourself what is best and find the technique you're most comfortable with.

POUNDING MASTIC

Mastic, the crystal resin of a tree related to the pistachio tree, is best pounded by hand in a small marble mortar. You need to pound it with either sugar or salt to keep it from sticking to the mortar. For use in sweet dishes, pound it with about ½ teaspoon sugar; for use in savory dishes, pound it with about ½ teaspoon of salt.

ACIDULATING WATER

Squeeze the juice of 1 large lemon into a bowl containing 3 or 4 cups cold water. Submerge vegetables such as artichokes and celery root, as well as fruits such as apples and quinces, to keep them from discoloring.

TOASTING NUTS AND SESAME SEEDS

Several recipes call for toasting nuts and sesame seeds. I find it easiest to do this in a dry skillet. Place the nuts or seeds in the skillet and stir over medium-low heat until light golden. Remove immediately and empty into a plate; they will continue to brown in a hot skillet even if it is off the heat.

SHELLING CHESTNUTS

Using the tip of a sharp paring knife, score an X on the flat side of each chestnut. Blanch the chestnuts in a pot full of boiling water for about 7 minutes. Turn off the heat, and remove a few nuts at a time with a slotted spoon. Let them cool enough to handle, then peel off their hard outer shells and the papery inner layers. If the shells on some are still too hard to peel, just drop them back into the hot water for a few more minutes.

CLARIFYING BUTTER

Heat unsalted butter in a small saucepan over medium-low heat. Skim the foam off the top with a spoon and discard. Use the remainder to brush on phyllo as indicated in individual recipes.

WORKING WITH YOGURT

The recipes that call for yogurt in this book call for drained, preferably Greek yogurt. There is now a drained Greek cow's milk yogurt produced by the Fage Company on sale in gourmet shops in some major American cities. It resembles sour cream in consistency and taste. There is also excellent thick Mediterranean-style sheep's milk and cow's milk yogurt available widely at specialty food retailers in the United States. If none of these is accessible, you can always drain your own.

To drain yogurt: Line a colander with a cheesecloth and place it in the sink or over a large shallow bowl. To obtain 1 cup of thick, drained yogurt, about the consistency of sour cream, empty 2 cups plain yogurt into the lined colander and leave it to drain for anywhere from 2 to 4 hours to reach the desired consistency. You can save and drink the whey, which, chilled, is a refreshing summer thirst quencher.

HOW TO GRATE TOMATOES

This is one of the great rustic techniques of the Greek kitchen. Have ready a hand grater, preferably one with coarse teeth. Make sure the tomatoes are washed and dried. Hold the grater over a plate or shallow bowl. Hold each tomato from the stem end and grate it along the coarse openings of the grater until all that remains is the tomato's skin, flat and wide open. What you are left with are the pulp, the seeds, and the juice. As for the seeds, most traditional cooks aren't bothered by them.

HOW TO CLEAN ARTICHOKES

Greeks almost exclusively use only the inner, bottom part of the artichoke and about an inch of the stem and almost never bother with the leaves, unless the artichokes are very young and tender. To prepare artichokes the Greek way, cut away most of the stem, leaving about an inch of it intact. Have 1 or 2 cut lemons handy as you work with the artichokes, rubbing them on cut surfaces to prevent discoloration. Also have a bowl of acidulated water on hand (see page 458). Snap off the tough leaves near the base. Hold the artichoke on its side on a cutting board and, using a sharp serrated knife (to facilitate cutting through the dense leaves), cut the artichoke crowns down to within 1½ inches of the base. With a paring knife, trim the tough green exterior off the stem. Rub the artichoke with lemon. Using a teaspoon, thoroughly scrape away the hairy choke on the inside. Holding the artichoke on its side again, trim away any leaf stubs by going around the artichoke almost on a bias with the knife. Using a paring knife, trim the stem so that only its inner, tender core remains. Rub the artichoke with lemon and drop into the acidulated water. Continue until all the artichokes are clean. At this point you can put the cleaned artichokes into zippered-top plastic bags and freeze them for several months. Defrost completely before using.

✳ NOTE If stuffing the artichokes, remove the entire stem so that the cuplike heart can sit upright in a pot.

HOW TO CLEAN CELERY ROOT

Cut away the stalks and leaves and reserve for another use. Have a bowl of acidulated water handy. Hold the root sideways on a large cutting board. Using a large, well-honed butcher's knife, cut thin slices off the root, working all around, until the celery root is clean and there is none of the hard, rough exterior remaining. Use a sharp paring knife to get at difficult spots. Cut according to the recipe and drop immediately into acidulated water to keep from discoloring.

HOW TO CLEAN FAVA BEANS

Young, tender fresh fava beans are usually cooked in their pods in Greece, unless a recipe specifies otherwise. Clean the beans as you would green beans: Using a paring knife, cut away the stringy outer and inner seams. If the beans are large, remove the pods completely.

Dried fava beans come in two sizes, large and small. The small ones are sometimes called by their Egyptian name, *foulia.* Small or large, dried favas need to be soaked overnight or for 10 to 12 hours. To clean them, remove the black "eye" with a sharp

paring knife. Peeling them is an issue of some debate. For mashed fava bean recipes, the beans should be peeled as well. For other stewed dishes, just remove the "eyes." However, if some of the beans are very large and tough, you can remove their skins as well. Cretans, who cook an inordinate amount of fava beans, say that the small ones are best because they have thin skins. Good-quality fava beans remain white when boiled.

HOW TO ROAST PEPPERS

Several recipes call for roasted red bell peppers. You may also roast red Anaheim peppers, which look more like the traditional Greek variety from Florina but have thinner flesh. Preheat the broiler. Place the peppers on a baking sheet in neat rows and roast about 8 inches from the heat source, turning until blistered on all sides. Remove from the oven and let the peppers cool until they can be handled. Place one pepper at a time on a small plate, holding it by the stem. Either with your fingers or with a small knife, peel away the skin. Remove the stem, split open the pepper lengthwise, and scrape away and discard the seeds and white veins, and place in a container.

HOW TO DRY PEPPERS

If you live in a hot, dry place, you can dry the peppers outdoors: String as many red bell or red Anaheim peppers as desired (make sure they are washed and patted thoroughly dry first) by the stem using a needle and strong thread. Hang them outside in a hot, sunny place or indoors, near a sunny window, for about 2 weeks, maybe longer, depending on the weather, until the peppers are shriveled and brittle. Store in a cool, dark cellar or other cool, dark place.

HOW TO ROAST EGGPLANT

The best smoky flavor comes from roasting the eggplant over a flame. I do this on my gas stove at home, but it can also be done on an electric burner or under a gas or electric broiler. Wash and pat dry the eggplants. Keep the stems on.

For stovetop roasting: Set the heat to low and place the eggplant directly on the heat source, turning with tongs, until charred and soft on all sides. Make sure it is soft at the fleshy part near the stem; there is a lot of "meat" at the top, and it should not be wasted.

For roasting under a broiler: Preheat the broiler. Place the eggplant on a sheet pan and puncture the surface of the skin in several places with the tines of a fork. Broil about 8 inches from the heat source, turning, until charred and soft all over. It takes longer to roast eggplant under a broiler than on top of the stove.

To Remove the Pulp Remove the eggplant from the oven and place on a large cutting board. Let cool enough to handle. Using a sharp paring knife, cut down the center of the eggplant, opening it like a butterfly. Score the flesh horizontally and vertically, being careful not to go down to the skin. Using a spoon, scoop out as many seeds as possible and discard them, then scoop out the pulp, going as close to the skin as possible. Remove any pieces of charred skin that you may scrape out accidentally.

HOW TO SHRED PUMPKIN

Cut the pumpkin in half and then into wedges. Place one wedge at a time on its side on a cutting board and, using a large, sharp knife, cut away the rind. Grate the pumpkin by hand on a cheese grater with large holes. You can also grate it in a food processor.

HOW TO COOK WILD MUSHROOMS

Many parts of Greece are a mushroom-lover's paradise. Epirus, Thessaly, especially Mount Pelion, some of the islands in the eastern Aegean, especially Ikaria and Samos, and Crete, among other places, are all known for the variety and wealth of wild mushrooms. Besides the run of the mill *Boletus* and wood ears, one finds chanterelles and morels in the Greek mountains, puff balls, shaggy ink caps, saffron milk caps, and many, many more, even more obscure mushrooms. In some parts of Epirus, cognoscenti claim that even the elusive white truffle exists.

Fresh wild mushrooms are generally not available at markets in Greece. Nevertheless, the foragers of these treasures are like a kind of culinary cult, savoring their little secret in the most simple preparations. The trick to cooking or preserving any wild mushroom is to do so while keeping its innate flavor intact. Smaller mushrooms, such as chanterelles and morels, are usually sauteed lightly in a little olive oil, sprinkled with salt, and served, sometimes with lemon on the side.

For large mushrooms, the favored way of cooking them, especially to be served as a *meze*, which makes up the way most mushrooms are treated, is to grill them. Oyster mushrooms, puffballs, large *Boletus,* and more all lend themselves to grilling. The mushrooms are generally brushed with olive oil and sprinkled with salt and grilled over a low fire. They are almost always served with lemon.

Some mushrooms are also cooked in omelets or stews. Try the smaller ones in omelets. In this part of the world they are blanched first and then added to the eggs. In a good year, the mushroom harvest will be far greater than any family can consume in a short amount of time, so many people also pickle mushrooms, usually in a vinegar brine.

HOW TO CLEAN GREENS

The hardest thing about cleaning greens is cleaning them well. That means getting rid of all the dirt, mud, or sand that might be stuck to them. Always cut or chop the greens as per recipe directions before you wash them. Discard any tough stems, dried or macerated leaves, etc. Place the cut greens in a large basin filled with cold water and swish them around with your fingers. Any dirt in the greens will fall to the bottom. Transfer the greens with your fingers to a separate bowl or basin, empty out the water, and rinse the basin. Repeat the soaking and swishing until the water comes out completely clean. Place in a colander and drain well.

HOW TO SALT GREENS

The experienced old cooks always tell me salting greens is preferred to sautéing for savory pies because the greens retain their nutrients that way. Place the cut, washed, and drained greens in a large colander set over a large, shallow bowl and toss with salt—about 2 scant teaspoons per pound of greens. Coarse sea salt is best. Rub the greens between your

fingers to soften and then rub and knead them against the sides of the colander so that they exude as much liquid as possible. Place a plate and a weight over them and let them drain for at least one hour. You can use the juice in lieu of water and salt in making any of the phyllo dough recipes in this book, although none of the recipes says so, because the phyllo will turn an odd green color if you do. It will, though, be more nutritious. The whole point of the salting is to rid the greens of moisture, so do not wash them after salting. Taste each filling or other dish for salt and adjust accordingly to taste.

HOW TO CLEAN OCTOPUS

If the octopus is frozen, defrost it in the refrigerator overnight. Wash the octopus under cold running water. Cut away and discard the hoodlike sac. Turn the octopus over and, using your thumb, forefinger, and middle finger, squeeze out the beaklike mouth and the two stublike eye sockets on the other side. If desired, peel away the purple membrane using a sharp paring knife. I prefer it intact, as I find a skinned octopus insipid.

HOW TO CLEAN SQUID AND CUTTLEFISH

Squid and cuttlefish have similar anatomies and so are cleaned more or less the same way. Wash the squid under cold running water. Grasp the head just below the eyes and pull it off from the rest of the body. Set it aside. Using your index finger, scoop out and discard the guts and the thin bonelike cartilage on the inside of the tail section. If desired, remove the thin purple membrane over the tail section. Rinse the tail section inside and out and use as directed in the individual recipes. Take the head section in one hand and squeeze out the beaklike mouth and eyes with your thumb, forefinger, and middle finger. Discard the eyes and mouth and use the tentacles as directed in the individual recipes.

HOW TO CLEAN SEA URCHINS

Cleaning a fresh sea urchin is simple: Cut around the bottom side of the shell, where the "mouth" is, with a sharp knife. Shake out and discard the viscera. The roe, *corali* to the Greeks, is on the top side. Scoop that out with a spoon. Depending on the species, it takes between 6 and 12 urchins to make a portion.

HOW TO REHYDRATE SALT COD

All of the recipes that call for salt cod in this book call for it to be a filleted piece. Salt cod usually comes with the black skin removed, and except for the salt itself, the cod is clean. If it has not been removed, remove it. Cod needs a lot of soaking, but it is an inexact art since there is no way to know exactly how salty a piece of cod is without first tasting it. To be on the safe side, I recommend soaking it for 2 days. Place the uncut fillet in a large basin with enough cold water to cover it by 2 to 3 inches. Change the water 3 or 4 times a day. You can keep the cod outside the refrigerator while soaking, unless the weather is very hot, in which case soak it in the refrigerator, changing the water with equal frequency. Remove any bones, rinse, and proceed with the individual recipes.

HOW TO CLEAN SNAILS

Snails, perhaps anathema to some American cooks, are nevertheless one of the healthiest foods in the world. In Crete, where snails feed off the island's formidable flora of wild greens, the snails are high in cancer-fighting omega-3 fatty acids.

Depending on the season, live snails are sold either in their hibernating state, during which time their shells are sealed with a hard, papery membrane, or in the foraging state, when they crawl around in search of food, in which case the shells are open.

At Greek markets in the States, they can be found either way, again depending on the season. Snails hibernate in the summer, and these are thought to be the most delicious, because they have fed on tender greens all spring. In the arid Greek summer there is little in the way of wild flora for them to feed on, so they sleep; then, in the fall, after the first rains, they wake and start their hunt for food. The same holds true in the United States, and you can easily pick your own snails and follow the instructions that follow for cleaning.

Foraging snails need to be fed a "clean" diet over several days so that they exude their waste and become fit for cooking and eating. Cretans, the masters of snail cookery in Greece, recommend placing the live snails in deep baskets with a few handfuls of flour, dried pasta, or bulgur. The starch helps fatten them up and also strengthens their shells. Place a long twig of thyme in the basket, too, to help the snails climb about. Be sure to cover the basket with a towel or cloth—not plastic, because they need to breathe—so that the snails don't escape. Feed them for about a week, after which time they will have exuded their waste and will be ready for cooking. Open snails need to be washed very well in several cold water baths, under a running tap. Discard any that smell bad. Then blanch them for 5 minutes in a large pot of lightly salted boiling water. Remove with a slotted spoon, rinse well, and follow the directions in the individual recipes. Blanching them helps rid them of their thick saliva.

You can also leave snails to feed for longer in the baskets. When the snails are full and nourished, they will begin to hibernate again, sticking close together and developing a membrane. This way you can have snails on hand out of their usual summer hibernating season.

When snails have developed a membrane, either naturally according to the cycles of the season or by being fed a diet of grains, the membrane needs to be removed. To do this, with a paring knife, scrape the grit and hard crustlike buildup off the shells. Using the tip of the knife, remove and discard the membrane covering the snail's opening. Bring a pot of lightly salted water to a rolling boil and blanch the snails for 5 minutes. Remove and rinse well.

Where to buy snails In the United States, fresh snails are not easy to find outside of ethnic markets. However, several suppliers now provide fresh purged snails. Luckily, the variety most easily available in the United States is also the one most esteemed by Cretan cooks, *Helix aspera,* or the petit gris. You can also find frozen snails, which have already been shelled and parboiled, and these may be used in place of fresh snails in any of the recipes in this book. Stay away from canned snails, which are bland.

GRAPE LEAVES AND OTHER LEAVES

Most of the commercially brined grape leaves available in the United States are dismal. The leaves are tough and stringy and the brine so strong that its flavor permeates everything well after the leaves have been blanched, stuffed, and cooked. Good Greek cooks are persnickety about their leaves and either pick their own or buy them fresh in the early spring, when they come to market, and blanch and freeze them for future use.

When working with commercially brined leaves, remove them from the brine and rinse in a colander under cold running water. Bring a large pot of water to a rolling boil and blanch the leaves, in batches if necessary, for 4 to 5 minutes. Remove with a slotted spoon and place back in the colander. Rinse under cold running water.

To freeze your own: Choose leaves that are young and tender. They should be a few weeks to a month old. Wash them in a colander. Blanch them for 2 to 3 minutes in lightly salted boiling water, then transfer to a colander and rinse well under cold running water. Pat dry and store in the freezer in stacks of thirty, wrapped very well in plastic. To use, bring back to room temperature and proceed.

Stuffed leaves are one of the great dishes not only of Greece but all over the eastern Mediterranean. In Greece cabbage leaves are stuffed and rolled, but so are a few other more esoteric leaves: chard, collard or cabbage greens, and cyclamen leaves are among them.

HOW TO ROLL DOLMATHES

I think it is easiest and fastest to do this assembly-line fashion: Place the individual leaves, vein side up, in as many rows as will fit on your work surface. Snip off the stems with a small knife or kitchen shears. Place a heaping teaspoon of filling (or more if the leaves are very large) on the center bottom of each leaf, leaving about ½ inch of space. Fold in the sides to cover the filling, then fold in the bottom. Roll up the leaves, gently tucking in the sides as you go. Always place the rolled leaf seam side down in the pot.

RUSKS

Lots of recipes in this book call for rusks, usually Cretan barley rusks. A rusk is a bread twice-baked to preserve it in times when women baked their own breads and when lighting an outdoor, wood-burning oven on a daily basis was not economical. Nowadays you can find many varieties of barley rusks in the United States mostly at Greek and Middle Eastern food shops. Since they are as hard as tacks, there is a certain technique for making them palatable.

Turn the faucet on so that the water streams out in a thin flow. Run the rusk under the water, turning it to moisten all over. Hold it up and let it drip on its own for a minute or so. When it releases the last drop of water, proceed with the individual recipe directions.

Where to Find Greek Food Products in the United States

Most Greek food products, especially dry goods, olives, capers, olive oil, *trahana* and other grains, beans, rice, typical cheeses such as Greek feta, *kasseri, graviera*, etc., and Greek-style or Mediterranean-style yogurt can be found in the many Greek and Middle Eastern food shops in most major United States cities.

Contacting one of the specialty Greek food importers might be useful in pinpointing a store in your area.

Euro-USA
3212 West 25th Street
Cleveland, OH 44109
Tel: 1-800-999-5939
Fax: 1-216-398-3680
E-mail: Eurousanick@aol.com
For organic and conventional high-quality Greek extra-virgin olive oils, olives, excellent spoon sweets, thyme honey, small capers, herbs, excellent vine leaves, unusual olive pastes, and the best-quality Greek heirloom beans on the market.

Krinos Foods
47-00 Northern Boulevard
Long Island City, NY 11101
Tel: 1-718-729-9000
Fax: 1-718-361-9725

Web site: www.Krinos.com
For a large variety of Greek products from olive oils, olives, capers, cheeses, dried herbs, and Greek traditional pasta to whole wheat kernels, confectionery, honey, and Greek coffee.

Liberty Richter Inc.
400 Lyster Avenue
Saddlebrook, NJ 07863-5910
Tel: 1-201-843-8900
Fax: 1-201-368-3575
Web site: www.libertyrichter.com
For a wide range of Greek olive oils, olives, and wild herbs.

A few mail-order sources

Dean & DeLuca
560 Broadway
New York, NY 11101
Tel: 1-212-226-6800
Toll Free: 1-800-999-0306
For an enormous selection of gourmet produce, greens, grains, herbs, olives, cheeses, and much more.

Kalustyan
123 Lexington Avenue
New York, NY 10016
Tel: 1-212-685-3888
Fax: 1-212-683-8458
For a wide range of Greek and Middle Eastern food products.

Zingerman's Mail-Order Department
422 Detroit Street
Ann Arbor, MI 48104-1118
Tel: 1-313-769-1625
E-mail: zing@chamber.ann-arb.mi.us

For specific specialty foods For excellent sheep's milk and Mediterranean-style yogurts:

Old Chatham Shepherding Company
Shaker Museum Road
Old Chatham, NY 12136
Tel: 1-518-794-7733
Fax: 1-518-794-7641
Toll Free: 1-888-SHEEP-60
E-mail: sheepcheese@worldnet.att.net

For frozen phyllo The best is made by Athens and is widely available across the United States:

Athens Pastries and Frozen Foods, Inc.
13600 Snow Road
Cleveland, OH 44142
Tel: 1-216-676-8500
Fax: 1-216-676-0609
Web site: www.athens.com

For toasted corn kernels:

The Great Valley Mills
1774 County Line Road
Barto, PA 19504
Tel: 1-800-688-6455
Fax: 1-610-754-6490

SOME USEFUL WEB SITES FOR ORDERING GREEK FOOD PRODUCTS

www.3Emarket.com
For an enormous range of Greek specialty foods.

www.medfooddirect.com
For a large range of excellent-quality Greek gourmet products.

A Selective Bibliography

GENERAL

Aligizakis, Manolis. *The Processing and Preservation of Table Olives* (in Greek). Athens: Aligizakis, 1982.

Athenaeus. *The Deipnosophists.* Loeb Classical Library. Cambridge, Mass.: Harvard University Press, 1971.

Averof-Tossitsas, Vangelis. *The Monastery of St. Nicholas* (in Greek). Athens: Estia, 1973.

Balatsouras, Yiorgios. *The Table Olive* (in Greek). Athens: Balatsouras, 1992.

Bauman, Helmut. *Greek Flora* (in Greek). Athens: Ekdosi tis Ellinikis Etairias Prostasias tis Physeos, 1993.

Braudel, Fernand. *The Mediterranean and the Mediterranean World in the Age of Philip II.* New York: HarperCollins, 1992.

Burkert, Walter. *Greek Religion.* Oxford: Blackwell, 1990.

Cultural and Technological Foundation of ETBA (National Bank for Industrial Development). *Olive and oil.* Lectures from the three-day seminar held in Kalamata, May 7–9, 1993 (in Greek). Athens, 1996.

———. *From Wheat to Bread.* Lectures from the three-day seminar held in Pelion, April 10–12, 1992 (in Greek). Athens, 1994.

Dagher, Shawky M., ed. *Traditional Foods of the Near East.* Rome: Food and Agriculture Organization of the United Nations, 1991.

Dalby, Andrew. *Siren Feasts: A History of Food and Gastronomy in Greece.* London and New York: Routledge, 1996.

Davidson, Alan. *Mediterranean Seafood.* Baton Rouge: Louisiana State University Press, 1981.

———. *The Oxford Companion to Food.* New York: Oxford University Press, 1999.

Deuteros, Angelos N. *Bread at Birth and Death: Its Symbolism and Magic Among Contemporary Greeks* (in Greek). Athens: self-published, 1978.

Diamanti, Stefanos. *The Mushrooms of Greece* (in Greek). Athens: Ekdoseis Ion, 1992.

Frangaki, Evangellia. *Symbolism of Common Greek Plants* (in Greek). Athens: Frangaki, 1969.

Fytrakis. *The Traditional Recipes of Greece* (in Greek). 6 vols. Athens: Fytrakis, 1987.

Heldreich, Theodore. *Dictionary of the Common Names of the Plants of Greece* (in Greek). 1909. Reprint, Athens: Adelfon Tolidi, 1980.

Imellos, Stefanos. "Food from a Folkloric Point of View." *Yearly Review of the Department of Philosophy* 28 (in Greek). Athens: Athens University, 1979–1985.

Kaneva-Johnson, Maria. *The Melting Pot: Balkan Food and Cookery.* Devon, England: Prospect Books, 1995.

Kardoulis, Alexandros. *Trilingual Dictionary of Food and Drink.* Athens: Kardoulis, 1989.

Kochilas, Diane. *The Food and Wine of Greece.* New York: St. Martin's, 1990.

———. *The Greek Vegetarian.* New York: St. Martin's, 1996.

Koukoules, Phaidon. *Byzantine Life and Civilization.* Vol. 1 and 2. Athens: Ekdoseis Papaziki, 1955.

Lambraki, Myrsini. *Greens* (in Greek). Athens: Ekdoseis Trohalia, 1997.

Loukatos, Demetrios. *Christmas and Holidays* (in Greek). Athens: Ekdoseis Filippotis, 1984.

———. *The Fall* (in Greek). Athens: Ekdoseis Filippotis, 1982.

———. *Introduction to Greek Folklore* (in Greek). Athens: Educational Institute of the National Bank of Greece, 1985.

———. *More Winter and Spring Customs* (in Greek). Athens: Ekdoseis Filippotis, 1985.

———. *Summer* (in Greek). Athens: Ekdoseis Filippotis, 1981.

Mamalakis, Ilias. *Greek Cheese* (in Greek). Athens: Ekdoseis Trohalia, 1999.

Miha-Lampaki, Aspasia. *The Diet of the Ancient Greeks, According to the Ancient Comedy Writers* (in Greek). Athens: self-published, 1984.

Mirodan, Vladimir. *The Balkan Cookbook*. Gretna, Louisiana: Pelican, 1989.

Motsias, Christos. *What the Byzantines Ate* (in Greek). Athens: Ekdoseis Kaktus, 1998.

Potamianou, Themos. *33 Greek Recipes* (in Greek). Athens: Ekdoseis Tachidromou, 1965.

———. *Fish and Cooking* (in Greek). Athens: Ekdoseis Estias, 1995.

Roden, Claudia. *The Book of Jewish Food.* New York: Alfred A. Knopf, 1996.

Savidi, Lena. *1989 Calendar with 209 Traditional Greek Recipes* (in Greek). Athens: Hermes Press, 1988.

Sfikas, George. *Medicinal Plants of Greece*. Athens: Efstathiadis Group, 1993.

———. *Trees and Shrubs of Greece*. Athens: Efstathiadis Group, 1993.

Simopoulos, Kyr. *Foreign Travelers in Greece* (in Greek). Vol. 1 and 2. Athens: self-published, 1984, 1991.

Trichopoulou, Antonia, and Tonia Vasilakou. *Food Availability in Greece per Capita 1981–1982 and 1987–1988*. Athens: National Nutrition Center, 1995.

Voutsina, Evy. *Greek Flavor* (in Greek). 4 volumes. Athens: Ekdoseis Kastanioti, 1998.

Wilkins, John, David Harvey, and Mike Dobson, eds. *Food in Antiquity.* Exeter, UK: University of Exeter Press, 1995.

Wolfert, Paula. *The Cooking of the Eastern Mediterranean*. New York: HarperCollins, 1994.

———. *Mediterranean Grains and Greens*. New York: HarperCollins, 1998.

Zografos, Demetrios. *The History of Greek Agriculture* (in Greek). Athens: Agricultural Bank of Greece, 1976.

Zouraris, Christos. *The Deipnosophist* (in Greek). Athens: Ikaros Press, 1993.

———. *The Second Deipnosophist* (in Greek). Athens: Ikaros Press, 1998.

Specific Regions

PELOPONNESOS

Andromedas, John N. "Maniot Folk Culture and the Ethnic Mosaic in the Southeast Peloponnese." *Annals New York Academy of Sciences.*

Clark Forbes, Mary H. "Gathering in the Argolid: A Subsistence Subsystem in a Greek Agricultural Community." *Annals New York Academy of Sciences.*

Fermor, Patrick Leigh. *Travels in the Southern Peloponnese*. London: Penguin, 1984.

Greenlaugh, Peter, and Edward Eliopoulos. *Deep into Mani: Journey to the Southern Tip of Greece*. London: Faber and Faber, 1985.

Jameson, Michael H. "The Southern Argolid: The Setting for Historical and Cultural Studies. *Annals New York Academy of Sciences.*

Kochilas, Diane. "The Artichoke, a Green Daisy." *Ta Nea* (Athens) (newspaper), May 7, 1993.

Kremmydas, Vassilis. *Commerce in the Peloponnesos in the 18th Century* (in Greek). Athens: self-published, 1972.

Liddell, Robert. *The Morea*. London: Jonathan Cape, 1958.

Miha-Lampaki, Aspasia. "Bread as a Bloodless Offering in Messinia" (in Greek). Athens: *Society of Peloponnesian Studies Annual,* 1984.

———. "Ritualistic Pies of Messinia" (in Greek). *Society of Peloponnesian Studies Annual.*

Regional Office of Agricultural Development for the Peloponnesos and Western Mainland Greece. *Traditional Cuisine from the Agricultural Areas of the Peloponnesos and Western Mainland Greece* (in Greek). Patras: 1987.

Topping, Peter. "Premodern Peloponnesus: The Land and the People Under Venetian Rule (1685–1715). *Annals New York Academy of Sciences.*

Tsimikali, Pipina. "Folklore of Mani, Christmas Eve" (in Greek). *Nea Estia* 503 (1953).

THE IONIAN ISLANDS

Corfu

Bounias, Ioannis. *Corfu, History and Folklore.* Vols. 1 and 2. Corfu: 1958.

Climis, Carolos. *The Activities and Customs of the Corfiot People* (in Greek). Corfu: self-published, 1987.

———. *The Illustrated History of Corfu* (in Greek). Corfu: 1994.

Hitiris, Gerasimos. *The Folklore of Corfu* (in Greek). Corfu: Etairia Kerkyraikon Spouthon, 1991.

Laskari, Ninetta H. *Corfu, a Look Over Time, 1204–1864* (in Greek). Athens: I. Sideris, 1997.

Louis, Diana Farr, and June Marinos. *Prospero's Kitchen: Mediterranean Cooking of the Ionian Islands*. New York: M. Evans, 1995.

Politis, Mihalis H. *Olive Oil Cultivation in Corfu* (in Greek). Corfu: self-published, 1982.

Salsanos, Gerasimos. *How to Make Barbarella* (in Greek). Athens: Laografika Yli ek Kerkyras, 1930.

Cephalonia

Debonos, Angelos-Dionyssis. *Argostoli Celebrates* (in Greek). Cephalonia: self-published, 1979.

Loukatos, Dimitrios. "The Twelve Days of Christmas and Their Three Holidays in Cephalonia" (in Greek). Eptanisiaki Laografika.

Lefkada

Kontomihis, Pantazis. *"Olive Gathering in Lefkada."* Lefkada, n.d.

———. *The Traditional Household of Lefkada* (in Greek). Lefkada: Exdoseis Grigori, 1985.

Mamaloukas, Takis L. "Mandolato and Pasteli" (in Greek). Athens: Laografika tis Lefkados, 1978.

Rontogianni, P. G. *The History of Lefkada* (in Greek).

Ithaca

Anagnostatou, Andreas L. *Istorika kai Laografika Analekta tis Ithakis*. Athens: Dendrinos.

Magoulas, Mihalis P. *The Cuisine of Ithaca* (in Greek). Athens: unpublished, 1993.

Zakynthos

Marinos, June. *The Food of Zakynthos* (pamphlet). N.p., n.d.

Zois, Leonidas Charalambos. *The Folkloric and Historical Dictionary of Zakynthos* (in Greek). Self-published, n.d.

EPIRUS

Campbell, John. *Honor, Family and Patronage in a Greek Mountain Village*. Ph.D. diss., University of Virginia, 1964.

Hobhouse, J. C. A. *Journey Through Albania and Other Provinces of Turkey in Europe and Asia, to Constantinople, During the Years 1809 and 1810*. 2nd ed. London: James Cawthorn, 1813.

Hughes, T. S. *Travels in Greece and Albania*. Vol. 2. 2nd ed. London: Henry Colburn and Richard Bentley, 1830.

Kavvadias, F. B. *Sarakatsans: A Greek Pastorial Society* (in Greek). Athens: Ekdoseis Lucy Bratzioti, 1991.

Makris, Euripides. *The Life and Traditions of the Sarakatsans* (in Greek). Ioannina: self-published, 1997.

Mammopoulos, Alexandros. *Epirus*. Vol. 1 and 2. Athens: self-published, 1964.

Nitsiakos, Vassilis. *The Mountain Communities of the Northern Pindus* (in Greek). Athens: Ekdoseis Plethron, n.d.

Papaioannis, Ioannis. *Papingo* (in Greek). Papingo: self-published, 1994.

Pouqueville, F. C. H. L. *Voyage en Moree, à Constantinople, en Albanie et dans plusiers autres parties de l'Empire Ottoman, pendant les années 1798, 1799, 1800 et 1801*. Vol. 3. Paris: Gabon et Camp, 1805.

Scheim-Dimen, Muriel. *Change and Continuity in a Greek Mountain Village*. Ph.D. diss., Columbia University, 1970.

Wace, A. J. B., and M. S. Thomson. *The Nomads of the Balkans*. London: Methuen, 1914.

———. "North Greek Folk Festivals and the Worship of Dionyssus." *Annual of the British School at Athens*, 1909–1910.

MACEDONIA

Bozi, Soula. *Capadocia, Ionia, Pontos—Flavors and Traditions* (in Greek). Athens: Ekdoseis Asterismos, 1997.

———. *The Cuisine of the Constantinople Greeks* (in Greek). Athens: Ekdoseis Asterismos, 1995.

Grigoriadou-Bakirtzoglou, Eufrosyne. *Traditional and Modern Pontian Cuisine* (in Greek). Thessaloniki: self-published, 1990.

Ioannidou, Nina. *Thessaloniki: The Crossroads of Flavors* (in Greek). Thessaloniki: A. Maliaris-Paideias, 1996.

Stavroulakis, Nicholas. *The Cookbook of the Jews of Greece*. Athens: Lycabettus Press, 1986.

Stavroulakis, Nicholas, and Esin Eden. *Salonika: A Family Cookbook*. Athens: Talos Press, 1997.

ROUMELI AND THESSALY

Holland, H. *Travels in the Ionian Isles, Albania, Thessaly, Macedonia During the Years 1812 and 1813*. London: Longman, Hurst, Rees, Orme, and Brown, 1815.

Lemiki-Morfopoulou, Kaiti. *Pelion's and Other Recipes* (in Greek). Volos: Ekdoseis Ores, 1995.

Leschi Gynaikon Karditsas. *Traditional Pies of Karditsa* (in Greek). Karditsa, 1993.

Polymeropoulou, Maria M., et al. *Traditional Recipes from Roumeli* (in Greek). Lamia: Ekdoseis Arsenidi, 1994.

The Women's Israelite Community of Volos. *Jewish Holidays and Traditions—Ideas for Cooking* (in Greek). Volos: self-published, 1993.

THE NORTHEAST AEGEAN

Samos and Ikaria

Dimitriou, Nikolaos. *Folklore of Samos* (in Greek). Vol. A. Athens: self-published, 1983.

———. *"The Kneading and Baking of Bread in Samos"* (in Greek). *Laografika* 31, 1976–78.

Kerpes, Ioulios. *"Popular Foods of Ikaria"* (in Greek). *Laografika* 32, 1979–1981.

Chios

Argenti, Philip P., and H. J. Rose. *The Folklore of Chios*. Vol. 1. Cambridge: Cambridge University Press, 1949.

"Chios, Monuments and Arts" (in Greek). *Kathimerini* (Athens) (newspaper), July 31, 1994.

Perikos, John. *The Chios Gum Mastic*. Chios, 1993.

Recipes with Chios Mastic (in Greek). Chios: Union of Mastic Producers, 1992.

Traditional Recipes from Chios (in Greek). Chios: Filoproodou Omilou Kambou, 1992.

Traditional Recipes from Chios (in Greek). Vol. A. Chios: Second Lyceum of Kallimasias, 1994.

Lesvos

Balaskas, Stratis. *"The Grand Festival of the Bull"* (in Greek). *Aiolika Nea* (Lesvos) (newspaper), July 3, 1994.

Hatziyiannis, Christofa D. *The Festival of the Bull, Saint Paraskevi, Lesvos* (in Greek). Georgiko Somatio of Ag. Paraskevi, 1987.

Platanos, Vassilis. *Greek Folk Festivals* (in Greek). Athens: self-published, 1963.

———. *The Dance of the Horses* (in Greek). Athens: self-published, 1962.

Tragellis, Christos I. *Gone but Not Forgotten, the Old Trades of Kalloni, Lesvou* (in Greek). Athens: Sigma Press, 1986.

THE DODECANESE

Lykeion Ellinidon Rodou. *Rhodian Recipes* (in Greek). Athens: self-published, 1985.

Perseli, Annas. *Kassos Cuisine* (in Greek). Athens: self-published, 1994.

THE CYCLADES

Antzoulatou-Retsila, Euridice. *Partridges and Birds in the Easter Tradition of Our Land* (in Greek). Athens: self-published, 1993.

Bent, J. Theodore. *Early Voyages and Travels in the Levant*. London, 1893.

Delatola, Zosefina. *Tinos Traditional Cooking* (in Greek). Tinos: Ekdoseis Delatola, n.d.

Dimitropoulos, Achilles. *Syros, a Guide for the Visitor* (in Greek). Athens: Kykladikes Ekdoseis, 1994.

Dubisch, Jill. "The Ethnography of Tinos." *The Ethnography of the Islands*.

Florakis, Alekos. *Tinos, Folk Culture* (in Greek). Athens, 1971.

Foskolou, Nikoleta. *Traditional Recipes from Tinos* (in Greek). Athens: Ekdoseis Tinos, 1996.

Kochilas, Diane. "In a Meager Pot, the Food and Cooking of Sifnos" (in Greek). *Ta Nea* (Athens) (newspaper), August 20, 1993.

———. "Santorini: Island of Plenty, Island of Dearth" (in Greek). *Ta Nea* (Athens) (newspaper), August 13, 1993.

Lambraki, Myrsini. "Gastronomical Travels in Ofiousa" (in Greek). *Kathimerini* (Athens) (newspaper), September 21, 1997.

———. "Tomato Juice and Confetti" (in Greek). *Kathimerini* (Athens) (newspaper), July 27, 1997.

Roussos, Evangelos. "Local Names of the Plants in Syros." *Syriana Grammata,* 26–27, April–July 1994.

Roussou, Ypanti, and Lefteris Menegos. *Delicacies of Paros*. Naoussa Paros (music-dance group), n.p., n.d.

Sarlis, Yiorgos P. "The Plants of Syros." *Syriana Grammata,* 26–27, April–July 1994.

Technical Lyceum of Syros (student collection). *Traditional Recipes of Syros* (in Greek). Syros, 1996.

Troullos, Antonis. *The Sifniote Panygyri* (in Greek). Sifnos: self-published, n.d.

Troullou, Eleni. *Sifniot Treats* (in Greek). Sifnos: self-published, 1996.

Tsiros, Yiorgos. "Syros, Loukoumia Forever" (in Greek). *Kathimerini* (Athens) (newspaper), May 3, 1992.

Venardou, Filio E., ed. *Traditional Recipes from Kimolos* (in Greek). Kimolos, 1997.

CRETE

Ankori, Zvi. "Jews and the Jewish Community in the History of Medieval Crete." Athens: B' Diethnes Kritologikon Synedrion, 1968.

Baladie-Triantafyllidou, Yiolanda. *Trade and Economy in Crete from the Beginning of Ottoman Rule to the End of the 18th Century* (in Greek). Herakleion: Ekdoseis Bikelaia Dimotiki Bibliothiki, 1988.

Dembinska, M. "A Comparison of Food Consumption Between Some Eastern and Western Monasteries in the 4th–12th Centuries." *Byzantion* (Athens), vol. LV, 1985.

Hopkins, Adam. *Crete: Its Past, Present and People.* London: Faber and Faber, 1977.

Kazantzakis, Nikos. *Alexis Zorbas.*

———. *Freedom or Death.*

———. *The Odyssey: A Modern Sequel.*

———. *Report to Greco.*

Kochilas, Diane. "Herakleion" (in Greek). *Ta Nea* (Athens) (newspaper).

———. "The Roots of a Unique Cuisine I"(in Greek). *Ta Nea* (Athens) (newspaper), May 22, 1998.

———. "The Roots of a Unique Cuisine II"(in Greek). *Ta Nea* (Athens) (newspaper), May 29, 1998.

Papadakis, Manolis. "The Foods of the Cretans in the 15th and 16th Centuries" (in Greek). *Kritilogia* 7 (July–December 1978).

Platakis, Eleftherios. "The Multisynonymous Plants of Crete" (in Greek). *Kritiki Estia*, vol. 1, Hania, 1987.

Politistikos Syllogos Anogeion. "Traditional Occupations in Psiloriti" (in Greek). Vol. 1. *Ktinotrofia*, Crete: Anogeia, 1995.

Psillakis, Nikos, and Maria Psillakis. *Kritiki Paradosiaki Kouzina.* 2nd ed. Herakleion: Ekdoseis Karmanor, 1995.

Stathaki-Koumari, Rodoula. *The Traditional Bread of Rethymnon* (in Greek). Rethymnon: Rethymnon Museum of History and Folklore, 1983.

Stillwell, Alice. "Crete, Where Sea-Kings Reigned." *National Geographic*, November 1943.

Trevor-Battye, Aubyn. *Camping in Crete, With Notes Upon the Animal and Plant Life of the Island.* London: Witherby, 1913.

Index